A Diplomatic History of
the Balkan Crisis of 1875-1878

The First Year

A DIPLOMATIC HISTORY OF THE BALKAN CRISIS OF 1875-1878

THE FIRST YEAR

By

D A V I D H A R R I S

ARCHON BOOKS
1969

SBN: 208 00792 X
LIBRARY OF CONGRESS CATALOG CARD NUMBER: 69-19213
PRINTED IN THE UNITED STATES OF AMERICA

1/72

PREFACE

THE BALKAN crisis of 1875–1878 marks an important stage in Europe's march toward 1914. It breathed a fresh vigor into some of the Continent's old suspicions and rivalries and—like so many diplomatic contests that have given way to war—it created a host of new dangers to peace which eventually exacted their toll.

The present volume is a study of the first year of that crisis. It is work done with the historian's microscope and fine pencil rather than with the artist's broad brush. A detailed narrative seemed to me desirable for two reasons. In the first place, no writer who has tried to hasten through these years has produced a satisfyingly accurate account; and, in the second place, some profit may accrue from a close reconstruction of this crisis as a case history in European diplomacy. I have written, therefore, with the desire to relate without too much selection and interpretation an accurate story of the year's varied currents of interest and events and to present an exposition of the many maneuvers and negotiations which were, in general, typical of nineteenth-century international relations.

A narrative of the crisis of 1875–1878 is at best a bewildering one because of the diversity of national and individual stakes involved and because of the long train of talk and action which those stakes inspired. The complexity of the year's happenings imposed on me a serious problem of organization, a problem which I attacked in the hope, not of presenting to my reader an easily mastered chronicle, but of keeping his confusion within tolerable bounds. My procedure has been to isolate certain themes—not without some violence perhaps and at the cost of certain inevitable repetitions—and to follow them through periods of logical development.

I have prepared this volume under the benefit of many courtesies and benedictions. I gratefully acknowledge my indebtedness to the Social Science Research Council for a special fellowship and to the Council on Research in the Social Sciences of Stanford University for its equally material support.

D. H.

STANFORD UNIVERSITY, CALIFORNIA
January 15, 1936

v

TABLE OF CONTENTS

CHAPTER I

THE BROTH AND THE COOKS

NEW TROUBLE IN TURKEY

In the early winter of 1874–75 new trouble was brewing in Turkey. The conflagration which eventually ensued began modestly enough—as troubles went in the decrepit Ottoman state. One hundred and fifty or more Christian Hercegovinians, finding life no longer tolerable in their homes, fled to the haven of neighboring Montenegro. Never would they return, they asserted, until Turkish rule was at an end, and they declared that a majority of their relatives and friends would follow them in the spring.

The arrival of the fugitives in Montenegro was no pleasant experience for Prince Nicholas. The bellicose spirit of his subjects was readily stirred by the stories of oppression which they heard from the lips of their refugee kinsmen, and the excitement of the men of the Black Mountain threatened to destroy the precarious truce which Nicholas had only recently patched up with the Sublime Porte. Furthermore, the presence of such a number of new mouths to feed placed a considerable burden on the scant resources of the tiny principality.[1] The refugees could not be easily maintained by the prince, nor could he, on the other hand, send them back to suffer the certain revenge of their Moslem masters. Nicholas consequently asked the Austro-Hungarian government to present the case of his embarrassing guests in Constantinople,[2] and through the good offices of Vienna[3] the fugitive Hercegovinians were given permission to return to their homes without fear of punishment.[4] Early in June 1875 the emi-

[1] Wassitch to Andrássy, Scutari, 13 April 1875; Austro-Hungarian Monarchy, *Ministerium des k. und k. Hauses und des äussern, Actenstücke aus den Correspondenzen des kais. und kön. gemeinsamen Ministeriums des äussern über orientalische Angelegenheiten (vom 16. Mai 1873 bis 31. Mai 1877)* (Vienna, 1877), Doc. No. 99. Hereafter cited as *First Red Book*.

[2] Prince of Montenegro to Andrássy, Cetinje, 14, 17 May 1875; *ibid.*, Docs. Nos. 100, 101, respectively.

[3] Andrássy to Zichy in Constantinople, Vienna, 22 May; *ibid.*, Doc. No. 103.

[4] Andrássy to the Prince of Montenegro, 29 May; *ibid.*, Doc. No. 104.

grants were led back over the frontier,[5] but they went back without illusions as to their security and without willingness to submit again to the old regime. For two years underground plans for revolt had been quietly hatching[6] and during the critical winter of the flight clan chieftains and old rebel leaders had met repeatedly in the little town of Nevesinje to pursue their grim counsels of action.[7] How far plans had been taken or what material preparations had been made, it is difficult to say. A journalist in Dalmatia, somewhat suspect because of his pro-insurgent role while American consul during the rebellion in Crete, insisted that there were no mature plans, no collection of arms and ammunition.[8] But at all events, the fugitives returned home dressed in the garb of the Black Mountain—and defiant. They stirred up their fellow Christians, threatened the gendarmes,[9] and soon were in open revolt. Justifying themselves on the ground of the oppression which they had long suffered, the insurgents refused to pay their taxes, drove away the police, and declined to bring their grievances before the local governor.[10] The Turkish authorities, reluctant to alarm public opinion by dispatching troops to the disaffected area, sent two notables of Sarajevo to reason with the rebels. Before these emissaries arrived, however, the Christians had resorted to violence. A pack train on the highroad had been captured; five Turks had been murdered; insurgent bands had repulsed the gen-

[5] Prince of Montenegro to Andrássy, 6 June; *First Red Book,* Doc. No. 105.

[6] At least this was the assertion made to a Western journalist by Ljubibratich, one of the leaders of the rebellion. Dispatch from Ragusa, 9 October, in *New York Herald,* 6 November 1875, p. 4, cols. 1–2.

[7] Harold Temperley, *The Bulgarian and Other Atrocities in the Light of Historical Criticism,* a reprint from the *Proceedings of the British Academy,* XVII (1931), 4–7. Mr. Temperley has found an interesting confirmation of the accounts of the origins of the revolt in a series of ballads, composed later, in true Serbian style, to celebrate the occasion.

[8] W. J. Stillman, dispatch from Ragusa, 3 September 1875; *The Times* (London), 13 September, p. 8, col. 1. See his *Autobiography of a Journalist,* 2 vols. (London, 1901), and his *Herzegovina and the Late Uprising* (London, 1877).

[9] Bourgoing to Decazes, Therapia, 29 June 1875; France, *Ministère des affaires étrangères, Documents diplomatiques, Affaires d'Orient, 1875–1876–1877* (Paris, 1877), pp. 1–2. Hereafter cited as *First Yellow Book.*

[10] Political Report No. 4, Holmes to Derby, Bosna-Seraï, 2 July; Great Britain, Parliament, Commons, *Parliamentary Papers,* 1876, Vol. LXXXIV, *Turkey No. 2 (1876),* Doc. No. 1. The *Parliamentary Papers* will be hereafter cited as *Turkey No. — (18—).* All the material in the *Papers* covering the years 1875–1878 has been checked against the manuscripts in the Public Record Office in London and, unless there is indication given in this study to the contrary, it is to be understood that the printed document is correct.

darmes and occupied all approaches to the Nevesinje area. The notables hastily abandoned their mission, and the district governor requested troops; meanwhile the excited Moslem population prepared their arms for settling the disturbance in the traditional manner.[11]

In the course of a few days a battalion was dispatched toward the neighboring Turkish center of Mostar, but before ordering an attack the governor-general of the territory made one further attempt to calm the disturbance through conciliation. Two officials on their way to settle a boundary dispute with Montenegro were sent to Nevesinje to negotiate.[12] While these dignitaries were proceeding to their new task under the hot July sun, the progressive spread of the rebellion was signaled by a growing list of fights.[13] When eventually the commissioners arrived and invited the insurgents to submit their grievances to a hearing, there was no common ground for an understanding. The Turks went expecting no result,[14] and their report to the Sublime Porte on the sixteenth confirmed their anticipation. They found the Christians defiant and they recommended prompt military action as the only means of preventing the further spread of a serious revolt.[15] On the following day two battalions of infantry and a squadron of cavalry set out from Sarajevo for the disturbed area,[16] but since this contingent could bring small aid to the seven or eight battalions garrisoned in Hercegovina,[17] the Turkish attempt to restore order soon ended in a series of defeats.[18] The initial advantage was plainly with the Christian rebels. They were challenging a brutal but inefficient authority; they had the zeal of desperate souls; and, although lacking all serious military equipment, their bands, like

[11] Political Report No. 5, Holmes to Derby, 9 July 1875; *Turkey No. 2 (1876)*, Doc. No. 2. Tel. No. 50 and Report No. 54B, Herbert to Andrássy, Constantinople, 8, 13 July; *First Red Book*, Docs. Nos. 108, 110, respectively. The documents printed in this collection have been checked against the originals in the *Haus-, Hof-, und Staatsarchiv* in Vienna, and variations between the original and printed texts will be indicated. Doc. No. 110 is printed with unimportant emendations.

[12] Elliot to Derby, Therapia, 13 July 1875; *Turkey No. 2 (1876)*, Doc. No. 5. Bourgoing to Decazes, Therapia, 14 July; *First Yellow Book*, pp. 3–4.

[13] Holmes to Derby, Bosna-Seraï, 16 July; *Turkey No. 2 (1876)*, Doc. No. 6.

[14] *Ibid.*

[15] Hassan Édib and Constant to Safvet, Nevesinje, 4/16 July; *First Yellow Book*, pp. 5–6.

[16] *The Times* (London), 21 July 1875, p. 7, col. 2.

[17] Political Report No. 7, Holmes to Derby, Bosna-Seraï, 24 July; *Turkey No. 2 (1876)*, Doc. No. 9. [18] *The Times* (London), 27 July 1875, p. 5, col. 2.

eddies in a flowing stream, appeared and disappeared before the be-wildered Turks could strike a telling blow.

In the first days of August all Europe was aware that the move-ment had assumed ominous dimensions.[19] On the fifteenth of that month, when the provincial troops were occupied in the mountains of Hercegovina, the flames of revolt burst out on the kindred soil of Bosnia.[20] In this wider expanse the revived struggle between Chris-tian and Moslem was continued with that bitterness which, seemingly, only religion could inspire. With rebellion directed even more against local oppressors than against a distant suzerain, brigandage and atroc-ity were inevitable.[21] The local pasha, with tears streaming down his cheeks, spoke of innocent Mohammedan babes roasted on spits,[22] and more disinterested reporters chronicled events scarcely less shock-ing. Arrayed against the insurgents were not only the Turkish sol-diers but also the provincial Moslem population. With insufficient troops for their protection, these latter took the law into their own hands and were soon recruiting mobs of bashi-bazouks, those irregu-lars who had already made themselves symbolic of all that is fiendish in the practice of killing men.[23] Civil war was the order of the day in Turkey.

[19] Tel., Theodorovich to Andrássy, Sarajevo, 8 August; Vienna, *Haus-, Hof-, und Staatsarchiv* MSS, Varia Turquie II, 1875. Materials from the *Staatsarchiv* will hereafter be cited as SA. Much of the Austro-Hungarian diplomatic corres-pondence in the first year of the disturbance has been arranged in two special col-lections, Varia Turquie I, 1875, and Varia Turquie II, 1875, and when used this will be so indicated. Other special arrangements of the Austrian MS documents will be indicated as used.

Report No. 22, Holmes to Elliot, Bosna-Seraï (Sarajevo), 6 August; London, Public Record Office MSS, FO 78/2402. The correspondence of the British Foreign Office will be indicated by FO —/—. The first figure after the initials indicates the series, the second the number of the volume in which the document concerned has been bound. The form of citation for correspondence used in this volume will be as indicated: from whom, to whom, place of writing, date; source either printed or manuscript. It is to be understoon that *ibid.* used in such a citation refers to the source indicated after the semicolon.

[20] *The Times* (London), 17 August 1875, p. 3, col. 3.

[21] Freeman to Elliot, Bosna-Seraï, 21 August; *Turkey No. 2 (1876)*, inclosure in Doc. 18.

[22] Report No. 2, Holmes to Derby, Mostar, 22 August; FO 78/2536. In 1859 this pasha of tender feeling, Dervish by name, had poisoned a supply of flour and sent it out into this same Hercegovina with the hope that the Christians, at the time in rebellion, would capture and eat it (Temperley, *Bulgarian and Other Atrocities*, pp. 9–10).

[23] Arthur J. Evans, *Through Bosnia and the Herzegovina on Foot during the Insurrection, August and September 1875* (London, 1876), pp. 260–61.

But mere atrocities heaped upon atrocities by the subjects of the Grand Turk would hardly of themselves have been a matter of moment for the foreign offices of Europe. The disturbing factor in this rapidly spreading revolt was its repercussion in the whole territory of the Southern Slavs. These people of like heritage and hopes were scattered under several flags, but the virus of nineteenth-century nationalism was working in their blood. From the beginning of the revolt Montenegrins had joyfully crossed the frontier. In Austrian Dalmatia enthusiasts were soon openly collecting money for the rebellion as well as taking part in it directly.[24] From Serbia came numerous bands prepared to do heroic duty for the cause of Christian Slavdom.[25] Before the end of August it was obvious that not only was the Ottoman Empire confronted with a grave crisis but also that sacrosanct political frontiers might not be respected if the trouble went much further.[26]

THE SICK MAN AND HIS FESTERING MEMBER

In 1875 the senile frame of Turkey seemed little able to stand the shock of new ailments. During the preceding hundred years sporadic, and often heroic, remedies had been applied; but, although purgings and amputations perhaps forestalled the end, their workings had not wrought the miracle of rejuvenation. The first of the serious reforming sultans, Selim III, in 1807 had paid with his throne and life for an attempt to modernize the land. His successor, Mahmud the Reformer, had seen the necessity for change and had made energetic attempts to halt the rapid pace of decomposition and to infuse into Turkey's veins the new blood of Europeanization, but his thirty-one years of stubborn brutality had not been able to conquer a resourceful opposition. Mahmud's son, Abdul Medjid (1839–1861), had had good enough intentions; when he had come to the throne he had inaugurated a new program of reforms whose object was professedly the security of life, liberty, and property for all of his sub-

---

[24] Report No. 22, Holmes to Elliot, Bosna-Seraï, 6 August; FO 78/2402. Safvet to Ali in Paris, Constantinople, 11 August; *First Yellow Book,* p. 10.

[25] *The Times* (London), 20 August 1875, p. 3, col. 1.

[26] In August the official Montenegrin newspaper reported: "The insurrection is fast assuming formidable proportions. Symptoms of serious design multiply. Men are yearning for war, and oily tongued diplomacy is impotent to prevent them. This time insurrection is sure to result in emancipation. . . . . If rebellion becomes general, Servia [*sic*] and Montenegro will not be idle spectators. Now or never. . . . ." (*The Times,* 30 August 1875, p. 5, col. 5).

jects regardless of religion. Internal progress was undoubtedly made under Abdul Medjid's rule; the army was reorganized, centralization was forwarded, and the ground work of an educational system was laid. Furthermore, the Crimean War and the Peace of Paris had given Turkey a new lease of life so far as protection against outside dangers was concerned. The special position of Russia in Ottoman affairs was ended; the empire's independence and integrity were guaranteed by the Great Powers, and the old pariah was formally admitted to the select society of European nations. But in spite of a well-meaning ruler and a reforming minister and a vigilant British ambassador, in spite of new declarations of improved ways, in spite of a theoretically privileged international setting, Turkey had continued to be Turkey. While Abdul Medjid had slowly succumbed to the fatal combination of Moslem indulgence and Christian alcohol, effective regeneration of the country had been made impossible by the dead hand of Islamic law and by the sullen resistance of a fanatical population.

When Abdul Aziz succeeded his brother in 1861, the imperial pressure for reform, however unenlightened and capricious it might have been, was abandoned. Abdul Aziz had passed his earlier years in a strict seclusion broken by hunting and sheep raising as a preparation for ruling an empire. A man entirely ignorant of the West and saturated with Mohammedan scholasticism, the new sultan was counted at the time of his accession as one of the reactionaries, a partisan of the Old Turks.[27] Once on the throne, however, he professed a desire to carry on the work of improvement.[28] Yet environment and heredity alike stood in the way of his mild good-will. A throng of corrupt officials used every device to push their lord forward along the pleasant paths of reckless spending, and soon the sultan was exceeding their most sanguine expectations. He had begun by giving up a considerable portion of his civil list and by announcing to an amazed world that, in the interests of economy, he was going to satisfy himself with one wife. The fate of these resolutions was typical of all the rest. Shortly two additional wives were added, and then,

[27] Felix Bamberg, *Geschichte der orientalischen Angelegenheit im Zeitraume des Pariser und des Berliner Friedens* (Berlin, 1892), p. 360; A. de la Jonquière, *Histoire de l'empire ottoman depuis les origines jusqu'à nos jours* (Paris, 1914), II, 1–2.

[28] A. Schopoff, *Les Réformes et la protection des Chrétiens en Turquie, 1673–1904* (Paris, 1904), pp. 82–84.

once the door had been open, the female population of the harem slowly mounted to nine hundred souls.[29]

It was not long before Constantinople knew that the house of Othman's taint of madness was upon this imperial wastrel. At his best he sat in the midst of all that an Oriental monarch could crave, yet with his dulled mind consummately bored.[30] The passing years tended to substitute for this self-engrossing passivity a long series of extravagant whims and follies which put Turkey far on the dangerous road to bankruptcy. For months at a time imperial business was at a standstill because the autocrat refused to read state documents not written in red ink. At other times his pyrophobia mounted to such a frenzy that he would not permit a single lighted candle in the vast expanse of the palace.[31] More and more the pleasant company of buffoons, the delights of a gourmand's table, and the fighting of pet cocks wearing the highest imperial decorations took the time of this successor of the Prophet, this shadow of God.[32]

Such a total neglect of the fortunes of his empire, however, would have been tolerable, even in the face of an unleashed horde of avaricious bureaucrats, had neglect been Abdul Aziz's only sin. But this chapter of Turkish history was once again the story of how the hidden forces of the seraglio could make and unmake ministers and dictate the most important decisions of state. It repeated, too, the story of the creeping paralysis of corruption and confusion.

Resort to the money markets of the West had permitted to Abdul Aziz a prodigality for which there was no parallel in earlier Turkish times. To the conventional expenditures of a thronging and gold-hungry harem the sultan added lavish building: a new mosque, designed to be the equal of any in Turkey, was begun, and millions were poured into additional palaces planned by his troubled brain.[33] And finally, when many of his subjects were naked and starving, Abdul Aziz, with a folly worthy of more advanced states in subsequent times, set out to build a navy second to none.

[29] Bamberg, *op. cit.*, pp. 360–61.

[30] A. Gallenga, *Two Years of the Eastern Question* (London, 1877), I, 136. Gallenga was for a time Constantinople correspondent of the London *Times*.

[31] Sir Henry George Elliot, *Some Revolutions and Other Diplomatic Experiences* (London, 1922), pp. 240–41.

[32] L. Raschdau, "Aus dem politischen Nachlass des Unterstaatssekretärs Dr. Busch," *Deutsche Rundschau*, CXXXVII (December 1908), 383–84.

[33] *The Memoirs of Ismail Kemal Bey*, edited by Somerville Story (London, 1920), pp. 93–96.

In the first decade of his disastrous reign the sultan had inter-
mittently used the services of two ministers who labored for reform,
Fuad Pasha[34] and Ali Pasha. But the former died in 1869 and the
latter two years later, and with their deaths the fortunes of Turkey
took a turn distinctly for the worse. The sultan, no longer hampered
by the reformers, openly delighted in being again free to pursue his
own inclinations. This emancipation was signaled by the appointment
to the grand vizierate of Mahmud Nedim, a member of the Old Turk
party. Two contemporary characterizations of the new functionary
are on record. The contemporary Russian ambassador, to whose influence Mahmud succumbed so completely as to be called Mahmudov,
considered him, while not the equal of Ali, at least a man of remarkable character, intelligence, and zeal for reform.[35] The British representative, on the other hand, pictured a calloused opportunist who
courted every whim of his master and of the seraglio in order to remain in power, a reckless waster whose excesses evoked a new party
of reform.[36] Disinterested appraisal would incline toward the second
opinion. Certain it is that Mahmud's regime could not last one year
because of the confusion which he created in the administration, the
enemies he made, and the suspicious debts which he heaped up in the
Ottoman treasury. In the end the reformers brought him low, in spite
of the fact that the sultan shared the spoils of his corruption; he was
temporarily ruined by being convicted of gross peculation.[37]

The chief of the enemies who had dethroned the high-handed
vizier was Midhat Pasha, a Moslem of Bulgarian descent who had
worked his way, through exceptional merit and administrative ability,
into the upper Ottoman bureaucracy.[38] But Midhat, disciple though
he was of the great reforming ministers, was unable to realize his
aims with regard to the central administration. In attempting to restore funds pillaged from the treasury he had the presumption to

[34] Fuad, "The Political Testament of Fuad Pasha (addressed to the Sultan
Abdul Aziz in 1869, one day before the death of its author)," *Nineteenth Century,*
LIII (1903), 190–97.

[35] Nicholas P. Ignatiev, "Zapiski Grafa N. P. Ignatyeva, 1867–1874," *Izvestiia
ministerstva inostrannikh diel* (1915), I, 145–48.

[36] Sir Henry George Elliot, "The Death of Abdul Aziz and Turkish Reform,"
Nineteenth Century, XXIII (1888), 277–79. This view is naturally shared by
Ismail Kemal Bey, a disciple of Mahmud's chief enemy (*op. cit.,* pp. 76–77).

[37] Bamberg, *Geschichte der orientalischen Angelegenheit,* pp. 427–28; *Memoirs
of Ismail Kemal Bey,* pp. 83–84.

[38] Ali Haydar Midhat, *The Life of Midhat Pasha* (London, 1903), pp. 32 ff.

ask the sultan himself to restore a large sum which had reached the palace through irregular means, and the imperial response was the dismissal of the grand vizier and his exile as a provincial governor.[39] The experience convinced Midhat that a thoroughgoing political renovation alone could save the Ottoman Empire. In the next years he and his Young Turk friends laid down the principles of a new type of reform for Turkey, a reform the basis of which was to be a constitution in the Occidental sense. Without restraint on a crotchety sovereign, without a legislature which took no thought of religion and class, without organized decentralization, these reformers felt that the empire could not survive.[40]

In these years, however, Midhat and his fellow enthusiasts had to bide their time while the health of the Turkish body politic grew worse. With reform considered such a disagreeable remedy at the heart of the state, the dangerous fever of spending went on. The Ottoman financial administration was practically all that a financial administration should not be. The only serious principle involved was discrimination against non-Moslems, and the major results were venality and ruin. Of the money collected from his subjects, a considerable proportion, because of inefficiency, dishonesty, and tax-farming, never reached the sultan's coffers. That which did arrive was handled in a haphazard fashion, for civil list and budget were largely meaningless terms which the Turks had copied from the West.[41]

But these malpractices were nothing novel in Turkey. The innovation which had aggravated the already serious state of finance was foreign borrowing. The new expedient was inaugurated in 1854, when a modest loan was floated in London for the conventionally acceptable purpose of financing Turkey's share in the Crimean War. Once the soothing draught had been taken, more and more seemed imperative. Once peace was established, new loans were needed to clean up the debris left by the war. Then came more loans to take care of a floating debt which was doubling itself every six years. Then came still other loans for other purposes, and then still others with

[39] *Memoirs of Ismail Kemal Bey*, pp. 83–89. One of Midhat's most unrelenting enemies, the Russian ambassador, claimed a share in his overthrow (Ignatiev, *Izvestiia*, 1915, I, 149–50).

[40] Elliot, *Some Revolutions,* pp. 227–29.

[41] Donald C. Blaisdell, *European Financial Control in the Ottoman Empire* (New York, 1929), pp. 11–15.

ever shortening intervals. Progressively the rate of interest mounted while the issuing figure declined. In 1854 the first loan, drawing six per cent, was issued at 80. In 1874 the interest had advanced to nine per cent and the bonds were initially offered at from 58.5 to 43.5. By 1875 the total foreign debt had climbed to 200,000,000 pounds sterling and the annual charge approached 12,000,000, nearly three-fifths of the entire revenue.[42] The budget for 1875–76, which was issued as the storm clouds w re breaking over Hercegovina, pictured, consequently, a well-nigh hopeless situation. Revenue was estimated at £19,000,000; expenditures were fixed at £23,500,000.[43] The ministers made optimistic promises to effect an equilibrium, and the grand vizier sent out new circulars ordering retrenchment and reform;[44] but the impossible could not be achieved. The government was unable to pay its employees; even in the arsenals and in the yards where more of Abdul Aziz's cherished warships were being built, the workers had not received wages for six months, and, too hungry to work, they struck.[45]

If such was the general internal state of Europe's sick man, it was a mild malady as compared to the condition of his festering member, the province of Bosnia and Hercegovina. For centuries the pursuits and passions of man had contributed to make of this territory a land of confusion. Before the final Turkish conquest Bosnia and Hercegovina had suffered a long history of political and religious misfortunes. A frontier region, the area was for so many centuries the object of cupidity and conquest from all sides that it would seem hard to find a land so harrassed by a succession of subjections and revolts. Likewise would it be difficult to point to a region where religion had left such a legacy of discord. The struggle between the Byzantine and the Latin churches had been bitter and indecisive in this borderland between East and West. Complicating the problem still more, the serpent of heresy had crept in; a doctrine of good and evil—the forerunner of the Albigensian belief—had flourished only

---

[42] Blaisdell, *op. cit.*, pp. 27–76.

[43] *The Spectator*, 17 July 1875, pp. 902–3. *Augsburger Allgemeine Zeitung*, 21 July 1875, p. 3173.

[44] The grand vizier to the governors-general of the empire, 21 July 1875; Italy, *Ministero degli affari esteri, Documenti diplomatici concernenti gli affari d'oriente presentati dal ministro degli affari esteri (Melegari) nella tornata del 3 marzo 1877* [Rome, 1877], annex to Doc. No. IV. Hereafter cited as *First Green Book*.

[45] *New York Herald*, 3 July 1875, p. 11, col. 6.

to set the people against each other and to provide new excuses for foreign conquest.[46]

In 1463 the Turks moved into Bosnia and the turbulent land became an integral part of the Ottoman Empire. Twenty years later Hercegovina suffered the same fate. At the time of the conquest the inhabitants were of South Slavic or Serbian language and culture.[47] Religiously they were divided between the Roman Catholic and Greek Orthodox churches and the Bogomil heresy. Socially there were two strata; at the top were the magnates or nobles, and below were the serfs and peasants. The conquerors did nothing to disturb this economic structure, but the nature of Moslem administration imposed a fateful religious problem upon this already divided society. While the lower classes remained largely dispossessed and Christian, the nobles who were left after the wars and flights were confronted with the necessity of choosing between the faith of their fathers and their hereditary domains. Many, and particularly those whose conventional Christianity had been undermined by heresy, elected to pile up treasure on earth, and rallied to the standard of the Prophet. The asperities of class differences henceforth were thus exacerbated by the superposition of a parallel religious hostility. Proud nobles became prouder still when their new Moslem faith allowed them to disdain and exploit their *rayahs*—their Christian "cattle"—of like blood and background though they were. The democratic traditions of Islam had no influence on these fanatical converts; apostasy served only to accentuate their feeling of aristocratic worth.[48]

In the long years between the conquest and the nineteenth century these lords, or *begs,* enjoyed not only their economic privileges but also a practical political autonomy. Vassals rather than conquered subjects, they held in their own hands the real authority over the land, and there it remained for three centuries. The new epoch, when reform was in the air, found the *begs* as hostile to interference from Constantinople as to any other outside influence, and

[46] W. Miller, "Bosnia Before the Turkish Conquest," *The English Historical Review,* XIII (October 1898), 643–66.

[47] For a discussion of the racial character of the so-called Southern Slavs, see Eugène Pittard, *Race and History, An Ethnological Introduction to History* (New York, 1926).

[48] Charles Yriarte, "Une excursion en Bosnie et dans l'Herzégovine pendant l'insurrection," *Revue des deux mondes,* XV (1 June 1876), 597–600; Ed. Engelhardt, *La Turquie et le Tanzimat* (Paris, 1882–1884), I, 90–93; Evans, *Through Bosnia on Foot,* pp. lvii–lix.

repeatedly these fanatics waged holy war against the infidel sultan who proclaimed the equality of all his subjects and who tried to disturb the good old ways. In 1850 the padishah's strongest general was sent to Bosnia to tame the rebels, and in two years the old feudal regime was broken. An attempt was made to establish new methods of taxation and to bring some system into the administration, but at best the reforms were only superficial. The old abuses quietly persisted and the old masters continued to sit in the seats of the mighty.[49]

After the turn of the century the critical problem of Bosnia and Hercegovina was no longer that of the unruly *beg,* serious though it was, but the welling wave of Christian complaint. Already the *rayahs* had mingled their revolts with those of their oppressors and the experience of the mounting years brought no hope of another route to tolerable life. The glowing promises of 1839, the regime of Omer Pasha in 1850–1852 which they had welcomed, the new reform pledges of 1856—none had brought a softening of their hard lot.[50]

---

[49] R. W. Seton-Watson, *The Rôle of Bosnia in International Politics (1875–1914)* (London, 1931), pp. 6–8; Theodor von Sosnosky, *Die Balkanpolitik Österreich-Ungarns seit 1866* (Stuttgart und Berlin, 1913–14), I, 108–11; Émile Haumant, *La Formation de la Yougoslavie (xv*ᵉ*–xx*ᵉ *siècles)* (Paris, 1930), pp. 298–302. The British consul in Bosnia described the post-1852 regime in these words: "The establishment of the *medjlisses* [councils] which possess in fact all the real power of the administration and which were, and are, formed by the most influential, and generally the most intolerant of the half-ruined native aristocracy, gave them still the power to neutralize the efforts of the best officials sent here from Constantinople; and if not always to carry out their own views, at least to prevent any satisfactory progress.

"Since I have been here, that is for the last 16 years, they have been mainly composed of the same individuals with the exception of those who have died and who have generally been replaced by relatives. They are all persons who have by their position and corrupt practices regained considerable wealth and influence, and, representing the principles of the most fanatical and ignorant part of the Mussulman community, that is to say, of the majority, they can always secure their re-election."

The comment thus quoted continued by pointing out that these leaders gained indirect control of the tax-farms and by mutual agreement pursued, each in his own way, the long-standing iniquities. The more enlightened Bosniacs refused to participate in their plunderbund and every governor-general had to come to terms with this unsavory coterie in order to reimburse himself for the heavy cost of his appointment (Political Report No. 20, Holmes to Derby, Bosna-Seraï, 30 June 1876; FO 78/2489).

[50] Zohrab to Bulwer, Bosna-Seraï, 22 July 1860; Great Britain, Parliament, Lords, *Parliamentary Papers, Reports Received from Her Majesty's Consuls Relating to the Condition of Christians in Turkey, 1860* (2810), 1861, Vol. XV–XVII, Doc. No. 14. Holmes to Bulwer, Bosna-Seraï, 1 September 1860; *ibid.,* Doc. No. 19. (Hereafter referred to as *British Consular Reports, 1860.*) Sosnosky, *op. cit.,* I,

In 1858, in the wake of a new revolt, the Christians addressed an appeal directly to the sultan himself, an appeal which listed a formidable array of grievances. Promises were made in reply, but only promises, and in 1861 the smoldering embers of rebellion burst again into flame. Omer Pasha, the conqueror of the *begs*, returned, this time to negotiate; but faith in Turkish promises could not flourish in blood-soaked ground, and the insurrection, aided by Nicholas of Montenegro, went on. When in the next year the Black Mountain was forced to capitulate, Bosnia likewise had to submit; but Turkish attempts at reconciliation failed because no basic satisfaction was offered to meet the claims of the *rayah* population.[51]

Although there had undoubtedly been some material improvement in the condition of the Christians, that improvement was offset by their new self-consciousness and self-confidence which a better fortune inevitably brought, and by the fact that the tendency of the oppressed to raise an increasingly vigorous voice of protest inspired renewed defiance in the hearts of the *begs*. The taproot from which grew Bosnia's sturdy tree of trouble was the religious problem. In these 18,000 square miles was a population of 1,200,000 souls divided between three hostile faiths. Of this total, Greek Orthodox Christians numbered roughly, according to available statistics, 575,000, Roman Catholics 185,000, and Moslems 440,000.[52] In political affairs the Catholics were relatively unimportant. Often their animosity toward the Orthodox was so great that they could be found with the Mohammedans giving pursuit to insurgent "Serbs," as the Orthodox ominously called themselves, and in time of trouble the Turkish authorities had sufficient confidence in the Christian schism to distribute arms in the "Latin" villages. The Catholic clergy in Bosnia had enjoyed special privileges dating from the days of Mohammed II and exercised a powerful influence over their flocks;

108–13. Nicholas Iorga, *Geschichte des osmanischen Reiches* (Gotha, 1908–1913), V, 556–57.

[51] Sosnosky, *op. cit.*, I, 115–19; Engelhardt, *op. cit.*, I, 190–92.

[52] A. P. Irby, "Bosnia in 1875," *Littell's Living Age*, CXXVII (1875), 646, quoting Turkish statistics for 1874. G. M. Mackenzie and A. P. Irby, *Travels in the Slavonic Provinces of Turkey in Europe* (London, 1877), I, 7. Miss Irby placed no faith in the figures; she considered the number of Moslems "enormously exaggerated" although the ratio between the two Christian groups was "fairly stated." In 1860 English figures reckoned the same total population divided as follows: Moslems 490,000, Catholics 160,000, Orthodox 550,000 (Zohrab to Bulwer, 22 July 1860; *British Consular Reports, 1860*, Doc. No. 14).

but never—and this was notoriously true of the Franciscans there—
had they made any effort to civilize their charges. While the Orthodox looked to his nationality first and to his religion second, the Bosnian Catholic had largely submerged his nationality in the Latin
church. In so far as he had a political inclination, it was identified
with that of his fellow Slavs of Austrian Croatia.[53]

Religious toleration had been one of the foundation stones of the
Turkish state, and indeed of the religion which the Turks had embraced. Repeatedly this principle had been affirmed at the Sublime
Porte, and the sultan had never presumed to interfere in the religious
affairs of his non-Moslem peoples. In Bosnia and Hercegovina this
freedom had never been denied in theory and never entirely subverted
in practice. Yet the ill-will of the local Moslem lords did much to
hamper it. Permits for remodeling churches and for building new
ones were extremely hard to extract from gold-hungry authorities;
the precious bells often could not be rung. But, after all, such petty
annoyances in themselves were not unendurable.

The Christians' vexation did not lie in the question of toleration
itself but in the principle and the practice that toleration had to be
bought by special obligations and by an inferior position in society
and state. Such a principle and such a practice in a land where fanatical Moslem lords had economic control over Christian peasants were
millstones of misfortune. One of the baneful discriminations suffered by the Christian from this regime was a practical inability to
secure justice without treating the machinery with the costly oil of
baksheesh. Christian evidence, quite naturally, was excluded from
the cadi's court. The cadi was a Moslem, and his duty was the administration of the sacred law of Islam. In the new councils, or
medjliss, however, the testimony of a Christian was admitted by law,
and the council was open to a non-Moslem plaintiff on the abstract
basis of theoretical equality as provided in the reform decrees of the
sultans. The breakdown of justice, then, was not because of theoretical right; it was due to the invariable control of the council by
Moslems who were characterized by foreign consuls at different times
as being among the most notorious and bigoted of their creed. In
each council there was usually one representative of each of the
Christian churches, but the non-Moslems were never able to defend
the interests of their co-religionists; their presence, in fact, seemed

[53] Irby, *op. cit.,* p. 649; Mackenzie and Irby, *op. cit.,* I, 16–17; Yriarte, *Revue
des deux mondes,* XV (1876), 626–29.

only to give Christian approval to injustices voted by the majority.[54]
The general result of Bosnia's pretense at legality was a practical
abandonment of the Christian to the merciless caprice of the *beg,*
although perhaps not so openly as in the dark days before Omer
Pasha.

Many of the indignities suffered by the Christians were whims
of bullies who knew they could express with impunity their inherited
disdain.[55] Others, such as distinctive dress, were sanctified by tradition and incorporated into the actual law of the land. The focal point
of *rayah* grievance, however, was economic discrimination. The
Christians had acquired the right to own landed property, but the
difficulties which they had to overcome in acquiring land were so
formidable that few non-Moslems had been able to surmount them.[56]
The overwhelming mass of the Christian population was made up of
peasants who with one hand doled out taxes to the state and with
the other paid off obligations to their rapacious lords. The oldest
of the dues paid to the government was the military-exemption tax,
levied on every male non-Moslem between the ages of sixteen and
sixty and often on infants still at the mother's breast. More oppressive was the tithe, actually an eighth, paid on the peasant's crop.
Heavy as it was alone, its burden was greatly increased by the method
of collection. The tax was farmed out to the highest bidder, and the
farmer, backed by the force of the law, entered every community
intent upon a maximum private profit. Regardless of ripeness or
condition of weather, the crop had to stand on the ground until the
assessor came, and when he did arrive deception and intimidation
were his usual stock in trade. On top of the exaction for the ordinary
crops were petty taxes on animals and specific produce which gave

[54] Zohrab to Bulwer, 22 July 1860; *British Consular Reports, 1860,* Doc. No. 14.
Mackenzie and Irby, *op. cit.,* I, 19–20. Evans, *Through Bosnia on Foot,* p. 255. For
details of the administration and the pains suffered by the Christian in this quest
for justice, see the excellent discussion in Yriarte, *Revue des deux mondes,* XV
(1876), 614–17. See also the memorandum inclosed in Holmes to Derby, 1 October
1875; *Turkey No. 2 (1876),* Doc. No. 33. The published document warns against
"a good deal of exaggeration" but suppresses the fact that the author of this description was the Catholic bishop of Mostar, "a very respectable man" who served
"during long years as a parish priest in the Herzegovina" (FO 78/2536, Report
No. 9).

[55] See, for example, the torments of the *rayahs* described by Evans, *op. cit.,* pp.
141–43.

[56] Zohrab to Bulwer, 22 July 1860; *British Consular Reports, 1860,* Doc. No.
14, p. 55. Mackenzie and Irby, *op. cit.,* I, 11.

endless opportunity to the collector to harass the country.[57] In addition, the owner of the land took the third or the half of the crop which legally belonged to him. During the first half of the century the *begs,* feeling themselves in straitened circumstances, imposed additional obligations in the form of work on their *rayahs.* This expedient led to revolts and emigrations, and the subsequent governmental intervention stabilized the peasant obligations at a higher level.[58] In the years immediately preceding 1875, however, the principal complaints of the subject-peoples were directed against tax-gatherers and against the Ottoman officials who had come in after Omer's conquest. In former times when the Christians were under the exclusive control of the *begs,* the local Moslems, in spite of spasmodic violence and steady pressure, were too wise to slay the goose which was laying at least copper eggs. But the tax-farmer passed over the ground like a plague of locusts without thought for the morrow. Bosniacs in the early 'seventies, consequently, were regretting the times gone by.

Socially the lot of the *rayah* had probably been improving after the middle of the century. Financially, both the natives and outside observers agreed, his position was worse because of the mounting burden of taxation and the increased obligations to the lord.[59] But whether or not the net result of the years was a tangible improvement or a retrogression it is difficult to state. In any case the culminating experiences of Bosnia and Hercegovina were a bad harvest in the year 1874, serious difficulties with the tax-gatherers which led to violence on the part of the gendarmes and flight on the part of many of the Christians, and, finally, the return of the refugees and mutual defiance and violence which in the early summer of 1875 flared into open revolt.[60]

The question of the causes of the new revolt which brought in its wake so many troubles and dangers to Europe is perhaps one that

[57] For details of these various taxes, see Yriarte, *Revue des deux mondes,* XV (1876), 606-14; also the memorandum in *Turkey No. 2 (1876),* Doc. No. 33.

[58] Yriarte, *Revue des deux mondes,* XV (1876), 601-5.

[59] Zohrab to Bulwer, 22 July 1860; *British Consular Reports, 1860,* Doc. No. 14, p. 55. Mackenzie and Irby, *op. cit.,* I, 12-14.

[60] Evans, *op. cit.,* pp. 333-34. "Christian Populations in Turkey," *London Quarterly Review,* XLVI, 81. For a description of the alleged violence suffered by the Christians of the Nevesinje area on the eve of the revolt, see *Augsburger Allgemeine Zeitung,* 20 July 1875, p. 3155.

cannot be answered categorically—and need not be. Several observers in the country at the time were unqualifiedly of the opinion that the immediate cause of the insurrection was to be found in rental obligations and more especially in the ruthless taxation suffered by the Christian population.[61] One of the Austrian consuls not far from the scene—although perhaps suspect—was of the same opinion,[62] while in Constantinople the Russian ambassador, who perhaps knew more than any other man of the intrigues in Turkey, was of the opinion that the outbreak was provoked by the irritation of a ruined population.[63] His British colleague's first explanation was likewise resistance to taxation,[64] and a similar view was held by the representative of Austria.[65] At the Sublime Porte, no less, there was a disposition to recognize as its cause the evils and abuses of the Turkish administration.[66]

Misery alone, however, has always provided meager nourishment for rebellion; there must be added to it a sense of injustice and a vision of better days either in the future or in the past. The state of feeling in the insurgent area readily met such requirements. The fact alone that the *rayahs* complained increasingly, that they undoubtedly exaggerated their griefs, would indicate that the ground was prepared for revolt. Moreover, the requisite hatred was there; and, too, glorious memories and tenacious hopes. Ballads recalling the heroic age of the Southern Slavs, ballads lamenting the "damned day of Kossovo," had been for centuries the daily expression of the people. More practical still, they had their own precedent for revolt; they saw the superior advantages of their relatives under Habsburg rule; their leaders had shared during the 'sixties in the ambitious schemes of Prince Michael of Serbia; they lived in closest contact with the free spirits of defiant Montenegro. No one need be surprised

[61] Evans, *op. cit.*, 256, 332–33; Yriarte, *Revue des deux mondes*, XV (1876), 605; Irby, *Living Age*, CXXVII, 648; Mackenzie and Irby, *op. cit.*, I, 15; *New York Herald*, 4 October 1875, p. 3, col. 4, and 13 October, p. 13, col. 1; *The Times* (London), 13 September 1875, p. 8, col. 1.

[62] Report No. 24, Dépolo to Andrássy, Banjaluka, 8 August 1875; SA, Varia Turquie II, 1875.

[63] Report No. 356, Ignatiev to Gorchakov, 22 November/6 December 1875; Count N. P. Ignatiev, "Zapiski Grafa N. P. Ignatieva," *Istoricheski Vyesnik* (St. Petersburg), CXXXV (1914), 828.

[64] Elliot to Derby, Therapia, 13 July; *Turkey No. 2 (1876)*, Doc. No. 5.

[65] Zichy to Andrássy, 7 September, *First Red Book*, Doc. No. 145.

[66] *Ibid.*

that these Christians deliberately laid plans for rebellion.[67] No one need marvel that acts, insignificant in themselves, set fire to northwestern Turkey. It was nothing more than Sancho's proverb over again: "Tell me what you have sown, and I will predict what you will reap."

THE OLD FRIENDS OF THE GRAND TURK

The declining years of the Ottoman Empire had been blessed with two friends, France and Great Britain. It was not, of course, that these two Western powers had any special love for the Turks; the Turk was an important counter in Europe's great game of equilibrium, and he had to be maintained. The fateful year of 1870, however, saw defeated one of those advocates who had rendered Turkey valiant service, particularly in the eighteenth century. After Sedan, France was too concerned with immediate problems, too enveloped in pain, to have energies left for an active part in international relations.

The major role in defending Turkey thenceforth belonged to Britain. All the great European powers were professors of, and believers in, the maintenance of Turkey, but on the Continent it was

[67] Mihailo D. Stojanovic, *Serbia in International Politics* (manuscript dissertation at the University of London, 1930), p. 8. The author, who has used generally inaccessible Serbian sources, states that the preparations for the revolt were begun in 1872 by leaders of previous rebellions. See also Temperley, *Bulgarian and Other Atrocities,* pp. 4–6, for the account preserved, in the form of songs, of the meetings of clan leaders during the winter of 1874–75. Ljubibratich, one of the chieftains in 1875, informed a Western correspondent of his preparations; these are the words placed in his mouth: "The whole thing has been entirely different in its course from our original design. Gusic and I (pointing to his brother-in-law) had at the moment of the outbreak been at work two years on a plan which we have not been able to follow out. All our work was in vain, and we found ourselves compelled to begin anew. . . . . We had prepared for a formidable uprising at a given period—an uprising in which fully 20,000 Herzegovinians were to be engaged. We had made arrangements by which at a given moment the Turk was to find himself displaced, was to see all around his forces and in all his strongholds in the province a standing army of officered [*sic*] and provided with munitions and provisions. We were to constitute a provisional government, with its delegates, and were to publish our programme at a moment when one or two sharp fights at frontier points should have determined our success. The conspiracy was well laid and progressed in a fair fashion, when the troubles and oppressions became so great that the people would wait no longer, and took up arms in irregular fashion" (*New York Herald,* 6 November 1875, p. 4, col. 1–2). It is difficult to accept at face value a story which comes to the reader through the mouth of a semi-Oriental rebel and the pen of a journalist; but, given the evidence from other sources, there was undoubtedly some truth in it.

largely a question of keeping the old creature on its feet until some satisfactory division of its members could be made. The English imagination could not go that far; so long as India was British, the eastern end of the Mediterranean was desirably Turk. However, when the swashbuckling Palmerston passed from the scene, English policy tended to slump back into the ease of splendid isolation. Glad-stone, that giant of ponderous conscience who directed the destinies of Liberal England, was no friend of bold policy abroad. In so far as he was interested in international affairs he was a man of peace, at least in the tepid manner of the nineteenth-century liberal. His moral zeal was largely consumed in fighting the dragon of govern-mental extravagance and in redressing the wrongs of national life. His cabinet went even to the drab extent of accepting an unfavorable verdict in the "Alabama" arbitration, and such meekness seemed indication enough to many people at home and to still more abroad that England had gone into eclipse. Prince Bismarck was alleged to have said that he had lost five years of political life by foolishly thinking that Britain was still a Great Power,[68] and the three em-perors on the Continent formed themselves into a new edition of the Holy Alliance which tacitly appropriated to itself a vague juris-diction over Europe.

Substantial though the internal achievements of the Gladstone ministry were, by-elections foreshadowed the doom of the Liberal regime. In 1874 came the dissolution; the prime minister had wanted to abolish the income tax by curtailing expense for national defense, and when he could not carry out his program a general election was called. Since 1869 the leadership of the Conservative party had been in the hands of Benjamin Disraeli, that unique and most exotic flower produced in the ancient garden of British statesmanship. Jew, sec-ond-rate romancer, coxcomb, in many respects un-British to the core, a man blinded to the distinction between *Wahrheit* and *Dichtung* by his boundless imagination, Disraeli none the less had the courage and the ability to march from ridiculous political beginnings in 1837 to the chief place in his party. In the campaign of 1874 he took his stand on the exact opposite of what his rival had been practicing in the preceding years: he promised repose in domestic legislation and more energy in the conduct of foreign relations. It was a program that had a strong appeal. The Gladstonian reforms had wearied the

[68] Mrs. R. Wemyss, *Memoirs and Letters of the Right Hon. Sir Robert Morier* (London, 1911), II, 330.

land and his diplomacy had depressed it. Britain's response in the election was a Conservative victory with a secure majority in the House of Commons.

The speech from the throne which marked the beginning of the new regime gave a mild warning of the new prime minister's intentions. "I shall not fail," the queen's message read, "to exercise the influence arising from these cordial relations [with other powers] for the maintenance of European peace, and the faithful observance of international obligations."[69] Respect for treaties, an impeccable basis for British policy, Disraeli undoubtedly hoped to maintain. Britain had dictated a large share of the world's treaties, and they sanctified British advantage. The balance of power likewise was a question of vital importance. The events of 1870–71 had, in Disraeli's opinion, upset that balance, and, to his great dissatisfaction, he saw England constrained to follow in the wake of the Continental alliance.[70] But a general resolution and a regret are not in themselves a foreign policy. Disraeli had great ambitions for his country; he wanted it to be powerful and glorious, yet he took up the reins of government with no concrete program to that end. While waiting, Micawber-like, for something to turn up, his interest centered on more appropriations for the army and navy, that highest combination in the international poker of prestige.[71] At the time it would have been easy to suspect the premier of Turcophile leanings, but it would have been difficult to fasten on him the label of a Russophobe. Like all good Englishmen, he had approved the Crimean War to dislodge the Russians from Turkey. Like Gladstone he had none the less shown no zest for continuing the war a year for the dubious advantage of closing the Black Sea to the tsar's warships.[72] In 1870, consequently, when Alexander II overthrew that restriction, Disraeli, although annoyed by the treaty violation, used the occasion only for an attack on Gladstone without expressing his own opinion.[73] As he took office in 1874 Disraeli was anxious about Russia's steady penetration into central Asia, a march which gave promise of bringing the two Great Powers face to face in the East.[74] But in preference to an

[69] *Hansard's Parliamentary Debates,* 3d series, CCXVIII, 22–23 (19 March 1874).

[70] W. F. Monypenny and G. E. Buckle, *The Life of Benjamin Disraeli, Earl of Beaconsfield* (New York, 1913–20), VI, 13; subsequently cited as *Disraeli.*

[71] *Ibid.,* V, 425–26.   [72] *Ibid.,* Vol. IV, chap. 1; V, 136.

[73] *Ibid.,* V, 130, 133–36.   [74] *Ibid.,* V, 409–11.

acceptance of growing friction as a matter of course, the new government invited the tsar to England, and Disraeli sought to promote friendlier relations. Furthermore, in the spring of the following year, when all Europe was thrown into a hysterical scare of renewed Franco-German war, Disraeli turned his thoughts to a Russian alliance as the best means of bridling Germany's reincarnation of "old Bonaparte."[75]

Although Disraeli's cabinet shared his political views and his concern for the balance of European power, its members were more representative of traditional stolidity. Of the two men who were to be intimately associated with the prime minister in handling foreign problems, one, the Earl of Derby, had been an old friend, while the other, the Marquis of Salisbury, had been formerly a difficult colleague and associate. Disraeli's championship of electoral reform in 1867 had produced a deep breach between him and Salisbury. The subsequent years of opposition had not healed the wounds, and the most delicate maneuvers had been required to bring the powerful nobleman back to the India Office where he had served in the previous Conservative regime.[76] Once in the cabinet, Salisbury overcame his animus and worked at peace with his chief.[77] In foreign affairs his long-standing orientation was sympathy for France — a sympathy which, after 1870, meant solid suspicion of Germany.[78] As minister responsible for India he, no less than the prime minister, was disturbed over the advance of Russia in central Asia,[79] but of iron-clad prejudices concerning either Russia or Turkey he exhibited no trace.

Lord Derby, in 1874, according to custom, went back to the Foreign Office, where, as Lord Stanley, he had been installed by his father in 1866 with the frank admission that he was a misfit. The most searching portrait of the foreign minister available as an introduction to his role in the Balkan crisis appeared as that role was assuming a considerable importance:

. . . . The late Lord Derby had a genius for taking up lost causes. The present Lord Derby dislikes no waste of strength so much. The late Lord Derby was a spirited statesman, who rather approved of one-sided enthusiasm. The present Lord Derby, as he told the Glasgow students six years ago, and has told the Edinburgh students now, prefers even "cultivated apathy," or to use his more modern phrase, "a wise but not unkindly scepticism," to anything

---

[75] *Disraeli*, V, 420–22.

[76] *Ibid.*, V, 111, 132, 284–90. Lady Gwendolyn Cecil, *Life of Robert Marquis of Salisbury* (London, 1921–32), II, 20, 43–46; hereafter cited as *Salisbury*.

[77] *Salisbury*, II, 64.   [78] *Ibid.*, II, 32–34.   [79] *Ibid.*, II, 69–71.

like earnestness of the one-sided sort. The late Lord Derby was . . . . a man of fiery eloquence. The present Lord Derby prefers to treat fiery thoughts, like fire itself, as "good servants, but bad masters," and we may admit at once that he quite succeeds in keeping the ardour of his ideas well under control. . . . . In short, we can hardly conceive statesmen at more completely opposite poles of the political world than the late and the present Lord Derby, except, indeed, in this,—that both of them have been in a high degree *manageable* in the hands of a skilful manipulator like Mr. Disraeli, who has known how to carry them with him as he shifted his position. . . . .

Lord Derby himself distrusts every policy which does not look hum-drum. He acts habitually on the theory that if you ever do a big thing, you should make the least of it in the world, and let it pass, if you can, for a small thing. Indeed, he is so habitual a "minimiser," that if he gets hold of a large policy —as in the Suez-Canal case—he pares it down till it seems a small policy; and if he is conscious that he does not intend much . . . . he will confess to all the world that he meant nothing, and loudly avows that it is a very undesirable thing to do what seems to mean something, and yet not mean anything by it. He once suggested that "war with limited liability" ought to be possible,— meaning, we suppose, that it ought to be possible for a State to say, "We will spend so much money and use up such and such a number of regiments or ships in this war, but we will not go beyond this." That has always seemed to us very characteristic of Lord Derby's sobriety of mind, and of his weakness as a politician. He would often like to sink a given amount of capital in a policy, but he would like to be off his bargain when that capital was used up. He forgets that that is just what is impossible, under any sort of popular government. . . . . He tells you very plainly that the political ends he advocates show a balance of advantage, but that the balance is not very great, and that you might easily squander too much energy in securing it. Consequently, his support, though it commands a certain amount of respectful adhesion from the thinking men, is not a great political power. It is the support of a political Laodicean, who thinks it the first of duties to be neither hot nor cold, and indeed he is so temperate that if he acted alone, he would never get up the steam necessary to ensure locomotion. . . . .

Lord Derby's weakness as a statesman is his radical timidity. With all his splendid good sense, his lucid intellect, his wholesome habit of looking steadily at all ideas presented to him, and his tendency to distrust extreme theories of any kind, you can see that he has little or no initiative; that he sees both sides too strongly to believe in either; and that his Conservatism, therefore, is due to that most profound of all sources of Conservatism, the want of any adequate motive-power to induce men to alter what is. But that is almost as dangerous a habit of mind as rashness itself, for any one who has really got to take great resolves. . . . . He is so timid of great professions, that he disavows the only adequate motive for his own policy, and so plays his adversaries' game. There is great wisdom in him of the negative kind, but it is not the kind of wisdom which a great leader wants who is piloting a great Government through stormy seas, and whose duty it is not only to breast the waves, but to raise in his crew the confidence and the courage which can alone bring them safely through.[80]

[80] "Lord Derby," *Spectator*, 25 December 1875, pp. 1616–17.

In 1875 the outlook of the British cabinet, which had proposed more energy in foreign relations, was clouded by the fact that the league of the three Continental emperors had quietly appropriated the direction of Europe. Particularly for the prime minister was this "tripartite confederacy" an unnatural alliance incompatible with England's "due and natural influence in the government of the world."[81] Feeling unable to defy the powerful combination, Disraeli desired to break it up by the subtle solvent of wooing. For almost a generation he had been a partisan of friendship with France, but his experiences with Napoleon III and then the Franco-Prussian War had led him to the belief that, in spite of misgivings as to Bismarckian policy, Britain was more naturally akin to Germany.[82] Hence the logical way to end the league was to lure Emperor William and his chancellor from it. In February, Disraeli spread his honeyed bait before the German ambassador. Denouncing France as an ally, the premier expressed a stirring conviction that Germany was the only state with whom England could go hand in hand; and, with ardor rising, he went so far as to deplore his country's failure to join Prussia in the war of 1870. For the future, he assured the ambassador, Berlin could count on London; the same interests, the same outlook would lead the two nations in the same direction.[83] Before this ambitious plan could bring results, the "war scare" of May had overcast the skies and the old suspicions of Bismarck returned in full force to Disraeli's mind. Casting aside the idea of a special understanding with Germany, the prime minister turned to the possibilities of a Russian alliance, and supported the tsar's peace remonstrances in Berlin.[84] As the clouds began to dissipate, the Russian ambassador could detect a marked current of public opinion in London favorable to strengthening relations with the tsar's government. Disraeli himself reiterated this inclination and again made a bid for clearing up the problems of central Asia.[85] But this hope was to be disappointed.

---

[81] Disraeli to Manners, 7 June 1876; *Disraeli*, VI, 31.   [82] *Ibid.*, V, 126.

[83] Winifred Taffs, "The War Scare of 1875," *The Slavonic Review*, IX (1930), 341, quoting unpublished dispatch from Münster to Bismarck, 28 February 1875. Disraeli had in the previous month been pleased at Bismarck's friendly attitude toward the new government (*Disraeli*, V, 420).

[84] *Disraeli*, V, 421–22.

[85] Shuvalov to Alexander II, London, 13 May; R. W. Seton-Watson, "Russo-British Relations during the Eastern Crisis," *Slavonic Review*, III, 424–25. British opinion toward Russia had undergone considerable modification since

As soon as the revolt of the sultan's *rayahs* loomed large on the horizon, London—and the rest of Europe—saw that the imperial league not only had survived the war scare but intended to solve the new Balkan problem in spite of the old words about non-intervention in Turkey.

If the years had done much to soften the asperity of British feeling toward Russia, they had also gnawed away at the old conviction of unqualified support of the dynasty of Othman. The degradation, the tyranny, the extravagances rampant in Turkey had taken their toll of British support. Even Lord Derby budged far enough from inaction to believe, in the 'sixties, that the breakup of Turkey might be a matter of no distant time.[86] Still, despite the evaporation of Crimean sentimentality, there remained India and its routes of communication as anchors to British consideration. On the eve of the Hercegovinian revolt the parlous state of the Turkish Empire was brought up for discussion in the House of Commons, and, although private members vigorously indulged their feeling of reprobation and called for interference, the response from the treasury bench was traditional. The Undersecretary for Foreign Affairs left no doubt as to official opinion: treaty obligation forbade interference in Turkey no less than did general principle. Apologizing for Turkish misrule on the ground of the complexity of the problem, the Undersecretary claimed that there was evidence of progress and assured his listeners that the British government continued to hope for a strong Turkey working out its own salvation, a Turkey free from the collective and separate interference of the great states of Europe.[87]

1856. Distrust flared up again when the tsar denounced the Black Sea restrictions of the Paris treaty, but even so neither government nor responsible leaders of the opposition in 1870 felt the prohibition to be an important factor in keeping Russia out of Turkey. Exception was taken more to the form than the content of the change. On the heels of the new arrangement in the following spring, however, came the Russian advance in Asia, an action which did much in England to revive the old hostility. Nevertheless, in 1874 the British had shown enough desire for a peaceful settlement to invite the tsar to London for a discussion. Reassuring promises were made and the improved relations were signalized by the marriage of the Duke of Edinburgh, second son of Queen Victoria, to the tsar's daughter Marie. (George Carslake Thompson, *Public Opinion and Lord Beaconsfield, 1875-1880* [London, 1886], I, 204-208.)

[86] Thompson, *op. cit.,* I, 204.

[87] *Hansard's Parliamentary Debates,* 3d series, CCXXV, 181-219. The debate took place on 18 June.

THE MOST INTERESTED NEIGHBOR

The neighbor of the ailing Turk most directly interested in his condition was Austria-Hungary. This interest of the Dual Monarchy, with a tumultuous story behind it, had become one of its most vital concerns.

From the first appearance of the Moslem hordes on the Danube, the Habsburgs had suffered the misfortunes of their geographical position and perhaps, too, of their character. Occupying the political watershed of Europe, they were unable for centuries to pursue a consistent policy. Exigencies in the west alternated so regularly with problems in the east that the harassed forces of the empire could never be concentrated long enough to render a task well done. Habsburg Balkan policy, consequently, formed a long chain of misadventures, some imposed, some invited by neglected opportunity, some precipitated by lack of plan. One need only recall the failure to exploit the victories of Prince Eugene of Savoy, the abandonment of Beograd in 1739, the discordant policies of Maria Theresa and her son Joseph, and, finally, the hesitations and blunders of the Crimean War.

The defeat of 1866 should have settled at last the monarchy's vexing problem of orientation. The Italian possessions were gone— and, more important still, gone too was the age-old hegemony of central Europe. The time had arrived to turn eastward, and there were influential voices calling in that direction; but Emperor Francis Joseph and Beust, his German chancellor, heard only the siren call of revenge. For five years more the Orient was neglected, while lively hopes inspired doubtful schemes. The great event of 1871 eventually destroyed both schemes and hope; the aging realm of the Habsburgs had no further prospect of challenging the might of united Germany. No one recognized this fact more plainly than the sovereign and the minister who had hoped and planned. The critical situation of the Danubian empire demanded reconciliation with Berlin, and, with heavy heart, Francis Joseph bowed before the inevitable. Beust began the preparations; but Beust was no man to inspire confidence in the Iron Chancellor of Germany, and so he had to go. In November 1871, Count Julius Andrássy moved into the Ballhausplatz as the common minister for foreign affairs.[88]

[88] Eduard von Wertheimer, *Graf Julius Andrássy, Sein Leben und Seine Zeit* (Stuttgart, 1910–13), I, 630–34; hereafter cited as *Andrássy*. This work is the "standard biography" of Andrássy. It contains invaluable information but it includes so much conventional adulation that it does considerable violence to truth.

It was no simple task that Count Andrássy took over. In the international setting the Dual Monarchy was in an unenviable position. The waverings of the Hofburg during the Crimean War had alienated Russia without winning a friend in the West; defeat in Italy had been only a prelude to a more humiliating defeat in Germany; and there was no clear-cut policy with regard to the Balkan problem. In internal affairs the polyglot empire was being increasingly embarrassed by the racial problem. The murmur of the dissatisfied nationalities was ever rising in volume while the mediocre-minded sovereign held tenaciously to things as they were because they were as they were. Invading the realms of both internal and external affairs was the problem of the Southern Slavs. These people of like language and supposedly kindred racial stock found themselves fortuitously distributed among several different political jurisdictions. Their developing sense of unity constituted one of the most vital questions for the empire; the possibility that this problem had in it the seeds of doom for Austria-Hungary had already been recognized. The union of these people within the bounds of the Habsburg state meant a dangerous expansion. Their union under the banner of some Piedmont of the Balkans meant, in turn, a fatal dismemberment.

The Austro-Hungarian foreign minister was a Magyar. That fact had shaped his previous career—rebel in 1848, refugee and condemned exile, negotiator of the *Ausgleich* of 1867 after his pardon, and minister-president of Hungary—and that fact was destined to dominate his conduct of Austro-Hungarian foreign relations. His inaugural statement was all that Europe could expect. Inspired by the vitality of the empire and convinced of the clarity of its interests, he proclaimed a program of internal development. It was a policy, he stated, which repudiated the dubious advantages of even the most successful war, of any territorial expansion.[89]

This declaration by Andrássy, meant for public circulation in Europe, naturally did not indicate his specific concerns nor reveal the ways and means which the minister had in mind. The problem of the Slav was of necessity the major preoccupation of the new Hungarian policy-maker. Neither his patriotism as a Magyar nor his personal

---

[89] Andrássy to the imperial and royal missions abroad, 23 November 1871; Austro-Hungarian Monarchy, *Ministerium des k. und k. Hauses und des äussern, Auswärtige Angelegenheiten, Correspondenzen des kais. und kön. gemeinsamen Ministeriums des äussern, no. 6 (vom November 1871 bis September 1872)* (Vienna, 1872), Doc. No. 1.

experiences could permit him to forget his animus toward and his fear of the lumbering Russian bear. Yet his outlook was not determined alone by the past. The tsar's repudiation of disagreeable treaty provisions in 1870 had announced a new forward policy in the Near East;[90] the doctrinaire sentiment of Pan-Slavism was a rising challenge to Austro-Hungarian control over their own Slavs as well as a challenge to imperative Austro-Hungarian influence in the adjacent lands of Turkey. Andrássy had two plans of procedure to meet the Slavic menace. His first, since he was no enemy of Berlin, was a close understanding with Germany. The Dual Monarchy, he knew well, needed the support of the first power of Europe if it should come to a reckoning with Russia, and he pushed his imperial master forward toward the painful reconciliation with Emperor William.[91]

The minister's second plan was a more active role in the Balkans. He had begun years before to resent Russia's pretensions to being the only protector of the Christian populations of Turkey. As he participated in the Suez Canal festivities in 1869 it had pained him to see that Austria-Hungary, whose peoples had poured out more blood than any other in resisting the Turks, had no prestige in the East and that no one thought of the Habsburg state as a vitally interested power when discussing Turkey.[92] Knowing well the danger that the Balkan Christians, and especially the Slavs, might be brought within the orbit of Russian influence, Andrássy sought to persuade these unfortunate people that their nearest and most unselfish friend was in Vienna.[93] At every opportunity he tried to promote the prestige of the monarchy and to win the gratitude of the sultan's Slavs by furthering their economic interests. Since the Orthodox Christians had a natural leaning toward Holy Russia, it was especially desirable for Catholic Austria-Hungary to offset that sentiment by fostering Latin interests over the frontier. This policy had been begun long before.

[90] Andrássy had been a bitter opponent of Beust in the latter's inclination to give way generally to Russia's action (*Andrássy*, I, 618–19).

[91] The outcome of this program—the league of the three emperors—will be discussed subsequently. Andrássy also nurtured the idea of a close understanding with England as a bulwark against French or Russian attack and as a means of preventing an alliance, fatal to Austria-Hungary, between Russia and Germany (*Andrássy*, II, 14–18).

[92] *Andrássy*, I, 457–58.

[93] *Ibid.*, II, 94–95; Elliot, *Some Revolutions*, p. 203; General H. L. von Schweinitz, *Denkwürdigkeiten des Botschafters General v. Schweinitz* (Berlin, 1927), I, 296–97.

Through a consulate established in Sarajevo in 1850 and a seminary set up some years later, Vienna had been able in numerous ways to play the patron of Bosnian Catholics.[94] Andrássy, more conscious than his predecessors of the possibilities of such a program, continued it. He did not hesitate to confess that he was going to use secret service money for schools and religious establishments in Bosnia among the Latin Christians in order to have as much influence over them as Russia had over the Orthodox. A portion of these funds evidently went to buy carriages for the higher Catholic clergymen, since the minister had found it highly displeasing that these notables should ride on donkeys while their Orthodox rivals enjoyed more elegant transportation.[95]

This prestige policy, however, Andrássy did not pursue as a direct preparation for an eventual annexation of Bosnia and Hercegovina. In repudiating a desire for expansion, the new minister was at least halfway honest. As one of the proud Magyars who had dealt ruthlessly with the Serbs and Croats of Hungary, he had the common view of his nation that the number of Slavs in the empire was already too great. His reasoned opinion, too, formed always with Russian maneuvers in mind, was that Turkish authority should be strong and that a good understanding should prevail between Ballplatz and Sublime Porte.[96]

But those were general views which Andrássy had not always held, and they also were views subject to change should circumstances so suggest. The complicating factor was Serbia. Years before it had been understood in Vienna and Budapest that the vital interests of the Habsburg monarchy forbade Serbia's becoming a Slavic outpost of Russia. Beust, despite his preoccupations in Germany, had appreciated the necessity for patronizing Serbia and had rendered Prince Michael considerable service.[97] During his regime as chancellor,

---

[94] Evans, *Through Bosnia on Foot,* pp. 181–82.

[95] Report No. 343, Buchanan to Derby, Vienna, 15 October 1875; FO 7/852.

[96] *Andrássy,* II, 52.

[97] For details of Beust's attitude and policy toward Serbia, see Austro-Hungarian Monarchy, *Ministerium des k. und k. Hauses und des äussern, Auswärtige Angelegenheiten, Correspondenzen des kaiserlich-königlichen Ministeriums des äussern, no. 1, vom November 1866 bis Ende 1867* (Vienna, 1868) ; also *ibid., no. 2, vom Januar bis November 1868* (Vienna, 1868). See Count Friedrich Ferdinand von Beust, *Trois quarts de siècle, mémoires du comte de Beust* (Paris, 1888), Vol. II, chap. vi (English translation by Baron Henry de Worms, *The Memoirs of Friedrich Ferdinand Count von Beust* [London, 1887], Vol. II, chap. xxxvii).

Beust had been converted to the idea of securing for the ambitious Michael the administration of the coveted land of Bosnia and Hercegovina as a means of fostering his sympathetic attachment to Vienna, and, apparently, the suggestion had been presented directly to the prince.[98]

Andrássy, influenced for the time by a pro-Serb consul in Beograd, shared the view that friendly relations were a necessity. The Hungarian, however, was not so generous as his German predecessor. He wanted to buy the good-will of Beograd and Cetinje with the eastern half of the provinces and acquire the remainder for Austria-Hungary.[99] He would accomplish this expansion, he told one of the Austrian generals in the month of his circular, not by war but *"in friedlicher Weise"*[100]—a cession by Turkey in exchange for protection against foreign attack.[101] The project in Andrássy's mind provided a stone which he could throw at two vultures. Not only was Michael to be won but an important domestic problem was to be settled. The Croats no less than the Serbs made pretentious claims to Bosnia and Hercegovina; should the latter acquire a portion of those lands, the former, he hoped, would be so provoked that there would be little likelihood of a Serbo-Croat union against Hungary.[102]

There were several reasons why this attractive plan fell through. When it was presented to the Serbs in 1870, they, believing that the whole of Bosnia and Hercegovina was virtually theirs, would not discuss a partition.[103] Andrássy himself seems to have been discouraged by the European consequences which the projected action might entail.[104] But the most probable explanation of its failure is to be found in the growing dissatisfaction felt in Vienna and Budapest with the Serbs. For their part the Serbs naturally felt no little apprehension when the project of Austrian expansion to the south was revealed; the Austrians, on the other hand, could only be irritated that the little principality, in its stubborn refusal, had revealed the

[98] R. W. Seton-Watson, "Les Relations de l'Autriche-Hongrie et de la Serbie entre 1868 et 1874," *Le Monde slave*, February 1926, pp. 215–16.

[99] *Andrássy*, I, 461.

[100] Anton von Mollinary, *Sechsundvierzig Jahre im österreich-ungarischen Heere, 1833–1879* (Zürich, 1905), II, 287. Wertheimer (I, 462 n.) would have it that Andrássy considered this plan in 1869 and that *"Im Jahre 1870 war nicht mehr die Rede davon";* this is erroneous.

[101] *Andrássy*, I, 461–62.   [102] *Ibid.*, I, 461.

[103] Haumant, *La Formation de la Yougoslavie*, p. 412.

[104] *Andrássy*, I, 462.

persistence of its own inflated hopes of expansion. Apprehension alone would have driven the Serbs toward Russia, but the agents of the tsar accelerated their approach. In the summer of 1871 they disciplined Serbia for her Austrian leanings[105] by placing Montenegro first on the patronage list; and the action was eminently effective. The Beograd politicians felt the pressure of Slavic opinion, and their reversal of position was heralded in October by a visit of Prince Milan, Michael's successor, to Russia. The Austrian agent in Beograd had soon to conclude that Serbia had become the blind instrument of Russian policy and was to be treated as such.[106] Such sympathy as Andrássy might have had for the Serbs was evaporated by the warmth of Serbo-Russian relations.[107] In his conversations with the Russian chancellor in 1872 he made no secret of his annoyance with the "Greater Serbia" idea nurtured in Beograd,[108] and, having failed through persuasion and offers of Turkey's territory to induce the Serbs to abandon their megalomaniac dreams, he was prepared to enforce his own decision. Should Serbia make an aggressive step toward Bosnia, the power of the Dual Monarchy would descend on her. Bitterly he spoke to the German ambassador of Russia's attempt to sponsor the Christians of Turkey; Serbs and all the others, he impatiently insisted, had to learn that they should lean on Austria-Hungary, that they could do nothing without her.[109]

In the following year, 1873, the rift in the lute of Austro-Serb relations was somewhat patched up. The new prime minister of Serbia and then the prince himself went to Vienna—trips at least reminiscent of the proverbial journey to Canossa—and the explanations and promises there made gave to Andrássy considerable satisfaction.[110] But the chief of the Ballplatz was not disarmed. Pan-Slavic agitation was still a dangerous reality, and Austria-Hungary

[105] For details of the good relations existing between Austria-Hungary and Serbia and how they were undermined in 1870 and later, see Slobodan Jovanović, "Serbia in the Early 'Seventies," Slavonic Review, IV (December 1925), 385–87. See also Vaso Trivanovitch, "Serbia, Russia, and Austria during the Rule of Milan Obrenovich, 1868–78," The Journal of Modern History, III (September 1931), 417–20.

[106] Seton-Watson, Le Monde slave, May 1926.

[107] Andrássy, II, 42–43; Seton-Watson, Le Monde slave, August 1926, pp. 273–76; Jovanović, Slavonic Review, IV, 387.

[108] A. Meyendorff, "Conversations of Gorchakov, Andrássy and Bismarck in 1872," Slavonic Review, VIII (December 1929), 402–403.

[109] Schweinitz, Denkwürdigkeiten, I, 296–97.

[110] Seton-Watson, Le Monde slave, I (August 1926), 278–88; Trivanovitch, Journal of Modern History, III, 432; Jovanović, Slavonic Review, IV, 388.

could not without jeopardizing its existence permit Serbia to ar-
rogate unto itself the role of the Piedmont of the Balkans. In the
years following the failure of his partition scheme Andrássy apparently returned to the conventional Magyar conviction that the empire could not profitably annex more Slavs. In 1875, consequently,
it may be assumed that he did not wish to acquire Bosnia and Hercegovina and throw on the European table the dozing demon of the old
Eastern question. An occupation, however, was not entirely excluded from his plans: if Serbia and Montenegro made a move in
that direction, he was prepared to go in.[111]

Quite different from the view of the foreign minister was the
long-standing opinion held in high military circles. In 1856 Field
Marshal Radetzky had proposed the occupation of Bosnia and Hercegovina, and following him one leading commander after another
had pointed out the—to them—pressing necessity for securing a
proper hinterland for the shoestring of Dalmatia.[112] Various motives other than considerations of defense inspired the agitation.
After the defeats of 1859 and 1866 Austrian military prestige was
at a low level—and an easy march into northwestern Turkey gave
promise of helping to refurbish the faded laurels. Internal political
desires also had a share. The Slavic population, hoping for a place
of equality within the empire, naturally felt that the more Slav subjects Francis Joseph had the better the chance of autonomous position. At the same time the Austrian conservatives hoped that the
annexation might lead to a destruction of the hated *Ausgleich* which
had given the Magyars such sweeping powers.

The desires of the expansionists found a genial response in the
Vienna Hofburg. As early as 1866, if not earlier, the emperor had
shown inclinations of his own in that direction. Shortly after peace
was made Bismarck allegedly offered German support for compensation in the south, but, whether that be true or not, the general commanding the frontier received orders to be ready to march into
Bosnia in the following spring.[113] Bismarck's suggestion, together
with a comparable one that apparently came from Napoleon III in

[111] *Andrássy*, II, 260.

[112] August Fournier, *Wie Wir zu Bosnien Kamen* (Vienna, 1909), p. 4; *Andrássy*, II, 256–57; Edmund von Glaise-Horstenau, *Franz Josephs Weggefährte,
das Leben des Generalstabschefs Beck, nach seinen Aufzeichnungen und hinterlassenen Dokumenten* (Vienna, 1930), pp. 179, 184–85; Mollinary, *op. cit.*, II,
285–87.

[113] Fournier, *op. cit.*, p. 4.

the following year,[114] was forestalled by the civilians, Beust and Andrássy; but Francis Joseph did not waver. In the spring of 1875 emperor and generals secretly contrived a scheme that had an ominous look: After a visit to the king of Italy, Francis Joseph was to make an extensive tour of Dalmatia. Baron Mollinary, the commanding officer in Croatia, learned of this prospect one day in March; on the palace steps he met three of his important colleagues, including Baron Rodich, the governor of Dalmatia, who announced to him with unconcealed joy that they had just completed the plans with his majesty for the journey. The surprised Mollinary, according to his own account, could scarcely believe his ears. When convinced, he exclaimed, *"Dann brennt's"* ("Then there's going to be fire"). He reminded his fellow officers of the smoldering embers over the frontier which needed little fanning to burst into blood-consuming flames, and he warned them of the dangers involved in the emperor's visit. The plotters merely smiled; their satisfaction was not entirely inspired by the thought that Francis Joseph was going to make an interesting journey.[115]

During thirty-three strenuous days the imperial party toured the beautiful coastland of the Adriatic while every interested individual hoped for the realization of his own particular wishes. The festivities seemed to the local British consul a Slavic celebration,[116] and less suspicious witnesses indicated a profound impression made on the Southern Slavs, regardless of political affiliation. For many Montenegrins the visit of the emperor to Dalmatia and his brief excursion into their own land was a culmination of Austria's genial interest and protection, and Prince Nicholas and his retainers received their great guest—so it is recorded—with requests for an Austrian occupation of Bosnia.[117] Turkey's Slavs and the Serbs saw that of the three great tsars in Constantinople, Moscow, and Vienna, the last was the nearest and the greatest.[118]

[114] Seton-Watson, *Le Monde slave,* I (1926), 215-16.

[115] Mollinary, *op. cit.,* II, 281-82.

[116] ". . . . The local demonstration, such as it was, appeared to me,—as also to many others,—thoroughly Slavish; the imperial visit having been, so to speak—utilized to express the popular national feeling of Pan Slavism; supreme in these parts. . . . ." (Political Report No. 5, Taylor to Derby, 15 May 1875; FO 7/860).

[117] Glaise-Horstenau, *Franz Josephs Weggefährte,* pp. 181-83; Fournier, *op. cit.,* p. 14.

[118] Sturdza to Rumanian foreign minister, Beograd, 17 June; *Aus dem Leben König Karls von Rumänien* (Stuttgart, 1894-1900), II, 443.

Back in Vienna in July, after the insurrection in Hercegovina had begun, Francis Joseph called in General Mollinary and informed him that the disturbance might compel an occupation of Bosnia. If Turkish authority failed, the emperor explained, the provinces should fall into none but Austrian hands.[119]

In the same days there was no doubt in the mind of the German ambassador. In his opinion the Austrians, through teasing the Turks and cajoling the Slavs, had created the impression that the Habsburg Empire was going to drive out the Moslems. Thirty-three days of imperial pageantry in Dalmatia could be interpreted by these illiterate people in only one way. The ambassador expressed his conclusion in an old proverb:

> "The donkey gave the dam a blow,
> And then there came an overflow."[120]

THE INSATIABLE BEAR

The most portentous shadow over declining Turkey was that of the Russian bear. Seemingly the gamut of those forces which shape history had turned Russia to the south and decreed hostility to the Turk. Geography had had its share; no barrier stood between the seat of Muscovy and the Black Sea; the slow-moving rivers made natural highways to the south, highways across which the Ottomans had established themselves. Economic interest, in turn, followed the dictates of geography; more than a thousand years before 1875 the Russians had attacked Constantinople because the masters of Byzantium had impeded their trade. Then religion had entered the field to add its attractive power. The faith of Byzantium had returned home with the early traders of Russia, and later, when Santa Sophia became a mosque, there fell to the Orthodox soul of Russia the obligation to protect and redeem those brothers in Christ who suffered the rule of the Moslem. And, finally, out of the womb of fate there came still another strong force to pull in the old direction.

This new force was the conviction that many of the subject peoples of the Grand Turk were brothers of the Russians not only

[119] Mollinary, op. cit., II, 288.

[120] Schweinitz to Radowitz, Vienna, 4 August; Joseph Maria von Radowitz, Aufzeichnungen und Erinnerungen aus dem Leben des Botschafters Joseph Maria von Radowitz (Berlin, 1925), I, 334.

in faith but also in blood. This belief, which seemed to the Russo-phobes of the eighteen-seventies to be a veritable wolf from the steppes of Russia, had quite innocent origins. Slavic racial con-ciousness and attempts at Slavic unity go far back into the past. If the reader is so inclined, he may see some such manifestations in the seventh-century ephemeral kingdom of Samo the Frank, in the title "King of the Slavs" taken by a tenth-century king in Poland, in the manifestoes of the Hussite wars, to say nothing of the poems and chronicles of the various peoples of the group.[121] These early re-minders of a community of blood came largely from non-Russian Slavs.[122] Indeed, the first apostle of Slavic unity who preached his doctrine on the great plains of the north was sent to Siberia for his zeal. This ardent missionary was a certain George Križanić, a na-tive of Bosnia, born in the early years of the seventeenth century. Partisan of religious conciliation, he wanted the quarrel between Latin and Greek Christian to be put into the background, and he called on the Russian tsar to save the five branches of the great Slav family who languished in foreign subjugation.[123] Križanić was a Roman Catholic who impoliticly informed the tsar that Russia could gain much by an understanding with the West; other Serbs, his contemporaries and successors, appealed to the great sovereign to aid them in resisting the aggressive Latins.

It has been claimed that Peter the Great read the memorial of the unfortunate Bosnian missionary. Whether that be true or not, it is certain that the bizarre history, *The Kingdom of the Slavs,* by the Dalmatian Orbini, a book that sang the greatness of the race, struck the fancy of that vigorous ruler.[124] Peter's interest in the Slavs, however, went beyond idle curiosity as to their origin; he had prac-tical ends to be achieved for Russia. In 1711, as he renewed his war on Turkey, he addressed an appeal to the Christians of the Balkan peninsula to join him in fighting for faith and freedom; and it is noteworthy that his summons to revolt reminded many of these people of their Slavic blood and former glories.[125]

[121] Louis Leger, *Le Panslavisme et l'intérêt français* (Paris, 1917), pp. 35–56.

[122] Alfred Fischel, *Der Panslavismus bis zum Weltkrieg* (Stuttgart and Berlin, 1919), pp. 14–19.

[123] Leger, *op. cit.,* pp. 58–70; Fischel, *op. cit.,* pp. 20–22; Haumant, *La Formation de la Yougoslavie,* pp. 144–45.

[124] Leger, *op. cit.,* p. 71; Haumant, *op. cit.,* p. 131; Fischel, *op. cit.,* p. 22.

[125] Fischel, *op. cit.,* pp. 22–23; Leger, *op. cit.,* pp. 74 ff.

The plans and work of Peter the Great were, in spite of his gestures, more imperial than Pan-Slavic. The same may be said of those of his successor, Catherine II. Both had foremost in mind the interests of the Russian state; both hoped to stir the Orthodox subjects of the sultan to revolt for Russian ends; both made special pleas to the Southern Slavs only incidentally. Russian opinion still saw the Balkan peoples primarily as participants in the same faith, not as representatives of a common race. Had Catherine had any special interest in saving the Southern Slavs she would nót have laid plans for a restored Byzantium nor would she have negotiated with Joseph II of Austria for a partition of the Balkan peninsula. The first stirrings of national awakening in the eighteenth century touched eastern Europe and inspired a fairly concrete Pan-Slavic program; but, so far as Russia was concerned, racial consciousness was essentially a product of the nationalistic nineteenth century. This newborn sentiment at home took the forms of Slavophilism and ruthless Russification, and transcended political boundaries as Pan-Slavism.

The aid rendered by Russia to the revolting Serbs in 1806 gave an impetus to the growing idea of Slavic kinship, and in the next generation each successive arrangement between tsar and sultan prescribed some benefits, albeit meager at times, for these Southern Slavs. Russia emerged from the Napoleonic wars strong and self-conscious. National glory, romanticism, the new-born interest throughout Europe in history—all inspired in the Russians a lively interest in their race and their kindred. Several Russian professors became interested in Slavic antiquities, and in 1826 three chairs of Slavic studies were established at Russian universities to carry on the scientific work which had been initiated by distinguished Western Slavs.[126] The new enthusiasm was by no means limited to the intelligentsia; soldiers had come back from the western wars inspired by the same sentiment, and in Kiev they organized a lodge called the Society of the United Slavs. The advent of Nicholas I and the political crisis which accompanied that event, however, brought an end to unofficial activity in Russia. The new tsar looked with suspicious eyes on Pan-Slavic ideology. It was tainted with liberalism and it gave promise, to his way of thinking, of jeopardizing purely Russian nationality on which he laid so much worth. During his reign the Slavic sentiment which was flourishing in Russia was essentially

126 Fischel, op. cit., pp. 25–52; Leger, op. cit., pp. 114–24; E. L. Mijatovics, "Panslavism: Its Rise and Decline," Fortnightly Review, XX (1873), 96–97.

non-political in its expression. A new secret Slavic organization, the Society of Cyril and Methodius, was organized in 1845. This fraternity had nebulous dreams of a loose association of free Slavic peoples; but before it could begin its activity the merciless hand of the autocrat fell upon it.[127]

The reverse suffered by Russia in the Crimean War dimmed considerably the prestige enjoyed by the great free state among the subjected Western and Southern Slavs. At home, none the less, the Slavic movement was pushed forward with renewed zeal. In 1857 a new society was organized in Moscow, the Slavic Welfare Committee, whose work was the promotion of the idea of unity and of the fortunes of fellow Slavs, especially those below the Danube. The more generous regime of Alexander II approved the organization and its aims; indeed, it was placed under the control of the Asiatic Department of the Foreign Office. The tsarevich was its patron and the tsarina a contributor to it.[128] The most famous of the activities of the Slavic enthusiasts in Russia was the organization under imperial favor of an ethnographic congress in Moscow in 1867 and the convocation of representatives of all the branches of the race— except the refractory Poles. There were shadows over the festive gathering: the Polish problem was an embarrassment; language difficulties, religious differences, and intraracial nationalism dampened the enthusiasm. Still, the gathering in Moscow, despite its difficulties, was a material impetus to Pan-Slavism in Russian society.[129]

During the next years branches of the Moscow society were established and the work for Slavic welfare and unity marched on. Motives for the gifts and labors were various: some participants were generous enthusiasts; some were enemies of the Occident; some were apostles of Orthodoxy; some were covert champions of Russian imperialism. All those motives, however, sanctioned a propaganda of words and deeds among the Southern Slavs. Pamphlets and periodicals were issued to carry the gospel a id, more practical still, Russian

[127] Fischel, op. cit., pp. 168–208; Thomas G. Masaryk, The Spirit of Russia, Studies in History, Literature, and Philosophy (London, 1919), I, 307–8.

[128] Fischel, op. cit., pp. 368 ff.

[129] Fischel, op. cit., pp. 381–94; Leger, op. cit., pp. 210–49; Mijatovics (Miyatovich), Fortnightly Review, XX, 109–10 (an anti-Russian account written by the English wife of a Serb politician). The Western world was apprised of the congress by the vitriolic pen of Julian Klaczko, a Lithuanian Jew who had transformed himself into a Polish Catholic: "Le Congrès de Moscou et la propagande panslaviste," Revue des deux mondes, 1 September 1867, pp. 132–81.

money was freely given for schools and churches and for scholarships in Russian institutions of learning.[130]

The years 1870 and 1871 saw the appearance of two books in Russia which articulated the faith and hopes of Pan-Slavism. The first, entitled *Opinion on the Eastern Question,* was written by General Rostislav Fadeiev, one of the leading supporters of the cause. This undiplomatic soldier made no attempt to conceal his innermost convictions. The old Eastern question, in his mind, had become a Slavic question, and so far as Russia was concerned it was a question of advancing to the leadership of a united race or of being driven back into Asia. He pictured an eventual confederation of the Slavs; he urged a more generous support of those cultural activities which in the meantime would bind the branches of the great family together. But his theme was a more practical one. The chief enemy of Slavdom, the barrier to imperative advance in Turkey, Fadeiev insisted, was Austria. The road to Constantinople, consequently, went by way of Vienna; the only choice for the ruler of all the Russias was to advance to the Adriatic or retire behind the Dniester.[131]

The second elaborate statement of the credo of Pan-Slavism was that of Nicholas Danilevski, student of fishes and dreamer of the eternal laws that govern men. Taking his stand on the belief in a cycle of successive civilizations and on the current Slavophil ideas about the West, Danilevski argued at considerable length the implications of the title of his book, *Russia and Europe.* Europe, he vehemently claimed, was not a geographic continent but the territory of a senile and rotting Germano-Romanic culture. Russia had nothing to do with its feudalism, its bourgeois evolution, or its false forms of Christianity, which in Protestantism was a negation of religion and in Catholicism was a product of lies, pride, and ignorance. European culture was not a general culture of mankind; it was merely one of the series in the world's history—the one which had supplanted

[130] Mijatovics, *op. cit.,* pp. 105–7; Arthur May Hyde, *A Diplomatic History of Bulgaria from 1870 to 1886* (Urbana, 1931), pp. 37–39; Michel Lhéritier, *Histoire diplomatique de la Grèce de 1821 à nos jours* (Paris, 1925), III, 322. The distinguished Bulgarian statesman, Stambulov, for example, applied to the Asiatic Department of the Russian Foreign Office for financial aid to study in Russia and received a scholarship established by the tsarina (A. Hulme Beaman, *M. Stambuloff* [London, 1895], p. 20). Masaryk (*op. cit.,* I, 314, note 1) claims that the chief object in launching the committee was to combat Roman Catholic activities in the Balkans.

[131] Fischel (*op. cit.,* pp. 400–4) gives an extended summary of Fadeiev's arguments.

the ancient, the one which was destined to be eclipsed by that of the Slavs. Danilevski's study of history gave him the laws governing these culture entities: Every race, indicated by a language or a group of related languages, forms such an entity. The civilization of each type, worked out by each according to its own nature without being able to draw on other groups, can develop only when the people who form it are free. This civilization reaches its greatest fullness, its greatest richness, when it has varied ethnographic elements and when these are joined in a confederation rather than swallowed up in one political whole. The cycle of a civilization is like that of a plant: after a period of growth comes a period of bloom and fruit which is relatively short and which leaves the organism used up. Europe's cycle, in the opinion of the impassioned Danilevski, was approaching its exhaustion. It had reached its peak in the sixteenth and seventeenth centuries; the achievements of the nineteenth century were merely the fruits that betokened the autumn season and the winter of extinction.

After examining the characteristics of the Slavs, Danilevski concluded that they formed a cultural type of their own, a type in many ways differentiated from the European and superior in its possibilities. The Eastern question had been fundamentally a struggle between the Germano-Romanic and the Graeco-Slavic civilizations; the role of the Turks had been an unwitting protection of Orthodoxy against the predatory Latin West. As the Ottoman Empire weakened, the Europeans renewed the attack, bent on further subjecting the Slavs and hindering the evolution of their cultural and political power. With the appearance of an independent Slav state, the destiny-prescribed service of the Moslems was at an end; the empire of Philip and Constantine had been resurrected on the plains of mighty Russia by Catherine the Great. After that time Turkey did not serve the purposes of destiny; its former defense of the Balkans became only pointless subjection. Slavdom's real struggle, however, Danilevski saw, as did Fadeiev, in the opposition of the West. Only with the Crimean War had this fundamental clash become apparent. The settlement of that antagonism he believed to be impending. The Slavs were faced with the question of their fate: were they to advance into their independent cultural entity, or were they to remain a vassal race? His answer was a stirring call for Slavdom to throw all its energy into the fight.

The highest development of the Slavic cycle, Danilevski continued, demanded a confederation of all the families of the race. Political union was as necessary as spiritual union if the Slavs were to take their part in history as a cultural group. It was Russia's obligation to assume the leadership in this struggle for freeing the conquered brethren. It was to be a warfare directed against Austria and Turkey, enemies whose very existence was an affront to Slavdom. After the victory had been won his plan called for redrawing the map of southeastern Europe and incorporating its several new divisions as autonomous states in the great Pan-Slavic union. The boundaries which the dreamy student of fishes proposed anticipated to a noteworthy degree the lines drawn by the post-World War diplomatists in their desire to make the Balkans safe for a number of things. Russia was to take for herself only Bessarabia and Galicia, along with the Ruthenian parts of Bukovina and Hungary. The autonomous units of the confederation were to include a Yugoslavia, a Czecho-Slovakia, a Bulgaria, an extended Greece, an exclusively Magyar Hungary, a Latin Rumania, and a metropolitan Constantinople.[132]

Danilevski's work appeared in a periodical in 1869 without attracting any special attention, but when it was published in book form two years later it created a sensation. Soon it captured the enthusiasm of the Pan-Slavists and became in its repeated editions the veritable bible of the movement.[133] None the less, popular enthusiasm cannot be identified with governmental policy. True it is that the Welfare Committee enjoyed imperial patronage, but the English consul who knew most about the Balkan Slavs was of the opinion, after years of study, that the committee had no specific end in view and that the tsar and his officials had no definite knowledge of such propaganda as was being carried on.[134] The chancellor of the empire

---

[132] Nicholas I. Danilevski, *Russland und Europa, eine Untersuchung über die kulturellen und politischen Beziehungen der slawischen zur germanisch-romanischen Welt* (Stuttgart and Berlin, 1920), *passim.* This German edition, the only one available to me, contains in its more than three hundred pages a little more than half of the original work. There is a good brief condensation in Fischel, *op. cit.,* pp. 395–99. For an incisive comment on the ideas of Danilevski, see Masaryk, *op. cit.,* I, 291–93.

[133] For an interesting statement of Dostoyevsky's reaction to the Slavic problem in general and Danilevski's thought, see Anton Florovsky, "Dostoyevsky and the Slavonic Question," *Slavonic Review,* IX (1930), 411–23.

[134] Political Report No. 15, White to Derby, Beograd, 9 July 1875; FO 78/2399.

himself scoffed at the importance ascribed to the work of the Pan-Slavs and, although he refused to take any steps to curtail their charity, he repeatedly professed his readiness to deal with political propagandists at work under the flag of benevolence.[135]

No assumption is more groundless than the belief that a personified Russia plotted grandiose plans and pushed her intrigues in season and out with a zeal no less devious than single-minded. Tsar Alexander II had come to the throne just as Russia's painfully wrought position in the Near East was being battered to pieces in the Crimea. It was only natural that in the next years he should have wished to destroy the restrictions and wipe away the humiliations which the war and the peace of 1856 had forced upon him.[136] Nurturing these same feelings was the chancellor of the empire, Prince Alexander Mikhailovich Gorchakov. Prince Gorchakov, after a long diplomatic career in Germany, had worked his way to the Vienna embassy at the time of the Crimean War. There and in Paris he fought his country's fight, attaining popular acclaim by his refusal to sign the calamitous treaty. Called then, as the logical man, to the St. Petersburg foreign office, the prince entered the limelight of Russian affairs. He took office with the announcement of a program of repose. *"La Russie,"* he said in an early circular, *"ne boude pas; elle se recueille."*[137] But the period of reflection did not last long; within four years Russia's restoration had gone so far that the minister reasserted his country's vital concern for the Christians of Turkey and proposed an international surveillance of the sultan. Such a proposal was quickly paralyzed by Great Britain; but Gorchakov, made chancellor of the empire in 1863, persisted in his ambition for the resurrection of Russia.[138] He restlessly sought the termination of the humiliating Black Sea regulation; he espoused the cause of the Orthodox Christians of the Ottoman Empire;[139] he went at least part

---

[135] General Fleury, *La France et la Russie en 1870* (Paris, 1902), pp. 94–96, citing one of his dispatches from St. Petersburg dated 31 May 1870; Gregory Trubetzkoi, "Les Préliminaires de la conférence de Londres," *Revue d'histoire diplomatique,* XXIII (1909), 113; Meyendorff, *Slavonic Review,* VIII, 403–8.

[136] Serge Goriainov, *Le Bosphore et les Dardanelles* (Paris, 1910), pp. 142–43.

[137] Julian Klaczko, *The Two Chancellors* (London, 1876), pp. 1–36, 79–103.

[138] See, for example, Fleury, *La France et la Russie en 1870,* pp. 43–46, 120–21.

[139] Gregory Trubetzkoi, "La Politique russe en Orient: le schisme bulgare," *Revue d'histoire diplomatique,* XXI (1907), 162–63.

way with the Pan-Slavs when, in 1867, he supported a plan for an extensive provincial autonomy in the Balkans.[140]

The motive which inspired the chancellor, one English diplomat observed, was "vanity tempered with patriotism." He was a patriot, a minister filled with a desire to restore his country to her former position and prestige. But the wit for which he was famous did not turn on his own person; he himself and Russia were twin gods to whom he constantly burned incense. The highest compliment he could pay was to compare a man to himself. "In many respects," said Gorchakov of Andrássy on one occasion, "he resembles me. He has the same pride, the same frankness, the same loyalty."[141] And as for Bismarck, the ever-mounting master of Germany had been his pupil. A polished master of French, Gorchakov permitted himself the vanity of style. The "Narcissus of the Ink-well" he was termed,[142] and one of the Russian ambassadors bitterly complained that in place of definite instructions, the chancellor, even in his telegrams, contented himself with the flowers of literature.[143] The aged statesman lived and died under the charge that his vanity called him to a brilliant role in international affairs, that he dreamed of eloquent speeches in great congresses of the powers, and that, while cherishing such dreams, he neglected to pursue independently the interests of Russia. And true it was that, before 1870, Prince Gorchakov held Russian policy to the *lentissimo* march of the European concert.[144] When the opportunity for isolated action arose in that year, however, he seized it. In the midst of the Franco-Prussian War there appeared a new polished circular in which the hated treaty clauses relating to the Black Sea were repudiated. With Prussia friendly and France broken, the tsar at last was able to rid himself of the old humiliation. The Austrian eagle fluttered angrily; the British lion roared enough to assuage a tender conscience; but the insatiable bear escaped from his shackles. The London conference ponderously laid down the prin-

[140] Henri Hauser, *Histoire diplomatique de l'Europe (1871–1914)* (Paris, 1929), I, 123; William L. Langer, *European Alliances and Alignments, 1871–1890* (New York, 1931), p. 67.

[141] Wemyss, *Morier,* II, 362–69.

[142] Sir Horace Rumbold, *Recollections of a Diplomatist* (London, 1902), II, 245–46.

[143] Gabriel Hanotaux, *Contemporary France* (New York, 1903–1909), IV, 95, note, quoting the unpublished memoirs of Count Peter Shuvalov, Russian representative at the Court of St. James.

[144] Ignatiev, *Istoricheski Vyesnik,* CXXXV, 51.

ciple that treaties could be changed only by the consent of all the signatory powers—and proceeded to ratify Russia's unilateral action.[145]

This bold excursion into the realm of isolated action satisfied the St. Petersburg authorities. After one successful venture, imperial policy returned to the former concert basis. But the program of the Europeanized capital with its coolness toward Pan-Slavism and its hampered march in international harness made little appeal to certain Russian officials who had fallen under the spell of racial enthusiasm. This attitude of impatience seems to have been especially characteristic of the consular agents who had been trained in the Foreign Office's Asiatic Department and sent into Asia and southeastern Europe.[146] But just how far these agents of the tsar took their Pan-Slavic enthusiasm in the Balkans it is difficult to determine. In 1877 the Turks published a series of documents alleged to be genuine Russian correspondence, which indicated a considerable Pan-Slavic agitation and political intrigue conducted by imperial agents in Austria and Turkey;[147] but, in spite of bits of confirming evidence, the dubious origins of the alleged documents and the purpose inspiring their publication place them under suspicion. At the same time, it is more than likely that individual consular agents had a share in

[145] For studies of the Black Sea question, see Goriainov, *op. cit.*, chap. xii; Kurt Rheindorf, *Die Schwarze-Meer Frage, 1856–1871* (Berlin, 1925) ; and Heinrich Mertz, *Die Schwarze-Meer Konferenz von 1871* (Stuttgart, 1927). The protocol of the conference and the text of the treaty may be found, among other places, in Gabriel Noradounghian, *Recueil d'actes internationaux de l'empire ottoman* (Paris, 1897–1903), III, 301–37. The texts of the important treaties are also available in Sir Edward Hertslet, *The Map of Europe by Treaty* . . . . (London, 1875–1891), and in Thomas Erskine Holland, *The European Concert in the Eastern Question* (Oxford, 1885).

[146] G. de Wesselitsky-Bojidarovitch, *Dix mois de ma vie, 1875–1876* (Paris, 1929), pp. 17–18.

[147] These documents appeared in Constantinople in a French edition by G. Giacometti entitled *Les Responsabilités* and an English translation by Edgar Whitaker entitled *Russia's Work in Turkey: a Revelation.* The publication is accepted seriously and digested in some detail by Felix Bamberg, *Geschichte der orientalischen Angelegenheit im Zeitraume des Pariser und des Berliner Friedens* (Berlin, 1892), pp. 429–43. Trubetzkoi (*Revue d'histoire diplomatique*, XXIII, 118–19), a Russian diplomat who has had access to the archives, does not deny specifically these documents in so many words but speaks of them as the result of the work of spies and gives the reader to understand that they have no factual basis. Certain of the ambassador's own statements, however, would indicate some groundwork of fact, at least in one episode revealed in the Turkish publication. (N. P. Ignatiev, "Zapiski Grafa N. P. Ignatyeva, 1867–74," *Izvestiia ministerstva inostrannikh diel*, 1914, pp. 128–31. This citation is to a long memorandum drawn up by General Ignatiev in 1874 to describe his policy and actions.)

Pan-Slavic propaganda and good works. No basis exists, however, for supposing these activities to have been expressions of imperial machination.[148]

The most important bridge between the solid land of Russian officialdom and the ethereal castles of the Pan-Slavs was the person of the ambassador to the Sublime Porte, General Count Nicholas Pavlovich Ignatiev. After winning his spurs on the rough terrain of Chinese diplomacy, Ignatiev in 1864 took possession of the Russian embassy on the Bosporus. Soon his vigorous speech and his intrigues, real and imagined, won for him the popular title of "Father of Lies"[149] and made him quite generally the *bête noire* of the Near East. But Ignatiev was far from being as Mephistophelian as his enemies in London and Vienna insisted. He was a man of wit and personal charm as well as a prevaricator, an intriguer, and a Pan-Slavic zealot, and his labors won devoted friends as well as bitter enemies.[150] The misrepresentations for which he was famous did not justly make him unique among European diplomatists. The most charitable of the British ambassadors who dealt with him passed off this reputation as being founded on a constitutional inability to be exact, largely in the minutiae of life, although Ignatiev was not entirely exonerated in the larger questions and answers. "As the lamb innocently and unconsciously bleats," this ambassador wrote, "so did the general tell his little fibs." When caught, Ignatiev alleged a hereditary failing. On one occasion when a friend complimented him for his excellence at fabrication, he replied, "You flatter me too

[148] For a complimentary estimate of the Russian consular service by an English resident for seven years in Bulgaria, see H. C. Barkley, *Bulgaria before the War* (London, 1877), pp. 168–69.

The difficulty of arriving at some exact information regarding consular activities is illustrated in the case of A. S. Yonine, the Russian consul general in Ragusa. The British were inclined to see him as an incarnation of cunning and intrigue. His colleague, her Britannic Majesty's consul, described him as "a thorough and celebrated Pan-Slav . . . . at the same time he is an assiduous successful political intriguer and neglects no opportunity or means to urge his government's policy on the disaffected Prince and people" of Montenegro (Political Report No. 4, Taylor to Derby, 13 April 1875; FO 7/860). Wesselitsky (*Dix mois de ma vie*, pp. 42–44, 82–83), pro-Serb relief-worker during the revolt, who on one occasion had a fistfight with the consul, charged him with working for the exclusive interest of Prince Nicholas, while the ambassador in Constantinople accused him of being under the spell of Austria (Ignatiev, *Istoricheski Vyesnik*, CXXXV, 72–73).

[149] Elliot, *Some Revolutions*, p. 186 n.; Radowitz, *Aufzeichnungen und Erinnerungen*, I, 367.

[150] A. Gallenga, *Two Years of the Eastern Question* (London, 1877), I, 97–98.

much, my dear sir; you didn't know my father."[151] Truth is the greatest weapon that a man of such renown can possess, and Ignatiev was too clever to ignore this fact.

The Russian ambassador took with him as his self-imposed instructions three "unchallenged principles of action"—principles inspired by his Russian patriotism and by his devotion to the cause of the Slavs. The first of these, which he shared with his superiors in St. Petersburg, was the destruction of the treaty of Paris at least to the point of overthrowing the Black Sea limitations and of recovering Bessarabia. The difference between Gorchakov and Ignatiev was one of means; while the chancellor wished to win Europe by his rhetoric at congresses and in dispatches, the ambassador, profoundly suspicious of the West, wished to throw overboard collective obligations and to deal independently and in unhampered sovereignty with Turkey. The second of the ambassador's principles concerned the old question of the Bosporus and the Dardanelles. Russia, he felt, was stifled in the Black Sea; political and economic considerations demanded that she have a way out, that the Straits should be directly or indirectly under her control. Direct control naturally was to be achieved by forceful seizure and annexation; but for the immediate future Ignatiev, mindful of the European complications, elected an indirect supremacy. This he proposed to attain through taking the sultan in hand. By maintaining friendly relations with the Sublime Porte he anticipated acquiring such influence that Turkey would become a satellite; the ambassador would control the Straits, would direct the Ottoman ministers, and would prepare for a definitive solution of the Eastern question to the satisfaction of Russia and the rest of the Slavs. The third of the general's principles was Pan-Slavism. The unity toward which he worked he saw obstructed by three hindrances: the particularism of the Slavs in general; the special stubbornness of the Poles with their Roman Catholic perversity; and, finally, the enmity of Austria-Hungary, where Germans and Magyars were denationalizing the Slavic majority of the empire. Like Fadeiev and Danilevski, Ignatiev believed the Habsburg state to be the real enemy of the Slavs, the state with which Russia had to fight to the death for supremacy in the East. In that inevitable struggle Ignatiev wished to enlist Russia's natural allies, the Austro-Hungarian and the Ottoman Slavs. For them Russia had to make

---

[151] Rumbold, *Recollections*, II, 311–13.

sacrifices; Russia had to free them from foreign masters and organize them into some close connection with herself.

In this third objective, as well as in the first, Ignatiev came into controversy with Prince Gorchakov. The Westernized chancellor enraged and embittered the ambassador by seeing no menace in Habsburg domination over Slavs. While the one interpreted the growth of the Slavic population of Austria as death to Russia, the other placidly thought that Turkey's Slavs could be made happy by Austro-Hungarian rule.[152]

The years between 1864 and 1875 saw the ambassador working with unflagging zeal for his aims, drawing down upon himself the lasting hostility of Europe and the frequent dissatisfaction of St. Petersburg. When he arrived in Constantinople, Ignatiev found little capital with which to work. The powers which had dictated the settlement of 1856—England, France, and Austria—were in complete ascendancy; although at odds among themselves, they were able to come together to defeat Russia. The Crimean War and Gorchakov's period of pondering had destroyed all Russian influence at the Sublime Porte. The immediate task of the tsar's new representative was clearly indicated. Using all his efforts to break up the Western coalition and regain the traditional influence of Russia over the sultan and his Christian subjects, Ignatiev set about embroiling the other embassies and provoking difficulties in order to make the sultan see the desirability of a good understanding with him. He interfered in the affairs of Rumania to discredit France; he argued with the Turks for the military evacuation of Serbia; he pleaded the cause of Montenegro; he contended at the Sublime Porte that close relations between Russia and the Christians of Turkey would save the latter from falling into the hands of Western revolutionaries; he courted the good-will of the ambitious khedive of Egypt both as a support for Russian policy in Constantinople and as a means of creating friction between England and France.[153]

---

[152] Ignatiev, *Istoricheski Vyesnik*, CXXXV, 50-56. These memoirs of the general, written after his fall and published in 1914, have been digested by Emmerich von Huszár, "Die Memoiren des Grafen N. P. Ignatiew," *Österreichische Rundschau*, XLI (15 November 1915), 166–74; Alexander Onou, "The Memoirs of Count N. Ignatyev," *Slavonic Review*, X (1931), 386–407, 627–40; also XI (1932), 108–25; and B. H. Sumner, "Ignatyev at Constantinople, 1864–1874," *Slavonic Review*, XI (1933), 341–53, 556–71.

[153] Ignatiev, *Izvestiia*, 1914, I, 100–35. The ambassador's intrigues with the khedive assume a conspicuous place in the documents published by the Turks in

In his own writings the ambassador gives an ardent, if at times perhaps distorted, account of his struggles to bring the European-minded Prince Gorchakov to an independent course of action, of his warfare against the Western powers, of his eternal vigilance for the Slavs, of his intrigues in every direction—all activities which give him a high rank amongst the proverbial Machiavellians of Old World diplomacy. Valiantly he worked for a settlement of the Cretan problem which would win for Russia the support of the Greeks. Before that problem was settled he was busy conniving with the Serbs for a union of the Balkan Christians. At the same time the ambassador, always on the alert to accelerate the centrifugal forces at work in Turkey, was busy aiding the Bulgarians to win an autonomous church.[154] In addition he initiated steps leading to Russian emancipation in the Black Sea. Faithful ever to the principle that Eastern affairs should be regulated directly between Russia and Turkey, Ignatiev had appealed to his foreign office to act independently, and when Gorchakov ignored his exhortation, he made his own instructions and began his arguments with the grand vizier. In the end Ignatiev saw his plan for isolated action adopted in St. Petersburg, and he himself was severely reprimanded for his initiative and his program was carried out without his having been consulted.[155] In the years which followed, the ambassador, still determined in the face of his disappointments, pursued his plans in Constantinople.

1877 (Bamberg, *op. cit.*, pp. 430–31). In the early part of 1871 the Turks bought from a Pole the alleged authentic text of a treaty between the khedive and the Russian consul-general in Cairo. When the grand vizier catechized Ignatiev about the alliance, the ambassador's answer was a laugh (Trubetzkoi, *op. cit.*, XXIII, 118–19). For Ignatiev's plans to deflect European attention from Constantinople and to embroil the Western powers in Egypt, see Max Hoschiller, "La Russie sur le chemin de Byzance," *Revue de Paris*, XXII (1 August 1915), 493–94.

[154] The murder of Prince Michael in 1868 gave the mortal blow to the first scheme of a Balkan League. The Bulgarian religious difficulty was settled in 1870 by the creation of the exarchate. Ignatiev's role in the settlement of the church controversy was, in final analysis, a very minor one despite the zeal which he put into it. For a discussion of his part in the league plans, see Ignatiev, *Izvestiia*, 1914, III, 99–105, also 1915, II, 166–72; an English digest in Sumner, *Slavonic Review*, XI, 566–71; Trubetzkoi, *Revue d'histoire diplomatique*, XXI, 186–98, 396–413; Hyde, *Diplomatic History of Bulgaria*, pp. 24–32; Émile Haumant, "Les Origines de la lutte pour la Macédoine (1855–1872)," *Le Monde slave*, October, 1926, pp. 57–58.

[155] Ignatiev, *Izvestiia*, 1914, IV, 95–102; Ignatiev, *Istoricheski Vyesnik*, CXXXV, 70–72; Onou, *Slavonic Review*, X, 399; Sumner, *Slavonic Review*, XI, 558–62; Goriainov, *op. cit.*, 149–50; Trubetzkoi, *Revue d'histoire diplomatique*, XXIII, 128–38, 271–89, 359–87.

After 1870 French influence disappeared; in the following year the last of the strong Turkish statesmen, Ali Pasha, died, and Ignatiev's star was in the ascendancy. He had won the good-will of Sultan Abdul Aziz by his charming plea for good relations, and important ministers, most notably Mahmud Nedim, found in the Russian ambassador Turkey's best friend.[156]

Successful though Ignatiev was on the Bosporus, his influence still fell short of the banks of the Neva. His dogma of hostility to Europe found no echo there. After 1870 the venerable chancellor of the empire had returned to his practice of marching with the West, and the patriotic general found himself ignored and his country bound hard and fast. While Ignatiev preached isolated action, Gorchakov helped to create the league of the three emperors.

THE NEW HOLY ALLIANCE

The Hercegovinian revolt began when Europe was under the constellation of the three imperial stars—William I, Francis Joseph, and Alexander II. The engineer of this imposing juxtaposition had been Germany's man of blood and iron. Prince Bismarck will ever be a controverted figure in history, but friend and foe alike will continue necessarily to see the action on the European stage of his day center about him. Such an observation has long been a commonplace, a platitude of the first magnitude; but it seems doubtful if it will be disturbed. One can well point out that he had no great flame of postwar idealism, that his ways were at times devious and that in the end his scheme of things went tumbling down because he did not rise high enough to find definitive solutions for his problem of peace. None the less, Bismarck had at his command the power of Europe's strongest state; he had the world hanging on his most informal word, and—above all—he was almost unique in knowing exactly what he wanted and in working to that end.

After 1871, of course, he had tremendous advantages which cannot be discounted. Greatest of these was the fact that Germany had gained its objectives and needed thereafter only to use its military strength and diplomatic prestige to maintain its position. The chancellor's attainments had given him advantages, yes, but they had not produced security. Germany's geographic position on a continent of sovereign, predatory states was eternally dangerous; Germany's history had raised up enemies who exacted eternal vigilance. Bis-

[156] Ignatiev, *Izvestiia*, 1915, I, 149, 157.

marck's greatness lies in seeing the German position and necessities with unsurpassed realism, in not leaving the analysis, as has been usually the case, to subsequent generations. Security demanded strong armed force and the prevention of hostile coalitions. The former was easy enough in a prosperous, patriotic state; the latter imposed care by day and troubled dreams at night.

Prussia fought its way to hegemony in Central Europe with the encouragement of one friend. Traditionally the Hohenzollern state had enjoyed good relations with Russia and that connection had been sealed by the kinship of the two sovereigns. But Bismarck was not shortsighted enough to entrust German fortune to the good offices of a single friend. In 1866 he was quite willing to wage war on Austria, to drive the Habsburgs out of Germany; but he was never willing to make a lasting foe of Vienna. At the close of the war his peace terms, although humiliating, were not intolerable; Francis Joseph paid no heavy indemnity and he ceded no land to Prussia. The purpose motivating the dictator of the peace was that Germany and Austria should ultimately achieve a close understanding. A close understanding was necessary in order to keep Austria from casting in her lot with France, and it was highly desirable as a counterweight to the waxing strength of Slavic nationalism.

But prostrate Austria was in no mood for advances from Berlin. Emperor Francis Joseph and Chancellor Beust continued for a time to cherish dreams of revenge. These were rudely broken by the guns at Sedan. Called back to reality by such a loud alarm, the *revanchards* of the Hofburg and Ballplatz set about preparing themselves for reconciliation.[157] In March 1871 Francis Joseph sent a special envoy to congratulate the new emperor on the occasion of his birthday, and in June a second representative went to Berlin for the unveiling of a monument to Frederick William III.[158] In August the next step was taken. After considerable persuasion Francis Joseph reluctantly suppressed his animosity and received his conqueror at Ischl.[159] Then came other meetings between sovereigns and chancellors at Gastein and Salzburg, meetings at which Bismarck and his august master pursued their suit for the good-will of Vienna.[160]

---

[157] *Memoirs of Count Beust*, II, 230–40.

[158] *Ibid.*, II, 256–57.   [159] *Andrássy*, I, 567.

[160] *Memoirs of Count Beust*, II, 257–82. For the earlier relations of the emperors, see Walter Platzhoff, "Die Anfänge des Dreikaiserbundes (1867–1871)," *Preussische Jahrbücher*, CLXXXVIII (1922), 283–306.

A further advance in Austro-German relations was made possible in November when Beust was dismissed and Count Andrássy was called from Budapest to be Minister for Foreign Affairs.[161] The two bases of the policy introduced into Ballplatz by the new minister were, as has been indicated, a more active role in the East and closer co-operation with Germany. The major care of Andrássy, the Magyar, was Russia. If the Dual Monarchy was to cope successfully with that great menace, the friendship of Emperor William was necessary. During the years of Beust's revenge policy Andrássy had set himself to combat vigorously any attempt to regain Austria's lost position in Germany. At the critical moment in 1870 it was Andrássy who saved the day for Austro-German peace and kept Francis Joseph from entering the lists on the side of Napoleon III.[162] In the following year when Andrássy, then minister-president of Hungary, went to Salzburg for the imperial meeting, he more than met Bismarck's desire for good relations by urging a combination against Russia.[163] As foreign minister, Andrássy entered upon his duties with a ready-made plan.

Usages of the time demanded that, if the goal of Austro-German entente were to be attained, Francis Joseph should go to Berlin to return the visit made by William. Beust considered such a project too humiliating to be contemplated,[164] but his successor called on the emperor to bury the hatchet of resentment and go to the capital where his defeat had been celebrated. The month of September was set for the epoch-making occasion,[165] and the ministerial press of Vienna and Budapest set to work at once to champion an Austro-German alliance which would paralyze both France and Russia and prevent their combination.[166]

These sanguine expectations were destined to disappointment. Much as Prince Bismarck valued an understanding with Austria-Hungary, he was not prepared to sacrifice for it the traditional

---

[161] *Memoirs of Count Beust,* II, 291–95; *Andrássy,* I, 629–31, 634.

[162] *Ibid.,* Vol. I, chaps. xiii–xiv; Sosnosky, *Die Balkanpolitik Österreich-Ungarns,* I, 98–100.

[163] Goriainov, *Le Bosphore et les Dardanelles,* p. 305.

[164] *Memoirs of Count Beust,* II, 283.

[165] *Andrássy,* II, 61.

[166] Banneville to Rémusat, Vienna, 10 August 1872; France, *Ministère des affaires étrangères, Commission de publication des documents relatifs aux origines de la guerre de 1914, Documents diplomatiques français (1871–1914), première série* (Paris, 1929), I, Doc. No. 148; hereafter cited as *Documents français.*

friendship of Russia. The bear was perhaps a bit difficult to handle at times, and it was desirable—to use the chancellor's figure—that Germania should mount the horse Austria in order to be equally tall,[167] but Bismarck was unwilling to make a definitive choice. He took the first opportunity to calm the susceptibilities aroused in the mind of Gorchakov by the imperial festivities at Salzburg[168] and in turn warned the Austrians that Germany had no intention of astonishing the world by its ingratitude toward Russia.[169] The chancellor, consequently, saw no little advantage in the desire of Tsar Alexander to be invited to the Berlin meeting. One of the members of the personal suite of Emperor William had taken it upon himself to urge Alexander to come and reaffirm the old entente between the three empires,[170] and in July Alexander descended on the German ambassador during a naval review and baldly asked if his Uncle William would not like to have him come along with Francis Joseph. The ambassador, in reporting this awkward situation, ascribed two motives to the tsar. Alexander was a lover of peace, and he believed that peace could best be secured when the three "northern powers" marched together. Less idealistic was the second motive—the tsar's fear that his uncle might in his absence enter into an understanding with Francis Joseph which would not be to the advantage or liking of Russia.[171] Under any circumstances it would have been difficult to ignore Alexander's bid for an invitation; but William sent his response all the more readily since he hoped that the enlarged reunion would calm the European warmongers and neutralize certain of Gorchakov's undesirable impulses.[172]

This arrangement, however, was not without its embarrassments for official Berlin. There remained the task of informing Francis Joseph that the tsar was coming.[173] General von Schweinitz, the Ger-

[167] Hans Lothar von Schweinitz, *Briefwechsel des Botschafters General v. Schweinitz* (Berlin, 1928), p. 84.

[168] Gabriac to Rémusat, Berlin, 11 November 1871; *Documents français*, I, Doc. No. 76. Marquis de Gabriac, *Souvenirs diplomatiques de Russie et d'Allemagne (1870–1872)* (Paris, 1896), p. 219.

[169] *Andrássy*, II, 24–25.   [170] *Ibid.*, II, 61–62.

[171] Reuss to Emperor William I, St. Petersburg, 16 July 1872; Germany, *Auswärtiges Amt, Die Grosse Politik der europäischen Kabinette, 1871–1914* (Berlin, 1922–1927), I, Doc. No. 121; hereafter cited as *Die Grosse Politik*.

[172] Bucher to Foreign Office, Varzin, 20 July 1872; *Die Grosse Politik*, I, Doc. No. 122.

[173] William I to Francis Joseph, Wiesbaden, 29 July; *ibid.*, I, Doc. No. 123.

man ambassador, was of the opinion that to Andrássy the news was very undesirable even though the minister had enough presence of mind not to give himself away.[174] Officially the reply from Vienna was an assertion of pleasure that Tsar Alexander was to be present.[175] It is possible that Andrássy still hoped to win Germany over to a close understanding directed against Russia, but there is likewise ground for believing the minister's denial of disappointment over the addition of another imperial presence. Despite Andrássy's national animosity and suspicion, relations between Vienna and St. Petersburg had improved during his regime. He himself, according to one story, had also paraphrased the famous prophecy of Prince Schwarzenberg by announcing as he took office that the world would be astounded by his friendly policy toward Russia.[176] Shortly thereafter he vindicated his joking words by inviting an understanding between the two countries; if the tsar, he suggested to the Russian ambassador, would not pursue a program of aggrandizement and if, further, Austria would not be suspected of designs on Turkey, he could see no question that might lead to strife.[177] St. Petersburg knew well the Austrian minister's reputation as a Russian-hater. Gorchakov in those first days was reserved; "We want to see Andrássy at work," he said.[178] But reassuring words spoken by Bismarck to the doubting chancellor,[179] and the peace-loving phraseology of Andrássy's inaugural circular[180] helped materially. "That is my program, exactly my program," commented the aged prince as he read the document.[181] By the following summer the mutual suspicions had been so lulled that for the first time since the Crimean War a Habsburg archduke visited the tsar,[182] and Prince Gorchakov was concluding that he and Andrássy had characters of great similarity.[183]

The brilliant festivities of the imperial gathering in Berlin took

---

[174] Schweinitz, *Denkwürdigkeiten*, I, 298.

[175] *Andrássy*, II, 64; Goriainov, *op. cit.*, p. 306.

[176] *Andrássy*, II, 25.   [177] Goriainov, *op. cit.*, pp. 305–6.

[178] *Andrássy*, II, 6, 28.   [179] *Ibid.*, II, 29.

[180] Andrássy to the imperial and royal missions, Vienna, 23 November 1871; *Red Book*, No. 6 of 1872, Doc. No. 1.

[181] Langenau to Andrássy, St. Petersburg, 27/15 November; Andrássy to Langenau, 11 December; *ibid.*, Docs. Nos. 7 and 8, respectively. *Andrássy*, II, 29–30. The quotation given above in translation is cited by Wertheimer as a part of Langenau's dispatch of 27/15 November, but it does not appear in the printed version of that document.

[182] *Andrássy*, II, 60.   [183] *Ibid.*, II, 71.

their charted course in September of 1872. But the importance of the occasion lay not in the attendance of humorless emperors at army maneuvers or in the dinners and receptions; while pageantry occupied the stage two chancellors and a foreign minister were behind the curtains exploring the dark corners of diplomacy. The discreet pace-setter in the hunt was Bismarck. Conscious of the diffidence and suspicions which his guests had brought with them, the German chancellor saw the necessity for proceeding slowly. It was no time for rushing into written accords; the feast of brotherhood required considerable incoherence in the conversations lest sharp points of difference be uncovered. He laid down as the basic condition of the reunion the exclusion of troublesome details and, to avoid any undesirable situations, he took care not to talk shop with his two guests together.[184]

One specific question was quickly settled; it was not difficult for emperors and their chief ministers to agree that the growth of socialism was an undesirable thing and that some study should be consecrated to it. Apart from that conclusion there was no tripartite understanding. The procedure, as engineered by Bismarck, was a series of bilateral discussions designed to soothe the frictions of the past. Once it was clear that Germany could not be won for some anti-Russian project, the newly wrought Austro-German harmony needed no special words. Andrássy went to Berlin convinced that in any eventual necessity for choice, Bismarck would be compelled to place himself on the side of Vienna.[185] It was enough that Francis Joseph should review the army that had defeated him and that chancellor and foreign minister should renew their congenial acquaintance. Russo-German cordiality, on the other hand, was more harmed than fur-

---

[184] Russell to Granville, Berlin, 12 September 1872; Winifred Taffs, "Conversations between Lord Odo Russell and Andrássy, Bismarck and Gorchakov in September 1872," *Slavonic Review,* VIII (1930), 701–7. In his report to Emperor William (*Die Grosse Politik,* I, Doc. No. 125), Bismarck stated that there had been no proposal made to him for a written agreement. In his conversation with Lord Odo Russell, the British ambassador, the chancellor claimed to have had difficulty with Gorchakov, who had brought with him "his best pens and his blackest ink" for the purpose of drawing up plans for "an ideal Europe." Russell's account of the conversation with Bismarck as reported to the French ambassador and recounted by him has it that the chancellor was far from pleased with *"ce vieux sot de Gortschakoff"* with his white cravat and his pretensions to *esprit,* who came prepared for treaties (Élie de Gontaut-Biron, *Mon ambassade en Allemagne [1872–1873]* [Paris, 1906], p. 168).

[185] *Andrássy,* II, 58.

thered when Gorchakov remonstrated with Bismarck in favor of *une France forte et sage.* The real achievement of the occasion was a material impetus to Austro-Russian understanding. Despite the advance which had already been made, there were still clouds on the Eastern horizon. The liberal gestures of the Hofburg toward the Poles had given considerable apprehension to St. Petersburg, and each government in turn was disturbed by the activities, suspected and real, of the other's agents in the Balkans.[186]

In the discussions between Andrássy and Gorchakov, the latter capitulated entirely to the suave Hungarian. He found Francis Joseph's minister "an honest, straightforward, sensible and earnest patriot, with whom he could establish a perfect understanding." Gorchakov was in agreement with Bismarck that it was a fortunate and happy thing to be rid of Beust. Andrássy had no trouble in convincing his new friend of the purely defensive character of the Dual Monarchy. He tendered the most reassuring explanations about the limits of Vienna's affability toward the Poles; he vigorously repudiated any aggressive intentions toward the Balkans. Maintenance of status quo in the East, said the minister, was Austria-Hungary's wish. Gorchakov's reply was a parallel declaration: Russia, too, wanted peace and status quo; he branded reports of Russian intrigue in Turkey as calumny and repeated the challenge made to Beust to prove the existence of such schemes. Russia, the chancellor said, did not propose to interfere in Turkish affairs; Russia was interested only in calling on the sultan to observe the rights and privileges guaranteed to the Ottoman Christians by treaty. So determined was his country in this course, concluded Gorchakov, that he would propose again, as he had proposed to Andrássy's predecessor, a common policy of strict non-intervention, a policy of leaving events in Turkey to take their course, come what might. Solemnly and formally the Austro-Hungarian minister accepted this proposal.[187]

[186] *Ibid.,* Vol. II, chap. ii.

[187] The two chief sources as to the Berlin meeting are Gorchakov's report to the tsar (Meyendorff, *Slavonic Review,* VIII, 403–8) and Russell's dispatch to Granville (Taffs, *ibid.,* VIII, 703–7). Wertheimer (*Andrássy,* II, 72) cites Goriainov (*op. cit.,* p. 307), who had access to the Gorchakov report. The Austro-Russian understanding was reported also by Gorchakov to the French ambassador (Gontaut-Biron to Rémusat, Berlin, 14 September; *Documents français,* I, Doc. No. 156; this dispatch is also given in Gontaut-Biron, *op. cit.,* 169–75). Bismarck's written account, a brief reply to a note from Emperor William, is in *Die Grosse Politik,* I, Doc. No. 125. For details concerning the externals of the reunion and the French position, see Gontaut-Biron, *op. cit.,* chap. v.

The results of the imperial meeting in Berlin were intangible. The international atmosphere had been too clouded to permit of sweeping settlements. Not all of the clouds vanished: Gorchakov took care not to offend the French; Bismarck refused to be pushed too far; Andrássy felt that if the Russians were quite honest they would remove General Ignatiev from the Bosporus;[188] everyone was ready with a deferential word to the English in the hope of eventual support. At the same time, the festivities and discussions were a victory for conciliation. The scars of 1854 were healed and the wounds of 1866 were given soothing ointment. In Andrássy Bismarck found all he could wish,[189] and Gorchakov now discovered in him his own picture in the mirror of youth.[190] Back in Vienna, Francis Joseph, greatly content with Andrássy's work for peace, raised his minister to the rank of general.[191]

This begining of a new concord, auspicious as it was, had not satisfied Count Berg, chief of the tsar's military men. Before the Berlin felicities the conqueror of Poland had set his heart on a defensive triple alliance. Alexander, however, thought that such a proposal would be premature in view of the newness of Austro-Russian intimacies; Berg was forbidden to mention his hope even to Prince Gorchakov, and, although he went along in the imperial suite, the old field marshal was restricted to the banalities of such occasions. But, having returned to St. Petersburg, Berg began to conspire for his plan. On his own initiative he took the project up with the German ambassador and sought aid in pushing on the sympathetic but hesitant tsar.[192] When Emperor William and Bismarck and Moltke came to the Russian capital for a return visit in the first days of May 1873, one half, at any rate, of the dream came true. If one can accept the impression of the French ambassador, the Germans arrived displeased with the turn of things in France. In St. Petersburg, further, they found not only that the atmosphere of Russo-German relations was cool but also that Gorchakov and the tsar were showing marked amiability toward the representative of the troublesome republic.[193] Bismarck thought it necessary, evidently, to be prodigal of

[188] Andrássy, II, 82.   [189] Taffs, Slavonic Review, VIII, 703–7.
[190] Andrássy, II, 76.   [191] Ibid., II, 77, 81.
[192] Reuss to Bismarck, St. Petersburg, 10 February 1873; Die Grosse Politik, I, Doc. No. 126.
[193] Le Flô to Rémusat, St. Petersburg, 2 May; Documents français, I, Doc. No. 200.

good-will toward his hosts. Not for twenty years, he assured his listeners, had he deviated from his absolute devotion to the tsar. An intimate understanding with Russia he held to be the only rational policy for Germany, a policy based not alone on a feeling of gratitude for Russia's role in 1870 but on calculated interest as well. The only way he knew to show Prussia's gratitude, Bismarck said, was to turn over to Russia all the credit which Germany had in the East.[194] The shadows passed and Berg's plan for a triple alliance to be begun by a dual pact won the day. On the sixth of May a military convention was signed by the two field marshals and ratified by their sovereigns.[195]

The imperial peregrinations were resumed when Alexander II accepted Francis Joseph's invitation to visit the universal exposition in Vienna in June.[196] When the St. Petersburg agreement was being negotiated, Gorchakov had intervened to oppose bringing the Austrians into the secret,[197] but his maneuver was fruitless. Count Berg accompanied his sovereign, and the same text for a dual convention was submitted to Emperor Francis Joseph with the proposal that it be signed by the two military commanders. Austrian reluctance to rush into further arrangements had already been indicated by the failure to include Prince Gorchakov in the original invitation,[198] and neither Andrássy nor Francis Joseph would accept the proposed alliance.[199] A counter-suggestion was put forward by Andrássy and, after some slight modifications,[200] his draft of a treaty was accepted. This new treaty, signed at Schönbrunn on 6 June 1873, was a personal com-

[194] Stremoükhov to Gorchakov, 18/30 April 1873; *Krasny Arkhiv*, I (1922), 10–18. Gorchakov to Alexander II; *ibid.*, I, 20–26. Goriainov (*op. cit.*, p. 308) used Gorchakov's report but made no mention of the convention which the visit produced.

[195] The text may be found in *Die Grosse Politik*, I, Doc. No. 127, and in *Krasny Arkhiv*, I, 28. Gorchakov was excluded from any participation in the negotiations.

[196] The Russians had been of the opinion that Francis Joseph ought to come to St. Petersburg first, but when Andrássy refused to consider the plan the tsar and his advisers gave way (*Andrássy*, II, 85–86).

[197] Gorchakov to Alexander II, 22 April/4 May; *Krasny Arkhiv*, I, 24–26.

[198] *Andrássy*, II, 86. Subsequently the disappointed chancellor received a special invitation and traveled with the tsar.

[199] Alexander II to William I, Stuttgart, 29 May/10 June [*sic*]; *Die Grosse Politik*, I, Doc. No. 128.

[200] Gorchakov drew up a project himself, but apparently it was abandoned in favor of Andrássy's scheme, on which the chancellor contented himself to *"peser quelques nuances de rédaction"* (*Krasny Arkhiv*, I, 26).

mitment between the two sovereigns alone. Their majesties agreed
to act in concert in order to dispel any such divergences as might
come between them, to stand united on the principles which they considered alone capable of assuring peace, and to impose on others the
maintenance of the peace of Europe if necessity should arise.

Their majesties agreed further that in case of aggression from a
third power the two powers would first of all seek a concrete understanding with each other, and if this entente necessitated military
action, they would conclude a special convention.[201] The generalities
of the document signed at Schönbrunn were a far cry from the convention produced a month before in St. Petersburg. No old discords
stood in the way of a Russo-German military alliance, especially
when the tsar personally was directing the negotiations. Austro-Russian relations, on the other hand, still were too delicate for specific
pledges to be acceptable in the Austrian capital.

The original plan of Emperor William was that he should go
directly from St. Petersburg to Vienna. A slight stroke, however,
dictated long repose and the visit was necessarily postponed.[202] In
October at last the aged sovereign was sufficiently recovered to make
the journey, and on the twenty-second at Schönbrunn he formally
gave his adherence to the Austro-Russian understanding.[203]

The June treaty together with Germany's ratification formed
the textual basis of the league of the three emperors.[204] To be established on a more solid basis, however, the newly wrought accord
necessitated an imperial Austrian visit to St. Petersburg. Braving
the reluctance of many of his own people no less than the rigors of a
northern winter, Francis Joseph went to the Russian capital in February 1874. The French ambassador in Vienna, after talking with
the emperor on the eve of his departure, decided that the journey

[201] The text of the Schönbrunn convention may be found in *Die Grosse Politik,*
I, Doc. No. 129; *Krasny-Arkhiv,* I, 30; and in Alfred Franzis Pribram, *The Secret
Treaties of Austria-Hungary* (Cambridge, 1920-21), II, 184-86. Francis Joseph was
not informed of the Russo-German military convention until after this treaty had
been signed.

[202] *Andrássy,* II, 101-4.

[203] *Die Grosse Politik,* I, Doc. No. 129; Pribram, *op. cit.,* II, 186; *Krasny Arkhiv,* I, 34.

[204] In Bismarck's opinion the St. Petersburg military convention was superseded by the subsequent triple understanding (Bismarck to William I, Vienna, 24
September 1879; *Die Grosse Politik,* III, Doc. No. 482). Before the convention
was signed the chancellor had declared that it would be non-effective unless accepted by Austria (marginal notation on Doc. No. 126 in *ibid.*).

was being undertaken merely out of politeness and that His Majesty went in a spirit of defiance.[205] But the report soon coming to Paris from Russia described a meeting permeated with *tendresse*.[206] Knowing how fresh in the mind of the tsar were the wounds of 1854, Francis Joseph made it his first duty to take a wreath to the tomb of Nicholas I, the tsar who—according to the Russian version—was done to death by the ingratitude of this selfsame Francis Joseph. Like a penitent pilgrim the emperor went from the grave to the gloomy death room where Alexander himself displayed the undisturbed relics of his father's last days. Through these acts of apparent contrition the visitor made his expiation; the thorn was removed from the tsar's spiritual flesh; the imperial reconciliation was allegedly complete.[207]

Practical politics, of course, was left to the ministers. Despite the toasts which hymned the blessedness of the unity of the three imperial majesties, the visit took place when both Vienna and St. Petersburg were agreed on a common annoyance with Bismarck for his feverish badgering of the French. Still not too certain of the exclusive merit of a triple harness, Gorchakov and Andrássy continued to look on a strong France as an essential weight in the European balance of power.[208] But naturally of far greater importance for Austro-Russian harmony was a re-examination of the problem of the East. Andrássy expressed his satisfaction with Russian conduct since the Berlin understanding,[209] and once again the policy of maintaining the status quo was affirmed. Expression of desire for the progressive improvement of the lot of Turkey's Christians was likewise repeated, but that solicitude, Austrian and Russian together agreed, would not transgress the bounds of European accord.[210] The relations between Gorchakov and Andrássy, one observer noted, had become almost tender.[211]

---

[205] D'Harcourt to Decazes, Vienna, 11 February; *Documents français,* I, Doc. No. 282.

[206] Le Flô to Decazes, St. Petersburg, 17 February; *ibid.,* I, Doc. No. 284.

[207] *Andrássy,* II, 108–19.

[208] Le Flô to Decazes, St. Petersburg, 17 February; *Documents français,* I, Doc. No. 284.

[209] *Andrássy,* II, 117.

[210] D'Harcourt to Decazes, Vienna, 2 March; *Documents français,* I, Doc. No. 291. Le Flô to Decazes, 1 June; *ibid.,* I, Doc. No. 306.

[211] *Andrássy,* II, 117.

The next months of the history of the imperial association were not without their difficulties, especially in Germany's relations with her two allies. Spanish troubles had again crossed international frontiers; Bismarck's crusade against the Catholic church had raised up a host of annoying corollaries; the Franco-German problem had been going from bad to worse. The European scene, in short, despite imperial visits and desires for peace, remained a chaos of indiscriminate suspicions. The most important of these prevailing ill winds which broke into periodic squalls was that which continued to blow over the frontier between Germany and France. The downfall of Thiers in May 1873 had been the signal for renewed difficulty. Bismarck from then on was in a perpetual state of nerves; the Duke Decazes at the Quai d'Orsay in Paris was laying plans to rally the whole of Europe to the side of France. The crisis came in May 1875, when excited rumor had it that Germany was about to renew the war. Only a few days after Decazes sent his long-planned appeal in all directions, St. Petersburg proved that Russian words about a strong France were not empty talk. On 10 May Alexander II and Prince Gorchakov returned to Berlin, this time not to pursue the amenities of imperial fraternity but to save the threatened French. The visitors found no imminent danger such as they had been led by General Le Flô to expect, but the Russian chancellor was moved, none the less, to compose a circular beginning with the unfortunate words, "Now the peace is assured."[212]

The war scare resulted in a serious shock to the weak joints of the league of the three emperors. When Bismarck realized that the French and the English and the Russians had all attempted to engineer an extensive European intervention into a war which he was not planning, his irritation was unbounded. His original gratitude for what he thought to be friendly British interest[213] changed to reproaches and bitterness when he pondered Lord Derby's gratuitous role.[214] Even more angry was the chancellor with the French,

[212] There is a considerable list of studies of the "War Scare" of the spring of 1875. See especially for bibliography and details of this episode Winifred Taffs, "The War Scare of 1875," *Slavonic Review*, IX (1930–31), 335–49, 632–49; William L. Langer, *European Alliances and Alignments, 1871–1890* (New York, 1931), chap. ii; N. Japikse, *Europa und Bismarcks Friedenspolitik* (Berlin, 1927), chap. iii.

[213] Bismarck to Münster, Berlin, 12 May; *Die Grosse Politik*, I, Doc. No. 176.

[214] Bismarck to Münster, 14 May; *Die Grosse Politik*, I, Doc. No. 180. Bülow to Münster, 3 June; *ibid.*, Doc. No. 184. Münster was of the opinion that the Brit-

and especially Ambassador Gontaut-Biron, whom he charged with a heavy responsibility for his humiliation. Before leaving Berlin for a six months' rest, Bismarck refused to see the ambassador,[215] and when he at last returned and received the trouble-maker his irritation had not abated.[216] The outcome was a request for the recall of this Catholic Frenchman who had from the beginning been a thorn in Bismarck's flesh.[217]

The effects on Russo-German relations were even more serious. In his conversations with Bismarck, Gorchakov received not only assurances of peaceful intentions[218] but also sharp reproaches and ironic commentaries as thanks for an attempt to save a peace which Germany had no intention of disturbing.[219] The chancellor made no secret of his irritation. He spoke bitterly to Lord Odo Russell about the conceit which inspired the aged Russian's desire to play a great

---

ish attempt to organize a European action was inspired by Beust, Austro-Hungarian ambassador in London (Münster to Bülow, London, 7 June; *ibid.*, Doc. No. 186). At all events, if Andrássy's statement can be accepted, Beust supported Austrian participation (Schweinitz to Bülow, Vienna, 19 May; *ibid.*, Doc. No. 183). Gontaut-Biron to Decazes, 28 May; *Documents français*, I, Doc. No. 434.

[215] André Dreux, *Dernières années de l'ambassade en Allemagne de M. de Gontaut-Biron, 1874–1877* (Paris, 1907), p. 174.

[216] *Ibid.*, pp. 176–85. See also Gontaut-Biron to Decazes, Berlin, 31 December 1875; *Documents français*, I, 478–79.

[217] *Die Grosse Politik*, I, 287 n.; Hauser, *Histoire diplomatique de l'Europe*, I, 111–13.

[218] Gontaut-Biron to Decazes, Berlin, 11 May; *Documents français*, I, Doc. No. 416.

[219] *Bismarck, the Man and the Statesman* (New York, 1899), II, 191: "I reproached Prince Gortchakoff sharply. It was not, I said, a friendly part suddenly and unexpectedly to jump on the back of a trustful and unsuspecting friend, and get up a circus performance at his cost; proceedings of this kind between us, who were the directing ministers, could only injure the two monarchies and states. If he was anxious to be applauded in Paris, he need not on that account injure our relations with Russia; I was quite ready to assist him and have five-franc pieces struck at Berlin, with the inscription *Gortchakoff protège la France;* we might also set up a theatre in the German embassy, where he could appear before a French audience with the same inscription, in the character of a guardian angel, dressed in white with wings, to the accompaniment of Bengal fire!"

That Bismarck spoke some such words would appear to be confirmed by Gorchakov's account of his interview given the next day to Gontaut-Biron. The self-appointed peacemaker suggested to the ambassador that the French should not appear too satisfied with the denouement of the scare in order to soothe the susceptibilities of Bismarck who was *un peu agacé* by the Russian intervention (Gontaut-Biron to Decazes, 11 May; *Documents français*, I, Doc. No. 416).

role,[220] and he complained to the tsar of his chief minister's "dishonest proceedings."[221] It was a rancor Bismarck was never to forget, a grudge which left its permanent mark of insecurity and distrust.[222]

Because of the discretion of Count Andrássy, the effects of the crisis on Austro-German solidarity were good. On the first of May Bismarck had given Károlyi, the Austro-Hungarian ambassador, earnest assurances of his peaceful intentions. Although Andrássy apparently was not as convinced as was his representative in Berlin, he concluded that his proper policy would be to keep clear of difficulty and leave the role of peace-preserver to Russia.[223] The fear of a possible Russo-German alliance to the exclusion of Austria was a material preoccupation in the Ballplatz, and it seemed to the foreign minister that the best way to destroy its ground would be for the Russians to take on themselves the entire odium of intervention.[224] There is some reason to suspect a rather devious maneuver on the part of Andrássy in his zeal to prevent too close a bond between Berlin and St. Petersburg. The tsar and his chancellor undertook the journey to Germany confident of Austrian support,[225] and rumor had it that Andrássy, distrusting Károlyi because of his submission to the spell of Bismarck, had authorized Gorchakov to speak for Austria in preference to making a direct remonstrance.[226] At all events, no steps were undertaken from Vienna. When the British requested an action comparable to their own, Andrássy declined on the ground that he had already had assurances of peace from Ber-

---

[220] Taffs, *Slavonic Review*, IX, 642.

[221] *Bismarck, the Man and the Statesman*, II, 191.

[222] Bismarck to Schweinitz, Berlin, 17 March 1876; *Die Grosse Politik*, I, Doc. No. 193.

[223] *Andrássy*, II, 230–31.

[224] *Ibid.*, II, 234.

[225] Russell to Derby, Berlin 8 May 1875; Lord Newton, *Lord Lyons: A Record of British Diplomacy* (London, 1913), II, 77. Same to same, 15 May; *ibid.*, II, 80. In June Gorchakov claimed that in his peace endeavors he had Austria's full powers for his action (Wemyss, *Morier*, II, 362). Wertheimer (II, 244), makes no reference to any possible encouragement given in St. Petersburg. He refers to warm words about Austria spoken to Károlyi by both Gorchakov and the tsar—words about the high value they laid on understanding with Vienna—and he asks his reader to believe that these expressions were inspired by Andrássy's reserve.

[226] Report No. 170, Secret, Loftus to Derby, St. Petersburg, 25 May 1875; FO 65/909. Gontaut-Biron to Decazes, 1 June; Dreux, *Dernières années de l'ambassade de M. de Gontaut-Biron*, p. 169.

lin[227] and he took care that Bismarck should know the Austrian stand.[228]

At the time the Austrian minister heard that Gorchakov was assuming the role of protector of France, his reaction was one of childish joy. Jumping on the table and waving his legs in the air, the sedate minister happily shouted: "Bismarck will never forgive him."[229] Time proved that Andrássy was right. But a second anticipation he had as well—that the bond between Austria-Hungary and Germany would be cemented by Bismarck's gratitude. And here again the minister was correct; "highest praise" and "full acknowledgment" were expressed in Berlin.[230] The crisis passed and the league of the three emperors continued to exist. But its nascent harmonies had been disturbed; one new confidence had been achieved for the price of an old.

SUMMARY

When the uprising began in Hercegovina in the summer of 1875 both the Turkish and the European backgrounds offered ample evidence that a minor disturbance in a remote corner of the sultan's domain might develop serious international consequences. The Ottoman Empire had come upon evil days with its old practice of irresponsible and inefficient rule complicated by the foolish extravagances of an insane sovereign. The province in question had become the hearth for those economic, religious, and nationalistic dissatisfactions which were engendering ruthless hatreds and were counseling acts of desperation. Each of the Great Powers of Europe had acquired an interest, either direct or indirect, in what might happen in Hercegovina, but none had a program free from doubts and qualifications. Of the most interested powers, Great Britain continued to oppose foreign interference in Turkey, but British public

[227] D'Harcourt to Decazes, Vienna, 11 May; *Documents français*, I, Doc. No. 414. Taffs, *Slavonic Review*, IX, 644. Andrássy also advised Italy to remain neutral (*Andrássy*, II, 232).

[228] Schweinitz to Bülow, Vienna, 19 May; *Die Grosse Politik*, I, Doc. No. 183. In talking with Schweinitz, Andrássy emphasized the difference between his own position and that of Beust. Andrássy telegraphed his rejection to Berlin on 10 May (*Andrássy*, II, 245).

[229] *Andrássy*, II, 243.

[230] *Ibid.*, II, 244. Schweinitz to Bülow, Vienna, 19 May; *Die Grosse Politik*, I, Doc. No. 183.

opinion had tended to forget the hysteria of the Crimean War days and the two most important men in the cabinet had profound differences of temperament which could not easily lie buried in times of international stress. In the Habsburg monarchy the German, Magyar, and Slavic elements found it difficult to agree on a common policy toward Balkan problems. But with a Magyar in the foreign ministry Austria-Hungary was committed to a political status quo in which the Slavs of Turkey were to be led to look to Vienna for meager and non-political aid, despite the leanings of the emperor and his generals toward territorial acquisitions. While the Austro-Hungarian ministers felt the necessity for curbing the growth of Slavic racial consciousness, the directors of Russian policy, on the other hand, were drawn by old political interest and the ties of assumed community of race to promote the disintegration of Turkey. The method whereby this aim was to be reached, however, was debated between a chancellor who held to the concert of the European powers and an ambassador in Constantinople who championed a course of independent action. In the counsels of the tsar co-operation won the day and Alexander II entered the league of the three emperors which had been promoted by a German chancellor who saw the dangers for his own land which would arise if ever Austria-Hungary and Russia went to war. In the course of the imperial meetings the Austrian and Russian ministers agreed upon mutual confidence and common efforts to maintain the status quo, but the Balkan interests of the two powers were so basically different that it was commonly supposed that the alliance would with difficulty survive the strains of a crisis in Turkey.

CHAPTER II

THE BEGINNING OF INTERNATIONAL
COMPLICATIONS

TURKEY AND THE OUTBREAK OF THE REVOLT

In the summer of 1875, when Turkey was seriously ill and when Europe was a welter of suspicions, the peasants of Hercegovina began their revolt. The provincial governor at Sarajevo first thought that it would be sufficient to surround the disaffected area with police and to send some of the local notables to negotiate.[1] On the second of July the two men selected for the work of peace set out, but the murders and depredations committed by the insurgents soon discouraged them from fulfilling their mission.[2] With the report of their failure in his hands, the governor, Dervish Pasha, requested authorization to use troops and to use the services of a Turkish commissioner who chanced to be on his way to the Montenegrin frontier.[3] At the Sublime Porte there was some fear as to the effects of opening military operations[4] and, although the sending of a battalion to Mostar was permitted, it was decided that first Constant Effendi, the frontier commissioner, should exhaust all peaceful means of conciliation.[5] The new peace agent went to his labors filled with a skepticism[6] which was soon confirmed. Two interviews arranged after considerable difficulty[7] failed entirely to find a common ground for Turk and *rayah,* and Dervish gave orders for the attack.[8]

---

[1] Political Report No. 4, Holmes to Derby, Bosna-Seraï (Sarajevo), 2 July 1875; *Turkey No. 2 (1876),* Doc. No. 1.

[2] Political Report No. 5, Holmes to Derby, 9 July; *ibid.,* Doc. No. 2.

[3] Herbert to Andrássy, Constantinople, 8 July; *First Red Book,* Doc. No. 108.

[4] Herbert to Andrássy, 6 July; *ibid.,* Doc. No. 107.

[5] Elliot to Derby, Therapia, 13 July; *Turkey No. 2 (1876),* Doc. No. 5.

[6] Holmes to Derby, Bosna-Seraï, 16 July; *ibid.,* Doc. No. 6.

[7] Report No. 356, Elliot to Derby, 20 July; *ibid.,* Doc. No. 8. Hassan Edib and Constant to Safvet, Nevesinje, 16 July; *First Yellow Book,* pp. 5–6.

[8] Holmes to Derby, 24 July; *Turkey No. 2 (1876),* Doc. No. 9.

The Turkish officials in those first days wanted to minimize the importance of the Hercegovinian rebellion. A week after the outbreak, Safvet Pasha, the foreign minister, still denied that there was trouble; true enough, he admitted, the returned fugitives had refused to pay taxes, had chased out the gendarmes, and had demanded many privileges; but the shooting had been merely to give vent to their joy on returning home. The Porte, he explained further, had not consented to send troops because of the bad effect such action might produce; it preferred to make all possible concessions.[9] Such an expression of generosity was, of course, not entirely sincere. The Turks knew very well that, Treaty of Paris or no Treaty of Paris, they had to proceed cautiously in dealing with their Christian subjects—even the rebellious ones.[10] Once, however, Safvet had received Constant's admonition of the sixteenth of July that force alone could end the affair, he was in possession of a good argument to give to the powers. Military action, he told the ambassadors, had been delayed as long as possible; now further hesitation would only increase the danger.[11] Promptly several Turkish battalions were dispatched to the scene of the insurrection.[12]

Well before the end of July severe fighting was common.[13] Its consequences were not to the satisfaction of the Turks; every new day saw the scope of the hostilities widening, until, by mid-August, the whole province was aflame.[14] Constantinople, none the less, was still reluctant publicly to attribute importance or proportions to the rebellion. The official bulletin of 5 August told of dispersal of the insurgents, of a generous amnesty, and of wholesale submission to the imperial authorities.[15] Actually affairs were quite different in Hercegovina and Bosnia, and, smarting under the sting of sharp reverses, the Turks a few days later were compelled to change their

[9] Herbert to Andrássy, 6 July; *First Red Book*, Doc. No. 107.

[10] Report No. 53AD, Herbert to Andrássy, 19 July; SA, Varia Turquie II, 1875. ". . . . Safvet Pascha versicherte mir letzthin, dass die Pforte so lange als möglich Truppensendungen vermeiden wolle, um nicht den Vorwurf auf sich zu laden, durch militärische Provokationen die Gemüter noch mehr erregt zu haben. . . . ."

[11] Tel. No. 52, same to same, 19 July; *ibid.* Report No. 356, Elliot to Derby, 20 July; FO 78/2384.

[12] *The Times* (London), 21 July 1875, p. 7, col. 2.

[13] *Ibid.*, 27 July 1875, p. 5, col. 2.

[14] *Ibid.*, 17 August 1875, p. 3, col. 3; 19 August 1875, p. 3, col. 4.

[15] *Ibid.*, 7 August 1875, p. 5, cols. 1–2.

tune. Complaining now of the failure of the insurgents to heed paternal counsels, they announced new measures of coercion.[16] The governor-general was ordered to send all his troops into action, and additional battalions were sent from Constantinople.[17] By the middle of August more than 30,000 men were in the field and additional thousands were marching.[18]

Tradition in the Ottoman state had it that responsibility rested very heavily on the shoulders of a Turkish official. Ruination of a public servant who had failed was for an Oriental autocrat the easiest means of meeting an unpleasant situation. So it came about that, in the sultan's eyes, Dervish Pasha was at fault. Quickly he disappeared from the scene, and, as usual, an allegedly more energetic governor took charge of operations[19] while a new commissioner of high position set out armed with wide powers to put things right.[20] At the same time the imperial dissatisfaction led to important changes in ministerial posts at the Sublime Porte. On 21 August three former grand viziers—all previously disgraced for one reason or another—were given critical positions. Midhat, the constitution-dreamer, became minister of justice; Hussein Avni took over the war office; Mahmud assumed the presidency of the council of state. All three were men noted for energy and resolution. Sir Henry Elliot considered them "the three most important persons in the Empire," and he permitted himself the old British hope that the administration of Turkey "will be distinguished by greater vigour than it has for a long time displayed." But Sir Henry was not swept away with enthusiasm. Although he had nothing but highest praise for Midhat, he saw in Hussein Avni the most venal man in Turkey; and he recalled that Mahmud, a friend of Russia, had only recently been convicted of gross peculation. In concluding his report of the ministerial change the ambassador confessed that his hope was a meager one; he acknowledged that united the three men could do

[16] Safvet to Musurus, Constantinople, 9 August; *Turkey No. 2 (1876)*, Doc. No. 10.

[17] *The Times* (London), 11 August 1875, p. 5, col. 2; 12 August 1875, p. 5, col. 2.

[18] Report No. 65B, Zichy to Andrássy, Constantinople, 20 August; SA, Varia Turquie I, 1875.

[19] Tel., Zichy to Andrássy, Constantinople, 19 August; *ibid.* (a suppressed portion of *First Red Book*, Doc. No. 125). The new governor, Redif, also had the reputation of being a poisoner of his enemies (Report No. 65B, Zichy to Andrássy, 20 August; SA, Varia Turquie I, 1875).

[20] Musurus to Derby, London, 11 September; *Turkey No. 2 (1876)*, Doc. No. 22.

great things, but he feared that each was out exclusively for his own interests.[21] His views were promptly vindicated. More bitter enemies could scarcely have been brought together than these three refurbished pashas; each had different views, different friends, different sympathies; each had had a share in tearing down the others from office. In place, therefore, of taking energetic measures for the regeneration of the empire, the triumvirate was soon engaged in internal strife. The first round of the battle went to Mahmud. Four days after returning to imperial favor he was back again in the vizierate, to the great surprise of those who recalled his previous career.[22]

During the next month the struggle between Mahmud and the vigorous Hussein Avni went on. In his desperation the grand vizier appealed to the ambassadors to use their influence in his favor at the palace. Elliot refused to intervene,[23] but Ignatiev plunged in on the side of his old friend.[24] In early October, at last, Mahmud won the duel with the minister of war, and the man who had energy enough to fight the insurgent Christians disappeared.[25] Three days later came an official confession of bankruptcy—merely another symptom of Turkey's plight. But long before these October days the difficulties brought to focus by the Hercegovinian uprising had outgrown the confines of the Ottoman Empire; Turkey was no longer left alone with her own problems.

AUSTRIA-HUNGARY AND THE OUTBREAK OF THE REVOLT

In the polyglot territories of the most interested neighbor, the outbreak of the revolt inspired widely divergent expressions of opinion. The Austro-Hungarian population most directly influenced by events over the border was naturally that of Dalmatia. Brothers in all but political control, the two peoples lived a common life and

[21] Report No. 469, Elliot to Derby, Therapia, 24 August; FO 78/2385.

[22] *The Times* (London), 27 August 1875, p. 5, col. 2; 4 September 1875, p. 9, col. 3. *Augsburger Allgemeine Zeitung,* 2 September, p. 3839. Bamberg, *Geschichte der orientalischen Angelegenheit,* pp. 444-45. L. Raschdau, "Aus dem politischen Nachlass des Unterstaatssekretärs Dr. Busch," *Deutsche Rundschau,* CXXXVII (December 1908), 390-93.

[23] Tel., Elliot to Derby, 20 September; FO 78/2387.

[24] Raschdau, *Deutsche Rundschau,* CXXXVII, 393.

[25] *Ibid.*

every disturbance in Turkish territory immediately had its repercussion on Habsburg soil. The revolt of the Hercegovinians and the
Bosnians was the revolt of the Dalmatians as well. From the beginning, committees in Dalmatia were at work providing arms and
ammunition; local authorities were entirely indifferent to the regulations of neutrality; the insurgents freely came over the frontier
to rest and to acquire new supplies.[26] The old sympathies of the
Dalmatians for the *rayahs,* the anti-Slavic British consul at Ragusa
insisted, provided "an indirect though powerful impulse to the rebellious movement." From early in July those sympathies were
stronger than ever. Despite press laws and declarations of neutrality,
the newspapers of the eastern coast of the Adriatic waged war
against the Turks.[27] A comparable voice was raised in the other
Slavic parts of the Dual Monarchy where hopes for annexation
accompanied imprecations on the blood-stained crescent. In neighboring Croatia news of the revolt was welcomed no less than in
Dalmatia. At the August meeting of the Croatian Diet the Hungarian masters of this Slavic land were nervous about compromising discussions, and it was a concern well justified. One speaker
voiced the feeling of his colleagues and of an applauding gallery
when he demanded large sums for the fugitives and warned the
dynasty that not only did the Croats fervently sympathize with their
oppressed brethren but also that Budapest and Vienna should take
their feeling into consideration.[28] In the few days of its session the
Diet was solemnly told that its existence might be jeopardized by
impetuous decisions, and it was only through such pressure that
the Diet's closing resolution was made moderate in its reference to
Turkey.[29] In Bohemia there prevailed a comparable opinion. A
Prague journal articulated the national view when it pleaded the
cause of the *rayah* and taunted the Germans with the reminder that
centuries earlier they had been saved by the Slavs from these same
wild Turks whom now they were allegedly supporting.[30]

The Germanic element of the Dual Monarchy could not share this
zeal for the insurgent cause. The liberals were opposed to expansion
of the empire because of the inevitable cost in gold and blood. Many

[26] Stillman, *The Autobiography of a Journalist,* II, 111.

[27] Political Report No. 7, Taylor to Derby, Ragusa, 4 August; FO 7/860.

[28] *The Times* (London), 28 August 1875, p. 3, col. 3.

[29] *Augsburger Allgemeine Zeitung,* 31 August, p. 3801; 2 September, p. 3837.

[30] *Ibid.,* 29 July, 3296.

of the more advanced Germans looked with disdain on the Slavs and felt that Austria and Turkey had a common problem in restraining these backward peoples.[31] Even more determined in anti-Slavic and pro-Turkish convictions were the Hungarians. A minority in the kingdom of St. Stephen, the Hungarians could maintain their proud supremacy only so long as the Slavs were in subjection. The influential *Pester Lloyd,* a journal allegedly in close contact with Count Andrássy, seized the first opportunity to maintain that the revolt had gone into ridiculous collapse. It was a publicity humbug, this newspaper insisted, to call the revolt a national movement. "Such tumults," one of its articles said, "are not to be considered as political or military events; they belong in the papers alongside notices of robbery, murder, theft and other interesting occurrences of the day. . . . ."[32]

Although Austro-Hungarian public opinion had many and divergent views about the revolt, the military men had only one. In it the soldiers betrayed the simplicity of the martial mind; the revolt should be used as the occasion for the annexation of Bosnia and Hercegovina without regard to possible complications. Francis Joseph had come back in May from his journey to Dalmatia—a journey arranged by the military men—apparently converted to the belief that the occupation of the hinterland could not be long delayed.[33] By the end of July the emperor saw the time for action approaching. The prospective commanding general was called to Vienna and notified of his selection—to his joyous satisfaction. However, the monarch was not yet ready for an unqualified decision. Intervention, he proposed, would follow only when Turkish authority really collapsed; when it did go under, Austrian occupation must follow.[34] The governor of Dalmatia, Baron Rodich, had little patience with such contingencies; he wished to march in immediately for the glory of Austria and for the salvation of his fellow Slavs. On the first of August, at last, Rodich was ordered to make a study of the anticipated advance of the imperial troops. Some days later he submitted a memorandum which argued the cause of occupation and which proposed—with annoying lack of understanding—to

[31] *Augsburger Allgemeine Zeitung,* 5 August, p. 3405-6; 11 September, p. 3978.

[32] *Ibid.,* 5 September, p. 3884.

[33] *Andrássy,* II, 259; Glaise-Horstenau, *Franz Josephs Weggefährte,* pp. 179-84.

[34] Mollinary, *Sechsundvierzig Jahre,* II, 288-89.

solve simply and quickly the attendant political problems.[35] While the governor of Dalmatia awaited the realization of his hopes, the easy-going tolerance in his province toward the insurgents evoked the suspicion of all those interested in the Turkish cause. The British consul in Ragusa, scandalized by the state of laxity about him, wrote: "With a bigotted Slav, Baron Rodich, as Governor-General and Commander-in-Chief in Dalmatia and an equally bigotted Slav General—Ivanovitch—commanding here—his brother-in-law, the rebels will always, I am afraid, succeed in introducing arms, ammunition and recruits from their friends this side of the border. . . . ."[36] The Turks, for their own part, found it desirable early in July to make the most polite communication to Vienna about the Dalmatian population,[37] and a month later sent an appeal to London for a friendly word to the same end.[38]

The principal barrier to Austrian expansion, the chief opponent of the Slav generals, continued to be the foreign minister. In contrast to the military authorities, Count Andrássy did not welcome news of the revolt. A disturbance on the Austro-Hungarian frontier was no happy occasion for a minister who recognized the dangers of the growing Slavic consciousness and who hoped to discourage Russian intrigue in the Balkans. As soon as the Vienna government learned of the uprising it exerted itself to prevent the extension of trouble and the participation of its own Slavs. In the first days of July orders went out to permit no refugees to cross the border with arms in hand[39] and two companies of infantry were dispatched to the frontier town of Metkovich to enforce the regulation.[40] Fearing lest the racial sympathies of the Slavic troops serving under the imperial flag compromise Austria's position, Andrássy had all Slavic units removed from the vicinity of the conflict. Any participation in the rebellion by Habsburg subjects, he warned his sovereign, would make Austria in the eyes of the world a combatant in the struggle

[35] *Andrássy*, II, 266–67.

[36] Political Report No. 10, Taylor to Derby, Ragusa, 21 September; FO 7/860.

[37] Report No. 55AD, Herbert to Andrássy, Constantinople, 16 July; SA, Varia Turquie II, 1875.

[38] Safvet to Musurus, Constantinople, 10 August; *Turkey No. 2 (1876)*, Doc. No. 11.

[39] Andrássy to Herbert in Constantinople, 3 July; *First Red Book*, Doc. No. 106.

[40] Derby to Ffrench in Vienna, 29 July; *Turkey No. 2 (1876)*, Doc. No. 7. Andrássy to Herbert, Terebes, 23 July; SA, Varia Turquie II, 1875.

rather than an arbiter and would revive the old talk of the instability of the monarchy.[41] As a further precaution, passage over Dalmatia was forbidden to all Serbs who wished to join the rebellion.[42]

While he was making these internal regulations, the foreign minister publicly repudiated the desires and the allegations of the Slavic press that the Dual Monarchy wished to annex the troubled provinces. The Austrian policy, he affirmed, was one of the strictest neutrality.[43] And further, in an effort to forestall all international interference in this territory where Austria had special interests, Andrássy proclaimed to the Turks and to the powers that he considered the rebellion to be exclusively an internal affair of Turkey.[44] In Constantinople the Austrian representative urged the Porte on to energetic action.[45]

The problem confronting Andrássy, however, was not so simple as to be disposed of by border regulations and declarations of neutrality and recommendations to put down the rebellion. Since coming to the Ballplatz, Andrássy had been making a determined effort to lead these people now in rebellion to turn to Vienna for aid. If he were to desert them now, that influence which he had been fostering would be instantly destroyed. On the other hand, he could not aid them without wrecking the fragile agreement with Gorchakov and perhaps without opening up the unwelcome Eastern question. In his instructions to the governor of Dalmatia, Andrássy attempted to straddle the razor's edge—and inaugurated a program of duplicity which he was not to abandon. Since it was desirable that the Turkish Christians should be neither deceived in their trust in Austria nor discouraged for the future, Baron Rodich was to inform them confidentially that the Austrian government did not believe the moment suitable for revolt and that, therefore, the insurgents could count on no support from the monarchy.[46]

The answer of Rodich to these instructions was his appeal for occupation previously mentioned. The impatient general was of

[41] *Andrássy*, II, 253–54.

[42] Andrássy to Wrede in Beograd, Vienna, 14 August; SA, Varia Turquie II, 1875.

[43] *The Times* (London), 27 July 1875, p. 5, col. 2.

[44] Andrássy to Herbert, Vienna, 10 July; *First Red Book,* Doc. No. 109, incomplete. Derby to Ffrench, London, 29 July; *Turkey No. 2 (1876),* Doc. No. 7.

[45] Report No. 385, Elliot to Derby, 26 July; FO 78/2384. Report No. 438, same to same, 10 August; FO 78/2385.

[46] Andrássy to Rodich in Zara, Terebes, 21 July; SA, Varia Turquie II, 1875.

the opinion that the whole action could be arranged to the satisfaction of everyone if Montenegro were bought off. Andrássy had the task, consequently, of pointing out the European complications which would ensue if Austro-Hungarian troops crossed the frontier: aiding Montenegro would be only raising up a Piedmont of the Balkans; an occupation would mean the destruction of the imperial league which was so essential to European peace. The best Austria could do, the minister argued, would be to march in and, after a short but costly occupation, march out.[47] In place of sympathy for his occupation plea, Rodich received new instructions to intern the insurgents who crossed the frontier and to see to it that Austrian subjects did not aid the rebellion.[48] In an additional political instruction Andrássy explained to the governor his attitude toward an occupation:

. . . . So long as the Turks are not driven from the land by the insurgents, so long as they remain masters of the land and the successes of the insurgents do not provoke the open participation of the neighboring principalities, it is not the intention of the government of His Majesty to think of any kind of occupation. Under other circumstances a complete expulsion of Turkish rule could be to our interest and we would do what we could to accomplish it. Today that is not desirable. Should events, contrary to expectation, lead to such a situation, we must be prepared for the eventuality; but we can do nothing that will place before us this undesired necessity.

A solution which would make Serbia and Montenegro masters of the hinterland of Dalmatia cannot be tolerated; the opposite solution [an Austrian occupation] would put our relations with Russia to a hard test. The maintenance of these relations, which culminate in Russia's non-intervention in these lands, is a European necessity and is demanded in the interest of our own position in the East. Our next duty is, accordingly, first, to establish our influence as a great power and as the most interested neighbor in every consideration; second, to keep up our treaty relations with Turkey; third, to retain the sympathies of the Christian populations in the East and make it clear to them that they can expect a final settlement of their fate only from us; and lastly, we must strive to prevent a definitive solution of the question at this time.[49]

As Andrássy drew up this statement of policy he was nervous about the failure of the Turks to push on with their military action,[50] but he had the comforting assurance that Russia wanted peace, that

[47] *Andrássy*, II, 267–68.

[48] Tel. No. 497, Andrássy to Rodich, Vienna, 10 August; SA, Varia Turquie II, 1875.

[49] "Political instructions for the governor, Baron von Rodich," 12 August; SA, Varia Turquie I, 1875.

[50] Report No. 248, Ffrench to Derby, Vienna, 11 August; FO 7/851.

Serbia was unprepared for intervention, and that Montenegro alone was too small to make much trouble. It was to Austria's interest to postpone definitive decisions, and the foreign minister saw in mid-August no reason to fear ill winds.[51]

RUSSIA AND THE OUTBREAK OF THE REVOLT

Although Austria-Hungary laid claim to being the most interested neighbor of Bosnia, Russia could not remain indifferent to a revolt in northwestern Turkey. The ties of race and religion as well as the bonds of political interest were too strong to permit a passive attitude. Such articulate opinion as there was in the great Slavic land was from the first days of trouble in favor of the insurgents. The welfare committees in St. Petersburg and Moscow gathered gifts and sent them through their own agents. Medical aid was organized for the sick and wounded; food and clothing were assembled for the refugees. Commensurably with the spread of the revolt, the concern of Russian society for these Christian victims of Turkish misrule increased.[52]

The complexities of international politics did not permit the St. Petersburg government so single-minded a view. Even if Russian officialdom had approached the rebellion with a unanimous opinion on procedure, Russian policy could not have been precipitate. In Constantinople the embassy began by discouraging the use of force and by urging the Sublime Porte to redress the just grievances of the Christians.[53] This sort of advice was strictly in accord with the old plan of General Ignatiev to avoid international complications

---

[51] Andrássy to Rodich, Vienna, 12 August; SA, Varia Turquie I, 1875.

[52] S. S. Tatishchev, *Imperator Aleksandr II, ego zhizn i tsarstvovania* (St. Petersburg, 1903), II, 316.

[53] A. Nelidov, "Souvenirs d'avant et d'après la guerre de 1877–1878," *Revue des deux mondes,* XXVII (1915), 303. Nelidov wrote these memoirs in 1896 after his chronology had become a bit shaky. He was chargé d'affaires of the embassy when Ignatiev went to Germany early in July for medical consultations (*Augsburger Allgemeine Zeitung,* 4 July, p. 2909). The general suffered from an eye malady which gave him a plausible excuse for journeys.

Sir Henry Elliot reported the Russian position in Constantinople in these words: "This afternoon Safvet Pasha read me a summary of the Consular reports from the Herzegovina which had been given to him by the Russian Chargé d'affaires. These reports are quite in accordance with the theory adopted by the Russian Government in all questions affecting the tranquillity of those districts. When lawless acts are committed within the limits of Montenegro or by Montenegrins, they are held to be merely attributable to the unruly character of the people, whom the wise conduct of the Prince fails to keep quite in check;—but when acts take

which would lead to collective intervention by all the powers; he wanted to dominate the Bosporus through his own personal influence and quietly to promote those centrifugal forces which would one day undermine the Turkish realm. But for several years quite another climate of opinion had been prevailing in the Russian capital. Although Ignatiev fought ardently for isolated action,[54] the Western leanings of Prince Gorchakov prevailed and Russia remained loyal to the imperial league.

Hence, when news came to St. Petersburg of the Christian rebellion, Baron Jomini, who was in charge of the foreign ministry, promptly concluded that the incident was a matter for collective attention. Fearing that the Turks could not keep order and that embarrassments for Europe might ensue, he anticipated that soon an understanding would be necessary if new conflicts were to be prevented.[55] And indeed, not many hours elapsed before it seemed to the Russians that the time had arrived for action. On 25 July Novikov, the ambassador in Vienna, proposed that common instructions be given to the consuls of the three imperial powers to work in the interest of reconciliation. Novikov emphasized the increasing gravity of the revolt and the danger that Montenegro might plunge into the fray if Turkey undertook extensive military operations, and he argued that a joint action of the allied powers might make it possible to avoid European intervention.[56] In St. Petersburg Jomini advanced other reasons in support of the Russian proposal. It was not an intervention, he assured the Austrian representative; it was

place on Turkish territory they are entirely the result of the tyranny of the Ottoman authorities, who have driven the unfortunate inhabitants to desperation.

"This is the spirit of the present report and it appears to be endorsed by the Russian Chargé d'affaires. The insurrectionary movement is represented as being merely a mode of bringing under the notice of the Porte grievances for which they would not otherwise obtain a remedy, and Mr. Nelidow consequently recommends that no measure of repression should be resorted to, but that full satisfaction should be afforded to the people, who would then return to submission. . . . I understand that while the Russian Chargé d'affaires advocates temporizing and treating with the insurgents, the Austro-Hungarian Chargé d'affaires continues to impress the necessity of vigorous repression. The united action of those two governments has mainly contributed to what is occurring but their interests are now seen not to be identical" (Report No. 385, Elliot to Derby, Therapia, 26 July; FO 78/2384).

[54] Ignatiev, *Istoricheski Vyesnik*, CXXXV, 72; Onou, *Slavonic Review*, X, 399.

[55] Report No. 36B, Langenau to Andrássy, St. Petersburg, 9/21 July; SA, Varia Turquie I, 1875; incomplete in *First Red Book*, Doc. No. 111.

[56] Tel., Orczy to Andrássy in Terebes, Vienna, 25 July; SA, Varia Turquie I, 1875.

merely an act of conciliation. "Besides," said Jomini, "it would be well to prove the persistence of the accord of the three courts and their vigilant solicitude for peace."[57] He followed this explanation by the flattering assurance that Emperor Alexander wanted to move the center of activity to Vienna, not only because of the proximity of the Austrian capital to the theater of the revolt but also because His Majesty wished to show a new proof of his confidence in Count Andrássy.[58]

The minister so honored did not share the Russian views, and rejected Novikov's vague proposal. He was quite willing, he said, to participate in a joint announcement to the insurgents that no help would be forthcoming from any one of the three powers; he was also ready to warn Serbia and Montenegro against supporting the revolt; but as for collective instructions designed to pacify the Christians, he was opposed to them. He saw neither ground for nor threat of European interference—all the more certainly if the three powers themselves strictly respected the principle of non-intervention.[59] Ambassador Novikov protested that such a limited role on the part of the three allies would be too cruel; he deemed it quite desirable that the consuls should act as intermediaries between the Turkish authorities and the Christian rebels.[60] But Andrássy, with suspicions aroused, remained unmoved and refused to recommend the Russian proposal. It seemed to him that the tsar had taken quite a fancy to the role of peacemaker since his recent descent on Berlin in that capacity, and it was possible, from the Austrian point of view, that he could overdo the part.

Even more disquieting than the conjectured ambitions of Alexander II was the implicit reappearance in this proposal of the tradition that Montenegro and the Turkish Christians were under the special protection of Russia. Acceptance would only increase the existing troubles; it would make more possible an intervention of the other guaranteeing powers; and, above all, it would tend to establish a permanent triple protectorate. He was not certain how much forethought the Russians had put into their project; but, whether the tsar had secret designs or no, the scheme threatened to

[57] Tel. No. 19, Langenau to Andrássy, 27 July; SA, Varia Turquie I, 1875. Also Report No. 37 of same date containing letter of Jomini to Langenau.
[58] Report No. 38, Langenau to Andrássy, 18/30 July; *ibid.*
[59] Andrássy to Orczy, Terebes, 26 July; *ibid.*
[60] Orczy to Andrássy, 27 July; *ibid.*

tamper with the special rights of the neighboring state—it would entail a guardianship over Austria-Hungary as well as over Turkey, and that could not be accepted without total loss of prestige for the Dual Monarchy.[61]

In reply to St. Petersburg the Austrian minister concealed these views behind a series of questions as to what was meant by the proposal. But knowing that he could not flatly refuse a Russian invitation, he resorted to a defensive offense and elaborated his own conditions for joint action. In place of the ambiguous Russian plan he suggested combined instructions to the Austro-Russian agents in Bosnia and in Constantinople: the consuls would use such means as seemed suitable to calm the insurgents, they would tell them that the powers would cause the Turks to remove just grievances, and they would urge the Christians to negotiate directly with the Ottoman authorities; the ambassadors would treat the revolt as an internal problem but would none the less warn the Porte of the dangers of military excesses and would call upon the Turks to make new attempts at pacification. Andrássy would not say that his counter-proposal was better or worse than a collective activity such as the Russians envisaged, but in favor of it were the considerations, he argued, that it lessened chances of European intervention and that it avoided moral obligations toward both Turks and Christians which could not be realized. On the basis of such a limited program Andrássy declared himself ready to negotiate.[62]

On 31 July Andrássy's conditions reached St. Petersburg. They did not go so far as the Russians would have liked, but in view of the necessity for early decision Jomini and the tsar could do nothing but accept them.[63] The Russian minister openly lamented that treaty provisions forbade a much-needed arbitration between sultan and subject,[64] but with a growing alarm prevailing in the Russian capital,[65] Novikov was authorized to collaborate with Andrássy on the

---

[61] Tel., Andrássy to Emperor Francis Joseph, 28 July; SA, Varia Turquie I, 1875.   [62] Tel., Andrássy to Langenau, 29 July; *ibid.*

[63] Tel. No. 21, Langenau to Andrássy, 1 August; *First Red Book*, Doc. No. 112. Report No. 39AC, same to same, 4 August; SA, Varia Turquie I, 1875. Tel. No. 23, same to same, 2 August; *ibid.*

[64] Report No. 255, Doria to Derby, St. Petersburg, 18 August; FO 65/910.

[65] Le Flô to Decazes, St. Petersburg, 5 August; *Documents français*, II, Doc. No. 2. Buffet to de Ring, Versailles, 6 August; *First Yellow Book*, p. 7. For some reason Hanotaux (*Contemporary France*, IV, 62–63) has it that Jomini "re-opened the 'Eastern Question'" on 5 August when he confessed to the French ambassador his worries and told him of negotiations with Vienna.

details of their action and the Russian agents in Turkey were ordered to accept instructions coming directly from Vienna.[66]

The identic instructions were drawn up readily enough on 5 August in a conference between Andrássy and Novikov and Schweinitz, the German ambassador. The consuls and their agents, the document read, were to go individually to the insurgents, warning them of lack of support from the powers, admonishing them to accept subjection, and promising to recommend at the Porte just treatment of the Christian population.[67] The meeting of the three negotiators, however, lost its unanimity when Andrássy proposed a new and hitherto unmentioned field for common action. The excitement and fever raging in the two principalities threatened a serious extension of warfare. Prince Milan of Serbia had just been to Vienna and had told Andrássy that if Prince Nicholas of Montenegro took the field, he could not restrain his own people. It was highly desirable, consequently, from the Austrian point of view, to take precautions against Montenegrin action. To that end Andrássy proposed that Nicholas should be advised to avoid all participation. He wished to inform the prince that if he and his subjects remained aloof, the powers would support his ambitions for more land, but if he compromised his neutrality he would be left to his own fate. Novikov, attuned to the traditional sympathy of Russia for the tiny principality, hastened to protest that the conference was concerned only with the revolted provinces of Turkey, that the question of Montenegro was beyond its sphere. It might be proper to give advice to Serbia, the ambassador contended, since Milan had come to Vienna to ask for it; but Nicholas had sought no opinions and none should be offered. It would be much better, he added with naive inconsistency, merely to inform the prince that the powers would aid him. Andrássy replied with long arguments for Russia's supporting a notice to Cetinje, and Schweinitz seconded his efforts, but Novikov remained obdurate. He refused to subscribe personally to such a declaration of distrust in the prince of Montenegro, and finally the whole question was referred to St. Petersburg.[68]

[66] Report No. 39E, Langenau to Andrássy, 23 July/4 August; SA, Varia Turquie I, 1875.

[67] "Instructions pour les Consuls et leurs Délégués," *First Red Book,* pp. 100–101.

[68] "Extrait d'un compte-rendu d'une conférence à Vienne le 5 août 1875 entre le ministre des affaires et les ambassadeurs d'Allemagne et de Russie au sujet des complications surgies en Herzégovine," in Andrássy to Langenau, Vienna, 9 August; SA, Varia Turquie I, 1875.

Novikov's defense of Prince Nicholas found for the moment no echo in the Russian capital and the ambassador was charged to agree to the projected remonstrance.[69] Tsar Alexander declared the Vienna instructions to be as "correct, prudent, and practical as the circumstances would permit."[70] The next step was then in order.

As the third member of the emperors' league, Germany was invited to participate in the negotiations at the same time that Novikov presented the Russian proposal in Vienna. Taking the position that the center of such a project belonged naturally in Austria, Secretary von Bülow in the Berlin foreign office promptly instructed General von Schweinitz to lend his co-operation.[71] Andrássy, ever anxious for a close understanding with Germany, informed the Wilhelmstrasse of each step in the negotiations,[72] and in response to these communications came assurances of Germany's full confidence in the Austro-Hungarian minister and unqualified willingness to subscribe to the Vienna decisions. Emperor William was delighted with the good understanding on this question.[73] Bismarck likewise was content. In a conversation on 20 August with a German official the chancellor spoke in the most friendly manner of Austria and of Andrássy in particular. At that time he enunciated a formula which he soon came to repeat almost mechanically: Germany had no immediate interest in the Eastern question and was concerned only with promoting Austro-Russian unity. When the two powers agreed, Germany agreed; if they did not, Germany could not cast the deciding vote. Within the league of the three emperors there could be no two-to-one decisions; each member enjoyed a *liberum veto*. But already Bismarck had misgivings as to the latent possibilities of the situation. He realized that so long as it was a matter of doing nothing, Germany's two allies could get along together, and he suspected that when they tried to do something positive their interests would collide. In case of trouble between Russia and Austria, Bismarck saw clearly that his position would be very difficult. Neutrality was a doubtful way out, while a choice between the two enemies would be hard. On the one side were strong traditional family policy

---

[69] Report No. 40B, Langenau to Andrássy, 4/16 August; SA, Varia Turquie, I, 1875.   [70] Jomini to Novikov, St. Petersburg, 4/16 August; *ibid.*

[71] Report No. 35B, Seiller to Andrássy, Berlin, 7 August; *ibid.*

[72] Tel., Andrássy to Seiller, 7 August; *ibid.,* incomplete in *First Red Book,* Doc. No. 114.

[73] Tel., Seiller to Andrássy, 10 August; SA, Varia Turquie I, 1875.

and the advantage of stability, while on the other were racial community and many valuable connections. If he chose Austria, Russia would become an irreconcilable opponent of Germany and an ally of France. If he sided with Russia, the tsar would become too powerful. But for the moment Bismarck believed that Gorchakov would be considerate of Austria, and hence he saw no reason at hand for apprehension.[74] The co-operation of the three imperial courts was a guaranty against disturbance.[75]

After the consular instructions had been prepared, Count Andrássy's idea of the next step was that the ambassadors representing the three powers in Turkey should present a request at the Sublime Porte for approval of the peace mission. Only subsequently, and then purely as a matter of courtesy, did he wish the ambassadors to inform their colleagues, the agents of the other Great Powers. Since it was, in his mind, exclusively a question of tendering good offices, the minister saw no reason for direct communication with the other European cabinets.[76] In other words, it was the Austrian view that the work of the consuls should be limited exclusively to the representatives of the three imperial powers. But Andrássy's plan of action soon came to an abortive end; before it could be arranged, Tsar Alexander had independently made a decision which entirely changed the complexion of the projected consular mission.

The disturbing influence behind the Russian action was France. The secondary role into which the disastrous war of 1870 had forced France had been an unmitigated humiliation. After marching at the head of Europe for so long, the French were pained and annoyed to see the three great imperial powers assume the hegemony of the world and to know, in early August, that these same powers proposed to settle the Eastern problem in which France had a vital interest.[77] From St. Petersburg came the disquieting news that the three empires were attempting to arrange a common action, and along with it a warning that the old *question d'orient* might burst

[74] Hermann Freiherr von Mittnacht, *Erinnerungen an Bismarck* (Stuttgart and Berlin, 1904), pp. 53–54.

[75] Bismarck to Emperor William I, Varzin, 13 August; *Bismarck-Jahrbuch,* IV, 37.

[76] Tel., Andrássy to foreign ministry in Vienna, Terebes, 16 August; SA, Varia Turquie I, 1875.

[77] Report No. 30, Kuefstein to Andrássy, Paris, 30 August; SA, Varia Turquie I, 1875.

at any moment like a bomb.[78] From Vienna came report of frequent meetings between Andrássy and the ambassadors of Russia and Germany. The French chargé d'affaires passed on Andrássy's assurance that the projected move would be in the interest of peace and status quo, but he added his own grave doubts as to the success of a moderate program of advice.[79] Official France made no secret of its worry lest the common interests of Europe—French interests —be jeopardized.[80] Calming explanations from St. Petersburg did not spare the nervous French minister misgivings as to the precise intentions of the empires nor keep him from complaining that the three Western powers had been excluded from the Vienna deliberations. France was as ready as any power, he said, to use its good offices for the restoration of peace in Turkey.[81]

In the Russian capital the French ambassador, General Le Flô, was determined to end the isolation of France. A strong partisan of understanding with Russia, he had had no little share in effecting the breach between Berlin and St. Petersburg during the war scare of May, and, inspired by that victory, he returned to the charge.[82] Seeking out Baron Jomini, the ambassador protested against his own country's being left beyond the pale of the deliberations and he sounded the warning that if France were not included she would

---

[78] Le Flô to Decazes, 5 August; *Documents français*, II, Doc. No. 2.

[79] De Ring to Decazes, Vienna, 9 August; *ibid.*, Doc. No. 3.

[80] Buffet to de Ring, Versailles, 6 August; *First Yellow Book*, p. 7. Buffet to Le Flô, 7 August; *ibid.*, pp. 8–9. The British ambassador in Paris reported: "I had the evening before last a conversation of some length with Marshal MacMahon. The Marshal seemed to be much disquieted by the intelligence he had received of the progress of the Insurrection in the Herzegovine. He appeared to apprehend that this Insurrection might raise the whole Eastern question at a time which would be very inopportune for France and for the Western Powers generally. He evidently feared that the understanding between the Emperors of Austria, Germany and Russia might prove a danger in such a contingency. The three Emperors might no doubt do pretty much as they pleased in the East, if they were all agreed, but this agreement might possibly, as I understood the Marshal, be purchased at the expense of the other Powers. Only two of the Empires were in his view directly concerned in the territorial arrangements in the East which might be the consequence of a serious disturbance of the Ottoman Power, but the Third would no doubt acquire some compensation for its acquiescence in any advantage to be acquired by the other two. In fact, if Germany left Russia and Austria to have their own way in the East, she would expect to be secured against any interference with whatever she, on her part, might choose to do in the West. . . . ." (Report No. 682, Lyons to Derby, Paris, 13 August; FO 27/2113.)

[81] Buffet to Bourgoing, Versailles, 13 August; *First Yellow Book*, p. 13.

[82] Hanotaux, *Contemporary France*, IV, 64–65.

seek a dual understanding with England.[83] The threat had its influence on the pro-Western Jomini; he went to the Austrian ambassador and told him that, since France's association would calm the disturbed nerves of Paris and give weight to the projected action, he proposed to advise the tsar to invite French participation.[84] Without waiting to consult his allies Alexander II gave his consent, and on 14 August the invitation was sent.[85] Count Andrássy was merely asked to second the invitation.[86]

Andrássy's response to this suggestion was a profound silence.[87] But the Russian invitation was sufficient. The Duke Decazes, France's foreign minister, accepted without delay. France was flattered to find herself again recognized as an essential partner in international undertakings and relieved that her sharing in the work of pacification would prevent the three powers from arranging the Eastern trouble to their exclusive satisfaction. The foreign minister was moved to compose several eloquent dispatches to the various ambassadors. There was pique in his words that Andrássy had not been sympathetic, but also exultation that "a noble European concert" had been established.[88] But there was still concern in his mind: he hoped that there would be no armed intervention of any kind in

[83] The French had already sought an exchange of information with the Italians (Visconti-Venosta to Cova in Constantinople, Rome, 10 August; *First Green Book,* Doc. No. VIII).

[84] Report No. 40C, Langenau to Andrássy, 4/16 August; SA, Varia Turquie I, 1875. *Documents français,* II, 3 n.

[85] Jomini to Le Flô, St. Petersburg, 2/14 August; *First Yellow Book,* pp. 14–15. Le Flô to Decazes, 14 August; *Documents français,* II, Doc. No. 4. This extension of the scope of the consular mission was plainly in keeping with the dominant view of the Russian foreign office, a Western outlook which supported a strong and co-operating France and which postulated further a common tune for the European concert. Prince Gorchakov, sojourning during the second half of 1875 in Switzerland, was a partisan of a procedure *à six* rather than an exclusive trio (Report No. 764, Adams to Derby, Paris, 13 September; FO 27/2114).

[86] Tel. No. 25, Langenau to Andrássy, 15 August; SA, Varia Turquie I, 1875.

[87] There is no document in the Austrian archives which reveals the minister's reaction. The French foreign minister wrote these revealing words after a few days: "The hesitations and uncertainties of Austrian policy in the presence of the Hercegovinian insurrection have not escaped us. They have become especially plain to us from the day Russia invited our participation. The Vienna Cabinet, we were told in St. Petersburg, would also ask our support. But its silence has been absolute, and far from inviting us to take part in its actions, has been astonished that we sent a delegate to the Hercegovina. . . . ." (Decazes to Vogüé in Vienna, 18 September; *Documents français,* II, Doc. No. 7.)

[88] Decazes to Vogüé, 18 September; *ibid.,* Doc. No. 7.

Turkey, and he sought close co-operation with England as a guaranty.[89] Very carefully in his communications he emphasized the peaceful, non-intervention character of the plan as presented by Jomini, and he attempted to define as carefully as possible the restricted duties of the consuls—not only to assure the desired co-operation of England and Italy but also to restrain Austria and Russia from going too far.[90] With all the Great Powers united on a rigidly defined program there would be no fear for the interests of France.

A few days after he decided to include the French in the projected action, Tsar Alexander ordered—again quite independently—invitations to be sent to London and Rome.[91] Already, however, the Italian Barkus had expressed his willingness. In fact, in his desire to proceed apace with the imperial powers, the Italian foreign minister had ordered his agent in Constantinople to do what the ambassadors did without further instructions from home.[92] The Italian position was comparable to that of the French. Largely by courtesy considered a Great Power, by happy fortune signatory to the Treaty of Paris, jealous of the other powers, ambitious for a role of her own in the Balkans, Italy had no desire to see the Eastern question opened at such an unpropitious time. Visconti-Venosta could with good conscience urge moderation and prudence on the Sublime Porte[93] and offer Italian co-operation to the other powers.[94]

Circumstances dictated that the British were to participate in the deliberations only after the center of activities had been transferred to Turkey.

THE FIRST STEP OF THE POWERS IN CONSTANTINOPLE

The next step, after the identic instructions had been drawn up in Vienna for the mission of the consuls, was to secure the consent

[89] Decazes to d'Harcourt in London, 18 August; *First Yellow Book,* pp. 15–17.

[90] Decazes to Le Flô, 20 August; *ibid.,* pp. 18–20. Decazes to Bourgoing in Constantinople, *ibid.,* pp. 20–22.

[91] The Italian *Green Book,* designed to give a minimum of important information, does not indicate the exact date of the solicitation. It was probably on 17 August, since the pertinent dispatch to London was sent on that day.

[92] Visconti-Venosta to Cova in Constantinople, Rome, 10 August; *First Green Book,* Doc. No. VIII.

[93] Visconti-Venosta to Robilant in Vienna, Rome, 9 August; *ibid.,* Doc. No. VII.

[94] Andrássy to Zichy in Constantinople, Terebes, 19 August; *First Red Book,* Doc. No. 126.

and support of Turkey. Armed with instructions and arguments, Count Zichy, the Austrian ambassador, returned to Constantinople from vacation to open the delicate negotiations.[95] Zichy, a diplomatic weakling who was entirely under the spell of General Ignatiev,[96] arrived at his post on 16 August and the next morning went to the Sublime Porte. Safvet Pasha and the grand vizier received the ambassador with thanks for his friendly intentions, but both declared the proposed mission an intervention in Turkish affairs forbidden by the Treaty of Paris and a dangerous precedent which might encourage the Cretans and the Bulgarians.[97] Zichy went away with a cool rejection. The next morning his Russian and German colleagues descended on Safvet, and the Turkish minister then awoke to the fact that the three powers were united. With that fact in mind, he saw nothing to do but give way and recommend the proposal to his superiors. The following day, 19 August, Zichy returned to the charge, calling the grand vizier out of council to press on him new arguments emphasizing the menace of Serbia;[98] but he was still unable to conquer all Turkish doubts. It was only

[95] Andrássy to Zichy, 7 August; *First Red Book,* Doc. No. 113, incomplete.

[96] Radowitz, *Aufzeichnungen und Erinnerungen,* I, 367. The British ambassador in Vienna wrote of him: ". . . . There is little doubt, however, that Count Zichy, acting under General Ignatiev's tuition, has done much to compromise the Austrian government at Constantinople; and my German colleague . . . . some days ago observed that Count Andrassy had much reason to regret having made such an unfortunate appointment, and that, were it not from a feeling of 'amour propre'—or unwillingness to acknowledge his error, Count Zichy would have been long since recalled. . . . ." (Report No. 327, Buchanan to Derby, Vienna, 5 October; FO 7/852.)
Elliot in Constantinople found him an undesirable colleague: "As it had long been with me an article of faith to look upon a cordial understanding between the two embassies as being especially desirable in all questions affecting this country, it was with the greatest regret that I found it impossible to continue with Count Zichy the confidential intimacy which I had maintained with his Predecessors. After finding that to speak to Count Zichy was in fact to speak to General Ignatiew, confidential intercourse became difficult." (Report No. 858, Elliot to Derby, 24 December 1875; FO 78/2391.) The British ambassador also had things little flattering to say of his colleague when he wrote his memoirs (*Some Revolutions,* pp. 205-6).

[97] Tel., Zichy to Andrássy, 18 August; *First Red Book,* Doc. No. 123, considerably modified. Report No. 65B, same to same, 20 August; *ibid.,* Doc. No. 131, incomplete.

[98] Zichy had received news that Prince Milan was on the point of declaring war on Turkey. Andrássy in sending this information had urged the Turks to immediate acceptance of the offer of the powers as a means of forestalling Serbia and to prepare troops for the impending encounter. Andrássy to Zichy, 17 August; SA, Varia Turquie II, 1875.

when General Ignatiev was received in audience by the sultan on the same day that the victory was gained.[99] Safvet seems to have been convinced that the action of the consuls might be beneficial in discouraging the insurgents if it remained within the projected scope,[100] and Essad, the grand vizier, was apparently converted to this view.[101] At all events it came to light in a few days, after he had fallen from office, that the grand vizier had recommended the mission to Abdul Aziz and had combated the sultan's reluctance to accept it by telling him—so it appears—the bald-faced lie that the proposal had the support of all the six Great Powers, that of Great Britain as well as of the rest.[102]

GREAT BRITAIN AND THE OUTBREAK OF THE REVOLT

The critical question, so far as the European concert was concerned, was the stand to be taken by the British cabinet toward the revolt in general and the international complications in particular. Sir Henry Elliot had gone to the Bosporus in 1867. There he made himself known as a cold defender of British interests and at the same time showed a deep-seated bias in favor of the Turk which was more than another aspect of his championship of his nation's cause. He was a man of unimpeachable integrity beneath his unfriendly exterior. But he occupied the most difficult of diplomatic posts and could never, had he been a genius among men, have won the sympathy of all the intriguers who ran rampant in the Turkish capital.

[99] Tel., Zichy to Andrássy, 18 August; *First Red Book,* Doc. No. 123, modified. Report No. 65B, Zichy to Andrássy, 20 August; *ibid.,* Doc. No. 131, incomplete. Zichy to Andrássy, 19 August; *ibid.,* Doc. No. 125, incomplete. Tel. No. 73, Zichy to Andrássy, 20 August; *ibid.,* Doc. No. 130, incomplete. Bourgoing to Decazes, Therapia, 25 August; *First Yellow Book,* pp. 22–24. Report No. 463, Elliot to Derby, Therapia, 22 August; FO 78/2385. Zichy's own accounts are not clear, and the printed versions are even worse. Elliot derived his account from conversations with Safvet and Ignatiev.

[100] Report No. 463, Elliot to Derby, 22 August; FO 78/2385. A few days later Safvet explained that the government had been led to abandon its opposition through fear of being accused of willfully refusing to stop bloodshed and through the belief that Russia and Austria could exercise a calming influence (Tel., Safvet to Musurus in London, 31 August; FO 78/2425).

[101] In reporting a conversation with Essad on the afternoon of 19 August, an official of the British embassy wrote: "Though it would in principle be admitting foreign intervention in the affairs of the Herzegovina, the Porte does not seem altogether averse to the course proposed. . . ." (Sandison to Elliot, 19 August; passage suppressed from inclosure in Doc. No. 17, *Turkey No. 2 [1876]*).

[102] Tel., Elliot to Derby, 29 August; FO 78/2385.

The Christians of the Levant, and even the English colony, had only complaints for him because of his aloofness and his disposition to favor the Turk. There was constant reproach against him that he did not plunge in, after the manner of his great predecessor, Lord Stratford de Redcliffe, and assume command of the internal affairs of the empire.[103] Rather than to work for the advancement of the Christian populations of Turkey the ambassador conceived it to be his British duty to fight all forms of foreign interference, particularly the influences emanating from his only important rival, General Ignatiev. The general, in his annoyance, charged that Sir Henry, *"homme bilieux et passionné,"* blindly became more Turkish than the Turks in his desire to combat the legitimate influence of Russia.[104]

English students have been inclined to emphasize the influence which Elliot enjoyed in Turkish circles[105] and that influence was indeed constantly visible as long as he remained in Constantinople. Stung by the talk—and by the reality—of Ignatiev's growing role in Turkish affairs, the British ambassador was moved, in early July 1875, to describe to the Foreign Office his own estimate of his position. "That many of those," he wrote, "who see His Excellency's [Ignatiev's] increasing activity, and hear every change of officials attributed to him by those about him should believe in his power is most natural; but I have no hesitation in repeating . . . . that upon questions of importance it is to Great Britain and not to Russia that

---

[103] Gallenga, *Two Years of the Eastern Question*, I, 108–10. Gallenga, it must be said as a control for the above borrowing, was correspondent of the *Times*, a man charged by Elliot with being in the service of Russia and excluded from the British embassy.

[104] In 1874 the Russian ambassador wrote: "L'ambassadeur britannique à Constantinople, homme bilieux et passionné, met un zèle tout particulier à combattre l'action de l'Ambassade Impériale. Appartenant à l'école palmerstonienne, il s'attaque systématiquement à notre influence légitime en intervenant dans les affaires où l'intérêt anglais n'est nullement engagé, comme, par exemple, dans la question gréco-bulgare, dans les affaires du Mont Athos, de Palestine, etc. Sans se donner la peine d'étudier à fond les questions religieuses et nationales, les anglais croient devoir prendre aveuglement le contre-pied de nos tendances et de nos vues réelles ou supposées. Pour nous nuire ils deviennent avec la Porte plus turcs que les turcs en les mettant constamment en garde contre des velléités imaginaires de notre part. . . . Les membres les plus respectables des véritables colonies anglaises dans le Levant se plaignent hautement d'être abandonnés au bon plaisir des turcs par l'ambassade britannique qui court après des mirages en se vouant à des intérêts étrangers à la nation anglaise. . . ." (Ignatiev, *Izvestiia*, 1915, I, 163).

[105] Sir Adolphus William Ward, editor, *The Cambridge History of British Foreign Policy* (Cambridge, 1922–23), III, 93–94.

the Porte turns for counsel." After reviewing several cases of Anglo-Russian contest which had proved the supremacy of his own influence, Sir Henry went on to argue against using that influence in the internal affairs of the Ottoman Empire. Of the two possible and opposed policies, he contended, that of non-intervention was "the safest and least likely to lead to dangerous complications."[106]

In Elliot's mind there was no doubt as to the causes of the rebellion in Hercegovina. Although he admitted that there were certain excesses under which the Christians suffered, he was convinced that foreign intrigue, baneful influences from Austria and Russia, lay at the bottom.[107] Without any hesitations, therefore, when his opinion was sought by the Turks the British ambassador turned his back on his recently vaunted policy of non-interference and urged the Porte not to permit fears of misunderstanding abroad to interfere with "the adoption of such measures as might seem necessary to prevent an extension of the spirit of insubordination."[108] Elliot kept close watch on the activities of the Turks, and in a few days, finding the Porte guilty of a "total want of energy," remonstrated with Safvet Pasha about employing no greater vigor in dealing with the insurrection.[109] Alarmed further over the harsh things said recently in the House of Commons about Turkey, the ambas-

---

[106] Report No. 322, Elliot to Derby, 4 July 1875; FO 78/2384. Lord Derby wrote on the margin of this dispatch: "Concur in view as to policy of interference and express confidence that he will maintain the past influence of Gt. Britain in all matters in which it can be properly exercised. Jy 20/75."

[107] Report No. 385, Elliot to Derby, 26 July; FO 78/2384. Jonin, the Russian consul-general in Ragusa, was the object of Elliot's special suspicion (Report No. 59B, Herbert to Andrássy, Constantinople, 30 July; SA, Varia Turquie II, 1875. Elliot, *Some Revolutions*, p. 207). In mid-July the ambassador wrote to London: ". . . . That the movement is due to the policy followed by the three Northern Powers during the last six months, scarcely admits of a reasonable doubt, although it is not to be supposed that Austria intended or desired it to be followed by any such result. Practically, but unconsciously that Power has been acting as a catspaw to Russia, and by adopting the policy of the latter, has been assumed by the populations to be animated by the same sentiments towards Turkey. That no great time would elapse without this leading to trouble in the Northern Provinces, had become a matter of certainty, and the reception given to the Emperor of Austria upon his visit to Dalmatia, had seemed to show that the late efforts of the Vienna Cabinet to conciliate the Slav populations had done less to secure their loyalty than to excite their hopes." (Report No. 345, Elliot to Derby, 14 July; FO 78/2384.)

[108] Report No. 345, Elliot to Derby, 14 July; FO 78/2384. This recommendation was approved in London (Draft No. 218, Derby to Elliot, 30 July; FO 78/2377).

[109] Tel., Elliot to Derby, 17 August; FO 78/2385.

sador went directly to the sultan and warned him that, if the interest of England was to be kept alive, he had to embark upon a serious program of reform.[110]

On 19 August Elliot learned of the overtures of Count Zichy and his imperial colleagues. The Austrian ambassador had been reluctant to write to Sir Henry because Sir Henry was so inclined toward misunderstandings, as he termed it; on calling at the embassy, however, he found Elliot, although somewhat sharp in his insinuations about Austria's relations to the insurgents, inclined none the less to approve the consular mission.[111] The queen's representative was suspicious of the "northern powers" and their proposal, and he was afraid the consuls might overstep their limited instructions. On the other hand, he trusted that the mission might discourage the insurgents in their hopes for Austrian aid, and he saw advantages in having an English representative in the field to keep the imperial consuls in check. The next day, the twentieth, the ambassador learned that the Turks not only accepted the proposal but invited British participation as well. Under such circumstances Elliot saw no further reason to hold aloof.[112]

Eleven years before the Hercegovinian uprising, Lord Derby, then Lord Stanley, had prophesied that the break-up of Turkey was a question of perhaps not a very long time and had confessed that England was not pursuing a wise policy toward the sultan's Christian populations.[113] But subsequent experiences had changed the opinion of the peer who was once again directing British foreign affairs, and the summer of 1875 found him entirely disposed toward

[110] Report No. 445, Elliot to Derby, 17 August; FO 78/2385.

[111] Report No. 65C, Zichy to Andrássy, 20 August; *First Red Book,* Doc. No. 132, incomplete.

[112] Report No. 460, Elliot to Derby, 20 August; *Turkey No. 2 (1876),* Doc. No. 17, printed with important emendations (FO 78/2385). Turkey's request for the co-operation of a British consul was undoubtedly desired for the same reason that moved Elliot—the conviction that a friendly Englishman could act as a restraining influence if the mission was tempted to exceed its instructions. The invitation is complicated by the fact that the grand vizier, in his desire to secure the approval of the sultan, had assured his sovereign that Great Britain approved of the proposal. Had British co-operation not been forthcoming, the grand vizier would have found himself in a delicate situation. Even so he was dismissed on 25 August. Elliot suspected that Ignatiev had presumed in his audience to inform the sultan that all the powers had agreed on the mission. Safvet agreeably replied that he had little doubt about it. (Report No. 504, Elliot to Derby, 30 August; FO 78/2385.)

[113] Thompson, *Public Opinion and Lord Beaconsfield,* I, 204.

Turkey.[114] Willingly the minister accepted the Turkish request to communicate with Vienna about the unruly Dalmatian population and to make remonstrances in Beograd and Cetinje.[115] But at the same time Derby regretted that the Turks should make the revolt a matter of international importance by such a request; it would be better for the sultan, he wrote to Elliot on 12 August, to rely on his own strength and treat the matter purely as an internal affair.[116] In this dispatch Derby laid down the official policy of Great Britain: He desired to keep foreign interference in all forms out of Turkey; he wished that this "local outbreak of disorder" should be put down— a wish that was not at all concerned with the justice or the injustice of the rebellion. Elliot's admonitions and remonstrances received his complete concurrence. "I approve your urging activity on the Porte," Derby telegraphed after a few days. "The consequences may be serious if the Porte allows its troops to be overpowered, or the insurrection to drag on unchecked for a length of time. Warn the Grand Vizier confidentially in this sense from H. M. Government.[117]

The British attitude toward the mission of the consuls was not at all improved by the fact that the tsar's invitation to participate was never delivered. The Russian chargé d'affaires found no one at the Foreign Office when he went to discharge his task[118] and London was left to act on Elliot's reports alone. Even so, the general disposition of English policy made it inevitable that the plan of the three emperors should meet with little response. Lord Derby, true to his suspicious and apathetic nature, did not like the plan and anticipated little good from it.[119] The prime minister shared this opinion. Disraeli was anxious about outside complications and he, like his colleague, wanted the sultan to crush the rebellion himself. No less than Elliot he was annoyed at what he termed a superhuman want of

[114] Bartholomey to Jomini, London, 4 August; *Slavonic Review*, III, 426.

[115] Safvet to Musurus, 10 August; *Turkey No. 2 (1876)*, Doc. No. 11. Derby to Ffrench, 12 August; *ibid.*, Doc. No. 12.

[116] Draft No. 235, Derby to Elliot, 12 August; *ibid.*, Doc. No. 13.

[117] Draft No. 254, Derby to Elliot, 19 August; FO 78/2377. Draft No. 218, same to same, 30 July; *ibid.*

[118] Report No. 288, incl., Jomini to Bartholemey in London, 5/17 August; FO 69/911. Report No. 49F, Mayr to Andrássy, St. Petersburg, 17/29 September; SA, Varia Turquie I, 1875.

[119] Ponsonby to Disraeli, Balmoral, 3 September; George Earle Buckle (editor), *The Letters of Queen Victoria, Second Series* (New York, 1926), II, 420 (hereafter cited as *Queen Victoria*, with *Second Series* understood).

energy at the Porte.[120] But the Foreign Office came to the reluctant conclusion that there was nothing to do but join with the other powers,[121] and on 24 August Disraeli gave his consent, protesting still, however, that he did not like it.[122]

The notice of the government's approval which went to Elliot the same day was no letter of cordiality and enthusiasm. Its important passage read:

. . . . Her Majesty's Government consent to this step with reluctance, as they doubt the expediency of the intervention of foreign Consuls. Such an intervention is scarcely compatible with the independent authority of the Porte over its own territory, offers an inducement to insurrection as a means of appealing to foreign sympathy against Turkish rule, and may not improbably open the way to further diplomatic interference in the internal affairs of the Empire.

Since, however, the Porte has begged your Excellency not to stand aloof, Her Majesty's Government feel that they have no alternative. They desire, at the same time, that the Turkish Government should understand that the assent of Her Majesty's Government is given at their own instance, and that Her Majesty's Government would have thought it better that the Porte should have dealt with the insurgents without foreign intervention of any kind.[123]

Thus England agreed; thus the harmony of the European concert was attained.

THE MISSION OF THE CONSULS

On 22 August the Turkish council of ministers formally approved the proposed mission of the consuls.[124] It was a decision

[120] Disraeli to Lady Bradford, 20 August; *Disraeli*, VI, 12. Also in Marquis of Zetland, *The Letters of Disraeli to Lady Bradford and Lady Chesterfield* (London, 1929), I, 275.

[121] "I suppose there is nothing to be done but to authorize Sir H. Elliot to join in this project of Consular mediation. The acceptance of it by the Porte seems to me to be exceedingly weak. They had much better have relied on their own power and suppressed the insurrection with a firm hand, as we advised them; but what can be expected of such a wretched system of personal Government except incapacity and consequent irresolution. I should expect this Consular mediation to be but another name for intervention—at all events it will be a direct inducement for the Christian populations to revolt wherever they have grievances. We cannot very well help joining, as, if we refuse, the other Powers would go on without us and we are probably the only Power on whom the Porte can at all depend for honest counsel or support. . . . ." (Memorandum of Lord Tenterden [Permanent Undersecretary of the Foreign Office], 21 August; FO 78&2385).

[122] *Disraeli*, VI, 12.

[123] Draft No. 258, Derby to Elliot, 24 August; *Turkey No. 2 (1876)*, Doc. No. 16.

[124] Zichy to Andrássy, 23 August; *First Red Book*, Doc. No. 135.

which caused Count Zichy considerable trouble. Only the day before the ministry had been changed to bring in the three mutually hostile ex-grand viziers, and rumor had it that the restored officials were going to reject the proposal in spite of the sultan's consent. Midhat was reported to be opposed to the dispatch of Server Pasha as commissioner, a man whom he termed a "wet-hen" and an "imbecile." Hussein Avni was said to be demanding rejection of the mission as an unwarranted interference in Turkish affairs and to be insisting on prompt suppression of the rebellion. In his despair the Austrian ambassador sought out his Russian colleague, and the two set about saving the plan. Ignatiev wrote a sharp note to the grand vizier and joined with Zichy in spreading a rumor, designed for the sultan's ears, that the new ministers were intent on defying His Majesty's imperial will. The desired effect was secured. Abdul Aziz sent an adjutant to the council of ministers and the mission was accepted.[125] The local authorities in Bosnia were informed of the coming of the consuls; a new military commander for the province was named, and Server Pasha was made president of the council of state and sent to the scene of rebellion with orders for the most generous righting of acknowledged wrong.[126]

[125] Report No. 66B, Zichy to Andrássy, 24 August; SA, Varia Turquie I, 1875. In talking a few days later with Zichy the sultan was very cordial toward the proposal. With great zest the naive ambassador reported to Andrássy and to his colleagues Abdul Aziz's words of thanks for the suggestion and his repeated expressions of appreciation for the good-will of the three imperial powers. (Tel. No. 82, Zichy to Andrássy, 28 August; *First Red Book*, Doc. No. 138, incomplete. Report No. 68AD, same to same, 31 August; SA, Varia Turquie I, 1875.) When Elliot asked Safvet about Zichy's account of the audience, the minister replied: "My dear Ambassador, you have been here long enough to know that the great object of the Sultan always is, that an Ambassador, who has an audience of him, should go away satisfied, even if it should be at the expense of his Ministers." (Report No. 504, Elliot to Derby, 30 August; FO 78/2385.)

[126] Instructions addressed to Server Pasha; *Turkey No. 2 (1876)*, Doc. No. 22, Inclosure No. 2. Ignatiev claimed credit for advising the sending of Server as commissioner charged with measures for pacification (Ignatiev, *Istoricheski Vyesnik*, CXXXV, 444). The character and work of the new peace agent inspired a number of varying opinions. One Austrian diplomat who knew Server well found the choice of doubtful wisdom. According to his view the pasha had never shown initiative and energy in any position he had ever held, while his slowness and hesitations were proverbial even at the Porte (Report No. 42, Mayr to Andrássy, St. Petersburg, 10/22 August; SA, Varia Turquie I, 1875). Stillman, the pro-insurgent *Times* correspondent, reminded his readers that a comparable mission undertaken by Server in Crete had been a complete fiasco, and he predicted that his mission now would meet the same end. The trouble was not the commissioner's personality, Stillman went on; the trouble was a total lack of faith on the part of the Christians

During these same days instructions to the six consuls were drawn up by the ambassadors in Constantinople, instructions varying somewhat in phraseology but all in conformity with the agreement that the foreign agents should warn the insurgents of their isolation and admonish them to submission.[127] All of the members selected for the mission had lived for some time in northwestern Turkey and were therefore fairly well acquainted with local conditions and persons.[128] On 4 September the Austrian, Russian, and German delegates arrived in Mostar, the starting point of the mission. Server Pasha, who had preceded them, took no notice of their coming—as if

---

toward promises emanating from the Turks, and the only solution was radical reform under European guaranty (*The Times* [London], 2 September 1875, p. 5, col. 4). The English consul in Mostar had quite contrary convictions: "Dervish Pasha [the provincial governor-general] is removed. Nothing could be more mistimed and injudicious. The revolution will acquire strength and the Turks be discouraged. Nobody is so fit to command here at this moment as Dervish. The Government should give him high rank and order him still to conduct operations here. Trebigne is relieved. Several thousand Servians are ravaging the Bosniac frontier. A capable governor is required at Serajevo. . . . . No one here can understand the mission of Server Pasha. The rebels were offered by Constant Effendi every possible concession but evidently would accept none. What more can Server offer? Now that they have been murdering, burning and robbing in all directions and have inflicted all the misery and destruction in their power on the Mussulman population, any talk of concessions to them would be felt by the Turks here as a humiliation not to be endured, and, as Dervish Pasha said to me, all control over them would probably be lost and each would seek his own vengeance as best he might. I think Server Pasha will at once see that he has no work to do here at present. He might on the contrary be useful if sent at once to Belgrade with an ultimatum." (Report No. 5, Holmes to Derby, Mostar, 2 September; FO 78/2536.)

[127] Tel. No. 478, Elliot to Derby, 25 August; *Turkey No. 2 (1876)*, Doc. No. 19. Report No. 479, same to same, 26 August; *ibid.*, Doc. No. 20. Tel. No. 76, Zichy to Andrássy, 23 August; *First Red Book*, Doc. No. 135. Tel., Hofmann to Zichy, 31 August; *ibid.*, Doc. No. 139. Ignatiev's instructions to the Russian consul are inclosed in Report No. 480, Elliot to Derby, 26 August; FO 78/2385. Bourgoing to Dozon in Mostar, Therapia, 20 August; *First Yellow Book*, pp. 25–26. Robilant to Durando in Galatz, Vienna, 28 August; *First Green Book*, Doc. No. XXVII. The agents selected were, for Austria-Hungary, Wassitsch, consul at Scutari; for Germany, Baron von Lichtenberg, consul in Ragusa; for France, Dozon, consul in Mostar; for Italy, Durando, Italian Danubian commissioner and consul-general in Bosnia; for England, Holmes, consul in Sarajevo (Bosna-Seraï); and for Russia, Jastrebov, consul in Scutari. There was some surprise at the time, and some suspicion among the anti-Slavs, that Jonin, the Russian consul-general in Ragusa and principal agent of the tsar in the western Balkans, was passed over on account of alleged illness (*The Times* [London], 31 August, p. 4, col. 3). The common assumption was that Jonin was in close contact with the insurgent leaders. Stillman denied it at the time (letter to editor, *Spectator,* 24 February 1877, pp. 245–46), but affirmed it later in his memoirs (*Autobiography of a Journalist,* II, 148).

[128] *The Times* (London), 7 September 1875, p. 8, col. 2.

to show, the Austrian agent remarked, the little importance he attached to their labors. Only on the next day were the conventional ceremonial visits dispatched. Server then took up the purpose of the mission, telling the consuls that the insurgents believed that the foreigners had come to protect them and asking them to begin their duties immediately by a proclamation to Hercegovinians, Bosnians, Montenegrins, and Serbs alike that would disabuse the rebel mind. For his own part, the commissioner was pessimistic; he intended to send out a proclamation calling the leaders to Mostar, and if they did not appear—and he expected that they would not—he would consider his own work concluded. The three consuls refused the invitation to issue a proclamation on the ground that they were instructed to talk with the insurgents in person. They too believed that no leader of the revolt would venture into Mostar, but urged the commissioner to go out to the frontier on specified days and there conduct his negotiations. After some hesitation, Server consented.[129]

On the seventh, the other delegates had arrived and a meeting was called to discuss procedure. The British agent, characteristically enough, began the deliberations by repeating Server's proposal for individual proclamations addressed to the two principalities as well as to the Bosnians and Hercegovinians. The suggestion was voted down five to one. Instead it was agreed that the duty of the mission was to support the work of the special commissioner, and on the following day two of the delegates called on Server to learn more of his plans. They found this worthy far from cordial or helpful. His instructions had it that the mission of the consuls was to end as soon as contact had been established between commissioner and insurgents. Since he was not to permit the foreign agents to participate in any negotiations, he proposed to keep away from them. He announced his intention to go to Stolaz and repatriate the refugees and then to set up a special mixed tribunal to which the insurgents would be called within a given time. As for the consuls, information coming to him from Constantinople promised that they would admonish the Serbs and Montenegrins as well as the rebels in Turkey proper; but whether they did or not, so far as Server was concerned the quicker they started to work on the insurgents, the better it would be.[130] The

[129] Report No. 1, Wassitsch to Andrássy, 6 September; *First Red Book,* Doc. No. 142.

[130] Report No. 2, Wassitsch to Andrássy, Mostar, 10 September; *First Red Book,* Doc. No. 146.

commissioner proceeded to issue his own eloquent plea for submission and went his own way, leaving the consuls to their own devices.[131]

In view of the instructions against the appearance of a collective action, the consuls divided themselves into two groups of three each and went forth to discourage the rebellion. The delegates of England, Russia, and France went to Nevesinje, and their colleagues set out toward the Dalmatian frontier. For the moment the province was relatively quiet. Turkish troops had been arriving in considerable numbers and the Christian bands had been retiring before them. So quiet was it, in fact, that the Porte had just triumphantly announced—with the consular mission undoubtedly in mind—that order had been completely restored.[132] This claim, of course, was only a Turkish pretension. The consuls interviewed numerous insurgent leaders and nowhere, as they progressed from one appalling scene to another, did they find Christian rebels who were willing to submit. Everywhere their official message met with the same response: it was impossible for the abuse-ridden *rayah* to have confidence in Turkish promises and to submit to the proclaimed mercy of the special commissioner; the insurgents would talk with Server Pasha only in the presence of the consuls and would return to their burned homes only when the European powers guaranteed security and genuine reform.[133] At best there was little possibility that the delegates, prom-

---

[131] Server's proclamation to the insurgents read in part as follows: ". . . . It is notorious that our magnanimous Sovereign is animated towards his faithful subjects with paternal sentiments, and also that, like an affectionate father, he never allows his children to be molested by anyone whoever it may be. I invite you, therefore, to come to me without delay to communicate to me all the facts that you allege have been communicated contrary to the laws and regulations in force in the Empire. Justice will be done you, and your legitimate demands will be favourably received. But to render yourselves worthy of this sovereign favour, you must immediately return to your homes which you abandoned upon insufficient grounds . . . . Your safest course is the one that I have just pointed out to you. As soon as you revert to it, you will recover both happiness and tranquillity. . . . ." (Text in *Turkey No. 2* [*1876*], Doc. No. 28, Inclosure No. 2, British Foreign Office translation.)

[132] *The Times* (London), 2 September 1875, p. 5, cols. 4–5; 6 September, p. 5, cols. 3–5; 7 September, p. 3, col. 1; 14 September, p. 6, col. 1. Charles Yriatre in September made a journey along the Austrian frontier and down in Bosnia and wrote a very interesting account of his experiences as well as a vivid description of the country in "La Bosnie et l'Herzégovine pendant l'insurrection," *Revue des deux mondes,* 1 March 1876, pp. 167–200.

[133] Report No. 47B, Seiller to Andrássy, Berlin, 22 October; SA, Varia Turquie I, 1875. Report No. 81C, Zichy to Andrássy, Constantinople, 19 October, *ibid.*

ising nothing definite and guaranteeing nothing at all, could influence the defiant Christians, but it was Turkish perfidy which gave the mission its coup de grâce. A considerable body of insurgents had on 19 September gathered in good faith near Nevesinje to meet the consuls, and the governor-general, knowing of the interview, ordered a surprise attack. Fortunately for the foreign representatives—and therefore fortunately also for the Turks—the troops made the assault before daylight on the twentieth, a few hours after the consuls had departed.[134] After such a gross abuse of good faith further negotiations between consuls and insurgents were quite naturally out of the question. The mission promptly ended in dismal failure. The foreign delegates went back to their starting point and the insurgents returned to the one support on which they could rely—their meager arms.

The consuls arrived again in Mostar with a profound sense of

Report No. 82, same to same, 22 October; *ibid.* Report No. 4, Wassitsch to Andrássy, 26 September; *ibid.* Same to same, Mostar, 13 September; *First Red Book,* Doc. No. 147. Same to same, Trebinje, 17 September; *ibid.,* Doc. No. 148. Same to same, Mostar, 24 September; *ibid.,* Doc. No. 150. Durando to Visconti-Venosta, Mostar, 28 September; *First Green Book,* Doc. No. L. Report No. 7, Holmes to Elliot, Mostar, 28 September; *Turkey No. 2 (1876),* Doc. No. 32, inclosure.

[134] Report No. 607, Elliot to Derby, 28 September; *Turkey No. 2 (1876),* Doc. No. 31. Consul Holmes's account (Report No. 7, to Elliot, 28 September; *ibid.,* Doc. No. 32, inclosure) was toned down in its reference to Turkish treachery when it was published in the following year. The printed version passes off the origin of the attack by a reference to the governor-general's claim that the encounter was provoked, contrary to Turkish plans, by the insurgents' seizure of a convoy. The pertinent part of Holmes's dispatch actually read as follows: ".... The Governor-General had been at Stolatz, and had only left for Mostar two hours before our arrival. That evening my colleagues and myself came to the conclusion that the Governor-General, who was perfectly acquainted with our whereabouts, had ordered the expedition to surprise the insurgents. He did not, however, know when we intended to leave them, and therefore he had acted without the slightest regard for the consequences which might result to ourselves and to our mission, and that this proceeding rendered perfectly useless our going to Bilekia or anywhere else, as the insurgents who might escape would naturally warn their comrades of the danger of meeting to confer with us. .... On the 23rd I spoke to the Governor-General. .... I said it might have been a very serious thing for us if it had happened one day sooner, and he immediately replied that he had given a certain Omer Bey, an officer on the staff, strict orders to attend to our safety. Now if he had done this before the expedition started from Stolatz where he was at the time, he must have contemplated the attack; and his statement as to its being a mere accident was clearly untrue. I mentioned it also to Server Pasha who seemed embarrassed what to say about it" (FO 78/2536). In Constantinople the British consul, who alleged himself to be a very indignant man, was accused of having an understanding with the Turkish commander (Tel. No. 97, Zichy to Andrássy, 25 September; SA, Varia Turquie I, 1875).

the inadequacy of existing plans to bring peace and order to the fury-ridden land. The German representative saw no hope for a direct understanding between Turk and *rayah;* the only possible solution appeared to him to be reorganization of the province under European control.[135] The British agent concluded that circumstances would impose either a European or an Austrian intervention and, although he thought the former better, he confessed that even collective action of the Great Powers could do little toward a genuine solution.[136] The Italian consul hoped that peace might be brought by the organization of Bosnia and Hercegovina on the model of the Lebanon district in Syria.[137] The Russian representative contented himself with a severe judgment of the Turks and a blanket vindication of the insurgents' demands.[138] The Austrian delegate reported the insufficiency of their instructions and likewise the improbability that Turkish arms could ever restore order.[139] In Constantinople on 26 September the three imperial ambassadors sat down to study five of the consular reports. That of the suspected Holmes was not circulated by Sir Henry Elliot. Under the leadership of General Ignatiev, the three diplomats—one capable man and two nonentities—proposed to move on to more positive steps. Recognizing the failure of the mission, the ambassadors went beyond the original agreement and instructed their respective consuls to discuss the problem of pacification with Server Pasha and present to them a practical solution which would be acceptable to both sides.[140] Ignatiev, as *doyen,* invited the other ambassadors to join in the instructions, but only Bourgoing of France responded.

Wassitsch, the Austrian delegate, seized on the new order as an opportunity to advance the insurgent cause. He argued to his colleagues the view that the only promising way out was a peaceful

[135] Report No. 82, Zichy to Andrássy, 22 October, giving substance of the German consul's report; SA, Varia Turquie I, 1875.

[136] Report No. 7, Holmes to Elliot, Mostar, 28 September; FO 78/2536. This dispatch is given with its most important passages deleted from *Turkey No. 2 (1876),* Doc. No. 32, inclosure.

[137] Tel., Durando to Visconti-Venosta, Mostar, 27 September; *First Green Book,* Doc. No. XLII.

[138] Report No. 81C, Zichy to Andrássy, 19 October, which gives extracts from two dispatches of Jastrebov of 15 and 19 September (old style); SA, Varia Turquie I, 1875.

[139] Report No. 5, Wassitsch to Andrássy, 27 September; *ibid.*

[140] Tel. No. 95, Zichy to Andrássy, 26 September; *ibid.* Report No. 76AC, same to same, 28 September; *ibid.*

meeting of Turk and Christian on neutral ground under the supervision of European agents. He converted the other consuls—even the difficult Holmes—and on the twenty-seventh the members of the mission formally recommended to their ambassadors a European intervention to effect an armistice and a conference in Ragusa in which the consuls would participate.[141]

The proposal lasted hardly over night. The grand vizier, with his jealous regard for the sovereignty of Turkey, refused to listen to the recommendation and hastily forbade his commissioner to enter into discussion with the European representatives.[142] The three imperial ambassadors were sullenly told that the consular mission was ended and that there could be no discussion of an enlargement of its duties.[143] No more success did the Wassitsch proposal have in other quarters. The ambassadors in Constantinople rejected it equally promptly[144] and the various foreign offices were no less hostile,[145] except that of St. Petersburg where Jomini betrayed sympathy for the insurgent cause.[146] In spite of the desperation of the revolted area, the repercussions abroad were still not strong enough to force a prompt intervention. For the time, consequently, the foreign agents remained inactive in Mostar and Server Pasha was left alone with the problem of pacification.

The Porte's special commissioner continued to pursue his triple program of reform promises, repatriation of refugees, and military operations. Not one of his measures, however, was successful. A new proclamation early in October contained glittering concessions, but even Holmes agreed that these measures were merely vague and

---

[141] Report No. 5, Wassitsch to Andrássy, 27 September; *ibid.* Durando to Visconti-Venosta, 27 September; *First Green Book,* Doc. No. XLII. Tel., Elliot to Derby, 28 September; FO 78/2387. Tel., Wassitsch to Andrássy, 27 September; *First Red Book,* Doc. No. 152.

[142] Safvet to Server, Constantinople, 28 September; FO 78/2425. Tel., Elliot to Derby, 28 September; FO 78/2387.

[143] Tel. No. 97, Zichy to Andrássy, 27 September; SA, Varia Turquie I, 1875.

[144] Bourgoing to Decazes, Therapia, 28 September; *First Yellow Book,* p. 32. Decazes to d'Harcourt, Versailles, 28 September; *ibid.,* p. 33. Corti to Visconti-Venosta, Therapia, 28 September; *First Green Book,* Doc. No. XLV. Tel., Elliot to Derby, 28 September; FO 78/2387.

[145] Andrássy to Wassitsch, 28 September; *First Red Book,* Doc. No. 153. Decazes to Bourgoing, 1 October; *First Yellow Book,* p. 34. Artom to Durando, Rome, 30 September; *First Green Book,* Doc. No. XLIV.

[146] Report No. 49C, Mayr to Andrássy, St. Petersburg, 17/29 September; SA, Varia Turquie I, 1875.

hastily written promises and would have no influence on the rebels.[147] "The utmost distrust prevails regarding any reforms," he wrote. "It avails nothing that Server Pasha announces them. They are not yet carried out and cannot be for a long time, and the people disbelieve that they ever will be. . . . ." It was a skepticism which the consul found well grounded. Incompetent officials and an unrepentant Moslem population were proof enough to convince him that there was little likelihood of real reform.[148] And, indeed, the passing weeks of the autumn proved only too well the validity of his prediction. "It is a fact," he wrote later in October, "that Server Pasha's reforms are even now not being carried out." The commissioner sat in his office and peacefully accepted any report brought to him by the corrupt local officials. The Moslems laughed at him—and the Christians continued to despair.[149]

With such eminently justified suspicion in the minds of the insurgents and refugees, Server's attempts to lead them back to their devastated villages were no more successful than his reforms. A few Christians did venture to return to their homes, but massacre was promptly their lot[150] and new flights into Dalmatia ensued.[151]

Server Pasha at the end of September had hoped to destroy the insurgents in two weeks as a prelude to pacification,[152] but this too

[147] Report No. 12, Holmes to Elliot, 11 October; *Turkey No. 2 (1876)*, Doc. No. 36, Inclosure I, with the consul's opinions deleted (FO 78/2536).

[148] Report No. 13, Holmes to Elliot, 13 October, in Report No. 11, Holmes to Derby, 14 October; FO 78/2536: ". . . . Even if the chief authorities are sincere, the matter virtually depends on the rich and influential Turks of the Herzegovine, who have formerly, and who will in future neutralise all the efforts of the Constantinople functionaries. Even now scarcely a day passes without indications of how little the native Mussulmans believe that they will have to change their conduct, and the population in general regard with incredulity bordering on contempt, all Server Pasha's announcements of reform. A feeble government like Turkey, however sincere, cannot change by a decree the nature and traditions of the ignorant, fanatic, corrupt and obstinate agents which it must necessarily employ, nor can it alter the sentiments of whole populations. I could give endless examples of how the laws are perverted and put aside in these countries, which would show your Excellency how little likelihood there is of the proposed reforms ever being carried out, except in a few cases of taxation which depend on the Government itself. . . . ."

[149] Report No. 16, Holmes to Elliot, 21 October, in Report No. 13, Holmes to Derby, 22 October; FO 78/2536.

[150] Report No. 702, Elliot to Derby, 26 October; *Turkey No. 2 (1876)*, Doc. No. 40.

[151] Holmes to Elliot, 23 October; *ibid.*, Doc. No. 42, inclosure.

[152] Tel., Wassitsch to Andrássy, 30 September; *First Red Book*, Doc. No. 157.

was a plan that failed. Encouraged by European notice, the insurgents were never more determined than they now were in the fall of the year. The troops killed such insurgents as they could find, but their minor enterprises led to no results.[153] The morale of Turkish officers and men was soon ebbing. Knowing nothing of the country, they dreaded to leave the highroads, and most of the victories they announced were compounded of exaggeration and pure invention.[154] As winter approached the soldiers were in a miserable plight—sick, ragged, without proper food and shelter. Server Pasha, however, continued to do nothing and to assert that all was well.[155] While the land was still full of insurgents, the commissioner insisted that the rebellion had been suppressed,[156] and in the face of serious Turkish defeats he blandly continued his cheerful reports. With military operations demoralized and reform measures a tragic fiasco, conditions in Bosnia and Hercegovina were going from a very bad bad to worse. Only European diplomacy, Consul Holmes warned his government, could prevent complete anarchy in the spring.[157]

In such a manner the first stage of the rebellion came to an end. The Turks had failed to pacify the insurgents, and so had the European powers. The Austrian foreign minister had wished that the uprising should be ended before international complications began and had laid plans to discourage the troublemakers; but he had been obliged to give way at least partially to Austria's ally, who had nothing to lose by a mild intervention in the internal affairs of Turkey. A second revision of plans Andrássy had had to make when Tsar Alexander, on his own initiative, had thrown overboard an exclusive move of the three imperial powers in favor of a common action of the European concert. Two of the remaining powers—France and Italy—had accepted the invitation eagerly, and the third—Great Britain—had accepted too, but with bad grace and hesitation. The

[153] Report No. 14, Holmes to Elliot, 14 October, in Report No. 11, Holmes to Derby, 14 October; FO 78/2536 (suppressed from *Turkey No. 2* [*1876*], Doc. No. 36, Inclosure No. 2).

[154] Holmes to Elliot, 23 October, in Report No. 14, Holmes to Derby, 25 October; FO 78/2536 (suppressed from *Turkey No. 2* [*1876*], Doc. No. 42, inclosure).

[155] Report No. 20, Holmes to Elliot, 11 November, in Report No. 17, Holmes to Derby, 15 November; FO 78/2536.

[156] Report No. 12, Wassitsch to Andrássy, Mostar, 23 October; SA, Varia Turquie I, 1875.

[157] Report No. 21, Holmes to Elliot, 19 November, in Report No. 18, Holmes to Derby, 22 November; FO 78/2536.

restricted consular effort which Andrássy had fashioned out of the Russian proposal had now failed and new measures were in order.

But before that work was under way two additional elements had complicated still further the problem of peace in the Balkans.

SERBIA AND THE OUTBREAK OF THE REVOLT

It was an axiom of the time that any disturbance in Bosnia and Hercegovina would have its repercussions in the principalities of Serbia and Montenegro. More than half a century earlier the former, and the greater, of the two had begun a turbulent and undesigned drive toward freedom by revolting in the name of the sultan. Subsequent times had led to autonomy, but Western ideas of a national sovereign state made slow headway through the brambles of domestic quarrels and traditional inertia.[158] Headway was made, nevertheless. In 1844 Milutin Garashanin wrote that the old Eastern question could be solved only by the Balkan people themselves through the erection of free national states on the soil of Turkey. As foreign minister of Serbia Garashanin set out to achieve that solution. Secret committees were formed; agents traveled up and down the peninsula; an innocuous-sounding literary society quietly spread its propaganda for a great south-Slavic state into Turkey and the Austrian Empire.[159] By the 'sixties Serbian sentiment had made a solid growth. The revolutionary year of 1848 had given a great impetus to Slavic nationalism and the progress of Italian unity inspired the felicitous thought that Serbia should become the Piedmont of the Balkans. In 1860 there had returned to sovereign authority in the little land a man who had the ambition, and less certainly the ability, to satisfy those dreams—Michael Obrenovich. In the next eight years Michael had laid the first real foundations of a modern state in Serbia, had brought to an end the humiliating Turkish occupation of his land,[160] and had skillfully laid a plot to set all the Balkan peoples against their Ottoman conquerors.[161] This last plan he was unable to realize; in 1868

[158] For a discussion of this question see Nicolas Iorga, "Origines des idées d'indépendance balkanique," *Le Monde slave,* IV (July 1927), 73–93.

[159] Stojanovic, *op. cit.,* pp. vii–viii.

[160] T. W. Riker, "Michael of Serbia and the Turkish Occupation," *Slavonic Review,* XII (1933–34), 133–54, 409–29.

[161] For sketches of Michael, see *ibid.,* pp. 133–34; Seton-Watson, *The Rôle of Bosnia in International Politics,* p. 10; Seton-Watson, *Le Monde slave,* I (1926), 212;

Michael paid the ultimate price for the enmities he had aroused and his schemes were spared the dubious test of application.

Michael left no heir and designated no successor. The conspirators hoped that the confusion of the day would permit the return of the Karageorgevich dynasty; but alert ministers forestalled a coup d'état, and Milan Obrenovich, a cousin of Michael and a boy of thirteen or fourteen then pursuing his studies in Paris, was made prince of Serbia. During the next four years Yovan Ristich dominated the prince, his fellow regents, and the land, despite the concession of a constitution labeled democratic. Ristich sprang from humble origins to become one of the outstanding men of his country. A Doctor of Philosophy from Heidelberg, he was saved from a professorship of history by a man who recognized his ability; after his return home he occupied several high positions in domestic and foreign service.[162] When Milan attained his majority in 1872 he bore a bitter grudge against the constitution-maker who had deprived him in his minority of the absolute power that had belonged to Michael. In the years which followed, the prince seized such opportunities as were offered to dispose of the detested Ristich; but the unwelcome minister's command of a parliamentary majority made him a formidable man to eliminate.

Prince Milan began his reign auspiciously. He was young, intelligent, and attractive, and the Serbs believed that their boy ruler would rise to the great occasion in store for their land. But Milan had severe liabilities in his family, his education, and his temperament. His putative father had died early as the result of a dissipated life, and his mother was beyond the pale of conventional respectability.

Harold W. V. Temperley, *History of Serbia* (London, 1919), pp. 242–47. A comprehensive story of Michael's Balkan alliance may be pieced together now from a number of studies: S. Th. Lascaris, "La première alliance entre la Grèce et la Serbia, le traité de Voeslau du 14/26 août 1867," *Le Monde slave,* September 1926, pp. 390–437; Émile Haumant, "Les Origines de la lutte pour la Macédoine," *Le Monde slave,* October 1926, pp. 52–66; Georges Y. Devas, "Les Origines de l'unité yougoslave," *Le Monde slave,* April 1918, pp. 532–49; Ed. Engelhardt, "La Confédération balkanique," *Revue d'histoire diplomatique,* VI (1892), 29–55; Michel Lhéritier, "Le Traité d'alliance secret entre la Grèce et la Serbia (1867–68)," *Revue des études napoléoniennes,* XXLII (1924), 133–41; Lhéritier, *Histoire diplomatique de la Grèce,* III, 222–38; S. Th. Lascaris, *La Politique extérieure de la Grèce avant et après le Congrès de Berlin (1875–1881)* (Paris, 1924), pp. 32–34, 217–20; Simeon Radeff, *La Macédoine et la renaissance bulgare au XIXᵉ siècle* (Sofia, 1918), pp. 233–42; Ignatiev, *Izvestiia,* 1914, III, 102–7, 112–14.

[162] Trivanovitch, *Journal of Modern History,* III, 415–16; Haumant, *La Formation de la Yougoslavie,* pp. 371–73; *Andrássy,* II, 251.

His schooling had been begun in Paris, but when he moved to Beograd his turbulence and laziness defeated the educational labors of a feeble tutor. He grew to man's estate in the corrupt atmosphere of his capital without family or friends and was mentally and morally neglected. In spite of his native intelligence, Milan well-nigh of necessity became frivolous, prodigal, and intriguing. Such hopes as the Serbs entertained for the future of their prince were soon being undermined by the growing conviction that Milan was ready to subordinate country to personal whim. Some of his subjects turned their thoughts to the exiled Peter Karageorgevich, and others looked to Prince Nicholas of Montenegro.[163]

Milan's irresponsibility and his animus toward the powerful Ristich, coupled with the party intrigues of unseasoned politicians, made Serbia the scene of heated political battles. Ristich's liberal party commanded a majority in the *skupshtina,* and Milan's repeated attempts to construct ministries from the opposition precipitated crises of growing frequency.[164] In March of 1875, after three cabinets had fallen in less than half a year, the prince felt obliged to dissolve the skupshtina.[165] As the time approached when revolt against Turkey was to flame up just beyond the frontiers of Serbia, the principality was torn by domestic discord.

Foreign policy in these first years of Milan's reign was similarly vacillating. The regents swung Serbia from a Russian to an Austrian orientation and then back again after the re-emergence of Russia in 1870–71 and the punishment of Beograd by Russian sponsorship of the Bulgarians and Montenegro.[166] But neither Great Power was ready to support the ambitions which survived the murder of Michael, and the Serbian position was still further weakened

[163] Trivanovitch, *Journal of Modern History,* III, 420–23; Haumant, *op. cit.,* pp. 375–76; Temperley, *History of Serbia,* pp. 263–64; William Miller, *The Ottoman Empire and Its Successors, 1801–1922* (Cambridge, 1923), pp. 336–37.

[164] Jovanović, *Slavonic Review,* IV, 389; Temperley, *History of Serbia,* pp. 261–62; Trivanovitch, *Journal of Modern History,* III, 425–27.

[165] Schulthess, *Europäischer Geschichtskalender,* 1875, pp. 477–82. Chedomille Miyatovich, *The Memoirs of a Balkan Diplomatist* (London, 1917), p. 109. For a description of Serbian politics in 1874 and 1875 see the reports of the Rumanian agent, Sturdza, of 30 November 1874, 27 January 1875, and 24 February in Nicolas Iorga, *Correspondance diplomatique roumaine sous le roi Charles Ier (1866–1880)* (Paris, 1923), pp. 326–28, 333–34, 335–36.

[166] Jovanović, *Slavonic Review,* IV, 385; Haumant, *Le Monde slave,* October 1926, pp. 58–69; Seton-Watson, *Le Monde slave,* May 1926, p. 199; Trivanovitch, *Journal of Modern History,* III, 420.

by bad relations between Beograd and Cetinje.[167] Despite discouragement from St. Petersburg and an absolute veto called out from Vienna,[168] Serbian hopes remained set upon Bosnia and Hercegovina, and secret societies carried on Michael's plan for an agitation in the interest not only of war on Turkey but also of the union of all the Southern Slavs. Shortly after the assassination in 1868 Benjamin Kállay, newly appointed Austrian diplomatic agent, made a tour of Serbia and reported to his government the close bond of sympathy between the principality and Bosnia, and repeatedly in the next years he warned Vienna of the enduring direction of Serbian aspirations.[169] Comparable accounts went to Bucharest from the Rumanian agents. The Serb press made no secret of the necessity for the eventual unification of Bosnia with Serbia. "Today," said the *Srbski Narod* in 1871, "we can console our friends as well as our enemies with the news that young Serbia has secured alliances thanks to which she will attain her aim in the East in the same manner that Piedmont attained hers in southern Italy and Prussia in central Europe. . . ."[170] In the next year the *Vidov Dan* proclaimed, "We the people, we have the duty and the right to prepare . . . . the powerful and vigorous material for the work of delivering our unhappy brothers in Turkey."[171] In the summer of 1872—as another illustration of this current of feeling—during a demonstration held in Beograd, banners were carried bearing such slogans as "Let the frontiers be extended: that is the desire of Serbs of all countries," and "Bosnia, Hercegovina and Old Serbia ought to be mine."[172] In 1874 another Serb journal maintained that "the vital question of our state is intimately bound up with the question of all the Serbs, and their emancipation and unity . . . . is the one condition of its existence . . . ." Later in the same year the skupshtina somewhat covertly embraced the same ideal; in an address to the throne the majority declared:

> To direct the scattered forces of our people toward a serious and common action, to come to an understanding with and draw close to our fellow peoples

[167] Ignatiev, *Izvestiia*, 1914, IV, 148.

[168] Seton-Watson, *Le Monde slave*, February 1926, pp. 217–20.

[169] *Ibid.*, May 1926, pp. 188–95; August 1926, pp. 273–88. Seton-Watson, *The Rôle of Bosnia in International Relations*, pp. 12–13.

[170] Report of Rumanian agent in Beograd, 3/15 July 1871; Iorga, *Correspondance*, p. 86. For earlier reports of the same tenor, see *ibid.*, pp. 54, 71.

[171] Report of the Rumanian agent in Beograd, 27 January (old style) 1872, *ibid.*, pp. 90–91.

[172] Report of the Rumanian agent in Beograd, 19/31 August 1872; *ibid.*, p. 93.

who have the same leanings, the same interests and the same dangers, that is the route which the national skupshtina ardently wishes to see its illustrious sovereign always travel.[173]

But as the early summer of 1875 approached, Serbia was too occupied with internal problems to think seriously of foreign adventures. Widespread dissatisfaction with Prince Milan's regime was apparent,[174] and an agitation in favor of calling Prince Nicholas of Montenegro began to make itself seriously felt.[175] A heated electoral campaign began as soon as the national legislature was dissolved in March and the outcome of the election, set for August, was in doubt. The newly arrived British consular agent in June described the state of affairs as "far from being as good as we might desire." The political situation which he described to Lord Derby was in marked contrast to the sedate practices of Westminster. "The large mass of the electors," he explained, "consists of uneducated Boors, and it is very much to be feared that many of the Deputies are not much better."

It will of course take me some time to form my own independent opinion of what is passing here, but all those persons with whom I have conversed on the subject are agreed in thinking that the time when the next Assembly will meet and the attitude of that body, will be critical events for Prince Milan, and his Dynasty.

Should the majority of the Deputies prove themselves well disposed towards their actual ruler, many difficulties may be got over. . . . . If however the reverse should take place, and contrary to the expectations of some of his supporters, should the new Assembly allow itself to be swayed by the evil counsels of the agitators, and to follow in the footsteps of the preceding "Skoupstchina," it is not impossible that the Prince may be induced to adopt some extreme measures or even have recourse to some desperate resolution.

I have been told that previous to my arrival here, the possibility of such a contingency as a "Coup d'Etat" was discussed privately by the Prince himself with some of the foreign accredited Agents, but the opinion appears to prevail that it is doubtful whether the Prince could rely on the support of the Army in any emergency, or on the efficient cooperation of any public man of notoriety, possessing both sufficient energy and influence to secure success, if serious complications were to arise.[176]

Such was the state of affairs in Serbia when revolt broke out in Hercegovina. The first news was received in Beograd with some

[173] Iorga, *Correspondance*, pp. 314–15, 323–24.

[174] Schulthess, *Europäischer Geschichtskalender*, 1875, p. 482.

[175] *Andrássy*, II, 251–52; *Aus dem Leben König Karls von Rumänien*, II, 443.

[176] Political Report No. 11, White to Derby, Beograd, 11 June 1875; FO 78/2399.

doubt. Then came confirmation, and the Serbs concluded that the rebellion was serious. For a moment, however, their spontaneous sympathy was dampened; reports had it that two villages had raised the Austrian flag and it was supposed that Austrian agitators had been at work in the wake of Emperor Francis Joseph's visit to Dalmatia. More information soon dispelled this assumption and Serb opinion rallied to the insurgent cause.[177]

The revolt, apparently unexpected in Beograd, naturally complicated the domestic political situation. The opposition group readily seized upon the disturbance as a welcome subject for agitation, and by the same token the government, fighting with all strength for its existence, was confronted with a new and formidable embarrassment.[178] Prince Milan, resentful toward Ristich's constitution and occupied with plans for his forthcoming engagement, was likewise disturbed by the news from Hercegovina. He was concerned lest Serb hotheads rush into the fray and thereby compromise the principality. But a greater anxiety to him was the possible role of Prince Nicholas of Montenegro. In the competition between the two for the leadership of the Southern Slavs, Milan could not afford to be less sympathetic toward the rebellion than his rival, and it became quickly apparent that Serbia could not stand aloof if Montenegro made war on Turkey.[179] Before the end of July Prince Milan and his government, seriously hopeful of avoiding a conflict, sought a statement from Nicholas concerning the attitude of Montenegro.[180]

It was at best a difficult moment for an important decision in Beograd, but a visit of the prince to Vienna made a definitive resolution for the time impossible. That the prince should go to the Austrian capital during such a crisis was for the press an "opportunity for indulging in the wildest flights of political romance." It was announced as Milan set out on 30 July that he was going to take counsel in the Ballplatz,[181] but the actual purpose of his journey was the formal settlement of his engagement to the daughter of a wealthy landowner of Bessarabia. Milan's mother had sought out the richest fiancée to be found for her debt-ridden son, and since his mother's unsavory

[177] *Augsburger Allgemeine Zeitung*, 22 July 1875, p. 3191.

[178] Report No. 47, Cingria to Andrássy, 22 July; SA, Varia Turquie II, 1875.

[179] Report No. 48, Wrede to Andrássy, Beograd, 26 July; *ibid.*

[180] Report No. 49, Wrede to Andrássy, 28 July; *ibid.*

[181] *The Times* (London), 2 August 1875, p. 5, col. 2. *Augsburger Allgemeine Zeitung*, 3 August, p. 3373; *ibid.*, 4 August, pp. 3392-93.

reputation made it impossible for her to appear in Serbia, the prince was obliged—and happy—to go to Vienna for the ceremony of betrothal.[182] But whether Milan wished these political counsels discussed in the press or no, the revolt made it desirable for the Austrian foreign minister to talk over Serbia's position with the prince. Committed from the beginning to the speediest pacification, Andrássy energetically admonished Milan to the maintenance of peace, emphasizing as was his wont the responsibilities which precipitate action would entail. The prince professed himself mindful of the minister's arguments but declared his inability to make a commitment. He promised to do what he could in the interest of tranquillity, but protested, first, that he would be compelled to follow Nicholas of Montenegro in case Nicholas went to war,[183] and, second, that agitation in Serbia had reached such heights that he feared for the decisions of the skupshtina. To the latter excuse Andrássy had a ready reply. He advised the prince to go before his turbulent deputies and remind them that only a few years previously another parliament had resolved on war on a neighbor state and that the result had been Sedan and the collapse of Napoleon III's empire. The little lesson in history appeared to impress the youthful ruler, and he repeated his pledge to work for moderation.[184] Refreshed by his vacation and

[182] Reports Nos. 243 and 245, Ffrench to Derby, 4 and 6 August, respectively; FO 7/851. The British chargé d'affaires in Vienna was not impressed with the prince and his country: ". . . . The life which this young Prince of 23 is forced to live at Belgrade would perfectly account for his desiring escape from it whenever an opportunity occurs for so doing—educated as he has been in Paris. He finds himself in his own country entirely cut off from any civilized intercourse, in hourly dread of assassination, seeing nobody but his Ministers and his military Aide-de-camps, and even these may be said to be but half civilized, for the country possesses neither proprietors nor a middle class; nothing beyond some 1,500,000 peasants, a few of whom have become Ministers and a certain number soldiers. Even field sports have been denied to him and he can never stir outside his so-called palace without a strong military escort from the constant danger of assassination. Those who knew him as a boy were charmed with the frankness and intelligence of his character but equally struck by the change which a few years of this life in Servia have wrought in him. He has grown suspicious; his intellect is dulled; and the only things he now cares for are the pleasures of the table. Yet this is the State which aspires to be the 'Piedmont' of the Principalities, which has raised the nucleus of an army destined according to Servian creed to march one day against Turkey and overthrow her, and found and become the head of a Southern Slavonia, which is to absorb all the other Danubian and Austro-Turkish provinces of that race!" (Report No. 243.)

[183] "Extrait d'un compte rendu d'une conférence à Vienne le 5 août 1875 . . . ."; SA, Varia Turquie I, 1875 (St.P. 75).

[184] Andrássy to Wrede, 14 August; First Red Book, Doc. No. 118.

enamored of the bride whom his mother had provided, Milan returned to his capital on 12 August to find that affairs had not stood still in his absence.

On the day after the prince departed, his ministry of second- and third-rank conservatives gave its benediction openly to the rebellion and the temper of Serbian feeling mounted to fever heat. The ban on popular subscriptions was immediately lifted and within a few days the equivalent of five thousand dollars was raised for the benefit of the sick and wounded. Circulars in great numbers were sent out bearing stirring appeals. "There is not one amongst us," said one of them, "whom the report of the Insurrection in Hercegovina has not reached and who has not heard of the bloody and heroic struggle carried on by our brothers on the Narenta. There is not one amongst us who has not heard at least from old folks of the heavy lot of misery and bondage which our Nation once suffered, when our Fathers and Grandfathers rose in arms and overthrew the yoke after a bloody and famous insurrection of which we reap the fruits this day . . . . The dreadful circumstances attending such a position have driven them to arms, and to take the chances of a decisive struggle to rid themselves of a tyrannical yoke, and they have cast their future destinies on a die . . . ."[185]

Committees were permitted to enroll volunteers to go to Hercegovina, and soon armed bands were en route to the scene of the rebellion.[186] The Beograd press was allowed free rein, while a semi-official

[185] Report No. 24, White to Elliot, 4 August; FO 78/2399. White introduced his account of the activities in Serbia in these words: "I have the honour to report to Your Excellency two circumstances which if they are not meant as a sop to the patriotic excitement prevailing just now at Belgrade, and as an election manoeuvre and were to be construed as indications of the actual intentions of the Servian Government, would have to be considered as extremely reprehensible."

[186] *Ibid.* White concluded his report: "The other circumstance would be still more serious if it were possible to trace the action of this Government in an undeniable manner in these proceedings. About one hundred individuals have left Belgrade with the intention it appears of joining the rioters, but I have been as yet unable to ascertain the existence of an enlistment office, and as these men are going through Hungary there is an impossibility to trace their destination." A dispatch from Beograd on 7 August to the *Augsburger Allgemeine Zeitung* read in part: "There is no talk of Serbian neutrality if the insurrection in Hercegovina is not soon suppressed. Already the waves are high, although there is a suspicion that Austria has a hand in the game, but it is hoped that with continuation the revolt will succeed, especially should Serbia and Montenegro intervene, if only through armed bands. Many officers and under-officers of the militia have already gone *via* Croatia and Dalmatia to the theatre of war" (11 August, p. 3501). A dispatch from Ragusa dated 19 August to *The Times* (London) (21 August, p. 5, col. 4) reported:

journal in an inspired article proclaimed its warning that Serbia and Montenegro could not remain indifferent to this new flow of Slavic blood. The war minister went to the interior to inspect military equipment; garrisons were ordered to undergo energetic exercises, and at night material alleged to be firewood was brought to the Beograd fortress.[187] The foreign minister for his part sought out the Greek diplomatic agent and made a first step toward reviving the alliance which Michael had made. The minister informed the agent that, in case the rebellion went on and Montenegro became involved, his own country would be obliged to follow and that, consequently, an understanding with Greece would be invited. To that end he proposed the sending of a secret representative to Athens.[188] The motives of the Serbian cabinet in adopting its semi-compromising measures were perhaps those of expediency and principle. The Austrian agent insisted that the government was appearing to support the rebellion in order to control and moderate the national zeal,[189] and there is no doubt that a government hoping to win an impending election had to make some concession to excited popular opinion. At the same time the rebellion brought to the fore the fundamental questions of dynasty and Serbia's leadership of the Southern Slavs. Furthermore, the desire for Bosnia was too inherent a part of Beograd ideology to permit indifference to what was happening there.[190]

Prince Milan thus returned on 12 August to a land rent by a political campaign and agitated by a tumult at its door. As he arrived at his residence three hundred volunteers ready to go to Hercegovina greeted him with the shout, "War with the Turks! Lead us against the Turks!"[191] Milan's first task concerned a reply to an annoying communication from the Sublime Porte. During his absence the grand vizier had addressed to the Serb agent in Constantinople a request that the Beograd government recall from the frontier a corps of 9,000 men which had been recently moved up and which was allegedly inspiring the rebels with renewed zeal. The Serb foreign

---

"Advices received here state that numerous bands from Servia have passed into Bosnia to join the insurgents."

[187] Report No. 51, Cingria to Andrássy, Beograd, 6 August; SA, Varia Turquie II, 1875.

[188] Lhéritier, *Histoire diplomatique de la Grèce*, III, 382.

[189] Report No. 51, Cingria to Andrássy, 6 August; SA, Varia Turquie II, 1875.

[190] Jovanović, *Slavonic Review*, IV, 390.

[191] *Augsburger Allgemeine Zeitung*, 18 August 1875, p. 3614.

minister curtly replied that no troops would be withdrawn because no troops had been sent to the frontier. Not satisfied with such a response, the grand vizier abandoned the accepted form of correspondence and sent a telegram direct to the prince himself asking him what measures had been taken to restrain the excitement in Serbia. Milan declared himself insulted by this Turkish slight to his princely dignity, and in the ministerial councils of the fourteenth and fifteenth of August feeling ran high. Confidential report had it that, with the exception of the war minister, all the members of the council spoke in favor of war on Turkey. Milan, however, with Andrássy's remonstrances fresh in mind, engineered a more moderate decision; and, although the grand vizier was rebuked for his presumption in addressing the prince directly, the Serbian government agreed to do what it could to maintain order.[192]

Three days after Milan's return to Beograd the long-anticipated election took place. The bellicose attitude of the conservative ministry had not been able to stay the tide of liberal sentiment, and on 16 August the vote resulted in a substantial victory for the opposition. Constitutionally the ministry was not responsible to the skupshtina, but convention dictated otherwise, and Danilo Stevanovich and his colleagues presented their collective resignation.[193] That the verdict of the voters was a verdict for action against Turkey there was no doubt. The powerful Ristich had come out openly for war, and his party won the election despite the prince's opposition.[194] "I regret to have to report to Your Lordship," the British agent wrote on the seventeenth, "that the affairs of Servia have assumed a much more critical aspect within the last few days. The question of Servia assuming openly a hostile attitude towards the Porte has been canvassed in the electoral Districts . . . . and wherever a decided advo-

[192] Report No. 53, Cingria to Andrássy, 16 August; *First Red Book,* Doc. No. 120, incomplete. Political Report No. 29, White to Derby, 17 August; FO 78/2399.

[193] *The Times* (London), 17 August, p. 3, col. 3. *Europäischer Geschichtskalender,* 1875, p. 485. A second cause for the resignation of the ministry was the lack of sympathy between prince and cabinet which had appeared when Milan opposed its zeal for war: "Matters have become more critical here. Late Ministry were ready to resign even before the result of the election should the Prince continue to be unfavourable to the drifting into an attitude hostile to Turkey. . . . ." (Political Report No. 28, White to Derby, 17 August; FO 78/2399). The Austrian consular agent ascribed the resignation exclusively to the difference between Milan and his cabinet (Report No. 56, Wrede to Andrássy, 19 August; SA, Varia Turquie II, 1875).

[194] Trivanovitch, *Journal of Modern History,* III, 427–28.

cate of a Revolutionary War against Turkey was confronted by a doubtful candidate, the preference was given by the electors to the former one. . . . ."[195]

Prince Milan's situation was rapidly getting worse. On one side was Andrássy speaking very plainly for the Great Powers in favor of peace; on the other was his own people clamoring for war. And confronting him as the next task was the selection of a new cabinet which could sail the ship of state between Scylla and Charybdis. The result of the election was so clear that the prince found it impossible to exclude Ristich from the ministry. Unwilling, however, to turn the country over to the militant liberals, Milan attempted to form a coalition ministry in which his conservative friend Marinovich would be an important member.[196] But Ristich and Marinovich were old and unrelenting enemies, and the building of a cabinet around them proved a difficult undertaking. One after another the leading politicians refused the prince's appeal, and the critical days went by without an agreement.[197]

In the meantime the resigned ministry continued in office. Six of its seven members had been converted to war before its fall; and the election results, although a personal repudiation, encouraged them in their inclinations. With public opinion increasingly hysterical in its demand for war, the ministers inaugurated a series of preparatory measures. Order went out for the autumnal maneuvers of the militia which would call 100,000 men to the colors; plans were drawn for an enormous money-raising operation; negotiations were begun for the purchase of army supplies.[198]

[195] Political Report No. 29, White to Derby, 17 August; FO 78/2399. Report No. 56, Wrede to Andrássy, 19 August; SA, Varia Turquie II, 1875.

[196] Report No. 57, Wrede to Andrássy, 19 August; *First Red Book*, Doc. No. 124, incomplete. Marinovich was alleged to have been the discoverer of the wealthy Russian fiancée and negotiator of the wedding contract as well as leader of the party which had Milan's support (*Augsburger Allgemeine Zeitung*, 26 August 1875, p. 3735).

[197] Political Report No. 34, White to Derby, 21 August; FO 78/2399.

[198] Political Report No. 33, White to Derby, 20 August; *ibid.* Report No. 56, Wrede to Andrássy, 19 August; SA, Varia Turquie II, 1875. *The Times* (London), 24 August 1875, p. 12, col. 1. In Constantinople the greatest concern of the moment, fraught as it was with difficulty, was the intentions of Serbia (Report No. 66AB, Zichy to Andrássy, 24 August; SA, Varia Turquie I, 1875). In anticipation of an attack the Porte began concentrating a large military force in the direction of Nish, and it was stated that the Ottoman minister of war would take personal command of the troops and would, furthermore, not hesitate to pursue his action, if need be, into Serbia itself (*The Times*, 25 August 1875, p. 3, cols. 3–4).

This anomalous situation continued until 31 August, when finally, after a crisis of two weeks' duration, Milan was able to build a cabinet. But it was not of the character he had wished; in a sense it was a coalition body but a coalition which excluded the conservatives and which included the chief liberals, all of whom were apparently members of the nationalistic society called the *Omladina*. Stevca Mihailovich became premier but, more important for the time, the foreign office was taken over by Ristich, the man who favored war. That evening there was a great torchlight parade in Beograd to do honor to the new ministers. After singing the national anthem before the prince's palace, the procession went on to the several homes of the ministers, serenading them with shouts for war with the Turks. During the next days great zeal was put into organizing new welfare committees, and the recruiting stations were swarming with volunteers for service in Bosnia.[199]

However, the first days of September did not bring the war that so many enthusiasts were anticipating. At the time fortune was not overly favoring the Hercegovinians and the spread of the rebellion to Bosnia had failed to achieve the desired results. The new cabinet, moreover, after having worked so earnestly to win office, learned the sobering lesson of responsibility. The ministers were embarrassed by their campaign promises and worried by the problem which they had to face. Prince Milan had acquired no new affection for the liberals and left his chief advisers to muddle along as best their uncertain lights would allow. It seemed to White, the British agent, that the danger of a Serbian declaration of war was passed.[200]

This foreign observer, only recently arrived in Beograd, did not know the tenacity of Serb feeling. The insurrection was not making great progress and the cabinet was embarrassed, but Ristich and his friends clung to the belief that Serbia ought to aid the struggling

---

Sir Henry Elliot's view of this delicate state of things he incorporated in a telegram of 29 August to Derby (FO 78/2385) : "The Servian agent has expressed anxiety about collection of Turkish troops at Nisch. I told him that the Porte has no thoughts of an attack upon Servia, but is forced to be prepared to resist aggression which seems threatened by them, and if Servia wantonly provokes hostilities she must be prepared to bear the consequences. Minister for Foreign Affairs has asked my opinion of the course to. be pursued. I said vigorously repel attack upon Turkish territory but avoid all action beyond it."

[199] *Augsburger Allgemeine Zeitung,* 5 September 1875, pp. 3886–87, 3892–93; 8 September, p. 3929. *Aus dem Leben König Karls,* II, 458.

[200] Report No. 51, White to Elliot, 6 September; FO 78/2399.

brothers of Bosnia and Hercegovina even if it led to war with Turkey. Milan, on the contrary, still was afraid to brook the wrath of
the powers and insisted that a military venture would be disastrous
for the land. The decision between prince and minister lay in the
hands of the national legislature.[201]

The skupshtina met in Kragujevatz on 1 September, but Milan
was so annoyed with his ministers that for more than a week he refused to appear for a formal opening session. On the tenth, at last, he
undertook the delicate task of meeting his turbulent deputies. His
speech was designed to appease both Serbia and Europe. He gave a
sop to the feelings of his people by a sympathetic comment on Bosnia
and Hercegovina: "The population of these provinces, despairing of
seeing the end of their sufferings, have risen, arms in hand, to defend themselves from the abuses under which they suffer notwith-
standing the humane and generous intentions of His Majesty the
Sultan." But beyond words of commiseration the prince did not go.
In place of advocating war he informed the assembly that Turkey and
the powers had undertaken to restore peace, and he pledged himself
to aid in the work of arranging a tolerable settlement.[202] Such words
were a clear warning to the excited delegates that Milan refused to
countenance an attack on Turkey.

The assembly listened to the speech in silence. The next day a
committee was set up to draft a reply to the address from the throne,
and until the twentieth the character of this document was vigorously debated in secret sessions. A strong minority of the committee
fought for a declaration of war. The ministers, however, despite
their pre-election belligerency, felt the necessity of moving more
cautiously,[203] and the committee majority, which they dominated,

---

[201] Jovanović, *Slavonic Review*, IV, 390–91.

[202] The text of Prince Milan's speech may be found in *Turkey No. 2 (1876)*,
inclosure in Doc. No. 26; *British and Foreign State Papers*, LXVI, 1054–56;
Hertslet, *Map of Europe by Treaty*, IV, Doc. No. 452.

[203] ". . . . It is evident that the new Government has slackened the warlike
preparations of their immediate predecessors in Office, and that they endeavour to
explain to their supporters that they require time and money, before they can
embark in so hazardous a venture. The Prince himself professes openly a peaceful
policy ever since the foundation of the new Cabinet and has modified his attitude
very strongly in that sense, but at the same time the language of the immediate
followers of the ministry and of their organs in the press, as likewise their uninter-
rupted relations with the leaders of the Omladina are of such a character as to
throw considerable doubt on the sincerity of their professions. . . . ." (Report
No. 56, White to Elliot, 19 September; FO 78/2399.)

proposed to entrust the final decision on war or peace to the wisdom of the prince. After more than a week of spirited debating, unanimity in the committee was still lacking and two drafts were accordingly presented on the twentieth to a plenary session of the assembly.[204] This body was still under the influence of the moderated Ristich and the peaceful Milan—by the terms of the constitution thirty-three deputies were nominees of the prince[205]—and the vote for the majority report stood seventy-one to forty-four. With the thirty-three votes of the nominated members subtracted from the total, the actual vote of the elected representatives was forty-four in favor of a declaration of war to thirty in favor of peace.[206] The text of the reply so voted was largely a recapitulation of the prince's speech dressed in the garb of brotherly sentiments for the insurgents and of self-sacrificing patriotism for Serbia:

. . . . The circumstances are serious, but not less serious is the firm will of the Servian people to rise equal to the difficulties of their position. Accordingly, the National Assembly declares solemnly, in the name of the people of Servia, that it is ready to protect its country, to defend its liberty, and to defend the inheritance of the great Milosch and of our ancestors. There is no sacrifice that Servia is not prepared to make on the sacred altar of the country in order to attain this end. At the call of your Highness the people of Servia will rise like one man to defend their beloved country.

Highness, centuries of suffering have determined our brethren of Bosnia and of the Herzegovina to appeal to arms and to fight for their rights as men and as a nation. The sight of their blood revolts our brotherly sentiments. Their cries of despair find a noble echo among other civilized nations. It is impossible that we should remain indifferent to their fate.

The National Assembly is filled with the deepest sense of gratitude for the efforts of your Highness to help to restore definitively tranquillity to these distracted countries, and to insure a lasting contentment to our cruelly tried brethren.

In this patriotic path your Highness may also count entirely on the support of the people of Servia. They are ready to put at your Highness' disposal all the means needful for the happy realization of this great work. The National Assembly, in the name of the people of Servia, give your Highness the assurance that, to this end also, it will not flinch from any sacrifice, being con-

---

[204] *The Times* (London), 17 September 1875, p. 5, col. 4; 20 September, p. 12, col. 1; 29 September, p. 3, col. 4. *Augsburger Allgemeine Zeitung*, 15 September 1875, p. 4033; 16 September, p. 4049; 20 September, p. 4117. *Aus dem Leben König Karls*, II, 460.

[205] Chedo Miyatovich, *Servia and the Servians* (London, 1908), p. 29.

[206] *The Times* (London), 21 September 1875, p. 3, col. 1; 28 September, p. 10, col. 1. *Augsburger Allgemeine Zeitung*, 21 September 1875, p. 4133; 25 September, p. 4194.

vinced that your Highness, together with the Government, will devise the means by which Servia may best respond to her duty. . . . .[207]

As September moved on the temper of the land became more bellicose. The concentration of some sixty Turkish battalions on the Serbian border[208] was countered by an order on 13 September for the mobilization of 24,000 men of the frontier brigades.[209] In the next days the military movements and preparations—all taken in the name of defence—were continued on a large scale. All the artillery and troops of the regular army were divided between the eastern and western frontiers—to face the Turks around Nish and to be ready for action in Bosnia—while the militia was kept under arms in camp. Reports circulated about plans for increasing the military forces and about the purchase and registration of horses.[210] Furthermore, and still more compromising, the new government continued the practice of arming volunteers and sending them into Bosnia.[211]

In the skupshtina, meanwhile, majority opinion continued to be restive under Milan's pacifism. It has been stated by a Serbian scholar that Ristich as leader of the ministry had not really decided on war; that what he wanted was to force Turkey by threats to permit Serbia's intervention in favor of the insurgents and, if war should come out of his maneuver, to put it off until the following spring.[212] But in his aim to achieve some advantage for his country he proposed to be limited only by a realistic estimate of what was possible. The task at hand, he told the deputies, was to decide on what was wanted and what could be done and to plot Serbia's course accordingly with utter disregard of the Great Powers.[213] In secret session the assembly voted by two-thirds majority a considerable war credit[214] and the government was authorized to use current resources

[207] The full text in French and English translations may be found in *Turkey No. 2 (1876)*, inclosure in Doc. No. 27, and in Hertslet, *op. cit.*, IV, Doc. No. 453. The translation above is that of the British Foreign Office.

[208] Report 68AD, Zichy to Andrássy, Constantinople, 31 August; SA, Varia Turquie I, 1875.

[209] *The Times* (London), 14 September 1875, p. 3, col. 5.

[210] Tel., White to Elliot, 25 September; FO 78/2387. Report No. 66, White to Elliot, 27 September; FO 78/2399. *The Times* (London), 23 September 1875, p. 3, col. 1; 30 September, p. 5, cols. 4–5.

[211] Stojanovic, *op. cit.*, pp. 15–16.

[212] Jovanović, *Slavonic Review*, IV, 390–91.

[213] Trivanovitch, *Journal of Modern History*, III, 427–28.

[214] *Europäischer Geschichtskalender*, 1876, p. 490.

in forwarding military preparations and in aiding the insurrection.[215] At the same time the government decided to attempt again to revive Prince Michael's Balkan alliance. An aide-de-camp of Milan was dispatched on a futile mission to Athens,[216] and a second emissary went to Cetinje to sound out Prince Nicholas.[217] When Milan still hesitated, the skupshtina passed several additional resolutions preparatory to war, among which was provision for a parliamentary committee to collaborate with the government in case hostilities did begin. This action appeared to the prince to be unpleasantly like the establishment of the committee of public safety during the French Revolution.[218] His difficulties were far from diminishing.

During these three months of excitement the relation of Serbia to the revolt had continued to be a matter of prime importance to those powers who had set out to restore tranquillity in the Balkans. When Count Andrássy had his conversation with Prince Milan early in August he inaugurated a series of admonitions destined to continue for almost a year. Not more than a day after the first exhortation was delivered in Vienna, Consul White discussed Serbia's conduct with the foreign minister in Beograd,[219] and less than a fortnight later, after Milan had returned to his capital, the consul carried Britain's formal advice against war directly to the prince himself.[220] White reported that he "exhausted every argument to show the Prince the great dangers to which such a course would expose himself and his Country, and the improbability of their deriving any advantage even if successful for a time, of which there was so little likelihood. . . . ." But these arguments were offered to Milan two days after the election and the resignation of the ministry, and he was in no position to make a binding promise.[221] Nor had his situation improved two days

[215] Stojanovic, *op. cit.*, p. 80.

[216] Lhéritier, *op. cit.*, III, 385.

[217] Stojanovic, *op. cit.*, pp. 80 f. On 6 September *The Times* (London) (p. 9, col. 3) commented on rumors of a Serbo-Montenegrin negotiation. On 24 November (p. 5, cols. 4, 5) the same journal reported the termination of the Serb agent's sojourn without a definitive understanding.

[218] Jovanović, *Slavonic Review*, IV, 390–91.

[219] Report No. 25, White to Elliot, 5 August; FO 78/2399.

[220] The Sublime Porte had made appeal for remonstrances in Beograd and Montenegro, and Lord Derby, in response, telegraphed to Elliot on 12 August: ". . . . Direct Her Majesty's Agent at Belgrade to use his best efforts to counteract any disposition which may be apparent in Servia to aid or foment the disturbances . . . ." (Draft No. 234; FO 78/2377).

[221] Political Report No. 30, White to Derby, 18 August; FO 78/2399.

later when Prince Wrede, the Austrian agent, repeated Andrássy's earlier opinions. At best Milan could only complain of his task in the face of a cabinet crisis and of an excited nation and confess that he had come to no final solution.[222]

Milan had indeed come back home to find the war spirit so rampant that it was difficult for him to hit upon a course of action. One thing, however, he had to clear up, and that as quickly as possible. Andrássy had claimed to speak in the name of the league of the three emperors and had in addition, apparently, dropped a hint about Austria's preparedness to defend her own interests in case of need. The question of the moment was the accuracy of those assertions. The answer he attempted to learn by sending up a trial balloon over Russia. Calling in the Russian consul, Milan told him that revolt would soon break out in Bosnia and that he would be obliged to respond to it by a declaration of war. In anticipation of such action, he wanted to know if Tsar Alexander would prevent an Austrian occupation of Serbia.[223]

The tsar and his advisers, as has been noted, had committed themselves from the beginning to pacification through common action of the imperial league. Rather, therefore, than enter into any understanding with the principality, Alexander sent word to Milan that if he declared war on Turkey, he would be abandoned to his own folly.[224] Loyally the prince's statement was passed on to Vienna, and Novikov, the Russian ambassador, proposed on his own initiative that the three imperial agents in Beograd should admonish Milan against a precipitate decision.[225]

Andrássy was obliged to consider immediately what attitude he should take toward the Serbian threat. The simplest means of preventing war, he informed Emperor Francis Joseph, would be a direct military intervention. If a demonstration across from Beograd succeeded in saving peace, as he thought it certainly would, Austria-Hungary would appear as the gendarme of Turkey and would be pulling the chestnuts out of the fire for Russia. And, furthermore, the destruction of the hopes of Montenegro, Bosnia, and Hercego-

---

[222] Report No. 57, Wrede to Andrássy, 19 August; *First Red Book*, Doc. No. 124, incomplete.

[223] Tel. No. 26, Langenau to Andrássy, 16 August; SA, Varia Turquie II, 1875.

[224] Tel. No. 28, Langenau to Andrássy, 19 August; *ibid.*

[225] Tel., Hofmann to Andrássy in Terebes, 17 August; *ibid.*

vina would be attributed to Austria. On the other hand, if a demonstration failed to restrain the Serbs, the Dual Monarchy would expose itself no less to the hatred of the Slavs and in addition would suffer a serious loss of prestige. A policy of forcible interference, therefore, he felt he could not recommend. He proposed to his sovereign rather a declaration to Milan that he might, contrary to Austrian wishes, declare war, but that if he did he would have to face the consequences of his action while Austria looked exclusively to the protection of her own interests. If this course were adopted the Vienna government would share with Russia the entailed hatred and would not lose prestige. But should such a warning fail to restrain the zealots of Beograd, and should the ensuing war take on the character of a South-Slavic nationalistic crusade, Austria would have to be ready to act. The minister thought it would be desirable to take possession of Beograd and, after the restoration of order, extract from the Serbs a satisfactory indemnity for the cost of operations.[226] He was inclined to suspect that the Serb radicals in control of the government would indeed attempt to push on into enterprises dangerous to the security of Austria-Hungary, and for such a contingency he had a special point of view. In so far as Serbia was a part of Turkey and in so far as the relations between vassal and suzerain were considered, Andrássy proposed to act in conjunction with the other guaranteeing powers. But those questions which involved strictly Austro-Serbian relations he held to be entirely beyond the province of the European concert; they were questions which the Dual Monarchy would regulate for itself.[227] Andrássy's basic idea was the same as that which prevailed in the Ballplatz in 1914—and was, in fact, the only idea logically compatible with the sacred dogma of sovereignty.

The Austrian foreign minister was, as he said, averse to pulling chestnuts out of the fire for Russia, but he was not averse to permitting the tsar to render that service to Austria. If Alexander was so ready to take upon himself the odium of restraining Serbia, Andrássy was more than willing to retire into the background. In preference therefore to accepting Novikov's proposal for a joint admonition to Milan, he suggested that the Russian government deliver an admonition of its own couched in the form of a reply to the prince's recent communication to St. Petersburg. He agreed to support that reply

[226] Tel., Andrássy to Emperor Francis Joseph, Terebes, 17 August; SA, Varia Turquie II, 1875. *Andrássy,* II, 252–53, 264–65.

[227] Tel., Andrássy to Langenau, 21 August; SA, Russia, 1875.

but declared that it was impossible, after the advice he had given to Milan in Vienna and its apparent lack of success, to do anything further for the time.[228] To encourage the tsar in his intention Andrássy sent an inflammatory telegram to Russia. It was not Milan, he said, who wanted war, but the Omladina, the revolutionary party; Ristich and his friends did not believe in a real understanding of the three imperial powers and he hoped to find support from one or the other of them for a war of revolutionary character.[229]

Novikov promptly withdrew his own proposal and urged that Vienna support the tsar's démarche immediately.[230] But at the Russian foreign office the unconscious zeal to serve Austrian interests was even greater. Baron Jomini was in favor of permitting the Serbs to continue to live in fear of an Austrian occupation and suggested that there was no need for the time being at least for Andrássy to support the Russian pronouncement.[231] Francis Joseph's chief minister seemed to be in a fair way to achieve his end with little cost.

The continued military preparations and the war spirit still prevailing in Beograd soon proved, however, that peace was not so easily saved. There was consolation for Andrássy, none the less, in the assurance that Serbia did not have the approval of St. Petersburg. Jomini, in expressing a severe judgment of Serbian conduct, readily agreed that the Dual Monarchy could not tolerate a turbulent and aggressive state on its frontier.[232] Tsar Alexander was equally emphatic. Whatever might be his sympathies for the Slavs, he said, he wished to have nothing in common with the revolutionary party which had come into power in August.[233]

Toward the end of September the situation in Beograd became critical. The regular garrison of the capital and the first-class militia were sent to the frontier without the knowledge of Prince Milan.

[228] Tel., Andrássy to Hofmann in Vienna, 19 August; SA, Varia Turquie II, 1875. Tel., Andrássy to Langenau, 19 August; ibid. As a further part of his program to keep Serbia from doing some irreparable harm Andrássy sent a confidential notice to the Sublime Porte of Milan's threatened declaration of war and urged the Turks to prepare a military force necessary for such an emergency as quickly as possible (Tel., Andrássy to Zichy, 19 August; ibid.).

[229] Tel., Andrássy to Langenau, 19 August; ibid.

[230] Tel., Hofmann to Andrássy, 20 August; ibid.

[231] Tel. No. 29 and Report No. 42, Mayr to Andrássy, St. Petersburg, 20 August and 22 August, respectively; SA, Varia Turquie I, 1875.

[232] Mayr to Andrássy, 24 August/7 September; First Red Book, Doc. No. 144.

[233] Report No. 47B, Mayr to Andrássy, 29 August/10 September; SA, Varia Turquie I, 1875.

Both the Austrian and Russian consuls warned their respective governments that only an immediate and energetic diplomatic interference could prevent the outbreak of war.[234] In response to this warning Jomini on the twenty-ninth telegraphed to Vienna proposing a collective threat to Milan's government. The text of the suggested declaration read: "It will be impossible for the powers guaranteeing the treaty of Paris to save the principality from a Turkish occupation if the Serbian government resorts to aggressive acts against the Porte."[235] Andrássy was in complete agreement and immediately sent orders to his agent in Beograd.[236] The minister, thinking always in terms of the imperial league, proceeded to invite German participation.[237] But in St. Petersburg the tsar's advisers were thinking, as in the case of the consular mission, of a common action of all the Great Powers, and it was accordingly suggested to Andrássy that he send invitations to the other capitals as well.[238] The Austrian minister could not very well refuse the request, and on 2 October he telegraphed proposals for a démarche to Rome, Paris, and London.[239] Yet Andrássy was far from reconciled to the Russian outlook. He explained to St. Petersburg:

. . . . We have addressed these powers as being interested in the general peace and have avoided appealing to them in their capacity of guaranteeing powers. I have so acted with the intention of doing nothing which might suggest the idea of a permanent organization of the six guaranteeing powers with province over the other eastern questions—an arrangement which would hinder the initiative and the previous understanding of the three courts which I hold to be so essential.[240]

Andrássy continued naively to believe that the league of the three emperors should and could lead the rest of Europe by a progression of *faits accomplis*.

The support of Germany in the declaration to the Serbs was a

<hr/>

[234] Wrede to Andrássy, 25 September; *First Red Book,* Doc. No. 151, incomplete. Tel. No. 34, Mayr to Andrássy, 29 September; *ibid.,* Doc. No. 154, incomplete.

[235] Tel. No. 35, Mayr to Andrássy, 1 October; *ibid.,* Doc. No. 159. Wertheimer (*Andrássy,* II, 269), as usual, puts the worst interpretation on Russian action by alleging that the tsar apparently held a Serbian declaration of war to be premature.

[236] Tel., Andrássy to Mayr, 30 September; *First Red Book,* Doc. No. 155.

[237] Tel., Andrássy to Seiller, 30 September; *ibid.,* Doc. No. 156.

[238] Tel. No. 35, Mayr to Andrássy, 1 October; *ibid.,* Doc. No. 159.

[239] Tel., Andrássy to Gravenegg, Kuefstein, and Beust, 2 October; *ibid.,* Doc. No. 161.

[240] Tel. No. 697, Andrássy to Mayr, 2 October; SA, Russia, 1875.

matter of course except for those formalities which guarded imperial dignity.[241] The French foreign minister had already anticipated the invitation with a remonstrance of his own[242] and readily subscribed to the collective declaration.[243] The Italian government, with obvious gratitude for the recognition, also added its support.[244] In London, as the negotiations for the consular mission ominously brought out, there prevailed a slightly different climate of opinion. Nowhere was there less sympathy for the rebellion than in Whitehall—but nowhere likewise was there less interest in dancing to the tunes called on the Continent. A collective condemnation of Serbian policy Lord Derby dismissed on the ground that the British consul had been charged since the outbreak of the revolt to oppose a hostile decision.[245] But three days later, on the sixth, the secretary relented and authorized White to join in making the common representation.[246]

Before all the requisite instructions reached Beograd the outlook there had suddenly changed. Prince Milan had come to the limit of his endurance when the skupshtina, without consulting his wishes, had called out the militia and sent it to the frontier. Although Ristich was not in Kragujevatz when this decision was made, the prince held the cabinet responsible for his intolerable position and determined to get rid of his ministers at all costs. In anticipation of that action he transferred the assembly to Beograd where he could keep it under his eye, and he telegraphed an appeal to his old conservative friend Marinovich, then in Rumania, to return and form a new ministry. Marinovich, however, had no zeal for so formidable a task and advised his sovereign to patience.[247] Unable to abide by such advice, Milan on 4 October repaired in person to the meeting hall of the

241 Tel., Seiller to Andrássy, 1 October; *First Red Book,* Doc. No. 158.

242 Decazes to Bourgoing, 1 October; *First Yellow Book,* p. 35. The French agent had also recommended strong pressure to prevent the outbreak of war (*ibid.,* pp. 31–32).

243 Decazes to de Laboulaye, 12 October; *ibid.,* pp. 38–39.

244 Gravenegg to Andrássy, Rome, 3 October; *First Red Book,* Docs. Nos. 165 and 166.

245 Tel., Wolkenstein to Andrássy, 5 October; *ibid.,* Doc. No. 170.

246 Tel., Wolkenstein to Andrássy, 6 October; *ibid.,* Doc. No. 173. Tel., Derby to White, 6 October; FO 78/2399. This authorization was given, not because of any representations from the powers, but in response to a telegram from White dated 4 October (*ibid.*).

247 Tel. No. 34, Mayr to Andrássy, 29 September; SA, Russia, 1875. *The Times* (London), 6 October 1875, p. 5, col. 4.

skupshtina. The ministers were taken completely by surprise as he walked into their private room and informed them that he was going to deal directly with the assembly without the intervention of his constitutional advisers. Some discussion ensued, at the end of which Milan, followed by the ministers, marched in to address the deputies. The prince was received without a word. As soon as everyone was seated he arose and announced that he had felt obliged to accept the cabinet's resignation. In utter astonishment the ministers got up and left the room. Milan then continued his speech. "Do you," he asked, "have confidence in me?" The skupshtina aroused itself from its stupefaction sufficiently to give an affirmative response. "Are you in favor of war?" was his next question. The deputies this time shouted their "Yes." Undeterred by the enthusiasm of their reply, Milan proceeded to lay before them his reasons for opposing their desire. When he had described the attitude of the Great Powers and the nature of their impending step, he left the hall. Not a voice was raised among the startled legislators as the prince calmly lighted a cigar, mounted his carriage, and drove away.[248]

Two days later, 6 October, when the five consular agents were ready to present their collective declaration, Serbia had no ministers. Solemnly the agents gave the text to a subordinate official of the foreign office, and solemnly in turn the official promised to convey the message to the incoming minister.[249] The British consul was inclined to think that the warning was "not likely to produce a sufficiently deterrent effect on those agitators who are looking forward to a general and combined rising of the Rayahs at no distant period,"[250] but for the time being, at all events, Prince Milan was master of Serbia. The day after the consular declaration he called all of the deputies into his palace and again put his question to them: "Who is for war, and who is not?" And taking up the roster of the assembly, he called the roll. Only twelve now had the courage to

---

[248] *Europäischer Geschichtskalender,* 1875, pp. 491–92. *Augsburger Allgemeine Zeitung,* 12 October 1875, pp. 4451–52. White had it that the ministers resigned during their discussion with the prince before he went into the meeting hall and that Ristich preceded him and announced their action (Report No. 76, White to Elliot, 6 October; FO 78/2399).

[249] Wrede to Andrássy, 7 October; *First Red Book,* Doc. No. 176. Joannini to Melegari, 6 October; *First Green Book,* Doc. No. XLIX. The text of the declaration is appended to each of the dispatches cited. On 8 October White notified the Serbian foreign office of the support lent by his government to the views of the other powers (Political Report No. 64, White to Derby, 8 October; FO 78/2399).

[250] Political Report No. 65, White to Derby, 9 October; FO 78/2399.

vote for war; the others—although most of them had been openly
belligerent until that moment—voted for peace. Then Milan put
a second question to the cowed representatives: "Who is in favor
of supporting the insurgents?" A second time he called the roll and
again the vote was to his satisfaction. This exercise terminated, the
prince graciously waved his hand to announce that the audience was
ended.[251]

It proved easier for Milan to intimidate the skupshtina than to
find a suitable set of ministers. With the conservatives still refusing
to take over the government, the prince had no alternative but to
turn again to the left. He found men more acceptable personally
than Ristich and his liberal associates; but except for that qualification the new cabinet which was installed on 9 October had a foreign policy not essentially different from that of its predecessor.
Kaljevich, the incoming premier, and his colleagues were likewise
members of the nationalistic Omladina society. "I find very little
real difference amongst public men here, whether Radical or Conservative," White observed in reporting the change of ministry; "of
whatever shade of opinion, all are equally imbued with the desire to
see Servian aggrandizement accomplished. . . . ."[252] The minister
of war in the preceding cabinet retained his position and the support
pledged by Ristich to the new government was indication enough
that policy was not going to be fundamentally changed, but, even
so, under the circumstances of its selection the new cabinet could
not plunge immediately into war. The ministerial declaration made
before the skupshtina on the tenth was a stirring oration on "the
holiness of patriotic duty," and on "Serbia the hope of our suffering
brothers"; but no hint of policy toward Turkey lurked behind its
impassioned phrases.[253]

Premier Kaljevich and his colleagues were doctrinaire liberals
to the point of radicalism, and immediately they engrossed the skupshtina in a program of reform legislation. Prince Milan approved
the action of Kaljevich, hoping that in these discussions of internal
problems the deputies would be distracted from their obsession with
war.[254] And, indeed, the prince's hope was fulfilled. In secret ses-

---

[251] *Europäischer Geschichtskalender,* 1875, pp. 493–94.

[252] Report No. 82, White to Elliot, 11 October; FO 78/2399.

[253] *Europäischer Geschichtskalender,* 1875, pp. 494–95. For a brief biographical
sketch of Kaljevich, see *Augsburger Allgemeine Zeitung,* 19 October 1875, p. 4563.

[254] Jovanović, *Slavonic Review,* IV, 392.

sions the assembly laid plans for a loan, but when that body was prorogued for a month at the end of October it had back of it little more than weeks of futile talk.[255] With the liberal reforms still under discussion and with winter at hand to make impossible any immediate military campaign, the feverish excitement of Serbia slowly abated. But the ambitions of the principality were not forgotten. The minister of war quietly continued his task of building up an army; financial agents went to the money markets of Europe to arrange a loan;[256] diplomatic agents were sounding Greece, Montenegro, and Rumania and establishing relations with Albanian and Bulgarian revolutionaries.[257] When snow covered the mountains of the Balkans there was "unanimous regret" in Beograd that the opportunity of August had not been seized, and there was a general feeling in Europe that, if the rebellion smoldered on until spring, only a military occupation could keep the Serbs from their long-delayed war.[258]

MONTENEGRO AND THE OUTBREAK OF THE REVOLT

In 1875 the tiny principality of Montenegro had back of it a long history of warfare against the Turks. Repeatedly in that blood-stained past the troops of the sultan had assaulted the steep cliffs of the Black Mountain, but never had Ottoman control been effectively asserted over the last defense of the Montenegrins, the lofty crags above Cattaro. Around the beginning of the sixteenth century the plight of his land had so discouraged the ruler that he had fled to a more comfortable life in Venice. Some submission to the Turks may have followed—the records are scant—but if true it was a compulsory act that was soon repudiated. With the reigning house gone, the stout-hearted Montenegrins had put their fortunes in the hand of the second most important man in their midst, the Orthodox bishop of Cetinje, and for three centuries Montenegro was a theocracy ruled by the *vladika* or prince-bishop chosen in the monastery of the chief town of the land. The wars had continued; again and again the Turks pushed up the mountain side—but were never able to remain. A more subtle enemy in the form of the religion of the

[255] Report No. 90, White to Elliot, 1 November; FO 78/2399. The Rumanian agent in Beograd had little respect for the Serbian legislators (see Iorga, *Correspondance diplomatique*, pp. 101–2).

[256] Report No. 98, White to Elliot, 4 December; FO 78/2399.

[257] Stojanovic, *op. cit.*, pp. 80–82.

[258] Report No. 100, White to Elliot, 8 December; FO 78/2399.

Turks had also invaded this last Balkan resort of free men, but Vladika Danilo had proclaimed and led a St. Bartholomew of renegades—and Montenegro had remained Christian. When this redoubtable man of God ended more than a generation of rule in 1735, sovereignty had become hereditary in his family of Petrovich, the old popular assemblies had disappeared, and a permanent bond of sympathy had been created between great Slavic Russia and this tiny land of kindred tongue and religion. In 1799 came the next major event for Montenegro. As the culmination of a number of defeats Sultan Selim III had signed a treaty which renounced all pretension to Ottoman sovereignty. But this recognition of independence became obscured in the old conflict which was carried on into the nineteenth century. Acre by acre the Montenegrins fought their way toward better land and step by step the Montenegrins admitted the ideas of the Western world. During the reign of the second Danilo from 1851 to 1860 the old theocracy was abandoned as out of keeping with modern times, and Montenegro became a hereditary secular principality. This revolutionary act and other reforms had strained the tolerance of Danilo's stubborn subjects and he paid the penalty of assassination for his rule.

Nicholas, his nephew, took possession of the uncertain throne and had the personality and ability to hold it successfully for fifty-seven years. As was to be the case of his brother sovereign of Serbia eight years later, the new prince was called from his studies in Paris to assume authority over a turbulent land. But, in contrast to Milan, Prince Nicholas had the advantage of years—he was nineteen in 1860—and the advantage of genuine character and of abilities which remained unspoiled. He was a man of poetic nature, but at the same time a poet whose feet never left the hard ground of reality. A man of giant physique, he had too those talents of mind which stamped him as a typical hero of the Slavic ballads of earlier times. He knew by name, in those years before his territory was expanded, every head of a Montenegrin family and he could trace their genealogy back to the "damned day of Kossovo" almost five hundred years before. Genial and diplomatic though he was, Nicholas in 1875 was an autocrat, a ruler who made personally every decision that concerned his tiny land.

His reign had hardly begun before Nicholas learned the difficulties inherent in the age-old quarrel with Turkey. The Ottoman forces had been badly defeated by Danilo in 1858, and four years later the sultan sought revenge, during a revolt in Hercegovina, by attacking the principality from three directions. The peace which the prince had to sign was more humiliating than injurious, and it settled nothing. Nicholas set out immediately to prepare for the next chapter of the history written in blood. He worked to heal the fresh wounds; he traveled through Europe in search of support; he sent agents into Albania and Bosnia and Hercegovina; he formed an alliance with Prince Michael of Serbia. In France in 1866 he was encouraged to negotiate with the Porte for a harbor and for an extension of territory to the south and east; but when the Montenegrin delegates went to Constantinople they soon discovered that there was little prospect for satisfactory arrangements, and the negotiations were abandoned. Friction continued and Nicholas proposed to seize the first opportunity for war. The situation on the frontier was particularly threatening in 1872 and hostilities were then only narrowly averted.[259] Two years later—in October 1874—there occurred at Podgoritza another of the border disturbances which once again raised the specter of war. Both sides now refused to give way in the question of punishment of malefactors, and a European intervention alone was able to save the peace.[260] Tremendous excitement in Montenegro ensued, and it was in the midst of this turmoil that a band of Hercegovinians sought asylum on the Black Mountain saying that they would never return home so long as the Turks continued to rule. After the murder of Michael of Serbia, Prince Nicholas emerged as the leader of the Southern Slavs and the harassed people of Hercegovina looked to him as their defender. In previous revolts the insurgents had received valiant support from the Montenegrins, who shared with them their religion and language and their undying hatred of Turks.[261]

Encouraged by the cordial receptions which he had received during his visits in Europe, Prince Nicholas drafted plans for enlisting the aid of the Great Powers in expanding his principality to its "natural limits" at the expense of Turkey. In 1873 he had been on the point of addressing to the powers a memorandum arguing this

---

[259] General Ignatiev in his memorandum published in *Izvestiia* (1914, III, 115–17; VI, 150–51; 1915, II, 169–70) describes Nicholas' activities from 1866 and 1872 and claims that he, through his private correspondence with the prince and through his influence over the sultan, prevented war.

[260] Austrian diplomatic correspondence on this crisis may be found in *First Red Book*, Docs. Nos. 55 ff.

[261] Stojanovic, *op. cit.*, pp. 7–8.

necessity. At the last moment this maneuver had been abandoned in favor of a new attempt at direct negotiations with the Porte. Moved by a new sense of strength, Nicholas had been ready to demand not only a territorial gift from Turkey but also the official recognition of an agent in Constantinople, a mixed tribunal on the frontier, commercial facilities, and comparable concessions. Through the moderating intervention of General Ignatiev the dangers of 1873 had been avoided,[262] but in May 1875, after the Podgoritza affair had heated the spirits of his subjects and had revealed a considerable sympathy for Montenegro in Europe, the prince refused to be restrained any longer and at last he prepared his memorandum of demands on Turkey and circulated it for foreign appreciation.

The expedient did not fare successfully. When the president of the Montenegrin senate presented the document in Vienna Andrássy dismissed it as an undesirable disturbance to order. The same fate met the memorandum in St. Petersburg; it was judged inadvisable to create at that time new embarrassments at the Porte. But Jomini's comments to the Austrian ambassador revealed nevertheless that sympathy which Russia had felt for the little principality since the days of Peter the Great. The foreign office director did not hide his conviction that Prince Nicholas should not be discouraged by a peremptory refusal, and the tsar himself, Jomini reported, had said that some settlement of the question at hand ought to be made which would not give umbrage to the prince and his people.[263]

These expressions of Russian opinion in June of 1875 indicated how difficult it was for the league of the three emperors, despite the good-will put into the pledges that created it, to overcome the disparities between sovereign views on Balkan problems. The Vienna government could not share this affection for the ambitious prince of Montenegro, and Andrássy was content with using polite language to take the edge off his categorical rejection of Nicholas' proposals. "I have been informed today," he told the prince late in June, "that his Majesty the Emperor Alexander shares my opinion that, at the present juncture, an action undertaken in the sense of the memorandum of May would not achieve the wishes of your Highness nor those of the friends of Montenegro."[264]

[262] Ignatiev, *Izvestiia*, 1915, II, 170–71.
[263] Report No. 34AF, Langenau to Andrássy, 11/23 June 1875; SA, Russia, 1875.
[264] Andrássy to the Prince of Montenegro, 28 June; SA.

In the face of such opposition Nicholas was obliged to withdraw his memorandum, but he was unwilling to abandon hope for his ambitions. His relations with the Porte, never good, were aggravated by the Podgoritza incident and by an impasse in litigations over frontier rectifications. The Turks were holding up the payment of a compensation for lands ceded to them until the boundary was definitively established, and Nicholas in turn was refusing to go on with fixing the boundary until the money was paid.[265] Taking advantage of existing negotiations, the prince presented a series of demands first to the frontier commissioners and then directly to the grand vizier in a letter dated 3 July. In this document Nicholas revived the concessions which he had been on the point of presenting two years before: a mixed commission on the frontier, regularly accredited diplomatic agents, and the rights of Montenegrin craft to use the Boyana River.[266] In essence it was a request for that recognition of independence given in 1799 and subsequently repudiated in the assumptions subscribed to in Constantinople.

Such was the outlook in Montenegro when the Hercegovinian peasants returned home and raised the standard of revolt. The long-standing tradition of the area was that hostility toward the Turks was common cause on both sides of the frontier; and immediately in July 1875 Montenegrin spirit identified itself with the rebellion. Prince Nicholas was consequently in a very difficult situation, even more so than his brother sovereign in Serbia. Each had an excited mass of subjects clamoring for action; each had clear intimations from the Great Eastern Powers that no complications were wanted from the principalities. But, in addition, Nicholas saw the revolt begin at his own door, and Nicholas remembered the misfortunes of 1862 which had arisen out of a comparable circumstance. Open

[265] Political Report No. 3, Holmes to Derby, 1 July; FO 78/2402. The question necessitating boundary negotiations had been left over from the European commission of 1858. That commission had given to Turkey several villages in Montenegrin territory, and, although Nicholas recognized Turkish ownership of the villages, he claimed Montenegrin sovereignty for the fields belonging to the villages. The negotiations in June had reached the point where the Turkish commissioners had consented to pay an indemnity for the fields but had failed to do so (Political Report No. 2, Holmes to Derby, 18 June; *ibid.*).

[266] Prince of Montenegro to the Grand Vizier of Turkey, 3 July; FO 78/2425 and SA, Varia Turquie I, 1875. Subsequently one of the British agents claimed to have discovered that Jonin, Russian consul-general in Ragusa, was the author of the letter (Political Report No. 11, Monson to Derby, 10 February 1877; FO 7/911).

participation was beyond his powers.[267] He assured the Turkish frontier commissioner that neither he nor his people could be held responsible for the revolt[268]—although the British consular agent in the area had contrary ideas[269]—and he published strict injunctions to his people to respect the neutrality of the land.[270] And it would seem that for a time Nicholas did attempt to discourage the rebellion, if for no other reason than that the Russian support which was essential to success was not forthcoming. But the aroused feelings of the Montenegrins were so intense that not even the autocratic Nicholas could be indifferent to them. The prince wanted to be the leader of the Southern Slavs and he could not afford to lose the good-will of those neighbors who looked to him for support. Furthermore, he could not be less sympathetic to the revolt than the Dalmatians who began from the first days of trouble to swarm over the frontier. Hence it was that the prince of Montenegro winked at his own subjects joining their brethren and quietly encouraged the sending of volunteers and ammunition.[271]

The assertion of Prince Milan that he would be obliged to follow the lead of Montenegro made the attitude of Prince Nicholas a matter of prime importance for those powers which were in August attempting to restore order in Turkey through a modest program of advice. In the middle of that month Andrássy, with the support of the Russian ambassador, dispatched to Cetinje a polite but clear

[267] Temperley, *The Bulgarian and Other Atrocities,* p. 5. The subsequent ballads, studied by Professor Temperley, describe Nicholas informing the insurgent leaders that his strength was not great enough to permit him to give the aid that he desired to render. The prince's memoirs, also studied by Temperley, substantiate the more poetic expression.

[268] Political Report No. 4, Holmes to Derby, 2 July; FO 78/2402. Nicholas in talking to Constant Effendi laid the blame on Serbian intrigue. Since the days of the negotiation of Michael's Serbo-Montenegrin alliance, Nicholas had been extremely jealous of Beograd's pretension to leadership of the Southern Slavs.

[269] Report No. 6, Holmes to Derby, 24 September; FO 78/2536: ". . . . It is a great mistake to attribute this insurrection entirely to Turkish misrule. The people have been persuaded and forced to rise by Servian and Montenegrin political intriguers who will not now permit their misguided victims to act otherwise than they think fit. When the Servians and Montenegrins are forced to be quiet the matter will end, but until then I do not think that any representations we can make to the people of the Herzegovine will have any effect. It was so in 1861 when Montenegro took the lead and I fancy it will be so now that Servia seems to take her turn."

[270] *Augsburger Allgemeine Zeitung,* 27 July, p. 3268; 29 July, p. 3299.

[271] Temperley, *op. cit.,* p. 5. Stillman, *Autobiography,* II, 125. *The Times* (London), 21 December 1875, p. 6, col. 3.

admonition to neutrality;[272] but as the days advanced the Russians preferred to concentrate attention on the obstinacy shown at the Porte and the dangers that might grow out of it. Before the end of August it was the certain conviction of St. Petersburg that Turkey was preparing an attack on Montenegro. Baron Jomini protested that such a result coming from the Austro-Russian understanding would be most painful:

. . . . We hope on the contrary that it [the entente] might demonstrate the two powers united in their interests and in their intention to maintain tranquillity and the status quo in the East on the only conditions possible; that is, through restraining both the foolish ventures of the Christians and the inept brutalities of the Turks.

We have so far fulfilled only the first part of this program. If we stop at this point we will have intervened directly to the profit of Turkish brutality. That would not be desirable from the Austrian point of view.

In order to avoid these extremities, it is urgent to agree on a common determination to exercise, if necessary, sufficient pressure on the Turks. They must be made to feel that at the basis of our peaceful accord there is a firm resolution that will not hesitate in the face of energetic measures. Such a conviction would suffice. . . . .[273]

Ambassador Novikov developed this introductory comment by a suggestion which departed rather materially from the excuse for the overture, the concentration of Ottoman troops on the Montenegrin frontier. As he expressed it, Novikov anticipated with regret a Serbian and Montenegrin participation caused by the failure of the Turks to make decent concessions to the insurgent populations, and from that axiom he went on to suggest that such a misfortune could be avoided only "through energetic action on the councils of the Porte" in the interest of the oppressed Christians. To the end of framing suitable measures he proposed discussions between Austria and Russia.[274]

Such a maneuver to push the intervention of the powers far beyond the limited activities of the consular mission was naturally unacceptable to the director of Austrian policy. Additional demands on the Porte Andrássy rejected as being neither necessary nor possible until the results of the current peace efforts were known. With

[272] Tel., Andrássy to Rodich, 13 August; SA, Varia Turquie I, 1875. "Vom russischen Botschafter mitgeteilter Entwurf des Telegrammes an den Fürsten von Montenegro"; ibid. Nicholas in reply promised unqualifiedly to maintain his neutrality (Tel., Andrássy to Wrede, 15 August; First Red Book, Doc. No. 119).

[273] Jomini to Mayr, 17/29 August, in Report No. 44B, Mayr to Andrássy; SA, Russia, 1875.

[274] "Aide-mémoire übergeben von Botschafter Novikow am 30-8-75," ibid.

a logic that could not be contested, he reminded Novikov that the object of the powers had been to start negotiations between the insurgents and the Turkish authorities and pointed out that there could be no valid ground for new interference until those negotiations were completed.[275] The minister distinguished sharply between new demands in favor of the insurgents and the dangers of a Turkish attack on Montenegro. He declared that he himself had no indication of such a threat but that, if danger were apprehended in Russia, he was quite willing to inform the sultan that the imperial powers would not tolerate a new war.[276]

Jomini was obliged to accept what Andrássy offered, and the three representatives at the Porte were instructed to use their judgment as to when a suitable declaration should be delivered. The director of the Russian foreign office still insisted that danger was imminent on the Montenegrin frontier;[277] but, as a matter of fact, the real danger of the moment was the concentration of Turkish troops in areas adjoining Serbia, and when the ambassadors found it desirable to remonstrate at the Porte within the week their remarks concerned the larger of the principalities. The Turkish response was all that could have been desired in its repudiation of aggressive intentions, and the crisis which had been seen from St. Petersburg disappeared in thin air.[278]

In the meantime a compromise on the frontier disputes between Montenegro and Turkey had been effected toward the end of July[279] and early in the following month the grand vizier sent Prince Nicholas a telegram promising to discuss the desires contained in the prince's letter.[280] The first of September, however, found the prob-

[275] Andrássy to Hofmann, Terebes, 30 August; SA, Russia, 1875.

[276] Tel., Andrássy to Hofmann, 30 August; *ibid.*

[277] Tel. No. 33, Mayr to Hofmann, 31 August; *ibid.* Report No. 44C, Mayr to Andrássy, 20 August/1 September; *ibid.*

[278] Reports Nos. 518 and 526, Elliot to Derby, 5 and 7 September, respectively; FO 78/2386. Tel., Safvet to Musurus, 9 September; FO 78/2425. Decazes to Bourgoing, 17 September; *First Yellow Book,* pp. 30–31.

[279] Political Report No. 9, Holmes to Derby, 30 July; FO 78/2402.

[280] Tel., Grand Vizier of Turkey to the Prince of Montenegro, 4 August, in Report No. 61AB, Herbert to Andrássy, Constantinople, 6 August; SA, Varia Turquie II, 1875. The British ambassador had expressed the hope that "the answer of the Porte would be dictated by a conciliatory spirit, and show a disposition to meet the wishes of the Prince." At the time the Porte was inclined to grant all of Nicholas' requests except that for a diplomatic agent in Constantinople (Report No. 423, Elliot to Derby, 4 August; FO 78/2385).

lem more complicated than ever. In Montenegro private support of the insurrection went on as before, and military preparations were being pushed vigorously in spite of the prince's declarations of peaceful intentions.[281] As the Serbian skupshtina was gathering under the leadership of a warlike ministry there was widespread and enthusiastic belief in Montenegro that both principalities would soon be at war. The prince himself sounded the warning that he could no longer restrain his people,[282] and when, a few days later, Prince Milan forestalled a Serbian declaration, Nicholas publicly confessed sharing the disappointment which hung over the whole of Montenegro.[283]

[281] Tel., Rodich to Andrássy, 5 September; SA, Varia Turquie II, 1875. *The Times* (London), 14 September, p. 6, col. 1.

[282] Report No. 46, Mayr to Andrássy, 24 August/5 September; SA, Varia Turquie I, 1875. The German foreign office was worried about Prince Nicholas' declaration and asked in St. Petersburg if it were desirable to maintain the veto on war recently announced in Constantinople. Jomini, always alert for Montenegrin interests, answered that it was. He characterized the prince's words as a mere trick to bring pressure to bear on the Turks in his negotiations. "Baron Jomini," Mayr explained, "does not blame severely the actions of the prince who is trying to gain the best advantage possible out of his situation and whose country has need of a territorial increase to be able to lead an honest and tranquil existence. In general, whenever it is a question of Montenegro and its ruler, it is easy to see the marked sympathy which they enjoy here. . . . ."

[283] The London *Times* correspondent wrote from Cetinje on 13 September 1875: ". . . . All that I could discover a week ago was that everybody was confident of war and anxious for it. To-day, however, the lack of news from Servia, and perhaps certain indications that she hangs back have influenced the public mind and produced an unwonted excitement, through which one gets glimpses of the real feeling, and the natural diplomatic reserve is thrown off to a certain extent. One would think that some great disaster had fallen on the nation, and in the bitterness of their hearts people speak out. . . . .
"The population of Cettinge is not large enough to be considered numerically as representing the opinion of Montenegro; but it must be remembered that it includes all the highest functionaries, a body guard of picked men from all the Principality, and many persons who have come here to await the decision of the Servian Skuptschina, including many chiefs of the Insurgents. This afternoon these were all in the streets as if waiting for a proclamation. All along the side of the street which leads to the Palace was a solid line of men composed of the elements I have named. . . . . The rumour was current everywhere that Servia had yielded to diplomatic pressure, and that the rising was to be abandoned. Dejection was on the face of everybody. . . . ." (27 September 1875, p. 6, col. 1.)
Later the same correspondent wrote from Cattaro: "Before leaving Cettinje I had an audience of Prince Nikita. . . . . The Prince expressed great disappointment at the inaction of Servia, and said that he was ready and willing to move with her had she moved, but that he did not feel justified, in spite of the desire and pressure of his people, in declaring war on Turkey alone. His soldiers were well organized

But with Serbia definitely removed from the lists, Nicholas was unwilling to assume the risks of undertaking war alone and the critical days of September passed without a rupture. Peace, however, was by no means on a sure footing. In November again the prince sent out his warning that it would be very difficult to restrain his people in case the Turks suffered defeat near the frontier.[284] This danger seemed equally real at the Porte, and a new appeal went out from Constantinople to the powers asking further interference in Cetinje.[285] Andrássy responded to the request and sent Nicholas an earnest representation.[286] The prince's reply was eminently correct: military preparations and movements were purely defensive; information had come to the effect that Turkish troops had been ordered to pursue their victims into Montenegrin territory; only in such a contingency would war ensue.[287]

Again formal peace had a narrow escape in spite of advancing winter, and relations between Turkey and the principality were the worse for the new experiences. Repeatedly in December protests were addressed to the powers from Constantinople complaining of

---

and armed with breechloaders and artillery, whereas in 1862 they had only old fashioned Albanian smoothbores. His supplies of ammunition were ample, and he did not apprehend defeat in the mountains from all the Turkish troops now in the field; but the part of a faithful ruler was to spare useless shedding of blood of his people, and he remembered that, though in 1862 they defended their valleys against 60,000 Turks and fought for eight months alone, they were finally obliged to yield to the greater resources of the Porte, their ammunition being exhausted and 3,000 of their number killed without any result whatever, and if now they were left to fight alone they would probably finally meet the same fortune, which he could not take the responsibility of risking. He disclaimed any ambition in connexion with the Insurrection, and was willing, in case the Powers should decide to guarantee an autonomy to the Herzegovinians, to exert his utmost influence towards the speedy cessation of the Insurrection, though without some such guarantee being given to the Insurgents it would be impossible for him to take any pacificatory action in the matter. The Insurgents were a kindred people; they looked to him for his moral support at least, and he could not refuse it. His own people would support him unanimously should he go further even; but in view of all the circumstances he regarded the cessation of bloodshed as the most important object if accompanied by concessions of the requisite security of the Rayahs. . . . ." (*Ibid.*, 28 September, p. 10, cols. 2–3.)

[284] Report, Zichy to Andrássy, 19 November; SA, Varia Turquie I, 1875.

[285] Corti to Visconti-Venosta, 21 November; *First Green Book,* Doc. No. LXVII. Tel., Zichy to Andrássy, 23 November; *First Red Book,* Doc. No. 186.

[286] Tel., Andrássy to Zichy, 26 November; *ibid.,* Doc. No. 187.

[287] Tel., Andrássy to Zichy, 27 November; *ibid.,* Doc. No. 188.

the participation of Montenegrins,[288] and the conviction was ever growing in Turkish circles that the insurrection could not be ended until the military action was taken into the principalities. The Turks anticipated a final settlement in the spring. But the Montenegrins too, like the Serbs and the Bosnians and the Hercegovinians, anticipated the time when cold weather would no longer interfere with killing.

[288] Tel. No. 168, Zichy to Andrássy, 15 December; SA, Varia Turquie I, 1875. Bourgoing to Decazes, 21 December; *First Yellow Book,* p. 57. Circular tel. of Rashid, 29 December; FO 78/2527.

CHAPTER III

THE ORIGINS OF THE ANDRÁSSY NOTE

THE SCHEME OF THE FATHER OF LIES

The Russian role in the mission of the consuls had been a reflection of the pro-Western policy prevailing in St. Petersburg. The transfer of directive authority over Turkey into the hands of Count Andrássy had been a decision contrary to the program of isolated action long championed by General Ignatiev and had taken place while he was absent from his post. At Ems in Germany the ambassador read a newspaper account of the projected consular deputation and in it recognized the defeat of his years of labor. The mission as he saw it meant a serious threat to the good relations he had slowly built up with the Turks; and, worse still, it recognized Austrian leadership and interest in problems which he wanted to make Russia's own. Promptly he returned to Constantinople intent on paralyzing Andrássy's initiative and saving as much for Russia as he could.[1] The ambassador's first task, however, was not in accord with his desires. Acting on instructions, on 19 August, he saved the fate of the proposed consular mission from the bungling hands of Count Zichy.[2] Of how disagreeable it was to him to promote Austrian interference in Bosnia, Ignatiev made no secret. With the zeal of a man struggling for a life cause he set out to defeat Andrássy regardless of the inclinations of St. Petersburg.[3]

---

[1] Ignatiev, *Istoricheski Vyesnik,* CXXXV, 443–44. Onou, *Slavonic Review,* X, 400–401. The Balkan truce consecrated in the league of the three emperors had not been accepted by the Russian ambassador to the Sublime Porte. The honeyed words of the Berlin feast had done nothing to assuage his defiance of Vienna. In his opinion Andrássy had not really renounced adventurous plans but had merely simulated an agreement with Prince Gorchakov to gain time the better to put his schemes into execution (Goriainov, *Le Bosphore et les Dardanelles,* pp. 307–8).

[2] Report No. 65B, Zichy to Andrássy, 20 August; *First Red Book,* Doc. No. 131, incomplete. Bourgoing to Decazes, 25 August; *First Yellow Book,* pp. 23–24. Report No. 463, Elliot to Derby, 22 August; FO 78/2385.

[3] With regard to Ignatiev's opinions and feelings, his British colleague wrote: "I saw General Ignatiew today for the first time since his return and had some conversation with him on the state of things in the Herzegovina, which gave me a

The prime necessity of the moment, as it appeared to Ignatiev, was to wrest the center of diplomatic action from the hands of the Austrian minister and move it to Constantinople, where he himself dominated his weak German and Austrian colleagues and where he himself exercised a strong personal influence at the Porte. Even before the consuls began their fruitless journey he had developed a plan looking to that end. The first point of his program called for a very important expansion of the duties of the consuls—the preparation of a report containing a statement of the grievances of the local population and a recommendation of practical remedies for the ills of the revolted province. The second step would be a set of identic

tolerable insight into the game which the credulity and blind confidence of his Austro-Hungarian colleague enables him to play with much prospect of success. Speaking confidentially to me, and knowing that what he said would not be repeated to Count Zichy, he did not hesitate to attribute the present rising in a great degree to the recent visit of the Emperor Francis Joseph to Dalmatia, and to His Majesty's attempts to conciliate the Slav populations, and to his acceptance of petitions from Christian subjects of the Sultan, setting forth their grievances and saying that they looked upon His Majesty as their protector. . . . . It is not to be doubted that the Russian Ambassador will endeavour to impress this view upon the minds of the Turkish Ministers, nor can it be denied that he may do so with much truth; but he will then be in a position to show that it is to himself, as practically directing the proceedings of the three Northern Embassies, that the Porte must turn to save it from the consequences of the ill-considered acts of the Austro-Hungarian Government. . . . ." (Report No. 454, Elliot to Derby, 19 August; FO 78/2385).

On 17 September the British ambassador reported: "It has been becoming more and more evident that whatever may be the outward understanding between Russia and Austria, there is no cordiality of feeling between them, at all events so far as regards the former Power. General Ignatiev has lately, on more than one occasion, spoken of the extreme anxiety of the Emperor to act cordially with Her Majesty's Government in the affairs of this country. The traditional policy of Russia, in regard to the Christian populations, has always been to proceed slowly, and with extreme caution, and it appears that His Majesty now sees with some alarm, that, by the impetuous rashness of Count Andrassy he is being hurried much faster than he wishes to go. There is an evident desire on the part of General Ignatiew, whether shared or not by his Government, I cannot say, to shew the reluctance with which he acts in concert with his colleague, and how he is obliged to restrain him in the execution of his instructions. According to the account given me by the General, the wish at Vienna would seem to be, that in everything connected with Turkey, the three Governments should proceed independently of all others, while that of Russia is, on the contrary, that, as far as possible, there should be a general understanding upon them. This, he said, was strongly exhibited when it was agreed at Vienna to propose that the Consuls should communicate with the Insurgents. He found that joint instructions, signed by Count Andrassy, and by the Russian and German Representatives, had been despatched to the Consuls: he had, however, at once called upon Mr. Novikow to explain by what authority he gave instructions to Russian Consuls in Turkey, as he himself believed them to be under his own control. The Emperor approved of his proceeding, and he at once took steps to

instructions to the ambassadors, based on the report, instructions which would direct them to make severe and even threatening remonstrances at the Sublime Porte in favor of reform. And finally, in his desire to prevent atrocities and consequent intervention, Ignatiev suggested that the Austrian military authorities on the frontier should threaten the Turks and even undertake action on Bosnian soil against troops guilty of excesses in the pursuit of the Christians.[4] The general was honestly opposed to opening the Eastern question with all its ramifications at that unfavorable moment and sought, therefore, an early end of the rebellion. If Austrian threats and even military sorties could restrain the Turks, he was willing to employ

---

prevent the appearance of an exclusive interference of the Three Powers, by proposing to the Porte that the Consuls of all the Great Powers should make the same communication to the Insurgents. . . . ." (Report No. 565, Elliot to Derby, 17 September; FO 78/2386).

A week later Elliot again reported a talk with his Russian colleague: "General Ignatiew has again spoken to me with anxiety of the proposals which might be made from Vienna with reference to the Herzegovina and Bosnia. It was only those, he said, who had been in intimately confidential relations with that Cabinet, who could be fully aware of the inconsiderate lightness with which Count Andrassy brought forward suggestions of the most serious and objectionable nature. The proposals, upon which, at various times, the Russian Government had had to throw cold water, would hardly be credited but, to do Count Andrassy justice, he was by no means tenacious of the views which he put forward, for he was generally able to abandon them with as little reflection as he had given to them in taking them up. In holding this language General Ignatiew is no doubt to a certain degree animated by a wish to make it appear that the difficulties which are created in Turkey by Foreign interference, are attributable to the Austrian rather than to the Russian Government, but any conversation which I have with him leads the more to the conviction that his feelings, which were never friendly towards Austria, are daily becoming less so. . . . ." (Report No. 586, Elliot to Derby, 24 September; FO 78/2387).

A few days later Elliot added: ". . . . I am myself unable to judge to what extent General Ignatiew may be considered as faithfully reflecting the policy of his Government, and Your Lordship is aware that I am not generally disposed to put too implicit confidence in him. I have, however, now been long acquainted with my colleague, and I do not think that I am mistaken in believing him to be deeply galled by the lead latterly taken by Austria in matters affecting this country. He has long been anxious to impress the Turks with the conviction that their safest policy is to place reliance on the Emperor and the Russian Government against the dangers with which they were threatened by Austria, and I feel little doubt that he would now be glad of an opportunity of giving such striking evidence of it, as would enable him to appear as the chief, if not sole protector of the Empire" (Report No. 608, Elliot to Derby, 28 September; FO 78/2387).

[4] "Les vues de M. Ignatiew," September 1875; SA, Varia Turquie I, 1875 (St. P.). "Copie d'une dépêche de S. E. M. le baron Jomini à S. E. M. le général Ignatiew, en date de St. Pétersbourg, le — septembre 1875"; ibid. Ignatiev, Istoricheski Vyesnik, CXXXV, 444-45.

them. Undoubtedly, however, he must also have considered that such means would effectively destroy Austrian influence in Constantinople and would throw the Turks more definitely than ever into the arms of the Russians.

Ignatiev's plan was approved by Tsar Alexander,[5] and while the St. Petersburg Foreign Office was trying to convert the imperial allies, the ambassador proceeded independently in Constantinople. As dean of the diplomatic corps he had organized at his embassy an informal conference, first of his Austrian and German satellites, and subsequently of the agents of France and Italy as well. Sir Henry Elliot remained defiantly aloof. With the consul's report of failure in his hands, Ignatiev converted Zichy and Werther to the first two points of his plan—the recommended program of reforms and ambassadorial pressure on the Porte[6]—and, as has been previously noted, the consuls were instructed to present to the embassies their opinions. The British ambassador characteristically refused to accept the invitation to participate in sending instructions[7] and did his best to

[5] Report No. 356, Ignatiev to Gorchakov, 24 November (O.S.) ; Ignatiev, *Istoricheski Vyesnik*, CXXXV, 822–23. Ignatiev showed Zichy a letter of the tsar's relative to the next step to be taken, which was of the following import: "Nous ne voulons que réformes réelles et pratiques. Mais nous sommes loins de proposer des solutions radicales, incompatibles avec les droits du Sultan. Nous voulons maintenir intacte l'entente avec le Cabinet de Vienne. Il faut faire entrer la Porte dans cette voie et l'y maintenir par une pression amicale. Constantinople doit rester le siège et le centre de l'action collective. . . . . La direction devrait être confiée aux représentants de Constantinople." Poor Zichy, in reporting these words, exultantly claimed that the tsar's words and Ignatiev's confidences to him proved that St. Petersburg had made Austria's policy its own and that Andrássy enjoyed the complete confidence of the tsar (Private letter, Zichy to Andrássy, 24 September ; SA, Varia Turquie I, 1875).

[6] Tel. No. 95, Zichy to Andrássy, 26 September ; *ibid*. Report No. 76AC, same to same, 28 September ; *ibid*.

[7] In reply to a note from Ignatiev, Elliot wrote: ". . . . I could join in the first part of the instructions which you propose for the Consuls, but the last part directing them to prepare a 'projet de solution' appears too great a departure from the original understanding for it to be possible for me to send it without instructions from my Government. The Turks consented to the Mission of the Consuls, and my Government took part in it on the understanding that as soon as they had communicated their instructions to the Insurgents and had recommended them to submit their grievances to the Turkish Commissioner, their task would be ended and they would return to their respective posts. It was especially insisted upon that they should not appear to act as a 'corps' or to have identic instructions, and it appears to me that it would not only be contrary to the understanding that they should assemble to discuss and propose a project of settlement, but also extremely undesirable, as being a decided step towards the European intervention which we deprecate. . . . . The information that we have from our Consuls is that the Insurgents sum-

dissuade his French colleague.[8] The consuls' reply from Mostar which advocated a conference in Ragusa under their supervision was not at all what Ignatiev was wanting and he rejected the proposal as readily as did the others.[9] To him this suggestion was nothing short of preposterous and he appealed to the French and British ambassadors for aid in restraining the Austrian government from the extremes to which it appeared ready to go. He warned Bourgoing and Elliot that if they did not support him the three imperial powers alone would undertake the solution and that such an action would probably result in Austrian intervention.[10] In his desperate

---

marily reject the advice given to them by our Consuls, which may be looked upon as putting an end to their mission. . . . ." (Elliot to Ignatiev, 25 September, in Report No. 597, Elliot to Derby, 26 September; FO 78/2387). In reporting to London the ambassador characterized the proposal of his colleague as "extremely objectionable." "Being apprehensive," he added, "that the instructions which were sent to the other Consuls might be taken by them as an encouragement to step beyond their proper line of action, I thought it right especially to warn Mr. Holmes against taking part in any collective project of arrangement if it should be suggested by his colleagues and to confine himself to exchanging his views with them for the information of Her Majesty's Government" (Report No. 596, Elliot to Derby, 26 September; FO 78/2387). In his negotiations with Elliot, Ignatiev made no mention of the second and third points of his program, viz., the role of the ambassadors and Austrian military action. Elliot, however, suspected that his Russian colleague had hopes of a conference of the ambassadors which would prepare a reform program (Report No. 693, Elliot to Derby, 22 October; FO 78/2389).

[8] Report No. 597, Elliot to Derby, 26 September; *ibid.*: ". . . . I may observe that General Ignatiew was not quite accurate in representing in his note to me that all our colleagues had consented to the course he proposed; for the suggestion which he had made to the Italian Minister, and in which Count Corti expressed his acquiescence, did not contain the part to which I took exception. Count Corti, moreover understood that the communication was to be made to our respective Governments and not to the consuls, and he consequently only telegraphed to Rome." The Italian consul, as a result, received no instruction (Durando to Visconti-Venosta, Mostar, 27 September; *First Green Book*, Doc. No. XLII).

[9] Tel., Elliot to Derby, 28 September; FO 78/2387.

[10] Ignatiev to Elliot, 26 September, in Report No. 597, Elliot to Derby, 26 September; FO 78/2387: ". . . . Nous sommes, ainsi que la Porte, en présence des demandes des insurgés que vous connaissez, et des complications ultérieures qui peuvent surgir. Préférez-vous que la question soit traitée à Vienne? Soit: Nous rendrions un véritable service au gouvernement Ottoman en autorisant nos consuls de rechercher, d'accord avec Server Pacha, une issue de l'impasse où se trouve cette question délicate. . . . ." Also Report No. 606, Elliot to Derby, 28 September; *ibid.*: ". . . . M. de Bourgoing was of the opinion, which I have myself several times of late conveyed to Your Lordship, that General Ignatiew was sincere in these professions, but if, as there is reason to suspect, the General wishes to obtain from the Consuls reports upon which he would suggest that the Ambassadors at Constantinople might concert some project of pacification and of future Government for Bosnia, I said I doubted whether it would be advisable to follow him. . . . ."

attempt to forestall this dreaded interference, the general abandoned his old policy of isolated Russian action and urged on his superiors the necessity for a conference in Constantinople participated in by all the powers.[11] When St. Petersburg showed signs of turning the entire question over to Austria, it seemed to Ignatiev much better to enlist the restraining aid of England and France than to allow Andrássy to dictate his own settlement. With the consular mission a failure and the rebellion more successful than ever, it was plain to be seen that new and more far-reaching projects would be shortly issuing from the Ballplatz in Vienna. In a few days that anticipation gave promise of realization. News reached the general that the Austrian minister was not in sympathy with his plan and had new schemes of his own. Loudly Ignatiev spread the warning that the question of reforms treated officially by the cabinets would arouse Turkish susceptibilities and lead to failure,[12] and quietly, it would appear, he whispered to the grand vizier rumors of an Austrian decision to call a conference or at least to take the lead in an intervention.[13]

These efforts of the ambassador proved fruitless. His French colleague was afraid of an independent position, having been instructed not to wander from the paths of concerted action; and Elliot was suspicious and obdurate. Ignatiev's first attempt to defeat his archenemy was, therefore, a failure. But with unflagging zeal he turned to another means. Recognizing plainly that a continuation of the chaos reigning in Turkey would soon lead to collective intervention with Andrássy taking a leading role, the general began a desperate effort to push the sultan into forestalling such a measure by spontaneous reform. Ignatiev had never been in such a commanding position on the Bosporus. His favorite, Mahmud Nedim, had been returned to the vizierate late in August[14] and the equivocal po-

---

[11] Ignatiev, *Istoricheski Vyesnik*, CXXXV, 444–45.

[12] Tel. No. 36, Mayr to Andrássy, St. Petersburg, 2 October; SA, Varia Turquie I, 1875.

[13] Tel., Zichy to Andrássy, 4 October; *ibid.* Andrássy hastened, in response to complaints from the grand vizier, to deny that he had any such intentions (Tel. No. 709, Andrássy to Zichy, 5 October; *ibid.*); but Ignatiev, aware of the denial, declared Andrássy's words to be in direct contradiction to his recent utterances to Novikov, and he urged his government *"de tirer son épingle avantageusement du jeu"* (Tel. No. 39, Mayr to Andrássy, 8 October; *ibid.*).

[14] Ignatiev, as has been noted, fought vigorously for the political life of his friend during the next month when the restored grand vizier was the object of

sition of Austria gave him an excellent storm-signal to exploit his own advantage. Taking his arguments directly to the sultan, Ignatiev won a most breath-taking response. Abdul Aziz, moved partially by his desire to be pleasant, and stirred too, in all probability, by fears of intervention, put himself into the hands of Russia. He overwhelmed the ambassador by announcing a desire to establish a close personal relationship with the tsar and a willingness to permit Russia, through the person of Ignatiev himself, to suggest a reform program on condition that Russia should not participate in any concerted European pressure. In talking with the dragoman of the embassy late in September, the grand vizier confirmed this new amity. The sultan had told him, he said, that he had made a great mistake in not following his father's friendly policy toward the tsar; he saw now that Russia was not his enemy and he was inclined to listen secretly to the ambassador's advice.[15]

Although the general did not have the confidence of his British rival in Constantinople, the two diplomats were entirely agreed in the opinion that Turkish reform was the only means of dispelling the menace of collective intervention. Sir Henry Elliot, therefore, was no less importunate than Ignatiev. In mid-August he went to the palace and informed the sultan pointedly that English sentiment, after years of disappointed waiting for reform, was becoming unfriendly, and he listed a number of abuses in sad need of rectification.[16] In September, when the international barometer was perceptibly falling, Sir Henry repeatedly called out a warning.[17]

---

embittered attack from both Midhat and Hussein Avni. The Russian ambassador attempted to persuade his colleagues to join him in defending his friend and even suggested to his German colleague that he give Mahmud the decoration of the Black Eagle in order to raise him in the sultan's eyes (Raschdau, *Deutsche Rundschau*, CXXXVII, 393).

[15] Ignatiev, *Istoricheski Vyesnik*, CXXXV, 453-55. Nelidov, *Revue des deux mondes*, XXVII (1915), 306. Nelidov, secretary of the Constantinople embassy, in recalling this remarkable moment gives this additional comment: *"Tel était du moins le sens des rapports que l'ambassadeur adressa à ce sujet au Ministère."*

[16] Report No. 445, Elliot to Derby, 17 August; FO 78/2385.

[17] "In the course of a confidential conversation with the Grand Vizier yesterday, I took occasion to represent to him how desirable it is that the Porte should lose no time in giving evidence of its determination to remedy the grievances complained of in the Northern Provinces. If this was not done, there is a probability that the Governments more immediately interested in the maintenance of tranquillity may propose some special measure for satisfying the people, and there could be no doubt how much better it would be that the initiative should be taken by

The Turkish answer to these exhortations was an imperial *iradé*, published on 2 October, which ordered the end of the grievances of which Elliot had been complaining. The increase of the tithe was withdrawn; claims on arrears of taxes were abandoned; the various communities were to be represented in the provincial administrative councils by delegates of their own choice; delegates from the provinces would be permitted to take their desires to Constantinople, where those desires would be used as the basis for further reforms; special agents would be dispatched to administer the tax laws in accordance with the principles of justice; investigations into the possibility of a more equitable system of taxation were promised.[18]

General Ignatiev was highly delighted with the sultan's prompt action. Now, he told Elliot in exultation, the wind would be taken out of Count Andrássy's sails.[19]

the Porte itself. . . . ." (Report No. 577, Elliot to Derby, 21 September; FO 78/2387). "My correspondence has made Your Lordship aware how urgent I have thought it that the Porte should not delay the adoption of measures for the immediate removal of the just cause of complaint of the populations of all parts of the Empire in reference to the collection of the tithes, and to the manner in which alleged arrears of taxes were being levied. I frequently represented to the Grand Vizier that in this and other reforms, he should endeavour to forestall the representations which might soon be made by foreign Governments. . . . ." (Report No. 625, Elliot to Derby, 2 October; FO 78/2388).

[18] *Turkey No. 2 (1876)*, Doc. No. 29, inclosure. *Ibid.*, Doc. No. 34, inclosure. *British and Foreign State Papers*, LVII, 1211–12. *First Yellow Book*, pp. 37–38. Hertslet, *The Map of Europe by Treaty*, IV, Doc. No. 454, pp. 2407–8. At the end of September, Elliot, at the request of the grand vizier, drew up a memorandum of the grievances which had been the object of his oral remonstrances, and the *iradé* was largely a recasting of the ambassador's proposals. The only one of his suggestions ignored in the official document was the one recommending regulation of abuses growing out of forced work on the roads and labor exactions by the proprietors (Report No. 614, Elliot to Derby, 30 September; FO 78/2387).

No indication is available which would reveal whether or not Ignatiev also made specific suggestions. If he did they would of necessity have closely paralleled those advanced by Elliot. In his memoir he merely states, "His work [i.e., Elliot's] and mine entered into the *iradé*. . . . ." (*Istoricheski Vyesnik*, CXXXV, 822–23). Three days later, after Mahmud had unhorsed the doughty Hussein Avni, came the official Turkish declaration of bankruptcy. One of the officials of the German embassy asserted (Raschdau, *Deutsche Rundschau*, CXXXVII, 393) that Ignatiev had been advising this for years as a means of breaking Anglo-French financial control of Turkey, but there is available no direct evidence that the ambassador's hand was in this decision. The condition of Turkish finance imposed better arguments than Ignatiev could possibly have advanced. Blaisdell (*European Financial Control*, pp. 79–80) misses the point altogether when he surmises that Ignatiev welcomed the declaration of bankruptcy as a contribution toward opening up the Eastern question.

[19] Report No. 625, Elliot to Derby, 2 October; FO 78/2388.

COUNT ANDRÁSSY'S COUNTER-PROPOSALS

In the meanwhile the St. Petersburg ministry had made Ignatiev's threefold program its own and a statement of the proposal together with a projected letter of instructions to the ambassadors was drawn up for communication to the imperial allies.[20] On 18 September the two documents were presented in Berlin—apparently in the hope of securing German approval before taking up the question in Vienna.[21] But if the Russians did hope to use German assent as a means of forcing that of Austria, they were disappointed. Bismarck had years before laid down the principle that the league of the three emperors would not function on the basis of a majority vote, and Emperor William informed his nephew that he would delay his decision until he learned the views of Vienna.[22] At the same time, 23 September, an even clearer response appeared in the *Reichsanzeiger,* the empire's public voice. Germany's interests, the article in question announced, were not concerned in the Eastern question; the imperial government intended merely to support the wishes of its two allies and it refused to take a friendly power under its tutelage in regard to the affairs of Turkey.[23] Privately at the foreign office, Bülow assured the Austrian ambassador that the emperor wanted to proceed hand in hand with Francis Joseph.[24]

On 23 September the Russian plan was presented in Vienna. In the next days Andrássy discussed the question at length with Novikov, the Russian ambassador, and on 2 October sent his opinions to St. Petersburg. The Austrian minister recognized quite clearly the limitations of his representative at the Sublime Porte and knew that any decision of the three imperial ambassadors left uninstructed would be the decision of General Ignatiev. Only the day before Emperor Francis Joseph had announced to the Austrian and Hungarian

[20] "Les vues de M. Ignatiew," September 1875; SA, Varia Turquie I, 1875 (St. P.). "Copie d'une dépêche de S. E. M. le baron Jomini à S. E. M. le général Ignatiew, en date de St. Pétersbourg, le — septembre 1875"; *ibid.*

[21] Report No. 43, Seiller to Andrássy, Berlin, 21 September; SA, Varia Turquie I, 1875 (Berlin).

[22] Tel., Seiller to Andrássy, 23 September; *ibid.*

[23] *Andrássy,* II, 270–71. "Germany and the Herzegovina," *Spectator,* 25 September 1875, p. 1195. *Europäischer Geschichtskalender,* 23 September 1875, pp. 168–69.

[24] Report No. 42AD, Seiller to Andrássy, 18 September; SA, Varia Turquie I, 1875.

delegations—and to the remainder of Europe as well—that his realm had a major concern in the rebellion[25] and his foreign minister had no inclination to abandon vital national interests to the dubious mercies of "the father of lies." With regard to the first of the Ignatiev proposals, Andrássy was willing for the consuls to recommend solutions, but he demanded that their report should go to their governments rather than to a local committee of the ambassadors. His rather lame pretext was that if the representatives of the allied courts acted on concerted instructions they would be able to carry the other ambassadors with them, but if they acted independently the agents of France, England, and Italy might lead the Porte in some contrary direction. As for an identic dispatch to the ambassadors calling on them to admonish and threaten the sultan into reform, he could consent to such a procedure only when the three cabinets had agreed on a program of reforms which seemed suitable to them. In other words, the specific measures to be exacted from Turkey he reserved for the home governments; he could not consent to giving Count Zichy carte blanche to push Abdul Aziz along any path that Ignatiev might wish. However, since Tsar Alexander had approved Ignatiev's proposal, the foreign minister professed a willingness to accept the idea of identic instructions but wished to make certain modifications in the Russian draft. He was very reluctant to threaten to abandon the Turks to their own fortunes and misfortunes if they did not satisfy their suffering populations. Such an action might well open the door to contingencies incompatible with Austria's vital interests. The military action which the Russian plan assigned to Austrian troops Andrássy rejected as armed intervention.[26]

Before the negotiations could proceed further there came the sultan's *iradé* and in its wake another attempt of General Ignatiev to forestall Austrian meddling. On 4 October, Baron Jomini in St. Petersburg sent a note to the Austrian chargé d'affaires asking him to come as quickly as possible. "I have great news for you," he an-

---

[25] *Europäischer Geschichtskalender*, 22 September, p. 240; *Augsburger Allgemeine Zeitung*, 23 September, p. 4169.

[26] Tel. No. 1, Andrássy to Mayr in St. Petersburg, 2 October; SA, Varia Turquie I, 1875. On the following day the foreign minister, ever alert to maintain intimate relations with the German government, forwarded his observations to Berlin (Andrássy to Seiller, 3 October; *ibid.*). Bülow replied with a complete endorsement of Andrássy's statement and emphasized the undesirability of allowing the ambassadors a free hand (Report No. 48B, Seiller to Andrássy, 8 October; *ibid.*).

nounced as Mayr appeared, and then proceeded to unfold Ignatiev's new plan. It also was composed of three points: (1) the sultan's reforms were to be formally noted; (2) the refusal of the insurgents to follow the advice of the consuls was to be recorded; and (3) the powers were to reserve their liberty of action for future decisions which might be imposed by the necessities of humanity and the interests of neighboring states.[27] Such a program, of course, would eliminate specific demands formulated in Vienna but would constitute a lasting threat over the heads of the Turks which the Russian ambassador could exploit for the advancement of his own influence and cause. No such avowal, naturally, was made; in explaining his ideas to Zichy, Ignatiev contended that it would be much better if the powers did not exact a definite program from the sultan but would leave the plan and execution of reforms to the Porte while reserving to themselves a general right of criticism and control.[28] The approval promptly given to the ambassador's new proposal[29] was indication enough that official Russia shared his desire to sidetrack Count Andrássy. Even Prince Gorchakov, with his penchant for Austro-Russian co-operation, added his voice of approval. From Switzerland, where he was spending his vacation, the chancellor urged moving the center of action to Constantinople. Hitherto, he said to an Austrian representative, Andrássy had been carrying the whole burden of the question, but now, since all six powers were engaged, it would be desirable to transfer the focal point of negotiations to Constantinople where the minister would have only one-sixth of the responsibility.[30]

This turn of the discussion was not at all pleasing to the director of the Ballplatz. Andrássy had just a few days before expressed his belief in Ignatiev's loyal support of the allied program,[31] and now his mind was filled with suspicion. "Out of these events," he wrote to Zichy, "I have won the conviction that beside the political action which General Ignatiev follows in common with Your Excellency

[27] Tel. No. 38, Mayr to Andrássy, 5 October; ibid., in First Red Book, Doc. No. 172, with "on" substituted for "L'Empereur Alexandre."

[28] Tel. No. 111, Zichy to Andrássy, 7 October; SA, Varia Turquie I, 1875.

[29] Report No. 50AJ, Mayr to Andrássy, 8 October; ibid. Jomini argued to the chargé d'affaires that this spontaneous act of the sultan would safeguard his dignity and at the same time would be a happy event for the powers, who would have great difficulty in imposing reforms on the Porte.

[30] Tel., Ottenfels to Andrássy, Berne, 6 October; ibid.

[31] Tel. No. 2, Andrássy to Zichy, 4 October; ibid.

and the German ambassador, he is pushing through a policy of his own which he keeps secret from you." The whole Russian activity pointed, as he saw it, to a private understanding between the ambassador and the grand vizier.[32] From the Austrian point of view it appeared less desirable than ever to shift the center of diplomacy to Constantinople.

On 10 October Andrássy made his second response to St. Petersburg. Points one and two of the new Russian program were quite innocuous; the minister accepted them. But as for the third—the indefinite threat—he proposed to "complete it by certain practical propositions for Bosnia and Hercegovina which would give consistency to the point and prevent as much as possible the return of analogous events." His reply, translated out of diplomatic parlance, meant that he was rejecting the suggestion of a vague pressure exercised by the ambassadors and was proposing the preparation of·a specific program of reform. And, further, he wished it to be the work of the imperial league in which he was taking the lead. "I hold more than ever," he added in his reply to St. Petersburg, "to the manner of procedure which we have followed up to the present, which consists in an accord between us before all. I have the conviction that in consulting à trois we shall execute à six, whereas in consulting à six we should arrive at having nothing to execute. The most profitable result of consultations à six would be to create difficulties for the entente and the action of the three."[33]

A week later Andrássy forwarded to St. Petersburg his "practical propositions." To prepare the ground for them he first entered into an analysis of the sultan's recent iradé, which was to be, according to the Russians, a starting point for a new era of reform. He found it motivated by the desire to escape the influence and counsels of the powers, and he anticipated that it, like all precipitate measures, would not achieve the objective which it had in view. The sultan's abandonment of delinquent taxes he characterized as nothing more than an invitation to further rebellion, and as for the promised reforms, their vague phraseology made them in part impossible and in

---

[32] Tel., Andrássy to Zichy, 15 October; ibid. The foreign minister added in this communication to his fellow-Magyar nobleman: "The events which I have just mentioned need not change your outward relations with General Ignatiev, but should moderate your excessive trust in him. In business assigned to you rely upon yourself rather than upon the general."

[33] Tel., Andrássy to Mayr, 10 October; First Red Book, Doc. No. 180, incomplete.

part conducive to renewed disturbance. The Turkish initiative, he suggested with no little irony, could have been inspired only by Sir Henry Elliot. For such reasons Andrássy declared himself unable to be content with the Turkish action; he deemed it impossible to stop at some illusory solution if the three powers were to keep their influence intact for future eventualities. Hence the necessity for proposals prepared by the imperial cabinets.[34]

It was easier for Andrássy to make destructive criticisms of Turkey's projects than to advance feasible proposals of his own. There were more solutions to the problem which he did not want than solutions which he could devise. He did not desire annexation of the insurgent province to Austria-Hungary, and he could not have effected it with impunity if he had wished to. He would not tolerate the expansion of Serbia and Montenegro, nor would he accept the formation of a new state on the southern frontier of the Dual Monarchy. A large and aggressive Slavic principality adjacent to the Slavic provinces of Austria-Hungary would constitute a serious threat to the internal peace and even the stability of the empire. The creation of a series of small autonomous units would raise up an impossible situation. In short, there was no political rearrangement which was at all possible; for the time it was imperative that the Bosnians and Hercegovinians remain under direct Turkish control. Prince Gorchakov, on the contrary, had expressed his own inclination for an administration of Bosnia analogous to that of Serbia and Rumania.[35] Andrássy, accordingly, was moved, in his talks with the Russian ambassador[36] and in his second telegram of 16 October to St. Petersburg, to combat such a solution.[37] The only reforms which he could offer to the insurgent Christians were of necessity limited to religious and economic conditions. In this second communication to the Russian foreign office Andrássy argued through many pages of manuscript the desirability—and by inference the sufficiency—of

[34] Tel. No. 1, Andrássy to Mayr, 16 October; SA, Varia Turquie I, 1875. Again in this introductory dispatch the minister emphasized his view that the preparation of reform measures and their imposition on Turkey would be the work of the imperial powers. E.g., he wrote, "Ma conviction que la Porte accédera à nos demandes repose sur le fait même que ces demandes lui seraient adressées par les trois cours et soutenues au besoin par le reste de l'Europe."

[35] Tel., Ottenfels to Andrássy, 26 August; SA.

[36] Goriainov, op. cit., pp. 312–13.

[37] Tel. No. 2, Andrássy to Mayr, 16 October; SA, Varia Turquie I, 1875, partially deleted in First Red Book, Doc. No. 183.

three concessions to be exacted from the sultan: absolute religious equality; elimination through state purchase of the corvée and the seigniorial tithes remaining from the old manorial regime; and the abolition of tax farming. Austria-Hungary more than any other state, Andrássy concluded in a tone of diplomatic warning, had to suffer the consequences of disturbance just beyond its borders, and, as a seriously affected neighbor, was forced to make her voice heard in Constantinople.[38]

The Vienna program was foredoomed to the most bitter opposition from General Ignatiev. From the moment he learned of Andrássy's objection to his first proposals, the ambassador, as has been seen, let no occasion escape to attempt to discredit his enemy. As the days passed and the lines of cleavage between foreign minister and ambassador became more marked, Ignatiev's hostility mounted to the point of frenzy. In his efforts to enlist the aid of Sir Henry Elliot he did not hesitate to attribute the most extravagant intentions to Andrássy,[39] and, when he saw his own foreign office weakening,

[38] *Ibid.*

[39] Several quotations from the dispatches of Elliot indicate the progress of Ignatiev's views. ". . . . Count Andrassy wishes, he says, that the report of the Consuls at Mostar of the impressions and views which they had formed during their mission should be sent to Vienna, where the three Governments should concert upon a project to be submitted to the Porte for the administration of Bosnia. . . . .Count Andrassy's object was plain. He was bent upon making it appear that every reform in the administration of the Northern Provinces and every amelioration of the condition of the Christians proceeded directly from himself, and to attain this end he was regardless of everything else. . . . ." (Report No. 627, Elliot to Derby, 3 October; FO 78/2388). "General Ignatiew called upon me this morning for the purpose of telling me very confidentially what had been passing at Vienna respecting the course to be followed in the question of the Herzegovina. . . . . It was only now that he had learned how extravagant, to use his own expression, that proposition was:—it was more so, in fact, than that of the Consuls who had suggested a conference at Ragusa with the Turkish commissioner and the chiefs of the insurgents; for Count Andrassy proposed that there should be such a conference at Ragusa, but that, out of deference to the feelings of the Insurgents, the Turkish commissioner should be excluded from it. The Austro-Hungarian minister considered the demands of the insurgent chiefs . . . . as perfectly reasonable, and had completely endorsed them, including that for a regular armistice. . . . ." (Report No. 649, Elliot to Derby, 8 October; *ibid.*). "General Ignatiew called upon me this afternoon. . . . . It had been understood that the Austro-Hungarian Government had agreed that there should be no interference in the affairs of Bosnia, but Count Andrassy afterwards insisted that a representation should be made to the Porte of the reforms required by the Powers, it being, he argued, impossible to put faith in those promised by the Turks. This had formed the subject of fresh discussions with the Vienna Cabinet, and he had had again to combat Count Andrassy's views and to show that whatever reforms should be theoretically

Ignatiev carried the battle directly to Emperor Alexander himself.[40] On 19 October he left Constantinople for the Crimea to lay his views in person before the tsar.[41] The basis of his argument was the sultan's offer to effect a close personal alliance with the emperor on condition that Russia refrain from international pressure on Turkey. If this opportunity were not seized, the ambassador predicted that Austrian diplomatic action would bring about a total eclipse of Russian influence in Constantinople and war would follow in the near future. But Ignatiev's desperate labors to break up the Austro-Russian entente were not successful, even though he did carry the day in certain of his objections to Andrássy's reform program. Alexander was loyal to the imperial league; when his ambassador argued that neutrality in Turco-European difficulties would not be incompatible with maintenance of the league, the tsar informed him that he had another understanding of fidelity. Nor was Alexander apparently disturbed by the specter of war which Ignatiev paraded before him; if Turkey was to collapse, the tsar held an understanding between the three emperors to be more imperative than ever. In discouragement Ig-

---

adopted, the execution of them must be left to the Porte, those imposed by the Powers would be less likely to be honestly carried out than any which might be voluntarily made by the authority of the Sultan. . . . . With regard to Count Andrássy's proposal, General Ignatiew again repeated that it became daily more evident that his real object was not to ameliorate the condition of the Bosnian population but to make it appear that they had obtained important concessions through the influence of Austria Hungary" (Report No. 665, Elliot to Derby, 14 October; *ibid.*). After Elliot had finished writing this dispatch, Ignatiev came to him "asking whether it would not be possible for Mr. Holmes to persuade Server Pasha of the necessity of giving immediate effect to the reforms sketched in the imperial Iradé and the vizirial instructions. . . . . Your Lordship will be struck with the strange position in which the Russian Ambassador is at this moment placed, in being forced to appeal to his English colleague to urge the adoption of steps which shall defeat the object of the Austro-Hungarian Government with which his own professes to be acting in concert. It may be doubted whether General Ignatiew would venture to telegraph to the Russian Consul in the same sense as he asked me to do to Mr. Holmes, but there cannot, I think, be a question that it is desirable for us to assist him at the present moment in resisting the extreme pretentions of Count Andrassy when it can be done in an open and straightforward way, and I have never concealed from the Austrian and German Ambassadors, any more than from General Ignatiew, that I was doing all in my power to urge the Porte to make administrative reforms in Bosnia and Herzegovina at the earliest possible moment" (Report No. 666, Elliot to Derby, 15 October; *ibid.*).

[40] Report No. 627, Elliot to Derby, 3 October; *ibid.* Nelidov, *Revue des deux mondes*, XXVII (1915), 308.

[41] *The Times* (London), 20 October 1875, p. 5, col. 1. Tel., Zichy to Andrássy, 19 October; SA, Varia Turquie I, 1875.

natiev resigned his position. The tsar, however, refused his request, and ten days after his departure the ambassador was back again on the Bosporus, fighting still to defeat Andrássy.[42]

[42] Ignatiev, *Istoricheski Vyesnik*, CXXXV, 457–60. Onou, *Slavonic Review*, X, 401–4. Nelidov, *Revue des deux mondes*, XXVII (1915), 308. Ignatiev's argument for a Russo-Turkish arrangement and the tsar's reply are confirmed in a private letter from the Austrian ambassador to Andrássy (19/31 December): "Auf einem offiziellen Bericht Ignatiews mit dem Vorschlag 'de s'entendre avec la Turquie et de laisser l'Europe à côté' antwortet der Kaiser 'de n'entendre pas la loyauté de cette manière.'" It must be pointed out, however, that in a letter written by Ignatiev to Jomini from Livadia on 12/24 October (Alexander Onou, "Correspondance inédite du baron Alexandre de Jomini," *Revue d'histoire moderne*, September–October 1935, p. 378), the general says that he went to Livadia because of "your mémoire and the direct propositions of Count Andrássy." Since the two men were not seeing entirely eye to eye at the moment one need not expect that Ignatiev would have necessarily told Jomini his whole scheme. After his return to Constantinople, Ignatiev told his Austrian colleague that, in spite of certain criticisms of the Andrássy program, he had insisted to the tsar on the necessity of co-operation between the two governments (Tel. No. 124, Zichy to Andrássy, 27 October; SA, Varia Turquie I, 1875). His story to the British ambassador was different: ". . . . He could tell me in very strict confidence that this [the Andrássy] proposal was of such a nature, that if adopted it could not fail to lead, if not to civil war, at least to constant massacres. The authority which has hitherto resided with the Mussulmans would be wholly transferred to the Christians in a manner which the former could not be expected tamely to submit to, and a power was to be put into the hands of the Bishops, who were to be entirely independent of the Porte. The Catholic Bishops, he observed, are for the most part Austrian subjects, and this will no doubt always be regarded by General Ignatiew and his Government as a strong and legitimate argument against their being put into a position to exercise an extended jurisdiction. . . . . The Emperor, General Ignatiew added, did not at all like the manner in which Turkish affairs were being treated, exclusively by the three Powers, and wished that all the guaranteeing Governments should be consulted in regard to them" (Report No. 728, Elliot to Derby, 6 November; FO 78/2390). "Every time that I see General Ignatiew he continues to dilate upon the anxiety of the Austro-Hungarian Government to make excessive demands upon the Porte, which he is obliged to combat. He told me yesterday that Count Andrassy now cites the occupation of Syria, by French troops after the massacres, as the precedent which might be followed in Bosnia, where a similar duty might be delegated to Austria-Hungary by the other Powers. The Ambassador says that he has done his best to show that in a country with a large Musulman population such as that in Bosnia, the first rumour of such an occupation would be a signal to them to rise and massacre the Christians" (Report No. 749, Elliot to Derby, 14 November; FO 78/2390). This last report from Elliot was forwarded to Vienna, and Sir Andrew Buchanan, the British ambassador, asked Andrássy about his alleged desire to use the French occupation of Syria as a precedent for Austro-Hungarian action in Bosnia. "His Excellency expressed some surprise at such a wish being attributed to him, and as I objected to giving him my authority for the report, he said if it came from General Ignatiew, I can only say it is untrue, adding with some excitement 'It is terrible to have to deal with such a man.' . . . ." (Report No. 383, Buchanan to Derby, Budapest, 16 November; FO 7/852). To the French ambassador Ignatiev claimed that Andrássy was intent on arranging the settlement between the three imperial

Novikov, the Russian representative in Vienna, was entirely under the spell of the gracious Hungarian count who directed Austrian policy. Novikov, consequently, adopted all of Andrássy's plans and commended them diligently to his own government.[43] Jomini, who was in charge of the St. Petersburg foreign office during the absence of Prince Gorchakov, took an intermediate stand. He could not bring himself to a break with Austria,[44] but he none the less appreciated Ignatiev's impassioned desire to call a halt to Vienna's unbridled leadership of the imperial league. When the Andrássy program arrived in St. Petersburg, Jomini uttered the proper diplomatic phrases about Andrássy's propositions being "the most propitious solution imaginable" and then went on with the all-important "but." When the verbiage was cleared away Jomini was seen to be supporting the plan of Ignatiev and not that of Andrássy.[45] In making his recommendation to the tsar Jomini's view was unchanged: the best program would be to leave the initiative to the grand vizier and to allow the ambassadors to push him down the road of reforms through menace of intervention.[46]

A preliminary dispatch of 24 October from the Crimea revealed the dominant influence of Ignatiev and Jomini in Russian councils: His Majesty the tsar appreciated well the perfect courtesy and intentions of Count Andrássy and found his propositions, in principle, entirely within the circle of Russia's traditional ideas; but, before assuming the responsibility for a plan which in some respects fell short of Ignatiev's recommendations to the Turks, the tsar wished to examine the situation from every angle. Two considerations, the message continued, imposed this hesitation. The Austrian minister had not seen all the consular reports and recent dispatches from Constan-

---

courts and then presenting their decision to the three other powers—which was, of course, the truth—and that back of all the plans was an impending Austrian occupation of Bosnia (Bourgoing to Decazes, 3 November; *Documents français*, II, Doc. No. 10).

[43] Tel., Hofmann to Andrássy in Terebes, Vienna, 21 October; SA, Varia Turquie I, 1875.

[44] In early October he had written to Ignatiev, in response to the latter's castigations of Austrian policy: "You are too severe on Andrássy. . . . . We must take him as he is and try to keep him. Only think what would happen if he resigned" (Onou, *Slavonic Review*, X, 402, quoted from Ignatiev, *Istoricheski Vyesnik*, CXXXV, 459).

[45] Confidential letter, Mayr to Andrássy, 9/21 October; SA, Varia Turquie I, 1875.

[46] Tel. No. 44, Mayr to Andrássy, 22 October; *ibid.*

tinople and the cabinets would be justly accused of haste if these documents were not maturely studied. Moreover, the *iradé* had anticipated the Andrássy program; it was desirable first of all to give the Porte sufficient time to prove its intentions.[47]

A week later Russia's formal response was ready for delivery. The essence of its long pages of polished French was that rejection of Andrássy's method of procedure which had been politely foreshadowed in the earlier dispatch. The Russians had no objection to the proposed reforms; indeed, they wanted to make Andrássy's propositions, in so far as they were practical, merely the starting point for others still to come. The question at issue between St. Petersburg and Vienna was whether the powers should prepare a specific list of reforms and exact their acceptance through direct intervention or whether, exercising a lasting vigilance, they should push the sultan into reform through less formal advice and a permanent menace.

In the final analysis this question had two aspects. There was at stake a real problem of agreeing on the procedure best suited to secure effective reform. Then there was the critical problem of leadership with its repercussions on national prestige and fortunes. Would the leader be Ignatiev directing Turkey from Constantinople, with his goal an eventual solution of the Eastern question to the satisfaction of Russia; or would it be Andrássy in Vienna at work to bring the Balkan Slavs within the orbit of Austria-Hungary? This second problem was the important one; the discussion, however, ignored it. Baron Jomini's pen brought to Andrássy's program searching questions as to substance, form, and possibilities of execution—questions which, be it said in the light of later events, clearly pointed out the weaknesses and dangers of the Vienna views. It would be necessary, Jomini contended, either to envisage more drastic means to conquer the ill-will of the Turks which an open intervention would inspire— to follow the precedent of intervention established in Syria, for example—or it would be necessary to modify the demands and more especially the form in which they were expressed. He proposed in the name of the tsar the second alternative, or, as he termed it, a combination of the ideas of Andrássy and the means suggested by Ignatiev. The Russian ministry still held to an identic dispatch such as the ambassador had proposed early in the month, a document which

---

[47] Hamburger to Novikov, Livadia, 12/24 October; *ibid.* Tel., Hofmann to Andrássy, Vienna, 25 October; *ibid.*

would take formal note of the *iradé* and which would raise aloft the ax of European reprobation in case the sultan did not initiate and carry through progressive reform. To satisfy Andrássy's insistence on his own three propositions the new Russian reply included a draft copy of confidential instructions to the ambassadors which would call upon them to warn the sultan that in the coming days of grace those special measures espoused in Vienna were to be pressed with requisite energy.[48]

In his desire to combat the Andrássy plan Baron Jomini declared himself to be most sanguine of what Mahmud Nedim, that notorious favorite of Count Ignatiev, could accomplish if given a free hand. In private conversation, however, he revealed the pessimism which was growing in Russia, and admitted to the Austrian chargé that he anticipated failure as the end result. In this event he leaned toward the collective intervention of all the guaranteeing powers, first through a conference, and then, if necessary, through a military occupation delegated to Austria and Russia under a European commission. Should this arrangement not be made, he proposed a policy of absolute non-intervention under which sultan and subjects would fight it out to the bitter end. Out of an attempt at non-intervention, however, Jomini claimed to foresee the certainty of a great European crisis.[49] These remarks addressed of course informally to Vienna, indicated again that, in contrast to Andrássy's desire to have the imperial league solve the problems of the East, the St. Petersburg government still thought in terms of the European concert. From the beginning of the crisis Russian policy had not been averse to a political approach to the cause and cure of Christian rebellion in Turkey, as was indicated, for example, by Chancellor Gorchakov's pronouncement in favor of an autonomous principality. Russia had nothing to gain by the palliatives which were necessarily the limits of Austrian concession. Franker yet was Jomini in talking with the French chargé d'affaires. The coming spring, the tsar's representative said, would

---

[48] Jomini to Novikov in Vienna, St. Petersburg, 19/31 October, together with a "Projet de dépêche identique ostensible" and a "Projet d'instructions confidentielles"; SA, Varia Turquie I, 1875. The ideas, if not the exact phraseology, of these documents, as in the case of the Hamburger dispatch cited above in note 47, were drafted by Ignatiev during his brief sojourn in Livadia (Ignatiev to Jomini, 12/24 October; Onou, *Revue d'histoire moderne,* September–October 1935, pp. 378–79).

[49] Report No. 55AF, Mayr to Andrássy, 15/27 October; SA, *Geheime Aktenstücke, Abmachung mit Russland, Baron Jominis Projekt.*

perhaps see a great extension of the rebellion, which might conceivably mean the ruin of Turkey; and it was imperative to anticipate this contingency. In her attempt to prevent bloodshed in the Balkans, Jomini went on, Russia had contracted a moral obligation toward her fellow-Christians, and, in a burst of confidence, he described their eventual fate as a federation of free states with a free city of Constantinople as their capital.[50]

In early November when the new Russian views were communicated to him, Andrássy believed thoroughly in the efficacy of his own program. One of the generals familiar with the insurgent provinces tried to convince him of the uselessness of such attempts, but the minister refused to be dissuaded.[51] His plans, he frankly admitted, might prejudice the independence of Turkey,[52] but he would not agree to a radical solution. The best course, he still insisted, was to prepare a list of feasible reforms and see to it that the Porte carried them out.[53] Most categorically, therefore, he refused Baron

---

[50] Hanotaux, *Contemporary France,* IV, 71–72. The dispatch of de Laboulaye used by Hanotaux is not printed in the official collections. Jomini's words to the French chargé d'affaires are merely another indication of that undercurrent of sympathy toward France which came to the surface in the war scare of the spring of 1875 and which was to appear repeatedly in the course of the developing crisis in the Balkans. It is seen in the tsar's independent invitation to France to join in the consular mission. It is seen in the prompt attempt in mid-September to secure French support for Ignatiev's original plan (Decazes to Vogüé in Vienna, Paris, 18 September; *Documents français,* II, Doc. No. 7, pp. 8–9). It appears again in October when the tsar announced that France, England, and Italy would be invited to help prepare a project for the pacification of Turkey (Gontaut-Biron to Decazes, Baden, 5 October; *ibid.,* Doc. No. 8).

In his conversation with Lord Augustus Loftus, the English ambassador, who had just returned to his post, Jomini was more discreet. He spoke freely of his fears for the spring and of the necessity for new measures, but merely said—just at the moment when he was preparing his rejection of the Vienna procedure—that Russia had given Count Andrássy carte blanche to plan a solution (Report No. 321, Loftus to Derby, St. Petersburg, 26 October; FO 65/911).

In talking to the Italian chargé d'affaires in St. Petersburg Jomini argued the superior morality and prudence of intervention as against a policy of non-intervention and hinted that the Syrian occupation might afford a suitable precedent. He claimed to speak, however, only his personal opinion (Di Collobiano to Visconti-Venosta, St. Petersburg, 9 November; *First Green Book,* Doc. No. LXV).

[51] Mollinary, *op. cit.,* II, 294–96. In his conversation with Mollinary on 4 November, Andrássy told him that a concert of all the Great Powers for the solution of the Eastern question was impossible and that only a *fait accompli*—without definition—could lead to results. For the time he proposed to remain neutral and to try not to lose the sympathies of the *rayahs.*

[52] Tel., Buchanan to Derby, Vienna, 7 November; FO 7/852.

[53] Andrássy to Wassitsch, Budapest, 9 November; SA, Varia Turquie I, 1875.

Jomini's invitation to consider more serious measures for the future. He discouraged the idea of a conference by informing the Russians that Austria, always the most concerned of the powers, had no intention of issuing a call; and he rejected flatly, in his conversations with Novikov[54] and in his communication to St. Petersburg, the idea of joint Austro-Russian armed occupation. The first consideration in that decision was his abiding determination to keep all forms of Russian interference out of this territory over which Vienna was entitled, in his view, to exercise an exclusive influence. Less fundamental objections, naturally, had to be sent to the tsar. Andrássy professed a fear that the adventure might lead to frictions such as the servants of Abraham and Lot raised between those men of old. But more important still, he stated in his reply to Russia, if the occupation led to an improvement it would be morally impossible to give the province back to Turkey, and if it did not lead to an improvement the experiment would have been useless. Thus military intervention by the two powers was, under all circumstances, beyond consideration.[55]

Andrássy's second task was to combat the Russian objection to his own reform program. On the sixteenth he did this in three dispatches to St. Petersburg. The first was a zealous defense of the three concessions he proposed to exact from Turkey, together with a tenacious reaffirmation of the necessity for and the efficacy of his suggested procedure. Throughout the dispatch it was clear that the major concern in Vienna was to bring the rebellion to an end before it spread to Serbia and Montenegro. The minister believed that his reforms would satisfy the insurgents and that they would return peacefully to their homes, grateful for what Austria had done. Dim and uncertain prospects of Turkish reform which did not achieve those ends left Andrássy unimpressed. Since, in his opinion, the Russian program gave no promise of pacification, he closed his first communication with the clearest intimation that he would insist upon his own.

The second official dispatch of the day consisted in a lengthy contrast between his views and those of General Ignatiev. The Austrian plan with its precise demands, Andrássy insisted, meant pacifi-

---

[54] Private letter, Mayr to Andrássy, St. Petersburg, 4 November; SA, Varia Turquie I, 1875.

[55] Andrássy to Mayr, Budapest, 18 November; SA, *Geheime Aktenstücke, Abmachung mit Russland, Baron Jominis Projekt.*

cation; the Russian plan meant vague demands and vague threats which would produce alarm and disturbance not only in Turkey but in Europe as well. Ignatiev's scheme, he felt sure, would suspend the sword of Damocles over the general peace no less than over Turkey. Andrássy reaffirmed his conviction that pacification could come only through specific concessions demanded by the powers and accepted by Turkey.

The third of Andrássy's dispatches of 16 November was a frank statement of his basic reason for insisting on his own means and measures. To his other objections he added one further ground

that makes it appear undesirable to me to see the center of action moved to Constantinople. After my previous experiences I must to my regret indicate the very serious doubts which the personality of General Ignatiev, in such a case, inspires in me. I have observed that this ambassador, in the first place, has without informing us simply abandoned conditions that we had accepted . . . . and that he, furthermore, has repeatedly made proposals and sent them to Livadia [to the tsar] with the claim that his projects had received the approval of the other two ambassadors, whereas the latter were not at all or insufficiently informed about them. In a word, the previous activity of General Ignatiev evokes in me the fear that he, even had he agreed on a step with his colleagues from Germany and Austria-Hungary, might undertake others behind their backs and deal independently with the Turks. In all of this I see hindrances, in view of which I can promise myself no beneficial effects from the interference of General Ignatiev, even if his proposals were feasible.[56]

When Baron Jomini received these communications he recognized that a prolongation of the discussion would lead to no profitable result and that the preservation of Austro-Russian unity demanded acceptance of the Austrian program.[57] Still unconvinced by An-

[56] Dispatches Nos. 1, 2, 3, Andrássy to Mayr, Budapest, 16 November; SA, Varia Turquie I, 1875. The animosity which Andrássy bore Ignatiev was no secret from St. Petersburg (Tel. No. 50, Langenau to Andrássy, 1 December; *ibid.*). Earlier in the month Jomini had tried to assuage this feeling, engendered, he supposed, by the suspicion that the ambassador was responsible for the sultan's *iradé*. If Ignatiev had used words which led to such a conclusion, Jomini explained, they were merely bravado; he had the habit of appropriating credit for everything that happened. Although his untimely initiative had repeatedly brought admonitions down on his head, Ignatiev was still, Jomini confessed, *persona gratissima* with the tsar and had mounted in imperial favor. Mayr, for his own part, reported that there was some coolness between Emperor Alexander and Prince Gorchakov and that there were persons predicting that Ignatiev would take over the direction of Russian policy if the Balkan situation became worse (Private letter, Mayr to Andrássy, 4 November; *ibid.*).

[57] Report No. 356, Loftus to Derby, St. Petersburg, 24 November; FO 65/912.

drássy's arguments and profoundly pessimistic about the future,[58] the minister recommended acceptance on grounds of expediency.[59] Four days later, 30 November, Prince Gorchakov stopped in Berlin en route home to resume direction of Russia's foreign affairs. Confessing to Prince Bismarck that there was some annoyance against Austria in St. Petersburg, he promised to remove it and to promote peace through a community of views and action.[60] "Tell Count Andrássy," he wrote to Novikov on the same day, "that it is our firm resolution to maintain an intimate understanding with Austria. . . . . Count Andrássy will have the proof of it as soon as I return to St. Petersburg. . . . ."[61] The Austrian foreign minister, it appeared, had won his battle.

THE TURKISH MANEUVER TO ESCAPE

General Ignatiev, it will be recalled, had returned to Constantinople late in October, dejected and defeated. The tsar had turned a deaf ear to his appeals for an independent action. Within a few days the general had to suffer additional humiliation at the hands of his own government. The Russian *Messager officiel* published a manifesto of sympathy for the insurgents:

> . . . . Russia has not sacrificed to the alliance its sympathies for the Sclavonic Christians, and the sacrifices made by the Russian nation for the oppressed Sclavonic population of Turkey are so great that Russia is justified in stepping forth with its sympathies before the whole of Europe. . . . . Russia was the first to raise her voice for the protection of the unhappy Herzegovinese, who had been forced by excessive burdens of taxation and oppression to resort to the most extreme measures. . . . .[62]

This proclamation was warning enough to Turks and Greeks alike that Ignatiev's protests of friendship were empty words. In Con-

---

[58] Ignatiev, *Istoricheski Vyesnik*, CXXXVI, 50-52. Onou, *Slavonic Review*, X, 403-4. Hoschiller, *Revue de Paris*, XXII (1915), 601. "It remains for me to tell you one thing," Jomini wrote to Ignatiev in December. "We are persuaded of our impotence to meet this great task opening before us like an abyss. We are sure that it will uselessly swallow up the purest Russian blood and exhaust us. We pray God that this cup may be taken from us. Be sure that we would prefer any outcome in preference to throwing ourselves into this abyss. . . . ."

[59] Tel. No. 48, Langenau to Andrássy, St. Petersburg, 24 November; SA, Varia Turquie I, 1875. Private letter, same to same, 24 November; *ibid.*

[60] Bülow to Alvensleben, Berlin, 8 December; *Die Grosse Politik*, I, Doc. No. 130.

[61] Gorchakov to Novikov, Berlin, 18/30 November; SA, Varia Turquie I, 1875.

[62] *Annual Register*, 1875, p. 290. *Europäischer Geschichtskalender*, 1875, p. 246. The translation is that of the *Annual Register*.

stantinople there was a storm of indignation. Mahmud Nedim, who had once earned the name of Mahmudov, now spoke bitterly of his old friend's duplicity and complained that Britain was Turkey's only ally.[63] Ignatiev valiantly argued at the Porte that the Russian government had published the article solely for home consumption and that it should not be taken seriously abroad.[64] Undaunted he continued his struggle to defeat his Austrian rival. The reports which the ambassador soon wrote to St. Petersburg indicate that he was successful in undoing much of the mischief that the *Messager officiel* had caused. In a two-hour audience of the sultan on 3 November he found Abdul Aziz—so he wrote to his government—still willing to embark on a reform program under the private advice of the tsar; and in his subsequent talks with the grand vizier Ignatiev convinced Mahmud of the pressing necessity of still more reforms to cut the ground from under Austrian intervention. Victory seemed assured when he put the insurgent demands into a memorandum and persuaded the pliant Mahmud to present it to his imperial master. This personal triumph in Constantinople inspired the ambassador to try again to convert his own superiors. Page after page of impassioned words Ignatiev sent to Gorchakov and to the tsar pleading for a private arrangement with the Turks and predicting that the Andrássy plan would bring catastrophe in its wake.[65]

But Prince Gorchakov made "no serious reply"; the chancellor, now pledged to the Vienna program, ordered the ambassador to follow his instructions and to abandon any further private initiative.[66] After this new repudiation Ignatiev, with broken heart, sat

[63] Report No. 739, Elliot to Derby, 11 November; FO 78/2390.

[64] Report No. 738, Elliot to Derby, 10 November; *ibid.*

[65] Ignatiev, *Istoricheski Vyesnik*, CXXXV, 805–36. See also report of Ignatiev to Alexander II, 3/15 November, and annexed report of Michael Onou, first dragoman of the embassy, concerning an interview with the grand vizier; A. Onou, *Revue d'histoire moderne*, September–October 1935, pp. 382–84.

[66] Ignatiev, *op. cit.*, CXXXVI, 50–53. Onou, *Revue d'histoire moderne*, September–October 1935, pp. 386–87. ". . . . General Ignatiew continued the conversation, and spoke with great soreness of the manner in which his Government had placed the whole direction of the Bosnian question in the hands of Austria. He did not understand a Government being willing, as his own appeared to be, to adopt any decision that might be come to by the Minister of another Power. He particularly distrusted the demands which Count Andrassy was supposed to make upon the Porte in reference to tenure of land in Bosnia. He had expressed his own opinion on that subject very freely, but there appeared to be an intention to recklessly rushing into a complicated question, which had better be avoided" (Report No. 781, Elliot to Derby, 24 November; FO 78/2390).

back to nurture his last hope that the new Turkish reform might in some way forestall disaster.

Sir Henry Elliot did not need the frequent importunities of his Russian colleague to join him in admonishing the Turks to new and more sweeping measures. A few days after Ignatiev had seen the sultan, the grand vizier sent word to Elliot that he was preparing "a very full project of reform" and wanted to consult with him.[67] Without awaiting a further invitation the British ambassador went to Mahmud and urged him to press on with his project before Andrássy could have time to present his demands.[68] In early November the honest but torpid Safvet Pasha was replaced in the foreign office by Rashid Pasha, Ottoman ambassador to Vienna. The new minister appeared to be in an advanced state of debility,[69] but Elliot promptly sought him out and enlisted his support for immediate ac-

[67] ". . . . Artin Effendi, at present Acting Minister for Foreign Affairs, who is Mahmoud Pasha's most intimate confidant, spoke to me yesterday in much the same strain, beseeching me to support His Highness against the intrigues by which he is beset. I told him to assure His Highness that any support I could give him depended upon himself. When I saw the measures that are called for applied to the Insurgent Districts, and efficient securities given to protect the Bulgarians from the outrages of which they are now the victims, and all classes of the Sultan's subjects throughout the Empire treated with the equality and justice to which they are entitled, I should give the warmest and most cordial support to the Grand Vizier and Ministers who endeavoured to inaugurate such reforms" (Report No. 739, Elliot to Derby, 11 November; FO 78/2390).

[68] Report No. 753, Elliot to Derby, 14 November; ibid.

[69] ". . . . Safvet Pasha was an honest but not very efficient Minister who, knowing that he was no favorite of the present Grand Vizier, has since the succession of Mahmoud Pasha to power, shewn himself so indisposed to assume the slightest responsibility that the most ordinary current business has been nearly at a standstill. Rashid Pasha was Minister for Foreign Affairs during Mahmoud Pasha's first Vizierat. He is a better man of business than his predecessor, but far less reliance can be placed on his sincerity and straightforwardness. . . . ." (Report No. 733, Elliot to Derby, 9 November; FO 78/2390). The British ambassador in Vienna wrote of the new Turkish minister in the following words: "Although Reschid Pacha has proceeded to his new post at Constantinople apparently aware of the influence which the present state of affairs in Bosnia and the Herzegovine may have on the interests of the Turkish Empire, his appointment as Minister for Foreign Affairs is far from being considered here a judicious one, as he is now suffering from physical debility, which must impair to some degree his mental powers and moral energy. His Excellency, according to his own statement, is only in his 45th or 46th year, but he has the appearance of an old man, and as he cannot carry on a conversation for a few minutes without frequent yawns, the fears entertained here may not be unfounded, that he will not be equal to the duties of a Turkish minister in the present critical position of his country" (Report No. 387, Buchanan to Derby, Vienna, 18 November; FO 7/852).

tion.[70] The sultan, apprised of the impending dangers to his sovereign pride, ordered the work forward.[71]

It was not long before the zealous Zichy got wind of what was happening. On 19 November he reported somewhat skeptically rumors of a new reform decree which the grand vizier was going to prepare.[72] A week later he learned that earnest discussions were going on at the Porte[73] and in an audience the day following the ambassador heard from Abdul Aziz himself that elaborate plans were being made, plans, the sultan hinted, which would be within the bounds of his imperial inclinations.[74]

This news from Constantinople was highly disagreeable to Count Andrássy. As he received Zichy's first warning the minister was in the act of drawing up arguments in favor of his own reforms which Zichy, renouncing his hampering intimacy with Ignatiev, was to advance to the Turks.[75] Immediately Andrássy directed all his efforts toward preventing an action in Constantinople that might rob him of his program—and of the credit in the eyes of the Slavs for satisfactory reforms in Bosnia. He sent Zichy elaborate arguments to be used in preventing the publication of the impending decree. "Regardless of whether the motive is to be sought in the promptings of General Ignatiev or in the attempt of the Porte to close the way to foreign interference, try to persuade the grand vizier to give up this intention," Andrássy telegraphed on the twenty-fifth. The insurgents, he went on, would not be pacified by concessions coming solely from the Porte, be they ever so extensive. Rather than lead to pacification, he insisted, such action would lead to new defiance, and he

---

[70] Report No. 783, Elliot to Derby, 25 November; FO 78/2390. The Foreign Office in London informed Elliot of its approval of his efforts (Draft No. 399, Derby to Elliot, 9 December; FO 78/2378).

[71] Report No. 789, Elliot to Derby, 28 November; FO 78/2390.

[72] Zichy to Andrássy, 19 November; *First Red Book,* Doc. No. 185, incomplete.

[73] Tel., Zichy to Andrássy, 26 November; SA, Varia Turquie I, 1875.

[74] Tel. No. 143, Zichy to Andrássy, 27 November; *ibid.*

[75] Tel., Andrássy to Zichy, Budapest, 21 November; *ibid.* Andrássy, in his determination to have his program accepted, was prepared to take the battle to Constantinople and argue to the Turks his own views as against those of the Russians. Warning Zichy that he could count on no aid from Ignatiev, the foreign minister instructed him to abandon his intimacy with the general in favor of better relations with Elliot and to exercise a direct influence on the Porte. "In view of the fact that Turkish distrust of Russia is greater than of us, Your Excellency's intimacy with Ignatiev renders our task more difficult. Your Excellency must abandon it."

warned the Turks that new promises from them would not move the powers to abandon further interference but would indeed produce a contrary result. The determined minister offered them the alternative of putting down the rebellion by a great military effort or of settling the problem in conformity to the advice of the Great Powers.[76]

Count Zichy telegraphed back to Vienna that he did not think he could induce the Turks to postpone their action and suggested that, in preference to his making the attempt, the Austrian press should intimate that the reform activity at the Porte was a result of his recent audience of the sultan.[77] Andrássy had only recently announced through the *Wiener Abendpost* that Ignatiev was working in the interest of a program made jointly by the Austrian and Russian cabinets; it was manifestly impossible for him now to proclaim to the world that Zichy had converted the sultan to Andrássy's reforms. In response to the ambassador's devious proposal Andrássy instructed him again to attempt to delay a new *iradé*. This time the minister added cajolery to threats: if the Turks waited, he promised that nothing would be done without the approval of all the powers and that no demands would be made which would injure the sultan's sovereign dignity. He called on Zichy to inform the Turks that the Austrian way was the only one by which to prevent serious complications in the spring, and that if they did not adopt it he in turn would not accept responsibility for the complications which he foresaw.[78] On the following day, 30 November, Andrássy sent Zichy a new argument: the insurrection was not at an end; indeed, the insurgents had greater hopes than ever, and if something was not soon done for genuine pacification the Montenegrins would plunge openly into the conflict. Consequently the Austrian measures ought to be awaited, and, said this minister, who was claiming the role of chief friend of the insurgent Christians, in the meanwhile the Turks ought to

---

[76] Tel. No. 834, Andrássy to Zichy, 25 November; SA, Varia Turquie I, 1875.

[77] Tel., Zichy to Andrássy, 28 November; SA, Varia Turquie I, 1875, in incomplete form in *First Red Book*, Doc. No. 189. Zichy was not certain how much the Russians had to do with the Turkish activities, but he felt sure that Ignatiev would pretend that the new reforms were at least partially his work, *"in welcher Richtung,"* the ambassador added, *"er weder gehindert noch controlirt werden kann."* He thought, however, that a press notice such as he was recommending would paralyze his colleague's schemes.

[78] Tel. No. 848, Andrássy to Zichy, 29 November; *ibid.*, in incomplete form in *First Red Book*, Doc. No. 190.

strengthen their military action at all costs.[79] People in serious plight are more inclined to be grateful for small favors.

On the heels of that additional telegram came still another admonishing Zichy strictly to carry out his instructions. To his other arguments the ambassador was charged to add the warning that Prince Gorchakov was on his way home and would not accept this artificial solution that was being prepared at the Porte. The ambassador was also to let Rashid Pasha know that the Russian chancellor would not support the intrigues of Ignatiev. "The contents of the new *iradé*," the telegram said, "make it more than likely that General Ignatiev wishes to make my plans miscarry; this can succeed, but the result will also be abortive for the Porte."[80]

Zichy made his first attempt to influence the Turks, and a very timid attempt it was, on the twenty-ninth. The sum total of results which he achieved was assurance that the reform program was marching forward and that, although no policy had been fixed with regard to communicating it to the powers, the foreign minister would be grateful for Count Andrássy's wise advice.[81] Two days later, with his additional instructions in hand, the Austrian ambassador screwed up his courage and asked the grand vizier to delay his action in the interest of a concerted work of pacification. Mahmud's reply was a peremptory refusal. The rebellion and the reforms were completely separate problems, he told Zichy, and the latter were not intended to move the insurgents to peace; they were for the improvement of the administration of the whole empire, and he was going to proceed to them without delay. As for the trouble in Bosnia, he saw himself obliged to confine his actions to military measures and proposed to concentrate there his strongest forces. But even if he could not quickly end the rebellion in this way, the grand vizier added, any attempt of the powers to interfere, no matter what form it took, he would consider an intervention in the internal affairs of Turkey. Just what the Porte would do in such a case he was not in a position to state.[82] The only consolation which Zichy could telegraph to An-

[79] Tel. No. 852, Andrássy to Zichy, 30 November; SA, Varia Turquie I, 1875.

[80] Tel. No. 853, Andrássy to Zichy, 30 November; *ibid.*

[81] Tel. No. 146, Zichy to Andrássy, 29 November; *ibid.*, in incomplete form in *First Red Book*, Doc. No. 191.

[82] Tel. No. 155, Zichy to Andrássy, 2 December; SA, Varia Turquie I, 1875. "The communication has inspired the Grand Vizier with deep distrust of Austria" (Secret telegram, Elliot to Derby, 3 December; FO 78/2391).

drássy was that if he hurried he could still present his demands before the Turks were ready to act.[83]

Three days later, 5 December, the ambassador ventured back to the Porte, this time for a confidential talk with the new foreign minister. Rashid was most sympathetic under the weight of Zichy's arguments and promised to go into the question of delay with the grand vizier—but again Zichy felt the necessity of closing his report to Vienna with admonitions for haste.[84] Andrássy, however, had not yet won the final consent of St. Petersburg and the only course open to him was to send his importunate representative back to the Turks armed with further arguments. The tone of the new message which he sent to Zichy was firmer than ever. Andrássy told the Porte that any independent maneuver of Ignatiev could not be interpreted as a sign of division between Austria and Russia, and that his own action would in no way be arrested if the Turks ignored their best interests and proceeded independently with their plan. The instructions continued:

At the same time point out that the language held to us by the grand vizier claiming that the projected reforms have nothing to do with pacification and that the counsels of a friendly power . . . . would be considered an illegitimate interference . . . . indicates in our eyes an absolute lack of confidence . . . . and say that I do not wish to expose the ambassador of His Majesty to the necessity of hearing again such observations. Add that the intentions of our august sovereign, as much by inclination as by the interest of the monarchy, are most sincere toward Turkey, but that if, in spite of all the proofs which we have given of our desire to be useful to Turkey and to Mahmud Pasha, we do not obtain results entirely different from those which we have seen up to the present, we shall be obliged henceforth to be guided exclusively by our own interests.[85]

[83] Tel. No. 157, Zichy to Andrássy, 3 December; SA, Varia Turquie I, 1875.

[84] Tel. No. 159, Zichy to Andrássy, 6 December; *ibid.*

[85] Tel. No. 870, Andrássy to Zichy, Vienna, 7 December; SA, Varia Turquie I, 1875. "I do full justice to Your Excellency's distinguished qualities and professional zeal, but I believe that if your words do not make more of an impression on the grand vizier, it is to be ascribed to your high opinion of him. Your Excellency sees in him an important statesman who looks to the honor of his state; I see him merely as a sly Turk who gives in only when he is afraid. I know that he has sold himself in his time. Ignatiev directs him in this stroke. Above everything he wants to hold onto his post. Please see him from this point of view; it is the correct one. . . . ."
Zichy refused to concur in Andrássy's low opinion of Mahmud; to the ambassador the grand vizier appeared the one man of progress in Turkey possessed of energy and prestige (Report No. 96AG, Zichy to Andrássy, 14 December; *ibid.*).

When Zichy presented this new threat to Mahmud and Rashid on 8 December he was convinced that it made a deep impression. Actually, however, the ambassador brought away no very tangible results. Once again he was informed that the sultan's reforms had nothing to do with special concessions to insurgent Christians and could not be delayed. As for the trouble in Bosnia, the Turks explained in a more moderate tone, if the three powers wanted to make suggestions some time, those suggestions would be readily taken into consideration if they did not injure the sultan's honor.[86] Andrássy, who repeatedly had to protest to Zichy that his communications were unintelligible, mistook the import of the ambassador's account of this reply and concluded with no little satisfaction that his efforts had induced the Turks to agree to promulgate at the moment only certain general reforms and to await the suggestions of the powers before dealing specifically with Bosnia.[87]

The foreign minister's satisfaction was very short-lived. While Andrássy and Zichy were working to prevent Turkish action, the British and the Russians, and even the German ambassador, were pushing in the opposite direction.[88] As for the Russians, the evidence would indicate that their position was equivocal. Gorchakov informed the Austrian ambassador on the sixth that the Turks had promised Ignatiev a confidential copy of the reforms for Russian criticism before their publication and that he, in response to this

[86] Tel. No. 160, Zichy to Andrássy, 8 December; SA, Varia Turquie I, 1875. On the same day the British ambassador reported to London: "The Austrian Ambassador has again been instructed to urge delay in the promulgation of Reforms, and to represent that it is asked in the interest of the Porte. The Grand Vizier again has answered that he could not withhold measures intended for the benefit of the Sultan's subjects in all parts of the Empire. . . . ." (Report No. 814, Elliot to Derby, 8 December; FO 78/2391). If the Turks had made any change of stand, Elliot would have known it.

[87] Tel., Andrássy to Beust in London, 9 December; SA, Varia Turquie I, 1875. Derby to Buchanan in Vienna, 11 December; Turkey No. 2 (1876), Doc. No. 47.

[88] Tel. No. 158, Zichy to Andrássy, 5 December; SA, Varia Turquie I, 1875. When Rashid Pasha asked the British ambassador's opinion of Zichy's step, according to Elliot, "I said that Her Majesty's Government had always recommended that the required reforms should be promptly given and unless the Austrian Government gave some satisfactory reason for wishing for delay, the measures could not, I thought, be published too soon. The German and Russian Ambassadors speak in favour of immediate publication but at the particular request of the Austrian Ambassador they have not been informed of his action. Raschid Pasha believes that Count Andrassy's object is to cause it to appear that the initiative of the concessions proceeds from him" (Report No. 814, Elliot to Derby, 8 December; FO 78/2391).

offer, had demanded communication to all three of the imperial powers so that they could agree on a common response.[89] On the same day, according to the Turkish ambassador in St. Petersburg, the chancellor urged the grand vizier on to the promulgation of the reforms as quickly as possible.[90] This information reached Andrássy probably on the tenth. On that day Zichy reported that Ignatiev had demanded communication of the impending Turkish *ferman* to the three powers and he informed Andrássy that, although the Turks would give confidential copies of the document to the three ambassadors, they would not delay publication until the opinion of the imperial governments was heard.[91] On the eleventh, when this information was in his hands, Andrássy was highly indignant. He had the impression that Ignatiev had induced the Turks to go back on their promise to make a difference between general reforms and special reforms for Bosnia and that they were proceeding with the type of measure which he was trying to prevent. By telegraph he

---

[89] Tel. No. 51, Langenau to Andrássy, St. Petersburg, 6 December; *First Red Book*, Doc. No. 192. On 13 December Gorchakov repeated this statement to the Austrian ambassador and claimed to have reiterated the demand several times (Report No. 68AC, Langenau to Andrássy, 3/15 December; SA, Varia Turquie I, 1875).

[90] Zichy reported these words as the Turkish ambassador's account of Gorchakov's statement: "... Il faudra donc les promulger un moment plus tôt et les porter à la connaissance des puissances. Le général Ignatiew a eu l'instruction d'engager le Grand Vizir à promulger ces réformes le plus tôt possible et à les porter à la connaissance des trois puissances. ..." On the margin of this report Andrássy wrote a revealing comment: *"Sehr eine schwache Auffassung—wenn selbe nicht zum Ziele hat, uns die Popularität der Initiative zu rauben!"* (Tel., Zichy to Andrássy, 9 December; *ibid.*).

The British ambassador was informed of this amazing situation. On 10 December he reported to his foreign office: "Raschid Pasha who called upon me today spoke of the perplexity in which the Porte was placed by the divergence in the language of the Austrian and Russian Governments. Count Andrassy had told the Turkish Ambassador at Vienna that the three Powers were perfectly agreed; and that if there was any apparent difference at Constantinople it was the Ambassadors who were answerable for it. At the same time the Turkish Ambassador at St. Petersburg telegraphed that the Russian Government recommended the Porte to issue their reforms as quickly as possible, and said that General Ignatieff had been instructed in this sense. Count Zichy, on the other hand, communicated a telegram from Count Andrassy urgently pressing for a postponement of the measures of concession. It appeared therefore that both Ambassadors were acting according to their instructions and the difference of language must be attributed to their Governments and not to themselves. ....." (Report No. 824, Elliot to Derby, 10 December; FO 78/2391).

[91] Tel. No. 163, Zichy to Andrássy, 10 December; SA, Varia Turquie I, 1875.

appealed to St. Petersburg to support his stand,[92] and he sent a new warning to the Turks that if they, in spite of promises, went on with their reforms he would see to it that his own proposals were not in vain.[93]

Secure in the belief that Austria and Russia were divided, the Turks continued their work. With immeasurable politeness they agreed to deliver the text of the document to the three imperial ambassadors before publication,[94] but as soon as the sultan gave his approval on the twelfth the *ferman* was quietly sent to the representatives of England, France, and Italy, while Zichy and his alleged allies had to wait until the morrow.[95]

The sultan's new decree was eloquent in its promises of reform, many of them re-echoes of the unfilled pledges of 1839 and 1856. "Civilized states," it began, "ought to concentrate their efforts on guaranteeing public rights." In noble language the generous will of

[92] Andrássy to Langenau, 11 December; *ibid.* In his anxiety to win Russian co-operation the Austrian minister confessed for the first time a slightly distorted version of the reason why he had been putting up such a struggle for the leadership in the reforms. "I can not explain the reasons," he said, "that could prompt Russia to give to the Porte in preference to the three powers the credit for the concessions to be obtained for the Christians."

On the twelfth, when Langenau took up this question in St. Petersburg, the tsar assured him that the sense of the instructions to Ignatiev had been the same as those of Zichy, and on the next day Gorchakov told him that he had repeatedly ordered the ambassador to ask for a communication of the Turkish program before its publication (Report No. 68AC, Langenau to Andrássy, St. Petersburg, 3/15 December; *ibid.*).

When Ignatiev heard that Andrássy had accused him of leading the Turks into breaking a promise to the Austrian minister he was irate. He informed St. Petersburg—and it seems quite apparent that he was correct—that the Turks had never agreed to delay concessions to the insurgent province (Report No. 69AB, Langenau to Andrássy, 5/17 December; *ibid.*), and he went in irritation to Zichy and asked him to inform Andrássy that, although since September he had been pushing the Turks on the road to reform, he had done nothing since he had heard that his colleague had made a very energetic step in the opposite direction (Report No. 96C, Zichy to Andrássy, 14 December; *ibid.*).

[93] Tel. No. 279, Andrássy to Zichy, 11 December; *ibid.*

[94] Tel. No. 164, Zichy to Andrássy, 12 December; *ibid.*

[95] Report No. 13, Elliot to Derby, 6 January 1876; FO 78/2454. "I am less disposed to attribute this to accident," Elliot wrote, "than to a wish that the Northern Ambassadors should not be the first to be able to speak of a measure which they might represent themselves as having obtained from the Porte." Tel. No. 165, Zichy to Andrássy, 13 December; *First Red Book,* Doc. No. 194.

The opinion at the time was that Ignatiev was largely responsible for the new Turkish measure (*Annual Register,* 1875, p. 280. Raschdau, *Deutsche Rundschau,* CXXXVII [1908], 395). *The Cambridge History of British Foreign Policy* (III, 96) gives the credit to Elliot.

God's shadow on earth was set forth. The origins of the *ferman* were in the desire to forestall European intervention in favor of the Christians, and the final document, regardless of what may have been told to Count Zichy, revealed that desire. There were in it provisions of a general nature for the whole empire, but in essence it was a series of concessions to the non-Moslems. The courts were to be re-ordered to lessen the influence of the *cadi* and his sacred law; members of provincial tribunals were to be elected by all subjects regardless of religion. As for taxation, the direct taxes were no longer to be collected by police agents but by representatives elected by the people. The provision regarding the tithe was less promising: the tax farmer remained, but steps were to be taken to guard against his arbitrary proceedings. The military exemption tax, which had long been a notorious abuse, was now to be limited to men between the ages of twenty and forty, and the men themselves were to choose the collectors. One further economic provision concerned the Christians. The *corvée,* or compulsory labor on roads and other public utilities, was no longer to be made "a source of annoyance and injury," although the practice was maintained. Christians were to be eligible for all offices and were to participate in local elections; they were allowed to own land anywhere in the empire. "All the subjects who live in the shadow of Our Imperial protection are, in Our eyes and in Our feeling of justice, on terms of complete equality." Free exercise of religion was guaranteed.[96]

The devil was trying to be a monk, no doubt, but was not, in spite of his zeal, reaching the higher rungs of monasticism. The heavy weight of the sacred law of Islam still gave promise of upsetting the scales of Turkey's justice; the rapacious tax farmer was to continue his annual round of the provinces; the Christian still had to leave his own fields and go out to forced labor on the roads; and, lastly, the offers of secure land titles and of representation and of freedom of worship had the appearance of being nothing more than a new edition of the old deceptions. These inadequacies were discredit enough, but the worst of the *ferman's* shortcomings was its failure actually to rob Andrássy of his cherished measures. Most certainly the Turks

[96] The text of the *ferman* may be found in *Turkey No. 2 (1876),* Doc. No. 50; *First Red Book,* Doc. No. 195; *First Yellow Book,* pp. 42–48; *First Green Book,* Doc. No. LXXIII; Hertslet, *Map of Europe by Treaty,* IV, Doc. No. 455; *British and Foreign State Papers,* LXVII, 1212–18; A. Schopoff, *Les Réformes et la protection des Chrétiens en Turquie, 1673–1904* (Paris, 1904), pp. 168–75.

were aware that the Austrian statesman was going to ask for the end of tax-farming and abolition of servile dues as well as a reaffirmation of religious equality, but at the Sublime Porte there was no inclination to anticipate that demand. Apparently the Turks thought that halfway measures would suffice to destroy the Vienna plan; at all events they informed Andrássy that, in their opinion, the *ferman* had eliminated "all the eventualities of a nature to lead to regrettable facts."[97] They suggested, in other words, that there was no further necessity for bringing forward his measures. Andrássy had other ideas. In the midst of his final preparations he took time to inform Zichy that publication of the Turkish decree was no longer disagreeable to him.[98]

THE PROGRAM OF THE IMPERIAL LEAGUE

While this diplomatic interlude was being played on the banks of the Bosporus, Prince Gorchakov was returning home to resume personal direction of Russian policy. During his brief halt in Berlin on 30 November the chancellor was prodigal in his expressions of good-will toward Austria's plans and of confidence in Andrássy.[99] Returned to St. Petersburg on 3 December, he reiterated his unshakable intention to act with Austria, but his conversations soon reflected the influence of Ignatiev's plans and pleas. While assuring the Austrian ambassador that he had accepted the Andrássy proposals in principle,[100] he indicated to Lord Augustus Loftus, the Brit-

[97] Rashid to Aarifi in Vienna, Constantinople, 16 December; SA, Varia Turquie I, 1875.

[98] Tel. No. 904, Andrássy to Zichy, 16 December; *ibid.*

[99] Report No. 490, Russell to Derby, Berlin, 1 December; FO 64/831. The British ambassador quoted Gorchakov as follows: ". . . . The Eastern Question was threatening again and had to be faced and dealt with. There were two ways of dealing with it. 1st a complete reconstruction or 2nd a mere replastering (*replâtrage*) which would keep matters together for another term of years. No one could possibly wish for a complete settlement—everyone must wish to put it off as long as possible. He for one could only consent to give his best efforts to the *'replâtrage à six et pas à trois'* and he hoped for and reckoned on the co-operation of England and France with the Northern Powers to make it as lasting as possible. He expected to find on reaching St. Petersburg, the plan drawn up by Count Andrássy for the pacification of the Herzegovina and he was prepared to find it good for he had the greatest confidence in Count Andrássy, and wished to co-operate cordially with him, not to say follow his lead. . . . ." Bülow to Alvensleben in St. Petersburg, 8 December; *Die Grosse Politik,* I, Doc. No. 130.

[100] Tel. No. 51, Langenau to Andrássy, St. Petersburg, 6 December; *First Red Book,* Doc. No. 192.

ish representative, that his interest for the moment was centered on Mahmud's forthcoming reforms and their formal communication to the six guaranteeing powers. Once the Turkish act was formally submitted, he felt that the powers would have the duty as well as the right to make further suggestions. If all the major powers acted in unison the Porte could not resist.[101]

During these same days Baron Jomini was equally lacking in real cordiality toward the Austrian project. He frankly told Langenau that he was proposing acceptance in order to save the entente,[102] and in talking with Loftus he still urged the desirability of having the consuls survey the progress of reforms and report to the ambassadors in Constantinople.[103] None the less, some satisfaction had to be accorded to Andrássy, who was demanding his own plan and a three-power leadership in preference to tossing the whole problem upon the general European table. When Ignatiev reported that Mahmud was going to give Russia and Russia alone an advance copy of the *ferman*, Gorchakov demanded its communication likewise to the two allies.[104] The general continued his warfare against his

[101] Report No. 367, Loftus to Derby, St. Petersburg, 8 December; FO 65/912.

[102] Report No. 65AB, Langenau to Andrássy, St. Petersburg, 3 December; SA, Varia Turquie I, 1875.

[103] Report No. 369, Loftus to Derby, 8 December; FO 65/912. Loftus had found Jomini reading the Treaty of Paris of 1856 and concluded that the Russian was revealing Andrássy's plan. "If my surmise is correct (for I must again repeat that Baron Jomini merely expressed the necessity of some guarantee) it would appear that Count Andrassy—acting in community with Prince Gorchakow—is meditating a guarantee of that nature which will establish a protectorate of the 6 Powers over the Christian population of the insurgent provinces. . . . . Any such action is contrary to Art. 9 of the Treaty of Paris.

"It is evident that Prince Gorchakow whose whole political object since his accession to power has been to tear up the Treaty of Paris, will find inordinate satisfaction in a measure of this nature, whilst he will indulge in a cynical exultation that the initiative should be taken by an Austrian minister. If the impression I have received is correct, Austria and Russia are now preparing to submit to Europe, as a guarantee necessary for the pacification of the insurgent provinces,—the proposal to abrogate the stipulations of the ninth article of the Treaty of Paris,— the effect of which will be not only the rescinding of another article of that Treaty, but the disavowing of the very principle on which the Crimean war was undertaken. . . . ."

[104] Tel. No. 51, Langenau to Andrássy, 6 December; *First Red Book*, Doc. No. 192. Until material is available from other Russian sources the exact nature of Ignatiev's actions during early December will remain obscure. If one accepts the ambassador's memoirs—and sources that permit checking vindicate them substantially—the sultan had earlier in the autumn agreed to submit his reforms for review by the tsar, as has been previously indicated. Ignatiev's position was shaken by the

enemy,[105] but the chancellor gave way to the obstinacy shown in Vienna. In making his response on 8 December Gorchakov left it entirely to Andrássy to decide if Turkey's reforms were sufficient or if he wished to continue with his own. Gorchakov let it be seen, however, that he himself would be content with a formal notification of the Turkish measures which would ipso facto give the powers the right of supervision.[106]

After this capitulation Andrássy was no longer disturbed by the sultan's *ferman*.[107] General Ignatiev and the Turks, he rejoiced, had failed in their attempt to cut the ground from under his specific proposals for the revolted province,[108] and with Russia following in Austria's wake he was prepared to go ahead. On 24 December the minister and Novikov completed their formal draft of the long-delayed reform program and sent it to St. Petersburg for approval. Four days later Gorchakov and the tsar accepted the document.[109] On the thirtieth it was sent to London, Paris, and Rome for what the Austrian foreign minister hoped would be a prompt response.

This document, subsequently known as the Andrássy note, was essentially a restatement of Andrássy's views and propositions of October with certain clarifications. Religious liberty with its corollary of equality before the law was the first of the demands. The abolition of tax farming remained likewise as a fundamental condition. Coupled with it was a provision that the returns from all direct

---

article of the *Messager officiel*, but from the Austrian dispatches it would appear that he recovered that position and in early December attempted again, with Turkish consent, to effect a private Russo-Turkish understanding on the *ferman* which was approved by the sultan on the twelfth. How honest, of course, the Turks were in making such an agreement—if they did make it—is another question. But at all events, any private agreement was given its death blow when Gorchakov refused to sanction it. The grief of Ignatiev can well be understood when he saw his life's ambition almost reached and then destroyed by his superiors' insistence on co-operation with Austria (Ignatiev, *Istoricheski Vyesnik,* CXXXV, 461–62; CXXXVI, 53). The existence of some kind of agreement between the ambassador and the grand vizier and the keenness of the former's disappointment are confirmed by the letters of Ignatiev to Jomini dated 19/31 November, 1/13 December, and 8/20 December (Onou, *Revue d'histoire moderne,* September–October 1935, pp. 385–87).

[105] Goriainov, *Le Bosphore èt les Dardanelles,* p. 313.

[106] "Copie d'une lettre particulière du prince Gortschakow à M. de Novikow à Vienne," St. Petersburg, 26 November/8 December; SA, Varia Turquie I, 1875.

[107] Tel. No. 904, Andrássy to Zichy, 16 December; *ibid.*

[108] Tel., Andrássy to Károlyi in Berlin, 17 December; *ibid.*

[109] Tel. No. 60, Langenau to Andrássy, 28 December; *ibid.* Report No. 71AB, same to same, 19/31 December; *ibid.*

taxes collected in the insurgent province should be used for local purposes. The last of the demands also originated in Andrássy's first "practical proposition"—state aid in the commutation of peasant obligations to their landlords.

Gorchakov had forwarded to Vienna certain suggestions of a minor nature to be included in the note. Most of them were included, but the Russian chancellor wanted to espouse more radical measures than Andrássy dared to espouse in the question of European control. That control, Andrássy thought, would be virtually assured by the Porte's official notice of acceptance, but he did not dare emphasize the point in a document to be submitted for the support of England and France. The only control of the concessions which the note mentioned, therefore, was that to be exercised by a special mixed commission made up equally of Moslems and Christians.[110]

Bulwarking the Andrássy program when it was dispatched to the other capitals were elaborate arguments to show the inadequacy of Turkey's previous reform efforts and to demonstrate the necessity of Europe's action. Present also in the note was the minister's optimistic belief that his measures and means would bring peace to northwestern Turkey.[111]

SUMMARY

Almost four months had gone by since the duel between General Ignatiev and Count Andrássy had begun. The former had been inspired by his old hope to exclude Austria-Hungary from Turkish affairs and to shape the destiny of the decadent empire to suit the interests of Russia and the Slavs; the latter had been inspired by his long-standing policy of winning the support of the neighboring population, by the resolve to prevent that same population from de-

[110] Tel., Andrássy to Langenau, Vienna, 26 December; *First Red Book*, Doc. No. 199, incomplete. On the day following, Andrássy sent a new telegram to the ambassador in St. Petersburg: "Please give to Prince Gorchakov only enough from my yesterday's telegram to make him satisfied with the contents of the draft dispatch. Give him the remaining arguments after he has read the dispatch. I am concerned lest he, if he receives the arguments before the dispatch, conclude that his suggestions have been ignored, which has not been the case" (SA, Varia Turquie I, 1875).

[111] The text of the Andrássy note may be found in several places and among others: *Turkey No. 2 (1876)*, Doc. No. 55; *First Red Book*, Doc. No. 202; *First Yellow Book*, pp. 59–71; *First Green Book*, pp. 82–89; Schopoff, *op. cit.*, pp. 176–86; Hertslet, *Map of Europe*, Doc. No. 456; *British and Foreign State Papers*, LXVI, 921–31.

veloping ambitions prejudicial to Austria-Hungary, and by the determination to exclude Ignatiev from an important role in the international dealings with Turkey. A common purpose to defeat Andrássy's intention had temporarily abated the hostility normally existing between Ignatiev and his British colleague, and the two, together and independently, had attempted to forestall the impending intervention by pushing the sultan into spontaneous reform. For a time the Russian government had supported the maneuvers of the general; but in the end, when confronted by an unyielding obstinacy in Vienna, the tsar had given way and committed himself to the Andrássy reforms. Allies and collaborators Russia and Austria remained; but the negotiations had revealed fundamentally divergent interests in Turkish affairs, and the new program, like the consular mission, had represented a Russian surrender to the Austrian point of view.

CHAPTER IV

EUROPEAN ACCEPTANCE OF THE ANDRÁSSY NOTE

GERMANY AND THE ANDRÁSSY NOTE

In the months following the outbreak of revolt in Hercegovina, Germany adhered to Bismarck's principle of endorsing any Austro-Russian arrangement. After the humiliation he had suffered in the war scare of May the German chancellor secluded himself in the country, leaving Bülow in charge of foreign affairs. As the winter came on Bülow became fearful of the outcome of the rebellion[1] but continued to reply to Andrássy's confidential reports that Germany's co-operation was assured in any steps on which Vienna and St. Petersburg agreed.[2]

Toward the end of November Bismarck returned to Berlin in anticipation of the visit of Prince Gorchakov. In the meantime Lord Odo Russell, the British ambassador, had been seeking everywhere to ferret out the chancellor's thoughts. From the Foreign Office he could learn nothing; Bülow would discuss anything with him except the Eastern question. Gathering bits here and there, however, Russell concluded that the chancellor was still nurturing the doubts and vexation which Gorchakov had inspired in May. Russia's gratuitous rescue of France at that time and her inclination to abandon an entente à trois in favor of a European concert were, the British ambassador thought, matters of annoyance in Berlin.[3] But when Russell talked with Bismarck on 29 November he was unable to confirm these suspicions. The prince reiterated his habitual words about Germany's disinterestedness and expressed his optimistic belief that Andrássy and Gorchakov would find a solution to the Turkish trouble which would be satisfactory to everyone.[4] Nor did he show concern

---

[1] *Denkwürdigkeiten des Fürsten Chlodwig zu Hohenlohe-Schillingsfürst* (Stuttgart, 1907), II, 173 (diary for 3 November). Hereafter cited as *Denkwürdigkeiten*.

[2] Report No. 59AB, Seiller to Andrássy, Berlin, 27 November; SA, Varia Turquie I, 1875.

[3] Russell to Derby, 12 November; Newton, *Lord Lyons,* II, 87–90.

[4] Report No. 488, Russell to Derby, 29 November; FO 64/831.

on the day following in his conversations with Prince Gorchakov. The aged Russian chancellor's cordiality toward Austria evoked again the promise of German support.[5] The same assurance Bismarck gave to Count Károlyi, the Austrian ambassador. He was indifferent, he said, to the means whereby an understanding was reached. His great concern was Austro-Russian co-operation, and he was ready to endorse any arrangement made concerning Turkey.[6] Andrássy's offer to receive any suggestions that Bismarck wanted to make[7] was declined and General von Schweinitz in Vienna was instructed to announce Germany's adherence to the impending agreement.[8] The immediate future, said Bismarck on 18 December to certain guests of his, was free from care; the only cloud in the skies, little Hercegovina, could not disturb Germany.[9]

This serenity gave way to considerable alarm toward the end of December. On the twenty-fourth, when Andrássy had completed the draft of his note, he sent a copy to General von Schweinitz at the same time that he dispatched one to St. Petersburg. Four days later, when he was in Budapest, the Austrian foreign minister learned to his surprise that Schweinitz was refusing to give that approval which had long been promised. Andrássy thought that the ambassador suspected an attempt to use Germany's support in forcing that of Russia and he hastened to write to the general, explaining that nothing was farther from his mind.[10] This protest that he was merely keeping Berlin informed was inspired by a mistaken notion of what the hitch really was. Schweinitz had been of the opinion that the note was to be sent exclusively to the three imperial ambassadors in Constantinople and that they would invite the support of their colleagues; only on the twenty-fourth apparently did he learn that the note was to be delivered to London, Paris, and Rome; and he refused to subscribe to the change until he had instructions from home.[11] The instructions

[5] Bülow to Alvensleben, Berlin, 8 December; *Die Grosse Politik*, I, Doc. No. 130.
[6] Report No. 60AB, Károlyi to Andrássy, Berlin, 2 December; SA, Varia Turquie I, 1875.
[7] Tel. No. 903, Andrássy to Károlyi, 15 December; *ibid.*
[8] Tel., Károlyi to Andrássy, 16 December; *ibid.*
[9] Hans Blum, *Fürst Bismarck und seine Zeit* (München, 1894–1899), V, 241.
[10] Tel., Andrássy to Károlyi, Budapest, 28 December; SA, Varia Turquie I, 1875. Andrássy to Schweinitz in Vienna, 28 December; *ibid.*
[11] Tel., Hofmann to Andrássy, Vienna, 29 December; SA, Varia Turquie I, 1875. When the foreign minister learned the nature of Schweinitz' objection he telegraphed to Berlin an explanation. He at first thought that only Schweinitz—and not the Berlin foreign office—was unaware of the Russian request to send the note

which came to Schweinitz on 29 December were all that Andrássy could have desired: Germany readily agreed to the plan of communicating with the other capitals and promised that her ambassadors would be instructed to support those of Austria.[12]

This new support promised from Berlin, however, was merely an expedient to gain time; Bismarck had suddenly abandoned passive drifting in favor of a plan of his own. The incentive to that change of attitude, it would seem, was the unpleasant news sent by Schweinitz that the Russians had gone beyond the league of the three emperors and had brought the other powers into the settlement of Turkish affairs. The significance of that action in Bismarck's eyes was an enlarged and important place for France in European councils. Of France alone Bismarck was not afraid,[13] but in a coalition between France and Russia or in a revival of Kaunitz' triple alliance against Germany there was tremendous danger.[14] The beginnings of a courtship between the republic and the tsar's autocratic state were clearly seen in the war scare of May, while the subsequent exchanges of cordiality between Prince Gorchakov and the French foreign minister in Switzerland presaged no good for Germany.[15] The Russians had continued the courtship by inviting French participation in the mission of the consuls, and report came to Bismarck in the last days of December that the politicians in Paris were so encouraged by

to the remaining Great Powers, and he wanted Bismarck, no less than Schweinitz, to understand that the change in procedure was ascribable to Gorchakov's letter of 8 December (Tels., Andrássy to Károlyi, Budapest, 29, 30 December; ibid.). A week later Andrássy learned that Bismarck as well as the German ambassador had doubts about changing the entente of the imperial league into an action à six. He instructed his representative in Berlin again to remind the Germans that the modification of procedure was long talked of by the Russians and that he accepted it supposing that the tsar's views were known in Berlin and there approved. Andrássy had from the earliest diplomatic action been a partisan of exclusive action à trois and continually advocated that policy in his conversations and communications with Russia; but, after his note had been sent to the other capitals, he confessed to Károlyi that he had nothing of which to complain. His great concern was close co-operation with Germany, and now that the diplomatic table was surrounded by "heterogeneous elements more inclined to Austria than to Germany," Andrássy deemed it more than ever to the interest of Berlin not to disturb the bonds with Vienna (Andrássy to Károlyi, Budapest, 11 January 1876; SA, Germany, 1876).

[12] Tels., Károlyi to Andrássy, 29, 31 December; SA, Varia Turquie I, 1875. The second of these telegrams is in First Red Book, Doc. No. 204.

[13] Hohenlohe, Denkwürdigkeiten, II, 177–78.

[14] Taffs, Slavonic Review, IX, 336; Bismarck, the Man and the Statesman, II, 255.

[15] Dreux, Gontaut-Biron, p. 203.

Russian attentions that President Thiers was talking of reviving French influence and power through participating in a settlement of the Eastern question under the patronage of the tsar.[16] The chancellor's concern about France could only have been increased, along with his ill humor, when on the thirty-first he had a baffling interview with the French ambassador, the intriguer who in Bismarck's mind was largely responsible for his ever-stinging humiliation.[17] At the end of the old year the French problem was disquieting.

Relations with Austro-Hungary, also, had suddenly become complicated. For some time Bismarck had been convinced that the maintenance of cordiality between Berlin and Vienna demanded the retention of Count Andrássy in power. There were two parties in the Austrian capital: that represented by the foreign minister stood for co-operation with Germany; that represented by Schmerling and supported by certain of the archdukes was anti-German and inclined toward expansion southward in connivance with Russia.[18] Bismarck's problem was rendered more difficult by the fact that Emperor Francis Joseph vacillated between the two influences. A year previous an archduke had written a pamphlet against Germany and Andrássy had persuaded the emperor to reprimand him. Subsequently, however, a certain Austrian colonel had produced a pro-German pamphlet and the archdukes had engineered a punishment for him.[19] To confirm the uneasiness in Bismarck's mind there came, then, the news that the imperial program was to be made, on Gorchakov's request, a European program, and along with it came an observation from Schweinitz that Andrássy was ready to yield to Russian wishes. It seemed clear enough to the chancellor that Andrássy and Gorchakov had effected an understanding which brought them closer to each other than to him and that they were bringing France into their plans. He could not understand the sudden shift in Vienna and he called on Schweinitz for an explanation.[20]

[16] Bülow to Hohenlohe, Berlin, 28 December; *Die Grosse Politik*, I, Doc. No. 195. *Andrássy*, II, 287.

[17] Gontaut-Biron to Decazes, Berlin, 31 December; *Documents français*, I, pp. 478–79. The chancellor was trying to get at the origins of the spring disturbance but was able to derive no satisfaction from the ambassador, who had long since become a thorn in his flesh.

[18] Hohenlohe, *Denkwürdigkeiten*, II, 178.

[19] Report No. 488, Russell to Derby, Berlin, 29 November; FO 64/831. *Andrássy*, II, 287.

[20] *Andrássy*, II, 288; *Die Grosse Politik*, II, 29 n. Both sources cite an unpublished dispatch from Bismarck to Schweinitz dated 2 January 1876.

Finally, as a climax there was added to Bismarck's feeling of uneasiness the conviction that Andrássy's reform program was destined to failure[21] and that, consequently, events might develop over which Germany would have no control.

The German chancellor had been not a little surprised and displeased at the role assumed by the British cabinet in the May crisis,[22] but the new year's gift of threatening clouds made it necessary for Bismarck to turn and turn quickly to that same cabinet which appeared to be the one possible hope of protection. On the second of January he made an advance of far-reaching potentiality to the representative of Queen Victoria. The kernel of the chancellor's talk with Lord Odo Russell was a desire to establish with London a thorough understanding, an understanding whereby German support would be given to England's wishes in case of future complications in Turkey. That understanding he wanted to inaugurate immediately by a common attitude toward the Andrássy reform program, but he wished to go still further in cementing good relations by attacking together the problems which he saw arising from the inadequate schemes framed in Vienna. In the course of this extended conversation Bismarck let it be known to Russell that he anticipated difficulties arising out of the Eastern question and that he was ready to take the lead, in harmony with British interests, in meeting those difficulties before they had jeopardized the peace of Europe. He confessed his concern over his position in face of Austro-Russian relations; he saw well, he said, that the two powers could not be permitted to become too familiar behind his back, and he saw equally well that conflict between them would be very serious for Germany. The chancellor reiterated his belief that the best guaranty against undesirable complications was the continuance of Andrássy's control of Austro-Hungarian foreign affairs. From that consideration Bismarck went on to the question of future arrangements. The opponents of Andrássy were vigorously urging an annexation policy on Francis Joseph and there was a possibility that they might carry the day. If they did, he anticipated a Russian demand for Bessarabia—and then, if there was not great circumspection, a wholly undesirable war might follow. It was clear in Bismarck's mind that circumspection meant Andrássy's confounding his anti-German enemies by the annexation of Bosnia,

[21] Bülow to Münster, 4 January 1876; *Die Grosse Politik,* II, Doc. No. 227.

[22] Bismarck to Münster, 14 May 1875; *Die Grosse Politik,* I, Doc. No. 180. Bülow to Münster, 3 June; *ibid.,* I, Doc. No. 184.

and further meant arranging a peaceful return of Bessarabia to Russia, a compensation for England in Egypt, and perhaps some bone thrown to France to keep her mind off her eastern frontier.[23]

Three days later Bismarck attempted to deal with the Russian phase of the problem. In a conversation with the tsar's ambassador, he began by attacking the Austrian reforms and by attempting to arouse doubts in St. Petersburg as to the honesty of Andrássy himself. The chancellor professed his inability to understand how a minister, ordinarily so lazy, should have put so much labor into a scheme that promised such meager results. He declared himself obliged to suspect that Andrássy had secret designs. He went on, however, to claim a critical interest in maintaining this suspected

[23] Reports Nos. 8 and 9, Russell to Derby, Berlin, 2 and 3 January 1876, respectively; David Harris, "Bismarck's Advance to England, 1876," *Journal of Modern History*, III (September 1931), 443–48 (FO 64/850). The telegram preceding these two reports which Russell sent on 2 January read as follows: "Secret. Prince Bismarck requests me to tell you in confidence that he would be glad to know Your Lordship's opinion on the Austrian proposals before he answers or deals with them. He wishes for a complete understanding with England in regard to Turkey and offers his cooperation should difficulties arise, if Her Majesty's Government is willing to accept it, in the general interest of peace, which he knows England desires as earnestly as himself" (FO 64/850). The German report of the conversation is in Bülow to Münster, 4 January; *Die Grosse Politik*, II, Doc. No. 227. Both these accounts leave much to be desired. Russell's reports, although the only official documents preserved in the Public Record Office, omit mention of those all-important provisions for the future which Bismarck in some manner, however indirect it may have been, let the ambassador understand he wanted to effect in co-operation with the British cabinet. Those prospective territorial changes which the chancellor suggested were conveyed to London—one can say with all assurance of certainty—in private correspondence which was not made a part of the official record. During the course of the Balkan complications there was a seemingly extensive exchange of private letters between the foreign office and the embassies which, to the great annoyance of students now aware of it, obviated the necessity for incorporating many very important acts and opinions into the official dispatches. Just what Russell reported in his personal messages is not known and may never be. In later years much of Russell's accumulation of papers was destroyed by his wife, and Lord Derby's nephew and successor to the title has not been moved to open his uncle's correspondence.

Bülow's account to the German ambassador was designed allegedly for his information rather than as an instruction to participate in subsequent negotiations. It was written in the form of a private letter, vague in phraseology and shockingly jumbled in content—a trellis on which Bismarck-fanciers have constructed elaborate schemes. The confusion of the document, whether studied or genuine, extends to the point of missing the date of the interview.

The clearest record of Bismarck's views on what should be done are drawn from a report of the Russian ambassador dated 24 December 1875/5 January 1876 (Goriainov, *Le Bosphore et les Dardanelles*, pp. 314–15).

minister in power and suggested his contemplated partition of Turkey as a means of saving him.[24]

Prince Gorchakov promptly rejected the ideas of his former pupil. He admitted in his reply that he had no illusions about Andrássy's reforms but held to the conviction that the experiment ought to be made; the main thing, in his mind, was unanimous agreement of all the powers. Bismarck's views, the Russian chancellor commented, made him think of the great tempter on the mountain—as well as of the Bismarck who had talked with Napoleon III at Biarritz. It appeared to Gorchakov that Berlin was still capable of producing devious plans that merited suspicion, and he advised the tsar against walking into any traps baited with the sweet morsel of annexation possibilities in understanding with England. The master of Germany, he observed, loved too well the grand role of arrangement-maker.[25]

The position of England and the machinery of her government did not permit such a ready disposal of Bismarck's suggestions. Lord Derby returned a polite reply,[26] and deliberations were begun. The immediate preoccupation of the queen's advisers was the action to be taken on the Austrian plans. But Bismarck's hands bore the stains of too many crafty intrigues to permit suspicious Englishmen to rush hastily into connivance with him. Clearer assurances as to the chancellor's intentions were imperative. Bismarck attempted to advance his cause on the first of February by renewing his offer of aid with new affirmations of a disinterested desire for peace.[27] Doubt, however, still ruled the Foreign Office. Lord Lyons, ambassador in Paris

[24] Goriainov, *op. cit.*, pp. 314–15. Bismarck predicted to the Russian ambassador that England would be ready to accept such an arrangement in order to be rid of her apprehensions concerning Constantinople and the Straits.

[25] *Ibid.*, pp. 315–16, citing Gorchakov's letter of 30 December (old style).

[26] Tel. No. 14, Derby to Russell, 6 January 1876; FO 64/846: "Secret. Thank Prince Bismarck for friendly communication. Assure him of friendly desire of H. M. Govt. to cooperate with that of Germany in regard of Turkish affairs. I will speak to Count Münster without reserve, but some days must pass before our opinion can be expressed since Colleagues must be consulted." The extender of this telegram was no more explicit (Draft No. 16, 6 January; *ibid.*). Bismarck received Derby's response a day or two later: "Upon receiving Your Lordship's telegram of the 6th instant, I wrote a private note to Prince Bismarck and conveyed to His Highness the expression of Your Lordship's thanks for his friendly communication and of the sincere desire of Her Majesty's Government to cooperate with that of Germany in regard to Turkish affairs" (Report No. 15, Russell to Derby, 8 January; FO 64/850).

[27] Report No. 56, Russell to Derby, 1 February; *Journal of Modern History*, III, 448–49 (FO 64/850).

and a confidant of Lord Derby, denounced the offer of friendship as a Bismarckian trick to gain British support in case Eastern complications expanded into a new Franco-German war,[28] and Lord Derby was inclined to share the suspicion. Russell, on the contrary, favored the understanding and urged a prompt reply.[29] Disraeli likewise was eager to proceed. He saw an arrangement with Germany as the portal through which England would march forward to regain that influence of which the aged romancer dreamed. Queen Victoria, in spite of her distrust of Bismarck, was converted by the mellifluous phrases of her prime minister,[30] and together the two attacked the suspicions and inertia of Lord Derby.[31] On 10 February the foreign minister reluctantly agreed that the German proposal of an unreserved exchange of ideas should be accepted, but he harbored still his doubts about Bismarck's real desire for peace and suspected still that the offer might involve hidden meanings. In the end Derby concluded that the best way to detect secret designs was to appear to be without suspicion,[32] and on the day following he called in the German ambassador for the conversation which he had promised more than a month before. The foreign minister began with words of politeness and explanations of the long delay, but the substance of his message offered little encouragement to an uneasy chancellor in Germany. His delay, Derby said, had been due to difficulty "in laying down principles which were to guide our action, when the future appeared so uncertain, and when circumstances might vary from day to day." Two principles, none the less, he was now ready to state: unqualified opposition to territorial changes, and unwillingness to interfere in the internal affairs of other countries whether it be a matter of advising Turkey or one of trying to save Andrássy.[33]

Disraeli found the foreign minister's account of the conversation "rather chilling" and urged some more cordial welcome to the proposed understanding,[34] but Derby insisted that his talk with Mün-

---

[28] Lyons to Derby, Paris, 14 January; Newton, *Lord Lyons*, II, 96–97.

[29] Queen Victoria to Derby, 9 February; Buckle, *Queen Victoria*, II, 443.

[30] *Ibid.*, II, 443 n. Disraeli to Queen Victoria, 12 February; *ibid.*, II, 444.

[31] Queen Victoria to Derby, 9 February; *ibid.*, II, 443.

[32] Derby to Queen Victoria, 10 February; *Disraeli*, VI, 20–21.

[33] Dispatch No. 115, Derby to Russell, 12 February; *Journal of Modern History*, III, 450–51. Derby's cordiality toward the overture and toward Bismarck was more apparent in Münster's account of the interview than in the minister's own (*Die Grosse Politik*, IV, 3 n.).

[34] Disraeli to Derby, 15 February; *Disraeli*, VI, 21.

ster and the account of it which he wrote were not yet a reply to Bismarck's advance; he was still waiting for more enlightenment from Germany.[35] Nevertheless, under the pressure of the prime minister's desire, he drew up a new dispatch. It incorporated Disraeli's favorable comment on an Anglo-German understanding; but a low temperature still prevailed. England, he wrote, would not and could not enter an exclusive alliance; a concerted action with Germany "cannot be definitively adopted without a clearer knowledge than we now possess of the motives which have led to Prince Bismarck's recent overtures, and of the expectations which he, and the Government which he represents, may have formed of the results of the understanding proposed by him. . . . . "[36]

On 19 February, when Russell presented the British response, Bismarck could only repeat his offer and reaffirm his desire for peace. He was ready to work with England for the preservation of the status quo; he was ready in case of need to make territorial adjustments. For the moment things had taken a turn for the better in his estimation; there was no immediate need for anticipating radical measures, and in the meantime he would only ask for a frank discussion with England when trouble arose.[37]

The chancellor had been obliged to abandon any thought of a thoroughgoing settlement of the Balkan question. Suspicion directed against him from both East and West made impossible anything but tentative and halting measures such as Andrássy had devised. As for the Vienna program in the meanwhile, Bismarck had waited for almost three weeks to learn the British opinion, and when he felt he could wait no longer he gave Germany's final approval.[38]

---

[35] Derby to Disraeli, 15 February; *Disraeli*, VI, 21–22.

[36] Dispatch No. 117, Derby to Russell, 16 February; *Journal of Modern History*, III, 451–52. The printed date is erroneous (FO 64/846).

[37] Report No. 76, Russell to Derby, 19 February; *ibid.*, III, 452–55.

[38] Report No. 41, Russell to Derby, 26 January; FO 64/850. There has been no little interest among certain historians in an alleged mission of Lothar Bucher, close friend and confidant of Bismarck, to England around the middle of December 1875 for the purpose of proposing an Anglo-German alliance. The one authentic reference to this mission is found in a letter from Münster, the German ambassador in London in this period, to Baron Eckardstein under the heading, Paris, 14 April 1898, in which he writes that the chancellor wanted an alliance with England and sent Bucher on a secret mission to London in 1875 to discuss its possibilities. Contrary to the advice of Münster, this letter has it, Bucher engaged the British ministers in a discussion and received a rejection for his efforts (Hermann Freiherr von Eckardstein, *Lebenserinnerungen und politische Denkwürdigkeiten* [Leipzig, 1919–20], I, 296). In this letter no mention is made of an exact date for the appearance of Bucher in London nor is the purpose of the alliance intimated. But Eckardstein,

ITALY AND THE ANDRÁSSY NOTE

The cabinet in Rome, jealous of the recognition of Italy as a Great Power, had eagerly participated in the consular mission and, as rumors of new negotiations between the three great continental

without advancing further evidence, states that the time was the middle of December ("*gegen Mitte Dezember*") and that the purpose of the discussion was to pave the way for an understanding with reference to Germany's future colonial and economic expansion in co-operation with the British Empire (*ibid.*, I, 308).

In the German archives, according to the editors of *Die Grosse Politik* (IV, 4, footnote continued from the preceding page), there is no reference at all to this mission. The foreign office archives in the Public Record Office in London likewise contain no confirming evidence.

Münster's letter and Eckardstein's elaboration of it are hardly convincing evidence of themselves. Before one can build up a satisfactory hypothesis, as Felix Rachfahl, for example, has attempted to do (*Deutschland und die Weltpolitik* [Stuttgart, 1923], I, 84), more information must be had. Münster's letter was written over twenty years after the alleged events occurred. Although he states that the refusal did not prevent Bismarck's making other attempts, he does not mention the conversation with Lord Odo Russell which Bülow reported to him on 4 January. Unless Bucher were directly involved in the January-February negotiations—and there is no evidence of that from either German or English sources—it seems strange that Münster, in this connection, should have ignored the January advance. The British prime minister in a secret memorandum of September 1879 to the queen, which discusses Bismarck's advance to England in January 1876, makes no mention of the presence of Bucher (*Disraeli*, VI, 487), nor is there any mention of him in any of the contemporary letters.

Friedrich Frahm ("England und Russland in Bismarcks Bündnispolitik," *Archiv für Politik und Geschichte,* 1927, Heft 4, p. 382) has advanced the hypothesis that Bucher was in England in January or February for the purpose of elaborating Bismarck's proposition to Russell. In the note exchange between Disraeli and Derby on 15 February, Frahm sees a special significance in these two sentences, the first from the hand of the prime minister, and the second from that of the foreign secretary: "I will not return the drt. despatch to Mr. V. Lister, but to yourself"; and "The draft I sent you is a mere record of a conversation which took place, and which I thought it as well to set down" (*Disraeli*, VI, 21-22). Frahm's comment is as follows: "Dies Protokoll kann sich nur auf eine Aussprache eines deutschen Vertrauensmannes mit Derby beziehen, also doch wohl Buchers im Dezember oder Anfang Februar." On 26 January, he adds by way of supporting evidence, Bucher was granted a special salary increase for certain useful services. In 1870 he was in Spain under an assumed name, and likewise incognito in England in 1881. Consequently, Frahm assumes, on this occasion he was the Mr. V. Lister to whom Disraeli did not return the dispatch. There are two objections to such a conclusion. The first is that Mr. V. Lister was assistant under-secretary of state in the British Foreign Office. The second, in the light of the documents which are now available, is that the "conversation which took place" was, in all probability, the one between Derby and Münster on 11 February and that the draft in question was Derby's Dispatch No. 115 of 12 February. Bucher was a guest of Bismarck in the country for four or five days in early November 1875 (Heinrich von Poschinger, *Fürst Bismarck, Neue Tischgespräche und Interviews* [Stuttgart, 1895], II, 77), but the available sources do not permit one to follow his subsequent activities.

courts spread, the ministers awaited anxiously another opportunity to take part in the European concert. Peace and good relations with the major powers were Italy's prime necessities in foreign policy, but those ambitions which had created a united state were by no means satisfied and there was evidence that Rome's desire for peace in the Balkans was only a temporary one. The Austrian representative at the Quirinal concluded from his observations that Italy had no real interest in the preservation of Turkey and would willingly see the Eastern question reopened in order to satisfy her own private desires.[39] But that role was one for the future; the immediate concern in Rome was friendly relations everywhere and, more important still, the rescue if possible of the Turkish question from the exclusive control of three powers and its restoration to where it rightfully belonged—in the hands of the signatory powers of which Italy was one among equals.[40]

It was with no little satisfaction, therefore, that in mid-December Rome received promise of a share in the negotiations.[41] On Christmas Day Andrássy abandoned the reserve which he had been maintaining since the crisis began, and in talks with the various foreign representatives, the Italian minister included, besought the support

[39] Report No. 69, Wimpffen to Andrássy, Rome, 25 December; SA, Varia Turquie I, 1875.

[40] Report No. 3, Paget to Derby, 5 January 1876; FO 45/284. King Victor Emmanuel was less discreet and modest than his ministers. On his New Year's visit to *il re galantuomo*, Paget, the British minister, asked the royal opinion. "His Majesty's reply was as nearly as possible in the following words: '*La question d'Orient—je la saurais bien arranger si l'on voulait bien m'en donner la permission. J'ai dit à l'Empereur d'Autriche et à l'Empereur d'Allemagne de me laisser faire. Je me chargerais de tout. Je prendrais le Sultan, je le mettrais dans quelque endroit de l'Asie centrale, et quand j'aurais tout fini, je dirais aux autres—Maintenant, messieurs, servez-vous. Vous, Autriche, Russie, prenez ce que vous voudrez; je prendrais quelque petite chose pour l'Italie. L'Angleterre prendrait aussi ce qui lui ferait plaisir.*' . . . ."
"Having had some experience of His Majesty's character, and of his disposition to indulge occasionally in what, if I may venture to employ the expression, can be best described as 'Braggadocio,' I am free to confess," the minister commented, "that the speech above reported made not the slightest impression upon me." Paget reported the conversation to Visconti-Venosta, the Italian foreign minister, who repudiated his sovereign entirely and maintained that a solution of the Eastern question was the last thing which he wanted at the time (Report No. 8, Paget to Derby, 8 January; *ibid.*).

[41] Barbolani to Visconti-Venosta, St. Petersburg, 29 November/11 December; *First Green Book*, Doc. No. LXXX. Robilant to Visconti-Venosta, Vienna, 16 December; *ibid.*, Doc. No. LXXVI.

of their respective governments as quickly as it could be given.[42] On 4 January the Austrian note was presented to the Italian foreign minister by the Austrian minister and supported by his German and Russian colleagues. There was no thought anywhere that Italy would not join, and Visconti-Venosta without hesitation accepted Andrássy's program subject to confirmation by king and cabinet.[43] Two days later the constitutional formalities were attended to and Italy accorded herself the distinction of being the first power to send its approval to Vienna.[44]

FRANCE AND THE ANDRÁSSY NOTE

In Paris no less than in Rome the major concern was that the Balkan complication should be treated as a problem common to all the signatory powers. This desire inspired the French government to join in the consular mission and to mediate between England and the Continent.[45] Anything short of a general concert meant, in French eyes, the great enemy pursuing diabolical designs. France, furthermore, wanted peace. The Franco-Prussian War had destroyed her pre-eminence and left her torn by domestic factions; she was decidedly not in a position to assume that role which she wished to play when the Sick Man's legacy was at last divided. France, in short, had no more opportunity than had Italy for an isolated stand in the face of the league of the three emperors. But in spite of that consideration, the Andrássy program did not receive in Paris the ready reception accorded it in Rome. On 2 January the note was presented to the Duc Decazes. The French foreign minister, declaring himself entirely in sympathy with the idea of exacting pledges from the sultan, intimated that his approval would be given. One point in the Vienna program, however, met with serious objection — that point which required that direct taxes should remain in the province.[46]

[42] Robilant to Visconti-Venosta, 26 December; ibid., Doc. No. LXXVIII.

[43] Visconti-Venosta to Robilant, 13 January; ibid., Doc. No. LXXXV. Visconti-Venosta to Corti in Constantinople, 8 January; ibid., Doc. No. LXXXI. Tel. No. 3, Wimpffen to Andrássy, Rome, 4 January; First Red Book, Doc. No. 208. Report No. 3, Paget to Derby, Rome, 5 January; Turkey No. 2 (1876), Doc. No. 59.

[44] Tel. No. 5, Wimpffen to Andrássy, 6 January; First Red Book, Doc. No. 211.

[45] E.g., Decazes to d'Harcourt in London, Paris, 18 August 1875; Documents français, II, Doc. No. 5.

[46] Tel. No. 1, 3 January, and Report No. 1, 5 January, Apponyi to Andrássy; SA, Varia Turquie I, 1875; the latter is given in modified form in First Red Book, Doc. No. 210.

Decazes had concluded that this provision was to be applied to all of the provinces of the Ottoman Empire. The enormous investments of French capital in Turkish securities made the duke hesitate to accept such a measure; if the sultan were denied the use of all the direct taxes of the empire the foreign bondholders would have still greater disappointments than the interest repudiation proclaimed in the preceding October.[47]

On the following evening the Austrian ambassador discovered Decazes' mistake and pointed out in a note that the tax provision was to apply to Bosnia and Hercegovina alone and could not entail any serious losses for the Ottoman treasury. Decazes replied immediately and cordially. Refusing to admit his mistake, he declared that a study of the Turkish budget showed the point to be insignificant and said that he was therefore giving the Andrássy note his entire endorsement.[48] Association with the projected step in Constantinople led by the three imperial powers was the only way France had of insuring herself a part in any future Balkan developments. It was, moreover, another step—and this was a vital consideration for the ministers in Paris—toward cementing those cordial relations with Russia which had already been so valuable for France.[49]

Real security for French interests forbade that France should follow merely in the wake of the three emperors. Those interests demanded that the Balkan problem be treated by the European concert of Great Powers. Consequently, from the moment he decided to participate, Decazes set out to win British and Italian co-operation.[50]

[47] Report No. 11, Lyons to Derby, Paris, 5 January 1876; *Turkey No. 2 (1876)*, Doc. No. 58.

[48] Report No. 2AB, Apponyi to Andrássy, Paris, 5 January; SA, Varia Turquie I, 1875. The official French documents give no hint of Decazes' hesitations. Subsequently Decazes told the British ambassador that he had for a time contemplated some reservations to Andrássy's proposed agrarian measures, "but on reading over the part of Count Andrassy's Note relating to them, he found that the suggestions were so little absolute and imperative, so platonic in fact, that he had desisted. . . . ." (Report No. 54, Lyons to Derby, Paris, 24 January 1876; FO 27/2160).

[49] Decazes to Vogüé in Vienna, Paris, 18 January; *Documents français*, II, Doc. No. 31.

[50] Decazes to Gontaut-Biron, 4 January; *Documents français*, II, Doc. No. 28. Another reason why the French were reluctant to separate themselves from England is perhaps to be found in a proposal regarding Egypt which was soon forthcoming. French investors were no less disturbed by the chaotic state of the khedive's finances than were the British, and in mid-February Decazes approached Lyons with a proposal for an understanding between France and England which might look

In long dispatches he made elaborate defenses of the Andrássy program[51] and in talking with the British ambassador he advanced certain considerations designed especially for Lord Derby. The chief of these was the possibility that Russia, finding her plans thwarted by the Western powers, would launch out to settle the Eastern problem in some way dictated exclusively by her own religious and racial interests.[52] With some concern Decazes awaited the decision to be made in London.

GREAT BRITAIN AND THE ANDRÁSSY NOTE

The role which Great Britain might play in the future problems of Turkey had been of secondary consideration in the councils of the imperial league. Count Andrássy had throughout the autumn remained unshaken in his belief that any arrangements agreed upon between him and Gorchakov would of necessity be concurred in by London no less than by Berlin. In St. Petersburg, it is true, there had been from the early days of the negotiations a disposition to proceed *à six*, but that inclination was inspired by no desire to be deferential to Lord Derby and his colleagues. There had been no direct communications between the London Foreign Office and the imperial capitals when the consular mission was being prepared, but a British agent had participated none the less. Consequently there was no indication that Andrássy was not correct in his assumption.

English opinion had not been disturbed by the imposing Continental alliance. Knowing well the jealousies and suspicions and incompatibilities only weakly leashed through imperial ceremonies, British editors were inclined to the view expressed by a conservative periodical early in July 1875 that the concert of the three empires was the best proof possible that no one of them was engaged in

---

toward the establishment of an international commission of control such as had been established in Tunis (Report No. 100, Lyons to Derby, Paris, 14 February; FO 27/2161).

[51] Decazes to d'Harcourt in London, Versailles, 4 January; *First Yellow Book*, pp. 71–73. Decazes to Vogüé in Vienna, 10 January; *ibid.*, pp. 80–81.

[52] Report No. 11, Lyons to Derby, 5 January; *Turkey No. 2 (1876)*, Doc. No. 58, incomplete. ". . . . In conclusion the Duke remarked that if Count Andrassy's proposals did in fact no more than patch up the rents in the Turkish Empire for a short time, still the preservation of peace in Europe, if only for a few years, was an object well worthy of the efforts of civilized Governments" (Report No. 12, 5 January; FO 27/2160).

enterprises of a nature to excite the others.[53] A month later this same journal was confident of the sincerity of the allies and saw no reason for foreign interference.[54] Austria, suggested another weekly, could not annex the insurgent territory; the only action of the Vienna officials would be to sell their neutrality to Turkey for additional railway concessions to Baron Hirsch.[55]

Debates in parliament had indicated that there were many people in Great Britain weary of the old unqualified support of Turkey, and it was not long after the revolt began before voices of sympathy were heard for the insurgent cause. The liberal *Spectator* described the miseries of the Christians of Hercegovina[56] but went on to lament the impossibility of interesting Englishmen in the fate of those people. This journal cynically remarked: "It is, in English judgment, better that iniquities of this kind should go on unchecked, than that Turkey should be beaten in a diplomatic contest."[57] *The Times* in July and August did much to vindicate that pessimism. The great daily deplored Turkish rule but insisted, none the less, that nothing could be done about the plight of the Christians lest the European peace be disturbed.[58] But late in August the editorial page experienced a change of opinion. Something had to be done, it announced, and it cast its vote in favor of autonomy: autonomy was the inevitable solution, and the more quickly the Porte granted it the better it would be for all concerned.[59] *The Spectator* hastened to agree. "There can be no peace," it claimed, "except the peace of exhaustion while the Sultan rules directly any province North of the Balkans." Autonomy, it admitted, was only a temporary expedient until the Turkish Empire collapsed, but autonomy appeared to be the best means of avoiding war.[60] But *The Spectator* soon decided that such a solution was hopeless; the powers, it wrote a fortnight later, were more interested in outwitting each other than in solving a serious

[53] "Germany and Russia," *The Saturday Review*, 10 July 1875, p. 34.

[54] "The Insurrection in Herzegovina," *ibid.*, 14 August 1875, pp. 188–89.

[55] "The Policy of Prince Milano," *The Spectator*, 7 August 1875, p. 999.

[56] *Ibid.*

[57] " 'Repression' in the Herzegovina," *ibid.*, 14 August 1875, pp. 1029–30.

[58] *The Times*, 14 August 1875, p. 9, cols. 2–3.

[59] *Ibid.*, 23 August 1875, p. 7, cols. 2–3; 27 August, p. 9, col. 2. Andrássy was much annoyed with *The Times* for its new stand (Tel., Buchanan to Derby, Vienna, 27 September; FO 7/851).

[60] "The Solution in the Herzegovina," *The Spectator*, 28 August 1875, p. 1080.

problem. As for England, England was no better than the others so long as Lord Derby had neither the courage nor the desire to change its traditional policy toward Turkey.[61]

A strong impetus to open sympathy with the rebellion was afforded in late August. In response to an appeal for aid printed in *The Times,* the venerable Lord Russell subscribed fifty pounds "on behalf of the Insurgents against Turkish misrule."[62] A public subscription list was set up, and early in September a meeting of British sympathizers with the Christians was held in London. It was nothing more than a cloud on the horizon,[63] perhaps, yet it was sufficiently an

[61] *Ibid.,* 11 September 1875, pp. 1136–37.

[62] *The Times,* 28 August 1875, p. 7, col. 6; Thompson, *Public Opinion and Lord Beaconsfield,* I, 221. "The articles in the Times and, still more, the letters of Lord Russell offering a subscription in favour of the insurgents in the Herzegovina have produced a painful feeling of surprise here among all classes," wrote Sir Henry Elliot from Constantinople. "They cannot understand how it can be possible that a former Prime Minister of England should thus openly encourage the revolt of the subjects of a friendly State for which, hitherto, it had shown constant sympathy. I have been appealed to from innumerable quarters for an explanation of this letter, but could only attribute it to advanced age and a generous sympathy for a population suffering from mis-government. Those who contribute to the cause of the Insurgents cannot have even a faint suspicion that they are in fact subscribing to the perpetuation of the most revolting barbarities, and to the continuance of a civil war in which the two parties will vie with each other in cruelty. . . . . Sympathy may be felt for men who openly take up arms against the Troops of what they regard as an oppressive Government, but that countenance and encouragement should be given in England to deeds such as are now being enacted can hardly be seen without a sense of humiliation" (Report No. 543, Elliot to Derby, 10 September; FO 78/2386).

[63] Said *The Saturday Review:* ". . . . It is to the credit of English good sense that the hasty language of prejudiced journalists has produced no result. Yet even the insignificant meeting of a few busybodies in London to support the rebellion may possibly mislead foreigners who have no means of appreciating the obscurity of the promoters. The chair was taken by a subordinate agitator of the days of Mr. Beales, and the principal speaker was a former Turkish official who could not have spoken with more violence if he had had some personal grievance to avenge on the Porte. It is not surprising that the managers of the affair made the most of a letter from Lord Russell, whose promise of a subscription in aid of the rebellion is said to have already misled the leaders of the insurgents. . . . ." ("The Insurrection in Herzegovina," 18 September 1875, pp. 345–46). This periodical had previously pronounced itself emphatically in favor of Turkish rule in Bosnia. In summarizing its position it stated: "It is not the business of England to protect Turkey against rebellions which the Porte will probably be always able to suppress; but there is no reason for departing from the established policy of discountenancing foreign intrigues which tend to the indefinite prolongation of anarchy. . . . ." ("The Insurrection in Herzegovina," 28 August 1875, pp. 253–54). *The Economist* found it almost inconceivable that a former foreign secretary and prime minister should have written such a letter, and referred to the "degrading eccentricities to which he has abandoned himself in his old age." It found the proposal to open a subscription not only unwise but probably illegal. *The Daily Telegraph* took its stand on the sultan's sovereignty; "sneered

indication of a contrary opinion to invite abuse from the conservative press and to cause annoyance to the Foreign Office.[64]

Many influences were at work against such pro-Christian sympathies. The Crimean War had been fought, thought Englishmen, to save Turkey, and only a few souls had the courage to renounce the war-bred sentiments of two decades before. Exasperated though some were by the incorrigible Turk, inertia and those suspicions inherent in full-blown nationalism made a change of policy difficult. Russia remained the national *bête noire*. The treaty of 1856 had broken "the Russ's" strangle-hold on Turkey, but in 1870 he had capitalized the Franco-Prussian War to make his first step toward shaking off the fetters imposed on him fourteen years before. Not content with a revival of activity in the Balkans, the Russians had been busy pushing forward their boundaries in Central Asia. In the summer of 1875 *The Times* printed numerous accounts of a Russian expedition to Krasnovodsk, which was reputed to be hiding political aims behind a façade of scientists. An editorial of late August charged that the real object of Russia was the occupation of Merv, only a few days' journey from the border of Afghanistan. Although there was no immediate danger, the article continued, the time might be foreseen when Russia and Britain would meet face to face.[65]

---

at the meeting and at Earl Russell's letters as 'the climax of ignorant credulity'; asked if the rayahs had 'any grievances substantial enough to justify rebellion,' and advised their sympathisers to clear their minds of cant, 'the cant of race, the cant of national faith, the cant of nationalities.'—(Sept. 10th.)." The *Pall Mall Gazette* of the same date made reference to the " 'unwise persons who assembled yesterday to hear an unwise letter from Earl Russell.' " (Thompson, *op. cit.,* I, 223.)

[64] The assistant undersecretary made this suggestion to his chief: "The publication of the account of cruelties perpetrated by the Insurgents might check the contributions to Ld Russell's Subs^n List." Lord Derby characteristically replied, "Yes, but though very likely true, it is all hearsay and apparently from Turkish sources" (Notes on the back of Report No. 2, Holmes to Derby, Mostar, 22 August; FO 78/2536).

One of the instigators of the public meeting was Lewis Farley, one-time Turkish consul-general in England. In October Farley approached the Russian ambassador and asked him to subsidize, to the extent of £100–£150 a month, a lecture and press campaign and propaganda directed to the protestant clergy to give religious color to the agitation which he was helping to inaugurate. Shuvalov thought the proposal *"judicieuse et habile"* and justified himself by a quotation from Talleyrand: *"Quand vous hésitez sur le choix d'une raison à donner ou d'une expression, dites 'humanité.' "* Despite the ambassador's enthusiasm, the proposal apparently came to nought (Seton-Watson, "Russo-British Relations during the Eastern Crisis," *Slavonic Review,* III, 430–31).

[65] *The Times* (London), 23 August 1875, p. 7, col. 1.

Time and new problems, however, had vitiated somewhat the old Russophobia. The war scare of May had given promise of introducing a new day of Anglo-Russian co-operation; the predominance of a united Germany made it desirable to review the question of foreign policy. Some there were, indeed, who wished to see a definite alliance with Russia to restore the balance of power. In proposing such a policy, one writer in the October *Fraser's* called on his fellow-countrymen to dismiss the old prejudices and forget the old notion that Russia was a bully standing over Turkey. Two things, he said, Russia wanted: the first was liberation of the Slavs of the Balkans who were languishing under foreign tyranny; the second was unrestricted access to the oceans for her trade. Neither of those aims, he insisted, was incompatible with the interests of Britain.

The necessity of maintaining the Ottoman Empire in its advanced and aggressive position on the outskirts of Christendom does not exist except in imagination, and therefore ought not to debar us from accepting the indispensable assistance of Russia in the arrangement of matters nearer home. We say the necessity does not exist, even for Turkish interests, because we believe that Turkey would prove much stronger within her natural frontiers, marked out by language, religion, and race, than in her present precarious position in the midst of an alien and hostile population. . . . .
    What, then, should be the policy of Great Britain if she is desirous of accommodating herself to the Future, instead of allowing herself to be overshadowed by the traditions of the Past? If she persists in shoring up the rotten worn-out edifice of Turkish dominion in Europe, she may indeed reckon on the co-operation and connivance of Austria, that fossil remnant of the Holy Roman Empire. . . . . But if we join her in trampling on the liberties of the nations she enthrals, we must be prepared to participate in the immense catastrophe that awaits her; for there is no room for her in the Europe of the future, whose constitution must rest on natural bases, and not on the artificial arrangements of diplomatists. On the other hand, by withdrawing our resistance to the programme of Russia in the East, we shall definitely abandon a policy full of peril, which endeavours to circumvent the inexorable Future, and pledges us to engagements which we can by no conceivable means fulfil.[66]

The Spectator likewise urged a reconsideration of British attitude toward Russia and the Southern Slavs. This periodical held it to be good policy, even from the most selfish standpoint, to support the emancipation of the oppressed peoples of the Balkans. It insisted that if England wanted to restrict the influence of Russia in southeastern Europe the way to do so was by joining Russia in aiding the legitimate ambitions of these peoples; so long as Russia alone was

[66] H. S., "Some Remarks on Our Relations with Russia," *Fraser's,* XCII, 450–55.

their champion, she alone would influence them. "Indeed," the article in question concluded, "Constantinople will be rather safer, instead of less safe from the Russian grasp, if the Herzegovina and Bosnia can be secured against the miseries which vex them into periodic insurrection. And even if it were not so, no good will ever come of the cynical policy which ignores the wretchedness of multitudes, in order to maintain against Russia the dominion of the seas."[67]

These utterances in favor of a new orientation of British policy found no echo in Whitehall. To the prime minister of Great Britain the rebellion of the Christians was merely a rebellion, and he and his colleague in the Foreign Office, like the ambassador in Constantinople, had no other thought than that it should be put down as quickly as possible.[68] Disraeli's major consideration was that no excuse should arise for foreign intervention in Turkey. He consented with reluctance to Holmes's share in the consular mission,[69] and he continued to express his concern for the future. This man, who had promised a more energetic foreign policy, experienced a moment of pessimism in early September. The fall of troublesome France had only made matters worse; the balance of power was upset, and England—to his great sorrow—seemingly could do nothing but follow in the path of the imperial league.[70] One conviction, none the less, made him answer Queen Victoria reassuringly when the sovereign showed signs of agitation: the Continental allies, he believed, were too jealous of each other to undertake an active step. In examining the problem with Lord Derby on 10 September, Disraeli came to the conclusion that there was no cause for alarm. The two ministers decided that they could consent to autonomy for the insurgent area, but the premier had no inclination to take the initiative in such a plan and did not think that anyone else would do so either.[71]

[67] "Russia and the European Powers," *The Spectator*, 18 September 1875, p. 1164.

[68] Disraeli to Lady Bradford, 20 August, and Disraeli to Lady Chesterfield, 21 August; *Disraeli*, VI, 12. Derby to Carnarvon, 13 September; Sir Arthur Hardinge, *The Life of Henry Howard Molyneux Herbert, Fourth Earl of Carnarvon, 1831–1890* (London, 1925), II, 326.

[69] *Disraeli*, VI, 12.

[70] Disraeli to Lady Bradford, 6 September; *ibid.*, VI, 13. Zetland, *Letters of Disraeli*, I, 279–80.

[71] Ponsonby to Disraeli, 3 September, and Disraeli to Queen Victoria, 10 September; Buckle, *Queen Victoria*, II, 420–21.

As the autumn moved on, Disraeli began to develop more concrete ideas of his own. Scarcely half a month passed before he modified his views on concessions to change in Turkey. "Fancy autonomy for Bosnia," he was saying on 1 October; such an arrangement there was to him more absurd than were it attempted in Ireland.[72] Endowed with an ability to believe anything he wished at any moment he wished, the prime minister expressed one thing and then its opposite without once having any real understanding of the new problem rising up to confront Europe. On the day that Andrássy was sending his "practical propositions" to St. Petersburg Disraeli was sure that the Balkan problem was virtually settled;[73] five days later he had it that the rest of Europe was perplexed and wanted Britain to make the first move.[74] Within a fortnight he saw the century-old "Eastern Question" arising for him to meet—and perhaps to settle.[75]

The Lord Mayor's banquet on 9 November imposed by tradition the necessity for the prime minister to review publicly the nation's foreign relations. The would-be recent history which the speaker on this occasion recited for his listeners was nothing but imaginative fiction. "It would be an affectation," he said in introducing the Turkish problem, "to pretend that a partial revolt in a province of European Turkey has brought about a state of affairs which in that part of the world becomes critical." A "wise forbearance," which he praised highly but did not define, had been so successful that there was hope "some months ago" that the rebellion would soon end. But the "unfortunate event" which revived the "expiring struggle" was "the financial catastrophe of one of our allies." Through the bankruptcy of Turkey the situation had become critical. The solution to this problem, he suggested, was that same forbearance which he had just extolled. Should it be maintained, he was certain that means—equally unspecified—would be "ascertained, which will bring about a satisfactory result." His peroration provided for the contrary contingency:

My Lord Mayor, I will not contemplate any other result, and therefore I will only say that the interests which the Imperial Powers have in this ques-

---

[72] Disraeli to Lady Bradford, 1 October; *Disraeli*, VI, 13. Also in Zetland, *op. cit.*, I, 288–89.

[73] Disraeli to Lady Chesterfield, 16 October; Zetland, *op. cit.*, I, 294.

[74] Disraeli to Lady Bradford, 21 October; *ibid.*, I, 296.

[75] Disraeli to Lady Bradford, 3 November; *ibid.*, I, 298–99. Also in *Disraeli*, VI, 14–15.

tion no doubt are more direct than those of Great Britain, but, though more direct, they are not more considerable; and those to whom the conduct of your affairs is now intrusted are deeply conscious of the nature and magnitude of those British interests, and those British interests they are resolved to guard and maintain.[76]

The speech was well received in England. Even *The Spectator,* Disraeli's sharp critic, had to admit that "it is not audacious, it is not epigrammatic, and it is not bombastic. . . . ."[77] No one, however, was more pleased with it than the prime minister himself. He considered the day "very successful" and believed that his words had effected their purpose. But the speech, he wrote, was only the break of day; soon probably there would be "a flaming sun and a sultry sky." He hoped that sixty years of peace (!) had not robbed England of all its spirit.[78]

The words and deeds of England's prime minister had left one observer unconvinced. He was Gavard, the French chargé d'affaires. A little more than a week after the Guildhall banquet Gavard wrote to Paris his troubled impressions of British isolation. Gladstone and his cabinet, he said, had permitted a Continental state to upset the European equilibrium, and the new government, although cognizant of the fault committed, thought it best to let things go. Gavard believed that the old policy toward Turkey was being abandoned. For Englishmen the Eastern question was India and the route to it from England. It seemed to him that on that future day when Turkey collapsed London statesmen would be interested in Egypt alone; a strong current of opinion appeared willing to leave Constantinople to Russia under the conviction that its possession would bring more

---

[76] *The Times,* 10 November 1875, p. 10, cols. 3–4. Thompson, *Public Opinion and Lord Beaconsfield,* I, 235. The following telegram from Elliot, dated 6 November, indicates how much Disraeli knew of the activities of the "Imperial Powers" at the time he made his speech: "General Ignatieff tells me in great confidence that Count Andrassy had sent to the Emperor of Russia a project of demands to be made upon the Porte in reference to the reforms for Bosnia. The proposal was, he said, extravagant and of such a nature as must if adopted lead to massacre and civil war. The Emperor had answered that as the Sultan had already begun to promulgate reforms, interference by Foreign Powers was not at present called for. His Majesty would, General Ignatieff says, prefer questions relating to Turkey being treated by all the Guaranteeing Powers" (Forwarded to Loftus in St. Petersburg, in Dispatch No. 331, 8 November; FO 65/906).

[77] "Mr. Disraeli at the Guildhall," *The Spectator,* 13 November 1875, pp. 1412–13; Thompson, *op. cit.,* I, 236.

[78] Disraeli to Lady Bradford, 10, 13 November; *Disraeli,* VI, 16.

handicaps than advantages.[79] In one observation Gavard was correct —the vital interest of England in controlling the passage to India. Four days before the chargé penned his thoughts, the British cabinet had been led by Disraeli to purchase the Suez Canal shares owned by the bankrupt khedive of Egypt. When the meeting had adjourned the prime minister's joy was boundless. "It is worth living in such times," he exulted.[80] Happily he speculated on the reactions of Gorchakov and Bismarck to the "great news" when the two met in Berlin supposedly to settle "everything" without consulting Great Britain.[81] Here indeed was the spirited foreign policy which Disraeli had promised, and the English press was lyrical.[82]

In the meantime it had been the task of the far less spectacular Lord Derby to conduct the day-by-day duties of external relations. The rebellion in Hercegovina and Bosnia, it has been indicated previously, did not command the sympathy of Britain's foreign minister. From the beginning he wished the disturbance to be crushed by Turkish military force and he was annoyed when the Turks, ignoring his advice, continued "their laziness and apathy" and permitted the revolt to go on.[83] This annoyance was increased by the consular mission in which the Turks themselves bespoke British participation when the powers who originated the proposal apparently ignored the London Foreign Office.[84] The secretary accepted the proposal, but his acceptance was at the same time a severe lecture to the Turks for agreeing to a foreign intervention.[85] During the next month—the

[79] Gavard to Decazes, London, 19 November; *Documents français*, II, Doc. No. 12.

[80] Zetland, *op. cit.*, I, 302. For details as to the purchase of the shares, see *Disraeli*, V, 439–54; Charles W. Hallberg, *The Suez Canal: Its History and Diplomatic Importance* (New York, 1931), chaps. xiv–xv, etc.

[81] Disraeli to Lady Bradford, 30 November; *Disraeli*, V, 450. Also in Zetland, *op. cit.*, I, 308.

[82] Thompson, *op. cit.*, I, 210, 237–42. "It is not easy to get the better of Mr. Disraeli," said *The Spectator*. "The slowly sinking reputation of the Government has been suddenly revived by one of those dramatic and yet statesmanlike *coups* in which the author of 'Alroy' delights. . . . ." (27 November, p. 1473.) "England and the Suez Canal," *ibid.*, p. 1476. "Mr. Disraeli from a New Side," *ibid.*, pp. 1508–1509. *The Saturday Review*, Disraeli's partisan, ecstatically wrote: "It is his own style of gorgeousness. In a moment he interferes in the East, he commits his country to a new adventure, he bandies about his millions like halfpence. . . . ." ("England and Egypt," 27 November, pp. 665–66).

[83] Derby to Carnarvon, 13 September; Hardinge, *Carnarvon*, II, 326.

[84] It will be recalled that although a Russian invitation to participate was sent to London it was not delivered.

[85] Derby to Elliot, 24 August; *Turkey No. 2 (1876)*, Doc. No. 16.

month of September when the consuls failed in their mission and when the insurgents marshaled their resources for the renewed struggle—Derby had no views except to approve the efforts of Elliot to inaugurate Turkish reform.

In Liverpool on 7 October Derby made the first public utterance for the government on the Balkan problem. The speech embodied the dull words of a man of apathy. The rebellion, he said, was greatly exaggerated; it had been discussed at some length in the press because it came in the slack season of the year when there was little news to print. And, with utter disregard of Holmes's reports, he added for the titillation of his audience: "I fancy one of the difficulties of the consuls who were lately sent on a mission of conciliation was to find the insurgents whom they were to conciliate." The powers had not proffered the expected aid and, said the secretary, "I don't think, therefore, we shall hear much more of the armed insurrection." As for steps to prevent "another outbreak," Derby thought that Turkey would consent to "considerable administrative reforms." About their success, however, he was not sanguine; there were no men to put them into effect, and regardless of what might be done to remove abuses and lighten taxation, discontent would remain. Autonomy he ruled out as impossible, thereby reversing, as Disraeli had done, his position of a month before.[86] Alleviation he thought possible through some unnamed means, but he saw no "good radical cure." The rest, he concluded, could be left to time, and meanwhile Turkey of the treaties was to be maintained.[87]

[86] Disraeli to Queen Victoria, 10 September; Buckle, *Queen Victoria*, II, 421: ". . . . Mr. Disraeli sees no difficulty, and Lord Derby agrees with him, in your Majesty's joining in any arrangement which would secure the autonomy of Herzegovina, under the sovereignty of the Porte. . . . ."

[87] *The Times*, 8 October 1875, p. 7, col. 6; Thompson, *op. cit.*, I, 227–28. *The Saturday Review* ("Russian Policy," 6 November 1875, pp. 569–70) acclaimed Derby's speech as a notice to those English journalists who were urging Russia on that there had been no change in British policy. *The Spectator* ("Lord Derby at Liverpool," 9 October 1875, pp. 1252–53) had only regrets: ". . . . But when we come to the part of his speech which has reference to Turkey, the intrinsic feebleness of the policy he is pursuing, appears. He defends the old doctrine that Turkey must be backed up, however bad her government, because you have nothing to substitute for it. . . . . England is probably almost alone in a position of real impartiality . . . . and England is represented by a statesman who is too timorous to take up any but the old traditional and exhausted policy of propping up 'the sick man' by the very useless expedient of mere advice and remonstrance. . . . . Lord Derby in assisting Russia and Austria to postpone the solution of an inevitable and every year more urgent problem, is really helping to make the catastrophe greater when it comes. It is a blind and weak policy. . . . ."

The same apathy Lord Derby revealed two days later in his first discussion of the Turkish problem with Count Shuvalov, the Russian ambassador. Shuvalov had recently returned to his post with instructions to enlist British co-operation in some immediate settlement of the question of the day and to justify Russia's right to secure an amelioration of the sad lot of Turkey's Christians. Finding no one in London with whom he could talk, the ambassador went to Knowsley, Derby's country seat, and, as he said, almost forced the door. The foreign minister and the ambassador found themselves in substantial agreement on the desirability of avoiding a serious Eastern crisis, but the former was reluctant to believe the latter's assurances that Andrássy shared their views. Nor could Shuvalov frighten his host by talking of the wide scope of the rebellion and the possibility of Serbian and Montenegrin participation in the spring. Derby persisted in his belief that the insurgents were better at isolated crime than at warfare with the Turkish forces and he refused to be concerned about the principalities. In his opinion the Serbs would not risk declaring war without foreign support, and the semi-barbarous Montenegrins could make no serious difficulties for the troops they would face. Again Derby refused to consider autonomy for Bosnia; the only thing to be done, he assured Shuvalov, was to approve the joint efforts of Elliot and Ignatiev to secure administrative and financial reforms, even though, he added, little was to be hoped from them.

The Russian ambassador concluded that it would be vain to expect any real sympathy from Lord Derby for the Christians of Turkey, and surmised that he would be entirely indifferent to the conflict were there not in London a fear for British position and for what might happen if the other powers acted without England. Despite the foreign minister's approval of Elliot's co-operation in Constantinople, Shuvalov sensed in Derby's conversation a feeling of ill-will as well as apathy. The ambassador explained to his home government that this feeling was the result of several considerations. The entente of the three courts and their common initiative in the Balkan problem, he believed, had incited and would always incite British defiance; he saw the ministers in England disturbed by France's flirtations with Russia and jealous and wounded in pride by the dominant role of Tsar Alexander in Europe.[88] Shuvalov had

---

[88] Shuvalov to Jomini, 2/14 October; *Slavonic Review*, III, 426–30. Derby's account is in Dispatch No. 326 to Elliot, 16 October; FO 78/2378.

little hope of winning British support and sympathy, but he thought he might induce Lord Derby to show more confidence and good-will if he were permitted to give from time to time some explanations of Russian policy such as were then being made in Paris.[89] The suggestion was well received in St. Petersburg. The ambassador was instructed to carry out his own suggestion,[90] and from that time forward Jomini kept the British ambassador well informed of the progress of the negotiations with Vienna.[91] Shuvalov found his tactics immediately effective; the defiance shown by Derby during his visit to Knowsley promptly gave way to "a more reasonable and equitable judgment."[92] When the ambassador next saw Derby a month after his first interview he was struck by the change which had come over him. The foreign minister confessed that he had been wrong in minimizing the rebellion and now anticipated that nothing would prevent co-operation with Russia, to whose moderation he gave full justice. Derby, however, continued to be pessimistic. He saw no hope for serious reform in Turkey and he let Shuvalov again see his suspicions of Austria.[93]

Distinctly less cordial were the November relations between London and Vienna. Count Beust returned to his post at the Austrian embassy late in October charged to maintain *"une grande réserve."*[94] It was Andrássy's intention to arrange his reform program with St. Petersburg and Berlin before discussing it with the other powers. Beust, therefore, was bound to silence, and Andrássy himself refused to divulge anything to the British representative in Vienna.[95] But to the Austrian minister's great dissatisfaction

---

[89] Shuvalov to Jomini, 22 October/3 November; *Slavonic Review,* III, 431. During these same days the Russian government received the proposal of the editor-proprietor of the *Standard,* an important London daily newspaper, to sell his journal for £250,000. The offer was taken to the tsar himself and was at last rejected because the price was considered too high and because of the probable impossibility of keeping the transaction secret (Jomini to Shuvalov, 16 October; *ibid.,* III, 430). For a discussion of the *Standard* episode, see R. W. Seton-Watson, *Disraeli, Gladstone and the Eastern Question* (London, 1935), pp. 24-25.

[90] Shuvalov to Jomini, 30 October/11 November; *Slavonic Review,* III, 431.

[91] Reports Nos. 338, 345, 350, Loftus to Derby, St. Petersburg, 10, 16, 22 November, respectively; FO 65/912.

[92] Shuvalov to Jomini, 30 October/11 November; *Slavonic Review,* III, 431-32.

[93] Shuvalov to Jomini, 1/13, 2/14 November; *ibid.,* III, 432-33.

[94] Report No. 93, Beust to Andrássy, London, 27 October; SA, England, 1875.

[95] ". . . . His Excellency [Andrássy] has become more reserved since I first knew him in his remarks upon public affairs, and it is only by occasional observations in frequent private conversations with him that I can form any opinion upon

there came news from London that Shuvalov had been giving away what he considered Austro-Russian confidences. With a transparent feeling of having been betrayed, Andrássy telegraphed to St. Petersburg to defend his idea of action *à trois* and to ask if the Russians were not willing to go on.[96] The reply was reassuring: Shuvalov had not been instructed to make any official communications but merely to answer Lord Derby's questions in general terms.[97] Shuvalov himself protested that he was merely trying to bring England into line with France in support of the imperial league.[98]

his views with respect to the Bosnian question;—I may state, however, that two days ago, in alluding to the country being misgoverned, he said it would be equally so if it were made independent—and, on my saying to him yesterday that at Vienna he was believed to be occupied here in drawing up a constitution for the Turkish insurgent provinces, he answered that the idea was entirely new to him, and that he certainly would not undertake such a task. . . . ." (Report No. 383, Buchanan to Derby, Budapest, 16 November; FO 7/852).

On 17 November Buchanan again asked Andrássy about his opinions and his intentions but the minister adroitly avoided a positive answer. ". . . . I observed that in what he had stated to me, he had only spoken of what he seemed to disapprove, but had abstained from adverting to his own views, as to how an arrangement might be come to. He answered that some persons looked to the ideal, and others suggested what would be insufficient to meet the difficulties of the situation, while he was of the opinion that a practical solution might be found between the two extremes, but as he had not yet been able to satisfy his own mind as to how this could be done, he must reserve any expression of opinion upon it until he had fully decided what to recommend. . . . ." (Report No. 390, Buchanan to Derby, Vienna, 18 November; *ibid.*) Thus spoke the minister who a month before had formulated his program and who had only the day before sent to St. Petersburg an obdurate insistence that it be carried through.

See also Derby to Buchanan, 20 November; *Turkey No. 2 (1876)*, Doc. No. 43.

Andrássy maintained the same aloofness toward the French ambassador, much to the latter's indignation (*Documents français*, II, 8, note 1. Vogüé to Decazes, Vienna, 28 December; *ibid.*, Doc. No. 25. De Ring to Decazes, Vienna, 15 November; *First Yellow Book*, p. 40. Vogüé to Decazes, Vienna, 28 November; *ibid.*, pp. 40–41).

[96] Tel. No. 266, Andrássy to Mayr, Budapest, 23 November; SA, Varia Turquie I, 1875. Shuvalov to Gorchakov, 4/16 December; *Slavonic Review*, III, 433–34.

[97] Tel. N. 48, Langenau to Andrássy, St. Petersburg, 24 November; SA, Varia Turquie I, 1875.

[98] Report No. 100AB, Beust to Andrássy, London, 24 November; *ibid.* Beust was not satisfied that the Russian answer, which was forwarded to him, was an authentic reply to Andrássy's question in view of the fact that Shuvalov was still saying that England would be asked for an opinion on Andrássy's reform program rather than mere support (Tel., Beust to Andrássy, 27 November; *ibid.*). The foreign minister was convinced that the Russians were accepting his plan and used Beust's comment as an opportunity to give his old enemy a sharp reproof: ". . . . I am quite astonished that your Excellency finds no genuine answer to my question in my communication; it is so clearly stated there that I must consider it unnecessary to repeat it. . . . ." (Tel. No. 844, Andrássy to Beust, Vienna, 28 November; *ibid.*).

By the time Andrássy had satisfied himself that Russia was not engaged in surreptitious dealings with England, he was confronted with a new annoyance. Lord Derby in talking with Beust had not the slightest word of sharpness or defiance toward Austria,[99] but from Jomini came news that the British secretary was attempting to arouse suspicions in Russia as to Austria's intentions.[100] To Andrássy it was merely another attempt of perfidious Albion to create difficulty between the two allies. He was persuaded that connected with this maneuver was a new change of opinion manifested by *The Times,* an abandonment of the proposal for autonomy in favor of an Austrian occupation as the only possible solution.[101] It was all a part of one scheme, the minister commented with bitterness, to separate Austria from Russia.[102]

There was no answer to Derby's seeming intrigues except to caution Jomini against them. And as for the British cabinet, there was nothing to do but try to win its support. Convinced that *The Times* in proposing an Austrian occupation was the voice of the government, Andrássy felt obliged to have the Austrian ambassador repeat in London the same arguments which he had recently used to combat Jomini's suggestion of a joint Austro-Russian military action.[103] Beust's reports continued to be encouraging. He saw no hint of British animosity. Derby did not seem to be impatient or

---

[99] Report No. 95AC, Beust to Andrássy, London, 6 November; SA, Varia Turquie, I, 1875.

[100] Report No. 62, Langenau to Andrássy, 12/24 November; SA, Russia, 1875. Lord Loftus in St. Petersburg had been raising the same question in talking with Jomini. Jomini commented: "Les insinuations sont trop cousues de fil blanc pour que j'aie besoin d'insister sur le but qu'elles poursuivent."

[101] *The Times,* 19 November 1875, p. 9, col. 2. "Nothing but a foreign army of occupation," said an editorial of that date, "can save Herzegovina from the risk of a catastrophe. . . . . Austria could not do a better service than by repeating in Bosnia and Herzegovina the act of police which she performed in 1854. The Porte would, of course, protest, and at first, perhaps, refuse to withdraw its own troops; but a State which exists on sufferance must be peremptorily informed that it wastes time by putting on airs of independence. The intervention must be made with the concurrence of the Great Powers; but all of them, we believe, will soon see that it is an absolute necessity. The work must be done by Austria because her territory adjoins the disturbed districts, and she is also the Power which this country at least would most confidently trust. She has no great purposes of ambition, nor has she any strength to spare for conquest. On the other hand, she would bring to the task the moral tone, as well as the authority, of a highly civilised Power. . . . ."

[102] Tel., Andrássy to Langenau, 4 December; SA, Russia, 1875.

[103] Report No. 105AF, Beust to Andrássy, London, 8 December; SA, Varia Turquie I, 1875.

concerned;[104] he listened sympathetically to arguments against an Austrian occupation.[105] Indeed, it seemed apparent to the ambassador that the British government did not expect to be consulted and would not be hostile to accepting what the other powers had agreed upon.[106] Andrássy's satisfaction with the British was complete when Beust telegraphed on 7 December that Derby was admitting Europe's right to intervene. Confident that all was well, he sent word to London that the British cabinet would be asked for an opinion just as soon as Gorchakov approved the text of the new program, rather than presented with an accomplished fact.[107] Derby received this message with the same sympathetic understanding which Beust had already described. According to the ambassador's next report the British foreign secretary, recognizing the right of Europe to concern itself with Turkey, promised to support the Austrian point of view in Constantinople.[108]

This attitude on the part of Derby came to public light on 18 December when the foreign secretary discussed the Turkish problem in Edinburgh. He was no longer content to minimize the rebellion as he had done in October. Following Disraeli's example, Derby erroneously attributed the revival of the revolt to Turkey's bankruptcy and predicted that Europe would not hear the last of the problem for a long time to come. But he professed the belief that the Continental powers, despite their swollen armies, wanted peace and, specifically, that Austria and Russia were anxious to see order restored in Bosnia. Lord Derby that he was, however, the speaker could not stop without emphasizing the shadows. General advice to Turkey offered him no hope, and he anticipated that concrete proposals might create divisions among half a dozen advisers, and, even if the advisers were agreed, the problem of peace was still gigantic.[109]

[104] Report 99AF, Beust to Andrássy, 19 November; SA, England, 1875.

[105] Report No. 105AF, Beust to Andrássy, 8 December; SA, Varia Turquie I, 1875.

[106] Report No. 102C, Beust to Andrássy, 1 December; *ibid.*

[107] Tel., Andrássy to Beust, Budapest, 9 December; *ibid.*

[108] Tel., Beust to Andrássy, 11 December; SA, Varia Turquie I, 1875. Derby in his own account of the conversation with Beust limited himself merely to repeating the substance of the ambassador's message (Derby to Buchanan, 11 December; *Turkey No. 2 [1876]*, Doc. No. 47).

[109] Sir T. H. Sanderson and E. S. Roscoe, editors, *Speeches and Addresses of Edward Henry XVth Earl of Derby, K.G.* (London, 1894), I, 276–78. Thompson, *op. cit.*, I, 254–55. Gavard to Decazes, London, 19 December; *Documents français*, II, Doc. No. 24.

Dispassionately appraised, the diplomatic situation in December offered no serious alarms for British statesmen. True it was that the rebellion in Bosnia was apparently beyond Turkey's control. The Foreign Office now had reports from Consul Holmes which depicted a very unhappy situation, a situation which in his view could be dealt with only by European action.[110] It was furthermore true that leadership in the dangerous project of intervention in Turkey was being assumed by the league of the three emperors. As a counterbalance, however, were other considerations. It seemed to Derby that, regardless of pledges to leave Turkey alone, some interference had to be made. The best guaranty that this interference would not go far—for the time at all events—was in the fact that it would be very difficult for Austria and Russia to combine on some positive program of radical action. Austria was too weak to embark on elaborate schemes and it was generally recognized that Andrássy did not wish to acquire any more Slavs for the Dual Monarchy. Russia, too, was unwilling to open the Eastern question and was desirous of maintaining the European concert. The British ambassador, taken into Jomini's confidence, reported that he had no doubts about Russia's wish to be moderate and conciliatory.[111] And, finally, the major points of Andrássy's program had come to London by way of St. Petersburg and were obviously not in themselves a radical measure.[112]

The beginning of the new year found England still not of one mind concerning the question of Turkey. The public addresses of the premier and the foreign secretary gave indication that the cabinet reflected divergent views, while in the press the poles of opinion were still farther apart. Conservative opinion, represented by *The Saturday Review,* had budged little from the feverish conviction of

---

[110] ". . . . I gave Your Excellency in my last despatch an idea of the miserable condition of the troops. The winter has commenced and they will soon be worse off, if possible, than they are now. I am assured that to procure a little money they sell their ammunition in the bazaars. Matters are certainly not improving;—to me they seem to be going from bad to worse, and if European diplomacy cannot during the winter bring about a pacification, I expect that in the spring both Bosnia and the Herzegovina will be in a state of complete anarchy, which will probably result in frightful massacres, and, as I have said before, Austrian military occupation. I am not an alarmist but all that I see and hear compels me most unwillingly to this conclusion" (Report No. 21, Holmes to Elliot, Mostar, 19 November, in Report No. 18, Holmes to Derby, 22 November; FO 78/2536).

[111] Tel., Loftus to Derby, St. Petersburg, 16 December; FO 65/912.

[112] Reports Nos. 396 and 397, Loftus to Derby, 21, 22 December, respectively; *ibid.*

Crimean War days. This journal seized with alacrity on the difficulties of foreign control over Turkey which Lord Derby had emphasized and found it easy to conclude that Turkey should be left to her own devices. "It is true that the liberal promises made in 1856 by the Sultan had not produced satisfactory results," the *Review* admitted; "but the reasons which dictated the provisions for maintaining the independence of the Porte are still to a great extent valid. In announcing by anticipation the expediency of the policy which is conjecturally attributed to Count Andrassy, the *Times* both consistently maintains the violent and one-sided doctrines which it has lately adopted, and directly thwarts and opposes the traditional policy of England. . . . ."[113]

Anti-Turkish feeling in England, on the other hand, had been materially augmented by the Porte's declaration of bankruptcy. With no little vehemence an Edinburgh magazine emphasized the extravagance of sultan and ministers which it suspected was probably increased by repudiation of half of the Ottoman debts. It declared that the money which went into Turkey after Britain had made her great expenditure in blood and gold during the Crimean War was lost. The Sick Man was on Europe's hands again, but the author of the article in question went on to take great satisfaction in the fact that Europe in 1876 was wiser than it had been in 1853. He found in retrospect that the diplomatic bickerings of that earlier period formed a "painful episode in European history" and, he said, "England most certainly has nothing to be proud of in respect to those transactions." Russia and Austria merited no hostility and, he concluded, there was no ground for England, with relatively small interest in decadent Turkey, to intervene. "The day is past when England will go to war to support the integrity and independence of the Ottoman empire."[114]

Other voices of British opinion were not content with passive hostility. An article in the January issue of *Fraser's* lashed the Turks with a crusader's zeal. The sultan's bankruptcy it considered "but one episode in the miserable drama, which for the sake of our common humanity, we may hope is drawing towards a conclusion." But Turkey alone was not responsible for the barbarous oppression which it inflicted on its subject peoples; all of the old evils

[113] "Turkey," *Saturday Review,* 1 January 1876, pp. 2–3.
[114] "Public Affairs," *Blackwood's Edinburgh Magazine,* CXIX (January 1876), 114–19.

were intensified after the Crimean war by the blind folly with which the English Government and the English people followed the Charlatan policy of Louis Napoleon. . . . . Purblind statesmen prated about the capacities of Turkey, her desire to found a civilized government, and her resources, until the people of this country believed it all, as they had believed it necessary for us to join Louis Napoleon in an expedition devised for his glory and the stability of his blood-stained throne. . . . . All that history had taught us about the cruelty, the rapacity, and the total absence of true governing faculty in the Turks was as clean forgotten as if we had just had a new revelation from Heaven. . . . . In a sense, and that by no means a light one, the post-Crimean policy of England has done more than anything else to bring matters to this point in Turkey. We have petted the Turk till he has tired of us, advised him till he seemed glad to open his arms to Russia, and, above all, we have given a spur to the reaction natural to his rule by lending him money, at first with full and ostentatious official sanction and approval, and then from the habit and traditions that this approval begot.

The hope for Turkey, as well as for Turkish bondholders, the indignant writer insisted, was to free Turkey from the Turks. The time seemed at hand for a change, for a solution to the Eastern question. Indeed, he contended, England herself, by purchasing the Suez Canal shares, had given the signal for partition. If, however, Europe hung back from the final rending of the Sick Man's withered carcass, the middle-course policy was the erection of a series of protected states—Bosnia, Bulgaria, Thessaly, for example—federated around a free city of Constantinople.

It might prevent war for a time at least, and would yet put so slight a barrier between either Russia or Austria and the gratification of their hopes, that they might be induced to postpone the struggle, now so inconvenient and dangerous. On the other hand, as the price of their emancipation, these states might take upon themselves a portion of the Turkish debt. . . . .[115]

Less violent but equally certain was *The Spectator:*

A Note proposing reforms to Turkey will do no more harm than a reading of the Eighth Commandment to a pirate ship, but let the statesmen, nevertheless, remain ready for the explosion, which, even if momentarily postponed, is as certain as the explosion of a magazine in which shells are perpetually falling. Nothing, as we believe, can avert it, except the detachment of Turkish provinces one by one, from Turkish direct rule. . . . .[116]

The most influential of the voices calling for a modification of

[115] "Turkey, Egypt and the Eastern Question," *Fraser's,* XCIII (January 1876), 1–12.
[116] "The Austrian Note," *The Spectator,* 8 January 1876, p. 36.

England's traditional policy toward Turkey was that of the venerable Lord Stratford de Redcliffe, the former ambassador of Britain who personally bore a material share of responsibility for the Crimean War. He could not be brought to suggesting the partition of Turkey, but in a letter to *The Times* written on the last day of the year, the great *Elchi* summoned England to step forth from isolation and join in active measures to solve the vexing problem of reform:

Under the circumstances, for England to be an idle looker-on seems hardly credible. Such an attitude with reference to interests so positive and perils so imminent would be a virtual abdication of her high position and its attendant duties. . . . . War on one side and an injurious dismemberment of Turkey on the other may surely be avoided by British influence, exercised from a suitable position. The Treaty of Paris gives us the right of acting with the other parties to it wherever the affairs of Turkey are concerned. If the three Northern Powers are left to themselves, they will, of course, be guided by their own views. There is no reason to mistrust Russia at present; but Russia is, nevertheless, one of the same triumvirate which partitioned Poland, and the retirement of England might be taken as her opportunity.

The moral insistence of England would in all likelihood be decisive in a conference of the five or the six Powers. Peace, the support of Turkey, its administrative, in particular, its financial improvement, and the equality of all classes of its population, would naturally be the main points of her policy; nor is there ground for apprehending opposition to such principles on the part of others. . . . . The measures in question are a superintendence of mixed organization internally, and a joint conventional pressure from without. The difficulties of this twofold arrangement would be far from insuperable, and the inconveniences would be compensated by the result.

These measures, reduced to a system, would doubtless amount to tutelage; but the Turkish Empire has long been virtually in that state, which, if it had been steadily as of right enforced, would have saved the Porte from its present embarrassments. . . . .

Stress has been laid in some newspaper articles on that clause in the Treaty of Paris which has an air of binding the Powers to abstain from interfering in the internal affairs of Turkey. But the engagement is, in truth, limited and conditional. The Christian plenipotentiaries promised only that the communication of the Sultan's reforms should not be held to warrant such interference. But other rights to interfere belong to the Powers, especially to those who either sided with the Porte in a moral sense or spent their money and shed their blood for the Sultan's cause in the Crimean War. The engagement, taken in its fullest interpretation, moreover, was an act of reliance on the Sultan's honour, and, consequently, resumable on the failure of that counterpledge. . . . . Their interference to the degree and in the manner proposed has no other object but that of saving Europe at large from a general war, and some of its States from the injurious effects of a rival's special aggrandizement; but the welfare of Turkey, as now circumstanced, would be a natural accompaniment of the plan herein suggested, and those who recommend it are the best friends of that Empire. . . . .[117]

On the same day that *The Times* published this penetrating view of England's relations to the problem—a letter which, be it noted, anticipated in general terms the Austrian program—Count Andrássy's note of 30 December was delivered at the London Foreign Office. The desire felt in Vienna for a prompt consideration was soon disappointed. Lord Derby had left London in mid-December and announced that local business in the north would not permit his return until 12 January, while the first cabinet meeting was scheduled to be held five days later. Beust suspected that it was a maneuver to gain time,[118] but his two colleagues, Shuvalov and Münster, looked upon the delay as an expression of British pique at the long wait to which London had been subjected.[119] Rather than leave the foreign secretary too long alone with the note, Beust sought an invitation to Derby's country estate and on the sixth journeyed to Knowsley to begin the arguments for British support. Before going he warned Andrássy not to expect him to return with "les poches pleines"; he knew that his host would not give a verdict before consulting his colleagues, and especially Disraeli, who was reported to be annoyed with Derby because of his speech in Edinburgh.[120] Despite the cordiality which the foreign minister had shown toward Austria, Beust was not at all convinced that the British cabinet would accept the Vienna proposals. On the eve of his departure he recalled again to Andrássy England's old tendency to isolation and reminded him that that proud state, once the arbiter of Eastern affairs, had been relegated to second rank with one power which was paralyzed if not entirely fallen and with another which was only recently born.[121]

The Austrian ambassador, consequently, was greatly surprised to find Derby sympathetic. Already the secretary had described the Andrássy note as "good in form and reasonable in tenour"[122] and to Beust he expressed his appreciation of the moderation which charac-

[117] *The Times,* 3 January 1876, p. 6, col. 6. Excerpts of the letter are in Thompson, *Public Opinion,* I, 260.

[118] Tels. Nos. 1 and 2, Beust to Andrássy, London, 3 January; SA, Varia Turquie I, 1875.

[119] Seton-Watson, *Slavonic Review,* III, 657.

[120] Report No. 2AF, Beust to Andrássy, 5 January; SA, Varia Turquie I, 1875.

[121] Report No. 2C, Beust to Andrássy, 5 January; *ibid.*

[122] *Slavonic Review,* III, 657–58.

terized it. In the discussion Derby wanted to go into the question of eventualities, but Beust sidestepped the issue by insisting that there could be no untoward eventualities if England supported the note, whereas if it were rejected England would be held responsible for whatever might ensue. The point regarding turning direct taxes back into the province—the point which had disturbed the French foreign minister—was the only one to which Derby seemed to take exception, and at the end of the day he promised to recommend British adherence to the prime minister.[123] That evening, evidently, Derby wrote his letter to Disraeli. In it he suggested that the time was past when Turkey's dignity and independence could be taken seriously; if the sultan could neither pay his debts nor keep order he had to suffer the consequences.[124]

The foreign secretary's willingness to co-operate did not find unanimous support among the British officials. Sir Henry Elliot had already telegraphed his condemnation of Andrássy's plan,[125] but the chief opposition was that expressed by the prime minister. Disraeli had nothing to say in favor of co-operating. The note he char-

---

[123] Tel., Montgelas to Andrássy, London, 8 January; SA, Varia Turquie I, 1875. Report No. 6 AG, Beust to Andrássy, 9 January; *ibid.*, in *First Red Book,* Doc. No. 214, with slight modification. Draft No. 27, Derby to Elliot, 14 January; FO 78/2448. Beust in reporting his conversation emphasized his understanding that a favorable response would be forthcoming at the end of the next week. Derby, on the other hand, made a special point in his account of his avoidance of a formal opinion or a commitment.

[124] Newton, *Lord Lyons,* II, 95.

[125] "I hardly see how such a note as proposed by Count Andrassy could be addressed to the Porte for most of the reforms suggested by him have already been adopted by the Porte. The Firman of the twelfth of December was officially communicated to the Embassies a day before it was promulgated, and they could not ask that it should be communicated a second time. A proposal to appoint a mixed commission of Musulmans and Christians to control the execution of the Reforms could not be made for one was appointed a fortnight ago, and sits daily to organize the details. Religious liberty is proclaimed except as regards rendering Christians liable to the military conscription. The abolition of the farming of the tithes is resolved upon. The Constitution and duties of the Provincial Councils are being defined. The remedies required for the improvement of the position of the agricultural population will come under the consideration of the Reform Commission, but they can only be judged by persons intimately acquainted with local habits and traditions, and I am not qualified to express an opinion upon those alluded to in Sir Andrew Buchanan's telegram. It is quite true that there is excitement and anxiety at Constantinople, and this should make the Powers careful not to do anything likely to produce exasperation among the Musulmans which might be the effect of an identic note such as is proposed" (Tel., Elliot to Derby, 3 January 1876; FO 78/2454).

acterized as "erroneous in principle and pernicious in practice"; and sending it to the Porte he thought "an act of imbecility or of treachery." He was afraid that accepting the Austrian program would embroil England in Turkey, and he foresaw considerable difficulty in Ireland if the cabinet urged on Turkey the principles of allocating direct taxes to local needs and of giving the peasantry the right to remove their ancient burdens when those principles were not applied beyond the Irish Sea. The premier had no counterproposals that would heal the Turkish malady, but at the same time he was reluctant to appear as Turkish or more Turkish than the Turks. "Could we not devise a course," he asked Derby, "wh. might avoid that?"[126]

Lord Carnarvon, the colonial secretary, joined Derby in urging acceptance, although he wanted to avoid the pitfall of pledging England to details.[127] The foreign office memorandum prepared by the permanent undersecretary raised no objections to English adherence except with regard to the embarrassing demands involving taxation and land rights.[128] Lord Salisbury, the secretary for India, found in the Andrássy text a danger that England would be led into a policy of intervention and he declared co-operation contrary to British tradition.[129]

These various objections came to light on 12 and 14 January when the ambassadors of France[130] and the imperial powers called on Derby, now returned to the foreign office, to urge his consent. The secretary expressed his personal opinion to Münster that England would accept the Vienna program with reservations as to its tax and land provisions,[131] but Shuvalov found him "timorous, hesitant, and little certain of the result" of the cabinet decision. In talking to the Russian ambassador Derby advanced numerous criticisms of the note, particularly for its attempt to regulate details of administration, and he stated that the two points under special attack were

[126] Disraeli to Derby, 9 January; *Disraeli*, VI, 18.

[127] Hardinge, *Carnarvon*, II, 327.

[128] "Turkish Reforms, memorandum by Lord Tenterden on Austrian Proposals, printed for the use of the Foreign Office, January 7, 1876"; FO 78/2529.

[129] Report No. 6C, Beust to Andrássy, 9 January; SA, Varia Turquie I, 1875.

[130] The French ambassador on the thirteenth left with Derby a résumé of the French foreign minister's arguments for British participation ("Précis of a despatch to H. E. M. d'Harcourt, dated Paris, January 4, 1876, and communicated to Lord Derby, January 13, 1876"; FO 27/2188). For text of the dispatch, see *First Yellow Book*, pp. 71-73.

[131] Tel. No. 11, Beust to Andrássy, 12 January; SA, Varia Turquie I, 1875.

"new and unknown in England." It was quite apparent to Shuvalov that the cabinet was divided between those who did not want to be isolated and those who did not want to be pulled along by the imperial league.[132] On the following day, 14 January, Beust went back to the Foreign Office armed with elaborate arguments from Andrássy with which to combat Lord Salisbury's fears of a military occupation[133] and renewed his plea for acceptance. The ambassador preached to Derby for an hour in every possible manner, as he reported to Vienna, but he came away from the interview feeling that he had accomplished nothing.[134]

Andrássy had already reconciled himself to accepting English reservations, "pourvu qu'elles soient véritablement légères,"[135] and after he had received Beust's report of his last interview he became so anxious for immediate action that he was willing for Derby either to support specific parts of his program or merely to advise the Turks not to reject it. Turkey was showing signs of tractability, and if there were no further delays in England to encourage the Porte, he hoped for success.[136] Beust carried this message to Derby and on the eve of the cabinet meeting he telegraphed to Vienna: "I have exhausted all the arguments possible and I have even resorted, not without success, to asking for personal reasons that the responsibility of a refusal should not be placed on me."[137]

On the morning of 17 January the leading editorial of The Times

---

[132] Slavonic Review, III, 658–59. Cf. Draft No. 26, Derby to Elliot, 13 January; Turkey No. 2 (1876), Doc. No. 62.

[133] Two unnumbered telegrams, Andrássy to Beust, Budapest, 11 January; SA, Varia Turquie I, 1875. Andrássy was at best no friend of Beust, but the latter's conduct of the negotiations in London had been highly unsatisfactory to the foreign minister and on several occasions he had subjected the ambassador to sharp reprimands for the content and phraseology of his reports. In one of the telegrams above Andrássy took Beust seriously to task for not representing properly his opposition to occupation.

Salisbury's objection had all the more point to it since, only a short time before, in the Hungarian diet Premier Tisza had given an equivocal reply to an interpellation regarding an eventual occupation. Andrássy's second telegram ordered Beust to explain the incident as being motivated by the necessity for holding the sword of Damocles over "the revolutionary Slavic elements" to prevent them from pushing Serbia and Montenegro into war on Turkey.

[134] Tel. No. 14, Beust to Andrássy, 14 January; ibid. Cf., Draft No. 23, Derby to Buchanan, 18 January; Turkey No. 2 (1876), Doc. No. 63.

[135] Tel. No. 46, Andrássy to Beust, 10 January; SA, Varia Turquie I, 1875.

[136] Tel. No. 72, Andrássy to Beust, 15 January; ibid.

[137] Tel. No. 16, Beust to Andrássy, 17 January; ibid.

called on the cabinet to accept Andrássy's note,[138] and before the day was over the Turkish ambassador himself did likewise.[139] The influential Lord Lyons had also by this time sent in his recommendation favoring adherence.[140] It is not certain which arguments and considerations determined the cabinet's decision. Disraeli later indicated that Turkey's request for British participation was the important factor; "we can't be more Turkish than the Sultan," he wrote[141] —but of course the indication is Disraeli's. At all events, Derby's prediction was confirmed: the cabinet agreed to give the Andrássy program "a general support" without committing itself to details.[142]

Beust was quite satisfied with the British decision; it was an indication at any rate that the cabinet would not pursue a policy of isolation.[143] Shuvalov, on the contrary, saw the shadows. In his opinion the cabinet was not moved by ideas of humanity and civilization; its acceptance had been forced by the influence exerted by the allied powers over Europe.[144] The Duke Decazes in Paris was no little pleased with the report from London,[145] but in Vienna it was deemed imperative to know just what "a general support" really

[138] *The Times* (London), 17 January 1876, p. 9, col. 1.

[139] Tel., Rashid to Musurus in London, Constantinople, 15 January, communicated to Derby 17 January; FO 78/2527. Elliot to Derby, 13 January; *Turkey No. 2 (1876)*, Doc. No. 60.

[140] Lyons to Derby, Paris, 14 January; Newton, *Lord Lyons*, II, 95–96.

[141] Disraeli to Lady Bradford, 18 January; *Disraeli*, VI, 19. Zetland, *op. cit.*, II, 11.

[142] Tel. No. 17, Beust to Andrássy, 18 January; *First Red Book*, Doc. No. 219, incomplete. "Foreign Office, Jan. 18/76. Private. Dear Count Beust, We have agreed to give a general support to the note of your government, details being reserved for further consideration. You can make use of this as you think fit. Very truly yours, Derby" (in Report No. 7AC, Beust to Andrássy, 19 January; SA, Varia Turquie I, 1875).

[143] Report 7AC, Beust to Andrássy, 19 January; SA, Varia Turquie I, 1875. The effect which the decision had on the relations between Beust and Andrássy is revealed in a letter which the ambassador wrote soon afterward: ". . . . At last came the despatch, and I was obliged to run after Derby at Knowsley and to spend three weeks here in making the greatest exertions in order to overcome the reluctance of the English Government to join the other Powers. I succeeded at last, and everybody complimented me here on my victory. But from Vienna not a word of thanks. I have done my duty—sapienti sat. I have supported energetically a policy which I did not quite understand; this was my duty . . . ." (Beust to Worms, London, February 1876; *Memoirs*, I, lxxxi).

[144] Shuvalov to Gorchakov, 21 January/2 February; *Slavonic Review*, III, 659.

[145] Decazes to d'Harcourt, 21 January; *Documents français*, II, Doc. No. 32. Cf. *First Yellow Book*, pp. 84–85.

meant and whether or not the English cabinet wanted to add an explanation before action was undertaken in Constantinople.[146] On 22 January Beust took these questions to the Foreign Office and repeated the intention of the allies to demand a written promise from Turkey. Derby's response was not very satisfactory to an impatient minister in the Ballplatz. He suggested that in a few days he would give Beust a full statement of British views and that, further, it would be better to delay the step in Constantinople until Elliot had received his instructions. He promised not to make specific objection to the points disapproved in London, but refused to join the other powers in demanding a written reply. The foreign secretary was untouched by Beust's protests of urgency. "It would not be kind of me," he said to the ambassador in a somewhat sharp but polite tone, "to tell you from whom came the delay."[147]

Andrássy, however, was in no mood for further loss of time. If Derby would support his demand for a written reply, he telegraphed to London, he was prepared to wait a few days; otherwise he proposed to go forward with his plan.[148] Prince Gorchakov had become no less impatient to proceed. On 24 January both Beust and Shuvalov attacked the British refusal to force a written promise from the Porte. The Austrian ambassador this time resorted to a note urging immediate support of this measure[149] and his colleague called in person. Shuvalov obtained nothing but a vague promise "that we should use our best endeavours to bring about an agreement between the Porte and the Powers who had undertaken to offer advice in the present juncture."[150] The reply to Beust, delivered on the following day, was a thirty-seven-page letter. One by one Derby analyzed the points of the Andrássy program, only to confirm the views which had

[146] Tel., Andrássy to Beust, 20 January; SA, Varia Turquie I, 1875.

[147] Tel. No. 18, Beust to Andrássy, 22 January, Report No. 8AE, 24 January; ibid. Dispatch No. 39, Derby to Buchanan, 24 January; *Turkey No. 2 (1876)*, Doc. No. 70. More than a week before, when Shuvalov was deploring the loss of precious time the English were causing, Derby reminded the ambassador that it had taken Vienna two and a half months to communicate the note and he did not see why England should not take a fortnight to frame a reply (*Slavonic Review*, III, 658).

[148] Tel. No. 3, Andrássy to Beust, Vienna, 23 January; SA, Varia Turquie I, 1875.

[149] Beust to Derby, 24 January; in Report No. 8B, Beust to Andrássy, 24 January; *ibid.;* also in FO 7/887. The note is paraphrased in Dispatch No. 44, Derby to Buchanan, 25 January; *Turkey No. 2 (1876)*, Doc. No. 71.

[150] Dispatch No. 35, Derby to Loftus in St. Petersburg, 25 January; FO 65/931.

been held in England for the previous fortnight. The three points acceptable to the cabinet were represented as being already granted or applied in Turkey. The other two measures, involving direct taxes and state aid for land purchase, remained still beyond the pale of British acceptance. As to the former, the note declared that it was "scarcely sufficiently explained for Her Majesty's Government to be able to appreciate its scope," and then proceeded to make it plain that Her Majesty's Government found the proposal distinctly undesirable. With regard to the demand for financial aid to the peasants it stated that the cabinet found "many difficulties both of principle and detail." The letter ended on a not unfriendly note, although it pointedly stated British expectation that Russia and Austria in exchange for "a general support" would do all that was possible to bring the rebellion to an end:

> Your Excellency will have observed from the foregoing remarks that Her Majesty's Government see nothing in the five points proposed by Count Andrassy to which they cannot give a general support; although, on the other hand, the proposed reforms relating to taxation and grants of land involve in their detailed application to districts like Bosnia and Herzegovina many questions upon which they are not prepared, in their present state of information, to offer a definite opinion. . . . .
>
> They rely upon the assurances contained in Count Andrassy's despatch, and upon those which your Excellency has conveyed to me, that, if these suggestions are carried into effect, the Austro-Hungarian Government will, in concert with the other Powers whose united action Count Andrassy has invited, use their best exertions to prevent the spread of the movement and to induce the insurgents to submit, or effectually preclude them from receiving assistance from beyond the frontier, should they persist in continuing the struggle.
>
> Her Majesty's Ambassador at Constantinople will accordingly be instructed to give a general support to the proposals of the Austro-Hungarian Government, and to act with his colleagues for this purpose.[151]

The British answer to the important question of the written guaranty from Turkey was contained in the instructions sent to Sir Henry Elliot on the same day. The tenor of these instructions was more friendly toward the Andrássy program than might have been expected. Indeed the whole responsibility for the existing situation was laid directly at the Sublime Porte on the ground that the Turks had not accepted the British advice of the preceding August and had not treated the rebellion as purely an internal problem. No mention was made of the points to which the cabinet had taken exception;

[151] Derby to Beust, 25 January; *Turkey No. 2 (1876)*, Doc. No. 72.

in fact, the whole Andrássy program was characterized as "little more than a request that the Porte will execute" its former pledges, and it was not deemed to be in conflict with the Treaty of Paris. Derby did not order Elliot to demand a written commitment, but he counseled the Porte not to raise any difficulties about the proffered advice and about "communicating to the Powers in some form the measures which may be proposed in consequence." Elliot was to recall to the Turks that numerous Turkish measures in the past had been so communicated. Derby himself would not suggest how this might be done, but, he added, "it would not be wise that too great regard should be paid to mere formalities. What appears to Her Majesty's Government to be essential is that the Porte should act promptly and vigorously in the execution of the reforms. . . . ."[152]

Thus a second time within a few months Great Britain had been drawn into an interference in the affairs of Turkey, an interference which had been presented in London after the details had been arranged in the capitals of the league of the three emperors. A second time, too, England accepted with bad grace because Turkey herself invited that acceptance and because there seemed nothing else to do.

TURKEY AND THE ANDRÁSSY NOTE

For some time before the completion of the Andrássy note the Turks had shown signs of aversion to a formal interference by the European powers. The reform proclamations of October and December had been inspired by the desire to circumvent such an attack on the sultan's sovereignty. Count Andrássy had given unmistakable warning at the Sublime Porte that, spontaneous reforms or no spontaneous reforms, he was determined to proceed with his own plans; but the ministers in Constantinople were not, as has been seen, intimidated. They published their *ferman* of 12 December in defiance of Vienna and, although they offered to hear friendly advice, they let it be known that they would not brook a foreign inter-

---

[152] Draft No. 52, Derby to Elliot, 25 January; *Turkey No. 2 (1876),* Doc. No. 73. A telegraphic summary of these written instructions was sent to Constantinople on the same day (Draft No. 61; FO 78/2448) with permission to act at once. Derby, seemingly moved by a desire to give Austria and Russia some of their own medicine of delay, asked the other powers to delay their action until the extended dispatch arrived on 2 February (Tel. No. 23, Beust to Andrássy, 29 January; SA, Varia Turquie I, 1875. Draft No. 68, Derby to Elliot, 29 January; FO 78/2448).

vention.[153] The grand vizier declared emphatically that if any written communication were addressed to him he would resign and his place would probably be taken by the doctrinaire Midhat or the bellicose Hussein Avni.[154] Threats and refusals, however, made Andrássy no less determined. He assumed the role of a wise mother preparing medicine for a reluctant child. He told the ailing Turk that, despite bad conduct in not heeding previous advice, he was intent on administering a draught which would improve his condition.[155]

The Porte was not disposed to be content with Andrássy's assurance that the medicine would be palatable.[156] On the contrary, Ottoman touchiness in the first days of the new year was more marked than ever. Rumor had come to the Turks that the powers were going to descend on them with an identic note, a procedure which would be an intolerable humiliation to imperial sovereignty. The grand vizier, in high indignation, again proclaimed his determination not to receive an official communication on the subject of reforms,[157] and the Turkish representatives abroad were instructed to protest against the rumored measure.[158]

[153] Report No. 105AF, Beust to Andrássy, London, 8 December; SA, Varia Turquie I, 1875.

[154] Letter No. 3, Gorchakov to Novikov, St. Petersburg, 20 December 1875/1 January 1876; ibid.

[155] Tel. No. 312, Andrássy to Zichy, 30 December; ibid. Tel. No. 175, Zichy to Andrássy, 31 December; ibid.

[156] Tel. No. 1, Andrássy to Zichy, 1 January 1876; ibid.

[157] Report No. 6, Elliot to Derby, 4 January; FO 78/2454: "The probability of an identic Note being sent by the Powers has produced a great sensation at the Porte. The Minister for Foreign Affairs is unwell and I have not seen him, but the Grand Vizier spoke to me with unusual energy of his determination not to receive any official communication on the subject of the reforms. If the Powers have remarks to make about them they may submit them unofficially but he declares that he will not lay any official communication before the Sultan, who, having upon his advice consented to important measures of reform, would regard it as an affront." The same language was held to Ignatiev (Bourgoing to Decazes, 3 January; Documents français, II, Doc. No. 27), to the Italian minister (Corti to Visconti-Venosta, 4 January; First Green Book, Doc. No. LXXXIV), and to the French ambassador (Bourgoing to Decazes, 5 January; First Yellow Book, p. 73).

[158] Report No. 4, Elliot to Derby, 4 January; FO 78/2454. The text of the Turkish protest as delivered in London (Rashid to Musurus, Constantinople, 3 January; FO 78/2527) is as follows: "Nous apprenons de différentes sources que le projet de réformes élaboré par le Comte Andrassy aurait été achevé et communiqué aux deux autres Cours Impériales, et que des pourparlers auraient été entamés entre les grandes Puissances pour arriver à une entente et nous communiquer ce projet avec demande d'exécution, sous la forme d'une note identique ou collective.

On the fifth and sixth, the various ambassadors undertook to carry out their instructions. In London Musurus Pasha was unable to win any victory. He had to talk with the undersecretary, Lord Tenterden, and his emphasis on the seriousness of the state of affairs could not elicit much comfort from a subordinate official without instructions. Nor could his request for a copy of the Andrássy note be met. The interview, Tenterden reported to his chief, "was not a very pleasant one. . . . . He [Musurus] seemed very much excited and annoyed. . . . ."[159] The pasha laid great hopes on England's refusal to join the other powers. He went about London offering arguments for the Turkish point of view;[160] he affirmed solemnly to Derby that his government would decline to accept the impending note.[161] There was anticipation at the Porte, apparently, that the

Quoique cette nouvelle ne nous ait été confirmée d'aucune part, nous croyons devoir, en prévision de l'éventualité à laquelle elle a trait, faire connaître dès à présent notre manière de voir et la façon dont nous envisageons une telle proposition, si elle venait à se produire dans les termes que j'ai indiqués. Votre Excellence sait avec quel sentiment de déférence la Sublime Porte a toujours accueilli les conseils qui lui ont été donnés par les Puissances amies et alliées du Sultan, toutes les fois que ces conseils lui sont parvenus sous forme d'avis amicaux. Mais nous déclarons dès à présent, pour ne laisser subsister aucun doute, aucune équivoque sur nos intentions, dont ces mêmes Puissances se sont toujours plu à constater la loyauté, que, si, contrairement à toute attente, et malgré nos efforts tendant à éviter une telle extrémité, une démarche de cette nature venait à se produire, nous nous verrions dans la pénible nécessité de la décliner, et cela uniquement en vue de sauvegarder le principe des droits souverains de la Sublime Porte. Je le répète, rien, jusqu'à l'heure qu'il est, n'est venu confirmer l'existence d'une telle combinaison, et l'assurance qui nous a été donnée par le Comte Andrassy, lors de la communication qui lui a été faite du dernier Firman, de ne point nous créer des difficultés et des embarras, nous permet d'en douter; mais je m'en crois pas moins devoir vous prier de vous énoncer dès à présent dans ce sens auprès de Son Excellence le Ministre des Affaires Etrangères."

159 Memorandum of Lord Tenterden, 5 January; FO 78/2527. Musurus also tried to secure a copy of the Andrássy note from Beust, but failed (Tel. No. 8, Beust to Andrássy, 8 January; SA, Varia Turquie I, 1875).

160 Report No. 6B, Beust to Andrássy, 9 January; ibid.

161 Draft No. 28, Derby to Elliot, 14 January; FO 78/2448: "The Turkish Ambassador called upon me on the 13th instant and proceeded to discuss the question of the Austrian Note. He argued in strong terms against the possibility of its being accepted by the Porte. Such a course, he said, would be suicidal: the certainty of war, or the loss of a province, would be a less evil than submission to what the Sultan could only regard as an insult. It would be fatal to his influence over his own subjects: and the discontent which would be produced by such a step would even endanger his throne. He assured me that whatever advice might be given, or whoever might give it, the Turkish Government must decline to accept the note."

British cabinet would hold aloof,[162] but it was an anticipation which soon proved groundless.[163]

In Rome the Turkish representative had no greater success with the declaration.[164] The Italian foreign minister politely denied any intention of doing anything derogatory to Turkish dignity,[165] but in a few days the king's representative in Constantinople lectured Rashid Pasha on the seriousness of Turkey's assuming the responsibility for a refusal.[166] In Paris the Turkish protest was equally futile. Decazes spoke in plain language to Sadik Pasha and his government about the inadvisability of their course and informed them of France's intention to maintain the European concert.[167] In Berlin Bülow summarily told Aristarchi Bey that since the Turks did not know anything about the negotiations they had no occasion to make a declaration.[168]

In St. Petersburg the answer given to Cabouli Pasha was equally categorical. Prince Gorchakov refused to listen to a Turkish protest and informed the ambassador that the Great Powers would accept no dictation as to the form of their communications.[169] In Vienna the caution of Andrássy spared Aarifi Pasha the pain of hearing

---

[162] Tel. No. 6, Zichy to Andrássy, 11 January; SA, Varia Turquie I, 1875: "Raschid Pascha, den ich soeben bei mir zu Tische hatte, teilte mir vertraulich mit, dass seiner Nachricht zufolge England sich den Propositionen der Mächte nicht anschliessen werde."

[163] While the British ministers were considering the note a rumor spread through the various capitals that Musurus, on his own initiative, had offered England certain concessions in Egypt in exchange for refusal to support the Andrássy note (Tel. No. 7, Zichy to Andrássy, 12 January; ibid. Tel., Andrássy to Beust, 15 January; ibid. Tel. No. 8, Langenau to Andrássy, 14 January; ibid.). Lord Derby denied the rumor emphatically (Tel. No. 16, Beust to Andrássy, 17 January; ibid.), and so did Rashid Pasha. The Foreign Office records have no account of such a proposal. See also Le Flô to Decazes, 9 January; Documents français, II, Doc. No. 29, and note.

[164] Tel. No. 5, Wimpffen to Andrássy, Rome, 6 January; First Red Book, Doc. No. 211.   [165] Report No. 6, Paget to Derby, Rome, 6 January; FO 45/284.

[166] Corti to Visconti-Venosta, 12 January; First Green Book, Doc. No. XC.

[167] Decazes to Bourgoing, 7 January; First Yellow Book, pp. 74–77. Decazes to Le Flô, 10 January; Documents français, II, Doc. No. 30. Ibid., p. 38, note.

[168] Tel., Károlyi to Andrássy, Berlin, 6 January; SA, Varia Turquie I, 1875. Aristarchi was embarrassed by his instructions and felt that his government had been precipitate in its decision. He devised a compromise proposal but, not having the courage to send it directly to the Sublime Porte, asked the British ambassador to forward it through British channels as an anonymous suggestion (Report No. 14, Russell to Derby, Berlin, 8 January; FO 64/850).

[169] Tel. No. 6, Langenau to Andrássy, St. Petersburg, 11 January; SA, Varia Turquie I, 1875. Circular Tel. from Andrássy, Budapest, 11 January; ibid.

an irritated and pointed comment. The Austrian foreign minister was determined that the Turks should not at such a late hour destroy his program. But, ever desirous of a united front of the three powers, he sought the approval of Germany and Russia before delivering his own peremptory reply.[170] Gorchakov was in entire agreement with Andrássy,[171] as was the German government,[172] and instructions were immediately sent to Constantinople to inform the Turks that they could not interfere with the intentions of the powers.[173]

The intimation of an impending collective step in Constantinople which had inspired the Turkish protests seems to be traceable directly to General Ignatiev.[174] The Russian ambassador was still intent on undermining the Andrássy program if he could. Now that his own government had gone so far as to approve the final draft of the note, his only means lay in stirring the Turks to resistance and in spreading the news that the Porte would not receive an official note from the powers. In Constantinople he made no secret of his hostility[175] and, when he saw a copy of the note, he telegraphed to Gorchakov that "in all his experience, he had never seen a diplomatic document drawn up in more unbecoming terms, or more calculated

[170] Tel., Andrássy to Langenau, 7 January; *First Red Book,* Doc. No. 212 incomplete: ". . . . There has never been a question of a collective démarche at the Porte, whose dignity has been taken into consideration. As to a protest against an identic communication, since the views were identic the communication could only be the same. At bottom it is immaterial whether the communication be made verbally or otherwise. But it is necessary to make it in writing or to deliver a copy of it in order to obtain a written response. I share completely the opinion of Prince Gorchakov and I consider it indispensable to obtain from Turkey an acknowledgement of receipt having the value of an engagement. This result cannot be obtained if we allow the Ottoman government to impose on us conditions regarding the form to be given to our step. . . . ."

[171] Tel. No. 3, Langenau to Andrássy, 8 January; SA, Varia Turquie I, 1875.

[172] Tel., Károlyi to Andrássy, Berlin, 12 January; *ibid.*

[173] Tels. Nos. 6, 7, Langenau to Andrássy, 11, 12 January, respectively; *ibid.* Tel. No. 40, Andrássy to Zichy, 9 January; *First Red Book,* Doc. No. 215. Gorchakov showed his telegram to Ignatiev (drawn up in the sense of Andrássy's communication of 7 January) to the representatives of Germany, France, and Italy, and asked them to invite their governments to send comparable declarations to Constantinople (Tel. No. 5, Langenau to Andrássy, 10 January; *First Red Book,* Doc. No. 217. Le Flô to Decazes, 9 January; *Documents français,* II, Doc. No. 29).

[174] Report No. 8, Elliot to Derby, 4 January; FO 78/2454. "There is reason to believe," the British ambassador telegraphed, "that the Porte learnt the intention of the three Powers to send an identic Note from the Russian ambassador. Several days ago he said to a person who has repeated his words to me that the Porte was resolved not to accept such a Note."

[175] Bourgoing to Decazes, 3 January; *Documents français,* II, Doc. No. 27.

to give offense and do mischief."[176] Meeting with no fortune in arguing against St. Petersburg's compliance toward Andrássy, the general resorted to alarms. He telegraphed to the Russian chancellor that the sultan was so nervous about the imminent intervention that he would not even see the grand vizier and that, further, the Turks would demand in return for acceptance a concession, an "equivalent," consisting of submission of the insurgents and the closing of the Montenegrin and Dalmatian frontiers.[177] It is quite possible that Ignatiev himself recommended some such conditions to the Turks, as rumor had it from an allegedly good source that he did.[178] At all

[176] "I had some conversation this afternoon with General Ignatiew whom I found as bitterly hostile as ever to Count Andrassy's proposal. I said I had not yet seen it, but was glad to hear that there was no intention of addressing an identic Note to the Porte. He replied, no, that that project had been abandoned, but he could affirm emphatically, tho' in strict confidence, that it had been dropped only in consequence of his own warnings that it would not be accepted.

"He had not received the project as it now stands as four Russian mails are detained at Odessa by the ice, but he had seen what had been sent to Count Zichy, and he had telegraphed to Prince Gortchakow that, in all his experience, he had never seen a diplomatic document drawn up in more unbecoming terms, or more calculated to give offense and do mischief. In the despatch accompanying the proposed instruction mention was made of the incompatibility of the Crescent and the Cross, of the necessity of putting the Christians upon an equality with Islam, and other expressions of a character offensive to the people of this country.

"If such a Despatch was made public, as it certainly would be, General Ignatiew would undertake to say that two years would not pass before we should have to repent of it. The first result to be expected from the communication of the instructions was evidently the dismissal of the Grand Vizier, and the interruption of all the reforms which he is now endeavouring to carry out. His successor would probably be either Hussein Pasha or Midhat Pasha neither of whom would be more disposed to listen to the Foreign Powers.

"When his instructions arrived, he should execute them with reluctance; but he hoped that in spite of what he thought objectionable in the scheme, Her Majesty's Government would consent to join in it, and put an end to the isolated action of the three Northern Powers. I replied laughingly that, if the proposal was at all such as he had depicted, I sincerely hoped that Her Majesty's Government would refuse to have anything to do with it, and leave its undivided patronage to those who had concerted it" (Report No. 29, Elliot to Derby, 9 January; FO 78/2454).

[177] Report No. 52, Elliot to Derby, 14 January; FO 78/2454. Tel. No. 7, Langenau to Andrássy, 12 January; SA, Varia Turquie I, 1875.

[178] There was a statement in Berlin, which the Austrian ambassador took seriously, to the effect that Ignatiev had advised the Turks to accept the reform note on two conditions: closing of the Dalmatian coast and a free hand against Montenegro (Report No. 3AB, Károlyi to Andrássy, 22 January; ibid.). Certain it is that Rashid discreetly raised the question to Zichy and Ignatiev whether Turkey, in exchange for acceptance, would be permitted untrammeled military operations against the insurgents and, in case the Montenegrins pursued their activities, against them as well (Report No. 3AH, Zichy to Andrássy, 11 January; ibid.). Gorchakov informed Constantinople that the Russian Empire would never

events he continued to do his utmost to inspire distrust of Andrássy[179] and represented Andrássy's project as "preposterous."[180]

permit a Turkish occupation of Montenegro (Tel. No. 10, Langenau to Andrássy,
18 January; *ibid.* Report No. 6AC, Langenau to Andrássy, 14/26 January; *ibid.*).
    [179] Report No. 41, Elliot to Derby, 12 January; FO 78/2454. One of the
Turkish officials held that Ignatiev was conspiring also to undermine the British
on whom he had been calling desperately for aid. "Having called today on Dervish
Pasha for the purpose of congratulating him on his appointment as Minister of
Marine, His Excellency said he had received a congratulatory visit from the
Russian Dragoman also charged with a confidential message from General Igna-
tiew. This was to the effect that Russia being now a true friend to Turkey, he
sincerely hoped to see Dervish Pasha placed very soon at the head of the War
Department, but that in the meanwhile he wished to put him on his guard against
the professions of sympathy and friendship which continue to proceed from the
English, and that no confidence should on any account be placed in Hobart Pasha
[the British commander of the Turkish fleet].
    "In requesting me to consider this communication strictly confidential, Dervish
Pasha wished me to understand that greater efforts were being made by the
Russian Embassy to excite suspicion and distrust of the English in the minds of
the other Turkish Ministers also, but that for his own part he had little difficulty
in discerning the real from the pretended friends of his country" (Report No. 7,
Sandison to Elliot, Pera, 10 January, in Report No. 80, Elliot to Derby;
FO 78/2454).
    In mid-January Count Zichy developed the idea that it would be a good thing if
Ignatiev were transferred to Vienna and his place taken in Constantinople by Novikov. "In order to see to it that no decisive activity takes place here, there is no
better means, in my opinion, than to get General Ignatiev away" (Private letter,
Zichy to Andrássy, 11 January; SA, Varia Turquie, 1876).
    Andrássy, however, was apparently so convinced of the support of Tsar
Alexander and Gorchakov that he was not overly concerned about the intrigues
of Ignatiev. The British ambassador after a talk with the minister late in December on the subject of Ignatiev made this report: ". . . . Count Andrassy appeared,
however, to think that the proceedings of the Russian ambassador had rather
injured than advanced the interests of Russia in the East, having alienated from
her the sympathies of the Greeks, and of the Bulgarians and of the Christians
generally, while he was looked upon with suspicion by the Turks. Therefore,
though he knew Count Zichy to be 'in His Excellency's pocket,' he had not found
upon the whole any great inconvenience from the relations existing between
them . . . ." (Report No. 441, Buchanan to Derby, 27 December 1875; FO 7/853).
    Andrássy, none the less, was moved once more to admonish his ambassador to
Turkey: ". . . . From St. Petersburg I am informed that General Ignatiev has
such complete knowledge of all events that he has seen the letters in which I
warned you not to place so much trust in him. I do not believe this, nevertheless
I request you, while maintaining intact your outward relations with Ignatiev, calming him with regard to our opinion of him, etc., to impose on yourself a *strict
reserve* in all communications with him. Your Excellency should give to him only
those communications necessary for the furthering of the common action, because
I am not convinced that he will not misuse other communications" (Andrássy to
Zichy, 26 January 1876; SA, Varia Turquie I, 1875).
    [180] "I found Raschid Pasha today extremely well disposed to receive the com-
munication by Austria in a good spirit. He said however that the Porte is greatly

Ignatiev's stratagems and threats were no more effective than his arguments. The tide of public opinion in favor of the oppressed Slavs was rising in Russia; Wesselitsky-Bojidarovitch was lecturing about his experiences in the revolted area,[181] and Red Cross delegates were enrolling for service there. But the higher officials remained committed to the Andrássy plan and hopeful of its success. Nelidov, secretary of the Constantinople embassy, tried to tell Gorchakov and Jomini of the dangers ahead, but, said Nelidov, their minds were closed.[182] Ignatiev was instructed to inform the Porte that the powers would not be dictated to about their communication[183] and that the Turkish answer had to be a promise to carry out the proposed reforms.[184]

Some time before all these sharp messages were received in Constantinople the Turks realized that their protest had been too hasty. It became apparent that the powers were going forward with their program regardless of what might be said at the Sublime Porte. The conventions of diplomacy made a collective step highly derogatory, and when it was learned, to the great relief of the sultan's trembling ministers, that not only was no such action to take place[185] but also that there was no overt desire to subject Turkey to a technical humiliation, a way was open for retreat. The Ottoman foreign minister and representatives abroad had the task, a week after launching their protest, of explaining that they had been misunderstood. It was far from his thought, Rashid wrote personally to Andrássy, to say that he would decline to receive any communication whatsoever:

What we wished to say, without even thinking of pretending to lay down conditions regarding the steps agreed upon by the powers, was that, at the

---

perplexed by the difference between the language held by Prince Gortchakow to the Ottoman Ambassador at St. Petersburg and that of General Ignatiew here. The former strongly urges a favourable reception, while the latter represents the project as preposterous. Raschid Pasha asked whether I thought the Ambassador was acting under instructions or upon his own impulse. I said that in my opinion General Ignatiew was actuated partly by personal feeling against Count Andrassy, and partly by the wish which he had always shown to inspire the Porte with distrust of Austria. The Porte ought therefore to listen to him with caution" (Report No. 47, Elliot to Derby, 13 January; FO 78/2454).

[181] See his *Dix mois de ma vie, 1875–1876, passim.*

[182] Nelidov, *Revue des deux mondes,* XXVII (1915), 308–10.

[183] Le Flô to Decazes, 9 January; *Documents français,* II, Doc. No. 29.

[184] Tel. No. 7, Langenau to Andrássy, 12 January; SA, Varia Turquie I, 1875.

[185] Report No. 16, Elliot to Derby, 6 January; FO 78/2454.

moment when our recent reforms are being put into execution and are receiving the benevolent approbation of the powers, a communication made in an official way [*faite d'une manière toute officielle*] . . . . would have placed us in the most embarrassing position in the face of the sovereign and of the country and would have been hardly in harmony with the sovereign rights of the Porte. But we have never wished to let it be understood that we would refuse to listen to the friendly counsels which would be given to us. . . . .

The trouble had arisen, the various foreign offices were told, from the "impenetrable mystery" as to the nature of the Andrássy project and from the threatening rumors of an identic or collective communication from the powers.[186] The combination of assurances regarding the sultan's dignity on the one hand and the obvious determination of the imperial powers on the other made the Turks more compliant. The one hope for security against excessive and humiliating pressure from the foreign states was that friendly England should be a party to the representations; there was good reason to believe that the government which fought for Turkey in the Crimean War would not permit the others to go too far. Consequently, on 13 January, when the contents of the Andrássy note were fairly well known in Constantinople,[187] Rashid invited British participa-

---

[186] Personal letter, Rashid to Andrássy, 19 January, in Report No. 6AD, Zichy to Andrássy, 21 January; SA, Varia Turquie I, 1875. Tel. No. 5, Zichy to Andrássy, 10 January; *First Red Book*, Doc. No. 216, incomplete. Rashid claimed to Zichy, according to the telegram cited above that the original instructions had been sent to Vienna during his illness. Rashid was apparently ill at the time (Report No. 6, Elliot to Derby, 4 January; FO 78/2454. Report No. 6AC, Langenau to Andrássy, 14/26 January; SA, Varia Turquie I, 1875).

[187] How the Turks learned the details of the Austrian reforms proved a puzzle in Europe for a time. Zichy claimed on 4 January that Elliot had told him in strict confidence that he had received from the British ambassador in Vienna knowledge of the substance and the form of the Andrássy note. Zichy also professed to have grounds for believing that Elliot had promptly informed the Turks and that Elliot's communication had inspired their circular protest of 3 January (Tel. No. 1, Zichy to Andrássy, 4 January; SA, Varia Turquie I, 1875). Elliot, on the other hand, attributed the Turkish protest to the machinations of Ignatiev (Report No. 8, Elliot to Derby, 3 January; FO 78/2454). The French ambassador was inclined to believe the same (Bourgoing to Decazes, 3 January; *Documents français*, II, Doc. No. 27). On 9 January Elliot stated in a dispatch to his government that he had told Ignatiev that day that he had not yet seen the Andrássy note (Report No. 29, Elliot to Derby, 9 January; FO 78/2454). A copy was sent to him from London on 3 January (Derby to Elliot, 3 January: *Turkey No. 2 [1876]*, Doc. No. 56). It would appear certain that Musurus did not secure any information from the British Foreign Office. On 5 January or later Derby wrote a marginal notation on Tenterden's memorandum of 5 January (FO 78/2527): "I do not think it is for us to communicate the note. It is an Austrian, not an English document." *The Times* in its second edition

tion[188] and two days later a formal request was telegraphed to London.[189] The grand vizier, however, felt himself slipping from his position of favor in the eyes of an excited sovereign, and on 20 January asked Andrássy to begin the negotiations without further delay.[190] Already the Porte, in anticipation of the demands, had begun to prepare

---

of 7 January printed a telegram from Constantinople which stated that Zichy had already confidentially given the note to the Porte. The Austrian chargé d'affaires, seeing that the news was creating no little danger to British support, hastened to make a formal denial at the Foreign Office (Tel. No. 6, Montgelas to Andrássy, London, 7 January; SA, Varia Turquie I, 1875). Andrássy denied it hastily but, evidently a little worried despite a belief in Elliot's culpability, asked Zichy for a denial (Tel. No. 35, Andrássy to Zichy, 8 January; *ibid.* Tel. No. 33, Andrássy to Montgelas, 8 January; *ibid.*). The ambassador categorically repudiated the charge (Tel. No. 3, Zichy to Andrássy, 9 January; *ibid.*) and Elliot reported Zichy's statement to London (Tel. No. 8, Beust to Andrássy, 8 January; *ibid.*). Beust did not believe Elliot had revealed the note, but Andrássy persisted in his conviction (Tel., Andrássy to Beust, 20 January; *ibid.*). By 9 January Ignatiev had not received the final draft of the note but he had seen Zichy's copy (Report No. 29, Elliot to Derby, 9 January; FO 78/2454), and had had for some time a clear notion of the Vienna proposals. It is perhaps safe to assume that the Porte's early knowledge came from the Russian ambassador.

[188] Report No. 45, Elliot to Derby, 13 January; *Turkey No. 2 (1876)*, Doc. No. 60. Two days later the Turkish foreign minister repeated the invitation prefaced by an explanation of the reasons for protesting against written communications. The statement of what the Turks would receive and would not receive was a little bolder in the note to London than in Rashid's personal letter to Andrássy which was written four days later. In the telegram destined for Lord Derby the Turkish minister announced his willingness to hear *"toute communication qui nous serait faite sous une forme non écrite, non signée et non remise ainsi officiellement entre nos mains, mais bien sans forme, par exemple, de communication verbale."* The form of communication which the Turks were specifying in London would have made impossible the written response having the character of a binding engagement which Andrássy was intent on receiving from the Porte. Pretending for the moment that there was to be only a verbal communication of the note, Rashid concluded his telegram: "Nous sommes donc, en présence du nouvel état de choses, tout disposés à écouter, sous la forme voulue que je viens de mentionner, les bons conseils des Puissances, et à faire nos observations là-dessus. Nous tenons avant tout que le Cabinet de St. James, s'inspirant de nos réserves qui vous ont été déjà exposées par mon dit Télégramme Circulaire, et que je viens de vous expliquer plus longuement, veuille bien ne pas se tenir à l'écart du concert que forment les Puissances garantes pour nous aider dans la pacification de l'Herzégovine, car c'est sur lui que la Sublime Porte a toujours compté *ab antiquo* dans toutes les questions vitales qui l'ont concernée, et c'est encore sur son concours puissant et son appui éminemment bienveillant que nous comptons" (Tel., Rashid to Musurus, Constantinople, 15 January, communicated to Derby, 17 January; FO 78/2527).

[189] *Ibid.*

[190] Tel. No. 13, Zichy to Andrássy, 20 January; SA, Varia Turquie I, 1875.

a regulation concerning land ownership in Bosnia,[191] and a report favorable to accepting the Andrássy proposals had been drawn up and presented to the sultan to prepare him for the next events.[192]

In the meantime negotiations were under way to settle the nature of the *démarche* in Constantinople. Gorchakov and Andrássy were agreed that the fundamental desideratum was the written reply from the Porte which would constitute a binding pledge to the powers. On the first day of the new year St. Petersburg had already received Ignatiev's reports that the Turks would make trouble—and specifically that the grand vizier would resign—if a written note or instructions were delivered to the Turkish foreign minister. In view of the danger of losing Mahmud, who still seemed desirable to the Russians, Gorchakov proposed that, instead of delivering the text of the note, its substance might be communicated in the form of an *aide-mémoire* and Turkish dignity thereby left intact.[193] Andrássy, however, was too jealous of his document to permit Ignatiev and his colleagues the privilege of tendering it in some abridged form. The note itself, he pointed out to Gorchakov, was as harmless a memorandum as an abstract, since it was not addressed to the Porte; therefore he wanted the Turks to have the original text. His own plan was that each of the imperial ambassadors should give the dispatch to Rashid and ask for a written acceptance of its provisions. To avoid the appearance of an identic form, he suggested that the other representatives should limit themselves to recommending Turkish approval.[194]

The Russian chancellor gave way to Andrássy's view[195] and eventually, after almost a fortnight of additional delay, the minister had the formal permission of St. Petersburg and Berlin to proceed with the negotiations at the Porte.[196] The governments in Paris and Rome likewise accepted the advisory roles which Andrássy had assigned them[197] and prepared dispatches of their own for communi-

[191] Report No. 3AH, Zichy to Andrássy, 11 January; SA, Varia Turquie I, 1875.

[192] Tel. No. 7, Zichy to Andrássy, 12 January; *ibid.*

[193] Letter No. 3, Gorchakov to Novikov, 20 December 1875/1 January 1876; *ibid.*

[194] Tel., Andrássy to Langenau, 8 January; *First Red Book,* Doc. No. 213.

[195] Tel. No. 6, Langenau to Andrássy, 11 January; SA, Varia Turquie I, 1875.

[196] Tel. No. 11, Langenau to Andrássy, 22 January; *ibid.* Tel., Károlyi to Andrássy, 21 January; *First Red Book,* Doc. No. 222.

[197] Andrássy to Apponyi in Paris and Wimpffen in Rome, 20 January; SA, Varia Turquie I, 1875.

cation to Rashid Pasha.[198] Only an explanation of what the British cabinet meant by "general support" was then delaying the long-planned step.

In the course of a few days it was learned at the Porte that, after all, the ambassadors were going to present written communications. Rashid claimed to have understood from Zichy that the desires of the powers would be given orally and had so informed the sultan. In his quandary the foreign minister went to Sir Henry Elliot for advice. After preparing Abdul Aziz for an oral communication, said Rashid, he was afraid to receive a written note which the conventions of diplomacy held to be incompatible with the sultan's sovereignty. Elliot, however, offered the distraught Rashid no comfort, reminding him, as he did, of "the serious consequences of such a refusal."[199]

Over night the plight of the Turks goaded them into finding a way out of the difficulty. It now appeared that the situation would be saved, the wrath of the sultan would be avoided, if, instead of having the documents peremptorily thrust into Rashid's hands, the minister could ask for the texts after they had been read. On 26 January this plan was sent to Andrássy with the solemn promise that Rashid would ask for the dispatch if the ambassadors' instructions did not prescribe its delivery.[200] The Austrian minister willingly

[198] Tel. No. 6, Apponyi to Andrássy, 23 January; *First Red Book,* Doc. No. 223, incomplete. The British ambassador in Paris reported in the following words an interview with the French foreign minister: ". . . . The Duc Decazes went on to say that he did not see how France could adopt the same course as that which was to be followed by the three Empires. It would, he conceived, be an extraordinary solecism in Diplomacy for a Foreign Ambassador to ask the Government to which he was accredited for a solemn written answer to a document neither emanating from his own Government nor addressed to himself. In the present case it would, in the Duke's opinion, be on all accounts much better that the French Ambassador at Constantinople should communicate to the Porte no more than a Despatch addressed to him by the French Minister for Foreign Affairs. . . . ." (Report No. 54, Lyons to Derby, Paris, 24 January; FO 27/2160.) A comparable expression of opinion was stricken from *First Red Book,* Doc. No. 223. Visconti-Venosta to Barbolani, Rome, 20 January; *First Green Book,* Doc. No. LXXXIX. Visconti-Venosta to Robilant, 26 January; *ibid.,* Doc. No. XCIV. Corti, Italian minister in Constantinople, was instructed to leave a copy of a special dispatch which had as its annex the text of the Andrássy note (Visconti-Venosta to Corti, 22 January; *ibid.,* Doc. No. XCII). Report No. 3AC, Wimpffen to Andrássy, 22 January; SA, Varia Turquie I, 1875. Tel. No. 12, Wimpffen to Andrássy, 23 January; *First Red Book,* Doc. No. 224.

[199] Report No. 104, Elliot to Derby, 25 January; FO 78/2455.

[200] Tel. No. 16, Zichy to Andrássy, 26 January; SA, Varia Turquie I, 1875. ". . . . General Ignatiew tells me that he has written to his government to recom-

accepted the proposal, although he ordered Zichy to leave a copy if it was not requested[201]—and more days were lost in arranging a common modification of the several sets of instructions.[202] It was only on the twenty-ninth that the last of these—the Italian—was dispatched to Constantinople.[203]

Count Andrássy had been unwilling, however, to wait until all

mend them to comply with Raschid Pasha's wish in this respect, but I believe I am doing him no injustice, if, in common with some others of my colleagues, I suspect him, at the same time of stimulating the susceptibility of the Turks upon these points of form" (Report No. 114, Elliot to Derby, 27 January; FO 78/2455).

"In the course of conversation with most of my colleagues upon Count Andrassy's despatch I have found them of opinion that it contains expressions which may be admissible in a communication to the Governments to which it was to be delivered, as explaining the position of the question of the Herzegovina, but which it would be unbecoming to put into the hands of the Porte.

"If the representatives of the Northern Cabinets are directed to read and give copies of that despatch exactly as it stands there is none of them who will execute his instructions without embarrassment" (Report No. 106, Elliot to Derby, 26 January; ibid.).

[201] Tel. No. 2, Andrássy to Langenau, 26 January; SA, Varia Turquie I, 1875. Tel. No. 99, Andrássy to Zichy, 26 January; ibid.

[202] Tel., Andrássy to Károlyi, 28 January; ibid. Tel., Károlyi to Andrássy, 29 January; ibid. Tel. No. 14, Wimpffen to Andrássy, 29 January; ibid. Tel. No. 7, Apponyi to Andrássy, 29 January; ibid. Gorchakov was at first inclined to reject Rashid's request but, after receiving Andrássy's view, gave his consent (Tel. No. 12, Langenau to Andrássy, 27 January; ibid.). From Ignatiev's report of the Turkish request Gorchakov had the impression that it was a matter of more than a mere formality and that agreement to it might compromise the result of the step. The ambassador had urged that a favorable reply be sent. The character of Langenau's report does not make it possible to see clearly what Ignatiev was attempting—if anything. If he had wanted to make trouble he would have recommended—so it would seem—rejection of Rashid's plan. It is quite possible, of course, that Gorchakov misinterpreted Ignatiev's telegraphic report, but the Austrian ambassador saw in the episode some dubious scheme. "It is not worth while to attach any great importance to the incident," Langenau wrote to Andrássy, "but I cannot refrain from being suspicious of anything, in the pending negotiations in Constantinople, which gives too much satisfaction to General Ignatiev" (Report No. 8AD, 21 January/2 February; ibid.).

[203] Visconti-Venosta to Corti, 29 January; First Green Book, Doc. No. XCVI. The French instructions were sent on the day preceding (Decazes to Bourgoing, 28 January; First Yellow Book, pp. 96–98). Decazes had his first draft ready on 23 January, in which, as the British ambassador in Paris expressed it, he did "his utmost all through to gild the pill for the Porte" (Report No. 53, Lyons to Derby, 23 January; FO 27/2160). He delayed sending his dispatch in order to know what the British cabinet was going to decide. After learning the contents of Derby's letter to Beust of 25 January, he told Lyons that he proposed to modify his instructions to Bourgoing to "see if he could not bring them into a somewhat closer resemblance to those which were sent to the English Ambassador. . . . ." (Report No. 63, Lyons to Derby, 26 January; ibid.).

six of the foreign representatives were ready. On 26 January, after having received a telegraphic summary of the British explanation,[204] the minister ordered Zichy to effect his *démarche* as soon as he received his instructions.[205] Not content with directing the ambassador to read his dispatch and wait for Rashid to ask for a copy,[206] Andrássy tried to provide for all contingencies. He recognized the inability of Zichy to present a convincing argument to the Turks and, consequently, drew up a detailed statement of how the ambassador was to act and what he was to say. First and foremost, Zichy was to avoid a discussion with the Turks of the substance of the proposals; Andrássy was intent on forcing the acceptance of his program *in toto* and he rightly was afraid that if any negotiations ensued, the unity of the powers, by which alone success was possible, would soon give way to discordant views of what was sufficient for the Turks to promise. For that reason the major task of Zichy was to secure a prompt acceptance of the note. He was to offer in exchange an Austrian guaranty that Russia and the other powers would work for peace, and he was to insist that it was to the best interest of Turkey to bind the powers, as Andrássy expressed it, by a promise to live up to the proposed reforms. Without such a contract, Zichy was to say, the insurgents would continue to hope for foreign aid— and the Turks were to be led to infer that, if they were stubborn, that hope might not be disappointed in days to come. Andrássy next provided the ambassador with replies tó the three conditions which the Turks, as rumor had it, were thinking of laying down for their acceptance of the reforms: that Austria assume responsibility for ending the rebellion; that the Dalmatian frontier be closed; and that the sultan be given a free hand with regard to Montenegro. The Vienna government, quite naturally, could not assume such responsibilities. The first was impossible except by means of an Austrian occupation, which Andrássy refused to consider; the second was practically enforced already; and as for the third, Russia had categorically refused to permit an attack on the Black Mountain, and the Dual Monarchy could not take a contrary stand. The foreign

[204] Tel. No. 19, Beust to Andrássy, 25 January; SA, Varia Turquie I, 1875.

[205] The German government asked him to delay until the arrival of Elliot's instructions, but Andrássy, usually so deferential to Bismarck, refused (Tel., Russell to Derby, Berlin, 31 January; FO 64/850).

[206] Tel. No. 1, Andrássy to Zichy, 26 January; *First Red Book,* Doc. No. 225. A slight change was made in the printed form of the last paragraph to avoid reference to forcing the note upon the Turkish minister if he did not ask for it.

minister disposed of each of the points with the conclusion that acceptance of his program would place Austria in a position to exert all the moral pressure at its command in the interest of pacification. It was Zichy's duty to argue, in short, that all possible conditions and developments would be improved if the Turks accepted the Austrian program. But the ambassador's task was not merely to secure an acceptance; he was called on to aid in the subtleties of Austrian high policy. "Engage the Porte," the instructions went on, "to have confidence in our action. Make the Turks understand that if, as we hope, the development of events turns to their advantage, it is to us that they owe it." And finally, if arguments seemed of no avail, Zichy was to resort to threats:

On the other hand if, contrary to every expectation, it is necessary, Your Excellency should declare with the same frankness that, in case the Porte deems it desirable to take refuge in stratagems such as have been practised in more than one circumstance to paralyze the moral effect of our action, if the Porte makes it impossible for us to count on the success of our conciliatory work, we can not avoid the thought that Turkey is condemned to perish and that nothing henceforth can stop her fall. In this contingency we shall see ourselves forced to consider only our own interests. Then the facilities which we now offer to the sultan's government to combat the insurrection would be withdrawn; the port of Klek would be closed to Turkish ships; we should not try further to restrain Serbia and Montenegro from entering the struggle; we should, in short, allow a free course to events.[207]

In order, further, to facilitate arrangements in Constantinople, Andrássy prepared a text of the reply which he wanted the sultan's government to make. Zichy was instructed to present it to the Porte "solely in the interest of preventing delays prejudicial to the result which it is desired to obtain." He was told to inform the Turks, if he thought it desirable, that the proposed response had been agreed upon by the "three courts," although there was at the time absolutely no basis for such a claim.[208] The text provided for a recognition of

[207] Dispatch No. 3, Andrássy to Zichy, 26 January; SA, Varia Turquie I, 1875.

[208] Dispatch No. 2, Andrássy to Zichy, 26 January; *ibid.* Only that day did the foreign minister send his draft-reply to Berlin (Tel., Andrássy to Károlyi, 26 January; *ibid.*) and two days later to Paris and Rome and still three days later to London for endorsement (Tels. Nos. 7, 8, Andrássy to Apponyi in Paris and Wimpffen in Rome, respectively, 28 January; *ibid.* Tel. No. 5, Andrássy to Beust, 31 January; *ibid.*). It was only on 4 February that Gorchakov approved the draft (Tel. No. 15, Langenau to Andrássy, 4 February; *ibid.*), and the German endorsement came one day later (Report No. 5C, Károlyi to Andrássy, 5 February; *ibid.*). Beust's conversation with Derby apropos of the text was not very satisfactory to the former: ". . . . The impression produced on him by my reading him the text, I

the friendly good-will of the powers and for a declaration of the
Porte's determination not only to accept the Andrássy reforms but
also to put them into immediate execution.[209]

Count Zichy's descent on the Porte had been prepared, in the first
place, by the agreement with Rashid regarding the manner in which
the note was to be delivered. Sir Henry Elliot had also paved the
way for a more finished enactment of the little diplomatic interlude.
As soon as he received a telegraphic summary of the cabinet's instructions, the British ambassador reported them to Rashid and
urged him again not to make any difficulty over matters of form.
With hope for English support destroyed, the Turkish foreign minister had to resign himself to the imminent visits of the foreign representatives.[210]

must confess, was not favorable in so far as I could judge by the expression on his
face. . . . ." Instead of arguing for British support of the text, Beust was reduced
to beseeching the foreign secretary to do nothing about the matter (Tel. No. 26,
Report No. 13, Beust to Andrássy, 2 February; ibid.).

[209] The text read as follows: "La communication que Votre Excellence a été
dans le cas de faire verbalement à la Sublime Porte en y ajoutant à titre d'aide-
mémoire la dépêche de M. le Ministre des Affaires étrangères d'Autriche-Hongrie
en date du 30 décembre 1875 a été de notre part l'objet d'un examen approfondi.

"La Sublime Porte ayant acquis la conviction que les Puissances sont disposées
à employer leurs bons offices pour contribuer à prévenir des complications qui
pourraient surgir de la continuation des troubles en Bosnie et Herzégovine et voulant
donner une preuve de son bon vouloir envers les conseils des Cabinets amis et
alliés, en même temps qu'elle est animée d'un désir de ramener les populations
insurgées, je m'empresse sur l'ordre de Sa Majesté le Sultan de faire part à Votre
Excellence de la résolution qui a été arrêtée à ce sujet.

"Le gouvernement impériale adhère aux propositions formulées dans la dépêche
susmentionnée du 30 décembre et se déclare fermement résolu à les mettre sans
délai à exécution.

"En portant de la manière la plus expresse cette détermination à la connaissance
de Votre Excellence je me flatte de l'espoir qu'elle sera accueillie par Votre Auguste
Cour [Gouvernement] avec une véritable satisfaction" (Supplement to Tels. Nos. 7
and 8, Andrássy to Apponyi and Wimpffen, respectively, 28 January; ibid.).

[210] Report No. 114, Elliot to Derby, 27 January; FO 78/2455. "I have communicated to Raschid Pasha the telegraphic summary of Your Lordship's instructions
which gave him great satisfaction.

"He says that the Sultan is so thoroughly convinced that Her Majesty's Government will not give him advice contrary to the interest of his Empire that it will
be more easy to induce His Majesty to receive the Austrian proposals favourably
when he knows that Her Majesty's Government do not regard them as objectionable
or dangerous.

"Raschid Pasha says that this communication will be of use in defeating the
attempts of those who are trying to persuade the Sultan that the Ministers who are
inclined to listen to the Austrian proposals are betraying him." (Report No. 117,
Elliot to Derby, 28 January; ibid. Cf. Turkey No. 2 [1876], Doc. No. 84.)

Count Zichy's instructions arrived on 30 January and, after notifying his various colleagues, he went the next day for his interview at the Porte. He read aloud the text of the Andrássy note and, true to his promise, Rashid asked for a copy as an *aide-mémoire*. After the polite banalities which the occasion demanded, Zichy produced the draft-reply and laid before the minister all the arguments which his superior had given him. Rashid made no objection to the suggested response and, although he raised some question about the provision for taxation, promised the ambassador that if he and his colleagues remained in office there would be no delay in a formal acceptance.[211] Then in rapid succession came the representatives of Great Britain, Russia, Germany, and Italy to offer the advice of their respective governments.[212] On the following day, after his instructions had arrived, the French ambassador added his word of counsel.[213]

When Europe had thus spoken, the problem was transferred to the sultan and his quaking advisers. The grand vizier and the foreign minister had been for some time the object of bitter attack from enemies both within and without the ministry. When the Andrássy program came before the council the session was used as occasion for a stormy scene, despite the fact that the Turkish translation of the note had been tempered to reduce its possible offense. Mahmud and Rashid were obliged to use all their energies in the frequently interrupted ministerial sitting to win approval for four of Andrássy's points and a qualified acceptance of the fifth concerning taxation reform.[214]

[211] Tel. No. 20, Zichy to Andrássy, 31 January; *First Red Book,* Doc. No. 228, incomplete. Report No. 139, Elliot to Derby, 31 January; *Turkey No. 2 (1876),* Doc. No. 86.

[212] Bourgoing to Decazes, 31 January, 2 February; *First Yellow Book,* pp. 98–99, 99–100, respectively. Tel. 21, Zichy to Andrássy, 31 January; *First Red Book,* Doc. No. 229. Report No. 151, Elliot to Derby, 3 February; *Turkey No. 2 (1876),* Doc. No. 87. Corti to Visconti-Venosta, 1 February; *First Green Book,* Doc. No. C. The Italian minister did not receive his instructions until 5 February, but went nevertheless on 31 January to the Porte to give his support and returned on the day his orders arrived to repeat his message. Corti to Visconti-Venosta, 6 February, *ibid.,* Doc. No. CIII. Report No. 162, Elliot to Derby, 6 February; *Turkey No. 2 (1876),* Doc. No. 90. *The Times* (London), 11 February, p. 5, col. 4.

[213] Bourgoing to Decazes, 1 February; *First Yellow Book,* p. 99.

[214] The finance minister had pointed out to his colleagues that all of the taxes, direct and indirect, collected in Bosnia and Hercegovina did not cover the expense of administering the province (Tel. No. 27, Report No. 11B, Zichy to Andrássy, 5, 8 February, respectively; SA, Varia Turquie I, 1875).

The Austrian foreign minister sent more instructions and arguments to Zichy,[215] but the Turks were not to be stampeded into complete capitulation. Throwing aside Andrássy's proposed reply,[216] Rashid on 7 February and the days following notified the foreign representatives in Constantinople of Turkey's approval of four of the five points.[217]

It was a notification, however, which was altogether premature; the sultan had not given his final approval. For some time the capricious mind of Abdul Aziz had been irritated by all the disturbances to himself and his empire which the rebellion had unleashed. True Oriental potentate that he was, he charged the grand vizier with the entire responsibility and commanded him not to appear at the palace until the insurrection was suppressed. The sultan impatiently reproached Mahmud with wasting his time by promulgating reforms when he should have been putting down the revolt. Abdul Aziz had no care, at all events in his moments of irritation, for the cautions necessitated by Turkey's position in Europe. He ordered his ministers to enroll a band of the notorious bashi-bazouks for service in Bosnia and seemed to be ready to attack Montenegro regardless of the Great Powers. To emphasize further his imperial wrath toward the grand vizier, the sultan removed a number of Mahmud's appointees, including the minister's own private secretary. Toward the end of January it seemed that Mahmud's days of grace were numbered.[218]

[215] Andrássy to Zichy, 5 February; *First Red Book*, Doc. No. 230, incomplete. Tel. No. 8, same to same, 6 February; SA, Varia Turquie I, 1875. Andrássy was unable to judge from Zichy's telegram, No. 27, the nature of the modifications which were looming in Constantinople, and he was obliged to leave it to the ambassador to save as much as he could. "I can only emphasize the wish," his telegram added, "that the decisions of the Porte vary as little as possible from the program. Make it understood that the difficulties of our task will only commence when the Porte has accepted. It is to the advantage of the Ottoman government to do nothing which might weaken the solidarity of the powers which is now in Turkey's favor. . . . ."

[216] "Upon my questioning Raschid Pasha as to the truth of the report that the Austrian Government had submitted to him a draft of the answer which they considered he should return to Count Andrassy's proposals, he laughed and said that he could not deny its correctness. It was not an answer that could possibly be adopted. It consisted of about three lines and simply stated that the Porte accepted without reserve the whole of Count Andrassy's proposals" (Report No. 193, Elliot to Derby, 14 February; FO 78/2455).

[217] Tels. Nos. 28, 29, Zichy to Andrássy, 7 February; SA, Varia Turquie I, 1875. Bourgoing to Decazes, 8 February; *Documents français*, II, Doc. No. 34. Rashid to Corti, 10 February; *First Green Book*, annex to Doc. No. CVI.

[218] Report No. 119, Elliot to Derby, 29 January; FO 78/2455.

Sir Henry Elliot had never had any affection for this Turk of pro-Russian leanings but, fearing that the fall of Mahmud would entail the fall of Rashid and "would greatly complicate matters,"[219] he sent a message to Abdul Aziz in which he expressed the hope that there would be no change. General Ignatiev, having learned of his colleague's action, likewise intervened and—to the great annoyance of the British ambassador—let it be known in Constantinople that he had saved Mahmud from destitution.[220] But Mahmud was saved regardless of who was responsible. On 2 February, when the sultan was informed of the foreign representations, he sent a secretary to the Porte to express his confidence in the ministry,[221] and the next day he invited his chief minister to the palace. In the discussion of the reform proposals as well as in his attitude toward Mahmud, the monarch was reassuring.[222]

But in a few days Abdul Aziz' revived geniality had entirely disappeared. At the time in the second week of February when supposedly he was to approve the decisions of the ministerial council, the sultan could not be induced to venture from behind the strong doors of his harem. A series of spiritual and physical tortures had seized him. The intervention of the powers, humiliating enough at best to his sovereign pride, had become worse when a German newspaper published the text of the Andrássy note; there was new trouble in Asia Minor to distress him, and, more serious still, Queen Victoria's recent speech from the throne had not met his expectations. To complicate his difficulties, Abdul Aziz had boils, and one of them, assuming the proportions of a carbuncle, had to be operated on—a service for which the grateful monarch gave the surgeon a present of 1,000 Turkish lire and advanced him to the rank of general of division. And, finally, to bring his woes to a climax, Abdul Aziz overindulged a fondness for hard-boiled eggs at breakfast—eighteen according to one account based on allegedly "good authority"— and, with little regard for apparent cause and effect, believed that he had been poisoned. On Thursday, 10 February, he rallied sufficiently to send Mahmud a message ordering the unhappy vizier to pay full value for the Ottoman bond coupons held by the ruler rather than on the basis of the bankruptcy payments entered upon in Oc-

[219] Report No. 120, Elliot to Derby, 29 January; FO 78/2455.
[220] Report No. 146, Elliot to Derby, 2 February; ibid.
[221] Tel. No. 24, Zichy to Andrássy, 2 February; SA, Varia Turquie I, 1875.
[222] Tel. No. 25, Zichy to Andrássy, 3 February; ibid.

tober. Such action—at a time when the public administration had no money for the most pressing necessities and when the troops in Bosnia were in a state of abject deprivation—was a measure of the appreciation which the descendant of Mohammed the Conqueror and Suleiman the Magnificent had for the problems of his state. Sir Henry Elliot in despair wrote home that "the prospects of the Empire may well be looked upon with dismay."[223]

The day following, Friday, the inhabitants of Constantinople were inclined to share the apprehensions of their British friend. "The Shadow of God" refused to go to the mosque for the weekly public prayers. That appearance was a sultan-caliph's most sacred duty; sultans at the door of death itself had felt obliged to use their last energies for the ride, and for a hundred years no sovereign had failed to perform this renowned ceremony. Yet Abdul Aziz did not appear, and the most ominous rumors circulated through Constantinople.[224]

Some of the ministers believed the sultan to be seriously ill, but Mahmud shared Elliot's suspicion that His Majesty was merely resorting to a little Turkish stratagem to delay accepting the Andrássy note,[225] and on Saturday the grand vizier attempted to win the imperial assent. He sent the first secretary of the sultan to the palace to press for an *iradé* and threatened resignation in case of refusal. The sultan's response was the appointment of a fanatical enemy of Mahmud as president of the ministerial council. The grand vizier then wrote a letter to the sultan repeating his request, and, when no new answer came, Rashid on Sunday morning went in person to the palace. Abdul Aziz refused to leave the recesses of the harem, and communications between monarch and minister proved difficult,

[223] Report No. 177, Elliot to Derby, 10 February; *Turkey No. 3 (1876)*, Doc. No. 8. Zichy laid the whole trouble between sultan and grand vizier to the impossible task of the latter to provide money for the insatiable desires of the palace. At this same critical moment Abdul Aziz was satisfying his love of fantastic building, was ordering great supplies of guns, when the previous deliveries had not been paid for, and was contemplating a new fleet of ironclads. When Mahmud tried to remonstrate that it would be better to pay for the guns already ordered and to buy warm coats for the troops, the sultan reproached him for his conduct of the military operations in Bosnia and urged him to attack Serbia and Montenegro (Report No. 13AE, Zichy to Andrássy, 15 February; SA, Varia Turquie I, 1875).

[224] Tel. No. 35, Zichy to Andrássy, 12 February; SA, Varia Turquie I, 1875. *The Times* (London), 24 February 1876, p. 8, col. 1. Report No. 185, Elliot to Derby, 11 February; *Turkey No. 3 (1876)*, Doc. No. 10.

[225] Report No. 188, Elliot to Derby, 13 February; FO 78/2455.

carried on as they were with the double intervention of a secretary and a harem guard. In the end, however, the energetic representations of the foreign minister won the day and the sultan gave his consent.[226]

That same evening the ambassadors received their second notification of Turkey's acceptance of four of the five points in the Austrian program. Only one paragraph of the new letter, a paragraph devoid of real meaning, was taken from Andrássy's draft-reply.[227] No one—not even Count Andrássy[228]—was inclined to take exception to the Turkish refusal to accept the entire proposal; and the long period of negotiations came to an end.

SUMMARY

By the time Turkey had formally accepted Count Andrássy's program, more than seven months had passed since the uprising had begun. So far as European diplomacy was concerned, the first three of those months had been lost in a futile attempt to admonish the insurgents into submission. The consular mission had represented a victory of the Austro-Hungarian minister's limited sympathies over the more radical inclinations of the Russian government. General Ignatiev, seeing the imminent defeat of a life's ambition in the important role assumed by Andrássy, had attempted to wrest that role from his enemy and to take it for himself; but in the subsequent competition between the two men St. Petersburg had eventually given in a second time to Vienna and Andrássy had framed the new plan for pacification. He had continued to think in terms of a leadership restricted to the league of the three emperors—in which he was dominating Prince Gorchakov and in which Prince Bismarck was pledged to ratify any Austro-Russian agreement—but Tsar Alexander and his ministers in turn had continued to think in terms of the concert of the six Great European Powers and, upon Russian insistence, Andrássy in December had sent his reform program to the other capitals for ratification. The weaker of the European powers—

---

[226] Tel. No. 36, Report No. 13AE, Zichy to Andrássy, 13, 15 February, respectively; SA, Varia Turquie I, 1875.

[227] Rashid to Elliot, Zichy et al., and Rashid to Musurus, Aarifi et al., Constantinople, 13 February; *Turkey No. 2 (1876)*, Doc. No. 93; *First Green Book*, Doc. No. CVI; *First Red Book*, Doc. No. 236; *First Yellow Book*, pp. 101–4

[228] Tel. No. 10, Andrássy to Zichy, 16 February; *First Red Book*, Doc. No. 237, incomplete.

Italy and France—had been gratified by the invitation to participate and they had proceeded to ratify the Vienna reforms. Germany and Great Britain, however, had not been so malleable. Prince Bismarck had become alarmed when he saw that the drift of European currents was bearing him into troubled waters, and he had suddenly in January sought English and Russian support for a partition of Turkey that would satisfy Austria and Russia and at the same time keep them closer to Germany than to each other and that would also give Germany some measure of British protection against France. But both governments had refused to join in such a far-reaching scheme—each for its own reasons—and Bismarck had given his consent to Andrássy's reform plan. In England both public opinion and the cabinet had been divided in their attitudes toward the old pro-Turkish policy and toward the league of the three emperors, but, after a period of deliberate delay, the cabinet, largely because there had been nothing else to do, had promised a "general support" of the Continental program. Then, at last, the foreign representatives in Constantinople had exacted from the Porte a formal promise to accept and institute the Austrian reforms, a promise given by the Turks only after they failed in an attempt to defy the collective will of Europe.

In mid-February the time had finally arrived to put Count Andrássy's second scheme of pacification to its practical test.

CHAPTER V

THE FAILURE OF THE ANDRÁSSY NOTE

TURKEY AND REFORMS

While the protracted labors of Mount Diplomacy had been in progress, Turkey had accomplished nothing toward her own solution of the problem of the rebellion. The rigors of winter and the deplorable state of the Turkish troops made a successful military campaign entirely out of the question. At best the commander was able, in the last days of the old year, to concentrate his half-starved men and carry through a new supply of provisions for the beleaguered fortress of Niksich and the blockhouses in the Duga Pass. The successful march was a victory for the Turks but at the same time a victory which did little more than permit Raouf Pasha to maintain his still desperate position.[1] Shortly thereafter the insurgents abandoned the Niksich area and moved westward to harass the road between Trebinje and Ragusa,[2] while to the north, in Bosnia, bitter fighting was renewed.[3] Mid-February witnessed no prospect for a military settlement of the rebellion.

Toward reform, in the meantime, there had been no serious steps. In late December Bosnia and Hercegovina were separated into two provinces and a large-scale change of officials ensued. Mukhtar Pasha became supreme military commander for both areas in place of Raouf[4] and Ali Pasha, former ambassador to France, was made

[1] *The Times* (London), 30 December 1875, p. 8, col. 3; 12 January 1876, p. 10, col. 1.

[2] *Ibid.*, 28 January 1876, p. 6, col. 1.

[3] Report No. 5, Freeman to Derby, 18 February; *Turkey No. 3 (1876)*, Doc. No. 24. Report No. 168, Elliot to Derby, 8 February; *ibid.*, Doc. No. 6.

[4] The British consul in Mostar attempted to persuade all of his colleagues to make a joint protest against the removal of Raouf. ". . . . Nothing could have been more ill-termed and unfortunate than the nomination of Ahmet Mouktar Pasha to the supreme command in Bosnia and the Herzegovina. Raouf Pasha had just done all that was possible to put matters in a better situation. He had infused courage and confidence into the troops . . . . and had inflicted severe losses on the insurgents. At the same time he had treated the latter with a consideration which gained their respect and almost their confidence. . . . ." The Russian consul refused to participate in a representation to Constantinople, and his Austrian colleague avoided the meeting of the consular corps in which the question was presented. (Report No. 3,

governor-general and commissioner for Hercegovina, the fourth within five months. Server Pasha returned to Constantinople, where he was soon to become president of the council of ministers; but in Mostar no one saw him go with regret. "It is the universal opinion," the British consul reported, "that no man has done so much to deprive the Christians of all confidence in reform as Server Pasha."[5] In January, shortly before Server's departure, the administration made its first steps toward redeeming some of the promises which had been given. Slavic scribes were attached to the local courts where Turkish was the official language, and the peasants were assured that thereafter their horses would be hired at the prevailing commercial rate rather than forcibly seized as heretofore for government service. In early January the official newspaper of the province announced that the authorities were already occupied with selecting reputable persons for tax-collectors and stated that the provincial council would be reorganized in March according to the law of the vilayets.[6] It was not until 1 February that the December *ferman* arrived in Bosnia. The document was taken in solemn procession with music and military escort to the government house, where it was read before an inert impromptu audience. "A short prayer was said; the troops cried, 'Long live the Sultan!' a salute of twenty-one guns was fired from the fortress, and the ceremony was ended."[7] The provisions of the *ferman* henceforth were a part of the law of the land—but no one took the document seriously. Christians and Moslems alike were convinced, and rightly so, that it would never become effective. The former were not inspired to believe any Turkish promise and the latter could not be persuaded that, as long as a caliph was on the throne in Constantinople, there would be equality between *rayah* and follower of the prophet of Allah.[8]

Holmes to Elliot, 17 January, in Report No. 4, Holmes to Derby, 21 January; FO 78/2537.)

[5] Report No. 2, Holmes to Elliot, Mostar, 6 January, in Report No. 3, Holmes to Derby, 10 January; *ibid*. Report No. 5, Freeman to Derby, Bosna-Seraï, 7 January; *Turkey No. 2 (1876)*, Doc. No. 64. Elliot to Derby, 30 December; *ibid.*, Doc. No. 68.

[6] Consular Report No. 6, Freeman to Derby, 7 January; *Turkey No. 2 (1876)*, Doc. No. 65.

[7] Consular Report No. 7, Freeman to Derby, 3 February; *Turkey No. 3 (1876)*, Doc. No. 9.

[8] Political Report No. 1, Freeman to Derby, 14 January; FO 78/2489. Freeman was as skeptical as the native population. "In any case," he wrote, "I fear that the Imperial Firman will in no way affect the present insurrection."

A few days before proclamation of the *ferman* the new governor had arrived in Mostar to take charge of the province. Ali Pasha admitted readily that the administration of Bosnia and Hercegovina was not only bad but unbearable, and he recognized as just the desire of the people for a regime which would permit them to live in decency. But with regard to the impending Andrássy reforms, he claimed to have received no instructions. In talking with the Austrian consul he professed to have neither interest in nor hope for the new program; General Ignatiev, he said, had assured the Turks that acceptance of the Vienna propositions would impose no obligations to carry them out, since the insurgents in all probability would not agree to them.[9]

At the Sublime Porte, however, the march of paper reforms had gone forward. In early January a permanent executive council was set up in order to institute "entirely and gradually" throughout the empire all the measures provided for in the December *ferman*. The council, composed of all the ministers and other high officials, was ordered to hold daily session and, in co-operation with a commission of control, to introduce and supervise a sweeping program of reform.[10] In addition there was a special commission which ground out a reorganization of the police system of the empire and a regulation against holding persons in prison without trial.[11] In the wake of those measures there came extensive "general instructions relating to the election of members of tribunals and of councils of vilayets." These regulations provided for equal representation of Moslems and non-Moslems in the local deliberative bodies; but the provision, in the case of every grade of officeholder, that the government would select the officials from an elected panel made the plan actually a derision.[12] From that alleged reform the Turks went on to inaugurate

[9] Tel., Report No. 26, Wassitsch to Andrássy, 28 January, 4 February, respectively; SA, Varia Turquie I, 1875.

[10] "Règlement respecting the Functions of the Executive Council"; *Turkey No. 2 (1876)*, Doc. No. 61.

[11] Report No. 37, Elliot to Derby, 11 January; *ibid.*, Doc. No. 77, inclosures 1 and 2.

[12] *Turkey No. 2 (1876)*, Doc. No. 80. The suffrage provisions gave the government an additional stranglehold on the province. Every male taxpayer above the age of 20 was declared to be an eligible voter, but his task was limited to selecting a group of electors subject to a series of easily manipulated qualifications: "(1), they must be of the age of 23 years; (2), they must never have undergone a criminal sentence; (3), they must never have molested anybody; (4), they must have no personal connection with the persons qualified to be elected," i.e., to the offices in the province.

a series of negotiations with the various patriarchs in order, as the intention was stated, to place the Christians on a more liberal footing. Three points were under discussion: the military exemption tax, conversion to Islam, and the matter of Christian bells. By the end of January, however, little substantial progress had been made with them.[13] An adjustment of the special tax on non-Moslems in accordance with the *ferman* proved to be very difficult. In times past the government had been levying an exaction on male Christians ranging in age from infancy to senility, and in relinquishing the assessments upon those not of military age the government was confronted with either losing considerable revenue or increasing materially the amount paid by those individuals who were still subject to the tax. The authorities, on the one hand, were unwilling to forego the revenue; and the Christians, on the other, protested vigorously against an increase in the tax. Some Christians proposed that the tax be abolished altogether and that non-Moslems be taken into the army on terms of equality with the True Believers, but the Turks were little inclined toward the plan.[14]

When the various propositions of the Andrássy program became unofficially known in Constantinople, the Porte began its preparations for the inevitable. In anticipation of the fifth point, which demanded a commission of control, two special commissions, one for Bosnia and one for Hercegovina, were projected for the institution and supervision of the other measures. The question of religious discrimination in land-owning was also taken up, and in early February its settlement was announced: all distinctions between Moslems and non-Moslems in the acquisition and ownership of land were theoretically swept into extinction.[15] These activities, thought Count Zichy, were proof positive that never before had the Turks been so busy with reform.[16]

A few days later Abdul Aziz gave his approval to four-fifths of the Andrássy program and his government formally pledged its word to the European powers that those reforms would be put into execution. On 15 February a telegram was sent from the Porte to Ali

[13] Report No. 8C, Zichy to Andrássy, 28 January; *First Red Book,* Doc. No. 226.
[14] Report No. 210, Elliot to Derby, 17 February; *Turkey No. 3 (1876),* Doc. No. 33.
[15] Zichy to Andrássy, 11 February; *First Red Book,* Doc. No. 232. Report No. 178, Elliot to Derby, 10 February; *Turkey No. 2 (1876),* Doc. No. 91.
[16] Report No. 11C, Zichy to Andrássy, 8 February; *First Red Book,* Doc. No. 231.

Pasha informing him of the acceptance of the four principles and ordering him to make a public proclamation of the concessions and to promise an amnesty for those who would return to submission.[17]

Already choice had been made of the two commissioners who were to go to the provinces to conduct the elections and act as presidents of the commissions. Haydar Effendi was designated as the commissioner for Bosnia and Wassa Effendi for Hercegovina. The former, long Turkish ambassador at Vienna, was praised by Elliot as a Moslem "of very liberal principles."[18] His colleague also enjoyed a good name in Constantinople; by birth he was an Albanian, by religion a Roman Catholic, by political persuasion a one-time member of Garibaldi's immortal thousand.[19] But in the province to which he was going his prestige was not so high. The Austrian consul recalled that twelve years earlier Wassa had come to Hercegovina to regulate abuses and that, after two years in which not one abuse was ended, he went away with the reputation of being an adventurer as talented as he was corrupt.[20]

The grand vizier formally promised that the instructions which the two new officials were to take with them would give them full power and that they were to have sufficient money to carry on the work of repatriation.[21] And, indeed, the fourteen articles of their special instructions did prescribe a generous mission of mercy: the refugees were to be escorted to their homes under protection; the sick were to be placed in hospitals; food was to be furnished until the new crops were harvested; material was to be provided for restoring churches and homes; taxes were to be relinquished for two years; and the proclaimed measures of reform were to be brought to realization.[22] Zichy lyrically claimed that in the annals of Turkish history

[17] Report No. 27, Wassitsch to Andrássy, Mostar, 25 February; *First Red Book,* Doc. No. 241, with annex. A new communication to the powers on 17 February confirmed this decision (*First Yellow Book,* pp. 105–6; *First Green Book,* Doc. No. CVIII).

[18] Elliot to Derby, 22 February; *Turkey No. 3 (1876),* Doc. No. 40.

[19] Elliot to Derby, 4 March; *ibid.,* Doc. No. 62. *The Times* (London), 11 March 1876, p. 8, col. 2. Zichy to Andrássy, 8 February; *First Red Book,* Doc. No. 231.

[20] Report No. 28, Wassitsch to Andrássy, Mostar, 4 March; SA, Varia Turquie I, 1875.

[21] Tel. No. 44, Zichy to Andrássy, 21 February; *First Red Book,* Doc. No. 239, incomplete.

[22] "Instructions spéciales aux commissions d'exécutions de Bosnie et de l'Herzégovine"; *First Red Book,* pp. 624–26. These concessions were inspired by Andrássy (Tel. No. 4, Andrássy to Zichy, 26 January; SA, Varia Turquie I, 1875).

no such instructions could be found.[23] Elliot, on the other hand, was disturbed for the future. He saw that when the commissioners arrived there would be three authorities in the provinces, each practically independent of the others, and he suspected—as was already true[24]—that the division of authority would give rise to jealousies and that as a result the returning refugees would be victims of their vengeful Moslem neighbors.[25]

These regulations for the repatriation of the insurgent and refugee Christians had a narrow escape before their final approval. The ministerial council drew them up on 22 February, and two days later Abdul Aziz sanctioned them. But later on the 24th a contrary influence prevailed over the sovereign's mind. Server Pasha had been able by exploiting his connections with the palace through marriage to see the sultan and justify his recently ended administration of the insurgent province. Abdul Aziz was convinced by this accomplished liar that, thanks to the Server regime, there was no longer in Bosnia and Hercegovina either rebel or refugee, that such trouble as persisted was exclusively the work of Serb, Dalmatian, and Montenegrin adventurers. In the evening, consequently, the grand vizier received a note from his imperial master ordering him to rescind the regulations as unnecessary in the existing orderly state of the land. The next day the question was again debated in a turbulent session of the council of ministers. Mahmud and Rashid pleaded for a renewal of the instructions, and when Server refused to make any comments, the council voted to resubmit the order to the sultan. Abdul Aziz was eventually prevailed upon to renew his approval, but his smouldering irritation against the grand vizier flared up to new heights. "What good is this empire," he was reported to have said, "when I cannot have the gold I need?"[26] General Ignatiev, having remarked the changed tide of imperial sentiment, had already begun private intrigues with Hussein Avni Pasha.[27]

[23] Report No. 17C, Zichy to Andrássy, 3 March; First Red Book, Doc. No. 243.
[24] Report No. 28, Wassitsch to Andrássy, 4 March; SA, Varia Turquie I, 1875. Report No. 15AC, Zichy to Andrássy, 22 February; ibid.
[25] Report No. 254, Elliot to Derby, 4 March; Turkey No. 3 (1876), Doc. No. 62.
[26] Tel. No. 48, Report No. 16, Zichy to Andrássy, 26, 29 February, respectively; SA, Varia Turquie I, 1875. Abdul Aziz gave his final approval on 29 February (Tel. No. 51, Zichy to Andrássy, 29 February; ibid.). The difficulties experienced by Abdul Aziz two weeks before had done much to undermine the grand vizier (Report No. 212, Elliot to Derby, 18 February; FO 78/2456).
[27] Report No. 203, Elliot to Derby, 15 February; FO 78/2455. Of the two candidates for the vizierate, Hussein Avni and Midhat, the latter was anathema to

In early March, after the delay imposed by the sultan's caprice, the two commissioners set out for the scenes of their labor. Two handicaps confronted them. First of all, the rebellion, to their surprise, was still going on; and, in the second place, there was no money available for the generous work of pacification to which they had been committed.[28] To make matters all the worse, Ali and Wassa gave little indication—at all events to a sympathizer with the rebels—of knowing what was actually expected of them or of wishing to do anything serious about it.[29] The predicted friction between the vari-

Ignatiev because of his reforming zeal, his pro-Western inclinations, and his reputation for energy.

[28] *The Times* (London), 11 March 1876, p. 8, col. 2; 16 March, p. 5, col. 2; 17 March, p. 5, col. 4; 25 March, p. 10, col. 1.

[29] W. J. Stillman, the *Times* correspondent, wrote on 28 March from Ragusa of the two men as follows: ". . . . Those who called on Ali Pasha yesterday left him none the wiser, because he said frankly that he did not know why he was here. Rodich had called on him, and this morning when I called he was not much wiser. From what I had heard of Wassa Effendi and Ali Pasha I had formed expectations of liberality and seriousness of intention in regard to the insurrection and the manner of dealing with it, which were entirely dispelled by a very brief conversation with each of them. It was not necessary to go into a lengthy discussion of affairs with either of them to find that either they did not know, or would not be allowed to act on the fact if they knew it, that the Insurgents are in a position to defy the Porte and its means of making head against them, and that the dangers are increasing in a manner which none but those wilfully blind could fail to appreciate. If their attitude is due to a *mot d'ordre* from Constantinople, the case is hopeless; if, which seemed to me more likely, it is due merely to the habit of shiftless waiting on events and hoping for what the Powers may do for them, it is scarcely more hopeful. To what seems to me the crucial question of what they were prepared to do to guarantee personal security to the refugees in case they could be induced to return to their country (homes they cannot be said to have), neither of them had any better reply than that they must trust to the promises and good intentions of the Imperial Government and the protection of the Ottoman troops. In Wassa Effendi I could see nothing but a very acute specimen of those Christian functionaries whose subservience to the Mussulman authority and supremacy makes their position a mere cloak and blind, behind which the old system can be carried on a little longer. He was not able even to discuss, without losing his temper, the suggestion of removing the Ottoman troops from the country, or either of the alternative projects of disarming the Mussulmans or allowing the Christians to go armed. The Insurgents were expected to lay down their arms and return to a country garrisoned by the troops whom they have lately so disastrously defeated, while the native Mussulmans, with all the new blood-feuds on their minds, were to be still allowed to retain their arms, and he did not seem to have the slightest conception that this was not personal equality before the law, much less that it was a condition no prominent Insurgent would dare to accept if he valued his tenure of life.

"Wassa Effendi left me angry, and, with more hope, I went to see Ali Pasha, for I have known really just and liberal Mussulmans in the Turkish service, and I

ous provincial authorities soon materialized and the native Mohammedan population began to show ominous signs of discontent.[30] In a
few days the utter hopelessness of the commissioners' work of pacification was apparent. The sum of money destined for aid to the
returning refugees disappeared into the pockets of the starving government employees; the grain which was to be used for food arrived,
after long exposure to the weather, sprouting through the sacks and
unfit for even animal consumption. Personal security remained a
paper fiction. In late March the troops, whose duty it was to protect
the returning fugitives, entered a Christian village, massacred several
of the inhabitants, and paraded severed heads on the points of their
weapons.[31] The authorities in Constantinople refused to consider
disarming the native Moslems,[32] and in Bosna-Seraï (Sarajevo) the
local authorities set about building a second minaret to tower above

---

had heard that he was much impressed with the difficulty of the work before him.
I was disappointed both with his tone and the views which he had of the affair.
His liberality was of the same kind as Server Pasha's, and, of the two, I think
I should expect more of the latter. Ali was equally glib, and even more polite,
but he was far less considerate in discussion than his predecessor. He smiled and
was cordial, and talked very frankly, but paid very little attention to what was said
on the other side. He showed simply as an adroit fencer on the defensive in argument, evading with great dexterity every embarrassing question, but impressing
me as quite incapable of a serious view of the matter, or of conceiving of his own
position that it was any other than that of one who must cover a matter which
could not be defended openly.

"He did not, like Wassa, lose his temper, but he assumed the same tone, and,
to the same questions, made the same replies. The Sultan's proclamation was in
his eyes a guarantee for all liberties and security; if the Insurgents wanted anything beyond, they were likely to want, for they would not be offered any other.
And when I assured him, from my personal knowledge of the people, that some
decided and tangible guarantee would be required, they not considering life sufficiently assured under the old conditions to induce them to venture back, he said—
Wassa had said the same—that was their affair—it was quite indifferent to the
Porte whether they came back or not. . . . ." (*The Times* [London], 6 April 1876,
p. 8, col. 1).

[30] Consular Report No. 10, Freeman to Derby, Bosna-Seraï, 16 March; *Turkey
No. 3 (1876)*, Doc. No. 96. Suppressed from the printed report was an additional
paragraph: "Unfortunately His Excellency cannot even rely on the cooperation of
the Governor-General and other local functionaries. I believe that he has already
reproached Ibrahim Pasha with having, up to the present moment, taken no steps
to execute the will of the Sultan, and it may be safely predicted that before long
two men of such opposite characters and sentiments as Haidar Effendi and Ibrahim
Pasha will be in open antagonism. . . . ."

[31] *The Times* (London), 6 April 1876, p. 8, cols. 1–2.

[32] Report No. 264, Elliot to Derby, 7 March; *Turkey No. 3 (1876)*, Doc. No. 63.

the Christian steeple, where still no bell was allowed despite proclamations of equality. Islam remained fanatical and superior.[33]

The insurgents were equally persevering. In that month which
was supposed to bring peace to Bosnia and Hercegovina the insurgents were moved by the same resolve which had been guiding them
for more than half a year—"a determination to fight to the last
rather than again submit to Turkish authority."[34] Instead of peace
the month produced a renewal of rebel action throughout the revolted
area. The refugees were "as unwilling to put themselves," as one of
the British consuls phrased it, "under the protection of a brutal and
ill-disciplined soldiery as to incur the risk of being driven from their
homes by the insurgents."[35] On 6 March the Christians caught a
body of two thousand soldiers straggling through a snow-covered
mountain pass and utterly routed them, acquiring in the fight, according to report, some eight hundred Ottoman noses.[36] With the
passing days the insurgents gained new victories[37] and soon the fortress of Niksich, the key to much of what remained of Turkish control of Hercegovina, was in critical straits.[38] As the end of the month
approached, the military situation was unchanged and nothing had
been done toward either repatriation or reform.[39]

AUSTRIA-HUNGARY AND PACIFICATION

Among the several complications which the uprising had for the
Austro-Hungarian monarchy was the fact that its subjects adjoining
the revolted area were practically identical in race and in culture with
the people in rebellion. The close relationship of the two populations
and the wild character of the arbitrary frontier made it impossible to
prevent a lively traffic across the border, and likewise impossible to
restrain the Slavs of Dalmatia from open participation. The Vienna
authorities had given restraining orders and had sent troops to enforce them, but the task was beyond their ability. Bands continued

[33] Political Report No. 6, Freeman to Derby, 2 March; *ibid.,* Doc. No. 45.

[34] *Ibid.*

[35] Political Report No. 7, Freeman to Derby, 10 March; *ibid.,* Doc. No. 79.

[36] Report No. 6, Holmes to Elliot, Mostar, 20 March, in Report No. 6, Holmes
to Derby, 20 March; *ibid.,* Doc. No. 98.

[37] Political Report No. 8, Freeman to Derby, 14 March; *ibid.,* Doc. No. 85.

[38] Report No. 296, Elliot to Derby, 19 March; *ibid.,* Doc. No. 91.

[39] Report No. 7, Holmes to Elliot, 30 March, in Report No. 7, Holmes to
Derby, 30 March; *ibid.,* Doc. No. 120.

in the early part of the new year to cross over the frontier despite Andrássy's promises that he would prevent the recurrence of such acts.[40] Arms and ammunition continued to pass into Bosnia and Hercegovina, and the insurgents continued to walk about unmolested in Dalmatia and hold their meetings openly in a Ragusan café. It was the boast of a local resident that artillery could be landed anywhere on the coast and taken across the border "with the greatest ease." "Everyone agrees also," said the British consul in his description of frontier laxness, "that the reason of this is the connivance of the Austrian officials, whose duty it is to prevent anything of the kind. From Baron Rodich down to the humblest douanier, all are more or less warmly in favour of the insurgents. All the officials are Slavs; and they take no pains to conceal their sympathies. . . . ."[41]

This failure to maintain strict neutrality exposed the Vienna government to the pain of remonstrances from Turkey and Great Britain;[42] but a more material pain to the empire was the growing burden of maintaining a large refugee population. Despite a heavy mortality—twenty-two per cent—the number of fugitives had been increasing until, in April, it was destined to reach fifty thousand, and they were all of necessity maintained by Austrian charity.[43] Caring for such a horde of miserable souls involved an expense which the Dual Monarchy could little afford to bear.

Count Andrássy's major preoccupation was, it has been repeated, to bring the insurrection to an end as soon as possible and to send the fugitive Christians back to the ashes of their homes. Recognizing that the refugees could not be induced to return unless they were offered security and aid, the minister in January outlined for the Turks a program of repatriation on which he was willing to co-operate. It was the program which the Porte was to adopt a month later for its commissioners: amnesty; protection against Moslem vengeance; material aid for rebuilding houses and churches; and seeds for the forthcoming spring sowing.[44]

[40] Elliot to Derby, 8 February; *Turkey No. 3 (1876)*, Doc. No. 6. Reports Nos. 266 and 271, Elliot to Derby, 8, 10 March; *ibid.*, Docs. Nos. 64 and 66, respectively.
[41] Report No. 18, Monson to Buchanan, Ragusa, 11 March; *Turkey No. 3 (1876)*, Doc. No. 57. Naturally, the quotation given above was stricken out before publication. The "Mr. ———" of the printed document was Stillman, correspondent of *The Times* (London).
[42] Draft No. 93, Derby to Buchanan in Vienna, 10 March; *ibid.*, Doc. No. 44.
[43] Mollinary, *Sechsundvierzig Jahre*, II, 292. Report No. 282, Elliot to Derby, 13 March; *Turkey No. 3 (1876)*, Doc. No. 71.
[44] Tel. No. 4, Andrássy to Zichy, 26 January; SA, Varia Turquie I, 1875.

Accepting this Austrian program of repatriation was almost as distasteful an experience in Constantinople as accepting the Austrian reforms had been. After swallowing the unpalatable reform pill the Turks were inclined to send Andrássy a pointed reminder of his promise to aid in ending the rebellion. Ottoman patience with Serbia and Montenegro was exhausted and the grand vizier, pushed by public opinion, wanted to serve notice of a declaration of war on the principalities in case Austria did not stop the sources of foreign aid. Sir Henry Elliot, when asked for an opinion, dissuaded Mahmud from giving any offense to Vienna,[45] and instead Rashid merely asked Zichy for some message from the Austrian capital which might be used to calm the sultan.[46] Andrássy's reply on 18 February was cordial and reassuring. He proposed as the first new step toward peace a Turkish summons to the insurgents to lay down their arms. For his own part he pledged the support of the Austrian border officials and agreed to appeal to the refugees to take advantage of the Porte's inducements and return to their homes.[47] He urged the Turks to send the commissioners at once and to proclaim both an amnesty for the insurgents and the concessions for the refugees which he had previously outlined. As soon as a given district was sufficiently pacified, he proposed to send home certain leaders who might exercise a peaceful influence over the insurgents and over Catholics of districts removed from the actual scene of the rebellion. But if the insurgents refused to submit under all of the guaranties that had been offered, Andrássy was not inclined to dally further with them. In such a case he recommended that the Turks should send out a body of troops strong enough to drive them over the Dalmatian frontier, where they would be seized by the Austrians and disarmed.[48]

[45] Report No. 201, Elliot to Derby, 14 February; FO 78/2455.

[46] Tel. No. 41, Report No. 13B, Zichy to Andrássy, 14, 15 February, respectively; SA, Varia Turquie I, 1875.

[47] Tel. No. 11, Andrássy to Zichy, 18 February; *First Red Book*, Doc. No. 238.

[48] Tels. 12 and 13, Andrássy to Zichy, 25 February; *ibid.*, Doc. No. 240, incomplete. The concessions for the insurgents and refugees suggested by Andrássy were accepted at the Porte (*ibid.*, Doc. No. 242), and delivered to the commissioners (*ibid.*, pp. 624–26) after the sultan had given his final approval on 29 February (Tel. No. 51, Zichy to Andrássy, 29 February; SA, Varia Turquie I, 1875).

A month later Andrássy sounded out the British on the possibility of London's assisting "the Turkish government to raise the money indispensably necessary for accomplishing the pacification of the Insurgent Provinces, and reestablishing the refugees in their homes under the new system of administration promised by the

During the same days Andrássy was preparing instructions for the various Austrian frontier officials. The governor-general of Dalmatia, notorious to more persons than suspicious British consuls,[49] was called to Vienna in mid-February and given precise written orders. The document in question emphasized the obligation to work for pacification imposed upon Austria by Turkey's acceptance of the reform program, and it stated the duties which Rodich was to perform. With regard to the insurgents, the governor was instructed to call their attention to the material improvement of their condition which the powers had won for them and to admonish them to make the reforms a reality through their own friendly co-operation. Those reforms, Rodich was charged to tell them, went far beyond what the insurgents could have hoped to win alone, and, consequently, fur-

---

Porte. On my inquiring whether he meant that Her Majesty's Government should join the other Powers in some transaction of the kind, he said there was no probability of the others listening to such a proposal, as Russia would do nothing, Prussia would say she had no interest in the question, and Italy is herself in difficulties for money.

"He said the insurrection had already caused very considerable expense to Austria-Hungary, and would, he feared, cause more,—but that he could not ask the Delegations, considering the deficits in both sections of the monarchy, and the disasters occasioned by the recent inundations, to enter into any engagements for assistance to Turkey,—and all he could do, therefore, for promoting the pacification of the provinces, would be to appropriate some secret service money to the rebuilding of the church at Duse, as, if the abbot would return to the convent there, he would be able to exercise a very favourable influence on the refugees. . . . ." (Report No. 164, Buchanan to Derby, Vienna, 24 March; FO 7/868.) The proposal came to nothing.

[49] ". . . . The name of General Rodich is by no means a very popular one with the public at large. In exercising the functions of Civil and Military Governor, he has more than once shown a disposition to follow a rather independent course in the way of applying money voted for one purpose to another, or authorizing expenditure which had not been voted at all by Parliament. This conduct has brought him repeatedly into collision with the Austrian Ministry, not less than with the Financial Committee of the Reichsrath. Moreover, it has been for a long time a complaint against him that, being himself of Slavonic descent, he was rather too much inclined to favour the claims and pretensions of the Slavonic inland population of Dalmatia, to the prejudice of the Italian population of the coast towns. With these antecedents, it was but natural that when the insurrection broke out, and complaints came of a certain laxity in the observation of the rules of strict neutrality, General Rodich should have been made responsible for what was up to a certain point but a consequence of the whole position of things. . . . .

"That General Rodich, with his sympathies for the Slavonic cause, should have most liberally interpreted his instructions is more than probable, but there has not been brought forward one authentic case which could be construed into anything resembling a real violation of neutrality. . . . ." (Vienna dispatch of 21 February, The Times (London), 25 February 1876, p. 11, cols. 1–2.)

ther rebellion was a useless and hopeless sacrifice of Christian blood. With regard to the refugees, Rodich was to summon them to return to their homes under the protection of the Turkish promise of security and aid, a promise made not to the fugitives themselves but to the Great Powers who were guaranteeing it. And finally, with regard to the administration of Dalmatia, Rodich was ordered to seize all suspected weapons and munitions and to prevent any foreign zealots from participating in the rebellion.[50]

Comparable directions were given to Baron Mollinary, commanding general in Agram and director of the Croat-Slavonian frontier: counsels of peace to the insurgents; admonitions to the fugitives to return home; closing of the border to munitions and fighting men.[51] Consul Wassitsch in Mostar was directed to aid the Turkish authorities in every way he could to induce the insurgents to lay down their arms and to prepare for the homecoming of the refugees.[52] His colleague, the Austrian vice-consul in Trebinje, was called upon to use his personal acquaintance with the rebel leaders to influence them to accept the amnesty and resume their peaceful pursuits. In case the insurgents were deaf to the Austrian exhortations, they were to be informed of stringent measures which would be taken against them: Andrássy proposed to blockade the insurgents and leave them to their own fate and to drive the refugees out of the Dual Monarchy without giving them any further material aid. On the other hand, those who submitted would receive every possible support and the leaders who were afraid to return home would be allowed to remain in Austria on a pension.[53] And, finally, as an additional precaution against foreign assistance for the movement, Andrássy appealed to the Italian government to do all that was possible to restrain Garibaldians from participation.[54]

On the part of the government in Vienna there was an honest and sincere desire to bring the rebellion to a speedy conclusion. In his

[50] "Directiven für den Statthalter von Dalmatien, Freiherrn von Rodich," Vienna, 21 February; SA, Varia Turquie I, 1875.

[51] Andrássy to Mollinary, 24 February; ibid. Mollinary, op. cit., II, 297.

[52] Andrássy to Wassitsch, 6 March; SA, Varia Turquie I, 1875. Specifically Wassitsch was charged to establish unofficial contact with the insurgents and induce them to send negotiators to the Ottoman officials.

[53] "Instruktion welche Herr Hauptmann Eugen Lazich mündlich den k. u. k. Vice-Consul Verčevich in Trebigne zu überbringen hat," Vienna, 28 February; ibid.

[54] Tel., Andrássy to Wimpffen—with Report No. 6 AD, Wimpffen to Andrássy, Rome, 19 February; ibid.

reform program Andrássy had done for the people of Bosnia and Hercegovina all that he thought possible. After the Turks had agreed to his propositions, the minister was obliged to exhaust every effort to persuade the Christians to accept them. If they did not, the last resort was force.

The tasks which official policy imposed on the Austrian functionaries turned out soon to be beyond their powers. Supervision of the frontier continued to be as difficult as before and at the Ballplatz itself it was admitted to be practically impossible.[55] Effort, none the less, was made. In early March, much to the excitement of the Dalmatian population, one of the most important insurgent leaders and his staff, together with a fanatical young Dutch woman who had come to see the prophesied end of Turkey, were arrested by Austrian troops and interned.[56] But despite this and other official acts, frontier traffic in food and munitions continued relatively unabated.[57]

It quickly proved impossible, moreover, to persuade the fugitives to return home. To General Mollinary, to General Rodich, and to the other Austrian agents their answer was the same: they would not go back because they could not trust the Turks for protection.[58] And indeed there was no little justification for the declared intention of some of the refugees to throw themselves into the river rather than return to Turkey. Despite promises, acts of violence and oppression continued to be almost daily occurrences. In one report in mid-March the British consul listed among recent villainies of the Moslem population robberies, burning of villages, violation of two young girls and of a woman in advanced pregnancy, impalements and behead-

---

[55] Report No. 60, Buchanan to Derby, Vienna, 10 February; FO 7/867.

[56] *The Times* (London), 23 March 1876, p. 10, col. 1. Report No. 277, Elliot to Derby, 13 March; *Turkey No. 3 (1876)*, Doc. No. 68.

[57] Political Report No. 19, Monson to Derby, Ragusa, 8 April; FO 7/882: "Apparent efforts are being made by the Dalmatian authorities to carry out with more strictness the orders received from Vienna to prevent the passage across the frontier of food and ammunition for the use of the Insurgents. I am, however, assured that such efforts are hardly more than ostensible; as in the case of food there is no difficulty in sending over supplies by employing women from among the refugees; and with regard to ammunition, the illicit trade is as rife as ever. . . . ."

[58] Mollinary, *op. cit.*, II, 297. Mollinary to Andrássy, Zara, 15 March; SA, Varia Turquie I, 1875. "Übersetzung eines Telegramms aus Alt-Gradisca," 22 March; *ibid.* (Const. 76). Report No. 29, Harriss-Gastrell to Buchanan, Budapest, 31 March; *Turkey No. 3 (1876)*, Doc. No. 111. Report No. 112, Buchanan to Derby, Vienna, 8 March; *ibid.*, Doc. No. 46. Report No. 143, Buchanan to Derby, 18 March; *ibid.*, Doc. No. 76.

ings, parading a schoolmaster's head through the street with musical accompaniment—all done with complete impunity.[59]

The crux of the whole program was, of course, the attitude of those actively engaged in the rebellion. Their position was foreshadowed in a manifesto dated 26 February. After a severe stricture on Prince Milan of Serbia for not taking "the direct road to poor Bosnia and Hercegovina," the statement turned somewhat poetically to the Andrássy plan:

. . . . On the other side we hear, but understand nothing in all these projects of reform that some European Cabinets have formed in order that the oppressed Christians of Turkey should obtain equality with the Mussulmans. For it is not only uncertain, but impracticable. In these projects of reform there is not a word said as to real liberty—liberty, independent and securely guaranteed by the Powers of Europe.

That is the project of reform we need. Such reforms suit us; if not, give us the tomb which will bury us, and where we may go down, quitting the world. . . . .

We repeat—only true liberty can disarm us, and to crush us there is need of more numerous arms than those of the Osmans, and then the women will remain after us to avenge us, receiving from our hands arms for our children that they may, even in dying, defend the liberty and rights of our people. . . . . Aid us! Hear us! now or never! . . . .[60]

[59] Political Report No. 9, Freeman to Derby, 17 March; FO 78/2489.

[60] Dispatch from Ragusa dated 29 February; *The Times* (London), 11 March 1876, p. 8, col. 1. Very little information is available which will give a clear idea of the intentions and ambitions of the insurgent leaders. W. J. Stillman, the *Times* correspondent, had intimate contacts with them, but his notorious sympathy for the rebellion makes his testimony somewhat suspect. In late December he made the following survey of his own conclusions: ". . . . Since I have been here I have made it my business constantly to obtain the opinions of every one I met who has had any experience in these Provinces, either as administrator, resident, or traveller, as to the advantages and objections of the various plans for a final solution of the problem how to dispose of the Slav Provinces, and the conclusion I draw from all indicates a very rational and what ought to be acceptable arrangement of the map. Any present re-formation of the old Serb Empire is, except in the eyes of Servian politicians, a solution utterly impracticable; and another matter in regard to which I find no doubtful judgment is that any kind of self-government is impracticable, and undreamt of by the people themselves. They have no political aspirations or affinities. What they want is simply law and order, and so long as these are maintained Austrian or Russian is equally acceptable. Whatever name the Government takes, it must assume all the duties and advantages of an autocracy. These people are as incapable of forming a Government as they are of creating a new religion, and nobody but a political visionary or a demagogue could propose any form or measure of self-government for them. An autocratic Prince with a small foreign force would maintain such order as these Provinces have not known for years, if ever, for the good reason that the whole population is well informed of one thing in regard to their political *status*—viz., that no movement they could make would

Baron Rodich's first interviews with the insurgents took place in Castelnuovo and Ragusa early in March before he learned of Turkey's concessions. He argued long and earnestly the guaranties for a better future—but without effect. The leaders presented in reply the reasons why they were unwilling to return to the old life: destruction of all their possessions, lack of faith in Turkish promises, doubt as to the ability of the consuls to protect them. Without discussing all their demands, they made it plain to Rodich that the fugitives could not return without their consent and that one condition of their own submission was the withdrawal of Turkish troops.[61]

As soon as the unpromising interview was over, Rodich received instructions to prepare a proclamation to the refugees and to supplement the notice with personal exhortations.[62] The governor had no faith in the effectiveness of such measures,[63] but Andrássy was still hopeful that the Turkish concessions would eventually be a compelling inducement[64] and he instructed Rodich to combat the distrust of the Christians by emphasizing the fact that Turkey's promise was made to Austria.[65] The immediate task, as the minister had planned, was to send back those refugees who might influence the insurgents, and along with them certain Catholics whose homes were not in the immediate area of the rebellion. The aid of the Catholic clergy was enlisted,[66] and special agents were dispatched to buy off the chief men

---

have any hope of success without more or less sympathy from the European Powers, and that if to-day they decided that the insurgent Provinces must go back to Turkey, the insurrection would be paralyzed at once. The only thing they have learnt by their long slavery is that the Turk has been supported by Europe, and that if Europe gives them another master they must accept him. . . . ." (*Ibid.*, 3 January 1876, p. 8, col. 1.)

Stillman continued to be a thorn in the sensitive flesh of British diplomacy. He had participated in a conference of the leaders in the Suttorina a week before they drew up their manifesto (Tels. of district captain in Lattaro to Rodich, 17, 19 February; SA, Varia Turquie I, 1875) and had advised apparently with the insurgents in the preparation of their document of the twenty-sixth. The British consul in Ragusa was fearful that Stillman had done "much mischief" among "the ignorant classes" who regarded the *Times* correspondent as the voice of opinion in England, and he promised to take every opportunity to discredit the correspondent's dangerous influence (Report No. 17, Monson to Buchanan, Ragusa, 11 March; FO 7/880).

[61] Rodich to Andrássy, Ragusa, 5 March; SA, Varia Turquie I, 1875.
[62] Tel., Andrássy to Rodich, 4 March; *ibid.*
[63] Tel., Rodich to Andrássy, 5 March; *ibid.*
[64] Report No. 112, Buchanan to Derby, Vienna, 8 March; *Turkey No. 3 (1876)*, Doc. No. 46.
[65] Tel. No. 221, Andrássy to Rodich, 6 March; SA, Varia Turquie I, 1875.
[66] Tel. No. 222, Andrássy to Rodich, 6 March; *ibid.*

by offers of subventions if they returned to Turkey or of permission
to remain on Austrian soil with a pension if they were afraid to go
back to their old homes.[67]

Just at this critical time in March the hopes for pacification were
jeopardized by a renewal of fighting. Carrying out their proclaimed
resolution to struggle on for freedom, the insurgents resumed their
operations. After a bloody and cruel victory over the troops near
Piva[68] and various encounters farther to the west,[69] the major body
of rebels moved north and fortified themselves directly on the Dalmatian frontier.[70] In conformity with Andrássy's suggestion,[71] Ali
Pasha sent his troops against them from three sides, intent on driving
them across into Austrian territory where they would be interned.[72]
But just at that moment the Austrian minister caught a glimpse of a
possible settlement through further negotiations and telegraphed to
Constantinople to urge delay until the work of Rodich and the Turkish commissioners had had a fair chance to succeed.[73]

The new hope inspiring Andrássy had come from Montenegro.
Since the beginning of the revolt Prince Nicholas had been under
pressure from the powers to maintain a strict neutrality, and now
that an attempt was being made to restore peace he was called upon
to lend his aid.[74] Baron Rodich went to Cetinje on the second of
March for a discussion of the Montenegrin position and found the
prince professedly desirous of heeding the admonitions of St. Petersburg and Vienna. Nicholas proposed to send two of his chief advisers to counsel the insurgents and fugitives,[75] and he told Rodich

[67] Andrássy to Rodich, 8 March; SA, Varia Turquie I, 1875. The Austrian
foreign minister suggested that it would be a good thing if the Turkish authorities
would also attempt to purchase the submission of influential men, but he was very
anxious that Russia should have no knowledge of his own action.

[68] Report No. 6, Holmes to Elliot, 20 March; *Turkey No. 3 (1876),* inclosure
in Doc. No. 98.

[69] Freeman to Derby, Bosna-Seraï, 10 March; *ibid.,* Doc. No. 79.

[70] Freeman to Derby, 14 March; *ibid.,* Doc. No. 85. Tel., Wassitsch to Andrássy, Mostar, 10 March; SA, Varia Turquie I, 1875.

[71] Tels. Nos. 12 and 13, Andrássy to Zichy, 25 February; *ibid.*

[72] Tel., Wassitsch to Andrássy, 8 March; *ibid.*

[73] Tel. No. 20, Andrássy to Zichy, 9 March; *First Red Book,* Doc. No. 253
with emendations. Rashid agreed that the moment was not suitable for an attack
but insisted on the necessity for operations when the insurgents concentrated en
masse in fortified positions (Tel. No. 60, Zichy to Andrássy, 11 March; *ibid.,* Doc.
No. 254, incomplete).

[74] The details of Montenegrin and Serbian affairs will be discussed below.

[75] Report, Rodich to Andrássy, Zara, 7 March; SA, Varia Turquie I, 1875.
Tel., Prince of Montenegro to Andrássy, 3 March; *First Red Book,* Doc. No. 244.

that he wished to arrange a new meeting between the governor-general and the insurgents.[76] Rodich naturally agreed to this plan, and Nicholas consulted the leaders. At the time the rebels occupied a strong position around Piva and the chieftains were unwilling to jeopardize their advantage by leaving their men without leaders. Hence they proposed that if the Turks would undertake no operations for ten days they would resume their discussion with Rodich. To facilitate the arrangement they agreed to permit the introduction of supplies into Niksich for that period. Prince Nicholas thought the proposal reasonable and asked Andrássy to make the proper arrangements with the Turks.[77]

The Austrian minister was reluctant to recommend the offer to the Porte but forwarded it to the Turks for their own decision.[78] Mahmud and Rashid were also unwilling to commit themselves for fear of the sultan's wrath, and passed on the responsibility to Mukhtar Pasha, the commanding officer in the field.[79] Andrássy, bent above all upon launching direct negotiations between the insurgents and the Turkish authorities, charged Rodich to recommend the proposed armistice only in case the leaders agreed to such negotiations.[80]

Already the insurgents had applied directly to Mukhtar Pasha for a twelve-day truce and had secured an informal agreement from him on condition of undisturbed access to the towns of Niksich, Piva, and Zubci. The insurgents, ever suspicious of what a Turk might do, proposed first that Prince Nicholas take charge of the revictualing of these places,[81] but later they changed their minds and on 21 March offered Mukhtar the choice of relieving Niksich with one battalion

[76] Tel., Rodich to Andrássy, 7 March; *First Red Book*, Doc. No. 249.

[77] Tel., Rodich to Andrássy, 14 March; SA, Varia Turquie I, 1875.

[78] Tel. No. 23, Andrássy to Zichy, 15 March; *First Red Book*, Doc. No. 259, incomplete. ". . . . Je ne voulais pas répondre affirmativement, car une pareille concession ne me semblerait opportune que si les insurgés demandaient cette trève pour s'aboucher avec les autorités ottomanes. D'un autre côté je n'ai pas voulu refuser, ne sachant pas s'il ne pouvait convenir à la Porte de consentir, soit pour des raisons militaires, soit afin que ses commissaires puissent profiter du délai pour se mettre en rapports avec insurgés, ce qui serait un acheminement à la pacification. Avant de répondre à Rodich, j'attendrai donc décision de la Porte; je m'y conformerai qu'elle qu'elle soit."

[79] Tel. No. 64, Zichy to Andrássy, 16 March; *ibid.*, Doc. No. 261.

[80] Tel. No. 263, Andrássy to Rodich, 14 March; *ibid.*, Doc. No. 263. Tel., Andrássy to Prince of Montenegro, 17 March; *ibid.*, Doc. No. 264.

[81] Tel., Prince of Montenegro to Andrássy, 18 March; *ibid.*, Doc. No. 267, incomplete. Tel. No. 65, Zichy to Andrássy, 17 March; *ibid.*, Doc. No. 265.

or of sending in a convoy from Montenegro. They gave their word of honor to accept such an arrangement but refused to permit Turkish military movements around Piva and Zubci.[82] Before the arrival of their proposal, however, the Turkish commander had proceeded with his business of fighting. In total disregard of the conditional armistice which he had accepted, a force of four battalions and 600 bashibazouks sallied forth to an attack near the town of Trebinje,[83] while in the Duga Pass Mukhtar himself tried in his own way to reprovision the garrison at Niksich.[84]

On 27 March, in response to Andrássy's desire for close co-operation between the Austrian and Turkish authorities, Mukhtar and Ali went to Ragusa to confer with Rodich. The governor-general concentrated all his energies on arranging the proposed armistice. In his discussions with Ali he was able to make no progress whatever. The commissioner was filled with suspicion toward the Slavic Rodich. Believing that if the governor were only honestly vigorous in words and action the whole problem would be quickly settled,[85] Ali limited himself largely to demanding thoroughgoing Austrian support in the suppression of the rebellion.[86] He refused to talk of a suspension of hostilities until Niksich was provisioned.[87]

Mukhtar was equally intransigent. He made no mention of his abortive negotiations with the insurgents; indeed, he declared himself opposed not only to an armistice but to any kind of dealings. Before the second day of the argument began, Rodich learned from Montenegro of the earlier negotiations, but even when confronted with his own acts Mukhtar refused to give way. Three hours of reasoning and threats did not succeed and Rodich finally retired to draft a written ultimatum: if the Ottoman commander did not agree to the steps considered necessary, Rodich proposed to report the impasse to Vienna and to consider the negotiations at an end.[88] In the evening

[82] Tel., Rodich to Andrássy, 21 March; *First Red Book,* Doc. No. 276. Report No. 55/gh, Rodich to Andrássy, 28 March; SA, Varia Turquie I, 1875.

[83] Tel. No. 522, Rodich to Andrássy, 20 March; *ibid.*

[84] Tel., Rodich to Andrássy, 23 March, incorporating Tel. of Mukhtar to Rodich; *First Red Book,* Doc. No. 280. Monson to Derby, Ragusa, 25 March; *Turkey No. 3 (1876),* Doc. No. 99. The Turkish commander as usual claimed to have repulsed the insurgents, but the contrary was actually the case.

[85] Political Report No. 6, Monson to Derby, 28 March; FO 7/882.

[86] Report No. 5, Monson to Derby, 28 March; *Turkey No. 3 (1876),* Doc. No. 109.

[87] Report No. 35, Wassitsch to Andrássy, 7 April; SA, Varia Turquie I, 1875.

[88] Reports 50/gh, 55/gh, Rodich to Andrássy, 30, 31 March, respectively; *ibid.*

Mukhtar capitulated. He agreed to an armistice during the first twelve days of April and to the suspension of troop movements. Zubci he proposed to provision by unescorted convoys, and he accepted the plan to relieve Niksich by way of Montenegro.[89] Prince Nicholas in turn agreed to this arrangement and ordered the president of the Montenegrin senate to supervise its execution.[90]

At the same time that Mukhtar accepted the armistice the Turkish authorities were at last ready to circulate proclamations of the amnesty and other concessions which had been agreed upon more than a month before in Constantinople. On 28 March there appeared a notice signed by Wassa, president of the Hercegovinian reform commission, and three days later another signed by Ali as governor was placed in circulation. Both documents notified the insurgents of the amnesty and tax exemptions which they might claim if they returned peacefully to their homes within four weeks; Wassa's went on to warn them that, in case of refusal, they would be excluded from "the Sovereign generosity" and would lose their worldly goods. The tone of the proclamations was not conciliatory and, though they spoke in general terms of tax concessions and of protection, there was no reference in them to reforms and to those guaranties which the insurgents held to be essential. Ali's circular showed neither repentance for Turkish rule nor sympathy for the cause of the insurgents—nor indeed great coherence for its reader:

.... You all know what measures were taken by the Imperial Government at the beginning of these disturbances and with what justice they have acted, so that neither your country nor any single one of you should suffer any loss; but in vain, for those who sought the accomplishment of their desire in the worth of your country, and those among you who followed these discourses gave another meaning to the well-intentioned initiative taken by the Government, and answered it at the point of the sword; it is thus that they compelled the Government, who were to re-establish peace, to repress and chastise them. .... Our illustrious Emperor, saddened in his imperial heart by this state of things, has not only consented to make you participate in the clauses of that just Firman, clauses which suffice to give safety and happiness to your country and to all her inhabitants, to compensate losses caused by the disturbances, and to realise some further important and essential improvements which are necessary in your country, and to make you enjoy legal advantages and to find there improvement; but he has also pardoned of the crime of disobedience all those among you who will lay down their arms and who will submit within

[89] Tels., Rodich to Andrássy, 28 March; SA, Varia Turquie I, 1875. One of these is given in *First Red Book,* Doc. No. 286.

[90] Tel., Rodich to Andrássy, 29 March; SA, Varia Turquie I, 1875.

four weeks from the day of this Proclamation. He will not fail to take care that measures are taken which will facilitate and insure your safety and well-being, as well as that of your families, when you return to your country. . . . . But if there are found those who know not how to appreciate so much sovereign grace, and who will persist obstinately to disobey, the Imperial troops will continue to repress them. . . . .

It was the same phraseology which the Turks had been using for a generation, and it therefore carried no conviction. Moreover, the proclamation was circulated a week after the period of amnesty formally began and one fourth of the time allowed for submission was thus cut off at a single stroke.[91] Baron Rodich was thoroughly displeased with the documents for their failure to specify the reforms and their insufficient reference to the amnesty and other concessions. He concluded from reading the proclamations and from his interviews in Ragusa that the Turks had no serious desire for pacification.[92] Mukhtar, on the other hand, reported that Rodich hoped for failure.[93]

As the critical moment for the great pacification offensive approached, Count Andrássy maintained his optimism. Boasting that he was accustomed to swim against the stream, he promised that, in spite of all the difficulties, "the pacification of the provinces and their improved administration would be accomplished."[94] The grounds for his confidence, however, were slight. The British consul in Mostar observed little at the time that would justify hope:

. . . . I assure your Excellency that when all the innumerable difficulties of the situation, both in the present and the future, present themselves in the reality which they assume to those on the spot, it is almost impossible to imagine any satisfactory solution of this wretched affair, whether there be pacification or not. When one witnesses the incompetency of the Government as evidenced in the appointments it makes, and the confusion of the orders it issues, and its total indigence,—the incapacity of most of the authorities, complicated by their jealousy and conflicting pretentions,—famine staring one in the face,—the insufficiency of troops, and the difficulty of maintaining even those now in the country,—the hopelessness of executing reforms with a divided population regarding each other with feelings of mutual fear, hatred

[91] Political Reports Nos. 12 and 14, Monson to Derby, Ragusa, 1 April; *Turkey No. 3 (1876)*, Docs. Nos. 117 and 119, respectively. (The quotation above is from the London Foreign-Office translation.)

[92] Report No. 51/gh, Rodich to Andrássy, 31 March; SA, Varia Turquie I, 1875. Monson to Derby, 30 March, 1 April; *Turkey No. 3 (1876)*, Docs. Nos. 116 and 118, respectively.

[93] Report No. 327, Elliot to Derby, 2 April; FO 78/2457.

[94] Report No. 141, Buchanan to Derby, 17 March; FO 7/868.

and vengeance, deepened by religious fanaticism,—and the continuance of political intrigues by agents of all kinds with or without the knowledge of their respective governments,—the man who can hope for any satisfactory result must be sanguine indeed. . . . .[95]

The armistice which was to open the door for peace proved to be a failure. Turkish and British reports described a marked renewal of the rebellion as soon as the truce began. On the first and second of April a strong band of insurgents made repeated attacks on the town of Nevesinje,[96] while at the same time several groups bringing two cannons were alleged to have crossed over from Dalmatia and Croatia into northwestern Bosnia. Turkish troops set out in pursuit of these latter insurgents; a passage at arms took place between the soldiers and Austrian patrols; and warm feelings resulted on both sides of the frontier.[97] Although the troublemakers in Bosnia were perhaps natives who had returned home to fight out their problem of peace,[98] the Turks insisted that they were Austrians, Serbs, and Montenegrins,[99] and made energetic protests in Vienna.[100] At the Porte there was great indignation; a majority of the ministers voted to withdraw all promises, to concentrate Turkey's military strength, and to send an ultimatum to Serbia.[101]

[95] Report No. 8, Holmes to Elliot, Mostar, 7 April; quoted portion suppressed from *Turkey No. 3 (1876)*, inclosure in Doc. No. 142.

[96] Tel. No. 76, Zichy to Andrássy, 4 April; SA, Varia Turquie I, 1875.

[97] Elliot to Derby, 3, 4, 7, 8, 13 April; *Turkey No. 3 (1876)*, Docs. Nos. 121, 128, 130, 145, 173, respectively. Report No. 199, Buchanan to Derby, 11 April; *ibid.*, Doc. No. 132.

[98] Report No. 18, Freeman to Elliot, Bosna-Seraï, 7 April; *ibid.*, inclosure in Doc. No. 137.

[99] *Ibid.* Report No. 45, Harriss-Gastrell to Buchanan, Budapest, 19 April; *ibid.*, Doc. No. 157.

[100] Aarifi to Andrássy, Vienna, 5 April; SA, Varia Turquie I, 1875. Tel. No. 77, Zichy to Andrássy, 6 April; *ibid.* "*Note verbale de la Sublime Porte en date du 8 avril*," in Report No. 28B, Zichy to Andrássy, 11 April; *ibid.*
Andrássy, who was not well-disposed toward Baron Mollinary, sent him a telegram accusing him of having violated his instructions and ordering him again to take measures for closing the frontier (Tel. No. 318, Andrássy to Mollinary, 6 April; *ibid.*). Mollinary, while admitting some abuses of neutrality, denied any serious attacks from his territory and promised to use more troops to prevent a recurrence of such border violations (Tels., Mollinary to Andrássy, 6, 9 April; *ibid.*). The Austrian foreign minister in turn denied to the Turks that there had taken place anything more than isolated acts, which would be corrected. Hayder, the commissioner for Bosnia, had been guilty of gross exaggeration, said Andrássy, and was, the irritated minister added, a simpleton (Tels. Nos. 319, 327, Andrássy to Zichy, 6, 8 April, respectively; *ibid.*).

[101] Tel. No. 77, Zichy to Andrássy, 6 April; *ibid.*

During the same days a second reverse in peace plans was suffered. The projected revictualing of Niksich was not accomplished. The supplies destined for the fortress were landed at Risano for transport through Montenegro, but it was then discovered that no pack animals were available. The Turkish authorities requested 500 horses from the Montenegrins and were told in reply that the number was not available. Effort was then made to purchase horses in Dalmatia, but everywhere the people stubbornly refused either to rent or to sell their animals for the movement of Turkish supplies,[102] and Niksich remained without provisions. New fuel was, of course, thrown on the fires of indignation already burning brightly in Constantinople. It was concluded at the Porte that the Turks had been duped in the recent negotiations by both Rodich and Prince Nicholas —that the two self-styled peacemakers were no less intent than the insurgents upon bringing about the fall of Niksich.[103] It appeared to the Turks also that the insurgents had merely utilized the armistice to concentrate their men along the highroad to that town with the intention of cutting off all communications.[104] To save the garrison Mukhtar was obliged to act promptly. Concentrating twenty or more battalions for the purpose, he set out on 13 April to drive his way through the Duga Pass. After six days of fighting he had to give up the attempt to reach Niksich; the forces against him had proved too formidable. But Mukhtar was not a man to admit defeat. On the eighteenth he telegraphed to the minister of war:

We have arrived at Gatzko [the point of departure] victorious. Engagements have been fought with the Insurgents continually during six days on our march towards and return from the neighbourhood of Niksics, and the Imperial troops gained striking advantages over the enemy, although the latter's forces were twice as numerous as ours, they numbering about 14,000. This time the Prince of Montenegro openly made war upon us. About 7,000 Montenegrins, well armed and regularly organized, had joined the Insurgents to fight against us.[105]

---

[102] Political Report No. 17, Monson to Derby, Ragusa, 6 April; *Turkey No. 3 (1876)*, Doc. No. 134.

[103] Rashid to Musurús, Constantinople, 13 April; *ibid.*, inclosure in Doc. No. 140. Report No. 386, Elliot to Derby, 17 April; FO 78/2457. Prince Nicholas in explaining the episode to General Ignatiev blamed the fiasco on Rodich (Report No. 416, Elliot to Derby, 23 April; *ibid.*). To Andrássy he laid the responsibility at the feet of the Turks (Tel., Nicholas to Andrássy, 13 April; SA, Varia Turquie I, 1875).

[104] Report No. 382, Elliot to Derby, 17 April; FO 78/2457.

[105] *The Times* (London), 20 April, 1876, p. 5, cols. 5–6. *Ibid.*, 28 April, p. 11, col. 1. Political Report No. 22, Monson to Derby, 14 April; *Turkey No. 3 (1876)*,

Despite the immediate failure of the armistice, the insurgent leaders had met on 6 April in the Suttorina for their conference with the governor-general of Dalmatia. Rodich went to the meeting equipped with new and elaborate instructions from Count Andrássy. The message for the insurgents had the tenor of the minister's recent utterances: Turkey had now pledged herself to the powers to carry out the reform promises, and the powers were resolved to see them fulfilled provided the submission of the insurgents made it possible; the Christians had to thank for these sweeping concessions not their own arms but the intervention of Austria and the other powers, and they could now return home secure in the conviction that Europe would attend to their protection; but should the leaders refuse this opportunity they would be shut off from all outside support.[106]

As Rodich set out for the Suttorina with this summons, the *Times* correspondent believed that the general was going somewhat mechanically to a task in the result of which he had no faith.[107] But, whatever might have been the dictates of his heart, Rodich delivered his message to the principal leaders. They heard him through but would venture only polite compliments to Emperor Francis Joseph before consulting with the lesser captains of the rebellion.[108] On the following morning Rodich received a written statement of the insurgents' conditions signed by thirty of their leaders.[109] Beginning

---

Doc. No. 148. Report No. 211, Buchanan to Derby, 19 April; *ibid.*, Doc. No. 149. Political Report No. 25, Monson to Derby, 19 April; *ibid.*, Doc. No. 171. Report No. 11, Holmes to Elliot, 20 April; *ibid.*, inclosure in Doc. No. 189.

[106] Tels. Nos. 285, 286, Andrássy to Rodich, 23 March; *First Red Book*, Doc. No. 281, with one line omitted: *"dass die von ihnen* [the insurgents] *erreichten Resultate ihnen eine ehrenvolle Stelle in der Geschichte ihres Landes sichern."*

[107] Stillman, *Autobiography*, II, 154: ". . . . I went to see Rodich, a shrewd, precise functionary, liberal, as far as one could well be in his position, and I saw at once that, while he was determined to obey his orders, and urge a pacification because it was in accordance with his orders, he had no faith in success, and had a great sympathy with the insurgents. He was peremptory, and had a soldier-like aversion to special correspondents; but he was very just, and might have done much had the situation admitted any other result than fighting it out. . . . ."

[108] Tel., Rodich to Andrássy, Castelnuovo, 6 April; *First Red Book*, Doc. No. 287, incomplete.

[109] *The Montenegrin Journal* of 1/13 April published an account of the meetings which represented Rodich as saying, in substance: "Montenegro is not in a position to help, and as for Russia, you know that twenty years ago, when she made war against Turkey she was beaten, so that, except for Austria, you have no hope, and if you do not listen to Austria, the blood hitherto shed will have been shed in vain." The British agent in Ragusa, in forwarding the extract, expressed his belief that

with the oft-repeated declaration of lack of faith in Turkish promises, the memorandum laid down the guaranties under which the rebels would return to submission:

1. That the Christians should be given at least a third of the land as their own property;
2. That all Turkish troops be withdrawn from Hercegovina except for garrisons in six stipulated towns;
3. That the Turks should rebuild the burned Christian houses and churches, give the Christians farm implements and food supplies for at least one year, and exempt them from taxation for three years;
4. That the Christians should not surrender their arms until the Mohammedans set the example and until the promised reforms had been entirely accomplished;
5. That, in case of the return of the Christians, their leaders should discuss with the Ottoman authorities the practical application of reforms, and that together the two groups should establish a constitution in harmony with the Andrássy principles, and that the reforms should be applied to all the inhabitants of Hercegovina and Bosnia;
6. That the control of the funds destined to aid the returning Christians should be given to a European commission, and that this commission should establish central depots supplied with necessities before the return of the émigrés; and
7. That in the six towns garrisoned by the Turks the governments of Austria-Hungary and Russia should maintain agents charged with surveillance of the progress of reform.[110]

the account of Rodich's meeting had been drawn up in the Russian consulate at Ragusa (Political Report No. 23, Monson to Derby, 17 April; *Turkey No. 3 [1876]*, Doc. No. 160). Private telegrams to the *Russki Mir* also reported uncomplimentary references to Russia (Report No. 136, Loftus to Derby, 9 April; FO 65/936). Naturally these were denied by Rodich (Tel., Rodich to Andrássy, 10 April; SA, Varia Turquie I, 1875) and by Andrássy (Tel. No. 19, Andrássy to Langenau, 12 April; *ibid.*).

[110] The text of an English translation of the Italian version may be found in *Turkey No. 3 (1876)*, inclosure in Doc. No. 144. A French extract of the memorandum is in *First Yellow Book*, pp. 117–18. The *First Red Book* (Doc. No. 289) gives only Rodich's telegraphic summary.

"Actually the whole affair was still in the hands of Prince Nicholas. He gave the insurgent leaders full instructions as to their answer to the Turkish Commissioners. Before the meeting in the Suttorina, Prince Nicholas told General Alimpic [Serb agent at the time in Cetinje] : 'Nothing will come of the reconciliation. The insurgents will put forward such proposals that the Porte will not be able to accept them.' " (Mihailo D. Stojanovic, "Serbia in International Politics, from the insurrection of Herzegovina [1875] to the Congress of Berlin [1878]," manuscript dissertation [1930] in the University of London, p. 52, citing source material from the Serbian archives.)

For a discussion of the activities of another peace emissary busy at the same time, see Appendix A.

From Baron Rodich's telegraphic summary of the insurgents' conditions Count Andrássy quickly formulated his opinion. On 9 April he telegraphed to Constantinople that he would not budge one hairsbreadth beyond the concessions already granted by the Porte; henceforth he proposed merely to instruct the insurgents to negotiate directly with the Turkish authorities and to urge the prince of Montenegro to give the same advice.[111] There was no other position that the Austrian foreign minister could take. He had pledged his word to the Turks that if they accepted his program nothing else would be asked, and there was no reasonable way around that pledge. His commitment, however, was undoubtedly subordinate to another consideration. Andrássy's basic objection to these conditions arose from the fact that they indicated economic and political ambitions which were beyond the limits of his toleration. He had set out to win for the Christians of the revolted province certain concessions, concessions which would restore peace, which would make the insurgents ever grateful for Austrian intercession, but which, at the same time, would not jeopardize the interests of the Dual Monarchy. The reform plan contained in his December note provided for the maximum which he felt he could give to his turbulent neighbors. When their demands exceeded what was to him judicious generosity, he had no course except to condemn them.

But Andrássy was only a partner, even if the leading one, in the negotiations; the first necessity, now as before, was an understanding with Russia. Already on the day before he expressed his opinion to the Turks he had sent a long telegram to St. Petersburg denouncing the insurgent terms:

. . . . Those conditions of an agrarian character are obviously inimical to the rights of property and therefore unrealizable. The guaranties demanded differ essentially from those which can be assumed by the powers. In general these demands go even beyond the recognition of the insurgents as belligerents and seem to me to be such as a victorious army alone might formulate. I do not think that, even if we wished to accept these conditions, we should have the least chance of making the Porte accept them. Furthermore, I think that, if

[111] Tel. No. 33 (329), Andrássy to Zichy, 9 April; SA, Varia Turquie I, 1875. Report No. 364, Elliot to Derby, 11 April; *Turkey No. 3 (1876)*, Doc. No. 146. On the morning of 10 April, before Zichy had delivered Andrássy's message, Ignatiev had volunteered the information to Rashid that both Rodich and Andrássy had characterized the insurgent terms as "perfectly reasonable." When Elliot, also in advance of Zichy, reported the real opinion held in Vienna, "Rashid Pasha was indignant at the artifices of the Russian Ambassador to create a distrust of Austria" (Report No. 367, Elliot to Derby, 10 April; FO 78/2457). Zichy saw Rashid later in the day (Tel. No. 80, Zichy to Andrássy, 10 April; SA, Varia Turquie I, 1875).

one wished to enter upon subsequent negotiations with the insurgents on these bases, it would be impossible to arrive at a result, whereas I believe, on the contrary, that if the two cabinets act together, the original conditions will undoubtedly be accepted.

We are therefore of opinion, and I have the conviction that this opinion will be shared by the imperial government of Russia, that there is no other response to make than that the powers maintain the views previously announced by them and that they decline every guaranty and every control other than those which they have pledged themselves before Europe to demand.

He concluded his message by proposing a joint Austro-Russian summons to Prince Nicholas of Montenegro, calling on him to advise the insurgents to accept *purement et simplement* the Andrássy proposals.[112]

AUSTRO-RUSSIAN NEGOTIATIONS OVER THE DEMANDS OF THE INSURGENTS

The Russian chancellor, it will be recalled, had been unswerving in his determination to co-operate with Vienna on the Andrássy program of reform. He had turned a deaf ear to the arguments and alarms of General Ignatiev; he had refused the devious plans of Prince Bismarck to cut the Gordian knot; he had peremptorily rejected the attempt of the Turks to protest against the impending measures of the powers. But in preparing the Turks for the presentation of the demands he had been cordial and conciliatory. "We wish to maintain the integrity of the Ottoman empire," the Turkish ambassador reported him as saying, "but it is necessary to introduce the reforms which I have been counseling in vain for twenty years. We shall do all in our power to relieve the Porte of the embarrassment of the rebellion. . . . ."[113] "As far as I am able to judge from appearances," Gorchakov wrote in early February, "the Porte, bowing to the advice of the Great Powers, wishes to proceed to the immediate application of the promises made in favor of Bosnia and Hercegovina. If she keeps her word and applies herself to a conscientious execution, we are obliged loyally to attempt to lead the insurgents to accept these favors. . . . ."[114] In pursuance of that obligation the chancellor sent the most serious admonitions to the princes of Serbia and Montenegro to maintain peace, and he gave a commission to Wesselitsky-

[112] Tel. No. 17, Andrássy to Langenau, 8 April; SA, Varia Turquie I, 1875. Report No. 197, Buchanan to Derby, 10 April; *Turkey No. 3 (1876)*, Doc. No. 131.
[113] Tel. No. 14, Zichy to Andrássy, 22 January; SA, Varia Turquie I, 1875.
[114] Private letter, Gorchakov to Novikov in Vienna, 7 February; FO 65/953 (communicated to Lord Derby in June).

Bojidarovitch to preach pacification in Hercegovina.[115] In February he was sympathetic toward a cessation of hostilities but sufficiently considerate of Turkey's position to oppose a formal armistice which might be interpreted as a recognition of the insurgents as belligerents.[116] When the Turks accepted the major portion of the Andrássy program, Gorchakov proclaimed his complete satisfaction and promised the Turks that as soon as the stipulated reforms were put into practice he would take effective action in the interest of a peaceful settlement.[117] As February moved on, the official world of St. Petersburg was inclined to consider the situation as good as could be expected.[118]

Before the month was over there had appeared a considerable gulf between the views of St. Petersburg and Vienna as to what should be the next step. At the time that Gorchakov was urging reforms as a preliminary step to pacification Andrássy was reversing the procedure and advising the Turks to hold in abeyance the organization of the commission until pacification had been effected.[119] A few days later, when Andrássy was suggesting to the Porte that a strong military attack should be launched in case the insurgents were obdurate,[120] Gorchakov was advising the Turks to slow their operations or, preferably, stop them altogether.[121] When in early March Andrássy was inclined to condone Turkish delay in the face of Montenegrin impatience to see something done,[122] Gorchakov leaned to the side of Prince Nicholas and again called on the Turks to proceed immediately with the institution of reforms, reminding them sternly that this work was a matter of honor for Austria and Russia.[123] In St. Petersburg there was no disposition to conceal a strong sympathy

[115] Wesselitsky-Bojidarovitch, *Dix mois de ma vie*, pp. 106–8; *La Bosnie-Herzégovine*, pp. 68–69, 86–87. Report No. 138, Loftus to Derby, 12 April; FO 65/936.

[116] Reports Nos. 29 and 43, Loftus to Derby, 2 and 4 February, respectively; FO 65/935.

[117] Tel. No. 17, Langenau to Andrássy, 14 February; *First Red Book*, Doc. No. 234. Tel. No. 42, Zichy to Andrássy, 15 February; SA, Varia Turquie I, 1875.

[118] Report No. 9B, Langenau to Andrássy, 4/16 February; *ibid*. Report No. 83, Loftus to Derby, 29 February; *Turkey No. 3 (1876)*, Doc. No. 31.

[119] Tel. No. 11, Andrássy to Zichy, 18 February; *First Red Book*, Doc. No. 238.

[120] Tels. Nos. 12 and 13, Andrássy to Zichy, 25 February; *ibid.*, Doc. No. 240, incomplete.

[121] Rashid to Aarifi, Constantinople, 27 February, with Aarifi to Andrássy, 29 February; SA, Varia Turquie I, 1875.

[122] Tel., Andrássy to Langenau, 4 March; *First Red Book*, Doc. No. 244.

[123] Tel. No. 20, Langenau to Andrássy, 6 March; *ibid.*, Doc. No. 246.

for Montenegro,[124] whereas in Vienna, when Novikov brought up in "an academic manner" the question of giving Prince Nicholas an increase in territory, Andrássy replied with a categorical refusal[125] and secretly warned the Turks against any such arrangement.[126] Gorchakov, still insistent in mid-March on the early realization of reform and anxious to keep Mahmud and Rashid in office for that purpose,[127] proposed that these two officials be given Austrian and Russian decorations; Andrássy preferred to wait until the work of pacification was accomplished.[128] Another portentous shadow appeared on the horizon of Austro-Russian unanimity when Andrássy presented Gorchakov with a fait accompli by sending an ultimatum to Serbia without previous understanding,[129] and still another when Gorchakov again announced "as a personal opinion" that autonomy for the two insurgent provinces was the only ultimate solution of the revolt.[130] Toward the end of the month, when Andrássy was concentrating all his efforts on persuading the insurgents and refugees to return to their homes, the Russian chancellor had become pessimistic and impatient. The chaos prevailing in Turkey left him with little hope. "I can say sincerely," he remarked to the British ambassador, "that we wish to maintain the Turkish Empire. It is our object and interest to do so, but we cannot struggle against destiny, and although we have used all our diplomatic efforts for the pacification of the insurgent provinces, we have no means of remedying the internal decay of the Empire."[131]

[124] Loftus to Derby, 29 February; *Turkey No. 3 (1876)*, Doc. No. 28.

[125] Andrássy to Langenau, 9 February; SA, Russia, 1876.

[126] Tel. No. 9, Andrássy to Zichy, 8 February; SA, Varia Turquie I, 1875. If Turkey embarked on a project of buying off the Christians, the Austrian minister stated: "elle se trouverait dans la position de la femme qui, poursuivie dans un traîneau par les loups, leur jeta ses enfants l'un après l'autre pour se sauver elle-même. Les premiers rassasiés, cessèrent la poursuite, mais la faim des autres ne fit qu'augmenter et la femme finit par être mangée."

[127] Report No. 95, Loftus to Derby, 14 March; *Turkey No. 3 (1876)*, Doc. No. 58.

[128] Andrássy to Langenau, 8 March; SA, Russia, 1876.

[129] *Vide infra*, chapter vii.

[130] Tel. No. 23, Langenau to Andrássy, 21 March; SA, Varia Turquie I, 1875. The foreign minister wrote on the margin of this document: "Der alte Herr radotiert schon wieder! was sehr unangenehm ist—er vergisst aber dass es sich nicht um Kokhand u. Samarkand handelt u. er diese Idee nie realisieren wird. Was ihm nach meiner gehorsamsten Ansicht auch klar gemacht werden muss."

[131] Report No. 115, Loftus to Derby, 28 March; *Turkey No. 3 (1876)*, Doc. No. 100.

In response to this slow but definite drift of official views the Russian press in late March suddenly burst forth with leading articles condemning Turkey, supporting the desires of the insurgents for material guaranties, and urging the territorial extension of Montenegro.[132] "The influence of a press which has no liberty is frequently mischievous," remarked a London weekly, "and its tone is habitually perplexing. When half a dozen semi-official papers at St. Petersburg and Moscow suddenly advocate a new line of policy, it may be inferred, not necessarily that the Government has changed its purpose, but that it is thought expedient to disturb the impressions which had previously existed. . . . ."[133] In a sense the climax of this press campaign at the end of March was an article in *Golos,* reproduced in the official *Journal de St. Pétersbourg,* an article which, said Loftus, "if not directly emanating from an official source, represents very faithfully the political views of the imperial government." It stated:

. . . . The powers who have made the Porte accept a program of reforms should continue their efforts to restore tranquillity in the south of Europe and to improve the situation of the insurgent provinces. Autonomy of the Christian communities ought to be the solid basis of this improvement; in assuming this autonomy as an objective, the great powers would follow a course in which there could be produced between them no conflicts of interests or views. One might say of this solution what M. Thiers once said of the republic in France: it is best because it divides the least. . . . .[134]

132 ". . . . Along the whole line of the Russian Press a change of tactics has suddenly set in. The maintenance of the *status quo* in the East and of the three Emperors' alliance in the centre of Europe is no longer the keynote of leading articles in the Russian capital. Very different ideas are being suddenly aired pretty freely. The inability of the Turkish Government to carry out the reform programme; the right of the Herzegovinese to ask for tangible guarantees; the possibility of aggrandizing Montenegro at the expense of the Porte—these and similar topics, tabooed but a short time ago, are unexpectedly on the tapis. The advantage of keeping on good terms with Austria is no more alluded to, and the Turk, yesterday the cherished ward of the Russ, is suddenly treated as a reprobate and given up to fate. . . . ." (Berlin dispatch of 1 April, *The Times* (London), 5 April 1876, p. 10, col. 1.)

133 "Turkey and Russia," *Saturday Review,* 8 April 1876, pp. 448–49. The article continued: "The Russian press has now renewed its chronic antagonism to Turkey; and it encourages Servia and Montenegro to take the aggressive course which they had hitherto been forbidden by the Russian Government to adopt. It is no longer thought expedient to insist on the necessity of maintaining the triple alliance; and Austria as well as Turkey is held up as an object of national jealousy. It is worth while to observe that England is simultaneously threatened with Russian aggression in Asia. One journal announces the necessity of an advance towards the Persian Gulf, and informs the English nation that, if it objects, it must take the consequences. . . . ."

134 Report No. 126, Loftus to Derby, 1 April; FO 65/936.

As a further—and ominous—articulation of Russian thought Prince Gorchakov wrote on 1 April: "I do not wish a rupture of our intimate relations with Andrássy. Too many persons have an interest in making a breach. It is to his interest to maintain the intimacy of our relations, of which Austria especially has need. . . . . If there is a divergence between us and Austria over the Eastern question. Bismarck has assured Shuvalov that we may count unconditionally on him. . . . ."[135]

Such was the independent swing of Russian feeling in April when Andrássy denounced the conditions laid down by the insurgents and called on Gorchakov not only to stand by the Austrian reform program but also to admonish Prince Nicholas to follow the same course.[136] After waiting in vain two days for a reply from St. Petersburg, Andrássy telegraphed again. He had seen in a message from Nicholas the possibility of extending the armistice for further negotiations, and he ordered his ambassador to Russia to press for an immediate reply.[137]

On that same day, 10 April, Baron Langenau called on Prince Gorchakov for his reply. He found the chancellor "fort occupé, très nerveux, et d'assez mauvaise humeur"—and opposed to Andrássy's opinions. The terms of the insurgents, he held in contrast to the Austrian minister, were not beyond the pale of discussion at all; he was in complete sympathy with their demand for dependable guaranties before returning to their homes. And as for the summons to the Prince of Montenegro, Gorchakov came directly out into the open and declared that he would send the desired telegram only on condition that along with the proposed admonition should go a promise of territorial aggrandizement including a port on the Adriatic sea. The chancellor went on to complain that the Austrian authorities had held up a supply of rifles purchased by Nicholas in Vienna, and characterized the embargo as proof of a suspicion which the prince certainly had not merited.[138]

Thus it appeared at a critical moment in the course of the rebellion that the Austro-Russian understanding which had been so labor-

[135] Gorchakov to Oubril, 20 March/1 April; Goriainov, op. cit., p. 316.

[136] Tel. No. 17, Andrássy to Langenau, 8 April; SA, Varia Turquie I, 1875.

[137] Tel. No. 18, Andrássy to Langenau, 10 April; ibid.

[138] Tel. No. 27, Report No. 18AC, Langenau to Andrássy, 10, 11 April, respectively; ibid. Report No. 138, Loftus to Derby, 12 April; Turkey No. 3 (1876), Doc. No. 138.

iously established and maintained was destroyed. The fundamental difference in approach to a revolt of Turkey's Christians had asserted itself despite the thin plaster of mutual confidence. Independently Gorchakov had, like Andrássy, expressed his views to the Turks[139] but at the same time he did not hesitate, when he learned of the Austrian minister's action, to voice his regret that Andrássy had not consulted him before sending an opinion to the Porte. It was to be feared, the chancellor told Langenau, that if this divergence of opinion were known in Constantinople it might be exploited by those eager to welcome a lack of complete Austro-Russian harmony.[140]

It was impolitic for Andrássy to widen the breach by throwing down the gauntlet to Gorchakov. Austro-Russian understanding was imperative in those uncertain days, and that necessity imposed on Andrássy the obligation to reconcile his own refusal to budge from his original program with the Russian demand that the insurgent terms be considered. This prodigious feat he attempted on 12 April as soon as he had heard from Langenau. Seemingly abandoning his views as expressed in Constantinople, he telegraphed to St. Petersburg:

. . . . Since, in my opinion pacification could not be effected except by a prolongation of the truce, and since it is to be feared that the Porte would refuse its consent to this prolongation if the powers supported the concessions demanded by the insurgents, since furthermore those of the insurgent demands which appear attainable can be the object of negotiations between us and the Porte, but not between us and the insurgents, I have thought it necessary to inform the Ottoman government that we should not go beyond the limits of what seemed to us necessary for putting into execution what we had already agreed upon with it. This declaration prejudices absolutely nothing. . . . .[141]

[139] Tel. No. 81, Zichy to Andrássy, 12 April; SA, Varia Turquie I, 1875.

[140] Report No. 18B, Langenau to Andrássy, 12 April; *ibid*. It was at this delicate juncture that the Russian newspapers, and notably *Golos* and *Russki Mir*, created a sensation unfortunate for opinion toward Austria by printing reports of Rodich's allegedly disparaging remarks to the insurgents about Russia (Tel. No. 28, Langenau to Andrássy, 11 April; *ibid*. Report No. 136, Loftus to Derby, 9 April; FO 65/936). The governor-general declared the report to be a willful distortion of his words by a Russian correspondent (Tel., Rodich to Andrássy, 10 April; SA, Varia Turquie I, 1875) and Andrássy telegraphed a denial to St. Petersburg (Tel. No. 19, Andrássy to Langenau, 12 April; *ibid*.). The official *Journal de St. Pétersbourg* politely doubted the authenticity of the report, but the director of the foreign office expressed his fear that the incident had served to revive anti-Austrian feeling (Report No. 138, Loftus to Derby, 12 April; suppressed in *Turkey No. 3 [1876]*, Doc. No. 138). *Vide supra*, p. 254, n. 109.

[141] Tel. No. 19, Andrássy to Langenau, 12 April; SA, Varia Turiquie I, 1875.

In a second telegram the Austrian minister took up the insurgent conditions one by one and gave his "matured" opinion. He concluded his critique by announcing that, in his view, these conditions were of three kinds: those already accorded, those which could not be accorded, and those which Austria was willing to join Russia in supporting in Constantinople. But the important category was the last; and it revealed, despite the telegram's phraseology of sweet reasonableness, that Andrássy had not strained the hairsbreadth very far. Of the seven conditions given to Rodich, the minister found two of a nature to warrant discussion, and these two were the least important of the group: concentration of the Turkish troops in garrisons; and the right of the Christians to bear arms along with the Moslems. The demands for one-third of the land, for a European commission, and for Austro-Russian surveillance were put into the category of the impossible.[142]

The second of the points of difference between Vienna and St. Petersburg, the extension of Montenegro, Andrássy disposed of without equivocation: he summarily rejected the Russian proposal.[143]

At the Ballplatz that same day Sir Andrew Buchanan was solemnly assured that, although there had been a "slight difference of opinion" between the two imperial capitals, Gorchakov had given way to Andrássy's opinion that no further demands could be made on the Porte.[144] But the statement was merely a childish—or diplomatic, if one will—fabrication. When Lord Augustus Loftus called on the Russian chancellor the day following, Gorchakov's opinions were unchanged and his annoyance with Andrássy's hasty action was easily seen.[145] Baron Langenau also found the venerable statesman unrelenting. Gorchakov had very definite views with regard to Montenegro. He preferred to make no move whatever in Cetinje, he told the Austrian ambassador, if it were not made in the manner he de-

---

The pertinent part of Andrássy's message to Constantinople read as follows: "Um etwaigen Besorgnissen in Konstantinopel vorzubeugen, wollen Ew. Raschid Pascha erklären, dass wir nicht ein Haarbreit über die von der Pforte gemachten Concessionen hinausgehen werden. . . . ." (Tel. No. 33 [329], Andrássy to Zichy, 9 April; *ibid.*).

[142] Tel. No. 20, Andrássy to Langenau, 12 April; *First Red Book*, Doc. No. 291.

[143] Tel. No. 19, Andrássy to Langenau, 12 April; SA, Varia Turquie I, 1875.

[144] Report No. 206, Buchanan to Derby, 13 April; *Turkey No. 3 (1876)*, Doc. No. 139.

[145] Report No. 146, Loftus to Derby, 14 April; *ibid.*, Doc. No. 151, incomplete.

sired. Langenau tried to persuade him to leave aside for the moment questions for future settlement, but the chancellor resolutely insisted that the extension of the principality was a problem of immediate concern.[146] He was grumbling still his regrets about the Austrian declaration, but seemed to be greatly pleased on the fourteenth when he learned that Andrássy had offered to support certain of the insurgent conditions. Plans were being made in those days for a personal meeting in Berlin between the directors of Russian and of Austrian policy and, now that the the latent divergency had appeared, Gorchakov considered an interview more imperative than ever.[147] In the meantime, Langenau observed, the tsar and his chief minister were occupied with three projects which they would probably take to Berlin: (1) to find guaranties that would permit the insurgents to go home; (2) to gain advantages for the prince of Montenegro; and (3) to prepare for the eventual autonomy of the insurgent area.[148]

The immediate problem in Austro-Russian relations concerned the insurgent demands. Gorchakov claimed to be too busy to discuss in detail the Andrássy arguments, but he did find time to insist, both through interviews with the ambassador in St. Petersburg and through instructions to Ignatiev, that the Porte renew negotiations with the rebels. The chancellor's patience was rapidly giving way to irritation against the Turks. He reminded them that Russia had never promised to suppress the rebellion in case the Andrássy note was accepted; he had promised his best efforts toward pacification, he stated, on condition that the reforms be executed, and he challenged Cabouli Pasha to cite one single measure which had been carried out.[149] Cabouli's account of the interview reported a declaration from Gorchakov to the effect that "Europe could not remain indifferent to the continued effusion of *Christian* blood in the Herzegovine." In Constantinople the expression created a veritable sensation; some people, wrote Elliot, regarded it as "foreshadowing an intervention in favour of the Christians, in whose sufferings alone

---

[146] Tel. No. 29, Langenau to Andrássy, 13 April; SA, Varia Turquie I, 1875.

[147] Tel. No. 30, Langenau to Andrássy, 14 April; *ibid.*

[148] Report No. 20, Langenau to Andrássy, 6/18 April; *ibid.* A short time before, when he was passing through Germany, Count Shuvalov had sounded Bismarck on the question of autonomy for the insurgent provinces but received a discouraging response (Report No. 20AB, Károlyi to Andrássy, Berlin, 29 April; *ibid.*).

[149] Report No. 156, Loftus to Derby, 22 April; *Turkey No. 3 (1876)*, Doc. No. 163.

the Russian Government appear to feel interest."[150] At the same time, none the less, it was plain beyond all question to the Turks that Austro-Russian unity was a thing of the past, and in that break they saw their freedom to do as they pleased. They informed Ignatiev on 17 April that they refused to accede to the wishes of Russia, and that, contrariwise, the rebellion was to be put down by force.[151] Cabouli was given the difficult task of reporting the Turkish decision directly to Prince Gorchakov. He was charged to express the Porte's regret at the chancellor's present language after he had promised support if the Andrássy proposals were accepted and after he had approved as sufficient the earlier concessions offered to the insurgents. And, finally, he was ordered to inform Gorchakov that the Turks considered military action the only route to pacification.[152]

The news of Mukhtar's renewed military activities reached St. Petersburg before the Turkish ambassador received his instructions. Prince Gorchakov, consequently, was already in a state of irritation and discouragement[153] when Cabouli arrived with his message. In unconcealed exasperation the chancellor replied, "Since the Ottoman Porte has itself by this declaration closed the negotiations, I have nothing to say to you for the moment; I shall come to an understanding with the northern powers on what there is to be done."[154] Turkey had appealed to the decision of arms, he said to Loftus, and the powers could only await the outcome: *"la parole est aux canons."*[155]

---

[150] Report No. 390, Elliot to Derby, 18 April; FO 78/2457. The disturbed ambassador continued: "Rashid Pasha says that the expression of a hope that an end might be put to the general suffering, caused by the Insurrection, would have been a very different thing from confining the interest shown to those who had themselves produced it."

[151] Melegari to Robilant, 22 April; *First Green Book,* Doc. No. CXXXII. Decazes to d'Harcourt, 18 April; *Documents français,* II, Doc. No. 40.

[152] Tels. Nos. 88 and 89, Zichy to Andrássy, 17 and 19 April, respectively; SA, Varia Turquie I, 1875. Report No. 384, Elliot to Derby, 17 April; *Turkey No. 3 (1876),* Doc. No. 174. Corti to Melegari, 18 April; *First Green Book,* Doc. No. CXXXIII.

[153] Melegari to Robilant, 22 April; *First Green Book,* Doc. No. CXXXII.

[154] Tel. No. 92, Zichy to Andrássy, 22 April; SA, Varia Turquie I, 1875.

[155] Report No. 154, Loftus to Derby, 20 April; *Turkey No. 3 (1876),* Doc No. 162. Elliot, when he read Loftus' account of Gorchakov's views, protested that the expression regarding inevitable conflict conveyed "a very inaccurate statement of the case." The ambassador at the Porte pointed out quite logically that Turkey had agreed to a suspension of hostilities on a stated condition and that, when that condition had not been met, it was necessary for Mukhtar to act (Report No. 412, Elliot to Derby, 23 April; *ibid.,* Doc. No. 202, incomplete).

RUMOR OF A TURKISH DECLARATION OF WAR ON MONTENEGRO

While Vienna and St. Petersburg were occupied with their discussion of the demands of the insurgents, new storm clouds were fast forming overhead. The focal point of this additional disturbance was Montenegro. Since the beginning of the rebellion the prince and people of the Black Mountain had been directly involved in the insurrection just beyond their borders, and for months Turkish wrath had been rising against them. In January Prince Nicholas quietly abandoned any pretense at maintaining a closed frontier, and his own subjects began to play an increasingly important role in the insurgent ranks.[156] In Constantinople conviction was ever growing that the principalities of Montenegro and Serbia were the real hearths of the rebellion and that war on them was the only way to restore peace to Bosnia and Hercegovina. In late January and early February there was real danger, consequently, that the Porte might open a formal war. In the next days that danger did not materialize, but there was no reconciliation between Montenegrin and Turk.

The critical moment in their relations came when the armistice of early April was arranged. Prince Nicholas pledged himself to aid in the transport of supplies to Niksich—and the supplies did not reach their destination. The prince readily blamed the Turks when communicating with Andrássy[157] and charged Rodich with the responsibility when corresponding with Ignatiev,[158] but consistently he exculpated himself. Rodich, too, although he felt unable to explain the failure, expressed belief in Nicholas' good faith.[159] At the Porte, however, the conviction was soon established that both Nicholas and the governor-general of Dalmatia had deliberately defrauded the Turks in the whole affair.[160] The Turkish foreign minister publicly charged that the failure to provision the garrison was due "to the disguised hindrances which Montenegro has taxed her ingenuity to multiply with a view to entirely prevent the accomplishment of this wish. . . . . Is it a very hazardous conjecture," he concluded, "if we

---

[156] Tel., Rodich to Andrássy, Zara, 13 January; SA, Varia Turquie II, 1875.

[157] Tel., Prince of Montenegro to Andrássy, Cetinje, 13 April; SA, Varia Turquie I, 1875. *Vide supra,* p. 253, n. 103.

[158] Report No. 416, Elliot to Derby, 23 April; FO 78/2457.

[159] Tel., Rodich to Andrássy, 13 April; SA, Varia Turquie I, 1875.

[160] Report No. 386, Elliot to Derby, 17 April; FO 78/2457.

suppose that advantage has been taken of our confidence and good
faith, and that the insurgent chiefs, in understanding with Montenegro, have made us lose time with a view to profit by circumstances?"[161]

In order to save the endangered fortress, as has been seen, Mukhtar on 13 April gathered his forces and started to march through the
Duga Pass. Defeated in the attempt, he returned to his base alleging
victory and reporting that seven thousand armed and regularly organized Montenegrins had participated in the battle.[162] However
much truth there was in the pasha's report, Mukhtar was primarily
bent on catering to the appetites for war which had recently become
so voracious in Constantinople. His affiliations in the capital were
with the party of vigorous action headed by the militant Hussein
Avni. For months this group had been urging the sultan to let them
go to the well-springs of the revolt but had been held in check by Mahmud and Rashid, who were laying great weight on the support of the
powers and on moderate measures of reform. The grand vizier and
his irenic colleague had been out of favor with the sultan since the
end of January and, as it became increasingly apparent in April that
there was actually little hope of pacification, the war party at the
Porte began to make rapid strides. For some time this element in
the Ottoman government had been planning to concentrate an army
at Scutari, just south of Montenegro, with a view to an eventual
invasion.[163] The grand vizier and foreign minister had been obliged
to admit that hopes of serious Austrian and Russian assistance in
quelling the uprising were an illusion. The intrigues of the Russian
consul-general in Ragusa, no less than the Slavic sympathies of the
Austrian frontier population, had long been notorious, but for the
Turks the climax of their disillusionment came when they learned
that Andrássy was apparently repudiating his first condemnation of
the insurgent terms and was joining Russia in a demand for new
concessions. Rashid could come to no other conclusion, he told his
friend Elliot, "than that the two Governments are trifling with the
Porte, which must therefore pursue its own course." He refused
any further "delusive negotiations carried on by Austrian or Russian Agents in whose good faith they [the Turks] can place no con-

---

[161] Rashid to Musurus, 13 April; *Turkey No. 3 (1876)*, inclosure in Doc. No. 140.
The translation is that of the British Foreign Office.
[162] *The Times* (London), 20 April 1876, p. 5, cols. 5–6. *Vide supra*, p. 253.
[163] *Ibid.*, 28 April 1876, p. 11, col. 1.

fidence," and he consented to the sending of troops to Albania in order to be prepared for an emergency which might be precipitated by the untrustworthy prince of Montenegro.[164]

Such was the state of feeling in Constantinople when Mukhtar's telegram arrived announcing open warfare on the part of the Montenegrins. Immediately the cry for war raised by ministers and all classes who made up Turkish public opinion became so insistent that there seemed little prospect of avoiding hostilities.[165] The sultan promptly—on 20 April—called a military council and ordered the dispatch of troops to Scutari "with a view to the adoption of immediate operations against the Principality." Sir Henry Elliot was at the Porte talking with the grand vizier when the order for the council meeting arrived. The ambassador was convinced that Turkey could not cope successfully with all the consequences of an attack on Montenegro. The Russian government had long since made it plain that an attack would not be countenanced, and Elliot consequently attempted to dissuade Mahmud from such a disastrous course.[166] But Mahmud was no longer able to command the confidence of his imperial master, as was proved on the eighteenth by the appointment of his enemy Dervish Pasha to the ministry of war. The council held on the evening of the twentieth was dominated by the belligerent spirit of the new minister; despite Mahmud's protest that there was no money for such an enterprise, a turbulent majority of the council voted in favor of war.[167]

On the following day, when the embassies in Constantinople learned of the decision, the trio of diplomatists of whom the Russian representative was the director decided that it was pressingly necessary to intervene. They drew up a sharp note of warning and authorized Ignatiev, as *doyen* of the corps, to elicit the approval of the other ambassadors and present the document at the Porte. The next morning—22 April—Ignatiev delivered his message to Mahmud and Rashid; the two despairing ministers were more than happy to receive the warning and use it to dissuade the sultan from the dangerous

164 Report No. 388, Elliot to Derby, 17 April; *Turkey No. 3 (1876)*, Doc. No. 175, incomplete.

165 Report No. 403, Elliot to Derby, 21 April; *ibid.,* Doc. No. 199.

166 Report No. 400, Elliot to Derby, 20 April; *ibid.,* Doc. No. 198, incomplete. Tel. No. 4, Károlyi to Andrássy, 23 January; SA, Germany, 1876.

167 Tel. No. 91, Zichy to Andrássy, 21 April; SA, Varia Turquie I, 1875.

course which the two were opposing.[168] Rashid went immediately to the palace with a written version of Ignatiev's message and laid before Abdul Aziz the overwhelming odds against a new military adventure. Before the audience was over the foreign secretary's earnest arguments prevailed;[169] the bellicose disposition quickly subsided and the ambassadors received formal assurance that Turkey wished no conflict with Montenegro and would welcome Nicholas' co-operation in the provisioning of Niksich.[170]

[168] The text of the declaration agreed upon by the three imperial ambassadors was as follows: "En présence des bruits de conflit avec le Monténégro répandus à Constantinople depuis jeudi dernier et des préparatifs de guerre ordonnés par la Porte, l'ambassadeur de Russie et ses collègues accrédités auprès de Sa Majesté le Sultan ont cru impossible de rester indifférents à cette situation.

"Ne connaissant pas encore l'impression produite par ces nouvelles sur leurs Cabinets et réservant entièrement l'opinion de ces derniers, ainsi que les démarches qu'ils jugeraient bon d'entreprendre, les représentants ont cru devoir signaler au gouvernement ottoman qu'en attaquant le Monténégro, il risquerait d'évoquer la question d'Orient toute entière et d'attirer les plus grandes calamités sur la Turquie" (Report No. 32A, Zichy to Andrássy, 25 April; SA, Varia Turquie I, 1875).

Zichy reported that Elliot, when asked to join in the declaration, declined on the ground that he had already given the grand vizier advice against war. Elliot stated merely that, when Ignatiev called on him on 21 April, he informed him of the remarks he had made to Mahmud. At all events it is certain that Elliot did not authorize his Russian colleague to speak for him, but Ignatiev took the responsibility upon himself to inform the Turkish ministers that he spoke for himself and his colleagues (Report No. 425, Elliot to Derby, 25 April; *Turkey No. 3 [1876]*, Doc. No. 206). "In mentioning this to me," the annoyed British ambassador subsequently reported, "the General said that he had considered himself warranted in speaking in the name of his colleagues, for although I had not authorized him to do so for me, he knew that I had already expressed the same opinion" (Report No. 438, Elliot to Derby, 28 April; *ibid.*, Doc. No. 210).

[169] Report No. 32A, Zichy to Andrássy, 25 April; SA, Varia Turquie I, 1875. Report No. 427, Elliot to Derby, 25 April; *Turkey No. 3 (1876)*, Doc. No. 207. Elliot concluded his dispatch with a new denigration of his old enemy Mahmud: "This is the second recent occasion upon which Rachid Pasha has, by a personal communication with the Sultan, exercised a marked influence over him, and it seems to confirm the truth of what is often said that, if His Majesty frequently takes ill-advised resolutions, it is because the present Grand Vizier never ventures to oppose him, or to inform him fully of the objections to the course His Majesty proposes to take."

[170] Tels. Nos. 92 and 93, Zichy to Andrássy, 22 April; SA, Varia Turquie I, 1875. Elliot's reports have it that on 21 April he sent a message to the new war minister emphasizing the imprudence of war, and that, before the day was over, he received a reply to the effect that the minister "was now inclined to avoid an attack upon Montenegro, and had spoken in this sense to the Sultan" (Report No. 407, Elliot to Derby, 21 April; *Turkey No. 3 [1876]*, Doc. No. 200*, incomplete). The following morning, at the time that Ignatiev was presenting the ambassadorial warning to Mahmud and Rashid, Elliot called in person on the new minister and received "the most positive assurance that there is no intention of attacking or de-

On 21 April the warning had gone out from Constantinople that war was threatening. British diplomacy without hesitation took its usual stand of justifying Turkey. Elliot readily believed Mukhtar's report of Montenegrin participation in the recent encounter and looked upon it as a moral obligation of Austria to force Montenegro, by a military demonstration if necessary, to keep the peace.[171] Elliot's opinion, couched in a telegram to London on the twenty-first, found its way by the next evening into the Ballplatz in Vienna. Buchanan, in a note forwarding to Andrássy his colleague's categorical statement of what Austria ought to do, was no less ready to place the onus of the crisis on Prince Nicholas. "Surely it would be monstrous," he wrote, "if the peace of Europe is to be compromised in consequence of assistance being given from Montenegro to the insurrection in violation of Prince Nicholas' promise. . . . ."[172]

The crisis was not as simple of solution for Count Andrássy as it was for the British. The Austrian minister was still concentrating his energies and hopes on effecting through his program the pacification of Bosnia and Hercegovina. He had been led to believe that Prince Nicholas of Montenegro was co-operating with him in promoting a reconciliation, and he could afford to bludgeon neither the prince nor the insurgents by a military action; the use of force would alienate sympathy which he hoped to win and it would create complications with Russia. Sweet reasonableness toward the Slavs, therefore, was still the order of the day. On the other hand, the Turks could not be permitted to destroy such prospects of a peaceful settlement as remained, regardless of how many Montenegrins fought in the Duga Pass. If the Porte resolved on no overt act, there was a chance for pacification; if war were declared on Montenegro, An-

---

claring war against Montenegro" (Report No. 409, Elliot to Derby, 22 April; *ibid.*, Doc. No. 201).

[171] Report No. 405, Elliot to Derby, 21 April; *ibid.*, Doc. No. 200, incomplete.

[172] Buchanan to Andrássy, 22 April; SA, Varia England, 1876; also in *Turkey No. 3 (1876)*, Doc. No. 167, inclosure No. 2. The critical portion of the original Elliot dispatch (No. 405 in *ibid.*, Doc. No. 200), suppressed in the printed version, read: "It seems to me, however, that when the Porte accepted Count Andrassy's proposals upon assurance that pressure would be applied to Montenegro which would terminate the insurrection, the Austrian Government incurred a moral obligation to ensure the neutrality of that Principality, and I am of opinion that under present circumstances the only means by which a rupture can be avoided between the Porte and the Principality would be a demonstration of an Austrian force in its immediate neighbourhood and an intimation to Prince Nicholas that if he cannot control his subjects Austria must assist him to do so."

drássy anticipated the entry of Serbia, Rumania, Greece, and Crete into the field at a time when the soldiers of the sultan were already involved beyond their abilities in the hills of Hercegovina. An enlarged area of hostility such as Andrássy saw opening before him would almost inevitably, it well seemed, mean the collapse of Turkey and the long-foreseen scramble for the spoils. It was most distinctly not to the advantage of Austrian policy to permit the break-up of the Ottoman Empire at that moment, and all the more so when Serbia and Montenegro gave promise of emerging with swollen gains. Austrian policy, as viewed by the foreign minister, demanded peace and renewed attempts to arrange an armistice and the provisioning of Niksich. Rather, therefore, than an armed demonstration against Montenegro, Andrássy sent a polite telegram to Prince Nicholas announcing opposition to Turkey's alleged decision and asking the prince to deny the charges made at the Porte.[173] Rather, therefore, than an acquiescence in any decision made by the Turks, Andrássy sent a stern telegram to Constantinople demanding peace. Mukhtar, he charged, was not reliable; the prince of Montenegro had not engaged his soldiers and there was no excuse on that score for war. Further, there was no excuse for war in the slowness of pacification plans, because, at worst, the joint work already undertaken had forestalled a spread of hostilities which could well have meant the end of Turkey. Andrássy sharply reminded the Porte that it could not master a local rebellion, to say nothing of a bitter warfare all over the Balkan peninsula. He closed his telegram with the threat which had now become well-nigh habitual when he was trying to influence the Turks:

If .... the Porte, contrary to all reason, decides on the course which you [Zichy] have indicated, it would not be the Porte's interests alone but also ours which would be compromised, and, moreover, there would be involved for us a question of honor. Your Excellency is therefore charged to declare in the name of the Emperor and King, our August Sovereign, that if this decision is put into execution, His Majesty, in spite of the personal friendship which he feels for the sultan and of which he has given many proofs, would be obliged to decline in advance all responsibility for the consequences which would result. You will add that in the face of such a policy on the part of Turkey which would rally to her enemies all the sympathies of Europe, we should be

[173] Tel., Andrássy to Prince Nicholas, 22 April; SA, Varia Turquie I, 1875. This denial was promptly forthcoming (Tel., Prince Nicholas to Andrássy, 23 April; *ibid.*).

led to examine the question of whether it is possible to permit further the debarkation in the port of Klek of the forces of Turkey which had become aggressive. . . . .[174]

In St. Petersburg the news of an impending war on Montenegro could not have come at a more unfortunate time for the Turks. *"C'est un soufflet qu'on me donne,"* the emperor wrote on the margin of the telegram which brought the report. Prince Gorchakov immediately ordered Ignatiev to protest energetically and to warn the Porte that a hasty step might lead to the destruction of the Ottoman Empire.[175] But, despite irritation against the Turks and firmness with regard to Montenegro, the Russian chancellor still held to the ideal of a concert of the six powers.[176] The report arrived in St. Petersburg on the evening of 21 April; at noon of the next day Gorchakov assembled the representatives of the guaranteeing powers and read them a telegram from Ignatiev describing the grave state of affairs in Constantinople. The threat of war, the agitated chancellor formally announced in the name of the emperor, was nothing less than suicidal folly, and if it materialized Russia could not honorably restrain the Serbs and other Balkan peoples from revolt. A common pressure of all the powers, he concluded, was the only means of forestalling such a crisis, and he appealed to the ambassadors to exhort their respective governments to send immediate protest to Constantinople. The foreign representatives, except that of Queen Victoria, assented with unqualified sympathy. Loftus, a personification of British policy no less than his colleagues in other capitals, intervened in the discussion to propose an investigation of Mukhtar's report before condemning it and to criticize Nicholas and the insurgents for their failure to meet their engagement; but at the same time Loftus admitted that his own information pointed to a serious crisis at the Porte.[177] Gorchakov, dressed in uniform to emphasize the solemnity of the oc-

[174] Tel. No. 368, Andrássy to Zichy, 23 April, 1 A.M.; SA, Varia Turquie I, 1875.

[175] Tel. No. 31, Langenau to Andrássy, 22 April; *ibid.,* Tatishchev, *op. cit.,* II, 303.

[176] Le Flô to Decazes, 21 April; *Documents français,* II, Doc. No. 41.

[177] Report No. 156, Loftus to Derby, 22 April; *Turkey No. 3 (1876),* Doc. No. 163. Barbolani to Melegari, 23 April; *First Green Book,* Doc. No. CXLV. Schweinitz, *Denkwürdigkeiten,* I, 322–23. Lord Augustus Loftus, *The Diplomatic Reminiscences of . . . .,* second series (London, 1894), II, 156. At the same time the Russian chancellor sent a circular telegraphic appeal for support to the other capitals (Tel., Gorchakov to Shuvalov, 22 April; *Slavonic Review,* III, 661, Doc. No. 22).

casion, indicated very plainly to the ambassadors that he looked upon the crisis as exceedingly grave. Privately to the Austrian representatives he protested again that the guns which Prince Nicholas had bought in Vienna should be released for immediate shipment.[178] "It is evident," Langenau wrote, "that the current of opinion in Russia, and even in governmental circles, is becoming more and more favorable to the Slavic coreligionaries." And as for Montenegro, *"C'est l'enfant chéri de la Russie, auquel on n'ose pas toucher."*[179]

The governments in Paris and Rome immediately sent their protests to Constantinople.[180] In the Wilhelmstrasse in Berlin there was little inclination to be alarmed by the prospect of war. Bismarck had only recently been urging the Russians not to be disturbed; a war, he thought, would lead to a Turkish defeat and that at least would precipitate some kind of dénouement. He considered almost any outcome preferable to prolonging the ruinous uncertainty which all Europe was suffering. Unofficially the German chancellor was marching *tambour battant* with the Christian Slavs,[181] but when he found Gorchakov so insistent, he instructed the German ambassador to participate in the warning.[182]

Andrássy had anticipated the Russian appeal by the ultimatum which he sent to Constantinople immediately after Zichy's alarming report had arrived. The new crisis appeared to the Vienna minister an opportunity to soothe the open wound in Austro-Russian relations made by the conflict over the insurgent demands, and Andrássy promptly assured Gorchakov that the two saw eye to eye with regard to the threatened attack. He submitted his sharp message to the Porte for the chancellor's edification, and, as an added proof of his solidarity, Andrássy reported that he had just rejected an official British proposal for an Austrian military demonstration against

---

[178] Tels. Nos. 31 and 32, Langenau to Andrássy, 22 April; SA, Varia Turquie I, 1875.

[179] Report No. 22AC, Langenau to Andrássy, 14/26 April; *ibid.*

[180] Decazes to Vogüé, 23 April; *Documents français,* II, Doc. No. 42. Decazes to d'Harcourt, 23 April; *First Yellow Book,* pp. 119–20. Report No. 144, Paget to Derby, 24 April; *Turkey No. 3 (1876),* Doc. No. 179. Corti to Melegari, 28 April; *First Green Book,* Doc. No. CXLVII.

[181] Private letter, Beust to Andrássy, 26 April; SA, Varia Turquie I, 1875. Beust got his information from Shuvalov, who had just returned to London from Germany (Schweinitz, *Denkwürdigkeiten,* I, 323).

[182] Launay to Melegari, Berlin, 26 April; *First Green Book,* Doc. No. CXLII.

Montenegro. No maneuver, this telegram to St. Petersburg insisted, could separate Austria and Russia in their common action.[183] In London the foreign office had heard from Elliot that peace was saved, and no action, accordingly, was taken. The Russian chargé d'affaires was informed of the British outlook on the twenty-fourth[184] and Shuvalov reported it to St. Petersburg.[185] Prince Gorchakov, having previously been forced to look out for obstructions erected by the British, feared that Derby was deliberately impairing the unity of European action. He was moved, therefore, to telegraph his protest on the twenty-sixth that British abstention was prejudicial to the maintenance of peace, and he besought some declaration from London that would prove to the Turks that England had not separated herself from the concert of Europe. The danger, he insisted, had by no means passed; the Porte was still concentrating forces at Scutari and such an action was bringing fire very close to the powder barrel.[186] He had already learned that the crisis had passed, but the principle of unity seemed to him the all-important consideration. The prince's apprehensions about British isolation proved unfounded; Derby, when confronted with the Russian importunities, finally cleared up the misunderstanding on the twenty-seventh by explaining that he had considered no further action necessary from the time he received Elliot's report that war would not materialize. There was no intention in London, he informed the Russians, to refuse to act in concert with the other powers when occasion was at hand.[187] The little episode was nothing more than an

[183] Tel. No. 22, Andrássy to Langenau, 23 April; SA, Varia Turquie I, 1875. Schweinitz, op. cit., I, 324. Gorchakov and the tsar looked upon the reported British proposal as an attempt to create friction between Russia and Austria (Tels. Nos. 33 and 34, Langenau to Andrássy, 24 and 25 April, respectively; SA, Varia Turquie I, 1875). The proposal for a demonstration was not presented to Andrássy as an official proposition from Lord Derby but was given in the form of a copy of Elliot's telegram which Buchanan presented as a reflection of his own personal views. Vide supra, p. 270 n.

[184] Draft No. 229, Derby to Elliot, 24 April; Turkey No. 3 (1876), Doc. No. 159. Draft No. 240, Derby to Loftus, 28 April; ibid., Doc. No. 177.

[185] Tel., Shuvalov to Gorchakov, 25 April; Slavonic Review, III, 661, Doc. No. 23.

[186] Tel., Gorchakov to Shuvalov, 26 April; ibid., Doc. No. 24. The chancellor's message was delivered to the parliamentary undersecretary on the following day (memorandum of Bourk, 27 April; FO 78/2531). Report No. 167, Loftus to Derby, 26 April; Turkey No. 3 (1876), Doc. No. 186. Report No. 171, Loftus to Derby, 26 April; ibid., Doc. No. 187, incomplete.

[187] Draft No. 239, Derby to Loftus, 27 April; ibid., Doc. No. 169. Tel., Shuvalov to Gorchakov, 29 April; Slavonic Review, III, 661, Doc. No. 25.

outcropping of the inevitable confusion incident to conducting sovereign diplomatic business in so many centers, but it was indicative of the temper of the moment in St. Petersburg. Gorchakov was irritated against the Turks, anxious for a united front, and fearful of the damage that English isolation might do.

In the meantime, as has been related, the Turks had been entirely dissuaded from their intention to attack Montenegro. The process began when Elliot sent his counsels to the new minister of war on the twenty-first. It was continued when Ignatiev on the day following took the collective admonitions of his colleagues to the grand vizier and when Rashid in turn carried the arguments to the palace. The next morning—the twenty-third—Mahmud was called out of a ministerial council still bent on war to receive a copy of Andrássy's threat. The ecstatic Zichy described the grand vizier's speech when he returned to the session in these words:

> I am, like you, all for war; we need war because war alone can save us. We shall have to organize four armies; the first against Russia, the second against Austria, the third against Montenegro, Serbia and Hercegovina, and the fourth for the maintenance of order at home. As for the expenses of war, the minister of finance will not fail to furnish us with the necessary money; you all know how much gold and silver is piled up in our treasury. In order to inform you of what we can expect from the powers I will read you a telegram which I have just this instant received.

Such zeal for war as remained, the ambassador reported, disappeared when Andrássy's message was read.[188] At about the same time Cabouli's report of the agitation in St. Petersburg arrived, and it left no doubt. Quite certain was it that Europe would not permit a declaration of war on Montenegro, however justified the Turks might think it. Before the day was over Rashid sent a circular message to the great capitals repudiating all bellicose intentions and describing the current report as nothing more than an erroneous rumor. The participation of Montenegrins in the recent fight in the Duga Pass, he explained, had imposed the sending of an observation corps to Scutari. If the powers strictly forbade Montenegrin participation in the insurrection he felt certain that there would be no necessity for military action.[189] The immediate danger, then, was forestalled and the fiction of peace remained intact. The first two weeks of April,

---

[188] Report No. 32A, Zichy to Andrássy, 25 April; SA, Varia Turquie I, 1875.

[189] Tel., Rashid to Musurus, 23 April; *Turkey No. 3 (1876)*, inclosure in Doc. No. 158.

however, had added materially to the complexity of the problem of the insurrection. Montenegro had emerged as an important factor, a factor far more important than the size of the diminutive principality might indicate. This fact was well proved in the second half of the month, when the Austro-Hungarian foreign minister was making a last and supreme effort to save his scheme of pacification.

ANDRÁSSY'S RENEWED EFFORTS FOR PACIFICATION

The breach between Austria and Russia over the insurgent demands and the Turkish threat of war on Montenegro had been for Count Andrássy painful annoyances to his all-important work of pacification. The insurgents had not, as he had once hoped, returned to their villages singing the praises of Francis Joseph. After that disappointment the minister had centered his energies on promoting an armistice and negotiations between the rebel leaders and the Turkish authorities. A second disappointment immediately materialized in the insurgent peace conditions, conditions which he could not support in Constantinople because of his inclinations and his previous pledges. Andrássy immediately sought Russian support in condemning the Suttorina demands in the hope that the insurgents, discouraged by a unanimous disapproval, would submit to a direct discussion with the Turks. That plan turned quickly into a third disappointment. But, in spite of it, he continued to work for pacification.

Very soon it was apparent that no good would come from the informal armistice during the first twelve days of April; a settlement of the differences between Turks and insurgents necessitated much more time. Before the truce expired, Prince Nicholas indicated a willingness to prolong its term,[190] and Andrássy instructed Rodich to take up the proposal with Mukhtar Pasha.[191] When he was on the point of recommending the measure to the Porte, however, the minister received complaints from Constantinople that Nicholas had not lived up to his promise to aid in the revictualing of Niksich and he felt obliged to have an explanation from the prince before sending new instructions to Zichy.[192]

[190] Tel., Rodich to Andrássy, 9 April; SA, Varia Turquie I, 1875.
[191] Tel., Andrássy to Rodich, 13 April; ibid.
[192] Tel., Andrássy to the Prince of Montenegro, 13 April; First Red Book, Doc. No. 292.

Nicholas responded on the same day—13 April—vehemently denying any responsibility for the failure to reprovision the fortress and proposing in the name of the insurgents a prolongation of the armistice for twenty days.[193] After two days of hesitation Andrássy recommended to the Porte an informal renewal of the truce. As an argument in favor of it he cited the renewed promise of Nicholas to aid in the relief of Niksich, and he pointed out that the offer indicated a peaceful inclination on the part of the insurgents.[194] At the same time Baron Rodich sent an appeal to Mukhtar to give up his impending second attempt to march into Niksich, and urged him to make a new arrangement with the prince of Montenegro.[195] Both Austrian efforts were doomed to failure; the Turkish commander had already set out on his unfortunate mission before the message arrived and in Constantinople the authorities, supporting the pasha's decision, sent a polite refusal to Andrássy's request.[196]

However, when Mukhtar's march was halted in the Duga Pass, the commander was obliged to reconsider the means of saving Niksich. On 21 April he at last acknowledged Rodich's previous telegrams and, by way of reviving negotiations, asked the general to state who would guarantee the provisioning of the garrison in case of a second truce.[197] Rodich referred the question to Prince Nicholas and, after consultation with the rebel leaders, the prince reported a new

[193] Tel., Prince of Montenegro to Andrássy, 13 April; SA, Varia Turquie I, 1875.

[194] Tel. No. 34, Andrássy to Zichy, 15 April; *ibid.* In response to an Austrian appeal for support (Buchanan to Derby, 13 April; *Turkey No. 3* [*1876*], Doc. No. 139), Derby on 13 April instructed Elliot to co-operate with Zichy in advocating the prolongation of the truce (Draft No. 216, Derby to Elliot; *ibid.*, Doc. No. 124). The next day when the British ambassador sought out his Austrian colleague he found to his amazement that Zichy had received no instructions. The whole procedure gave Elliot a new opportunity to defend the Turks: ". . . . We both consider that we should assume too serious responsibility if we advocated it [the prolongation of the truce]. The suspension was agreed to by the Porte on the understanding that Niksich was to be revictualled by the Prince of Montenegro, which has not been done, and the fortress has now provisions for very few days. It is for the purpose of throwing in supplies that the Commander-in-Chief insists upon the necessity of immediately resuming operations. Even now if the place should be obliged to capitulate the Governments which urged the first suspension will be considered responsible for the disaster" (Report No. 379, Elliot to Derby, 14 April; FO 78/2457).

[195] Tel., Rodich to Andrássy, 15 April; SA, Varia Turquie I, 1875.

[196] Tel. No. 86, Zichy to Andrássy, 16 April; *ibid.*, Tel., Rashid to Aarifi in Vienna, 15 April; *ibid.*

[197] Tel., Rodich to Andrássy, 22 April; *ibid.*

statement of the insurgent stand. Declaring that the Turks had profited by the former suspension of action to prepare another attack—the same kind of accusation made by the Turks—Nicholas' message laid down two conditions for renewing the truce: that the Turks should guarantee that they would neither reinforce their troops nor change their positions, and that the Porte should accept, through Austria as an intermediary, the discussion and the eventual realization of their seven demands. As for provisioning Niksich, the prince renewed the original offer to permit passage through Ostrog and he himself guaranteed the arrangement.[198]

Before these negotiations in Hercegovina could come to a conclusion there flamed up in Constantinople the threat of war on Montenegro. Finding their action forestalled by the intervention of Europe, as has been indicated, the Turks showed a marked moderation of temper; and on the twenty-second, under direction from the sultan, the ministers took up the negotiations. They proposed that if Nicholas agreed before the twenty-fifth to permit a convoy through Montenegro and to guarantee its security, they in turn would suspend Mukhtar's new march to the fortress.[199] Nothing was said about renewing the truce; in the minds of the Turks for the moment the important problem was sending food into Niksich. On the twenty-fifth, then, Andrássy had in his hands the offers of both sides of the controversy. Of the two, that of the insurgents was the more difficult because it stipulated acceptance of their original demands which the Austrian minister had rejected two weeks before. In his desire for resumption of negotiations, however, Andrássy tried, as he had tried with Gorchakov, to cover his views with words. To Nicholas he telegraphed that he would send the new conditions to Constantinople not as insurgent terms but as the suggestion of the prince himself, who was still disturbed by the menace of Turkish attack. With regard to the original seven demands of the insurgents Andrássy maintained the position that he had assumed when Gorchakov refused to join him in his condemnation: he promised Nicholas that Austria and Russia during the new armistice would submit to the Porte "those of the wishes of the insurgents which seem to them susceptible of realization. Once these points are clarified between the cabinets and the Ottoman government, Your Highness will be informed and

[198] Tel., Rodich to Andrássy, 23 April; SA, Varia Turquie I, 1875.
[199] Tel. No. 93, Zichy to Andrássy, 22 April; ibid.

the insurgents can enter into direct relations with the Turkish authorities."[200] He did not confess that of the seven demands he was willing to discuss only two, and those two the least important of the seven.

Andrássy's message to the Turks on the same day was of a different character. The insurgents, he telegraphed, had laid down certain conditions for the renewal of the truce, but "since these conditions do not seem to me to be acceptable by the Porte as they are, I shall try to modify them and shall not delay making known the results." In the meantime, he wished above all things to delay a new expedition by Mukhtar. Citing the promise of Prince Nicholas to guarantee the relief of the Niksich garrison, he called on the Turks to allow the pasha to make no move without further instructions.[201]

The reply from Cetinje to the latest communication was all that Andrássy could have wished. Nicholas agreed, on condition of Turkish inactivity during the truce, to guarantee the free passage of supplies through Podgoritza and Ostrog, and he accepted with thanks the Austrian offer to present the insurgent wishes at the Porte. The prince took no exception to Andrássy's limited concession but merely recommended the adoption *"aussi complète que possible"* of the insurgent demands.[202]

The Turks were not so amenable to Andrássy's desires. In response to Zichy's appeals the grand vizier consented to delay the projected march until the twenty-seventh, but set that as the last possible day to which action could be deferred. With regard to a new suspension of hostilities, Mahmud refused to take any step without specific orders from the sultan. The stumbling-block so far as the Turks were concerned was the nature of Nicholas' guaranty. As it was understood at the Porte, the prince promised security for the supply train only to his own frontier; between that point and Niksich they supposed that the caravan would be at the mercy of the insurgents and, in consequence, that in all probability it could not reach its destination.[203] Turkish apprehension was only increased by the conduct of Count Ignatiev who, in the eyes of his British and Austrian colleagues, was intent on hindering any peaceful settlement in Herce-

---

[200] Tel., Andrássy to the Prince of Montenegro, 25 April; *ibid.*

[201] Tel. No. 38 (375), Andrássy to Zichy, 25 April; *ibid.*

[202] Tel., Prince of Montenegro to Andrássy, 25 April; *ibid.*

[203] Tel. No. 99, Zichy to Andrássy, 26 April; *ibid.* Report No. 431, Elliot to Derby, 26 April; *Turkey No. 3 (1876)*, Doc. No. 208.

govina. Persistently the general argued in his conversations at the Porte that Prince Nicholas could not be held responsible beyond his own frontiers. The warning was made all the more effective by Mukhtar's reports that a large insurgent force was collecting in the immediate neighborhood of Niksich.[204] On the twenty-sixth there came to the Porte an additional incentive to defiant independent action—a peremptory summons from St. Petersburg to consent to the new truce and to the provisioning of Niksich.[205] In the ministerial council that day the forthcoming instructions to Mukhtar evoked, as was usual in the Turkish council, a lively debate. The warlike Dervish Pasha, leading the charge for the party of action, stressed the urgent necessity of relieving the fortress and in his confident zeal wagered his head that the commander had sufficient forces for the task. His heated arguments, coupled with the equivocal actions of Ignatiev and the growing suspicion of Russia's proclaimed disinterestedness, won the day for war. The council voted to send Mukhtar forward, and its decision was immediately approved by the excited sultan.[206] On the

---

[204] Report No. 453, Elliot to Derby, 2 May; *Turkey No. 3 (1876)*, Doc. No. 268.

[205] Tel. No. 103, Zichy to Andrássy, 26 April; SA, Varia Turquie I, 1875.

[206] Report No. 33AB, Zichy to Andrássy, 28 April; *ibid.* The accounts of Zichy and Elliot agree in giving a major influence to Russian activities in the Turkish decision. Said the former: ". . . . *dass das Vorgehen General Ignatiews in der Verproviantierungsfrage von Nikšić von grossem Einfluss war . . . .*" (Tel. No. 107, Zichy to Andrássy, 28 April; *ibid.*). The British ambassador's views were expressed in two reports on 27 April (No. 434 and No. 435 [FO 78/2457]) as follows: ". . . . It is understood that the language of the Russian Embassy in insisting that the Prince could not answer for the safety of the convoy beyond his own frontier has greatly contributed to this decision"; and ". . . . the distrust of Russia, whose influence over the Prince is known to be absolute, is so great that it was therefore decided at all hazards that the revictualling must be attempted by the Commander-in-Chief." There was no doubt in Elliot's mind of the justice of the Turkish decision: ". . . . Had either the Austrian or Russian Ambassador been able to engage that it [the proposed armistice] would be promptly agreed to by the insurgents, so that the arrival of provisions from Scutari could be safely calculated upon, the Porte would certainly have acceded readily to that mode of revictualling the place; but as they were unable to give any assurance upon that point, it became an absolute necessity to order Moukhtar Pasha to relieve it before it should be forced to capitulate. . . . ." (Report No. 453, Elliot to Derby, 2 May; *Turkey No. 3 [1876]*, Doc. No. 268.) The ambassador looked upon the moment at hand as the most critical the rebellion had produced: "If the attempt to relieve Niksich fails affairs will become very serious, for even should Montenegro not openly join the insurgents, it will probably require the united pressure of Europe to prevent the Porte from attacking the Principality. In order to avoid an imminent danger to the general peace it may be justifiable and proper to apply such pressure, but if the Allied Governments interpose their authority to prevent Turkey from adopting what she holds to be the only means of suppressing the insurrection, they will I believe as a necessary conse-

same day a circular telegram went out notifying the powers and asking their support in restraining Montenegro from participation in the impending fight :[207]

Taking into account . . . . the state of affairs which we see daily growing more and more marked around us, and considering the friendly and unchangeable disposition shown by the Powers, we make a last appeal for their upright moral support, with a view to put an end to these calamities, and to the crimes of high treason against humanity, daily committed by the ferocious

quence be forced to take the settlement of the whole Bosnian and Herzegovinian question into their own hands and to insist upon its being referred to a European conference" (Report No. 440, Elliot to Derby, 28 April; FO 78/2457).

The Turkish decision was taken without attempting to find out whether Nicholas would or would not guarantee the passage beyond his frontiers. On the twenty-sixth, when Andrássy learned of the doubts about this question, he sent a telegram to Nicholas asking him to give the proper assurances (SA, Varia Turquie I, 1875) and the prince replied the next day with a cordial agreement to protect the convoy all the way into Niksich (*ibid*.). Zichy, however, was later inclined to doubt the honesty of Nicholas' reply. The chief dragomans of both the Austrian and Russian embassies, he explained, spent the entire afternoon of the twenty-sixth at the Porte awaiting the Turkish decision. At five o'clock they informed their chiefs that Mukhtar was to be ordered to move, and shortly after six o'clock Ignatiev sent a cipher telegram to Jonin, the Russian consul in Ragusa, who was in close communication with Cetinje. At six-thirty the two dragomans returned to their respective embassies with details about the Turkish decision, and toward eight o'clock a second cipher telegram was dispatched to Ragusa. The next morning the Russian embassy sent still a third. Zichy suspected, therefore, that Nicholas probably knew of the Turkish decision on the evening of the twenty-sixth and was in a position on the day following to make the most glowing promises in the certain knowledge that nothing would come of them. His suspicions were all the more aroused because of the attitude of Ignatiev, who allegedly exercised a dominating influence over the prince. The general, according to Zichy's information, went to Rashid on the twenty-ninth and assured him that the Turkish decision met with the complete approval of the Russian embassy. Ignatiev went on allegedly to tell the Turkish minister that Nicholas' promises were not to be taken seriously, since they were made after the prince had heard of the instructions sent to Mukhtar. Ignatiev's words were relayed to Zichy by Rashid himself, but it is not at all certain how trustworthy the sultan's foreign minister was. The Austrian ambassador, however, took them at their face value and was very proud of having won the confidence of this important official. "Your Excellency will see," he wrote to Andrássy, "how occupied I am in watching Ignatiev." Their external relations were still good, he reported to his chief, and he warned most seriously against letting his secrets come back to his Russian colleague for fear of "war to the knife." Ignatiev would always have to be taken into consideration, Zichy concluded, and he wanted authorization to try to win him over from enemy to friend of Austria. The way to accomplish this work, he thought, was to exploit his vanity (Private letter, Zichy to Andrássy, 2 May; *ibid*.). The Austrian foreign minister, it need not be added, did not share the ambassador's illusions about how easy it would be to conquer the redoubtable general.

[207] Rashid to Musurus *et al.*, 26 April; *Turkey No. 3 (1876)*, Doc. No. 165.

rebels, to the destruction of our unhappy and inoffensive subjects. All this appears undoubtedly to give us the right of feeling convinced that the common action of the Great Powers must have been, or is at least on the point of being, brought to bear on the Prince of Montenegro, with a view to induce His Highness to confine himself to the strictest neutrality, and to urge him to act vigorously in the interest not only of pacifying this revolt, but in that of general peace; to prevent an armed participation of his subjects in the insurrection; and to secure the revictualling of Nichsich. . . . .[208]

The predilections of British policy inclined the foreign office in London to receive this appeal sympathetically. On the twenty-eighth Lord Derby sent a telegraphic message to the various European capitals endorsing the Turkish view and proposing a summons to Prince Nicholas "to maintain an efficient neutrality."[209] But the unanimity of opinion which had just a few days earlier condemned war on Montenegro was now a thing of the past. The French, indeed, made a suitable affirmative response,[210] but in Berlin Prince Bismarck was still unwilling to go beyond the limits of Austro-Russian agreement and excused himself on the pretext of having no consul in Cetinje.[211] In Vienna Count Andrássy, engrossed in his own affairs, dismissed the proposal on the ground of Nicholas' satisfactory explanations.[212] Andrássy had had occasion to see the influence which the ruler of Montenegro exercised over the insurgents and he could not afford, in the interest of his program, to alienate the prince's good-will. As soon as he heard of the resolution taken in Constantinople, the minister telegraphed to Nicholas a warning of what to expect and assured him of Austrian protection so long as he did not take the initiative in war.[213] The prince by his astute policy of outward compliance

[208] Tel., Rashid to Musurus *et al.*, 26 April; *Turkey No. 3 (1876)*, Doc. No. 176. Also in *First Green Book,* Doc. No. CXXXVIII, and *First Yellow Book,* pp. 123–24. The quotation is from the British Foreign Office translation.

[209] Draft No. 241, Derby to Loftus *et al.*, 28 April; *Turkey No. 3 (1876)*, Doc. No. 178.

[210] Report No. 299, Adams to Derby, 29 April; *ibid.,* Doc. No. 193.

[211] Report No. 180, Russell to Derby, 28 April; FO 64/851.

[212] Report No. 243B, Buchanan to Derby, 28 April; *Turkey No. 3 (1876)*, Doc. No. 211.

[213] Tel., Andrássy to Prince of Montenegro, 27 April; SA, Varia Turquie I, 1875. Nicholas was abounding in thanks when acknowledging this comforting message and denied in advance any fresh charges that Mukhtar might make (Tel., Prince of Montenegro to Andrássy, 28 April; *ibid.*). On the day following, when Mukhtar launched his attack, which could be heard in Cetinje, Nicholas, alleging an excited population and *"la présence d'une grande force turque si près de mon territoire,"* sent two battalions *"en observation"* to the frontier. "I should not be

maintained a strategic position; the Turks, on the other hand, were living up to their reputation of doing the wrong thing. After having been forced into accepting Andrássy's program, they were now in late April resolving on an action which gave promise of irreparable harm to that cherished plan. Andrássy, consequently, began anew his badgering of the Turks. He informed them that he had made all the arrangements the Porte had wished regarding a peaceful relief of Niksich; he had sustained the Turkish point of view in the armistice negotiations; he had arranged, in short, the acceptance of all the conditions laid down in Constantinople. After all that he had done, he refused any further responsibility and—coming to the real point of his message—he called upon the Turks to countermand Mukhtar's march.[214] A second telegram in the same spirit immediately followed,[215] but both were without result. Mahmud and Rashid were eloquent in their regrets that the impression made on Count Andrássy by the latest decision was so painful and they promised to go directly to the sultan with the Austrian message—but a counter order to Mukhtar they refused to consider.[216]

If Lord Derby, in sending to St. Petersburg his proposal for a joint summons to Montenegro, hoped for anything more than an irritation of the thin Russian skin, he was doomed to disappointment. The Turkish circular proposal on which he acted so sympathetically merely inspired Prince Gorchakov to add more vitriol to his language. When Cabouli brought the Porte's message to the chancellor, he received anything but a cordial reception. The view advanced by the Turks Gorchakov dismissed with the caustic observation that it

surprised," he explained to Andrássy, "if this defense measure, which is as just as it is natural, were misinterpreted, but I know that your Excellency will understand it and consequently approve it" (Tel., 29 April; *ibid.*). Quite obviously Nicholas' message was a notice to Andrássy that on the excited frontier where two undisciplined and hostile forces were facing each other war might burst out at any moment. And it is equally obvious that if war did burst out its beginnings would be obscured by such a cloud of lies and denials, charges and counter-charges, that each side could claim with considerable vehemence that the other was the aggressor. Andrássy, however, did not hesitate. On the thirtieth he replied: "Telegram of yesterday received. If your Highness sends only two battalions with orders not to cross the frontier, as I do not doubt is the case, we shall see in it only a measure of precaution which could not arouse any objection on our part" (Tel., *ibid.*). Equally obvious is it that Andrássy was taking a brave gambler's chance—with the lives of other people, and perhaps even with the fortunes of his own state.

[214] Tel. No. 393, Andrássy to Zichy, 28 April; *ibid.*
[215] Tel. No. 394, Andrássy to Zichy, 28 April; *ibid.*
[216] Tel. No. 106, Zichy to Andrássy, 28 April; *ibid.*

"n'était qu'un roman tandis qu'il demandait de l'histoire," and the overwhelmed ambassador went away to telegraph to the Porte that his interview was "far from encouraging."[217] Lord Augustus Loftus received a more polite response when he shortly thereafter presented his country's anti-Montenegrin proposal, but he was no more effective than his belabored Ottoman colleague. The chancellor had nothing but sympathy for the Montenegrins and nothing but abuse for the Turks. The menaces from Constantinople appeared to Gorchakov so unwarranted that he held it impossible further to restrain the prince and his people from action. Turkey had given a written promise to carry out reforms; not one had been put into effect, and at the moment when Austria was heroically working for an armistice and pacification the Turks had destroyed all hopes by their insensate appeal to arms. Gorchakov agreed heartily that all Europe should use energetic action, but in his insistent view the place to use it was Constantinople, not Cetinje.[218]

Russian policy, as it existed in the mind of the chancellor of the empire, was becoming more clarified. He still clung to hopes for pacification and for the European concert, but his Slavic sympathies were becoming crystallized. Montenegro was indeed his *enfant chéri,* to be protected and pampered at the expense of the Porte; the insurgents were no longer rebels to be pushed back into subjection but oppressed beings who had demands worth considering. The failure to arrange an armistice and the failure to arrive at a satisfactory agreement with Andrássy over the insurgent conditions[219] had thrown Gorchakov into a profound pessimism regarding the chances for

[217] Report No. 445, Elliot to Derby, 30 April; *Turkey No. 3 (1876),* Doc. No. 267.

[218] Reports Nos. 183 and 185, Loftus to Derby, 30 April; *Turkey No. 3 (1876),* Docs. Nos. 249 and 250, respectively. Report No. 23AF, Langenau to Andrássy, 2 May; SA, Varia Turquie I, 1875. Schweinitz, *Denkwürdigkeiten,* I, 325.

[219] In Vienna Andrássy and Novikov were busy toward the end of April, trying with considerable difficulty to iron out the differences in the Austrian and Russian appreciations of the insurgent demands. The foreign minister refused to budge from his first views of the conditions, and before the month was over he and the Russian ambassador patched up an arrangement embodying the two points Andrássy had originally accepted—concentration of Turkish troops and the right of the Christians to keep their arms. The one concession made by the Austrian minister was on the final paragraph: *"Les consuls ou délégués des Grandes Puissances exerceront leur surveillance sur l'application des réformes en général et sur les faits relatifs au repatriement en particulier"* (Tel. to Andrássy in Berlin, Vienna, 10 May, including document labeled "Von Novikow der das vereinbarte Projekt mir übergeben"; SA, Varia Turquie I, 1875).

peace. Unwilling to restrain Serbia and Montenegro any longer, the chancellor was envisaging, as he told Loftus, the desirability of erecting a wall of non-intervention around the Balkan peninsula and permitting Christian and Moslem to fly at each other's throat, even though, in the end, he anticipated that the Great Powers would have to stop the flow of blood.[220] As what he termed the first step in this strict non-intervention, Gorchakov vigorously and repeatedly urged the Austrians to close the port of Klek to the Turks inasmuch as the frontier had been closed to the insurgents. Impatiently he waved aside the Austrian observation that equal treatment of the enemies would mean recognition of the rebels as belligerents; Turkey, he said, had shown too much bad faith to permit Europe to be restrained by such considerations.[221]

When report came to the foreign office in London of the tide of Russian feeling, the undersecretary wrote a brief comment for his chief : "This looks serious. . . . . Prince Gortchakoff is evidently very angry at the failure of the plans for bringing about the surrender of Niksich to the insurgents, under pretext of renewing the armistice." Lord Derby was inclined to agree—but Lord Derby was Lord Derby : "This looks like a new move on the part of Russia but we can do nothing at present."[222]

While these expressions of opinion were being aired in the capitals of Europe, in Hercegovina Andrássy's hopes were drowned in blood. On 28 April Mukhtar Pasha marched triumphantly into Niksich, left provisions, and fought his way out again.[223] The first reports made no mention of what the chancelleries wanted most to know —whether or not Montenegro was to be a second time accused. After two days Mukhtar sent a detailed account of his expedition to the Porte; but apparently the pasha had learned from his earlier experience a modicum of discretion; the new report contained only innuendo. After describing a well-nigh miraculous increase in enemy numbers during his three days of victorious fighting, Mukhtar contented him-

---

[220] Report No. 185, Loftus to Derby, 30 April; *Turkey No. 3 (1876)*, Doc. No. 250.

[221] Tel. No. 37, Langenau to Andrássy, 1 May, and Reports Nos. 23B and 23F, same to same, 2 May; SA, Varia Turquie I, 1875.

[222] Notations on back of Tel., Loftus to Derby, 30 April; FO 65/943.

[223] Tel., Rashid to Musurus, 30 April; *Turkey No. 3 (1876)*, Doc. No. 180. Tels., Ali to Musurus, Mostar, 30 April; *ibid.*, Docs. Nos. 181, 182. Tel., Rashid to Musurus, 30 April; *ibid.*, Doc. No. 188. Tel., Rashid to Musurus, 1 May; *ibid.*, Doc. No. 190. Tel., Rashid to Musurus, 2 May; *ibid.*, Doc. No. 194.

self with observing that "as the forest was very thick, we could not determine how many Montenegrins were among the insurgents." Sir Henry Elliot promptly put Mukhtar's two and two together and concluded that "a very large proportion" of the reinforcements "must have come from Montenegro."[224] But at the Porte, whatever might have been believed about the men of the Black Mountain, there was no longer a desire to precipitate all the troubles which would inevitably materialize from an attack on Montenegro. The danger, then, of open war between Turkey and the principality was averted for a time. But the march of Mukhtar was none the less a catastrophe for Andrássy's meager hopes for pacification. After the renewal of fighting there was little possibility for an armistice and for discussion between Turkish authorities and rebel leaders. Bosnia and Hercegovina continued to be the stalking ground of anarchy;[225] Turkish officials returned to their fable about the extinction of the rebellion; Turkish commissions daily sat in sterile consultations, and the guerrilla warfare continued to take its toll of blood and ashes.[226]

SUMMARY

The task which Andrássy had given himself had proved too difficult; there were too many factors beyond his control. He had continued to lead and, at times, to drive the Turks farther than they wanted to go, and his efforts inevitably provoked their ill-will and inspired them to resistance and defiance. The Turks wanted neither to reform nor to be reformed. The Austro-Hungarian foreign minister had also failed in his endeavor to lure the rebels into submission. The spring months had revealed the broad chasm between his maximum concessions and their minimum demands, but the absence of any satisfactory alternative had forced Andrássy into the gamut of a diplomat's maneuvers to keep his own program intact. Those same months had witnessed an even more serious problem: Despite the cordiality with which Prince Gorchakov had eventually embraced the Austrian reform proposals, the Russian chancellor was finding it

---

[224] Report No. 455, Elliot to Derby, 2 May, inclosing dispatch of Mukhtar to the Porte of 1 May; *ibid.,* Doc. No. 269.

[225] Political Report No. 14, Freeman to Derby, Bosna-Seraï, 12 May; *ibid.,* Doc. No. 281.

[226] Political Reports Nos. 15 and 19, Freeman to Derby, 19 and 26 May; *ibid.,* Docs. Nos. 314 and 391, respectively.

increasingly difficult to see eye to eye with the framer of the December program. Events had tended to throw the two statesmen in opposite directions. While Andrássy remained steadfast in his determination to block the ambitions of the insurgents, Gorchakov was giving way to the rising current of Slavic sympathies in Russia. At the end of April, therefore, not only were the reform program and the armistice project a complete failure but divergent purposes threatened to strain the bonds between St. Petersburg and Vienna.

CHAPTER VI

THE BERLIN MEMORANDUM

THE BERLIN COLLOQUY AND MEMORANDUM

A month before the final breakdown of Andrássy's attempt to pacify Bosnia and Hercegovina it had become apparent in St. Petersburg that Austro-Russian relations were not without points of material difference.[1] Such a wide gulf, in fact, had appeared between the views of the two powers that Prince Gorchakov had begun to envisage a possible rupture between them and to rejoice that Russia could count unconditionally on German support.[2] But the aged chancellor had no thought of abandoning a policy of co-operation with Austria before it was absolutely imperative; for years he had been committed to the European concert and, from his place of major responsibility, he recognized, more clearly than Count Ignatiev was able to do, the dangers of a Russian program of isolated action. When he saw that Andrássy's hopes and plans could not be realized, Gorchakov was disposed to chart a new course in collaboration with Bismarck and the Austrian minister for foreign affairs. In early April he invited Andrássy in the name of the tsar to a consultation in Berlin during the first days of the following month:

. . . . His Majesty would like very much to meet with him in order to express his satisfaction with the perfect accord which has never ceased to preside over the march of the two cabinets in a crisis which interests both of them to the same degree. His Majesty thinks that it would be useful to exchange ideas in private conversation with regard to the eventualities which might have to be envisaged for the maintenance of general peace. . . . .[3]

Before Andrássy could reply to this cordial message, that perfect accord in which the tsar delighted had received a severe blow through

[1] *Supra*, pp. 258–59, 261–64.

[2] Gorchakov to Oubril, 20 March/1 April; Goriainov, *op. cit.*, p. 316.

[3] "Extrait d'une lettre du chancelier Prince Gortschakoff à M. de Novikow à Vienne," Livadia, 23 March/4 April; SA, Varia Turquie, 1876. Wertheimer, *Andrássy*, II, 276. On the same day that Gorchakov's letter was written to Novikov, Emperor Alexander sent to his imperial uncle in Berlin a telegram notifying him of the proposed gathering of the three directors of foreign affairs (Schweinitz, *Denkwürdigkeiten*, I, 321).

the divergence of views as to the merits of the seven insurgent demands. In the circumstances the first thought of the Austrian minister was the same as that in Gorchakov's mind—to enlist the aid of the great man in Berlin.[4] In order to be fortified for the next Russian move, Andrássy let it be known confidentially in the German capital that he wished to arrive early in time for a preliminary understanding with Bismarck.[5] Andrássy had reached the limits of his concessions when in mid-April he budged a portion of a hairsbreadth in the question of the insurgent terms, but his discussions with the Russian ambassador and the reports coming directly from St. Petersburg were evidence enough that Gorchakov would come with plans that went beyond those limits. In the previous autumn he had fought off a Russian proposal for a joint military occupation;[6] in March he had attempted to dissuade Gorchakov from talking about autonomy;[7] two weeks later he had summarily disposed of a suggested increase in territory for Montenegro.[8] In spite of these rebuffs Gorchakov and Emperor Alexander persisted in favoring more substantial guaranties for the returning refugees, in planning advantages for Prince Nicholas, and in anticipating an eventual autonomy for the provinces in revolt.[9] No Austrian minister confronted with such an unwelcome outlook could have done otherwise than seek the support of the third power of the imperial league.

Prince Bismarck was no more inclined than before to make an open choice between the two contending allies. After the failure of his January project to divide the Turkish spoils, the German chancellor had returned to his earlier role of endorsing any Austro-Russian agreement. In February the Turks sent an English nobleman on a special mission to Bismarck to denounce the alleged duplicity of

[4] *Andrássy*, II, 276.

[5] Tel., Andrássy to Károlyi, 29 April; SA, Varia Turquie I, 1875.

[6] *Vide supra,* chap. iii, pp. 150–52.

[7] "Je vois par votre télégramme No. 29 que le prince Gortchakow a peu d'espoir que les insurgés se prêtent à la pacification. Moi, au contraire, je ne vois rien qui puisse me faire désespérer d'un résultat satisfaisant. Les idées du prince, touchant à l'autonomie, sont à mes yeux une marque de confiance, pouvant servir à provoquer un échange d'idées entre nous. Je me réserve de faire connaître à Votre Excellence mes appréciations à ce sujet. Veuillez en attendant, si vous le jugez utile, prier le prince de ne pas faire mention envers des tiers de ses impressions. Si elles transpiraient, elles pourraient selon moi réagir d'une manière défavorable sur notre action commune auprès des insurgés" (Tel., Andrássy to Langenau, 23 March; SA, Varia Turquie I, 1875).

[8] Tel. No. 19, Andrássy to Langenau, 12 April; *ibid.*

[9] Report No. 20, Langenau to Andrássy, 6/18 April; *ibid.*

Austria and Russia and to seek a more active interest on the part of Germany in the preservation of the Ottoman Empire.[10] But Bismarck had refused to listen to such a plea; European peace and Austro-Russian amity were all-important to him, and Turkey, as he said with brutal frankness, meant nothing. The events of March served to justify the prince's doubts about the Andrássy scheme of reform, and he anticipated that the insurrection would go on until measures were adopted which would effectively restore peace. The best means to that end seemed to him to be an Austrian occupation, and when Count Shuvalov was passing through Germany toward the end of March the chancellor presented the idea to his old friend and persuaded him to approve it.[11] Bismarck was not unmindful, however,

[10] Reports Nos. 59 and 68, Russell to Derby, 3 and 9 February, respectively; FO 64/850.

[11] Secret Reports Nos. 137 and 145, Russell to Derby, 28 March and 5 April, respectively; FO 64/851. The first dispatch recounts Shuvalov's version of his conversation. The pertinent paragraph reads as follows: ". . . . He had talked the question over with Prince Bismarck and had found him indifferent to the ultimate fate of the Ottoman Empire, but very anxious about the maintenance of European Peace. Prince Bismarck had said to him that he would willingly support any arrangement respecting Turkey calculated to maintain and promote general peace which Russia might propose in concert with the European Powers, and that all he asked for was that Germany should not be involved in a quarrel with Austria, the integrity and welfare of which he attached the greatest importance to. . . . ."

The second dispatch reports Bismarck's version: ". . . . As far as I could gather, his account of the interview and conversation agreed with that given by Count Schouvaloff. . . . . He was inclined to think Count Schouvaloff correct in his views on the Herzegovina insurrection, which would probably continue in some shape or other to baffle the united attempts of Turkey and her friends at conciliation, and would finally render the adoption of other measures necessary to give peace to those unhappy populations. The administrative Powers of the Turkish Government were declining, and their financial resources diminishing, so that the Sultan would gradually require more and more support on the part of the Protecting Powers;— and he was therefore sincerely glad to learn from Count Schouvaloff that the Russian Government would, in his opinion, view without jealousy and give a cordial assent to an Austrian occupation of those Provinces whenever it became evident that the Turkish Government could no longer administer them without the material assistance of a neighbouring and friendly power.

"I said that as far as I knew, the Austrian Government had neither wish nor intention to undertake the task of occupation, and I was surprised to hear him speak of it as a contingency likely to occur.

"Prince Bismarck replied that I was correctly informed; but that in his opinion a continued state of disturbance and insurrection in those neighbouring Provinces on the one side, and the increasing impotence of Turkey to keep order and govern them on the other, would sooner or later compel Austria in self-defense, and in the interest of her own frontier populations to lend a helping hand to Turkey. This was a mere question of time, and the best solution to a threatening difficulty in the general interest of peace and order in Europe. . . . ."

that it was desirable, if not necessary, to offer to St. Petersburg some form of quid pro quo. To Shuvalov he was eloquent in his courtship of Russia. Acknowledging Prussia's indebtedness to the tsar for his support in 1866 and 1870, the chancellor declared his desire to put the German Empire at the beck and call of Russia.[12] Either at the same time or shortly afterward he went even further along the road of compensations and held out to the Russians the possibility of restoration of Bessarabia.[13]

But Bismarck's professions, as the Russian ambassador warned the enthusiastic Gorchakov, were only platonic.[14] He was by no means ready to leave Austria-Hungary in the lurch. On the contrary, he felt the need of a preliminary understanding with Andrássy no less than did the minister himself, and on the same day that Andrássy expressed a wish to arrive in Berlin ahead of Gorchakov, Bismarck communicated the same desire to Vienna. The Russian chancellor, he said, was bringing his chief advisers with the obvious intention of drawing up some document and, in order to be prepared for a surprise, he suggested that Andrássy come two days in advance.[15] A few days later Bismarck extended the time to three days,[16] but at the last moment Andrássy was taken ill and was unable to reach Berlin until the morning of the tenth, the day before the tsar and his suite were to come.[17]

Bismarck immediately went into conference with the first of his distinguished guests. The chancellor began with his oft-repeated phrases about Germany's disinterestedness and unwillingness to make proposals, but went on to suggest his approval of an Austro-Russian partition of the desirable portions of Turkey. Andrássy reported the discussion to his emperor in these words:

Wednesday I had a three-hour conversation with Bismarck. The kernel of it was as follows: The imperial chancellor holds fast to the necessity of the alliance of the three powers in the interest of the monarchical principle. Germany makes no proposal, will accept anything on which the two allies are

[12] Goriainov, op. cit., p. 316.

[13] Tel., Andrássy to Emperor Francis Joseph, Berlin, 12 May; SA, Varia Prussia, 1876.

[14] Goriainov, op. cit., pp. 316–17.

[15] Private letter, Károlyi to Andrássy, 29 April; SA, Varia Turquie I, 1875.

[16] Tel., Károlyi to Andrássy, 1 May; ibid.

[17] Tel. No. 428, Andrássy to Károlyi, 7 May; ibid. The Times (London), 8 May 1876, p. 7, col. 3; 9 May, p. 5, col. 3; 11 May, p. 5, col. 2.

agreed. He will request Emperor William to persist in this point of view and will explain to Gorchakov that between the three powers there can be no pressure brought to bear on any one. For that reason no one can force Germany into the embarrassing position of being obliged to decide between the two. He has himself taken the view that the demands of the insurgents should be taken into consideration, because he believes that this course would be more agreeable to us than the creation of autonomous states. After I had pointed out to him the difficulties of the various solutions without drawing any conclusions, he asked me if we considered an intervention, either alone or with Russia, acceptable. I answered, "Neither of them." Then he said that King Victor Emmanuel, nurturing the wish to try out his army somewhere, had offered himself in Milan as pacificator but that Keudell had received the offer in silence. I answered that it would be well to dissuade the king from this idea because Austria could never consent to it, and that the attempt could easily turn out badly. Thereupon Bismarck said that Germany, when another solution was impossible, had nothing against Austria's taking a portion [of the Turkish empire] and Russia's doing likewise. He had already inquired in St. Petersburg whether Russia would be satisfied with the return of Bessarabia. This was certainly no great territory of great importance, and in the interest of a settlement Germany could consent to the return of the mouth of the Danube to Russian hands. The idea seems not to have been displeasing in St. Petersburg, but as yet he has received no positive answer. He wished to know if your Majesty would accept it. I answered that I believed yes, but that we could not expose ourselves to a rejection, and would therefore have to await such a proposition rather than present it . . . .[18]

In warning the Porte in February not to give up any territory, Andrássy had written a little fable about a woman in a sleigh who, to save herself, threw her children one by one to the wolves but was herself finally eaten by the hungry beasts whose appetites had grown with the eating.[19] By May, Andrássy had, in spite of prevailing opinion in the Dual Monarchy, joined the pack of wolves. The only condition he laid down was that some other wolf should extend the invitation to the feast.

The Russians, in anticipation of the Berlin meeting, were indeed hoping, as the Austrian agent reported, to procure more satisfactory arrangements for the insurgents and the Montenegrins than Andrássy had been inclined to grant. Despite the pessimism which hung over St. Petersburg in late April, Prince Gorchakov looked forward to making some new attempt in Berlin to forestall the war that was threatening to envelop the Balkan Peninsula. He was considering sev-

[18] Tel., Andrássy to Emperor Francis Joseph, Berlin, 12 May; SA, Varia Prussia, 1876.

[19] Tel. No. 9, Andrássy to Zichy, 9 February; SA, Varia Turquie I, 1875. *Vide supra,* p. 259, n. 126.

eral possible solutions of the problem, and he sent out feelers to test the currents for and against them. The simplest settlement, from the Russian point of view, was a body of concessions to the insurgents in harmony with their demands; the most desirable arrangement, considered an ultimate necessity, was local autonomy. Andrássy had from the beginning been hostile to the latter solution, and his hostility gave no sign of abating. If no settlement satisfactory to the insurgents was possible, there remained the resort to a military occupation. But a military occupation introduced into the problem of pacification very serious complications. A purely Austro-Hungarian action was naturally undesirable, and the Russians used the alleged opposition of Austria to such a course as an argument against it. To the same end St. Petersburg emphasized the possible complications and difficulties that an Austrian occupation might engender and pointed out the provisional character of any peace imposed by such means.[20] While Prince Gorchakov was reluctant to commit himself too far before the meeting, it was known that he was contemplating the possible necessity of an occupation but was inclined toward a distinctly European rather than an Austrian action.[21] In early May the Russians apparently leaned toward an Italian mandate. An article in *Golos,* reprinted in the official *Journal de St. Pétersbourg,* advanced this proposal. It discussed the undesirability of an exclusive Austrian occupation and, citing the unfortunate Schleswig-Holstein experiment of the previous decade, pronounced against a joint Austro-Russian venture. The solution it found in giving the task to Italy; Italy was near, was not directly interested, and would not create complications.[22]

As a further preparation for the coming Berlin meeting the chancellor ordered General Ignatiev to prepare an exhaustive memorandum of his views on the Eastern question.[23] The general's reply was a curious mélange of would-be principles and practical suggestions. He began by enunciating the principle of non-intervention, the principle the violation of which he held to be the cause of the prevailing impasse in Turkey. He believed it certain that only force could bring the insurgents back to submission and that, before such

[20] Draft No. 270, Derby to Loftus, 8 May; *Turkey No. 3 (1876),* Doc. No. 218, incomplete.

[21] Report No. 194, Loftus to Derby, 9 May; *ibid.,* Doc. No. 251.

[22] Schweinitz, *Denkwürdigkeiten,* I, 327–28.

[23] Private letter, Zichy to Andrássy, 2 May; SA, Varia Turquie I, 1875.

an end could be accomplished, Montenegro would be attacked and Serbia would enter the fray. Unless non-intervention were proclaimed, he foresaw an Austrian occupation and a British penetration of the Straits. But, Ignatiev contended, non-intervention would not exclude energetic diplomatic steps and even material pressure if necessary. He suggested, as the first step to be taken under the banner of non-intervention, a warning to the Porte that an attack on Montenegro would result in denunciation of the guaranties of Turkish territorial integrity. Even this step would not, in his opinion, lead to a peaceful settlement and, before he concluded his memorandum, the ambassador had taken his proposed diplomatic action to the point of advocating a conference in which the united powers of Europe would attempt to settle the difficulties not only of Bosnia and Hercegovina but also of Montenegro and Serbia and the Ottoman Christians in general as well. His own scheme of arrangements may be summarized as follows:

1. There were only two ways of solving the problem of the insurgent areas. The first was to constitute them into an autonomous principality under Prince Nicholas of Montenegro. The second was to cede to Montenegro the mountainous part of the province adjacent to the principality and endow the remainder with broad immunities consonant with its peculiar conditions.

2. Montenegro should be recognized as independent and receive an increase of territory either in Hercegovina or on the coast, together with certain areas which had long been the object of contest between the principality and Turkey.

3. Serbia should be given Little Zvornik, which had for many years been a source of friction between vassal and suzerain states.

4. The *ferman* of December should be progressively extended under vigilant supervision for the benefit of the Christians.

The ambassador, anticipating strong opposition in Constantinople to a conference, proposed a sharply worded ultimatum to the sultan from the three imperial powers.[24]

---

[24] "Mémoire du général Ignatiew," in private letter, Zichy to Andrássy, 5 May; SA, Varia Turquie I, 1875. The text of the ultimatum proposed by the ambassador was as follows:

"Si le gouvernement ottoman désire continuer à jouir de la garantie territoriale qui lui est assurée par les puissances, il doit admettre l'examen en conférence des questions pendantes qui constituent un danger pour sa sécurité et pour la paix européenne. Si la Turquie réfuse, elle sera privée de la garantie d'intégrité et livrée à ses destinés. Les puissances se réservent de ne consulter désormais que leurs intérêts respectifs."

By some means, perhaps through the agency of the German ambassador, Zichy secured a copy of Ignatiev's memorandum and sent it to Vienna with a renewal of

As was usually the case with the recommendations of General Ignatiev, his superiors at home found the memorandum too extreme. The St. Petersburg foreign office drew up a document of its own which was packed in the luggage for Berlin. This long and carefully drafted paper began with a review of the negotiations concerning the insurgent demands and developed out of it the conclusion that the crux of the whole question, no less than the principal obstacle, lay in the problem of external guaranties and controls. On the one hand, the Turks rejected foreign interference as a violation of Ottoman sovereignty, while, on the other, the insurgents demanded it as a sine qua non of submission. This problem, therefore, was the one which demanded the principal attention of the European cabinets. Moral control—advice and exhortation—had not proved effective, and the tsar's government found it only reasonable that the leaders of the rebellion had demanded European surveillance and protection. The time was past for dallying with impotent words; if pacification was to be achieved, the powers would have to turn from moral to material control. To that end, accordingly, the Russian program called for a formal European conference, a conference which should invoke the Syrian precedent of 1860 and should prescribe for the revolted area an international commission supported by a foreign military occupation.[25]

On 11 April Tsar Alexander and his entourage arrived in Berlin, and for two days the rituals of uniformed and medaled majesty alternated with the business of conferring.[26] Count Andrássy reported the negotiations to his emperor by telegraph:

. . . . The tsar received me with unusual graciousness and friendliness. First he pointed to his uniform on which he wore Austrian and German decorations and said, "Here is my program." Then he stressed the wish for a conference between the six powers. During my audience he was given several

---

the plea that his Russian colleague be brought through flattery into the service of Austria: "Er ist ein Faktor mit dem gerechnet werden muss, da er bei guter Stimmung sehr nützliche Dienste leisten, andernfalls aber sehr schaden kann."

Andrássy remained unimpressed. On the eve of his departure for Berlin he wrote on the margin of the secret communication from Zichy: "Dies ist das berühmte Elaborat des Gen. Ignatieff! Wenn nichts Gescheiteres in das Feld geführt wird, mit dem hoffe ich zuversichtlich fertig zu werden."

[25] "Original des ursprünglichen Vorschlages, welcher vom Fürsten Gortschakoff in Berlin gemacht wurde und im Namen der 3 Mächte den Grossmächten mitgeteilt werden sollte"; SA, Varia Russia, 1876. The text of this document may be found in Appendix B.

[26] *The Times* (London), 12 May 1876, p. 5, col. 3; 13 May, p. 7, cols. 2–3.

dispatches from Ignatiev, all to the effect that Turkey is in the act of falling into ruin. Emperor Alexander commented that Turkey could easily surprise us by her collapse, whereupon I emphasized the even greater necessity for a close union of the three powers and added that I was convinced that we could also come to an understanding in our intimate circle with regard to this eventuality. He received this idea warmly and said, "Yes, before all, we two."

Up to this point everything had gone well. From him I went to Gorchakov, who read me a prepared memorandum and proposed to me to call together the representatives of the six powers, excluding the Turkish ambassador, and to communicate the memorandum to them in our names. Contents of this document absolutely unacceptable. Along with incomprehensible phrases it contains ideas of an occupation, coercive measures against Turkey to be prepared by a conference, a panegyric of the insurrection, and so forth. In the evening Gorchakov, Bismarck and I discussed it. I declared that under no circumstances could I accept these proposals. I fell back on my lack of instructions, whereupon Gorchakov objected that there was no time to wait for instructions and that I possessed the confidence of my monarch. He granted me the privilege of making modifications in the memorandum, but I must work out a formal counter-proposal before we resume our negotiations.

I have a strong conviction that the proposition came as unexpectedly here as it has come to me. I am counting on the support of Bismarck and Emperor Alexander. Whether with success I cannot say, but in the full consciousness of my responsibility I cannot consent at any price to the communication of this memorandum to the representatives of the other powers. Gorchakov yesterday proposed the intervention of a third power, which he did not name, and the entry of a fleet into the harbor of Klek. Both propositions I resolutely rejected and was supported by Bismarck. . . . .[27]

Later in the day the Austrian minister made a further report:

After I have, in conformity with your Majesty's instructions, rejected an occupation by us as well as by a foreign power, unanimity is possible only on the plan for the great powers to send war ships to Turkish waters for the protection of their subjects and the Christians in general. The idea seems to be approved here. France and Italy will probably agree to it, and we can therefore not stand in opposition. I must consequently request your Majesty to direct the dispatch temporarily of a second ship to Constantinople and to send the necessary orders to the naval command to hold several ships ready in order that they can be used when necessary if an agreement in this direction is reached.[28]

In the evening Andrássy drew up a more jubilant dispatch:

Situation totally changed. Gorchakov, as soft as butter, has completely given way on all the points unsatisfactory to us. Now I am hoping that the

[27] Tel., Andrássy to Emperor Francis Joseph, [12] May; SA, Varia Prussia, 1876.

[28] Tel., Andrássy to Emperor Francis Joseph, 12 May, 3:00 P.M.; ibid. The disturbances in Turkey which inspired the sending of warships will be discussed below.

entente and our own interests will come out of this meeting undamaged. In the morning Gorchakov will read in his own name to the representatives of the other powers the proposal which he accepted from me. This proposal contains two points: a two-months' armistice for the execution of reforms and an agreement to send the warships. Agreement on Montenegro will come later. I have talked with Gorchakov about plans for the future and have brought him around to declaring that he has no objection to the annexation of Turkish Croatia. Enough for the beginning.[29]

The situation had, indeed, totally changed. Prince Gorchakov, who had given way in the negotiations of the preceding autumn, again abandoned Russian plans in the face of Austrian opposition. The chancellor's memorandum was thrown away, and for it was substituted a document which, with the exception of a closing sentence, was dictated by Andrássy himself.[30] Moreover, it was a document which was essentially a restatement of the author's former views. After disposing of the problem of current outbursts of Moslem fanaticism by recommending the sending of warships under common instructions, the memorandum took up the old question of the insurrection and proposed to settle it by a two months' armistice and by a restatement of the meager concessions which Andrássy had been willing to make. During the new armistice, in other words, Turkish authorities and insurgent delegates were to seek an agreement through discussion of the original seven demands as sifted and sorted in Vienna. These were incorporated in five points:

1. Provision by the Turkish government of materials for rebuilding houses and churches and the furnishing of subsistence until the next harvest;

[29] Tel., Andrássy to Emperor Francis Joseph, 12 May, 10:00 P.M.; *ibid.*

[30] The text in SA is labeled: "Original der von mir dem Baron Jomini dictierten Note unter dem Namen Berliner Memoire des Fürsten Gortschakoff. A." (Varia Russia, 1876). The British ambassador in Berlin subsequently gathered rumors about the negotiations, some of which were far from accurate, but he did get the truth about the authorship of the memorandum. The document, he reported, embodied "the ideas of Count Andrassy and was dictated by him to Baron Jomini after a long discussion with the Czar in which he successfully persuaded His Majesty to adopt his views in preference to those of the Russian Chancellor.

"The memorandum which Prince Gortchakoff brought with him from St. Petersburg for submission to the Conference at Berlin was a bulky document of nearly 70 pages in which he advocated the establishment of autonomic States under the suzerainty of the Sultan like Roumania or Servia as the best means of pacifying the revolted provinces.

"This memorandum was at once rejected by his colleagues and Count Andrassy undertook the drawing up of the memorandum. . . . ." (Report No. —, Russell to Derby, 5 June; FO 64/852.)

2. Distribution of this aid in collaboration with the mixed commission provided for in the Andrássy note;

3. Temporary concentration of Turkish troops;

4. Right of the Christians to bear arms; and

5. Surveillance by foreign consuls or delegates of the application of reforms in general and repatriation in particular.[31]

At the end of the memorandum was a "tail" which was Gorchakov's sole contribution:[32]

If, however, the armistice expires without the effort of the powers successfully attaining the object they have in view, the three imperial courts are of opinion that it would be necessary to add to their diplomatic action the sanction of an understanding, with a view to effective measures which would seem to be demanded in the interest of the general peace, in order to arrest the prevailing evil and prevent its development.[33]

The triumph of Andrássy was almost complete. He had won a reprieve for his minimum program of concessions to the insurgents —largely it would seem through flattery of the tsar and of the eminently susceptible chancellor of the Russian Empire[34]—and he had secured Russian agreement to a substantial Austrian annexation of Turkish territory in case future conditions made such action desirable.[35] In only one respect did he fail: Gorchakov refused his re-

[31] The first and second of these measures Andrássy substantially recommended to the Turks in January (vide supra, p. 241). The third and fourth he had accepted on 12 April when he was seeking a compromise with St. Petersburg (vide supra, p. 262), and the last he conceded toward the end of the month when he was discussing the insurgent terms with Novikov, the Russian ambassador in Vienna (vide supra, p. 284, n. 219). The text of the five points in the memorandum is almost a verbatim reproduction of the agreement reached between Andrássy and Novikov, a text of which was telegraphed to Andrássy in Berlin on 10 May. In the telegram the document is referred to as "die vor 14 Tagen mit Novicov vereinbarten, lithographirten Punctuationen . . . .," and at the top of the text in SA is written, "Von Novikov, der das vereinbarte Projekt mir übergeben." (SA, Varia Turquie I, 1875.)

[32] When Gorchakov accepted the Andrássy version, he is alleged to have cried out: "But it is no longer my work" (Wertheimer, Andrássy, II, 297). Later he said to the German ambassador in St. Petersburg, "I do not understand why the memorandum has been named after me; Andrássy had a much greater share in it than I did; I only added the tail" (Schweinitz, Denkwürdigkeiten, I, 329-30).

[33] The text of the Berlin Memorandum may be found in Turkey No. 3 (1876), Doc. No. 248; First Red Book, Doc. No. 326; First Green Book, annex to Doc. No. CLX; and First Yellow Book, pp. 129-31.

[34] Andrássy, II, 297-98.

[35] Wertheimer in his biography of Andrássy writes much nonsense about his hero. Among his egregious blunders is his treatment of the Berlin meeting (II, 296-300). The object of Gorchakov's original memorandum was not, as he insists, an

quest to recall General Ignatiev from Constantinople.[36] Before leaving Berlin he sent another telegram to Francis Joseph: ". . . . Contrary to my expectation," he said, "the result is in a high degree satisfying."[37]

On the day following the agreement of the three imperial negotiators—13 May—the representatives of France, Italy, and Great Britain were called in to hear the results of the meeting. Bismarck and Gorchakov in turn explained the object of the deliberations as a new attempt to solve peaceably the difficulties prevailing in Turkey, and copies of the memorandum were distributed. When asked for expressions of opinion, the diplomats were naturally unable to go beyond the banalities of such an occasion. Russell expressed his belief that the British cabinet would agree to the memorandum but accepted the text only *ad referendum*. Gontaut-Biron's reply was essentially the same, and the Italian minister elaborated a comparable theme with variations regarding King Victor Emmanuel's sentiments of friendship toward the sovereigns of the three "northern powers." Gorchakov then concluded the meeting by announcing that he and Andrássy would remain two more days in Berlin and that they both hoped to have comments from the other capitals before they left.[38]

The advocates of the memorandum supplemented this brief and formal ceremony by personal appeals for support, with each appeal garnished in the most appetizing manner. In talking to the French ambassador Prince Gorchakov renewed his courtship of *la belle*

Aufteilung der Türkei. Both the tsar and his chancellor did discuss the necessity for an understanding which would prepare the powers for Turkey's collapse, but the revival of that old and unfortunate idea was probably not so much an indication of the tsar's desire to take immediate initiative in a partition of Turkey with a lion's share going to Russia as it was the result of Bismarck's recent maneuver to end the rebellion before Russia and Austria were at war. Wertheimer indignantly suggests that Gorchakov was expecting too much if he thought that the author of the reform note of 30 December would agree to the destruction of Turkey until all hope was gone. Andrássy, he says, was most unpleasantly affected by the proposal and was determined at no price to go into it!

[36] Report No. 209, secret, Russell to Derby, 15 May; FO 64/852.

[37] Tel. No. 104, Andrássy to Emperor Francis Joseph, 14 May; SA, Varia Prussia, 1876.

[38] Report No. 204, Russell to Derby, 13 May; *Turkey No. 3 (1876)*, Doc. No. 248. Tel., Gontaut-Biron to Decazes, 13 May; *Documents français*, II, Doc. No. 51, and *First Yellow Book*, pp. 127–29 (with deletion). Tel., Launay to Melegari, 13 May; *First Green Book*, Doc. No. CLII. Report, Launay to Melegari, 13 May; *ibid.*, Doc. No. CLXI.

France with more ardor than he had shown since the Balkan disturbance began. The chancellor proclaimed his earnest hope that France should return to a preponderant role in European affairs, and offered, as a means to that end, French leadership in the projected naval demonstration. A French admiral, he suggested, could take command of the united fleets, and France would once again assume her just position in the forefront of Europe.[39] Both Andrássy and Gorchakov argued the memorandum with Lord Odo Russell. Andrássy shrewdly based his bid for English support on a common hostility toward General Ignatiev and on opposition to any disturbance of the status quo in Turkey. The minister told Russell that he was still certain that his December program would bring pacification and explained that the new proposals were directed exclusively toward that end. The ambassador replied that England was always ready to support the integrity of Turkey, but went on to raise a question as to the meaning of the last sentence of the memorandum—that "tail" which Gorchakov had added. Andrássy "preferred not to enter upon conjectures and speculations" for the moment. Prince Gorchakov in turn pitched his words to Russell in the alarmist key. Europe, he said, stood before the unknown and only a cordial understanding of all the Great Powers could prevent a collapse; he attached the greatest importance to an *"entente à six et pas seulement à trois,"* and, lowering his voice, added, "more so than my allies who do not see the importance of it as I do." The chancellor was much more willing to discuss his contribution to the memorandum than was the secretive Andrássy: measures were to be agreed upon by all the powers according to the necessities of any given moment; ships, for instance, could be sent to all the ports of

---

[39] Dreux, *Gontaut-Biron*, pp. 211–12. Hanotaux, *Contemporary France*, IV, 104. Gontaut-Biron concluded that Gorchakov had not come out of the conference with as much as he had anticipated.

Somewhat later, after the British government had rejected the memorandum, the chancellor proved himself to be inconsistent, if nothing more. The queen's ambassador in St. Petersburg reported him as saying: ". . . . It has been his wish and object to reserve for England what he termed a 'leading part' in its execution, namely, if necessary the maritime action, as the British Fleet was more numerous and more powerful than all the other fleets combined. He should even have proposed that the Command in Chief should have been given to the eldest Admiral, in order to ensure its being given to an English Admiral. . . . ." (Report No. 329, Loftus to Derby, 19 July; FO 65/938). Andrássy in May ascribed to Gorchakov the same inclination toward British leadership in naval affairs (Report No. 324, "secret, strictly private and confidential," Buchanan to Derby, 26 May; FO 7/870).

Turkey to become "temples of refuge" for the Christian victims of
Moslem persecution. But, concluded Gorchakov, time would decide;
for the moment "unity in thought and purpose on the part of the
six guaranteeing powers" was the all-important consideration.[40]

THE POWERS AND THE BERLIN MEMORANDUM

In Italy the government of the Right fell in March, but its successor made no change in foreign policy. The state of the kingdom
still imposed on its leaders the acceptance of any decisions made at
the three imperial courts, but Italy's role in the chronic crisis was not
cheerfully accepted. The Berlin memorandum was to the Roman cabinet the same problem that the Andrássy note had been, and the Italian
outlook was the same: Italy needed peace and Italy wanted to defer
the Eastern question until the state was in a better position to defend
its own interests east of the Adriatic Sea.[41]   In the meantime
the new cabinet hoped that the Turkish question could be thrown
upon a table surrounded by six chairs.

In April, Melegari, the new foreign minister, sounded out the
British as to the possibility to joining them in a more active participation,[42] while the king, to the embarrassment of his ministers, persisted in quixotic talk. He volunteered the service of his army in
Bosnia to the German minister, and in an audience with Paget, the
British ambassador, Victor Emmanuel was equally indiscreet. "It
could not be displeasing to England," His Majesty said, "to see Italy
taking a more active part than she. had done in the settlement of
these questions,—for Himself he could not remain passive, it was

[40] Report No. 209, secret, Russell to Derby, 15 May; FO 64/852. The text of
this document may be found in Appendix B.

[41] Report No. 20AE, Wimpffen to Andrássy, Rome, 27 May; SA, Varia Turquie I, 1875. *Vide supra,* pp. 179–80.

[42] Report No. 143, Paget to Derby, 20 April; FO 45/286. The foreign secretary's reply was not encouraging: ". . . . In reply to His Excellency's request to
be informed of the opinion of Her Majesty's Government on the present position
of affairs in order that the two Governments may be able to act in concert, I should
wish you to assure M. Melegari that Her Majesty's Government sincerely share his
desire for concerted action and will be glad to find that the line of policy pursued
by the two Countries is identic. At this moment however the state of affairs seems
so unsettled, and changes so rapidly, and the information received is of so partial
and confused a character that it seems difficult to form a positive opinion as to any
course of action which would be productive of good results" (Draft No. 241, Derby
to Paget, 2 May; FO 45/281).

contrary to his nature not to be doing something. . . . ."[43] Melegari
wormed himself out of an embarrassing situation by assuring Paget
that he had never heard, except through the newspapers, of a *joint
Austro-Italian* occupation and by describing his sovereign as a man
of "active temperament and prone to generous impulses." The policy of the responsible ministers he held to be opposition to an occupation or to any other course which might jeopardize the interests of
the nation.[44]

On the eve of the Berlin meeting the only confessed concern of
the Roman cabinet had been that the deliberations in the German
capital should, if possible, be an affair of the six guaranteeing powers
rather than of the three empires alone. At the same time it was
readily recognized that Italy could do nothing but court the good-will
of the emperors if they did decide to act alone, and the Italian
ambassador was given a flattering speech to use when opportunity
was at hand. Melegari, in anticipation of a discussion of the insurgent demands, wrote down the Italian views; but his statement was
·so noncommittal that Italy was in a position to ratify any conclusions
that might be made.[45] On the afternoon of 14 May, the day after
the memorandum was circulated in Berlin, the Italian government
telegraphed its formal adherence to the new scheme of pacification.[46]

[43] Report No. 168, Paget to Derby, 5 May; FO 45/286. The ambassador read
the king a rather strong moral disquisition: ". . . . I replied that I was sorry to
hear this, that I had always been under the impression that, the unity of Italy completed, Italy was to be an element of peace in Europe—such at least had always
been the policy which had been proclaimed, and I thought that any departure from
that policy would be a great misfortune for Italy, as it would certainly be a subject
of sincere regret to Her Majesty's Government.

"The King interrupted me by saying, 'But does England hold very much to supporting the Turks?' I replied that I certainly believed that Her Majesty's Government held very much to the maintenance of the territorial arrangements of the
Turkish Empire as being not only part and parcel of the present system of Europe
as established by treaty, but because they foresaw that any disturbance of these
arrangements would inevitably be attended by the most serious complications. . . . .

"Returning to the general question, I ventured to remark that even supposing
His Majesty's doubts as to peace being ever restored between the Turks and the
Christians being well founded, it was certainly not the part of Italy to introduce an
additional hand of discord into the existing complications. Italy, I continued, of all
countries in the world, was the one which had the most need of peace and repose
for the improvement of her finances, which were not even yet in a satisfactory condition;—for the consolidation of her institutions—and for the development of her
resources. . . . ."
[44] Report No. 181, Paget to Derby, 19 May; FO 45/286.
[45] Melegari to Launay, 7 May; *First Green Book,* Doc. No. CXLVIII.
[46] Melegari to Launay, 14 May, 6:15 P.M.; *ibid.,* Doc. No. CLIII.

The French position continued to be substantially that of the Italians. France was a power whose might was not great enough to command an important role in deciding what was right. The interest of France had just been dramatically aroused in the affairs of Turkey by the murder of the French consul in Salonika. The tragedy was additional proof in Paris of the necessity for hastening the work of pacification. French support was pledged to this work with the hope that the Berlin deliberations would not exclude an informal consultation with the three outside powers. But any decision short of a military occupation France was ready to accept.[47]

As the Italian foreign minister was at the same time doing, on 14 May Decazes telegraphed French approval of the Berlin program.[48] A short time before, when Decazes had become worried over Austro-Russian differences, he had appealed to London to join him in aiding to reconcile these divergences;[49] but, confronted now by the request for an immediate reply, the minister did not solicit British opinion. He excused himself to London—because he had tried for the last half year to promote British co-operation—by alleging the pressure of time and by stating his supposition that England, as judged from the reported words of Gorchakov and Russell, had already promised its support.[50]

Great Britain's position was different from that of Italy and France. After its grudging "general support" of the Andrássy note in January, the cabinet returned to an aloofness seemingly greater than ever. The speech from the throne in early February contained the most conventional and colorless of phrases with regard to foreign relations.[51] A week after the reconvening of parliament, the prime minister introduced the bill making Queen Victoria empress of

[47] Decazes to Gontaut-Biron, 8 May; *Documents français*, II, Doc. No. 48. Cf. *First Yellow Book*, pp. 125–27.

[48] Decazes to Gontaut-Biron, 14 May; *Documents français*, II, Doc. No. 52. Subsequently Decazes was embarrassed by his hasty action and when his telegram was published in the *First Yellow Book* (p. 131) in 1877, the date was given as 15 May and the text indicated *"adhésion aux principes généraux de l'exposé . . . ."* whereas the actual telegram itself, if one supposes that the texts in *Documents français* are honest, states that *"le Cabinet français approuve l'exposé et les propositions qui vous ont été présentés et que son concours leur est assuré."*

[49] Decazes to d'Harcourt, 18 April; *Documents français*, II, Doc. No. 40.

[50] Decazes to French representatives abroad, 14 May; *ibid.*, II, Doc. No. 53. Report No. 330, Adams to Derby, 16 May; *Turkey No. 3 (1876)*, Doc. No. 264.

[51] Hansard, *Parliamentary Debates*, third series, CCXXVII, 2–3. *London Gazette*, 11 February, p. 587.

India, and for the ensuing month a goodly share of public attention was absorbed in this measure which was so ardently desired by the queen and so infelicitously handled by her chief minister. The press had little to write concerning the affairs of Turkey, and the Foreign Office did nothing. Lord Derby in mid-April looked on the insurrection as a malady which might last indefinitely, but showed no desire to do anything about it.[52] Count Shuvalov returned to his post in London just when Gorchakov was feverishly trying to organize a united resistance to a declaration of war on Montenegro, and the ambassador, as has been seen, found the foreign secretary unmoved. There prevailed in London, Shuvalov reported on 27 April, a "state of inertia," and he foresaw that it would have to be reckoned with in coming times of stress.[53] Derby finally bestirred himself enough to propose a collective remonstrance with Prince Nicholas of Montenegro; but when nothing came of it he relapsed into apathy. In early May Shuvalov sounded the foreign secretary on Britain's stand but derived little satisfaction from the attempt. Speaking for his government, Shuvalov deplored a possible Austrian occupation and urged some material concessions for the insurgents; speaking allegedly for himself in a private capacity, he favored complete autonomy for the revolted area and an extension for Montenegro. Derby in reply likewise deplored a possible Austrian occupation but thought it would be hasty to despair of the original Andrássy plan. When it was time to respond to the ambassador's private remarks, "I did not think it expedient," he subsequently wrote, "to offer an opinion on either of these two points."[54] Shuvalov went away from his interview believing that the foreign minister was disposed toward maintaining an accord between the powers and that he sought through it a solution to the question of the day,[55] but the ambassador was not edified by affairs in London. He anticipated that the British government would quickly reject a common European program if it were not faced by a united front of the other powers, and he was well aware that Lord Derby, despite his passive

[52] Report No. 38B, Beust to Andrássy, 12 April; SA, Varia Turquie I, 1875.

[53] Shuvalov to Gorchakov, 15/27 April; Slavonic Review, III, 661–62, Doc. No. 26.

[54] Report No. 270, Derby to Loftus, 8 May; Turkey No. 3 (1876), Doc. No. 218, incomplete (FO 65/932).

[55] Tel., Shuvalov to Gorchakov, 22 April/4 May; Slavonic Review, III, 662, Doc. No. 28.

good-will, disparaged every solution under discussion and had none of his own to propose.[56]

The most disturbing actor on the British scene in April, as the Russian chargé d'affaires surveyed it, was the premier. Disraeli, he noted, was more and more inclined to cast off restraints, to spring surprises, and to resort to his large majority in parliament in pushing through measures. But, this uneasy foreign observer went on, Disraeli had carried his cavalier tactics a little too far in the royal titles bill and it was more than likely that he would soon attempt some new action to regain his influence in parliament and his ascendancy over public opinion. The chargé d'affaires feared that he was going to try this maneuver in the field of Britain's foreign relations; the Suez Canal triumph and the debates on the royal titles bill, in which Disraeli made hints about Russian exploits in Asia, combined to point the direction of his thoughts.[57]

A week after the chargé d'affaires had chronicled his impressions, the prime minister was seeing "something cynical" in Gorchakov's treatment of the Turkish problem; the Russian policy, Disraeli felt, was "not exactly respectful to us."[58] When he learned that Gorchakov and "the Austrian" were coming to Berlin, he regretted that the cabinet had not exploited more fully Bismarck's desire to exchange opinions. The foreign office, after rejecting the original German proposition in January, had shown little interest in Bismarck's proposal. Only once afterward did Derby and his staff stir themselves; then they dressed up a rumor of Russian troop concentrations in the garb of a confidential question as to what was known in Berlin.[59] In May Disraeli realized that it would have been good to be on such friendly terms with Bismarck that he would not act without consulting England,[60] but by that time it was too late.

Lord Odo Russell's report of the Berlin proceedings reached London on the afternoon of 14 May,[61] and the premonitions that the prime minister was going to assume a leading role in the negotiations were quickly realized. The next afternoon Disraeli met the Russian ambassador at a reception in St. James Palace. "We have nothing to

[56] Shuvalov to Gorchakov, 26 April/8 May; *ibid.*, Doc. No. 29.

[57] Bartholomai to Gorchakov, 31 March/12 April; *ibid.*, pp. 659–61, Doc. No. 21.

[58] Disraeli to Derby, 20 April; *Disraeli*, VI, 22.

[59] Draft No. 137, Derby to Russell, 23 February; FO 64/846.

[60] Disraeli to Derby, 8 May; *Disraeli*, VI, 22–23.

[61] Disraeli to Derby, 15 May; *ibid.*, VI, 23.

reply to the Berlin propositions," he said brusquely, "since England has been treated as if we were Montenegro or Bosnia," and he went on to explain that "Prince Gorchakov and Count Andrássy have informed us that they will remain in Berlin until Monday and that they give us twenty-four hours to formulate England's reply." Shuvalov, taken aback by Disraeli's *"ton si peu parlementaire,"* attempted a calming response; but his suggestion that the discussion of a pressingly necessary armistice did not require weeks was not fortunate. "What armistice do you want?" the prime minister asked; "an armistice on the part of Turkey alone?" Shuvalov's stricture on Turkey which followed was interrupted by the arrival of the Prince of Wales, and in a few moments Disraeli, conscious of the heat of his remarks, returned to the ambassador and said, "Let's shake hands before everyone, because our discussion has been noticed and it should not be believed that it was unpleasant."[62]

From that infelicitous experience the Russian ambassador repaired to the Foreign Office, recalling to himself that only a few days before Lord Derby had expressed his satisfaction with the proposed meeting in Berlin and his hope to be able to support the projects formulated there. But, as Count Münster had learned only a few minutes earlier,[63] and as Count Beust was to learn a few minutes later,[64] the foreign secretary's good-will had evaporated in the heat of Disraeli's emotions. In general and in its specific points Derby condemned the Berlin memorandum. He criticized the armistice for being as favorable to the insurgents as it was prejudicial to the regular troops of the sultan, and he rejected the proposed peace terms as impracticable and impossible of support. He went on to suggest that the three statesmen who drew up the memorandum evidently anticipated a second failure in their reform plans, since otherwise they would not have added the last paragraph promising new measures if the Berlin program were not a success. Derby characterized that concluding paragraph as nothing more than a notice to the insurgents not to put down their arms, because, at the end of two months, they could expect some further solution. Shuvalov saw at once that there was no hope of saving the five bases of peace and he threw them overboard in an attempt to rescue the armistice, which

[62] Shuvalov to Gorchakov, 7/19 May; *Slavonic Review,* III, 664–65, Doc. No. 31.
[63] Draft No. 365, Derby to Russell; 15 May; *Turkey No. 3 (1876),* Doc. No. 259.
[64] Tel. No. 30, Beust to Andrássy, 15 May; *First Red Book,* Doc. No. 336, incomplete.

was in his opinion the principal point in the memorandum. The idea of separating the two parts of the program seemed to be agreeable to Derby, and, despite his first condemnation of the armistice, the secretary agreed to support it in the cabinet meeting set for the following day.[65]

In that council, however, the prime minister called the tune. The basis of the discussion and of the resultant decision was a memorandum which Disraeli had prepared in advance. The fundamental idea of his document was the belief that, step by step, England was being drawn into a scheme which was leading rapidly to the disintegration of Turkey and that the cabinet should call a halt to this untoward march. Disraeli took exception to the "mockery" of a European concert when three powers were excluded from the deliberations and were then requested, after a plan had been made, to give a reply on the basis of a telegraphic summary. He had nothing good to say for any one of the measures proposed: The sultan could not possibly reconstruct buildings for the insurgents and feed the refugees; distribution of relief through a commission would mean "a huge system of indiscriminate alms-giving, totally beyond the power of the Porte to effect, and utterly demoralizing to any country"; concentration of troops in specific places would result in anarchy; and consular supervision "would reduce the authority of the Sultan." After the current proposals had failed, England would be invited to join in "taking more efficacious measures to break up the Empire." In the prime minister's opinion it was better for Turkey to lose outright the insurgent provinces. The limit of his concession was—provided Turkey agreed—an armistice and a European congress pledged to reconsecrate the status quo.[66]

Such were the views of the chief of the government of Great Britain. The document was eloquent testimony to Disraeli's total lack of any sense of reality, of any comprehension of the problem confronting Turkey and Europe, of any sympathy for the people of Bosnia. He would not see—what any reasonably open-minded person could not escape seeing—that that lamented "disintegration of Turkey" was in full swing, that the evidence of the past ten months indicated that the sultan was unable through his own force to stop it,

[65] Shuvalov to Gorchakov, 7/19 May; *Slavonic Review*, III, 665–66. Draft No. 299, Derby to Loftus, 15 May; *Turkey No. 3 (1876)*, Doc. No. 260, incomplete (FO 65/932).

[66] *Disraeli*, VI, 24–26.

and that the measures proposed were an honest attempt to take away a knife from the throat of Turkey rather than put it there. Anyone objectively seeking a solution of the rebellion could see that the Berlin proposals had little chance of success; but no sensible man could possibly have sincerely believed that a reaffirmation in conference of "territorial status quo"—whatever that might have meant under the circumstances—could have ended the rebellion or have served the best interests of Turkey—as Disraeli would undoubtedly have liked to serve them. It is incredible that an honest man should have feared the utter demoralization of Bosnia and Hercegovina through a "huge system of indiscriminate alms-giving," that an honest man should be worried over the anarchy that would spring up in the revolted provinces if the troops were concentrated in certain places, and that an honest man should regret the loss of the sultan's authority to a consular commission. If ever there was an area inhabited by an utterly demoralized population and living in a state of anarchy, that area was Bosnia and Hercegovina at the time that Disraeli was reading his memorandum.

And yet the prime minister's rejection was ratified by the cabinet, and his arguments became the official opinion of England. The ministers were already drifting farther and farther apart on the Eastern question; between Disraeli's aroused hostility to the imperial league and Derby's constitutional inability to do anything, there were independent trends of opinion; but at the end of a deliberation lasting an hour and a half the consideration which determined the decision was that which was the basis of Disraeli's opposition—the cavalier treatment of proud England. "It is rather cool to ask it by telegraph," Gathorne-Hardy wrote in his diary, "as if they were to discuss and decide, and we only to assent."[67] A year later another cabinet member, Lord Carnarvon, wrote in retrospect: "With most of us there was, I think, a desire to resist what we considered insolent dictation, and there was also a sort of reaction against Derby's extreme irresolution—to which must be added that Disraeli was by this time strong in opposition to Russia."[68] After the meeting Lord Derby drew up in his own hand a laconic telegram and sent it to the British embassies:

[67] Alfred E. Gathorne-Hardy, editor, *Gathorne-Hardy, First Earl of Cranbrook* . . . . (London, 1910), I, 365.

[68] Hardinge, *Carnarvon*, II, 329–30.

Her Majesty's Government see grave objections to the plan put forward by the three Powers and are not prepared to press its adoption on the Porte.[69]

There was some feeling in the cabinet discussion that Britain's response should not be purely negative but that a counterproposal should be made. The chancellor of the exchequer presented a plan for a constructive suggestion,[70] but it was defeated and the British government resolved to stand entirely aloof.

That evening in Berlin Lord Odo Russell was apparently dazed by the news. Immediately he telegraphed:

Am I to communicate the rejection of Her Majesty's Government of the plan put forward by the three Northern Powers officially to the German Government? The consequences may be very serious.[71]

On the following day came an additional warning from Vienna:

. . . . During my conversation with Count Andrassy today . . . . His Excellency spoke of a rejection by the Porte of the Berlin proposals as likely to have dangerous consequences; and he gave me to understand that he had some difficulty in keeping them within the limits which he hoped could be supported by Her Majesty's Government.[72]

On the eighteenth, Russell explained his earlier telegram:

The serious consequences I apprehend from the refusal of Her Majesty's Government to join in the proposal of the three Powers are:

The encouragement it may give to the Porte to a policy of resistance or inaction.

The difficulty of supporting with success a policy in Turkey in opposition to the three Powers.

The more energetic action in Turkey it may in consequence necessitate on the part of the three Powers.

The tendency it may thereby create to hasten on events it would appear desirable to postpone in the East.

The alarm it will produce in the Commercial World.[73]

---

[69] Tel., Derby to embassies, 16 May; FO 78/2450. Queen Victoria was not pleased with the decision of the cabinet. She at this stage of the crisis was willing to acknowledge that the three imperial powers had a more intimate and vital connection with the problem of Turkey than did England, France, and Italy, and she was afraid that the encouragement given to the Turks in London might "precipitate rather than prevent the catastrophe" (Ponsonby to Disraeli, 16 May; Buckle, *Queen Victoria*, II, 453–54).

[70] Andrew Lang, *Life, Letters, and Diaries of Sir Stafford Northcote, First Earl of Iddesleigh* (London, 1890), II, 101; *Disraeli*, VI, 27.

[71] Report No. 214, Russell to Derby, 16 May; FO 64/852.

[72] Report No. 299, Buchanan to Derby, 17 May; FO 7/870.

[73] Report No. 216, Russell to Derby, 18 May; FO 64/852.

But Disraeli, quaffing deeply the heady wine of spirited foreign policy, remained undisturbed. "There is nothing in Lord Odo's remarks of significance," he informed the queen,[74] and, although he turned around and told Derby that anything done henceforth would have serious consequences, he nurtured for some time his annoyance with an ambassador who did not comprehend the situation.[75] The prime minister had some notion in his mind about the meeting of a European congress and he believed that Germany and England should go into it with a united program,[76] but there is no evidence that he had any constructive ideas as to what a congress should do.

Thus the stand of the British cabinet under the leadership of Disraeli was purely negative. On 19 May Derby sent a formal statement of its resolution to the various capitals in the form of two dispatches. The first was in substance Disraeli's cabinet memorandum, toned down in places, plus a refusal to support the demand for an armistice.[77] In the face of the prime minister's assault, Derby's professed sympathy for a truce had been unavailing. The second circular dispatch was a mildly phrased but meaningful commentary on the tactics of the imperial powers:

. . . . None of these proposals had previously been discussed with Her Majesty's Government, or, so far as they are aware, with the other Powers signataries [sic] of the Treaty of Paris; and the inconvenience has consequently arisen again, as in the case of Count Andrassy's note, of a set of Articles being submitted for the acceptance of Great Britain without any opportunity having been afforded for a preliminary consideration of their details by Her Majesty's Government, or for the possible objections of Her Majesty's Government to be considered by the three Governments concerned.

Her Majesty's Government attach little importance to forms in matters of this kind, and would readily have accepted the present proposals had they appeared to them to afford a feasible plan for the pacification of the insurgent districts; but they cannot accept, for the sake of the mere appearance of concert, a scheme in the preparation of which they have not been consulted, and which they do not believe calculated to effect the object with which they are informed it has been framed. . . . .[78]

The only descent from these Olympian heights was in a "very confidential and secret" message to Bismarck. Disraeli, ever hopeful

[74] Disraeli to Queen Victoria, 18 May; Buckle, *Queen Victoria,* II, 454–55.
[75] Disraeli to Derby, 18, 29 May; *Disraeli,* VI, 27–28.
[76] Disraeli to Queen Victoria, 18 May; Buckle, *Queen Victoria,* II, 454. *Disraeli,* VI, 27.
[77] Draft No. 385, Derby to Russell, 19 May; *Turkey No. 3 (1876),* Doc. No. 275. *Ibid.,* Doc. No. 276.
[78] Draft No. 387, Derby to Russell, 19 May; *ibid.,* Doc. No. 277.

of some undefined Anglo-German co-operation, induced Derby to convey to the chancellor Britain's regrets and the expression of what must have been to Bismarck a hollow-ringing desire to act in concert with Berlin in the interest of "the maintenance of the territorial status quo and the preservation of European peace."[79]

At the same time that the notification of the cabinet's decision was being sent about Europe, Derby dispatched a special message to the Sublime Porte. In it the secretary charged Sir Henry Elliot to inform the Turks that the British government had collaborated in the consular mission and had given a reserved endorsement of the Andrássy note at the request of Turkey itself, but that in this new proposal British approval would not be forthcoming regardless of the Porte's decision. Such a communication was obviously a tremendous encouragement to the Turks in their contest with the imperial powers; Disraeli would have let it stand unqualified, but Derby continued his old habit of taking back with one hand what he had given with the other. In a concluding paragraph the foreign secretary attempted to destroy Turkish illusions. The gravity of the existing situation Derby attributed to "the weakness and apathy of the Porte in dealing with the insurrection in its earlier stages," and to "the want of confidence in Turkish statesmanship and powers of government," and the responsibility for the plight of the empire Derby laid at the feet of the sultan and his ministers. Her Majesty's government would aid only in "such friendly counsel as circumstances may require. They cannot control events," the message concluded, "to which the neglect of ordinary principles of good government may expose the Turkish Empire."[80]

[79] ". . . . Her Majesty's Government request that Your Excellency will take an opportunity of mentioning personally to Prince Bismarck the regret they experience in having to separate themselves from the action of the German Government in regard to these proposals.

"Count Münster will no doubt have reported to His Excellency that I told him at the earliest moment the views which had occurred to me in order that Prince Bismarck should receive timely intimation of them.

"Her Majesty's Government have no reason to suppose that these proposals originated with the German Government. Their objections to them are founded on general principles and they would be glad to act in concert with the German Government in all matters so far as it may be possible to do so, since they believe that the interests of Germany and of Great Britain are equally directed to the maintenance of territorial status quo and the preservation of European peace." (Draft No. 386, "very confidential and secret," Derby to Russell, 19 May; FO 64/848.)

[80] Draft No. 308, Derby to Elliot, 19 May; *Turkey No. 3 (1876)*, Doc. No. 278. See also Draft No. 302, Derby to Elliot, 16 May; *ibid.*, Doc. No. 263.

As soon as the attitudes of Disraeli and Derby were reported about Europe on the sixteenth and seventeenth, Andrássy, as the most interested defender of the Berlin memorandum, took the lead in organizing an offensive against the British refusal. He defended his painfully wrought bases of peace; he sounded a warning to the British ambassador that he had had trouble holding Gorchakov down to a moderate program and that the failure of the new plan would mean increased difficulties;[81] with growing desperation he sought to salvage the armistice by abandoning his bases and, as in January, he pleaded with the English at all events not to oppose the memorandum even though they would not support it.[82] The armistice had to be saved if possible, and he telegraphed a call for aid to Berlin, Paris, and Rome.[83] In response, three additional foreign ministers and three additional ambassadors took up the cause of British participation.[84] None of them, however, was more successful than Beust, who went to the Foreign Office on the eighteenth to deliver Andrássy's messages and pleas. Derby now had several arguments to advance against the projected suspension of hostilities and the counterarguments that the ambassador advanced against them had no effect. The best that Beust was able to win from the secretary was a promise not to attack the decision of the remaining cabinets. As for the armistice, Derby would agree only to advise the Porte to do what seemed best.[85] Andrássy, quite naturally, was worried by the attitude prevailing in London. Two more telegrams to Beust flatteringly professed understanding for the British objections but urged the

[81] Report No. 299, Buchanan to Derby, 17 May; FO 7/870.

[82] Report No. 301, Buchanan to Derby, 17 May; *Turkey No. 3 (1876)*, Doc. No. 283. Tel., Andrássy to Beust, 17 May; *First Red Book,* Doc. No. 342.

[83] Tel., Andrássy to Károlyi, Kuefstein, and Wimpffen, 17 May; *ibid.,* Doc. No. 343, incomplete.

[84] Tel. No. 51, Wimpffen to Andrássy, 18 May; SA, Varia Turquie I, 1875. Tel. No. 9, Kuefstein to Andrássy, 18 May; *ibid.* Tel. No. 500, Mülinen to Andrássy, 19 May; *ibid.* Tel., Seiller to Andrássy, *First Red Book,* Doc. No. 349, incomplete. Report No. 177, Paget to Derby, 18 May; *Turkey No. 3 (1876)*, Doc. No. 280. Report No. 186, Paget to Derby, 22 May; *ibid.,* Doc. No. 307. Decazes to d'Harcourt, 19 May; *First Yellow Book,* pp. 133–38. Adams to Derby, 22 May; *Turkey No. 3 (1876)*, Doc. No. 291. Melegari to Menebrea in London, 20 May; *First Green Book,* Doc. No. CLXIV.

[85] Draft No. 224, Derby to Buchanan, 18 May; *Turkey No. 3 (1876)*, Doc. No. 266. Tel. No. 32, Beust to Andrássy, 18 May; SA, Varia Turquie I, 1875. Report No. 49B, Beust to Andrássy, 19 May; *ibid.* Shuvalov to Gorchakov, 7/19 May; *Slavonic Review,* III, 667.

pressing necessity for an armistice regardless of other considerations. If the Turks refused it, Andrássy argued, it would be very difficult to restrain Serbia and Montenegro from open war.[86] But when the ambassador took the new arguments to the Foreign Office on the twentieth, he was unable to make any impression. Derby still promised that he would not encourage the Turks to resist, but the dangers of Serbian and Montenegrin entry into warfare did not disturb him; nothing could be better for Turkey, he observed, than bringing the hostility of the principalities out into the open in place of their secret war.[87]

Andrássy attempted to rebut Derby's attacks on the memorandum and, perceiving the real reason for the British rejection, denied that he and Gorchakov and Bismarck had attempted to set a time limit for the reply from London, a claim which was not well founded.[88] But the minister's arguments for his peace terms were

[86] Tel. No. 11, Andrássy to Beust, 18 May; *First Red Book,* Doc. No. 344, in materially altered form. Tel. No. 12, same to same, 19 May; *ibid.,* Doc. No. 348, incomplete.

[87] Tel. No. 33, Beust to Andrássy, 20 May; SA, Varia Turquie I, 1875.

[88] Report No. 323, Buchanan to Derby, 26 May; *Turkey No. 3 (1876),* Doc. No. 347. The last part of the second paragraph should read: ". . . . but he supposed, as the French and Italian Ambassadors appeared to have no doubt that the proposals would be at once accepted by their respective Governments, *and as Lord Odo Russell expressed a personal opinion that they contained nothing contrary to the views of Her Majesty's Government* [italics mine], Prince Gortchakow may have intimated a wish to receive an answer before his departure from Berlin. . . . ."
The reports from Berlin of the ambassadors concerning this point would indicate very clearly that Andrássy was on unstable ground. Russell wrote: "Prince Gortchakow observed that he and Count Andrassy would remain till Monday at Berlin, and that they hoped the Governments of England, France, and Italy would be able to express an opinion on the telegraphic summary of their proposal before they left" (Report No. 204, Russell to Derby, 13 May; *ibid.,* Doc. No. 248). The French ambassador wrote: ". . . . *les trois Ministres, qui resteront réunis ici jusqu'à lundi soir nous ont pressés de leur donner une réponse et nous nous sommes engagés à l'avoir le plus promptement possible. Je vous prie donc de me transmettre la vôtre demain dans la matinée"* (Gontaut-Biron to Decazes, 13 May; *Documents français,* II, Doc. No. 51, and *First Yellow Book,* pp. 128–29). The Italian representative reported: ". . . . *Le chancelier russe nous a vivement engagés à provoquer, le plus tôt possible, les ordres nécessaires de nos gouvernements. Il lui serait agréable d'obtenir des réponses dans le plus court délai, et, si possible, dans la journée de demain. . . . ."* (Launay to Melegari, 13 May; *First Green Book,* Doc. No. CLXI).
When Buchanan's Report No. 323 was read by Russell, the latter took exception to Andrássy's statement that he had expressed his personal opinion that the memorandum contained nothing contrary to the views of the British government. "As the statement I made in the Conference," he explained to the foreign office, "was to the effect that having no instructions from Your Lordship, I could only take their proposals *ad referendum,* I fear that some misapprehension may exist in Count An-

really words of self-justification rather than attempts at persuasion. In private conversation with the British ambassador, Andrássy, indeed, expressed his satisfaction that the proposals of the memorandum had been rejected, because of the greater freedom that rejection would give to the London cabinet in defending common Anglo-Austrian interests. This confidential communication dismissing the peace bases as relatively unimportant went on to plead for the armistice as the basic necessity: without it England could not exploit an advantageous situation; without it Gorchakov would perhaps advance again his dangerous but unnamed Berlin proposals; without it the principalities would perhaps set the whole Balkan Peninsula on fire.[89] For the moment, while waiting for his secret

---

drassy's mind. . . . ." (Report No. 445, Russell to Derby, 2 June; FO 64/852). His report was actually to that effect: ". . . . On receiving a copy of this document for transmission to Your Lordship, I said that in absence of special instructions I did so *ad referendum*. . . . ." (*Turkey No. 3* [*1876*], Doc. No. 248). The Italian ambassador wrote in the dispatch cited above: "*Lord Odo Russel* [sic], *tout en reconnaissant le bon esprit qui animait ces communications, a déclaré, en l'absence d'instructions, qu'il devait se borner à en référer à son gouvernement.* . . . ." But in the report of the French ambassador one reads: ". . . . *Sur une observation du prince Gortchakow que, d'après ses lettres, il était fondé à compter sur l'approbation de lord Derby, lord Odo Russell a dit qu'il croyait, en effet, qu'elle serait donnée.* . . . ." See also *Disraeli*, VI, 28.

[89] Report No. 324, "secret, strictly private and confidential," Buchanan to Derby, Budapest, 26 May; FO 7/870: "On my writing to ask Count Andrassy for an interview this morning, he answered that he was delighted at my arrival, as he wished to charge me with 'certain confidential communications' for your Lordship, and that he would call upon me after attending a sitting of the delegations.

"When he came I communicated to him Your Lordship's Despatch to Lord Odo Russell, No. 385 of the 18th Instant.

"After he had made the observations upon it which I have reported in my official despatch of this date [Report No. 323, *Turkey No. 3* (*1876*), Doc. No. 347], he said he wished to state, for Your Lordship's private and confidential information, what must never appear in a Blue Book, and what he cannot communicate to you through Count Beust.

"He said, two powers whose interests are so conflicting, as those of Austria and Russia, can only maintain peace by compromises. Latterly their views with regard to the Turkish Insurgent Provinces had been divergent, and as they could not reconcile them by telegraphic correspondence, he went to Berlin where Prince Gortchakoff advocated measures which he could not approve,—but which the late events at Constantinople and Salonica and hourly sensational Telegrams from General Ignatieff rendered it extremely difficult to entirely reject—; more especially as the Russian Chancellor professed to have already secured the adherence to his views of France and Italy, and to know that Her Majesty's Government were disposed to concur in them. He was therefore obliged to make some concessions, but he insisted on those contained in the Berlin Memorandum being considered as his ultimatum; and in making them, he stated his conviction that they would be rejected by England. That they had been so he considered fortunate, although he cannot avow it;

arguments to convince the British, Andrássy was limited to warning the Porte that the London cabinet would not encourage Turkish resistance.[90] But his gratuitous message rested on no substantial foundation. When Beust took the latest Austrian communications to the Foreign Office he found Lord Derby polite but still unmoved.[91]

On 18 May the German government, without any hope of success, had responded to Andrássy's appeal and instructed Münster to attempt to bring about a reconsideration of the British decision.[92] When Münster's anticipated failure materialized, the role of the Wilhelmstrasse changed to that of mediator. Bülow and Bismarck did not defend the absolute merits of the Berlin proposals; they emphasized the desirability of a common understanding and an early settlement of the now long-standing difficulty through any means that was quick and feasible. If the British cabinet took exception to the program of the memorandum, Berlin was ready to entertain any sug-

and he looks forward to the independent attitude of Her Majesty's Government being most useful in promoting Austrian as well as English interests, as circumstances are sure to arise, when Her Majesty's Government will be able to exercise greater control over the course of events, than if they were embarrassed by the stipulations of the Memorandum.

"To secure this advantage, however, he considers that a suspension of hostilities will be absolutely necessary, for reasons which I have stated elsewhere; and in order to prevent the united action of Servia and Montenegro in the probable event of the former embarking in a war with Turkey. He has still confidence in the loyal and peaceful intentions of the Emperor Alexander, but he places less reliance than hitherto on Prince Gortchakoff, who has become impulsive from age or some other cause, and seems to be influenced by dangerous advisers and by General Ignatieff, to whose intrigues His Excellency attributes the present threatening state of affairs in Servia; and who, as his position has become untenable at Constantinople, seems determined to bring on a general convulsion throughout the Turkish Empire.

"His Excellency was still unwilling to give me any information as to the measures proposed by Prince Gortchakoff, but he represented him to be very greatly excited by the state of affairs in Turkey, one of his ideas being that a combined Christian fleet should be sent to the Levant, which he had no objection to place under the command of an English Admiral, to curb Moslem arrogance and fanaticism. . . . ."

Two days after the Austrian minister gave to Buchanan his secret opinions, the *Neue Freie Presse* printed a story to the effect that Andrássy had offered a wager to Gorchakov that England would reject the memorandum and that the chancellor characterized accepting the wager as tantamount to taking the money out of Andrássy's pocket. Andrássy's naïve biographer loftily rejected the story on the shaky ground that his hero had made a statement in the contrary sense before the Austrian delegation (*Andrássy*, II, 300–301).

[90] Tel. No. 56, Andrássy to Zichy, 28 May; *First Red Book*, Doc. No. 373.

[91] Draft No. 261, Derby to Buchanan, 1 June; *Turkey No. 3 (1876)*, Doc. No. 348. The date is incorrectly printed as 2 June.

[92] Tel., Seiller to Andrássy, 19 May; *First Red Book*, Doc. No. 349, incomplete.

gestions for improvement that might be proposed.[93]   The German defense of the manner of action of the three imperial powers was less convincing. Queen Victoria had supplemented Derby's comments on their method of procedure by informing the German empress, with a request that the message be passed on, that England should have been consulted before the memorandum was prepared and not afterwards.[94] Bülow insisted that the document prepared in Berlin was looked upon as a "preliminary discussion only, to enable the two Governments more directly interested to agree on the measures best calculated, in their opinion, to bring about the pacification of the Herzegovina." However, neither he nor the emperor, who made a written reply to Victoria's remonstrance, saw any reason why the imperial powers should not assume the leadership in arrangements. Neither apparently understood that in British eyes there was a material difference between offering objections and suggestions to a program already drawn up and sharing in the original formation of a common program.[95] Emperor William felt that the preliminary *entente à trois* had sufficient justification when he recalled to the queen that the same procedure had been followed at the time of the Andrássy note to which the cabinet gave its "general support."[96] The lesson that the league of the three emperors might have learned from British action in the preceding January had gone entirely unheeded.

Prince Bismarck, on the other hand, went to the heart of the question. In a private talk with Russell the chancellor presented the case for the cabinet's support in a realistic light which, coupled with the parallel declaration made by Andrássy, might well have been considered in London had Disraeli and his colleagues been inclined to realism. The peace in which England and Germany were interested, Bismarck explained, was for the moment contingent upon a friendly understanding between Austria and Russia. Andrássy was defending a moderate program against "a broader plan" urged by Gorchakov; the Austrian minister had won his fight in Berlin, and

[93] Reports Nos. 219, 221, 224, 228, Russell to Derby, 18, 20, 20, 22 May; *Turkey No. 3 (1876)*, Docs. Nos. 284, 286, 289, respectively.

[94] Queen Victoria to Disraeli, 8 June; Buckle, *Queen Victoria,* II, 458.

[95] Report No. 236, Russell to Derby, 27 May; *Turkey No. 3 (1876)*, Doc. No. 320.

[96] The German Emperor to the German Empress, 3 June; Buckle, *Queen Victoria,* II, 459–60.

the proposals patched up there were the cement of Austro-Russian peace. If those proposals failed, Andrássy might be hard pressed by Russia, and for that eventuality he needed the moral support and encouragement of England. Austria could ill afford a conflict with the tsar's forces—and European peace could ill afford to witness the end of Austrian strength and independence.[97] Bismarck had himself made his choice between Germany's two allies. If it came to war between Austria and Russia, he would stand with Austria; but since he did not want war, since he wanted to defer that unfortunate day as long as possible, he supported, and he besought English support of, a program, however poor, which was a basis of Austro-Russian co-operation. But no serious response came from London, where ruled a defiant prime minister and a suspicious secretary for foreign affairs.

The direct comments in St. Petersburg regarding the British refusal were limited largely to expressions of regret. Giers, temporarily in charge of the foreign office, attempted to explain to Lord Augustus Loftus that the unfortunate final paragraph of the memorandum had been meant as a confidential communication to the powers and was not to be made known to the insurgents at all,[98] but Giers had no instructions. Tsar Alexander and Prince Gorchakov had gone on from Berlin to Ems and it was from there that Russian policy was being directed. The news coming from Shuvalov to the sovereign and his chief minister was not encouraging. British suspicion of Russia, Shuvalov reported on 19 May, had mounted to the point where Russian intrigues were seen in everything; if it went on there would soon be no more insurgents in Hercegovina—the fighters would be nothing less than disguised Russians. The ambassador believed that British abstention was absolute, but warned the tsar that it might turn out to be of either a Derby or a Disraeli kind. If it were the former, it would be honest and willing to applaud the success of others; if it were Disraelian, this British abstention would probably lead to fishing in troubled waters, and, if a possibility came to hand, would produce some dramatic move that involved Egypt. Shuvalov concluded that, if success were to crown the efforts

[97] Report No. 234, "very confidential and secret," Russell to Derby, 26 May; FO 64/852. The text of this dispatch may be found in Appendix B.
[98] Reports Nos. 222, 223, 230, and 245, Loftus to Derby, 24, 24, 26, and 31 May; *Turkey No. 3 (1876)*, Docs. Nos. 317, 318, 357, and 360, respectively.

of the powers, the question of the revolt would be settled not only without England but in spite of her.[99]

Emperor Alexander and Prince Gorchakov had been anticipating British approval of the Berlin program. It had not occurred to them any more than it had to the sovereign and chancellor of Germany that Queen Victoria's cabinet might resent the role of the imperial league. The tsar, conscious of no unworthy motive, could not understand why the British suspected him, and he found it difficult to believe that they, after accepting the Andrássy note, should reject the memorandum.[100] Alexander, however, was not too dazed to share his chancellor's irritation at what seemed to them to be a British betrayal of the document to the Turks. It was necessary, Gorchakov decided, to make England's isolation as uncomfortable as possible.[101]

Gorchakov's reply to the reports from London was pitched in a high moral key. Russia and the other powers, he wrote, were committed to an honest improvement of the condition of the Christians of Turkey, and he was ready to have that position and the British position weighed in comparison, even by the British parliament, to decide "which responds more scrupulously to the obligations of humanity and civilization and which would contribute most to the maintenance of the Ottoman empire." "With head high" he defied anyone to prove unworthy thoughts or deeds either on the part of his sovereign or of himself, and he announced to Disraeli and his colleagues that Russia was going forward, that Russia would not sacrifice her convictions to charges that were unjust.[102]

THE PROBLEM OF PRESENTATION AT THE SUBLIME PORTE

Before hearing on 18 March of the final decision of the British cabinet Prince Gorchakov had already proposed to Andrássy that the five powers proceed with the imposition of the Berlin memorandum on Turkey. When, within a few hours, he learned the full extent of the English rejection his annoyance was extreme. He forthwith dispatched a new telegram to Vienna urging a forward

---

[99] Shuvalov to Gorchakov, 7/19 May; *Slavonic Review*, III, 664–67.

[100] Schweinitz, *Denkwürdigkeiten*, I, 338.

[101] Tel. No. 2, Károlyi to Andrássy, Ems, 23 May; SA, Varia Turquie I, 1875.

[102] Gorchakov to Shuvalov, 14/26 May; *Slavonic Review*, III, 667–69, Doc. No. 32.

march and branding "further negotiations with London as useless and not entirely compatible with the dignity of the powers."[103]

On the same day Andrássy had independently announced that it was necessary in the interest of saving time to carry on without England. In conformity with his previous views on procedure, the minister suggested incorporating the Berlin program in identic instructions to be read at the Porte.[104] Gorchakov was so impatient to proceed that he did not wish to delay long enough for the five directors of foreign policy to formulate among them a set of instructions. He proposed that the ambassadors in Constantinople be charged to deliver the memorandum as it was, together with a note of their own composition which would be "if not collective at least identic" for each of the foreign representatives.[105] Thus the same divergence of views on mode of action appeared that had long delayed the preparation of the Andrássy note. The Austrian policy still prescribed that all decisions and formulations of expression be restricted to the home governments in order that Ignatiev's influence might be placed under control; the Russian policy remained sufficiently under that influence to try again to delegate some discretionary authority, however slight, to the ambassadors in Constantinople. But on this occasion there was nothing critical at stake as there had been in the autumn negotiations; the new program was already made, and the difference between identic instructions containing that program paraphrased from the memorandum and a textual communication of the memorandum itself was so slight that Andrássy could well afford to give way with words of flattering respect to Tsar Alexander.[106] Andrássy believed that Tsar Alexander with his good intentions stood between him and a Gorchakov moved by dangerous desires and intentions, and he wanted therefore to court him on every occasion. To the effectiveness of the method the results of the meeting in Berlin were excellent testimony.

Andrássy at the same time began a courtship of England in the hope of aid if ever Austro-Russian relations came to a crisis. After

[103] Mülinen to Andrássy in Budapest, Vienna, 18 May; SA, Varia Turquie I, 1875.

[104] Tel. No. 15, Andrássy to Seiller in Berlin, 18 May; *ibid.* Tel., Andrássy to Károlyi in Ems, 19 May; *ibid.* Tel., Andrássy to Mülinen in Vienna, 19 May; *ibid.* Wertheimer's claim that Andrássy refused to agree to a march à cinq (*Andrássy,* II, 302) is incorrect.

[105] Tel., Károlyi to Andrássy, Ems, 20 May; SA, Varia Turquie I, 1875.

[106] Tel., Andrássy to Seiller in Berlin and Károlyi in Ems, 22 May; *ibid.*

agreeing with Gorchakov to go on, he paused to make a new attempt to secure British support for the armistice. Believing that the French might have more influence than anyone else, he telegraphed on 23 May to Paris to enlist the aid of the Duc Decazes.[107] It was, of course, a hope doomed to failure. The French minister addressed a "pressing appeal" to London,[108] but Derby merely sent his thanks to Andrássy for "the disposition thus shown by his Excellency."[109] When the new refusal was known in Vienna on 28 May,[110] Andrássy had no course open to him but to proceed with the presentation of the memorandum.

The one concern of the German government in the new phase of the question was, as before, Austro-Russian agreement. However, that agreement was no longer an arrangement by two powers toward whom Prince Bismarck was as neutral as he professed to be. Berlin's first act after Gorchakov indignantly proposed to go on without England was to seek the views of Vienna.[111] Andrássy's own proposal of identic instructions was approved on the day it was presented,[112] 19 May, and when on the next Gorchakov's slightly different plan of procedure was presented, Bismarck sought to learn the Austrian attitude[113] while delaying an answer to the Russian proposal on the plea of having first to consult the emperor.[114] Only when Andrássy's approval of Gorchakov's identic notes was given to the Germans[115] did Baron Werther in Constantinople receive his instructions. The one comment in Berlin was a regret sent to Andrássy that his own inclinations were not earlier known so that they might have been supported.[116]

The Italian policy was, as usual, to follow in the wake of the imperial powers. Before any decision on mode of procedure was

107 Tel. No. 13, Andrássy to Kuefstein, 23 May; SA, Varia Turquie I, 1875.

108 Decazes to d'Harcourt in London, 23 May; Documents français, II, Doc. No. 56. Report No. 353, Adams to Derby, Paris, 24 May; Turkey No. 3 (1876), Doc. No. 300.

109 Draft No. 245, Derby to Buchanan, 25 May; ibid., Doc. No. 302.

110 Tel. No. 7, Mülinen to Andrássy, 28 May; SA, Varia Turquie I, 1875.

111 Tel. No. 500, Mülinen to Andrássy, 19 May; ibid.

112 Seiller to Andrássy, 19 May; ibid.

113 Tel., Mülinen to Andrássy, 21 May; ibid.

114 Gontaut-Biron to Decazes, Berlin, 20 May; Documents français, II, Doc. No. 55.

115 Tel., Andrássy to the foreign ministry in Vienna, Budapest, 22 May; SA, Varia Turquie I, 1875.

116 Tel. No. 52, Mülinen to Andrássy, 24 May; ibid.

made the Roman government instructed the minister to the Sublime Porte to co-operate,[117] and when these same powers proposed identic notes, the Italian foreign minister concurred.[118]

By virtue of attempting to bridge the gulf between England and the Continental allies, France was again in a difficult position. The cabinet in Paris had approved the Berlin memorandum on 14 May without consulting either London or Rome.[119] Decazes had sent apologies for his failure to discuss the document with them, alleging the pressure exerted in Berlin for a prompt response;[120] but his apologies had failed to save the French considerable embarrassment when it became known that the British cabinet had rejected the memorandum. That embarrassment increased when Gorchakov, the protector of France, proposed to march forward à cinq.[121] Fearful of wounding British susceptibilities, Decazes wished to allow Disraeli and his colleagues more time,[122] but none the less on 22 May he felt obliged to give reluctant assent to the Russian proposition.[123] The next day, however, came Andrássy's appeal for a new French approach to London, and Decazes seized the opportunity to delay his final instructions[124] and to persuade the Italians to defer their own consent.[125] The minister had already written a long argument to London[126] and had expressed his surprise and grief to the British chargé d'affaires,[127] and now, seeing new possibilities in the Austrian offer, he renewed the attack both through the embassy in

---

[117] Melegari to Di Collobiano in St. Petersburg, 20 May; *First Green Book,* Doc. No. CLXVII. Melegari to Corti in Constantinople, 20 May; *ibid.,* Doc. No. CLXVIII.

[118] Melegari to Italian representatives abroad, 24 May; *ibid.,* Doc. No. CLXXVIII. Melegari to Corti, 27 May; *ibid.,* Doc. No. CLXXXIII.

[119] Tel., Decazes to Gontaut-Biron, 14 May; *Documents français,* II, Doc. No. 52.

[120] Decazes to French representatives in London, Vienna, Rome, and Constantinople, 14 May; *ibid.,* Doc. No. 53.

[121] Tel., Gontaut-Biron to Decazes, Berlin, 20 May; *ibid.,* Doc. No. 55.

[122] Hohenlohe-Schillingsfürst, *Denkwürdigkeiten,* II, 190.

[123] Tel. No. 10, Kuefstein to Andrássy, 22 May; SA, Varia Turquie I, 1875.

[124] Report No. 21, Kuefstein to Andrássy, 23 May; *ibid.* Tel. No. 11, Kuefstein to Andrássy, 23 May; *First Red Book,* Doc. No. 363. Tel., Decazes to d'Harcourt, 23 May; *Documents français,* II, Doc. No. 56. Report No. 347, Adams to Derby, 22 May; *Turkey No. 3 (1876),* Doc. No. 294.

[125] Report No. 347, Adams to Derby, 22 May; suppressed from *ibid.* (FO 27/2163).

[126] Decazes to d'Harcourt, 19 May; *First Yellow Book,* pp. 133–38.

[127] Reports Nos. 345 and 346, Adams to Derby, 22 May; *Turkey No. 3 (1876),* Docs. Nos. 291 and 292, respectively.

Paris[128] and through the French agent in London.[129] On the twenty-third, when d'Harcourt saw Derby, the secretary merely replied that he could say nothing that day;[130] but on the day following any hopes that might have been built on Derby's equivocation were destroyed by a categorical refusal to review the British position.[131] It was useless, the ambassador decided, to renew the discussion.[132]

Decazes reluctantly concluded that he would be obliged to participate in the action in Constantinpole,[133] but he was still not reconciled to seeing England remain aloof. A few days earlier he had directed the French ambassador to induce the Porte if possible to invite British participation, as had been done twice before since the outbreak of the rebellion, and, although Bourgoing was not successful in that mission, Decazes charged him on the twenty-sixth to repeat his plea. In case the Turks still proved adamant, the ambassador was instructed to raise indirectly the idea of a conference called on the initiative of Turkey.[134]

Neither of Decazes' plans for the solution of the problem of England's isolation traveled far. The Turks refused to ask Britain's association with the other powers,[135] and in a few days when the question of a conference was informally raised in London Lord Derby crushed it under the weight of his skepticism and inertia.[136]

[128] Report No. 353, Adams to Derby, 24 May; *Turkey No. 3 (1876)*, Doc. No. 300.

[129] Tel., Decazes to d'Harcourt, 23 May; *Documents français*, II, Doc. No. 56.

[130] Tel. No. 12, Kuefstein to Andrássy, Paris, 24 May; SA, Varia Turquie I, 1875. Report No. 51, Beust to Andrássy, 24 May; *ibid.*

[131] Drafts Nos. 529 and 536, Derby to Adams, 24 May; *Turkey No. 3 (1876)*, Docs. Nos. 293 and 304, respectively. Decazes to Vogüé, 25 May; *First Yellow Book*, pp. 145–46.

[132] d'Harcourt to Decazes, 25 May; *Documents français*, II, Doc. No. 58, note 1.

[133] Tel. No. 14, Kuefstein to Andrássy, 26 May; SA, Varia Turquie I, 1875.

[134] Tel., Decazes to Bourgoing, 26 May; *Documents français*, II, Doc. No. 57 and note.   [135] Report No. 552, Elliot to Derby, 29 May; FO 78/2458.

[136] ". . . . I replied that I saw no objection to the idea of a Conference in principle, but that I thought it would be useless without a basis. If the Powers were not agreed beforehand, there was not much prospect that they would agree any the more when the Representatives met around a Conference table. . . . ." (Draft No. 540, Derby to Adams, 27 May; *Turkey No. 3 [1876]*, Doc. No. 305). Disraeli had already brought up the idea of a conference in the cabinet meeting of 16 May (*Disraeli*, VI, 25), and when the French suggestion was made he took kindly to it "as the only practical solution in the long run." His program for it was still a "territorial status quo" which excluded increasing the territories of Turkey's existing vassal states but which admitted the creation of new ones (Disraeli to Derby, 31 May; *ibid.*, VI, 30, and Disraeli to the Prince of Wales, 29 May; Sir Sidney Lee, *King Edward VII*,

The French foreign minister, having then exhausted all possible means of mediating, on the twenty-eighth ordered his representative in Constantinople to share in the presentation of the identic notes.[137] Before all the final arrangements could be made, Prince Gorchakov had become pessimistic. He was fearful that the French would capitulate to English influence[138] and he anticipated that, through the same influence, Turkey might be led to reject the proposals of the memorandum. Hence he found it urgently desirable to consult with Andrássy on the attitude to be assumed by the powers in the face of the impending check. In his first conversation with the Austrian ambassador the prince was reluctant to commit himself beyond intimating that he was inclined to some middle course between complete abstention and the coercion of Turkey;[139] but Jomini, Gorchakov's aide, elaborated the Russian position by suggesting as a basis for future negotiations a Montenegrin memorandum which looked toward an "equitable administration" under the surveillance of a European commission.[140]

a Biography [New York, 1925], I, 419). The prime minister felt, however, that the time was not yet at hand (Disraeli, VI, 27), and there was, consequently, no favorable response from London.

The congress idea had no more success on the Continent. Bismarck agreed with Derby that practical bases were impossible (Derby to Russell, 10 June; Turkey No. 3 [1876], Doc. No. 402); Andrássy called it "eine monstruose Idée" (marginal notation on Report No. 27C, Kuefstein to Andrássy, 31 May; SA, France, 1876); and the Italians concurred (Report No. 24, Wimpffen to Andrássy, Rome, 18 June; SA, Italy, 1876, and Esarco to Rumanian foreign minister, Rome, 23 May; R. V. Bossy, Politica externă a Romăniei [Bucharest, 1928], 138, Doc. No. XXXII). The Russian chancellor, it may be assumed, was still inclined toward a congress, but there is no available reference to his reaction to the French proposal.

[137] Decazes to the French ambassadors in London, Vienna, St. Petersburg, and Berlin, Documents français, II, Doc. No. 58 and note 2.

[138] Tel. No. 4, Károlyi to Andrássy, 25 May; SA, Varia Turquie I, 1875.

[139] Tel. No. 2, Károlyi to Andrássy, 23 May; ibid.

[140] Tel No. 3, Károlyi to Andrássy, 24 May; ibid. "Projet de la réinstallation des réfugiés en Herzégovine proposé par M. Bojedar Petrovič-Negosch conformant aux idées de son altesse le prince de Monténégro"; ibid. (Rodich). The major points of the program of Nicholas were four in number: (1) withdrawal of Turkish troops; (2) provision of a sum of money sufficient to sustain the refugees for one year; (3) the formation of an "equitable administration"; and (4) the establishment of a European commission to supervise the repatriation of the refugees. In elaborating these points the memorandum suggested that slowly local autonomous governments in the hands of commissions containing Christian majorities should be formed and that eventually some kind of central government could be created above them. If these concessions were granted, Prince Nicholas—and by extension the insurgents—would consent to defer the question of dividing up the land which the insurgent chiefs had raised in their conference with Baron Rodich.

Andrássy was unwilling to envisage the future. He pleaded absorption in the business of the Austrian and Hungarian delegations; but, in spite of that absorption, he took enough time to telegraph to Ems a lengthy defense of his hopes for the Berlin program. The Turks, he said, had threatened to reject his December note in the same way that they were threatening at that moment, and he was confident that the new threat would disappear as did the first one. England, he had been repeatedly assured, was going to do nothing to encourage Turkish opposition, and he felt certain of success if the five powers proceeded with the notes. The only danger of the moment was in Serbia's war preparations, and he was convinced that if Prince Gorchakov would speak severely in Beograd the program of the memorandum would be realized.[141]

Gorchakov, once again confronted with Andrássy's obstinacy, had to abandon his desire to discuss the future. He refused in his turn, however, to exercise any pressure on Prince Milan of Serbia, on the ground that it would do no good. Before anything could be done about the Serbian problem he wanted to know what answer would be made at the Porte to the identic notes from the powers. Hence in his view the only thing to do was to present the memorandum in Constantinople as quickly as possible and await eventualities.[142]

The ambassadors had been collaborating on the text of their note, and the document, somewhat delayed by the slowness of instructions from Rome and Paris, was finally completed at a conference on the evening of the twenty-ninth. It was agreed that the communication was to be presented at the Sublime Porte at noontime of the following day. During the night, however, a dramatic event took place which made impossible the presentation of the note. Abdul Aziz, supreme lord of the Ottoman Empire and shadow of God on earth, was deposed.[143]

---

[141] Tel. No. 4, Andrássy to Károlyi, 27 May; *First Red Book,* Doc. No. 374, incomplete.

[142] Tels. Nos. 6 and 7, Károlyi to Andrássy, 29 May; SA, Varia Turquie I, 1875.

[143] Report No. 42F, Zichy to Andrássy, 30 May; *First Red Book,* Doc. No. 386. Corti to Melegari, 29 May; *First Green Book,* Doc. No. CLXXXIX. The text of the note prepared by the ambassadors may be found in annexes to each of the documents cited. Corti to Melegari, 1 June; *ibid.,* Doc. No. CXCIII.

TURKEY IN THE MONTH OF MAY

When the attempts at pacification based on the Andrássy note failed so dismally, it was clear to all discerning Ottomans that new interference on the part of the Great Powers was to be expected. As rumors of the impending meeting in Berlin began to circulate about Europe, Sultan Abdul Aziz became apprehensive that the critical time was at hand. Discreet questions were asked as to the purpose of the meeting,[144] but quite naturally no one was disposed to give the Turks a reassuring reply. Andrássy admitted that the affairs of Turkey would be the subject of discussion in Berlin and, although he expressed the hope that no radically new arrangements would be made, he intimated that the Porte's haste with reform would be the best guaranty against such an eventuality.[145] Gorchakov, in his mounting irritation, was not so polite. "I cannot predict what will be decided in Berlin," he replied to the Ottoman ambassador, "but I think we shall make arrangements to hasten pacification without more shedding of blood."[146] Clear notice was thus given that Turkey was most certainly to be subjected to new intervention and humiliation at the hands of Europe.

The fears and exasperations shared between palace and Porte were also making themselves felt in the Moslem population at large. The insurrection had gone into its tenth month, and its constant drain of imperial energies was rapidly bringing to a climax the unrest and deep-seated discontent already provoked by the universal distress of the empire. If the conference about to be held in Berlin framed hard demands, Sir Henry Elliot warned on 7 May, the safety of the Christian populations would be jeopardized.[147]

Indeed, as the ambassador penned his warning the empire was already the scene of horrible violence. In the north of European Turkey—in Bulgaria—events were taking place which were soon to outrage the conscience of the world. For the moment, however, those revolting deeds were unknown and attention was concentrated on a less wholesale but serious outbreak of mob fury. The fact that

---

[144] Tel. No. 112, Zichy to Andrássy, 6 May; *First Red Book,* Doc. No. 296, incomplete.

[145] Tel. No. 46, Andrássy to Zichy, 7 May; *ibid.,* Doc. No. 305, incomplete.

[146] Tel. No. 125, Zichy to Andrássy, 9 May; SA, Varia Turquie I, 1875.

[147] Report No. 467, Elliot to Derby, 7 May; *Turkey No. 3 (1876),* Doc. No. 253.

it arose out of a relatively trivial occurrence, as things go in Turkey, was all the more proof of the prevailing excitement reigning over the land. On 5 May a Christian girl of Bulgarian descent and dubious character arrived by train in Salonika. She was accompanied by two negresses and the *imam* of her village, and the purpose of her visit was to declare her conversion to Islam before the authorities. Her mother, according to one story, was on the same train, and at the station she appealed to the Christians gathered about to aid in rescuing her daughter. As the girl was being taken by the Moslems to the governor's house she was seized by a band of Greeks, stripped of her new veil, and taken in the carriage of the American vice-consul to the American consulate, where, to the great rage of the Mohammedan populace, she was kept for the night. The next morning as throngs were milling about the streets in anticipation of an attack on the consulate, the French and German consuls fell into their hands. Since the foreign agents were looked upon as protectors of the hated Christians, the enraged mob, discovering the two men in a mosque where they had sought refuge, murdered them brutally.[148]

The immediate demand of the powers concerned for prompt and severe punishment of those responsible for the crime,[149] the collective pressure of all the ambassadors in Constantinople for energetic action,[150] and the dispatch of warships to Salonika and other Turkish waters by all of the powers[151]—all these evidences of Euro-

---

[148] Tel., Czikann to Andrássy, Salonika, 6 May; *First Red Book*, Doc. No. 298. Chiari to Andrássy, Salonika, 6 May; *ibid.*, Doc. No. 299. Chiari to Andrássy, 25 May; *ibid.*, Doc. No. 368. Zichy to Andrássy, 9 May; *ibid.*, Doc. No. 313. The blue book, *Turkey No. 4 (1876)*, "Correspondence Respecting the Murder of the French and German Consuls at Salonica," is devoted to this incident and its immediate consequences. The first official report from Turkish sources (Rashid to Musurus *et al.*, 7 May; *ibid.*, Doc. No. 1) maintained that the American vice-consul, a Hellenized Levantine of Russian origin, had organized the Christian party that had abducted the girl. The British consul at Salonika exculpated his colleague (Blunt to Elliot, 14 May; *ibid.*, inclosure 2, in Doc. No. 49), while this agent himself in his own reports established his entire innocence (Lazzaro to Maynard, Salonika, 25 May; United States, Department of State, *Papers relating to the Foreign Relations of the United States* . . . . , 1876, pp. 569–72). Elliot, *Some Revolutions*, pp. 219–26.

[149] Tel., Bourgoing to Decazes, 7 May; *Documents français*, II, Doc. No. 46. Tel., Decazes to Bourgoing, 8 May; *ibid.*, Doc. No. 47.

[150] Tel., Zichy to Andrássy, 7 May; *First Red Book*, Doc. No. 306. Elliot to Derby, 7 May; *Turkey No. 4 (1876)*, Doc. No. 13. Corti to Melegari, 8 May; *First Green Book*, Doc. No. CLV.

[151] Tenterden to Secretary of the Admiralty, 8 May; *Turkey No. 4 (1876)*, Doc. No. 2, *et al.* Andrássy to Zichy and Chiari, 9 May; *First Red Book*, Doc.

pean determination failed either to calm or to intimidate the Moslems of Turkey. Repercussion of the murders was promptly felt in Constantinople, where both Christians and Moslems, in the grip of mounting fear, were buying firearms of every available kind. The former were arming for defense; the latter showed signs of aggressive intentions. In the ranks of the Prophet there was great irritation against the Christians; but observers soon noticed the possibility that their aroused hostility might be turned against the grand vizier and even the sultan himself as well. Among the most active buyers of arms and ammunition were several thousand *softas*, or professional students of the sacred law. So fraught with danger did the capital seem that on 9 May the ambassadors asked that warships be brought to Besika Bay at the mouth of the Dardanelles.[152] The next day as the atmosphere became more tense—although the Moslem movement began to appear more anti-governmental than anti-Christian—the ambassadors telegraphed to their respective foreign offices for a second gunboat to supplement the *stationnaire* ordinarily kept at Constantinople.[153] The uneasiness of the foreign quarter continued to grow, and during that and the following day deputations from the various European colonies called on their ambassadors to seek protection. The English were so concerned for their safety that they proposed to Elliot the calling up of warships, alleging that the dangers of the time justified ignoring the treaty provisions against such a measure.[154] During the excitement the hostility of a considerable group toward General Ignatiev reached a bitter intensity which was not assuaged by a comment made allegedly by the general's wife to the effect that in Constantinople it was her husband and not the sultan who reigned.[155] When rumors of a plot to burn and pillage

---

No. 310. Chiari to Andrássy, 9 May; *ibid., Doc.* No. 316. Andrássy to Zichy, 19 May; *ibid.,* Doc. No. 319. Melegari to representatives abroad, 18 May; *First Green Book,* Doc. No. CLXII. Russell to Derby, 18 May; *Turkey No. 4 (1876),* Doc. No. 32.

[152] Tel. and Report No. 475, Elliot to Derby, 9 May; *Turkey No. 3 (1876),* Docs. Nos. 224 and 256, respectively. Zichy to Andrássy, 9 May; *First Red Book,* Doc. No. 315.

[153] Tel. and Report No. 480, Elliot to Derby, 10 May; *Turkey No. 3 (1876),* Docs. Nos. 226 and 271, respectively. Tel., Zichy to Andrássy, *First Red Book,* Doc. No. 322.

[154] Tel., Zichy to Andrássy, 10 May; *First Red Book,* Doc. No. 322. Report No. 485 (tel.), Elliot to Derby, 11 May; *Turkey No. 3 (1876),* Doc. No. 237.

[155] Private letter, Kosjek to Schwegel, 15 May; SA, Varia Turquie, 1876.

the European quarter began to circulate on the tenth and eleventh, Ignatiev filled the Russian embassy with several hundred Croats and Montenegrins and prepared for siege operations,[156] while his immediate neighbors, the ambassadors of Austria and France, also made preparations.[157] On the tenth Ignatiev, as *doyen* of the diplomatic corps, called his colleagues together to advise on means of defense. Elliot was disposed to take exception to Ignatiev's assembling his retinue of Southern Slavs because of the increased danger of collision which it entailed, but he permitted the British consul to participate in a meeting of the consular corps. However, it was a meeting which so reflected the ambassadorial jealousies and suspicions that nothing was done for the eventual protection of the foreign inhabitants.[158]

By the tenth, however, the indications that the mounting storm would be directed against the government were being confirmed. On that day several thousand *softas,* all armed to the teeth, began milling up and down the streets shouting "down with the grand vizier" and demanding a comparable fate for General Ignatiev and the Sheikh-ul-Islam. Formal demands were addressed to the sultan, and the next day, as the excited theologians still were surging about the

---

[156] Nelidov, *Revue des deux mondes,* XXVII (1915), 314–16. On 13 May the *Levant Herald* of Constantinople published a "coarse and intemperate" attack on the Russian ambassador which led to the suspension of that journal but which, according to Elliot, was "hailed by universal expressions of delight by the whole of the Turkish and a very large majority of the Christian public." All of the Turkish papers and some of the Greek, the British ambassador further reported, planned to have comparable articles the next day but were restrained at the last moment by governmental authority. Representative sentences from the attack read: "The Russian ambassador appears to be alarmed at the pitch of unpopularity to which his political activity *per fas et nefas* has brought him. . . . . Conscience makes cowards of us all, and the great diplomatist, when he reflects upon all the agony and death, the misery and desolation, which his subtle dealings have brought, must sometimes feel a dart of compunction penetrate through the joints of his armour of cynicism. Circumstances, at all events, seem to indicate that the General is oppressed with apprehensions about his own safety at this moment, for his excellency fills his palace at night with a bodyguard of several hundred Montenegrins and Croats, to protect him from the vengeance of the Turkish populace. . . . . But the Russian Ambassador may rest assured that the Turkish populace will not hurt a hair of his excellency's head; Turkey has no crown of martyrdom to offer to General Ignatieff! . . . ." (Report No. 495, Elliot to Derby, 15 May; FO 78/2458).

[157] Zichy to Andrássy, 9 May; *First Red Book,* Doc. No. 315.

[158] Report No. 518, Elliot to Derby, 19 May; *Turkey No. 3 (1876),* Doc. No. 341.

Sublime Porte, the Sheikh-ul-Islam and then the grand vizier were dismissed.[159] That afternoon Mehemet Rushdi Pasha, a man universally respected for his integrity but too infirm for high position,[160] was made grand vizier and Hussein Avni, who had recently fallen into disfavor, was recalled to the war office.[161]

It was becoming clear to the foreign observers that the demonstration of the *softas* was no mere outburst of thoughtless Moslem fanaticism. These ultra-conservative students of the sacred law, by a most curious paradox, had become champions of a Western constitution for Turkey. The seeds of the movement had been sown in the previous autumn when Midhat Pasha, the ex-grand vizier noted for his reforming zeal, came to the conclusion that the salvation of the empire lay in placing restraints on the arbitrary power of a capricious sultan. In December when Mahmud was preparing his reforms designed merely to escape European intervention, Midhat had resigned on the ground that the grand vizier's measures did not go to the roots of a bad administration;[162] and in the months which followed he worked quietly for his cause. Several important officials were converted to the constitutional program, but the reformers immediately ran into the relentless opposition of Sultan Abdul Aziz to any limitations on his power. In looking about for support Midhat and his friends discovered in the discontent of the *ulemas* and the *softas* a golden bridge for understanding, and a vast conspiracy, based on the demand for constitutional government, was hatched.[163] The question of instituting a radical change of political organization seems to have come up for discussion in the ministerial council, and the grand vizier, already in general disfavor from his alleged subservience to Ignatiev, stood out as the major opponent of

---

[159] Zichy to Andrássy, 11, 11, 12 May; *First Red Book*, Docs. Nos. 323, 324, 327, respectively. Report No. 492, Elliot to Derby, 12 May; *Turkey No. 3 (1876)*, Doc. No. 288, incomplete. Corti to Melegari, 12 May; *First Green Book*, Doc. No. CLXIII. Bourgoing to Decazes, 17 May; *First Yellow Book*, pp. 132–33. *The Times* (London), 18 May, p. 10, col. 1; 20 May, p. 8, col. 1. Gallenga, *Two Years of the Eastern Question*, II, 53–54. Nelidov, *loc. cit.*, XXVII, 316.

[160] Bourgoing to Decazes, 17 May; *First Yellow Book*, p. 132. Elliot, *Some Revolutions*, p. 231.

[161] Tel. (Report No. 487), Elliot to Derby, 11 May; *Turkey No. 3 (1876)*, Doc. No. 236. *The Times* (London), 13 May 1876, p. 7, col. 3.

[162] Reports Nos. 831, 832. Elliot to Derby, 14 December 1875; FO 78/2391. Sir Henry Elliot, "The Death of Abdul Aziz and Turkish Reform," *Nineteenth Century*, XXIII (1888), 280. Elliot, *Some Revolutions*, pp. 228–29.

[163] *The Times* (London), 6 June 1876, p. 8, col. 1.

a plan acceptable to all but two or three of his colleagues.[164] The crisis came in the middle of May, in so far as various stories can be sifted, when the grand vizier attempted to have Midhat removed from the capital by the usual means of appointment to a provincial governorship.[165] Contrary to Mahmud's calculations, Mahmud and the Sheikh-ul-Islam departed and Midhat remained.

The elimination of two unsatisfactory officials was, of course, only a small first step toward constitutional government, and no one seriously supposed that the movement would stop at that point.[166] The *softas* had apparently not attempted to dictate Mahmud's successor in the grand vizierate, and when the name of the aged Mehemet Rushdi was announced the leaders of the demonstration were sympathetically inclined toward this worthy man although they doubted if he possessed the energy requisite for subduing a mad sultan. Midhat was the acknowledged leader of the constitutionalists and in the days following the ministerial changes it was confidently anticipated that Midhat would forthwith return to power.[167]

This expectation was soon fulfilled. Upon the insistent demand of the new grand vizier, Abdul Aziz on 19 May reluctantly appointed the reform leader minister without portfolio. The sultan, however, had no intention of capitulating so readily. Without consulting his chief minister, he put into the cabinet as a check upon Midhat two additional ministers, Namyk Pasha, a representative of the strict Mohammedan group, and the swashbuckling Dervish Pasha, who had only two weeks before been removed from office. It was a policy of giving with one hand and taking with the other, a policy which the monarch had seemingly already followed in putting the allegedly anti-constitutional Hussein Avni in harness with Mehemet Rushdi.[168]

[164] Report No. 534, Elliot to Derby, 25 May; FO 78/2458.

[165] Report No. 543, Elliot to Derby, 27 May; *ibid.* Mahmud after his fall alleged to the British dragoman that he had attempted to get rid of Midhat on the advice of General Ignatiev. It seems probable that the Turks knew how well Elliot liked to hear bad things about his Russian colleague—although it is quite possible, of course, that Ignatiev did suggest the elimination of a man who was as undesirable in his eyes as he was desirable in those of Elliot.

[166] Report No. 512, Elliot to Derby, 18 May; *Turkey No. 3 (1876),* Doc. No. 338.

[167] *The Times* (London), 23 May 1876, p. 8, col. 1.

[168] The role of Hussein Avni is not at all clear during these days. He was notoriously an opponent of Midhat, and was reported by certain of the British ambassador's confidants to be so opposed to the liberal agitation that he offered to drive away the *softas* at the point of bayonets (Report No. 38, Sandison to Elliot, 24 May, in Report No. 534, Elliot to Derby, 25 May; FO 78/2458).

In Mehemet Rushdi's ministry, consequently, there was such a diversity of interests that a common purpose at first seemed impossible. But Namyk was no sooner in office than he professed his support of the desired constitution,[169] and at the same time it became known that the calculating Hussein Avni, out of a desire to advance his own interests, had established quarters in the reform camp.[170]

As the next days came and went, the atmosphere of Constantinople was tense. In a common discontent Christian and Moslem arrived at a new understanding; all classes of society, from porters in the street to pashas in high office, were open in their expressions of hostility to the sultan. Everyone, it seemed to Elliot, was talking about a constitution, while Koran texts were being cited to justify condemnation of a negligent caliph and to denounce the sultan's absolutism as a violation of sacred law. The demand for fundamental reform was so insistent, the ambassador observed, that the reformers would not hesitate to attempt the deposition of Abdul Aziz if he proved recalcitrant. The attitude at such a juncture of the minister of war—Hussein Avni—would mean the difference between bloodless revolution and the "frightful consequences" of civil war.[171] Murad, the sultan's nephew and heir apparent of the house of Othman, had been in communication with the leaders of the new movement and had affirmed his readiness to proclaim a constitution on the day that he mounted the throne.[172] Abdul Aziz soon heard of these negotiations and placed Murad and his younger brothers in close confinement; but the public heard of that action, and their irritation mounted the more.[173]

The events of the turbulent week in Constantinople did not incline the Turks toward docility in the face of Europe. It was symbolic of Ottoman policy that Zichy on 11 May met the fallen Mahmud as he was walking out of the Sublime Porte and upon entering the building found that Rashid, the foreign minister, did not know that

[169] Reports Nos. 521, 532, Elliot to Derby, 19, 24 May, respectively; *ibid.* Zichy had it that Namyk was brought into the cabinet at the behest of the grand vizier (Zichy to Andrássy, 20 May; *First Red Book,* Doc. No. 353); but Elliot's reports followed in the text appear more convincing.

[170] Zichy to Andrássy, 19 May; *First Red Book,* Doc. No. 352.

[171] Report No. 536, Elliot to Derby, 25 May; *Turkey No. 3 (1876),* Doc. No. 345.

[172] Report No. 535, Elliot to Derby, 25 May; *ibid.,* Doc. No. 344.

[173] Report No. 512, Elliot to Derby, 18 May; *ibid.,* Doc. No. 338.

anything had happened.[174] The murder of the two consuls had been, of necessity, another blow to such toleration as the Ottoman Empire enjoyed in Europe. Gunboats of all the powers were anchored at the mouth of the Golden Horn and many other warships were moving into Turkish waters. It could not have been otherwise than that the Turks should be apprehensive of the meeting of Gorchakov and Andrássy as the guests of one of the governments whose agents had just been brutally killed by a Moslem mob. Apprehension, however, had not engendered meekness; the Porte, elated over Mukhtar's recent victory in Hercegovina, gave no indication of accepting arrangements made in Berlin which were not to Turkey's liking.[175]

Those arrangements, supposedly to be held secret by the powers, were scarcely made before they were known in Constantinople.[176] But the wounds to sovereign dignity inflicted by the Berlin memorandum were soon anointed with a soothing balm. On 16 May Lord Derby informed the Turkish ambassador that the British government would not join in forcing the new proposals on the Porte,[177] and three days later, after the cabinet's formal decision, that statement was emphatically confirmed.[178] Rashid took over bodily the arguments which Derby had furnished and used them in his conversations "with much emotion and some indignation."[179] Inspired—at all events in the opinion of Zichy—by the attitude of the London cabinet and its reflection in the person of Elliot, the Turkish ministerial council resolved to reject the Berlin memorandum before its

[174] Zichy to Andrássy, 12 May; *First Red Book,* Doc. No. 327.

[175] *The Times* (London), 27 May 1876, p. 7, cols. 5–6.

[176] It was generally supposed, and for Russia it was a matter of no little irritation, that Elliot had betrayed the contents of the memorandum to the Turks (Tel. No. 2, Károlyi to Andrássy, Ems, 23 May; SA, Varia Turquie I, 1875). Such knowledge regarding the memorandum as was available in London on 14 May was forwarded to Elliot, but there is no evidence in his official reports to indicate that he did share his knowledge at the Porte. When the German and Russian ambassadors subsequently asked Derby the straightforward question whether or not the British had revealed the proposed demands, the secretary claimed that he had found Musurus Pasha on 16 May "acquainted with the general purport of the proposals before our conversation" but confessed that the Turkish ambassador might have gleaned some details from their discussion together (Draft No. 423, Derby to Russell, 30 May; *Turkey No. 3 [1876],* Doc. No. 321 and Draft No. 340, Derby to Loftus, 30 May; *ibid.,* Doc. No. 322).

[177] Draft No. 302, Derby to Elliot, 16 May; *ibid.,* Doc. No. 263.

[178] Draft No. 308, Derby to Elliot, 19 May; *ibid.,* Doc. No. 278.

[179] Reports Nos. 515 and 517, Elliot to Derby, 19 May; *ibid.,* Docs. Nos. 339 and 340, respectively.

formal presentation at the Porte.[180] On the twenty-first a lengthy telegram incorporating that decision went out from Constantinople to the European capitals. Rashid's document declared that Turkish effort had brought the rebellion to "one of the last stages of pacification," an achievement which the Berlin conference gave promise of completely undoing. His government, he announced, could not give up the advantages gained through so much bloodshed; it would not, therefore, accede to an armistice. A paraphrase of Derby's objections to the peace bases of the memorandum followed, and the telegram ended on the high note of refusal to go beyond the Andrássy note.[181]

The responses which the Turkish ambassadors gleaned during the next days in the various foreign offices were far from encouraging. From Rome came mild remonstrance befitting Italian impotence;[182] from Paris came advice to invite England to support the memorandum.[183] At the Berlin foreign office Bülow refused to listen to comments on a program officially unknown to Turkey.[184] In Budapest Andrássy likewise rejected the proffered observations but vigorously advanced his own in the form of his old threat, dressed with a new garnishment or two, that the Porte would have to bear alone the weight of responsibility for ill-advised action.[185] Not even in London did the Turkish circular meet with encouragement. Derby admonished Musurus against "any precipitate action" and limited himself to advising a decision consonant with what the Turks concluded "after due consideration" to be their own best interests.[186] But such a remark, the secretary added, was not to be considered in Constantinople as a pledge of unqualified support; "both the circumstances and the state

[180] Report No. 41AF, Zichy to Andrássy, 26 May; SA, Varia Turquie I, 1875.

[181] Tel., Rashid to Musurus et al., 21 May; Turkey No. 3 (1876), Doc. No. 290.

[182] Melegari to Corti, 27 May; First Green Book, Doc. No. CLXXXIV.

[183] Report No. 22, Kuefstein to Andrássy, 24 May; SA, Varia Turquie I, 1875. Tel., Decazes to Bourgoing, 26 May; Documents français, II, Doc. No. 57.

[184] Report No. 22C, Károlyi to Andrássy, 27 May; SA, Varia Turquie I, 1875. Report No. 443, Russell to Derby, 1 June; FO 64/852.

[185] Tel. No. 4, Andrássy to Károlyi, 27 May; First Red Book, Doc. No. 374, incomplete. ". . . . Count de Vogüé then told me that the Turkish ambassador came back from Budapest with l'oreille basse. He denied having wished to present an anticipatory protest against the démarche of the five powers and pretended to have limited himself to several observations. He was greatly disturbed by the energy with which your Excellency called his attention to the probable consequence of a refusal by the Porte. . . . ." (Tel., Mülinen to Andrássy, 29 May; SA, Varia Turquie I, 1875).

[186] Draft No. 319, Derby to Elliot, 24 May; Turkey No. 3 (1876), Doc. No. 295.

of feeling in this country," he said, " were very much changed since the Crimean War and the Porte would be unwise to be led by recollections of that period, to count upon more than moral support of Her Majesty's Government in the event of no satisfactory solution of the present difficulties being found. . . . ."[187] Elliot seconded his chief in adding his own warning that Britain's rejection should not be construed as a recommendation to do likewise.[188] These words of discouragement coming from all over Europe had little effect. The grand vizier let it be known that, despite foreign opinions, the memorandum would be rejected;[189] and the foreign minister, as proof of why Turkey could not accept an armistice, sent out a new circular telegram describing the revolt as being in the throes of collapse.[190]

Still, important though the impending action of the powers was for Turkey, the problem of the Berlin memorandum was eclipsed by that of constitutional reform. While the Turkish protest was being summarily dismissed in the European capitals, Midhat and his colleagues in Constantinople were engaged in the task of bringing Abdul Aziz to reason—as they saw it. The sultan was well aware of the temper of popular feeling; but, as his ministerial appointments indicated, he refused to permit his fears to drive him to capitulation. He placed his scheming relatives under rigid surveillance and himself moved nervously from palace to palace in the hope of escaping danger. From the streets came persistent reports of resentment against his person, and as he looked out his window he saw lined up before him in the harbor a double row of foreign ships of war. He trembled for his own safety; and, as a Russian vessel took up its position under his very eyes, his impotent rage inspired him, so gossip had it, to smash the window with his fist[191]—but Abdul Aziz still refused to grant a constitution.

Hence it developed that on 28 May the ministerial cabinet resolved on the deposition of the obdurate padishah. The key man, the minister of war, joined Midhat and Mehemet Rushdi in the con-

---

[187] Draft No. 324, Derby to Elliot, 25 May; *Turkey No. 3 (1877)*.

[188] Report No. 524, Elliot to Derby, 23 May; *Turkey No. 3 (1876)*, Doc. No. 342. Draft No. 363, Derby to Elliot, 6 June; *ibid.*, Doc. No. 375.

[189] Report No. 541, Elliot to Derby, 27 May; *ibid.*, Doc. No. 374. Tel. No. 140, Zichy to Andrássy, 26 May; *First Red Book*, Doc. No. 366, incomplete. Tel. No. 141, Zichy to Andrássy, 27 May; *ibid.*, Doc. No. 371.

[190] Tel., Rashid to Musurus, 29 May; *Turkey No. 3 (1876)*, Doc. No. 324.

[191] *The Times* (London), 26 May 1876, p. 8, col. 1.

spiracy, and together they laid their plans to carry out a *coup d'état*. An authorization for the deposition was obtained from the Sheikh-ul-Islam to give sanction to the act in the eyes of good Mohammedans, and Hussein Avni took charge of the military precautions. During the twenty-ninth some rumor reached the palace of what was about to occur, and the sultan twice ordered Hussein Avni to report to him in person. In a hasty conference the three chief conspirators agreed that they could delay no longer, and in the pitch blackness of a stormy midnight they separated to their several tasks. Midhat went to the war office to harangue the troops, and Hussein Avni went with a body of loyal soldiers to the palace. The war minister proceeded immediately to the pavilion which was serving as a prison to Prince Murad. With two revolvers in his hands Hussein Avni forced his way into the presence of the terrified prince and sent him, overcome though he was by hysterical fear, to the war office. In the meantime soldiers had surrounded the whole palace, and Hussein Avni's chief aide marched into the bedroom of Abdul Aziz to announce to him his deposition. For a time Allah's vicar on earth refused to submit, but in the end the roar of the conspirator's cannons was persuasive.[192] When daylight came, the deposed sultan and his harem—women enough to fill fifty-three boats—were escorted to the old seraglio,[193] and Murad was head of the house of Othman. The next day there appeared an imperial *hatt* announcing the change of sovereign. "By the will of God and the unanimous wish of all our subjects," Murad was alleged to be saying, "we have just ascended the throne of our ancestors." "Full and complete liberty" the document proclaimed for every subject; a *"bona fide* system of legislation" was promised; the whole administration of the state was to reorganized.[194] A long stage in the constitutional journey seemed to have been made.

THE FATE OF THE BERLIN MEMORANDUM

The deposition of Abdul Aziz necessarily forestalled the delivery of the identic notes at the Sublime Porte. In the confusion prevailing

---

[192] Report No. 559, Eliot to Derby, 31 May; *Turkey No. 3 (1876)*, Doc. No. 393. Zichy to Andrássy, 2 June; *First Red Book*, Doc. No. 398. Elliot, *Some Revolutions*, pp. 232–36. Ali Haydar Midhat, *Life of Midhat Pasha*, pp. 82–86.

[193] *The Times* (London), 1 June 1876, p. 5, col. 1.

[194] Text of the imperial *hatt* of 1 June may be found in *Turkey No. 3 (1876)*, Doc. No. 394; *First Yellow Book*, pp. 147–48; *First Green Book*, Doc. No. CXCII; Noradounghian, *Recueil*, III, 395–96.

on 30 May no one knew if the ministers were to remain in office or what policy, if any, was going to be followed. The ambassadors therefore abandoned their démarche at the last moment—Zichy sent out a messenger to overtake his dragoman who was on the way to the Porte with the note—and they invited their governments to send new instructions.[195]

The news of the *coup d'état* was received in Paris with a certain relief. Decazes had most reluctantly separated himself from the British and consented to the five-power procedure; to him the change of sultans offered an avenue for escape from his embarrassing position and the opportunity for a new attempt to bring Disraeli's cabinet back into the European concert. Promptly he instructed the French ambassador in Constantinople to await further orders before acting, and he sent new overtures to London urging reconsideration of the British decision.[196] At the same time he proposed to the three imperial governments that the powers defer the notes until official relations had been established with the new regime. It was possible, Decazes suggested, that this new government might really accomplish some tangible peace of its own accord.[197]

On that same day—31 May—Andrássy agreed with the French foreign minister that it would be desirable to postpone the notes. He felt, as did Decazes, the injustice of descending on a new-born administration with such sweeping demands as were incorporated in the Berlin memorandum. As a practical consideration, moreover, Andrássy did not want to jeopardize his program by giving the Turks a chance to worm their way out of it on the grounds of the temporary disturbance in Constantinople. He recommended to Bismarck and Gorchakov, consequently, that they should wait.[198]

In Berlin Bülow was struck by the fact that Abdul Aziz was pulled down from his throne on the day that the ambassadors were planning to deliver their notes, and he felt it eminently desirable to proceed cautiously until something more was known of what was

[195] Zichy to Andrássy, 30 May; *First Red Book,* Docs. Nos. 382 and 386.

[196] Reports Nos. 375 and 376, Adams to Derby, 31 May; *Turkey No. 3 (1876),* Docs. Nos. 351 and 352, respectively. Draft No. 587, Derby to Lyons, 6 June; *ibid.,* Doc. No. 377.

[197] Tel. No. 15, Kuefstein to Andrássy, 31 May; *First Red Book,* Doc. No. 384. Report No. 27AC, Kuefstein to Andrássy, 31 May; SA, Varia Turquie I, 1875. Dreux, *Dernières années,* p. 208.

[198] Tel., Andrássy to Károlyi and Seiller, 31 May; *First Red Book,* Doc. No. 389, incomplete.

happening in Turkey.[199] Gorchakov and the tsar, still residing in Ems, also consented,[200] and the ambassadors were instructed to defer their action.[201]

The immediate problem then confronting the chancelleries of Europe was the attitude to be taken toward this change of Turkish sovereigns which had been effected by violence. Prince Gorchakov, who in his anger had refused further to consider England, proposed that official recognition of Murad should be preceded by a common understanding of the remaining powers.[202] Andrássy professed agreement with the plan but immediately belied his gesture by ordering Zichy to continue his relations at the Porte and to hold out hopes that recognition would follow a formal notification of Murad's accession.[203]

In London, of course, there was no inclination to consult with the European powers about the turn of Turkish events. The French suggestion that the moment was favorable for a closer understanding between all the powers—that, in other words, there was a new opportunity for England to co-operate—evoked from Derby only the laconic remark that "we must wait."[204] The foreign office did send out a circular telegram to the embassies on 31 May announcing that "it is important for Her Majesty's Government to know how the change of rulers has been taken by foreign Governments,"[205] but as soon as Turkey's formal announcement was made in London,[206] Elliot was instructed first to congratulate the new sovereign[207] and then, on 2 June, to proceed with recognition.[208]

[199] Report No. 24, Károlyi to Andrássy, 2 June; SA, Varia Turquie I, 1875.

[200] Tel. No. 10, Károlyi to Andrássy, 1 June; *ibid.* Dreux, *Dernières années,* pp. 209–10.

[201] Tel. No. 64, Andrássy to Zichy, 2 June; *First Red Book,* Doc. No. 397.

[202] Tel., Decazes to Gontaut-Biron, 2 June; *Documents français,* II, 67, note 2.

[203] Tel., Andrássy to embassies abroad, 1 June; *First Red Book,* Doc. No. 391.

[204] Marginal comment on Tel., Adams to Derby, 31 May; FO 27/2163.

[205] Draft No. 343, Derby to Loftus *et al.,* 31 May; FO 65/932.

[206] Tel., Rashid to Musurus, 31 May; *Turkey No. 3 (1876),* Doc. No. 330; communicated to the foreign office on 1 June.

[207] Draft No. 345, Derby to Elliot, 1 June; *ibid.,* Doc. No. 331. This telegram actually read: "In reply to your telegram of yesterday, Her Majesty's Government authorize you to congratulate the Sultan as you propose."

[208] Draft No. 356, Derby to Elliot, 2 June; *ibid.,* Doc. No. 354. The second order to Elliot followed a telegraphic appeal from Constantinople to hasten formal recognition (Tel., Rashid to Musurus, 2 June; FO 78/2527). This appeal was soon followed by another urging that Britain be the first to recognize the new sultan: ". . . . Mais Votre Excellence comprendra combien est légitime notre désir

In the French capital Decazes hastened to give a second proof that the fall of Abdul Aziz had ended his complaisance toward Russia. Not only did he cancel France's share in the presentation of identic notes at the Porte, but on 1 June, without consultation with Ems, he authorized Ambassador Bourgoing to enter immediately into semiofficial relations with the new government.[209] An understanding with regard to recognition by the five powers to the exclusion of England he rejected without qualification; it was out of this question of recognition that he hoped to build a bridge for British return to the European concert.[210] Very quickly the foreign minister was emerging from that effacement in which the swaddling clothes of the third republic had bound French policy. But Decazes' action, the British chargé d'affaires noted, did not fail to inspire a

certain uneasiness in influential quarters . . . . owing to what is considered to be another instance of his precipitate action. . . . . It is feared that the Duke, in his anxiety to assume the character of mediator, as it has been expressed to me, and to make it appear that France is acting a prominent part in the present crisis, is not serving her true interests; that he may therefore offend Prince Bismarck, and it is considered that the true policy for France, in her actual state, is to keep in the background and to await events rather than to attempt to lead them.[211]

The Italian government found itself in an uncomfortable position with regard to the recognition of Murad. The first impulse of the Quirinal cabinet was to wait for a signal from Ems.[212] On 1 June the British ambassador saw the foreign minister and made an attempt to induce him to abandon Russia in favor of an independent action with England and France, but Melegari was chary of such a venturesome

---

de voir que l'Angleterre soit la première à reconnaître officiellement notre nouveau souverain et à accréditer son ambassadeur auprès de lui. Indépendamment des considérations morales découlant de la position de l'Angleterre vis-à-vis de la Turquie, de l'impression et de l'effet favorables que cela produira sur l'opinion publique, la priorité de cette accréditation donnera, croyons-nous, à Sir Henry Elliot le droit d'être doyen du corps diplomatique. C'est là une particularité qui a un grand prix pour nous, et je ne saurais assez recommander à Votre Excellence de déployer ses efforts dans ce sens. Veuillez donc en entretenir d'urgence Lord Derby, afin que les lettres du représentant de la Reine lui soient envoyées les plus tôt possible" (Tel., Rashid to Musurus, 6 June; FO 78/2527).

[209] Decazes to Bourgoing, 2 June; *First Yellow Book*, pp. 149–50. Tel. No. 17, Kuefstein to Andrássy, 1 June; *First Red Book*, Doc. No. 394, incomplete. Report No. 380, Adams to Derby, 1 June; *Turkey No. 3 (1876)*, Doc. No. 353.

[210] Decazes to Gontaut-Biron, 3 June; *Documents français*, II, Doc. No. 60.

[211] Report No. 381, Adams to Derby, 1 June; FO 27/2164.

[212] Tel. No. 58, Wimpffen to Andrássy, 31 May; SA, Italy, 1876.

course.[213] By the next day, however, the minister was becoming nervous and fearful of falling between two stools. Having failed to learn anything as to the intentions of the imperial courts, he sent notice to them that the conservation of Italian interests in the East would permit no further delay, and he proceeded to instruct Count Corti to congratulate the new sultan.[214]

Any hope that Prince Gorchakov might have had for exploiting the change of sovereigns in Constantinople had been crushed by the precipitate action of France and England and Italy. When the desired unanimity of the Continent was lost, he was forced to go through the face-saving gesture of asking if Berlin and Vienna were content with the Turkish announcement and then, with affirmative answers in his hand, to proceed with recognition.[215] By 3 June the problem of regularizing relations with Turkey was disposed of except for the formalities and the inevitable platitudinous advice to reform.

As soon as that problem was cleared from the diplomatic table Prince Gorchakov wished to proceed immediately with the identic notes. When he addressed this proposal to the ambassadors in Ems on 4 June, he had just heard that the new regime in Turkey was planning to announce an armistice of six weeks' duration. Now the Berlin memorandum was based on an armistice, but the Russian chancellor saw a profound difference between the type of armistice which the memorandum demanded and that which the Turks were about to grant of their own accord; the latter was projected "not with the object of pacification but with a warlike policy in view."

---

[213] Report No. 204, Paget to Derby, 3 June; *Turkey No. 3 (1876)*, Doc. No. 406.

[214] Tel., Mülinen to Andrássy, 3 June; SA, Varia Turquie I, 1875. Tel., Paget to Derby, 3 June; FO 45/286. Melegari to Corti, 3 June; *First Green Book*, Doc. No. CLXXXVI.

[215] Memorandum of Novikov, with Tel. No. 42, Langenau to Andrássy, 2 June; SA, Russia, 1876. Gontaut-Biron to Decazes, 2 June; *Documents français*, II, Doc. No. 59. The coup d'état was eminently regretted by General Ignatiev, who saw Midhat and Murad replace Mahmud Nedim and Abdul Aziz, respectively, to his great disadvantage, despite the fact that he had been in secret contact with the new sovereign (Nelidov, *Revue des deux mondes*, XXVII [1915], 325). The ambassador refrained from political relations with Murad's government and tried to persuade his colleagues to remain aloof; but the failure of his hope was soon apparent, and on the third he joined the other foreign representatives in taking the first steps toward recognition (Report No. 570, Elliot to Derby, 3 June; FO 78/2459).

Moreover, he found the accession proclamation quite vague and without either promise or guaranty. The time had arrived, in his opinion, when the five powers should hesitate no longer in presenting their demands.[216] This zeal for proceeding with Andrássy's program cannot be set down to belief in the concrete measures which it contained; Gorchakov had recently looked upon them as being far from adequate in the existing turmoil. The presentation of the identic notes involved questions of policy and of prestige. The policy was that of European tutelage of Turkey; and prestige was at stake inasmuch as it was essential for Europe, and specifically for Russia, to see to it that the desires of Europe were not thwarted by Ottoman trickery. In the chancellor's view, the powers could not afford to embark on a proposal for Turkish reform and fail to see it through. With great earnestness Gorchakov sought the consent of Andrássy for immediate action. The talk of armistice and amnesty at the Porte he damned as a new scheme inspired by England to circumvent the memorandum, and again he denounced the lack of guaranties. But Gorchakov was not content to rely on the objective merits of his request. The chancellor reminded Andrássy that he had made great concessions at Berlin, and, as a final inducement, he agreed to remonstrate again with the Serbs. "He talked to me with such vigor," the Austrian ambassador reported, "that I do not doubt but what a refusal or even hesitation on our part would make a very bad impression on the Russian cabinet."[217] Confronted with such insistence, the Austrian minister was obliged to agree. He failed to see Gorchakov's distinctions between the two types of armistice, and he feared that the moment was the worst possible for presenting the memorandum demands; but Russian co-operation had to be bought by concessions, and he grudgingly consented to the Russian request.[218]

In his reply Andrássy predicted that the French would not collaborate; and, indeed, as he drew up his telegram, Decazes had already confirmed that surmise. That special intimacy which the Russian authorities had shown toward France since the war scare of the previous spring had received a first and rude jolt by the haste with which Decazes independently established relations with the new regime in Turkey. On 1 June Gorchakov discussed the *coup d'état* with

[216] Tel. No. 13, Károlyi to Andrássy, 4 June; SA, Varia Turquie I, 1875.
[217] Tel. No. 14, Károlyi to Andrássy, 5 June; *ibid.*
[218] Tel. No. 8, Andrássy to Károlyi, 6 June; *ibid.*

Gontaut-Biron, the French ambassador to Germany. The chancellor pretended that he was consenting to delay the identic notes out of respect for the views of Decazes, but at the same time the ambassador was allowed to feel the Russian displeasure at France's immediate recognition of Murad without previous agreement.[219] The next day Gontaut-Biron resumed the conversation, arguing the correctness of French action and the desire to maintain an identity of views with Russia. Gorchakov, without entirely abandoning his dissatisfaction, responded favorably to the ambassador's defense and renewed his earlier offer of an important role to France if a French fleet were sent to Turkish waters.[220] It was beyond doubt annoying that France should succumb to what appeared to be British influence, but at the same time Russia had need of French naval strength and France therefore was still worth courting.

On 4 June, when the Russians were desirous of proceeding with the notes, the tsar made a personal request to the ambassador that France should continue her support.[221] After the audience Gontaut-Biron had a long conversation with Koloshin, a subordinate Russian diplomat who, the French representative thought, spoke with the highest authority. Koloshin's demeanor was most grave; convinced that new measures would have to be taken when Andrássy's plans were again a failure, he begged that France should come forward with some program which would rescue Russia from great embarrassment. Gontaut-Biron wondered why it was that the tsar and his advisers were seeking a new maneuver when they had no solution for the anticipated difficulties, but he reminded Decazes that Russia had saved France from great peril just a year before and he urged that France should now do all that her honor and interests would permit to show her gratitude.[222]

On the next day Prince Gorchakov himself renewed the appeal to the French ambassador. The chancellor declared that the armistice announced by the Turks would be a failure and that, indeed, the whole program of the new government was unsatisfactory; in the face of such a farce as was being staged in Constantinople he held

---

[219] Dreux, *op. cit.*, pp. 209–10.

[220] *Ibid.*, pp. 210–12. Gontaut-Biron to Decazes, 2 June; *Documents français*, II, Doc. No. 59.

[221] Tel., Gontaut-Biron to Decazes, 4 June; *ibid.*, II, 67, note 3. Dreux, *op. cit.*, pp. 213–14.

[222] Dreux, *op. cit.*, pp. 214–16.

that the powers had either to present the identic notes or descend to the level of third-class states. His patience with England was exhausted; there could be no more time lost in deferring to the cabinet in London, and he besought Gontaut-Biron to write immediately to Decazes reminding him that the tsar's government had recently given way to his wishes and pressing him not to remain aloof. "I am counting on you," Gorchakov said in conclusion. "Write earnestly so that the fascicle of the five powers shall not be broken. It is not a question of Russian interests but of those of humanity and of Christianity."[223]

Decazes, however, was not swayed by the appeals and advice from Ems. He was still hoping and working to bring England into the new negotiations[224] and he had succumbed to the fear, moreover, that French opinion would not be sympathetic toward an impatient descent on the new government in Constantinople. Rather than accept the Russian proposal, therefore, the foreign minister on 5 June telegraphed to Ems his opinion that the recent events had made desirable a re-examination of the whole question of the note.[225]

Gontaut-Biron was anxious about the Russian reaction to this message, but the following morning—the sixth—when he delivered it he was able to defend with success the French position in a long conversation with Baron Jomini. The outcome of the discussion was a compromise plan: if the notes were adjourned and their contents modified, the five powers—with England ignored—would reaffirm the identity of their views as to the desirability of attaining the program contained in the original notes. Jomini in the course of the day converted his superiors to this moderated program, and that evening Gorchakov sent out a formal proposal which embodied it:

that it be declared to the Ottoman Government that the five powers, in maintaining their intimate and complete understanding with regard to the pacification of the insurgent provinces, consent to suspend their *démarche* until they

---

[223] Dreux, *op. cit.*, pp. 216–18.

[224] Report No. 397, Lyons to Derby, 6 June; FO 27/2164. The British ambassador was not impressed with Decazes' arguments: ". . . . The Duke continued for some time to speak of the ill effects which must in his opinion be the consequence of the existence of suspicions between England and Russia, but the only suggestion he seemed able to make with a view to removing any suspicion that might exist was that steps should be taken by England to be agreeable to Russia in the present crisis. . . . ."

[225] Tel., Decazes to Gontaut-Biron, 5 June; *Documents français,* II, Doc. No. 61.

have obtained proof that the Porte has proceeded to the realization of the important reforms of which the Porte has promised spontaneous and prompt concession.[226]

Even this well-nigh abject capitulation on the part of Tsar Alexander's advisers did not satisfy the Duc Decazes. Gorchakov persisted in talking of the five powers; Decazes persisted in talking in terms of the six. Hence the reply from Paris was reserved. The basic idea of the new Russian proposal Decazes approved, but he went on to announce that he was going to use it as a formula to which all the powers—by which, of course, he meant England—might be led to agree. In other words, the French minister intended to pursue his negotiations with London before making a final decision.[227] He recognized France's gratitude toward the tsar, but he was unwilling to follow Russia blindly; he was afraid of public opinion at home, where Thiers was the influential champion of an English alliance. In order to be free to act, Decazes felt it necessary to assert his independence and to effect at least the semblance of a *rapprochement* between London and St. Petersburg. Decazes was also inspired to prudence by the frank revelation of Russian views. He had months before laid it down as one of the conditions of French collaboration that there should be no talk of intervention or occupation; but now in these early days of June it had been confessed by a Russian diplomat that the Russian outlook envisaged an armed occupation. A common stand of all the powers still seemed best for French interests and at the same time seemed to offer the best means of aiding Russia out of a grave embarrassment; and Decazes sat down with the text of the identic note and with Gorchakov's latest plan before him to work out a new text that might be adopted by England.[228]

By the following afternoon Decazes had produced not one text but two, and these he gave to Lord Lyons for transmission to London. One document was an amended and modified draft of the identic note which the ambassadors had prepared in Constantinople. The other was a short declaration to the effect that the powers took cognizance of the armistice and amnesty proclaimed by the sultan and

[226] Tel., Gontaut-Biron to Decazes, 6 June; *ibid.*, II, Doc. No. 62. Dreux, *op. cit.*, pp. 219–22. Novikov to Andrássy, 7 June; SA, Varia Turquie I, 1875.

[227] Dreux, *op. cit.*, p. 222.

[228] Decazes to Gontaut-Biron, 6 June; *ibid.*, pp. 222–25.

were resolved to await the outcome of Murad's professed intentions "before presenting to him the friendly suggestions which the continuation of the struggle might counsel." In tendering his documents to Lyons the duke claimed that it was through his own offices that the Berlin memorandum and the resultant note had been set aside. The ground was therefore cleared, he argued, "for a return to united action by all the six Powers," and he contended that advantage might be taken of the existing situation through a common endorsement of either one or the other of his draft dispatches. The projected identic note, he went on, turned out to be such a far cry from the Berlin memorandum on which it was professedly based that it seemed to him "that it might not be difficult to make such alterations in it as would on the one hand adapt it to present circumstances and on the other render it acceptable to all the six Powers."[229]

The French foreign secretary was optimistic as he prepared his documents. He hoped that, at all events, he might elicit some formula or counter proposal from Lord Derby, and, should such be the case, the most difficult part of the battle would be gained.[230] But Decazes' hopes were cruelly dashed on the eighth when his documents came to the hands of Lord Tenterden, permanent undersecretary of the London foreign office. Tenterden's commentary was far from sympathetic:

. . . . These Projects of Notes account for the alarming intimations about Russia and the necessity of conciliating the Emperor Alexander which the Duc Decazes has been making to Lord Lyons; and which were no doubt intended to prepare the way for his proposals which we may fairly suppose to have a Russian colouring.

As we have heard that the Berlin Memorandum is indefinitely suspended it seems hardly worth while discussing another Edition of it. The new draft has been carefully worded but it really contains the essence of the old one—which we have found to be merely a repetition of the insurgents' demands in their letter to the Russian Agent.

The principal alteration consists in changing the grammar from the indicative to the subjunctive and making the different points suggestions instead of direct recommendations. . . . .

The whole thing is however so obviously a mere pretext that the Duc Decazes could not seriously suppose that H M Govt will accept it.

The other identic Note Project seems to be almost equally unacceptable. H M Govt have no suggestions to offer and have refused to concur in offering those proposed at Berlin. How then can they say that they wait "avant de

---

[229] Report No. 403, Lyons to Derby, 7 June; FO 27/2164.
[230] Decazes to Gontaut-Biron, 6 June; Dreux, *op. cit.*, p. 225.

présenter les suggestions amicales que la continuation de la lutte pourrait leur conseiller"—

Moreover this is both a menace to the Porte and an encouragement to the insurgents to continue the struggle in the expectation of intervention. . . . .[231]

Only after a delay of six days were the comments and suggestions of Tenterden incorporated in a formal reply.

. . . . Her Majesty's Government have great satisfaction in recognizing the friendly desire of the Duc Decazes to obtain the cooperation of Great Britain in the concerted action of the other Powers who had agreed to the Berlin proposals. They feel, however, bound to point out that the Draft of this present note varies rather in language than in substance from those proposals to which Her Majesty's Government with much regret felt themselves unable to assent.

Her Majesty's Government are still reluctantly compelled to abide by that decision and since the previous identic note is confessedly superseded to so great an extent by the recent proclamation of the Porte and the new state of things arising from the deposition of the late Sultan, and has been indefinitely suspended, Her Majesty's Government cannot take part in any project which would revive it. . . . .[232]

While waiting for this chilling reply from London, the French foreign minister had the difficult task of further negotiations with Ems. It was a matter of no little annoyance to Prince Gorchakov, after having reshaped his course along lines suggested by the French ambassador, to receive a temporizing response from Paris. Gontaut-Biron attempted to justify his government's policy, but he was unable to reason away the chancellor's irritation. Gorchakov spoke harshly of the contrast between Decazes' hesitations and loss of time in sterile negotiations with England on the one hand and, on the other, of his own care to make provision in the Berlin memorandum for an important French share in the naval demonstration. Decazes, he said sternly, had been attempting too important a role in his endeavor to mediate between Russia and England. Later in the day—8 June— Gontaut-Biron received Decazes' letter of the sixth and called again on the Russian statesman. But the explanations of the letter, far from assuaging the princely humor, made matters the worse. At every turn of the conversation the chancellor made deprecating remarks: France was on a false path which did her great harm in Eu-

---

[231] Memorandum of Lord Tenterden accompanying Report No. 403, Lyons to Derby, 7 June; FO 27/2164. At the end of Tenterden's comments Derby wrote: "I agree in all the above."

[232] Draft No. 599, Derby to Lyons, 14 June; FO 27/2157.

rope and delighted her enemies; England was profiting by the time lost through French delay; he had been counting on something better from France; and so on. None the less it was to the advantage of Russia to keep France in the concert, and impatiently Gorchakov consented to wait a few more days for a final decision.[233] Gontaut-Biron was seriously disturbed. "Try to find a formula, to obtain a counter-proposition from England," he wrote to Decazes. "Send me a sentence at least which will prove that our views remain in conformity with those to which we have already adhered. It is very important in my opinion. . . . . Successive delays will not bring a good result, I fear, but will make us lose the confidence of the other powers and our enemies will exploit them."[234] Decazes responded with as much cordiality as his position would permit; but there was in his answer no agreement to march forward without Great Britain.[235]

While the French government was proving itself obstinate to an exasperating degree, the allies of Tsar Alexander were entirely sympathetic. Andrássy had very reluctantly assented on 6 June to a prompt delivery of the identic notes, and was greatly relieved the day following to receive Gorchakov's proposal for a declaration of delay.[236] Immediately he announced Austro-Hungarian approval[237] and confidentially sent a copy of the new document to Rashid Pasha with the advice to accept it with suitable expressions of thanks and with promises to effect the proclaimed reforms.[238] Bismarck no less readily gave his consent to the declaration,[239] and the Italian government likewise fell immediately into line.[240] By the eighth, four of the six Great Powers had committed themselves to the declaration. Further delay, however, ensued, and it was not until the fourteenth that the last of the instructions were sent to Constantinople.[241]

[233] Tel., Gontaut-Biron to Decazes, 8 June; *Documents français*, II, Doc. No. 64, Dreux, *op. cit.*, pp. 225–27. Tel. No. 20, Károlyi to Andrássy, 8 June; SA, Varia Turquie I, 1875.   [234] Dreux, *op. cit.*, p. 227.

[235] Tel., Decazes to Gontaut-Biron, 9 June; *Documents français*, II, Doc. No. 65. Dreux, *op. cit.*, p. 227.

[236] Novikov to Andrássy, 7 June; SA, Varia Turquie I, 1875.

[237] Tel., Andrássy to embassies, 7 June; *First Red Book*, Doc. No. 427.

[238] Tel. No. 67, Andrássy to Zichy, 8 June; SA, Varia Turquie I, 1875.

[239] Károlyi to Andrássy, 8 June; SA, Prussia, 1876. Dreux, *op. cit.*, p. 228.

[240] Tel. No. 68, Wimpffen to Andrássy, 8 June; SA, Varia Turquie I, 1875. Melegari to Italian ambassador in St. Petersburg, 7 June; *First Green Book*, Doc. No. CXC.

[241] Tel. No. 176, Zichy to Andrássy, 14 June; *First Red Book*, Doc. No. 455, incomplete. Tel. No. 71, Andrássy to Zichy, 14 June; SA, Varia Turquie I, 1875.

The next evening there occurred an event in the Turkish capital which brought to an end any hope of salvaging something out of the original Berlin memorandum, which ended indeed any hope of profiting by the declaration of watchful waiting. While the Turkish council of ministers was in session, a wild young Circassian officer burst into the room armed with four revolvers and a sword. His grievance was a personal one against Hussein Avni—Hussein Avni had ordered him out of Constantinople because of his turbulence—but, maddened with fury and fortified by strong drink, this Tcherkess Hassan was not halted until seven persons, including his enemy and the innocent Rashid, lay dead and eight others were wounded.[242]

Dead likewise was the scheme of Turkish pacification which Count Andrássy had been fostering since the autumn when he set out to induce the Christian insurgents of Bosnia and Hercegovina to go back to their ruined villages singing the praises of Austria's great emperor for the blessings he had given them. In mid-June, almost a year since the rebellion had begun, peace was more remote than ever. The European concert was nothing more than a growing din of discords, and there was no agency able to cope effectively with the problem that had thrown into the balance the fate of Turkey and of the peace of Europe as well.

THE EMERGENCE OF GREAT BRITAIN

The two important events of early May, the turbulent disorders in Turkey and the Berlin memorandum, served to bring into high relief the position of England. The refusal of the cabinet to indorse the program framed by Andrássy and Gorchakov was, as has been noted, a serious blow to its prestige and its possibility of success. During the second half of the month when attempts were repeatedly made to win a reconsideration of at least a part of the memorandum, the importance of British collaboration in exerting pressure on Turkey became clearly apparent to the Continental powers. All the clearer was this lesson before the end of May when a concentration of warships in Turkish waters indicated the possibility that the London cabinet might not limit itself to a passive role.

[242] *The Times,* 28 June 1876, p. 10, cols. 1–3. Gallenga, *Two Years of the Eastern Question,* II, 105–14. Elliot, *Some Revolutions,* pp. 243–45. Maynard to Fish, 17 June; *Foreign Relations,* 1876, pp. 572–73. Report No. 634, Elliot to Derby, 17 June; *Turkey No. 3 (1876),* Doc. No. 509. Zichy to Andrássy, 16 June; *First Red Book,* Doc. No. 462.

The outcropping of public tumult culminating in the murders in Salonika and in the demonstrations in the capital provided the incentive for the appearance of the naval pieces on the international chessboard. As soon as the fanatical attack on the consuls was known, the British, along with the other powers, dispatched a ship to the scene of the riot.[243] Two days later—9 May—the ambassadors in Constantinople became so alarmed by the currents of public feeling that they asked for warships to come to Besika Bay at the mouth of the Dardanelles, and Sir Henry Elliot sent his request directly to the commander of the British Mediterranean fleet then at Jaffa.[244] The next day the foreign representatives joined in recommending the dispatch of an armed gunboat for each power to supplement the ships usually maintained at the capital itself.[245] In London the slow-moving Derby wanted fuller reasons than Elliot had given in his telegrams for sending the fleet to Besika Bay,[246] and while awaiting his explanation the foreign office was unwilling to send the fleet any closer than Smyrna.[247] Elliot immediately replied that it was a question of security for the endangered Christians of Constantinople,[248] and the next day he repeated his requests for the fleet at the mouth of the Straits and for an additional vessel at Constantinople, on grounds again of the prevailing danger.[249] The new importunities, however, left Derby still hesitant. His immediate response was to ask Elliot how sending a second ship to Constantinople would conform with the treaty of 1841,[250] but on the thirteenth, after Elliot had reported that all the ambassadors agreed that such an action was not contrary to the treaty,[251] the secretary agreed to the dispatch of a second gun-

---

[243] Tenterden to the secretary of the admiralty, 8 May; *Turkey No. 4 (1876)*, Doc. No. 2.

[244] Tel. and Report No. 475, Derby to Elliot, 9 May; *Turkey No. 3 (1876)*, Docs. Nos. 224 and 256, respectively.

[245] Tel. and Report No. 480, Elliot to Derby, 10 May; *ibid.*, Docs. Nos. 226 and 271, respectively.

[246] Draft No. 268, Derby to Elliot, 10 May; *ibid.*, Doc. No. 228.

[247] Tenterden to the secretary of the admiralty, 10 May; *ibid.*, Docs. Nos. 230–32. Secretary of the admiralty to Tenterden, 11 May; *Turkey No. 4 (1876)*, Doc. No. 9.

[248] Tel. and Report No. 479, Elliot to Derby, 10 May; *Turkey No. 3 (1876)*, Doc. No. 229.

[249] Tel. and Report No. 485, Elliot to Derby, 11 May; *ibid.*, Doc. No. 237.

[250] Draft No. 287, Derby to Elliot, 12 May; *ibid.*, Doc. No. 239.

[251] Tel. and Report No. 489, Elliot to Derby, 12 May; *ibid.*, Doc. No. 240.

boat.[252] On the same day—the day on which the Berlin memorandum was delivered to the ambassadors in the German capital—the foreign office finally requested the admiralty to send the fleet to Besika Bay as soon as possible,[253] despite the fact that it was known in London that the storm clouds had taken an anti-governmental rather than an anti-Christian direction.

The day following, it will be recalled, the provisions of the Berlin memorandum were received in London. There ensued those brief informal and formal discussions dominated by an aroused and defiant prime minister which culminated on the sixteenth in the cabinet's decision to remain aloof. The Berlin document suggested a common understanding of the powers for the protection of their subjects through the sending of warships under common instructions, but this proposal aroused Disraeli's opposition no less than those involving Bosnia and Hercegovina. On the sixteenth, as he wrote out his arguments to present to the cabinet, Disraeli was emphatic in stating that no power should send warships to Constantinople "on the pretence of protecting the Christians."[254]

During the next week the prime minister's mind was occupied with this question of naval enterprises in Turkish waters. He had patently no sympathy for Elliot's alarmed appeals to send the fleet for the purpose of restraining Moslem mob violence. In sanctioning the dispatch of ships to Besika Bay Disraeli was mobilizing pieces in his game of checkmating Russia. As the days went by, his imagination warmed to the possibilities of the occasion. At the cabinet meeting on 22 May he proposed to his colleagues that the strength of the fleet at Besika Bay should be materially augmented and went on to suggest the possibility of seizing the Turkish fleet and even Constantinople itself if necessity arose. Such an expansive program was startling to a body of ministers who heretofore had been content to do nothing, but it was agreed at that session to send three additional ships,[255] and two days later two other ironclads were ordered to Turkey.[256] On the twenty-third, meanwhile, Elliot had been instructed by telegram to report on the state of the Turkish navy.[257]

[252] Draft No. 293, Derby to Elliot, 13 May; *ibid.*, Doc. No. 245.

[253] Tenterden to the secretary of the admiralty, 13 May; *ibid.*, Doc. No. 247.

[254] *Disraeli*, VI, 25.   [255] Hardinge, *Carnarvon*, II, 330–31.

[256] Disraeli to Queen Victoria, 24 May; Buckle, *Queen Victoria*, II, 454.

[257] Draft No. 313, Derby to Elliot, 23 May; FO 78/2450. The text of the telegram reads: "How many Turkish ships in commission? How many are ready for commission? Is personnel efficient and reliable?"

When these decisions had been taken Disraeli declared himself to be "well satisfied with what we have done since Monday,"[258] but he was none the less looking forward to other measures still. The Turkish fleet was, in his eyes, such a desirable prize that its sudden seizure by the Russians was not beyond the possible; indeed, he professed to have heard that two weeks earlier Ignatiev was attempting to persuade the sultan to turn over the fleet to him and to call in a Russian garrison. Disraeli hoped that the personal influence of Elliot would be able to prevent new efforts in that direction, but in his agitation he swiftly forgot his own schemes to take the sultan's ships and concentrated his anxieties on possible violations of the treaty of 1841. Now he took his stand on the closure of the Straits as a "cardinal principle," and in the next days revolved in his mind a set of instructions for the commanding admiral to maintain the treaty by force. An admiral ready to fight and at the same time a competent ambassador with considerable latitude for independent decision—such an admiral and ambassador would provide that "stiffness" which would allow Britain to gain "all our points." It was a policy that might mean war, he admitted in response to Derby's criticism to that effect; but Disraeli measured its virtue by the fact that if war did come it would not be a war into which the contestants had drifted. He felt, however, that a strong ambassador and admiral would be able to win the game without war.[259] "All our points" were not, so far as the student is able to find out, clear in the prime minister's mind. Foremost was the desire to block Russia in those designs which he attributed to the tsar and his chancellor. Another facet of the same desire was a brilliant diplomatic victory to be won on a gamble with Mars. Also he was determined to save Turkey from what he chose to believe was dismemberment, although at the time Disraeli in his willingness to create new vassal states[260] was going far beyond the program contained in the Berlin memorandum. But, vague though the prime minister's ideas were, his imagination was stirred by great plans and bold stratagems. He wrote to his sovereign:

Your Majesty's fleet has not been ordered to the Mediterranean to protect Christians or Turks, but to uphold your Majesty's Empire. Had your Majesty sanctioned the Berlin Memorandum, Constantinople would, at this moment,

---

[258] Disraeli to Derby, 25 May; *Disraeli*, VI, 29.
[259] Disraeli to Derby, 28, 31 May; *ibid.*, VI, 29-30.
[260] *Ibid*, p. 30.

have been garrisoned by Russia, and the Turkish fleet have been placed under Russian protection.

It was knowledge of this advice, given to the Sultan by General Ignatieff, that led to the revolt of the Softas. The policy that we are advising your Majesty to pursue, prudent and conciliatory, but perfectly firm, will ensure your Majesty, and your descendents, always adding to the sign-manual R & I. . . . ."[261]

Disraeli's plan for a forcible defense of the treaty of 1841 ran into Derby's stubborn resistance, and in place of categoric instructions to keep the Straits closed the admiral received merely a statement of the international regulations governing the Dardanelles;[262] Elliot was charged to report any proposal to call the various fleets to Constantinople;[263] and a few days later—5 June—the foreign office proposed to the other powers having ships in Turkish waters that they should likewise instruct their commanding officers to respect the common treaty obligations.[264]

---

[261] Disraeli to Queen Victoria, 29 May; Buckle, *Queen Victoria,* II, 455–56. The queen had been out of sympathy with the policy of her government since the ministers had rejected Bismarck's overtures in January. She had recently acquiesced very reluctantly in the rejection of the Berlin memorandum and at the time of Disraeli's letter was taking exception to the concentration of the fleet at the mouth of the Dardanelles (Queen Victoria to Derby, 27 May; *ibid.,* II, 455).

[262] Tenterden to the secretary of the admiralty, 13 May; *Turkey No. 3 (1876),* Doc. No. 247.

[263] Draft No. 341, Derby to Elliot, 31 May; *ibid.,* Doc. No. 328. Cf. Dwight E. Lee, *Great Britain and the Cyprus Convention Policy of 1878* (Cambridge, 1934), p. 25, note 59.

[264] Draft No. 583, Derby to Adams *et al.,* 5 June; *ibid.,* Doc. No. 371. This draft was prepared by Tenterden and submitted to Derby with a memorandum which reads in part as follows (FO 65/954):

". . . . The question now arises—whether any and what, communication should be made to the other Powers.

"I see grave objections to asking them for an assurance to observe the Treaty of 1841.

"1. Because asking for an assurance implies a doubt of the force of the Treaty and weakens its authority.

"2. Because such an application exposes us to a retort which it would be difficult to meet since . . . . each time the Treaty has been broken it has been at our instance and in 1853 we claimed a right to break through it in case of necessity—a plea which is never likely to fail.

"3. Because it may lead to an argument as to the effect of the Treaty as read with the (Black Sea) Treaty of 1871.

"The Treaty of 1841 provided that foreign fleets should not pass *except in case of war.*

"The Treaty of 1871 enables the Porte . . . . to summon friendly fleets *in time of peace* 'in case the Sublime Porte should judge it necessary in order to secure

Before this venture into an active policy had been dealt with, the deposition of Sultan Abdul Aziz had momentarily obscured it. Queen Victoria, opposed on regal principle to "these violent depositions," felt no little sympathy for a fellow monarch who had been her guest and who had made a practice of inquiring about her,[265] but the queen and her ministers were not of one mind regarding the fate of an insane sovereign any more than they had been on foreign policy for the past year. With his usual readiness of pen the prime minister suggested that the leader of the *coup d'état* in Constantinople should have been none other than the British ambassador himself. Disraeli, however, was not ready with a program to capitalize the changed circumstances in the Turkish capital. He had some plan for an eventual congress, but international negotiations had not yet reached a stage sufficiently acute to induce him to act vigorously against the opposition of his own colleague in the Foreign Office and against the sentiment prevailing in the chancelleries of the Continent. While waiting to see what would happen, Disraeli took satisfaction in the thought that a constitution proclaimed in Constantinople would enhance Turkish prestige in Europe.[266] Lord Derby was equally content with the change of Ottoman rulers—but still saturnine. The deposition he

---

the execution of the stipulations of the Treaty of Paris of March 30, 1856.' This evidently opens a wide field of controversy.

"4. Because the demand for such an assurance may precipitate matters—supposing as is very likely, that we receive ambiguous answers or even a flat refusal—what is to be done then? It would be easy enough to deal with an overt act. Other Powers, out of jealousy, would join in protesting or even possibly resisting by force, but an ambiguous refusal would put us in the difficulty of either accepting or slurring it over or else making a declaration or threat of force which public opinion might not be ready to support. It would be going to war for an argument.

"5. Because such an assurance, if received would not be of the slightest value.

"If any Power saw an advantage in breaking it, broken it would be and the excuse of necessity, supported by our own words used in 1853, would be a ready answer to remonstrance.

"If the Powers won't abide by a Treaty to which they are jointly pledged, they certainly won't abide by an assurance to observe it given to us singly.

"The accompanying draft endeavours to meet the difficulty of asking for an assurance by suggesting that the Admirals of the other Powers should have their attention called, as a matter of convenience, to the Treaty of 1841 so as to be in the same position as our own Admiral.

"I confess that I should have advised not communicating with the other Powers at all, but if it is considered well to do so, I submit that this, or some similar form would be the least exposed to objection.

"TENTERDEN   June 2/76."

265 Queen Victoria to Disraeli, 3 June; Buckle, *Queen Victoria*, II, 456.

266 Disraeli to Derby, 31 May; *Disraeli*, VI, 30.

tentatively called a "fortunate event," but amplified his view by saying that "the misgovernment of the late Sultan had been notorious and
extreme, and his successor, whatever he might turn out to be, could
hardly do worse and would probably do better."[267]

A more tangible satisfaction derived from the fall of Abdul Aziz
was the inevitable annoyance which that event would create for Russia and the other European powers who were in the act of imposing
the Berlin memorandum on the Porte. As has been related, the London ministers, eminently satisfied with the results of their obstruction and the power of their position, failed to share the French desire
for Britain's return to the concert. Entirely without reference to the
views of the Continental foreign offices, Derby authorized Elliot to
recognize the new sultan. At the same time the British abandoned
their earlier aloofness toward the memorandum in favor of aggressive opposition. In the House of Commons on 1 June Disraeli announced that "the Note described generally, I believe, as the Berlin
memorandum" had not been presented in Constantinople and went
on the express hope "that it may not be necessary that it ever should
be so brought."[268] Lord Derby, in turn, took the position espoused
by Decazes and Andrássy that Europe "was bound to allow the new
Administration at Constantinople some breathing time." Still opposing any concerted advice or action as an encouragement to the
insurgents, the foreign secretary seized on the Russian change of
program on 6 June as an occasion to consider the Berlin program—as
indeed it was—abandoned and defunct.[269]

As the first days of June went by, the prime minister, stirred by
his gambling with the high stakes of international relations, liked
"the look of things."[270] Austria had offered to await British participation; France was courting British support and refusing to budge
without it; there was alarm in Germany lest an Anglo-French alliance be revived in opposition to the imperial league.[271] England had
emerged with a policy of rejecting the memorandum, of sending the
fleet to Turkish waters, and of warning the other powers about the
treaty of 1841. It seemed to Disraeli to be a "policy of determination,

[267] Derby to Paget, 1 June; *Turkey No. 3 (1876)*, Doc. No. 332.

[268] *Hansard*, third series, CCXXIX, 1521–22.

[269] Draft No. 465, Derby to Russell, 10 June; *Turkey No. 3 (1876)*, Doc.
No. 402.

[270] Disraeli to Lady Bradford, 6, 7 June; *Disraeli*, VI, 30–31.

[271] Tel. and Report No. 255, Russell to Derby, 6 June; FO 64/852.

but also conciliatory," which would preserve peace and restore England to a proper place in the councils of the world. Most satisfactory of all for the moment, that "unnatural alliance" of the three emperors was "as extinct as the Roman triumvirate."[272]

In his speech in the Commons on the first of June Disraeli talked of England's interest in peace—the conventional phrases of any minister or executive in a public utterance—but Disraeli likewise resorted to those disturbing words, "Her Majesty's Government have taken such measures of precaution as they thought were necessary to maintain the honour and the interest of this country; and that policy of precaution they intend to pursue."[273] When he discussed foreign affairs again in parliament on the ninth his mood had entirely changed; the dangers of the situation and the jealous watching of national honor had entirely disappeared. There were in this second speech only calming words. There was no gibe at Russia and Austria for the adjournment of the Berlin memorandum: "The remarkable events which have occurred in Constantinople would in a great measure account for that withdrawal." There had been no ill-will engendered by British abstention from supporting the memorandum. Quite the contrary, in fact, was true. The Continental powers had not only expressed their regret but had shown "a lively desire" that the cabinet reconsider its decision. With the abandonment of the memorandum, the prime minister continued, all the powers were united—"or rather the other Powers may be said to have concurred entirely with us"—in a threefold action: it was agreed that the new ruler of Turkey should be given time to work out independently his policies and measures; it was unanimously decided to recognize this new ruler; and it was the common will of Europe again to press upon Serbia its counsels of moderation.[274]

The purpose of the prime minister's stock-raising remarks came to light that very evening when he took the initiative of a conversation with the Russian ambassador. After the British rejection of the memorandum Shuvalov had held himself aloof, and their meeting on the evening of the ninth was the first since the chilling encounter at the Prince of Wales' levee almost a month before. When asked by Disraeli for a comment on his speech in parliament, Shuvalov—to

[272] Disraeli to Queen Victoria, 7 June; Buckle, *Queen Victoria,* II, 457–58. Disraeli to Manners, 7 June; *Disraeli,* VI, 31.

[273] *Hansard,* third series, CCXXIX, 1521–22.

[274] *Ibid.,* CCXXIX, 1606–9.

quote his own report—replied brusquely: "I am speaking no more, my dear minister; I have nothing to say in the face of the mistrust aroused against Russia and of the injustice with which you judge her action. I am sure that in these circumstances you will approve my silence." Disraeli vigorously denied the correctness of the ambassador's observations, assuring Shuvalov that he at all events did not share this alleged suspicion and that British silence had been due, not to any animus toward Russia, but to uncertainty of the future. Shuvalov in turn defended the Russian policy, declaring it to be centered entirely on securing an improved life for the Christians of the Balkan Peninsula. The thought that the tsar was conspiring against the integrity of the Ottoman Empire the ambassador repudiated with animation. This reply gave Disraeli the opportunity toward which he was working. "I am going to think it over," he said. "It seems to me that if Russia would tell us this time what she wants, we should yet be able to make an arrangement between us. But let her speak it directly to us, and not through the mediation of Harcourts and Münsters and Beusts."

Shuvalov was not certain whether these words were merely "after-dinner talk" or an attempt to abandon British isolation.[275] But when the conversation was renewed the next evening at Disraeli's instance, the premier seriously developed his bid for a private Anglo-Russian understanding. Denying again any distrust on the part of either himself or his government, Disraeli offered the best of goodwill in their common problems in Central Asia and in Turkey. As for Central Asia, he would feel no suspicions and he would offer no objections to any Russian action so long as Afghanistan was not involved. He proposed to observe the same friendly attitude in regard to Turkey. He made no accusations, the premier said; he had no doubts as to the honesty of Russian intentions. There was only one difficulty in the way of confidential relations, and that difficulty was the person of General Ignatiev, the embodiment of an unfortunate policy and a constant maker of trouble. Shuvalov rose so quickly and energetically to the defense of his colleague that Disraeli turned his guns from the tsar's ambassador in Turkey to the Austro-Hungarian minister for foreign affairs. Andrássy, he stated without hesitation, had been responsible for the insurrection by advising Emperor

[275] Shuvalov to Gorchakov, 29 May/10 June; *Slavonic Review*, III, 669–71, Docs. Nos. 34 and 36.

Francis Joseph to make his journey down the Dalmatian coast.[276] "When one is a Bismarck," he went on, "one can arouse such agitations, since one has the intelligence and energy requisite for mastering the ensuing events, but when one is an Andrássy one embroils affairs and one exposes the whole of Europe to dangers." Yet this was the man whom the Russians had permitted to take a leading hand in the Turkish problem. His original note had only complicated the problem, and it had been impossible to approve that second edition of his work prepared in Berlin. England, said Disraeli with an air of finality, had lost confidence in Andrássy and England refused to follow him.

From those opinions the prime minister went on to state the British attitude toward future developments: the insurgents were not fighting for reforms, but for independence; in such a state of affairs struggle and bloodshed were inevitable; neither Russia nor England could prevent it. Gorchakov had done wrong in trying to restrain Serbia and Montenegro because an enlarged conflict was imminent and because a solution could come from it alone.

> We believe a bleeding to be necessary and we shall consult together. If the Christians win the upper hand we shall then only have to register the accomplished facts; if Turkey defeats the Christians and the repression becomes tyrannical, it will then be the turn of the great powers to interfere in the name of humanity; then the intervention of Europe will be legitimate.

Shuvalov hastened to point out the dangers of a policy based on "bleeding." The Russian and the other courts, he explained, had from the beginning attempted to do something for the Christians without throwing the Eastern question on the table, whereas in each of the eventualities named by Disraeli that old trouble-making problem would rise to harass Europe. If the Christians won, Turkey would collapse, and the powers would be obliged to step in and regulate the settlement; if the Turks won and attempted to exploit their victory, the armed intervention of Europe would of necessity follow. In either case, Shuvalov argued, the degree of European interference and the character of the problems ensuing would of necessity be much more complex than would be the case if the powers united promptly on a less radical decision.

Disraeli listened to these objections in silence. Without attempt-

---

[276] The statement that Andrássy had advised the journey was incorrect. *Vide supra*, pp. 31–32. Disraeli in talking with Münster made the same kind of attack on the Austrian minister (*Andrássy*, II, 316).

ing to refute them he went on with his own views—with his attempt
to lure Shuvalov and his superiors into an Anglo-Russian understanding to the exclusion of Russia's friends on the Continent. "I
have confidence in Russia," he repeated, "and if she has a solution to
propose to us, we shall examine it in a spirit of conciliation and good
will." The one condition which Disraeli laid down was that the proposal be from Russia alone; for that reason the Berlin memorandum
and any new Austrian measures were ruled out of consideration and
the agitated Duc Decazes was bluntly rejected as an intermediary.
To confirm this new British policy, Disraeli invited Shuvalov to discuss the whole question with Lord Derby when the foreign secretary
returned to his office two days later.[277]

On the fourteenth, when the conversations were resumed, Derby
did indeed confirm in his manner the opinions clothed by his colleague
in more spectacular words. Derby too professed faith in Russia except for the language and conduct of certain agents; he likewise
denied any determined policy of isolation; and he repeated the apparent necessity for more fighting before a settlement could be made,
basing his position on the alleged desire of the insurgents for independence. In one point the foreign secretary was more specific than
the prime minister had been: if, in the coming fighting, the insurgents
were defeated, he would be willing to grant them a settlement comparable to that made for the Cretans in 1867. But, true to his nature,
Derby's main emphasis was on waiting three or four weeks before
anything was done.[278]

Shuvalov found it difficult to make a convincing explanation of
this British overture. One possible motive, he thought, was Disraeli's
desire to separate Austria and Russia and perhaps take the place of
Austria in the triple alliance. Another motive seemed to be a wish
to establish an accord with Russia and join her in determining future
decisions. Another motive which seemed more plausible to the ambassador was the desire of Disraeli, after having won popularity by
rejecting the Berlin memorandum and sending the fleet to Turkish
waters, to return to a policy more conducive to European peace.[279]

[277] Shuvalov to Gorchakov, 29 May/10 June and 30 May/11 June; *Slavonic
Review*, III, 669–70, 672–75, Docs. Nos. 34 and 38, respectively.

[278] Shuvalov to Gorchakov, 31 May/12 June; *ibid.*, III, 675–76, Docs. Nos. 40
and 41. Draft No. 378, Derby to Loftus, 14 June; *Turkey No. 3 (1876)*, Doc.
No. 427.

[279] Shuvalov to Gorchakov, 30 May/11 June; *Slavonic Review*, III, 675, Doc.
No. 38.

It is difficult to believe, however, that Shuvalov's last hypothesis was correct. Those two British actions of the previous month had certainly not entailed uneasiness or remorse; and there had been nothing uncomfortable in England's isolation. It is more reasonable to believe that the conversations were prompted by the prime minister's desire to give the *coup de grâce* not only to the Berlin memorandum but also—and more important—to the alliance which had produced it. The memorandum itself meant nothing; its merits and demerits had never been objectively studied in London; it had been sufficient that the document was drawn up by a combination of powers that had relegated England to a secondary position and that it was presented in a manner unworthy of a great state. So long as the document was alive its sponsoring league was alive; if it could be thrown into the waste-paper basket, there would be an opportunity for new arrangements. It was well known in London that the tsar and his chancellor had been defeated in the Berlin negotiations and were not content with the minimum program which the stubborn Andrássy had forced them to accept. When finally that program was thrown overboard by the Russians on 6 June, one is constrained to suppose that Disraeli saw his opportunity to drive a wedge between Gorchakov and Andrássy and destroy what he termed their "unnatural alliance." No better means was possible than to denounce the Austrian minister as an incompetent bungler and hold out hopes to the Russians for a settlement with them that gave promise of going farther than Andrássy would hear of going. Disraeli's first choice of a means of breaking up the league of the three emperors had been an understanding with Germany. He had made an attempt in that direction during February of the preceding year,[280] but the war scare of May had destroyed his plan. He had in January of 1876 received Bismarck's overtures with delight,[281] but the suspicious opposition of Derby had thwarted that hope and prevented any serious exchange with Berlin before the German chancellor gave his blessing to the memorandum. In the subsequent negotiations the inept explanations from Emperor William and others failed to conquer the annoyance felt in London. Messages direct and indirect invited the British cabinet to take the lead in proposing a settlement of the Eastern question with the assurance that German support was pledged in advance; but Disraeli nurtured his grievance against Bismarck for ignoring Eng-

[280] *Vide supra*, p. 23.   [281] *Vide supra*, p. 177.

land when the memorandum was in preparation, and Derby persisted in believing that the Iron Chancellor was "not exactly the person whom one can implicitly confide in."[282]

Russia, therefore, appeared the most likely mark in the new attack on the imperial league. But it is impossible to conclude that in the overtures to Count Shuvalov Disraeli and his colleague had more than destructive intentions. Shuvalov was of the opinion that the cabinet had no program of its own and was unable to formulate one that would be practicable for the problems at hand in June.[283] The evidence available would tend to confirm at least a part of that conviction. At all events the calloused indifference to the spread of the embittered warfare to Serbia and Montenegro and to the grave consequence for European tranquillity that might grow out of it proved clearly enough that the British ministers had no solution that they wished to present. The argument that more bleeding was necessary because the insurgents were fighting for independence was not an honest one; not a single report had come to the Foreign Office from consuls in Bosnia and Hercegovina that gave grounds for such an assertion. The dominating inspiration of British policy appeared still to be hostile obstruction to reform plans matured without British collaboration, a willingness or even a desire that everyone concerned should reap the full harvest of disaster associated with those plans, and a resolute determination to paralyze any attempt to impose on Turkey a foreign program regardless of how mild it was or how effectively it might forestall threatening complications. There was no thought that the achievement of Britain's objective—keeping the old Turk on his feet—might best be attained through sufficient external interference to impose a rational regimen on him. Disraeli and his cabinet, in their defiant suspicions of the three empires, had confused their idea of the means of saving Turkey with the end which they had in view. In protecting Turkey from collective interference they were rapidly making it a vulnerable object for individual attack. But in the London Foreign Office in 1875 and 1876 jealousy and suspicion obscured such simple axioms.

This overture from London came at a time, it will be recalled,

---

[282] The German Crown Princess to Queen Victoria, 13 June; Buckle, *Queen Victoria*, II, 464. Disraeli to Queen Victoria, 18 June; *Disraeli*, VI, 32–33. Derby to Ponsonby, 20 June; *ibid.*, VI, 33–34.

[283] Shuvalov to Gorchakov, 30 May/11 June; *Slavonic Review*, III, 675, Doc. No. 39.

when official Russian feeling was very bitter against England for its treatment of the Berlin memorandum. In reply to Shuvalov's telegraphic summary of his first conversation, Gorchakov instructed the ambassador merely to listen, to find out what "practical propositions" the Foreign Office had for the pacification of Turkey.[284] The ambassador, in return, informed his chief that such tactics were bound to fail and recommended the advancement of some exclusively Russian proposal.[285] The chancellor then came out into the open and instructed Shuvalov to work informally for "tributary autonomy" of the insurgent provinces and for concessions to Serbia and Montenegro— for the former the long-contested area of Little Zvornik and for the latter some adjacent territory and a port on the Adriatic. Gorchakov, however, had less doubt about Disraeli's motives than did Shuvalov. To his way of thinking, the British were up to their old trick of attempting to injure the friendly relations existing between Russia and Austria and France. He refused, out of loyalty to his friends, to keep the overture from London a secret.[286] Within a few days Paris knew all about the negotiations[287] and a *"notice confidentielle,"* summarizing Shuvalov's reports except for the strictures on Andrássy, betrayed the bid to Vienna.[288]

Gorchakov's suspicions, none the less, did not prevent his taking seriously the new attitude in England. When he saw the French ambassador on the fourteenth and fifteenth his smiling face revealed his satisfaction: he was awaiting the messenger bearing a full report of Derby's communication. England, he told Gontaut-Biron, had begun to understand the perils of disunion.[289] In the expectation that Shuvalov's dispatch was going to reveal some positive proposal from Derby, the chancellor on the fourteenth sent a most cordial message to London. The purely negative character of Disraeli's words gave Gorchakov opportunity to take again the role of an earnest searcher after a peaceful settlement: from the beginning of the insurrection

---

[284] Gorchakov to Shuvalov, 29 May/10 June; *Slavonic Review,* III, 670, Doc. No. 35.

[285] Shuvalov to Gorchakov, 30 May/11 June; *ibid.,* III, 675, Doc. No. 39.

[286] Gorchakov to Shuvalov, 2/14 June; *ibid.,* III, 667, Doc. No. 43.

[287] Decazes to d'Harcourt, 21 June; *Documents français,* II, Doc. No. 69.

[288] Without date or other descriptive label; SA, Varia Turquie I, 1875 (St. Petersburg, 1876). Tel. No. 21, Károlyi to Andrássy, 17 June; SA, Prussia, 1876.

[289] Gontaut-Biron to Decazes, 15 June; *Documents français,* II, Doc. No. 66. Dreux, *op. cit.,* p. 229.

His Majesty the tsar had made it his chief objective to maintain the political status quo by an improvement in the lot of the Ottoman Christians because he held such an improvement to be indispensable for the existence of the sultan's empire; His Majesty had wished always to work toward this end in collaboration with all the other powers and had regretted the recent decision of the British cabinet; the Russian policy was based on the desirability of avoiding at that time a serious crisis; the Russian government felt it desirable and necessary to resume efforts for pacification. For such reasons Gorchakov notified the British that the tsar's ministers would accept any kind of a proposal made in London, provided only that it would not provoke a war of extermination in the East or a general conflagration in Europe.[290]

Three days later, after learning of the murder of the ministers in Constantinople, Gorchakov wrote again to London. Piqued at Disraeli's attack on Ignatiev, the chancellor could not resist the impulse to attribute the recent activities in the Turkish capital to the intrigues of Sir Henry Elliot. But he had more serious purposes than personal recriminations. The lesson of the new tragedy, he maintained, was the urgent necessity for a general understanding. The English proposal to wait a month while events took their course he decried as one which ignored the gravity of the crisis and he reaffirmed the tsar's desire to discuss any program which London might propose.[291]

Not content to await a move from England, Gorchakov proceeded immediately to write a formal dispatch in reply to the report of Derby's conversation. The prince again made the most of the superior morality of the Russian desire to effect a peace before the fanaticism of Moslem and Christian had made an even worse shambles of the Balkan Peninsula; to see the quarrel settled by force, he insisted, would be to consign both victor and vanquished to ruin. The best interest of Europe and humanity would be served by prompt agreement on practical solutions. These solutions were still those which had been in process of formulation in Russia for some time: tributary autonomy for the insurgent area; a port for Montenegro; and a small bit of territory for Serbia. Gorchakov did not propose to exercise any undue pressure in imposing these terms on the Porte; he felt sure

---

[290] Gorchakov to Shuvalov, 2/14 June; *Turkey No. 3 (1876)*, Doc. No. 472. Derby received this dispatch on 19 June.

[291] Gorchakov to Shuvalov, 5/17 June; *Slavonic Review*, III, 677–78, Doc. No. 44.

that if England would join in recommending them the Turks would not hesitate to accept them.[292]

Before receiving these arguments from Ems, Shuvalov was already at work in London on behalf of the Russian objectives. When he saw Derby again on the eighteenth, he found the secretary quite willing to accept autonomy and territorial concessions but at the same time Derby declared that his political principles forbade interference between sovereign and subject. Shuvalov went away thinking there was hope of success if he could just assure the British that the Russian program called for unanimous advice rather than vigorous intervention.[293] The next day he was back at the Foreign Office to read a letter from Gorchakov in which the chancellor had already taken his stand on advice rather than coercion.[294] The ambassador returned two days later—21 June—to bring his chief's arguments for a prompt settlement. But the new conversation brought no tangible results. Shuvalov thought—and he had the report of someone close to the secretary, presumably Lady Derby,[295] to confirm his belief— that Derby was greatly disturbed by the challenge to clear-cut action contained in the communication. Both Shuvalov and his confidential informant felt that Derby was sympathetic but paralyzed by his inability to come to a decision.[296] The minister himself, naturally, had a somewhat different interpretation. As the dangers of a Serbian declaration of war were looming larger, he decided that England could not be too cautious. He insisted to the queen, who was worried about an anti-Russian and pro-Turkish policy, that he did not wish any antagonism with Russia; he paid tribute to the good faith of the tsar and "his responsible advisers," but felt that the "great administrative weakness" of the tsar's government and the "great duplicity" of certain Russian agents made it impossible to know if

[292] Gorchakov to Shuvalov, 5/17 June; FO 65/953 and SA, Varia Turquie I, 1875 (St. Petersburg, 1876). The document is paraphrased in Draft No. 381A, Derby to Loftus, 21 June; *Turkey No. 3 (1876)*, Doc. No. 476.

[293] Shuvalov to Gorchakov, 7/19 June; *Slavonic Review*, III, 678, Doc. No. 45.

[294] Tel., Gorchakov to Shuvalov, 7/19 June; *ibid.*, Doc. No. 46. The letter in question was Gorchakov's of 14/26 May in *ibid.*, Doc. No. 32.

[295] There are repeated evidences that during the crisis Lady Derby spoke more freely of political matters with the Russian ambassador than certain officials would have approved. Through Shuvalov confidential cabinet problems passed not only to the Russian government but to the liberal opposition as well. *Vide*, e.g., A. G. Gardiner, *The Life of Sir William Harcourt* (New York, 1923), I, 311, and Shuvalov to Gorchakov 15/27 June; *Slavonic Review*, III, 681, Doc. No. 55.

[296] Shuvalov to Tsar Alexander, 10/22 June; *ibid.*, III, 678–79, Doc. No. 48.

they were "telling truth" and, consequently, impossible to deal with them. Neither, in his way of thinking, was there any reliance to be placed on the shifting Andrássy nor any trust to be put in Bismarck; and as for France, France would conform to Russia's wish.[297]

Both the prime minister and the foreign secretary, however, wanted to keep the discussion going, and they asked for an explanation of what the Russians meant by "vassal and tributary autonomy" and what they would do if the sultan rejected such a plan. Shuvalov pointed to Serbia and Rumania as the examples to follow, and insisted that the refusal of the Porte to take advice from the powers would entail only non-interference in subsequent events. These statements appeared to him to be satisfying at least in regard to non-intervention, but the ambassador noted an ominous change of opinion in the mind of the premier: Disraeli, from being sympathetically inclined toward autonomy, was beginning to look upon a new Slavic vassal state in the Balkans as an outpost of Russian domination.[298]

Shuvalov urged the necessity for immediate action to forestall Serbian and Montenegrin entry into the struggle; he defended the purity of Russian intentions; he still besought any kind of a counter-proposal that the British wanted to make. But his efforts were of no avail. When he met Disraeli at a dinner on the twenty-third the prime minister dismissed the Russian proposals on the ground that, in spite of confidence and good-will, they "suggested, or proposed a good deal," and he ignored the challenge for a British solution.[299] The ambassador had a hard and discouraging task. "It is very difficult, sire," he wrote to the tsar on the twenty-third, "to conquer English slowness,"[300] and he added bitterly the next day:

. . . . If I were anywhere but in England, where experience has proved to me that it is always necessary in politics to expect bad dealings and never good, I would have the right, sire, to expect a favorable outcome in the negotiations that I am pursuing by your Majesty's order: but here everything can change from one day to the next. A telegraphic dispatch, a movement on the stock exchange, a fluctuation of public opinion suffices to modify the convictions of those who direct the destinies of England.[301]

[297] Derby to Ponsonby, 20 June; *Disraeli*, VI, 33–34.
[298] Shuvalov to Tsar Alexander, 10/22 June; *Slavonic Review*, III, 679, Doc. No. 50. [299] Disraeli to Derby, 24 June; *Disraeli*, VI, 34–35.
[300] *Slavonic Review*, III, 679, Doc. No. 51.
[301] *Ibid.*, III, 679–80, Doc. No. 52.

But in spite of the passivity which he encountered, Shuvalov continued his campaign. On the twenty-sixth he was again in the Foreign Office to explain the modest character of Russia's definition of autonomy,[302] and on the twenty-seventh he wrote a letter to Derby defending the sincerity of the tsar's policy and inclosing letters to show how the Russian consuls were working for peace in Beograd and Cetinje.[303] Lady Derby told him that he had almost converted the two British ministers to the Russian proposals—but also that, at the last minute, rumors of Russian agents secretly inciting Serbia and Montenegro to war had caused them to hesitate once more.[304]

Another influence no less formidable was at work to restrain a commitment in London. Andrássy, from the moment he heard of the campaign which Shuvalov was waging, began an active campaign of his own against autonomy for Bosnia and Hercegovina; and his condemnation of autonomy, which Beust delivered to the foreign office on the twenty-seventh,[305] was undoubtedly effective. If Andrássy was correct, Derby observed, the remedy which Russia proposed "seemed to be worse than the disease."[306]

Gorchakov was, of course, ignorant of the maneuver of his ally; he knew only that Russia was charged with intrigues in the Balkans and, in reply to Shuvalov's report, he protested that he was making honest remonstrances to Serbia.[307] On the following day, the twenty-eighth, he made a new appeal for prompt British support as the only way to save the peace.[308] But in London there was still no conversion. The suspicions which Disraeli had restrained in an effort to break up the Austro-Russian alliance had returned to inspire his thoughts. He did not—apparently—really want a Serbo-Turkish

[302] Draft No. 398, Derby to Loftus, 30 June; *Turkey No. 3 (1876)*, Doc. No. 519.

[303] Shuvalov to Derby, 27 June; FO 65/953. Gorchakov to Shuvalov, 15/27 June; *Slavonic Review*, III, 680, Doc. No. 53.

[304] Shuvalov to Gorchakov, 15/27 June; *ibid.*, III, 681, Doc. No. 55.

[305] *Vide infra*, p. 373.

[306] Report No. 435, Buchanan to Derby, 4 July; FO 7/872. ". . . . and I said that after your Lordship had communicated to me the serious objections which His Excellency had submitted to you through Count Beust against the adoption of such an arrangement, you had observed, that if they were well founded, the proposed remedy seemed to be worse than the disease."

[307] Gorchakov to Shuvalov, 15/27 June; *Slavonic Review*, III, 680–81, Doc. No. 54.

[308] Gorchakov to Shuvalov, 16/28 June; *ibid.*, III, 681, Doc. No. 56.

war; yet he had never seriously considered preventing such a conflict by remedying the situation that was bringing it rapidly to hand. As the danger loomed larger he conceived that the best way to dispel war was through a vigorous threat, not to Turkey or Serbia, but to Russia. If the tsar were warned that Britain would not permit a Russian intervention to save Serbia in case of defeat, he believed that the talked-of hostilities would not begin. That very day he was ready to launch the warning[309]—but the timorous Derby refused to be pulled along at such a rapid pace.

When Shuvalov saw the foreign minister again on the twenty-eighth, the day of the premier's bold proposal, Derby had no articulate anti-Russian feelings; but he none the less dealt the mortal blow to any hopes of an Anglo-Russian arrangement. There was one small consolation in the fact that Derby approved of Turkey's trying to separate Montenegro from the Serbs and insurgents by offers of concessions, but in the case of Serbia the secretary was adamant: with Prince Milan threatening war it was impossible for the Porte to make concessions. If the prince did not attack, Derby admitted that he might have some claims for consideration, but even so British policy could not be pledged; in case Milan gave clear proof of having abandoned his war plans there was a possibility that he might be given Little Zvornik, but most certainly nothing more. When the conversation passed on to the question of the insurgent area, Shuvalov discovered that the sympathy once shown for autonomy had entirely disappeared. Derby now doubted if autonomy would satisfy the rebels; he refused to suggest a plan for the government of the provinces without knowing opinion at the Porte; he doubted if "free institutions" would function in a land of such pronounced "religious differences" and of so many "natural animosities"; and he thought it unfortunate and inconvenient to use "vague and general terms" such as "local autonomy." For the moment he could not go beyond saying that the cabinet would approve "any practicable proposal for the amelioration of the local government" of Bosnia and Hercegovina.[310]

The next day these views were elaborated in a letter which was addressed by Derby to the Russian ambassador but which betrayed

[309] Disraeli to Derby, 28 June; *Disraeli*, VI, 36.

[310] Draft No. 393, Derby to Loftus, 28 June; *Turkey No. 3 (1876)*, Doc. No. 502.

the thought and phraseology of the prime minister. In this letter the insurrection was not at all a revolt against local oppression but a disturbance "fomented and maintained for purposes which are obviously of a general and political" character; the refugees were afraid not of Mohammedan vengeance but of Orthodox violence. The letter continued:

. . . . It is obvious that, while this state of things is allowed to continue, the efforts of the Powers in recommending schemes for the better administration of these districts must be fruitless. It was in this conviction that I have stated to your Excellency my opinion that the insurrectionary movement must be suppressed, and order restored, before any such schemes can be advantageously treated . . . .

The repeated explanations by Shuvalov and Gorchakov regarding autonomy were now entirely lost. The letter stated that Her Majesty's cabinet did not "clearly understand what is the particular plan which the Russian Government have in view." Nor could they frame "a scheme of administration" for a Turkish province because of local problems which only local knowledge could illuminate.

. . . . It is for this reason, among others, that Her Majesty's Government see so much objection to pressing on the Porte at the present moment, and without close and careful inquiry, projects of reform going beyond those already promised . . . .

The British government, contrary to that of the tsar, could not see any serious difficulties incident to the suppression of the rebellion. At a time when thousands of Christian bodies were rotting under the sun of Bulgaria, Shuvalov was assured that

Her Majesty's Government have no reason to anticipate that the suppression of the insurrection would be followed by the extermination or persecution of the Christian races. There are no signs of any such intention on the part either of the Porte or the Mahometan population, and Her Majesty's Government do not believe that any apprehension of the kind need be entertained.

In its concluding paragraphs the letter recapitulated Derby's statements regarding Montenegro and Serbia. As for the former, England had done all that was possible; as for the latter, the attitude of Prince Milan's government forbade the recommendation of any concession. The great necessity for the moment, in British opinion, was a new and energetic remonstrance by Russia in Beograd.

It is desirable that the Servian Government should be warned that if they attempt to secure territorial aggrandizement under the pretext of Slavonic sympathies, they must not expect to be protected from the consequences of failure and defeat.[311]

Her Majesty's Government are convinced that if this were done in a tone which did not admit of misconstruction, and the Turkish insurgent provinces were freed from the instigations to revolution of the foreign Slav Committees and agitators, the work of pacification would be so greatly advanced as to render the completion of it an easy task. . . . .[312]

During the greater part of a critical month Disraeli, with Derby in his wake, had toyed with the Russians. He had in the beginning promised the Cretan settlement as a minimum for the Bosnian rebels; he had agreed to prevent atrocities; he had raised high the hopes of Russia for sympathetic British co-operation. Before the month was over he had stopped his protestations of confidence and good-will, had abandoned the fiction that England would do something for Bosnia, and had terminated the sterile discussion by a letter of patent malice, brazen lies, and studied insult.

In the meantime the Austro-Hungarian foreign minister had been busily occupied in his attempts to win the British cabinet to his views. Count Andrássy had continued to hold tenaciously to his program of negotiations between insurgents and Turks during an armistice; and this program in turn embodied the hope that the insurgents would yet submit on the basis of the terms incorporated in the Berlin memorandum. The refusal of England to endorse that document did not discourage him from sending one argument after another to Constantinople in favor of a truce and negotiations with the rebel leaders. At the end of May he attempted to capitalize the rising menace of war from Serbia and Montenegro, urging that the best way to forestall new dangers was to end the old.[313] As soon as he heard of the fall of Abdul Aziz he sent another telegram. In it he contended that the new regime would do much better to hasten on with pacification than to become embroiled in a theoretical constitution which would make Turkey's troubles only the worse for reck-

[311] The thought of this last sentence and practically the whole of its phraseology Disraeli had attempted to introduce into Derby's dispatch to Loftus of the previous day (*Turkey No. 3* [*1876*], Doc. No. 502), but the secretary had removed it on the ground that the dispatch was a record of his conversation with Shuvalov and that he had not said the words added by the prime minister.

Disraeli was quite willing to see the Serbs lose their autonomous state and return to an undifferentiated part of the Turkish Empire in case of defeat.

[312] Derby to Shuvalov, 29 June; *Turkey No. 3 (1876)*, Doc. No. 506. Disraeli to Queen Victoria, 29 June; *Disraeli*, VI, 35–36.

[313] Tel. No. 57, Andrássy to Zichy, 29 May; SA, Varia Turquie I, 1875.

less experimentation.[314] The only hope of pacification à l'Andrássy lay in an armistice, and Andrássy continued, despite the collapse of the concert, to urge it; a respite of only eight days, he told the Turks, would be acceptable.[315]

On 5 June the grand vizier prepared a proclamation ordering a six weeks' armistice and submitted it to Andrássy for comment.[316] The minister scornfully refused to discuss the document on the ground that it ignored Turkey's earlier promises and failed to recognize the armistice as a contract with the great powers.[317] Such reasons, however, were only excuses. At the moment he received notice of the armistice proclamation Andrássy was reluctantly agreeing to Gorchakov's proposal to go forward à cinq with the memorandum.[318] His predicament, therefore, was real. He could not approve Turkey's armistice and at the same time send Zichy to the Porte to demand another. In replying to the Russian proposal Andrássy had nothing but good to say of the grand vizier's proclamation, but, being obliged to proceed with Gorchakov, he had to reject the armistice announced from Constantinople. It is not surprising that the British ambassador found him "vexed and agitated."

On the seventh, affairs looked better for Count Andrássy. News arrived that Gorchakov had abandoned his first proposal in favor of a harmless declaration of watchful waiting,[319] and the Turkish ambassador gave him a formal notice of the armistice which constituted in a sense that promise to the powers which Andrássy considered essential in dealing with the insurgents.[320] Freed from the

---

[314] Tel. No. 60, Andrássy to Zichy, 31 May; SA, Turkey, 1876. Report No. 78, Harriss-Gastrell to Buchanan, 2 June; FO 7/880.

[315] Report No. 89, Harriss-Gastrell to Buchanan, 5 June; FO 7/880.

[316] Tel. No. 161, Zichy to Andrássy, 5 June; First Red Book, Doc. No. 413, incomplete.

[317] Report No. 356, Buchanan to Derby, 6 June; FO 7/871.

[318] Tel. No. 8, Andrássy to Károlyi, 6 June; SA, Varia Turquie I, 1875.

[319] Novikov to Andrássy, 7 June; ibid.

[320] Aarifi to Andrássy, 7 June, inclosed in Report No. 366, Buchanan to Derby, 10 June; Turkey No. 3 (1876), Doc. No. 425. Aarifi's letter was written at the instigation of Buchanan. "Having ascertained today that it was decided yesterday at an interview between Count Andrassy and M. de Novikow that the ambassadors at Constantinople should be instructed to deliver a note to the Porte asking for an armistice, I have advised the Turkish Ambassador, if his instructions permit it, to address a note to Count Andrassy communicating to him officially the letter of the Grand Vizier to the commissioners in the Herzegovine and Bosnia and expressing a hope that His Excellency will see in it a desire of the Porte to meet

Russian pressure, the minister was able to examine the Turkish armistice proclamation in a more objective light. The document did not contain an express pledge to live up to the promises made by Abdul Aziz. In other words, it ignored the Austrian reform program to which the former sultan had bound himself. Andrássy, therefore, informed the Turks that they had the alternative of confirming the old pledges or of having them imposed a second time. Otherwise he approved the armistice proclamation.[321] At the Porte it was readily agreed to add a specific statement about previous engagements,[322] and the necessary orders were sent to the governors of Bosnia and Hercegovina.[323]

At last it seemed that Andrássy was making some progress with his long-standing plan to inaugurate peaceful negotiations between rebel and Turk. An armistice was now in effect; the various pledges and promises made in Constantinople had been reaffirmed; the next step was to begin the discussions. As the chief intermediary, Andrássy was unwilling to leave those discussions entirely to the litigants, and in order to insure their success, he returned to the active role of peacemaker. He sent Baron Rodich to deliberate anew with the insurgents;[324] he sponsored plans in Constantinople to disinterest the prince of Montenegro through territorial concessions;[325] he studied again the bases of peace settlement. In the new examination of the insurgent demands Andrássy was no more sympathetic than he had been before. His objective for the moment was to persuade the Turks to accept his own views on concessions to the insurgents,

the wishes of the Austro-Hungarian Government and the other Powers for a suspension of hostilities, and that His Excellency will give orders to the Austrian local authorities to cooperate with those of the Provinces, in making the necessary arrangements for the return of the refugees to their homes.

"The Turkish Ambassador has decided to adopt this course and proposed submitting the note to my approval but I said it appeared to me that my being acquainted with its contents before its delivery would be objectionable. . . . ." (Tel. and Report No. 359, Buchanan to Derby, 7 June; FO 7/871).

[321] Tel. No. 66, Andrássy to Zichy, 7 June; *First Red Book*, Doc. No. 424, incomplete.

[322] Tel. No. 169, Zichy to Andrássy, 9 June; *ibid.*, Doc. No. 439. Report No. 610, Elliot to Derby, 12 June; *Turkey No. 3 (1876)*, Doc. No. 447.

[323] Aarifi to Andrássy, 13 June; *Turkey No. 3 (1876)*, inclosure in Doc. No. 450. *Ibid.*, Docs. Nos. 421, 480, 503.

[324] Report No. 397, Buchanan to Derby, 15 June; *ibid.*, Doc. No. 467.

[325] Tel. No. 57, Andrássy to Zichy, 29 May; SA, Varia Turquie I, 1875, in garbled form in *First Red Book*, Doc. No. 377.

and on 9 June he sent to Constantinople a restatement of his program dressed in a raiment of attractive explanations. Gorchakov, he wrote, had recently wanted to present the identic notes and had asked for Austrian support on the ground that he had made great concessions to Austrian views in Berlin. It was an opening remark, of course, to show the Turks who was to be regarded as a moderate friend. Then, on the assumption that the insurgents in the forthcoming negotiations would repeat their demands of April, he proceeded to suggest to the Turks what their answer should be. It was an outline of the five provisions of the Berlin memorandum with an indication that here and there the Porte might interpret for itself certain of the concessions, as, for example, to whom sustenance should be given and the extent to which troops were to be concentrated in garrison towns. The one and only way for the Ottoman Empire to save itself from the prevailing crisis, Andrássy warned in conclusion, was through acting promptly on his advice.[326]

These hopes and plans of Count Andrássy were rudely disturbed when Beust telegraphed to him on the twelfth a summary of what Disraeli and Derby had just said to Count Shuvalov.[327] During the next few days the Austrian minister plunged into the task of attacking the British position. He confessed that the cabinet's point of view was to him a riddle for which he could think of only one explanation—that London anticipated a Turkish victory. Fearful of what a *laissez-aller* policy might produce, he instructed Zichy to intimate to the Turks that it would not be wise for them to count on British support,[328] and he suggested to his ambassador that he had better shake himself free from Ignatiev's domination and cultivate good relations with Elliot in order to win his powerful influence for the support of Austrian interests.[329] But, more important still, Andrássy began at the same time a direct assault on the British position by telegram and letter to Beust. He insisted in these messages that, contrary to the views of Disraeli and Derby, the insurgents did not want independence; indeed, many had gone back to their homes and many others wished to do the same; the moment was ripe for renewed attempts at pacification. But should the insurgents and the

---

[326] Andrássy to Zichy, 9 June; in considerably deleted form in *First Red Book,* Doc. No. 438.

[327] Tel. No. 42, Beust to Andrássy, 12 June; SA, Varia Turquie I, 1875.

[328] Andrássy to Zichy, 15 June; *ibid.*

[329] Tel., Andrássy to Zichy, 19 June; SA, Turkey, 1876.

Serbs and Montenegrins hear that England was willing to give them independence if they won it in battle, there would be no stopping them. Prince Gorchakov, he suggested for British edification, would be pleased with a passive attitude during the next weeks because he had been disappointed lately by Andrássy's moderation; the tsar honestly wanted peace, but if the struggle were resumed in Turkey it would be very difficult to restrain the rising current of Russian opinion and, in turn, difficult to keep the imperial government from capitulating to it. Andrássy deemed it imperative to know just exactly what the British had in mind, and he ordered Beust to inform him as quickly as possible. If Disraeli wanted to let things go, Andrássy professed to have no objection, because he was confident that on most questions England and Austria would stand together. He preferred that England should espouse the cause of pacification; but, regardless of which policy was chosen in London, the minister besought prompt notice of one choice or the other in order that positive decisions could take the place of hesitations and contradiction.[330] The tone of Andrássy's message betrayed the greatest agitation which he had suffered since the crisis began. Every argument that seemed at all plausible he sent to influence the British statesmen in the hope of a clear-cut response on which he could rely.

But if the Austrian minister in his agitation really thought that he could elicit a categorical statement from London he was soon disappointed. The next day—16 June—Beust sent a reply of two unsatisfactory sentences: "Have spoken with Lord Derby in the sense of yesterday's telegram and found a good reception. He insists that the Porte is ready for any concession except independence."[331] When Beust's written report arrived several days later Andrássy learned that England was not disposed to put any pressure on the Porte in regard to Turkish dealings with the insurgents.[332] On the twentieth, when the ambassador returned to the Foreign Office with a more elaborate message from Andrássy, he was unable to persuade Derby to go beyond his first refusal of commitments. There was nothing, Derby said, that could be done at the moment.[333]

[330] Tel. No. 19 and dispatch, Andrássy to Beust, 15 June; SA, Varia Turquie I, 1875. The dispatch is paraphrased in Draft No. 305, Derby to Buchanan, 22 June; Turkey No. 3 (1876), Doc. No. 481.
[331] Tel. No. 44, Beust to Andrássy, 16 June; SA, Varia Turquie I, 1875.
[332] Report No. 57D, Beust to Andrássy, 16 June; First Red Book, Doc. No. 463.
[333] Tel. No. 46, Beust to Andrássy, 20 June; SA, Varia Turquie I, 1875. Report No. 58, Beust to Andrássy, 21 June; ibid. Tel. No. 47, Beust to Andrássy, 22

Beust's failure to secure a positive commitment was only one of Andrássy's difficulties created by Great Britain. Shuvalov's negotiations with Disraeli and Derby were under any circumstances disturbing for Vienna, but all the more so when Andrássy learned that the British were quite willing professedly to give the insurgents independence if they won, and to give them a constitutional regime similar to that of Crete in case of defeat. The discussion in London threatened to produce arrangements quite undesired by Austria, and the foreign minister launched a new campaign. One part of it was an attempt to undermine the new Anglo-Russian amity. "It appeared to me," the British ambassador wrote in summarizing a talk with Andrássy on the eighteenth, "that His Excellency is very doubtful as to the expediency of accepting proposals which Prince Gortchakoff has approved."[334] However, the menace of the creation of a new Slavic state on the Habsburg frontier required more vigorous tactics than the fomenting of suspicions. On the twentieth, in talking with the British chargé d'affaires, Andrássy revived his attack on the proposal of independence or autonomy for Bosnia, insisting that the mixed character of the population would make for incessant fighting.[335] A few days later Andrássy concluded that it was impossible further to restrain Serbia and Montenegro,[336] and he became more determined than ever to forestall an agreement between England and Russia as to autonomy.

On the twenty-third Beust telegraphed that, in spite of all his arguments, Derby was still suggesting the possibility of self-government for Bosnia under a governor appointed from the Porte.[337] A new offensive from Vienna was therefore essential. On the twenty-fifth Andrássy sent another long telegram to the ambassador in London: autonomy for the insurgent area was out of the question; between Christian and Moslem there would spring up a war of extermination; other provinces, and notably Bulgaria, would promptly demand the same concession and the insurrection would be extended rather than pacified; Serbia and Montenegro, moreover, would not be discouraged from war; and, finally, Turkey would never consent

---

June; *First Red Book,* Doc. No. 480. Draft No. 305, Derby to Buchanan, 22 June; *Turkey No. 3 (1876),* Doc. No. 481.

[334] Tel. and Report No. 411, Buchanan to Derby, 18 June; FO 7/871.
[335] Tel. and Report No. 412, Ffrench to Derby, 22 June; *ibid.*
[336] Tel. No. 22, Andrássy to Beust, 22 June; SA, Varia Turquie I, 1875.
[337] Tel. No. 49, Beust to Andrássy, 23 June; *ibid.*

to such an arrangement. Andrássy still pleaded for his own program. Anything which went beyond it would have grave consequences; the insurgents would be encouraged to fight for better terms; the Turks would refuse further demands and the Moslem population would in turn be encouraged to oppose all reform; the revolt would spread to other parts of the empire.[338] The one practical hope which the moment afforded for the Austrian minister was the hope that the insurgents, when beaten on the field of battle, would accept the reforms prepared for them. He had abandoned faith in his long-sought armistice and now concentrated his energies on trying to prevent an Anglo-Russian agreement which would prejudice the Austrian future. Things had gone a long way from that point where Andrássy had planned a series of concessions for which the rebels would render thanks unto Vienna, but the developed political ambitions south of the Save and Danube made it more imperative than ever for the Dual Monarchy to go no further. If the rebels refused to accept Andrássy's reforms with jubilation, there remained the hope that a sound beating at the hands of the Turks would make them more receptive to small favors. For such reasons the Austrian minister urged the London Foreign Office to attempt no new diplomatic action so long as the Eastern question was localized in the mountains of northwestern Turkey.

On the twenty-seventh Beust presented these views in London. At the time, the Foreign Office was alarmed over reports that Russian

[338] Tel. No. 24, Andrássy to Beust, 25 June; *First Red Book,* Doc. No. 487. This telegram was elaborated in a written dispatch two days later (*ibid.,* Doc. No. 497). At about the same time the Russian ambassador presented to Andrássy his government's proposal—as made to England—to proceed immediately with establishing autonomy rather than awaiting the outcome of the contest at arms. Andrássy repeated all the arguments which he had sent to London and added others which had a direct bearing on Austro-Russian relations. The major point of his reply to Novikov was the compromising position in which the powers would find themselves if they abandoned one program before they had attained its objectives. The foreign minister reminded the Russians that he had acceded to every one of Gorchakov's wishes since the Berlin memorandum was written and intimated that the time had come for a change of roles. But, concluded Andrássy, if the whole Eastern question was thrown on the table, Austria would remain loyal to the program of compensatory annexations which had been informally set at their last meeting. Andrássy, with his usual care to keep Bismarck informed of the Vienna point of view, sent a detailed account of the recent negotiations to Berlin (Draft No. 1, Andrássy to Károlyi, 27 June; *ibid.,* Doc. No. 496. Draft No. 2, Andrássy to Károlyi, 27 June; SA, Varia Turquie I, 1875). He kept from the German government only the reaffirmation of his agreement with Gorchakov to take slices of Turkey (Tel. No. 28, Andrássy to Károlyi, 29 June; *ibid.*).

agents were pushing Serbia and Montenegro into war.[339] Disraeli spoke of "Count Andrássy's very sensible arguments,"[340] and Derby concurred in Andrássy's rejection of a new vassal state.[341] The next day, as has been seen, the British foreign secretary terminated the Anglo-Russian discussion.[342]

Austrian anxiety, however, was not yet composed. Beust's telegraphic summary of his interview was not clear, and Andrássy thought that Derby was still approving some kind of local autonomy for Bosnia and Hercegovina. In considerable excitement the minister once more protested to London that autonomy was impossible and that the proclamation of such a program would mean that pacification would not be accomplished short of a thoroughgoing solution of the whole Eastern question. Again he ordered Beust to find out whether Derby wanted a conservative solution of the crisis or a radical one: "We can understand both, but it is essential for us to know which of them the English cabinet wishes. State this clearly and attempt to get as clear a response as possible."[343]

Beust hastened to correct Andrássy's mistake, giving him this time the distinct assurance that it was the Austrian communication that had converted Derby.[344] He none the less went to the Foreign Office to present again Andrássy's demand for an unequivocal statement of British policy. But he was no more successful in his new mission than he had been on the previous occasion. Derby dismissed the alternative between a radical and a conservative settlement as permissible theory but impracticable reality, and would make no further commitment.[345]

SUMMARY

The month of June came to an end, consequently, with the problem of the insurrection farther from solution than it had ever been.

[339] Shuvalov to Gorchakov, 15/27 June; *Slavonic Review*, III, 681, Doc. No. 55.
[340] Report No. 61C, Beust to Andrássy, 5 July; SA, England, 1876.
[341] Tel. No. 51, Beust to Andrássy, 27 June; *First Red Book*, Doc. No. 491, incomplete. Derby in two dispatches (Nos. 311 and 312) to Buchanan (27 June; *Turkey No. 3* [*1876*], Docs. Nos. 497 and 498, respectively) reproduced all of Beust's contentions but did not reveal his own response.
[342] *Vide supra*, pp. 365-67.
[343] Tel. No. 28, Andrássy to Beust, 30 June; SA, Varia Turquie I, 1875, given in considerably altered form in *First Red Book*, Doc. No. 505.
[344] Tel. No. 54, Beust to Andrássy, 1 July; SA, Varia Turquie I, 1875.
[345] Tel. No. 55, Beust to Andrássy, 1 July; *ibid.*

This latest phase of the waxing crisis had begun when the Russians, feeling the inadequacy of previous measures and hoping still for an international treatment of the problem, had invited Count Andrássy to Berlin and had there tried to induce him to accept a European conference and a military occupation of the insurgent area. During the conference Prince Bismarck had taken the side of Andrássy, having really made his choice between Austria-Hungary and Russia, and the Austrian minister had consequently been able to discard the projects of Prince Gorchakov and to dictate what was little more than a restatement of the limited concessions he had been ready to make to the insurgent demands.

As in the case of the framing of the other two programs of the imperial league, the Berlin memorandum had then been submitted to the other capitals with request for an immediate reply. Italy and France had responded with more alacrity than usual; but in London Disraeli, enraged by the treatment meted out to England, had led his cabinet to reject the memorandum without any serious consideration of the objective merits of its program, and subsequently the British government had steadfastly refused to pay any heed to the explanations and the requests for other proposals coming from Vienna and Berlin.

The five remaining powers had then resolved to proceed with the task of imposing the new program on the Sublime Porte, but at the last moment malcontent and revolutionary Turks had dethroned their sultan and the powers had been obliged to suspend their plans and start afresh. Gorchakov's desire for a common European stand on the problem of recognizing the new sultan had been made impossible by the independent action of England, followed by that of Italy and France, and after that defeat the Russian chancellor had been unable to persuade the French to return to the Berlin memorandum. He had then agreed with the French ambassador on an innocuous substitute declaration which was a virtual capitulation to Paris; but even so the French foreign minister had decided not to leave the British. Consequently, in mid-June the governments of the three imperial powers with the government of Italy in tow had prepared to deliver the substitute declaration of watchful waiting in Constantinople. But even that step had been forestalled when an infuriated Circassian had attempted to murder the entire Turkish council of ministers.

The events of May and June had brought a new prominence and

a new importance to Great Britain's role in the Balkan crisis. The cabinet had defiantly rejected the Berlin memorandum when the Continental powers had failed to learn a lesson from the British attitude toward the Andrássy note, and the cabinet had sent a preponderant naval force into Turkish waters. In the excitement of the time the prime minister had flitted from one dramatic idea to another, but his only plan which had materialized had been an attempt to lure Russia into some understanding, or at least some discussion, prejudicial to the Continental alliance. Whatever the objective at stake, after almost a month of negotiations with Shuvalov, Disraeli and Derby had agreed with the excited Andrássy in rejecting local autonomy for Bosnia and Hercegovina and had abandoned any pretense at an understanding with Russia.

The insurgent area was still in chaos and anarchy, and Serbia and Montenegro were on the eve of war against Turkey.

CHAPTER VII

THE END OF THE FIRST YEAR

SERBIAN PLOWSHARES INTO SWORDS

In Serbia the rigors of a Balkan winter had come to add Nature's own veto to the prince's opposition to war on Turkey. The miracle of peace, however, was not wrought in the hearts of the Serbian people. The national legislature was the scene of varied debates and intrigues in December and January; there was talk about free press, about old scandals; aroused passions and personal abuse were the usual stock in trade of the nation's representatives.[1] But these tumults were essentially a thing apart for the deputies. The major thought of these worthies no less than of their electors was the coming of spring and the possibility of war. Every item in the budget was the inspiration for a wrangle in the assembly until army estimates were reached in late January, and then, without discussion and without opposition, appropriations were passed for large ordinary and extraordinary expenses.[2] The vote was a clear announcement that the militant spirit of Serbian patriotism was reviving. In less than a week the skupshtina, with rising fever of war expectation, voted a forced loan of two million dinars,[3] and when it concluded its regular session on 2 February it delegated secret powers to a committee in the interest of keeping control over the cabinet and over money matters in case hostilities broke out before the next regular session.[4]

Even Prince Milan, who had taken on his own shoulders the odium of an almost single-handed opposition to war, gave signs of abandoning his position. In conversations with the consular agents he freely admitted that one of several contingencies—an advantage to Montenegro or an Austrian occupation, for example—might force

[1] Report of the Rumanian agent in Beograd, 10/22 January 1876; Iorga, *Correspondance*, pp. 101–2.
[2] Political Report No. 4, White to Derby, 24 January 1876; FO 78/2486.
[3] *Europäischer Geschichtskalender*, 1876, p. 474. Tel., White to Derby, 31 January; FO 78/2486.
[4] Political Report No. 7, White to Derby, 4 February; *ibid.*

him into action.[5] It remained an axiom in Beograd that Serbia had to lead the Southern Slavic movement and that under no circumstances could Bosnia be lost to the great neighboring power. Moreover, Milan was a very young man of unsettled nerves incapable of standing up indefinitely against the arguments of his liberal ministers and the manifestations of public opinion.[6]

The British consul in early February raised the danger signal:

. . . . The confidential conversations of the Prince with myself and with some of my colleagues here, the preparations which have been steadily going on for some months, and which are now prosecuted with renewed vigour, the extraordinary powers voted by the "Skoupstchina," and demanded by the Servian Administration, the activity of numerous unofficial agents, whose connections are well known, all confirm the supposition that something important is in contemplation.[7]

Before the end of February military preparations had been materially advanced. Militiamen of the first and second classes were ordered to hold themselves ready; reserve lists of able-bodied men were made up; new commissions were granted; a staff was being prepared; horses, weapons, and uniforms were being bought.[8]

Parallel with the energetic work of making the fighting force ready, the Beograd authorities made new attempts to organize, after the manner of Prince Michael, the scattered Christian forces of the peninsula. In early February Prince Milan proposed to send an agent to Athens to revive the old alliance and he urged the Greek consul in Serbia to support the plan. But the Greek consul and his government were not disposed to make common cause with the peoples who were the greatest challenge to Greek hegemony in the Balkans. Consequently the Athens cabinet rejected completely the offer of negotiations. The alleged reason for the Greek refusal was lack of proper military preparation, but back of such an excuse was a growing consciousness of the rivalry between Greek and Slav for the possessions of old Turkey. Ever mindful of the fact that Serbia

[5] Report No. 3, Wrede to Andrássy, 15 January; SA, Beograd, 1876. Tel., White to Derby, 31 January; FO 78/2486. Report No. 172, Elliot to Derby, 8 February; *Turkey No. 3 (1876)*, Doc. No. 7.

[6] Jovanović, *Slavonic Review*, IV, 394.

[7] Political Report No. 8, White to Derby, 5 February; *Turkey No. 3 (1876)*, Doc. No. 2, incomplete.

[8] Report No. 17, White to Elliot, 21 February; *Turkey No. 3 (1876)*, inclosure in Doc. No. 50. The Serbian government's decree of 24 February on military organization may be found in translation in *ibid.*, inclosure in Doc. No. 384.

had not aided Greece in the Cretan disturbance of 1867, Greece was not ready in 1876 to rush into war for the sake of Serbia.[9]

[9] Lhéritier, *Histoire diplomatique*, III, 385–86. Lascaris, *La Politique extérieure*, p. 37. Report No. 28, Wrede to Andrássy, 14 March; SA, Beograd, 1876. The British consular agent's report of the negotiations in Beograd was as follows:

". . . . In February last when it became evident that Servia was pushing on her preparations with renewed vigor . . . . my Greek colleague, M. Doscos, had several interviews with the Prince of Servia.

"From what I could learn at the time it appeared to me that there was a mutual desire on both sides to learn something of each other's plans. My colleague wished to find out what Servia contemplated and the Prince to ascertain how far Greece was disposed to assist in a general rising of Eastern Christians against Turkey.

"So far the result of these interviews must have been discouraging for the Prince.

"I was not aware however that actual stipulations had been either proposed by the Prince or rejected by the Greek Consul General and certainly I would not be disposed to credit that part of the proposal in which the Prince is said to have spoken of securing the independence of Servia, for I have reason to believe that his ambition lies by no means in that direction, and that he and all parties agree in deprecating such a result as greatest danger instead of being a boon to Servia.

"My own impression from what I heard of these interviews was that there was a good deal of oriental finessing on both sides, and that the Prince and my colleague in treating of the turn of disturbances in different Provinces in European Turkey, addressed each other somewhat in the way (though in a different sense) related in the famous anecdote of one of our greatest Battles with the French, 'Après Vous, Messieurs.'

"My Greek Colleague has often spoken to me of the way in which the Servians had kept aloof from all participation during the Cretan Insurrection and he has frequently repeated to me that the lesson of 1867 has not been lost on his Government, which had no reason to disturb their good relations with the Porte, and would certainly discourage by every means, any disturbance in Turkish Provinces largely inhabited by Greeks, unless they saw first the Slavs fairly committed and the conflagration assuming a general character and one presenting a reasonable chance of success" (Report No. 37, White to Elliot, 4 April, in political Report No. 26, White to Derby, 4 April; FO 78/2486).

Available documents do not permit a satisfactory understanding of the role of General Ignatiev, if any, in these negotiations. That the Russian agents knew much more of what the Balkan states were doing than did the other agents there can be no doubt, but whether or not Ignatiev took a part in promoting a new Balkan alliance is another question. This brief report from Elliot on 14 February (No. 196; FO 78/2455), however, is interesting in that connection: "I learn confidentially that General Ignatiew has informed the Greek Minister that an alliance has been concluded between Servia, Montenegro and Roumania, and that one of the late Servian Ministers is about to proceed to Athens to procure the accession of the Greek Government to it. I have great doubts of the accuracy of this information."

Consul White in Beograd was certain of a Russian hand at work: ". . . . There is every probability that Russian Agents here, and by Russian Agents I mean those of General Ignatieff, having been urging Prince Milan to prepare for

The renewed negotiations with Montenegro, which were inaugurated at the same time, proved for several months to be no more fruitful than the dealings with the Greeks. Serbo-Montenegrin cooperation was clouded from the very beginning by the old contest for Slavic leadership, but in the early part of 1876 their relations were made all the more difficult by virtue of the fact that Prince Nicholas was mounting in Slavic favor to the disadvantage of Milan. The intimate and confessed connections between Nicholas and the insurgents, the marked contrast in the treatment meted out to the two principalities by Russia, the fact that the powers had interfered in Beograd and not in Cetinje—all these indications pointed definitely to the ascendancy of the popular Nicholas. In February there was circulated in Beograd a rumor to the effect that Austria was making arrangements to give Montenegro an increase of territory at the expense of the Porte.[10] Under such circumstances some forward action became a vital necessity for Prince Milan. The Serbo-Montenegrin negotiations of the preceding October had resulted in an informal understanding to do no more during the winter than aid the insurrection.[11] Such an arrangement was of course inadequate for the coming spring, and, on the invitation of Nicholas, a new Serbian agent went to Cetinje about the middle of February with a letter from Milan proposing a secret treaty of alliance and a war convention committing the two principalities to be ready at the end of March.[12]

These February activities of Serbia, it will be recalled, were being reported to Vienna just at the time when the sultan had accepted Andrássy's reform program. It was in those first days when experience had not played havoc with the minister's plans. Andrássy had no intention of permitting the Beograd politicians to do

---

every emergency . . . ." (Report No. 18, White to Elliot, 25 February, in Political Report No. 13, White to Derby, 28 February; FO 78/2486; deleted from *Turkey No. 3 [1876]*, inclosure in Doc. No. 51).

10 Report No. 14, White to Elliot, 17 February; *Turkey No. 3 (1876)*, inclosure in Doc. No. 49. Report No. 18, White to Elliot, 25 February; *ibid.*, inclosure in Doc. No. 51.

11 Stojanovic, "Serbia in International Politics, from the Insurrection in Herzegovina (1875) to the Congress of Berlin (1878)" (manuscript dissertation, University of London, 1930), pp. 80-82.

12 Tel., Novikov to Gorchakov, 2/14 February, communicated by Shuvalov to Derby, 27 June; FO 65/953. Report No. 13, Wrede to Andrássy, 14 February; SA, Beograd, 1876.

harm to those plans, and the Russians supported him in his determination. On the fifteenth Gorchakov ordered that both Milan and Nicholas be informed that Russia would support neither the one nor the other if they undertook actions which jeopardized peace,[13] and two days later Andrássy wrote a warning that was even more severe: the two imperial powers were resolved upon pacification and expected the principalities to abide by that decision; if Milan proceeded with his alliance and his war plans in defiance of the will of the powers, Austria would blockade the Serbian border.[14]

On 17 February Kartzov, the Russian consular agent, delivered Gorchakov's remonstrance. But the background of recent Serbian-Russian relations was of a nature to minimize the new démarche. During the preceding month St. Petersburg had not been averse to Serbian preparations; on the contrary, the Russian government had warned Milan not to stop them lest pacification fail and the rebellion spread over the Balkan Peninsula. The personal activities of the consul were, moreover, encouraging. Officially Kartzov was very stern; privately, as a friend, he took a hand in the sending of a diplomatic agent to Montenegro and he urged the Serbs on to war, assuring them allegedly that Russia would follow. Milan was entitled to be surprised and annoyed when this same man, three days after dispatching the agent to Cetinje, came to the palace to condemn war preparations and the pending alliance. The prince told Kartzov he could not understand why the Russian government had one face in Beograd, another in Constantinople, another in Vienna, and still

[13] Tel., Gorchakov to Novikov, 3/15 February, communicated by Shuvalov to Derby, 27 June; FO 65/953. Elliot sent the following account of the Russian remonstrance: "General Ignatiew received this morning a copy of the last message sent by the Emperor of Russia to the Princes of Servia and Montenegro which he considered to be drawn up in terms much more harsh than was at all called for, at least as regards Prince Nicholas.

"He observed, however, with exultation that the pacification of the Herzegovine would after all be due to Russia, as this message of the Emperor had only arrived at Cettigne just in time to prevent the signature of an arrangement by which the two Princes were on the point of engaging themselves in a joint action.

"He read the communication to me, and its terms were certainly stringent, or as he called them, harsh . . . .

"The mortification felt by General Ignatiew at this evidence of the energy with which his Government is seconding the efforts of Count Andrassy to bring about a pacification was very evident" (Report No. 305, Elliot to Derby, 24 March; FO 78/2456; cf., *Turkey No. 3* [*1876*], Doc. No. 104).

[14] "Instruction für den k. und k. diplomatischen Agenten und Generalconsul in Belgrad," 17 February; SA, Beograd, 1876.

another in St. Petersburg.[15] Five days later the British consul in some agitation telegraphed his superiors that the Russian message had been of no avail, that military preparations were going on just as before.[16]

Wrede, the Austrian consul, returned to Beograd only on 25 February, eight days after the declaration of his Russian colleague. Before the diplomatic agent arrived, Milan had boasted that he knew what Wrede was going to say and that, regardless of what he himself might reply, war was inevitable. But in his conversation with Wrede the prince was more circumspect. The starting point of his reply was his belief that the insurgents would not lay down their arms to receive Andrássy's reforms because the revolt had developed political ambitions. Milan, in the face of continued disturbance, had no confidence in the stability of the Ottoman Empire and he declared it to be an inescapable obligation to complete his military organization and be ready for all eventualities. He would not, he told Wrede, launch his country upon some venturesome policy; he was determined to resort to a belligerent action only when circumstances were favorable. He went on to explain that circumstances would be favorable for Serbia's participation if the insurrection continued, if Montenegro openly went to war, and if he were assured that the powers would not intervene. Those qualifications were minimum predicates of Serbian success, and Milan would not bind himself if they were met in the future. There was in his reply no humble submission to the wishes of Russia and Austria.[17]

[15] Stojanovic, *op. cit.*, p. 87, citing Serbian sources. Jovanović, *Slavonic Review*, IV, 394-95. Russian complicity in the sending of an emissary to Montenegro is indicated by the following telegram from Kartzov to Novikov, forwarded by the latter to Gorchakov on 2/14 February, and given in the form below by Shuvalov to Derby on 27 June (FO 65/953): "In accordance with your instructions, I delayed the despatch of the Servian Delegate to Montenegro in order not to imperil the success of the negotiations of Europe with the Porte. However, in view of their termination, Prince Milan and his Ministers, on the strength of the arrangement already come to between the Principalities, does not think it possible to postpone the Mission. . . . ."

[16] Tel., White to Derby, 22 February; *Turkey No. 3 (1876)*, Doc. No. 16. See also *ibid.*, Docs. Nos. 22 and 32.

[17] Report No. 19, Wrede to Andrássy, 25 February; SA, Beograd, 1876. Report No. 19, White to Elliot, 26 February; *Turkey No. 3 (1876)*, inclosure in Doc. No. 52. The French foreign minister, hearing of the admonitions addressed to the principalities, instructed his agents to lecture Milan and Nicholas in the same sense (Decazes to Bourgoing, 25 February; *First Yellow Book*, pp. 106-7). Milan, on 28 February, assured the French agent that there was no connection

This response was indicative that Milan had gone a long way toward capitulating to popular feeling. His half-year of opposition to war had resulted in his almost complete isolation in Serbia. The conservatives on whom he had reckoned had been intimidated into silence; some of them, indeed, had come out openly for action. His unpopularity became increasingly marked; threatening letters were sent to him; plots against him were being uncovered by the police. And, as if to emphasize his timidity and the insecurity of his position, his rival for the throne of Serbia, the pretender Karageorgevich, was leading a band of Bosnian insurgents and making a popular hero of himself. Further opposition to the national clamor for war was rapidly becoming more dangerous than actual war itself could be. At the same time the prince was losing faith in the pretensions of the league of the three emperors. There seemed to be no honesty and consistency in Russian policy; and Austria, it was believed in Beograd, had not only allowed Karageorgevich to enter Bosnia but had also prevented the arrangement of a foreign loan.[18]

The next days produced new fuel for the Serbian fire. As a result of recent liberal legislation the socialist party grew rapidly, and about the first of March certain of its members made a demonstration in Kragujevatz. On the occasion of a municipal election in that place a mob of one hundred persons carrying a red flag marched on the town hall shouting for a republic. This expression of heterodox opinion was quickly lost in the louder noise of patriot rifles; but the importance of the event was soon indicated in the arrests and investigations which allegedly pointed to a widely organized plot to seize the country.[19] The ministers as well as the prince were frightened by the specter haunting Serbia and they persuaded themselves that they had only the old choice between war abroad and revolution at home. Every element except Marinovich and his frightened conservatives found reasons for war: the prince to save

whatever between Serbian military precautions and the insurrection just beyond the border, the extension of which he would regard with disfavor (Decazes to ambassadors abroad, 4 March; *ibid.,* pp. 113–14). See also Political Report No. 15, White to Derby, 1 March; *Turkey No. 3 (1876), Doc. No. 53.*

When in the same days the Turkish foreign minister asked the Serbian agent about his country's military preparations, the latter was instructed from Beograd to inform Rashid that all news about Serb armaments was without foundation (Tel. No. 47, Zichy to Andrássy, 24 February; SA, Varia Turquie I, 1875).

18 Stojanovic, *op. cit.,* pp. 85–86.

19 *The Times* (London), 21 March 1876, p. 8, cols. 1–2.

himself and his dynasty, the ministry to save their offices, the liberals for political advantage, the socialists for an opportunity to capture the state. Then, too, there was the common reason of all patriots. And, finally, there was a widespread feeling that a poor principality could not go on indefinitely pouring the greater part of its revenues into preparing for war.[20]

Around the twelfth of March Milan, feeling that the crisis in Serbia's future was close at hand, called together the ministers and representatives from the various parties and groups of the country. After describing to this assembly the difficulties of the time, the excitement of the people, and the paralysis of normal life imposed by the prevailing uncertainty, the prince put to his hearers the alternative of continuing the military preparations in order to be ready to attack Turkey at a time of Serbia's own choosing or of declaring for peace and adjourning to a more favorable day the great work of the nation. The assembly unanimously chose the first plan. Its members voted against doing anything that would lead to an immediate rupture with Turkey, but at the same time they enthusiastically advised Milan to continue perseveringly with the military organization in order to be prepared when war became inevitable.[21]

In contrast to Milan, Nicholas of Montenegro responded to the admonitions given him with assurance of his determination to conform to the wishes of the emperors of Austria and Russia.[22] On 9 March Nicholas' profession was communicated to Milan by the Austrian consul as a further argument in favor of Serbia's neutrality. But Milan was now too far committed to war and too exasperated with his Montenegrin rival to be restrained. Dismissing

[20] Jovanović, Slavonic Review, IV, 392–94.

[21] Kartzov to Gorchakov, 16/28 March (o.s.), communicated by Shuvalov to Derby, 27 June; FO 65/953.

[22] Report, Rodich to Andrássy, 7 March; SA, Varia Turquie I, 1875. Rodich went to Cetinje on 2 March and had a long discussion with the prince concerning the policy of Montenegro. The burden of Rodich's message was that Austria and Russia wished peace and wanted Montenegro in turn to do nothing to jeopardize their work of pacification. Nicholas was told that peace could not last more than a few years and if he heeded the imperial desires his interests would not be forgotten on the day of reckoning. In his reply Nicholas, like Milan, advanced the difficulties of his position. On one side were his subjects; on the other were the Great Powers, and especially Russia, which gave him a personal subvention. He confessed that he was inclined toward the treaty with Milan then in process of negotiation, but confessed too that his own lot would be easier in his attempt to submit to the will of the powers if Serbia was kept at peace; if Serbia made war, Montenegro would have to make war as well.

Nicholas' promises as insincere, the prince repeated the language which he had used in talking with Wrede a fortnight before.[23]

The annoyance felt in Austria-Hungary at this continued defiance of the Great Powers was intense. Two days later the Hungarian minister-president, Tisza, replied to an interpellation in the Budapest Diet with a guarded threat against Serbia. His statement, arranged previously with the minister for foreign affairs, merely announced that the Dual Monarchy, in case the Serb government defied the interests of Europe, would be guided by those interests. Back of Tisza's words lurked the hint of a possible Austrian declaration of war should Milan's troops invade Bosnia.[24] The next day Andrássy sent to Beograd a categorical summons to submission. He instructed Wrede to inform the prince that, in view of the fact that Europe was guaranteeing Turkey's denial of aggressive intentions, Serbian military preparations were without justification, and should they be continued they would provoke the collective intervention of Europe. Andrássy informed Milan that if he wished to spare himself that measure he had to assert his authority over his cabinet and turbulent assembly and to halt his arming. It was not mere advice that Andrássy was now offering; he required Milan to state without equivocation whether he proposed to accept or reject that advice.[25]

On 16 March the Austrian agent delivered Andrássy's message. The prince refused to give a definitive answer, alleging the necessity for a few days of grace to discuss the question with his cabinet and to await an official confirmation from Russia in view of the fact that Kartzov had not prepared him for such a pointed message. In the meantime he had justifications and many complaints. He protested that he did not want war; the military preparations were essential to the reorganization of his army. He declared that the Turks were building batteries on the frontier; he complained that Prince Nicholas was receiving much better treatment at the hands of the powers than he was; and, dwelling on the difficult position in which he found himself, Milan threatened to abdicate.[26]

[23] Tel., Wrede to Andrássy, 9 March; SA, Beograd, 1876.

[24] Report No. 131, Buchanan to Derby, 12 March; *Turkey No. 3 (1876)*, Doc. No. 54. Report No. 132, Buchanan to Derby, 12 March; FO 7/868.

[25] Andrássy to Wrede, 12 March; *First Red Book,* Doc. No. 257.

[26] Tel., Wrede to Andrássy, 16 March; *ibid.,* Doc. No. 260, incomplete. Report No. 29, Wrede to Andrássy, 17 March; SA, Beograd, 1876. The Austrian reports are not clear on the fact that Milan took exception to Wrede's proposing to

Such a reply, which not only said nothing but which challenged Wrede's right to speak on behalf of Russia, created new irritation in Vienna. As soon as it arrived Andrássy dispatched two long telegrams to St. Petersburg appealing for immediate instructions to Kartzov.[27] Gorchakov had already learned from Kartzov of the Beograd incident; immediately after Wrede's threatening visit, Milan had called in the Russian consul to ask him if his Austrian colleague had full powers to speak for tsar as well as for kaiser, and, to be certain, the prince requested a notice from St. Petersburg. The Russian chancellor was not pleased that Andrássy should couple the tsar's name to a serious threat without previous understanding, and on 19 March he so expressed himself to Baron Langenau. But the dangers of the moment forced Gorchakov to accept the Austrian *fait accompli* and he agreed to instruct Kartzov to support it.[28] It was an agreement made grudgingly and before the day was over the chancellor repudiated it. A report from Kartzov indicated that Milan had broken off his alliance negotiations with Montenegro; and Gorchakov, declaring that Milan's action marked the end of the incident, canceled the promised instructions.[29]

Andrássy found himself in very trying circumstances. On the heels of the telegram from Langenau announcing the Russian refusal to support his threat came telegrams from Wrede to the effect that new orders had gone to the Serbian militia to assemble in the

---

speak in the name of the tsar of Russia as well as in that of Emperor Francis Joseph. The British agent learned that this was true, and a passage in Wrede's report bears it out. Report No. 26, White to Elliot, 18 March; *Turkey No. 3 (1876),* inclosure in Doc. No. 86, incomplete. Political Report No. 21, White to Derby, 20 March; *ibid.,* Doc. No. 88.

[27] Tel. No. 2, Andrássy to Langenau, 17 March; SA, Russia, 1876. Tel. No. 12, Andrássy to Langenau, 17 March; *First Red Book,* Doc. No. 262. The Austrian minister recognized that he was, as Milan objected, presumptuous in associating the name of the tsar with his threat; but he explained in his Tel. No. 2, where he instructed Langenau to give Prince Gorchakov a copy of his dispatch of 12 March to Wrede: ". . . . Son Altesse y remarquera le passage où il est dit que, si la sommation des puissances devrait rester infructueuse, nous nous verrions probablement dans la nécessité d'agir en qualité de délégués de l'Europe vis-à-vis de la Serbie. Il va sans dire que nous sommes loin de vouloir nous charger d'une intervention pareille, mais un langage énergique m'a paru être le seul moyen de calmer l'effervescence guerrière qui s'est emparée des esprits dans la principauté."

[28] Tel. No. 21, Langenau to Andrássy, 19 March; SA, Russia, 1876. Report No. 14AB, Langenau to Andrássy, 25/13 March; SA, Varia Turquie I, 1875.

[29] Tel. No. 22, Langenau to Andrássy, 19 March; *First Red Book,* Doc. No. 271. Tel. No. 23, Langenau to Andrássy, 21 March; SA, Varia Turquie I, 1875.

appointed stations,[30] that the government had ordered a large compulsory loan,[31] and that Milan was unwilling to give the required peaceful declaration before he was notified directly from St. Petersburg that such was the will of the tsar.[32] On the twenty-third Andrássy telegraphed again to Russia, arguing that the acts of the Serbian government, despite the recall of the agent from Montenegro, still indicated the imminence of war. Prince Milan, he insisted, was counting on the division of Austria and Russia and the minister urged Gorchakov to prove to the prince that he was mistaken in his calculation.[33]

The Russian chancellor had by no means in these days retracted his desire that the principalities should not go to war. He had repeatedly warned Nicholas and Milan; he had sermonized Kartzov; he had discouraged the Greeks from negotiations with a Serbian agent.[34] It was Andrássy's means—a sharp threat given without previous understanding and without professedly being willing to carry it out—rather than his end objective to which Gorchakov took exception. However, on the twenty-fourth, when Andrássy's latest plea came to him with its proofs of the continued danger of a Serbian attack, the Russian chancellor was moved a second time to support the Austrian message to Beograd.[35]

---

[30] 19 March; SA, Beograd, 1876.   [31] 22 March; *ibid.*

[32] 22 March; *First Red Book,* Doc. No. 277, incomplete.

[33] Tel. No. 15, Andrássy to Langenau, 23 March; *ibid.,* Doc. No. 279.

[34] Report No. 14B, Langenau to Andrássy, 25/13 March; SA, Russia, 1876. Report No. 198, Wyndham to Derby, Athens, 5 August; FO 32/466. For example, on 18/30 January Novikov sent the following telegram to Consul General Jonin in Ragusa: "I cannot hide from you that the explanations of Prince Nicholas appear to me not clear, and unsatisfactory. The Prince regrets the tone of his note, but that is not the question, but his action with regard to Servia, which, from authentic information, we learn is being led on, and every fresh step is said to be justified by engagements made by us. At the same time he is prodigal of pacific assurances to us. The Chancellor remarks that 'Prince Nicholas is playing a double game,' and one wanting in bona fides as regards Russia" (English translation communicated by Shuvalov to Derby, 27 June; FO 65/953).

On 1/13 March Gorchakov telegraphed to Novikov in Vienna: "Instruct Jonin to inform Prince Nicholas that the emperor is not unaware of the latest overtures to Serbia, and that his Majesty had learned with as much surprise as regret the decisions as dangerous to Montenegro as contrary to the assurances of which Prince Nicholas is so lavish with us. Our august sovereign should not have to expect this ingratitude so contrary to the constant benevolence of which the prince has been the object. Demand a categorical explanation, adding that its character will decide our subsequent relations" (*ibid.*).

[35] Tel. No. 25, Langenau to Andrássy, 25 March; *First Red Book,* Doc. No. 282, incomplete.

On the day following this concession, the Serbian foreign minister, despite his claim that no word had come from Russia, gave his response to the Austrian question put to Milan on the sixteenth. "The Serbian government," his declaration read, "has no intention of attacking Turkey nor of hindering in any way the work of pacification undertaken by the Great Powers and inviting thereby their collective intervention. The military preparations which have been made up to the present are only for the development of the military organization which has been very much retarded in recent years."[36] It was a reply which, as Andrássy expressed it, did not bespeak much enthusiasm for the idea of pacification, but the Austrian minister accepted it in the conviction that Milan's new knowledge of Austro-Russian unity would restrain him.[37]

Sir Henry Elliot, on the other hand, was indignant at the Serbian response. It was his incensed opinion that "the transparent inaccuracy of this explanation in the face of the efforts which have been made to purchase arms and horses requires no comment, and the Prince's assurances of his pacific intentions are equally open to doubt."[38] During the weeks which followed, evidence supported the views of Sir Henry. Soon the Turkish governor of Bosnia reported that Serb preparations, far from being suspended, were being more openly conducted than ever before and that agents were in Bosnia preparing the Christians for revolt around Easter time.[39] There was

[36] Tel. and Report No. 35, Wrede to Andrássy, 25 March; *First Red Book*, Docs. Nos. 283 and 284, respectively. The latter is printed in deleted form. The British agent in the Serb capital had on 23 March urged "that the Servian Government should put an end to this most unsatisfactory state of things, and should at once give the Austro-Hungarian Representative a reply removing the suspicions which might attach to their silence. . . . ." (Report No. 29, White to Elliot, 23 March; *Turkey No. 3* [*1876*], inclosure in Doc. No. 102).

[37] Tel. No. 24, Andrássy to Langenau, 27 March; *First Red Book,* Doc. No. 285, incomplete.

[38] Report No. 307, Elliot to Derby, 27 March; *Turkey No. 3* (*1876*), Doc. No. 105. The ambassador goes on to prove his point by a telegram "received at the Porte" which announced a Serb violation of the Bosnian border. Elliot had been in Constantinople long enough to know that he had to discount Turkish sources, but it was a mental exercise requiring some will-power for him to do so. His attitude was well epitomized in the last paragraph of his report: "These accounts will probably be found as usual to be exaggerated, but Raschid Pasha says that there cannot be any doubt that what is going on on the frontier is greatly at variance with the assurances given by the Prince."

[39] Reports Nos. 343 and 345, Elliot to Derby, 3 and 4 April; *ibid.,* Docs. Nos. 127 and 128, respectively. Tel. No. 47, Zichy to Andrássy, 3 April; SA, Varia Turquie I, 1875.

indeed no doubt, no secrecy, about the work of making the Serbian army ready for war. That organization had been neglected since the murder of Michael and when the revolt began in Hercegovina the Serb force was far from prepared to enter the fray. Between that time and April a formal reorganization of divisions, brigades, and lesser units and of a general staff and service of supplies had been effected. The acquisition of equipment had proved more difficult than a paper arrangement of manpower. In assembling materials not of a patently military character—cloth, animals, saddles, and the like—considerable advance had been made. Weapons had been more troublesome; in times past the government had been buying arms wherever they could be found, and a heterogeneous collection had resulted. During the winter an order had been placed for 50,000 Chassepot rifles discarded by the German army, but Austrian and Russian regulations had prevented their importation.[40] However, such supplies as could be purchased out of the meager funds of the principality continued to arrive. It seemed to the British consul toward the end of April that the preparations were sufficiently advanced to permit the launching of a campaign on short notice. Neither prince nor ministers, of course, would admit aggressive intentions, but at the same time no one denied that sooner or later Serbia would be at war with Turkey.[41]

The revived feeling of South-Slavic unity which showed itself with the approach of spring and of more immediate war possibilities brought home to the minds of many Serbs the fact that Austria-Hungary as well as Turkey stood in the way of complete realization of national aspirations. The desire of Count Andrássy to do something to win the gratitude of the Southern Slavs had long since given place to the desire to thwart their apparent political ambitions. He denounced the insurgent peace terms; he attempted to close Austro-Hungarian sources of aid; he ordered the arrest of Ljubibratich, one of the best known of the Hercegovinian leaders. Toward the prince and people of Serbia he was no more conciliatory; Karageorgevich,

---

[40] Beograd dispatch of 19 April; *The Times* (London), 26 April 1876, p. 5, col. 1.

[41] Political Report No. 35, White to Derby, 28 April; *Turkey No. 3 (1876)*, Doc. No. 221, incomplete. ". . . . This much I may say, that I have not met a single politician of any note in Servia who did not contemplate sooner or later hostilities with the Porte, not with a view to independence, but for the purpose of the acquisition of Bosnia, and through the deeply rooted desire of making the present Principality the nucleus of a larger Slavonic State under the suzerainty of the Porte, as long as European Turkey forms a compact State. . . . ."

Milan's rival for the unsteady throne, was allowed by the Dual Monarchy—according to Serb accounts—not only to lead insurgent bands in and out of Hungary unmolested but also to send agents and proclamations into Serbia,[42] and it was hinted from Vienna and Budapest that any attempt on the part of the Serbs to take possession of Bosnia would be met with an Austro-Hungarian occupation. On Palm Sunday, the anniversary of that hallowed day in 1815 when Milosh Obrenovich raised the standard of revolt and also the anniversary of the Turkish surrender of the Serbian fortresses in 1867, the long-smouldering grievances of the Serbs against their powerful neighbor came to a head. In the morning there was a religious celebration and military review; in the evening Beograd was illuminated and the prince attended a patriotic play at the theater. Afterward a band of half a hundred hoodlum patriots assembled in front of the Austrian consulate and set up a din of yelling and howling. The episode assumed no serious proportions; it was conducted by a small group in the presence of a crowd of indifferent idlers, and the hostilities did not progress beyond sporadic rock-throwing. But however insignificant the actual event, the fact remained that the agency of a Great Power had been insulted by subjects of a small neighbor state. Prompt apologies were in order, yet the Serbian government failed to volunteer those apologies and to promise punishment for the offenders.[43] Consequently Andrássy found it incumbent upon him to send an ultimatum to Beograd on 10 April. He summoned Milan's government to make apology, to give a formal guaranty against a repetition of the insult, and to promise strict punishment of the administrative organs that had so signally failed in their duty. Serbia faced a choice between complete reparation in such a manner and war.[44] The Austrians' demands were promptly met and Andrássy expressed his satisfaction,[45] but the incident did not improve Austro-Serbian relations. "I consider it my duty," the British agent soon wrote, "to notice what appears to me to be the deplorable decline of Austrian influence in Servia. That Power is looked upon here

[42] Report No. 41, White to Elliot, 21 April; *Turkey No. 3 (1876)*, inclosure in Doc. No. 219. Andrássy had promised to intern Karageorgevich, but the Hungarian authorities claimed to know nothing of the pretender's whereabouts.

[43] *The Times* (London), 20 April 1876; p. 10, col. 3.

[44] Tel. No. 332, Andrássy to Wrede, 10 April; SA, Beograd, 1876. The next day the minister specified a written apology (Tel. No. 343).

[45] Tel., Andrássy to Wrede, 26 April; *ibid.*

by Prince, Ministers and people in the light of an enemy, her reprimands and threats are not heeded; and certainly her moral influence appears slumbering. . . . ."[46] The military preparations continued and Beograd took on a defiant mood. Before the end of April White again reported the Serbian outlook:

> . . . . To one of my colleagues the Prince said quite unreservedly the other day that he was not going to be either awed or deterred by any threats proffered at Vienna or Pesth from doing whatever he considered his duty to Servia and to his people, and if at any time circumstances should make him consider that he must take up arms he would certainly have no hesitation in doing so.
> In a similar way Mr. Ristich whose influence is said to be great at this moment, said to me last night in answer to some observations of mine that Austria was not likely to be a consenting party to any aggrandizement of Servia at this time, "Let her then prevent us by force."[47]

Convinced of the hostility of Austria and doubtful if Russian official statements about peace were to be taken literally, Prince Milan in April capitulated entirely to the popular pressure for war,[48] and the people of Serbia, a short time before openly hostile toward him, now took him to their bosom.[49] Milan's government formally

[46] Political Report No. 31, White to Derby, 25 April; FO 78/2486.

[47] Political Report No. 35, White to Derby, 28 April; FO 78/2486, quotation suppressed in *Turkey No. 3 (1876)*, Doc. No. 221.

[48] Jovanović, *Slavonic Review*, IV, 395. Trivanovitch, *Journal of Modern History*, III, 430.

[49] White wrote to Elliot on 21 April (Report No. 43, in Political Report No. 32, White to Derby, 25 April; FO 78/2486):
"There is no doubt that since Prince Milan has shown a disposition to lend an attentive ear to the suggestions of the War party and has to a certain extent taken upon himself the direction of the military preparations, he has gained immensely in influence and popularity, not only amongst his own people but even amongst the Slavs in Hungary.
"The active opposition which existed here against him twelve months ago, is gradually disappearing and dwindling into insignificant proportions, and it is probable that if matters go on in this way the only remaining irreconcilables will consist of the few unscrupulous secret adherents of the dynasty of Cara George. This Pretender, who was accused of having been concerned in the murder of Prince Michael of Servia, and his son, reside both in Austria.
"The Slav 'Omladina' party used to consider Prince Milan as a lukewarm supporter of the National cause, but since he has merited the reproaches of Count Andrassy's Government, and the abusive language of the Hungarian press it is evident that they are rallying round him, and completely new and dangerous combinations amongst various Slav elements, hitherto hostile, would appear to be preparing in the dark, which may acquire a much more revolutionary character, whenever Austria should feel impelled to cross the Save into Ottoman territory with a military force."

adhered to the Geneva Red Cross convention; the military preparations quickly used up the funds attained by the forced loan; toward
the end of the month it became known that the prince had opened
negotiations looking toward a more bellicose group of ministers.[50]
On 5 May the change was effected. The new cabinet was the one
which had been dismissed the preceding October for its warlike
intentions, and Ristich was again vice-president and minister for
foreign affairs. Immediately the restored officials were proclaimed
the ministry of action.[51] But even before its formation had been announced the new cabinet suffered a severe internal dissension. The
war minister demanded complete liberty to hasten his preparations
with a prompt declaration of war in view. His colleagues refused to
bind themselves so completely and turned in their resignations. The
new government was ultimately saved when the war minister gave
way and accepted a regulation that he could not take any important
steps without formal cabinet decision.[52] The incident suggested that
it was likely to be a ministry of moderation rather than of action.

Ristich, however much he was inclined in early May toward war,
was too confirmed a realist to indulge in quixotic actions. In support of his new policy of caution he had the advice of General Ignatiev, who had recently counseled Prince Milan "not to allow himself
to be drawn too precipitately into a conflict with the Porte."[53] When
the new foreign minister called on the Austrian consular agent a few
days after resuming office he betrayed no new dangers to the precarious peace. Asked if he and his colleagues were going to respect
the declaration of non-aggression given to Austria on 25 March,
Ristich readily replied in the affirmative. Like his predecessor, how-

[50] *Europäischer Geschichtskalender,* 1876, p. 490.

[51] Tel., White to Derby, 8 May; FO 78/2486.

[52] Report No. 60, Wrede to Andrássy, 10 May; SA, Beograd, 1876.

[53] Report No. 53, White to Elliot, 10 May; FO 78/2486. Elliot was of the impression that his Russian colleague was making no attempt to aid Serbia. On 6
April he had written to Derby (Report No. 349, *Turkey No. 3* [*1876*], Doc. No. 129,
incomplete) : "The Russian Ambassador makes no concealment of the interest he
feels in the Prince of Montenegro, but he almost ostentatiously proclaims his indifference toward Prince Milan." White replied to Elliot's statement in these words :
"I have every reason to believe that the Prince of Servia has not during the last
seven months taken a single step of any importance here without consulting that
Ambassador previously, and that both his negotiations with the Prince of Montenegro and the military preparations carried on here, have been regularly and
strongly recommended by General Ignatieff. I am unable to account for this contradiction in his language. . . . ."

ever, he ignored the assurances from the powers that an unoffending Serbia would not be attacked and he paraded the old phrases about the necessities of defense. The concentration of Turkish troops on the frontier, Ristich contended, imposed "certain measures of precaution in order not to be taken by surprise." He declared that Serbian territory had been repeatedly violated, and he showed telegrams from frontier commanders to prove it. Wrede concluded from the words and the manner of his visitor that previous promises would have little influence on the eventual decision made in Beograd.[54] But Ristich as foreign minister espoused the belief that, before resorting to war, he should first explore the avenues of diplomacy in the interest of Serbia's ambition, and in defending this policy against Prince Milan's readiness for action the roles of the preceding summer were now exchanged. The minister proposed as Serbia's next move the dispatch of a special agent to Constantinople to ask for the cession of the insurgent provinces in the name of the peaceful preservation of Ottoman territorial integrity. It was Ristich's idea that this agent should point out to the Turks that the bad administration of the two provinces was a constant threat to the unity of that empire of which Serbia was a loyal part and should argue that the difficulties confronting the sultan could be entirely eliminated if the monarch placed Bosnia under the administration of Serbia, and Hercegovina under that of Montenegro. Ristich held that after the Porte had rejected this fair proposal the principalities would have a legitimate ground for war. This scheme, whatever its merits, could not be tried. Milan was strongly opposed to it; and Prince Nicholas, who looked upon himself as an independent sovereign, refused to become a vassal of the sultan even at the price of all Hercegovina. Thus it developed in May that the door was closed to diplomacy.[55]

The war fever was materially increased during this same month by the acquisition of a distinguished military man in the person of the Russian General Chernaiev. General Chernaiev had earned for himself a great name in Central Asia; indeed his career as a conqueror had been so much more successful than his government at the time desired that he was given a gold sword and retired from the active list. With the army closed to him, Chernaiev became a militant journalist and, when the Hercegovinian revolt began, he con-

[54] Reports Nos. 57 and 61, Wrede to Andrássy, 6 and 10 May; *First Red Book*, Docs. Nos. 301 and 317, respectively.

[55] Trivanovitch, *Journal of Modern History*, III, 431.

ducted a pen campaign for the Slavic cause. Just as Prince Milan was installing his ministry of action the general appeared in Beograd in the capacity of a private journalist.[56] The prince received him promptly and warmly and invited him, according to the general's story, to inspect the military organization of Serbia. Within a few days Chernaiev accepted a commission in Milan's army—to the professed disapproval of the Russian consul and the Russian government.[57] "I dare not pass in silence," Kartzov reported to the tsar, "the disastrous effect this incident is producing in the already thin ranks of the partisans of peace. It threatens to entail consequences of greatest gravity by establishing in the minds of the naïve Serbian people the erroneous conviction that the moment for action has at last arrived since Russia herself has sent one of her generals to lead them to the field of battle."[58]

Toward the end of May the Serbian preparations for war were well advanced. Bonds were imposed on the taxpayers in accordance with estimated ability to buy;[59] a three months' moratorium was proclaimed on private debts;[60] by decree of the prince liberty of the press was suspended as a blow at the conservative opposition.[61] Purchase of horses had been completed; pontoon bridges were ready; the army was organized; all that remained was the last act of calling out the national militia. The military authorities professed to need only the prince's command to begin the war.[62]

In spite of rebuffs which they had already received from several sides the Serbs inaugurated new negotiations for foreign alliances as

[56] *The Times* (London), 11 May 1876, p. 5, col. 2.

[57] Political Report No. 48, White to Derby, 26 May; *Turkey No. 3 (1876)*, Doc. No. 336, incomplete. Report No. 227, Loftus to Derby, 24 May; *ibid.*, Doc. No. 319. Schweinitz, *Denkwürdigkeiten*, I, 332. Chernaiev left it to Ristich to inform the Russian consul that he had espoused the Serbian cause, and when Kartzov saw the general subsequently he informed him that relations between the two were henceforth broken. The general's own account of his going to Serbia was written in the form of a letter to his newspaper, the *Russki Mir*, dated Beograd, 16/28 May (*Turkey No. 3 [1876]*, inclosure in Doc. No. 492).

[58] Kartzov to Emperor Alexander II, 14/26 May, communicated by Shuvalov to Derby, 27 June; FO 65/953.

[59] Political Report No. 41, White to Derby, 13 May; *Turkey No. 3 (1876)*, Doc. No. 279. Political Report No. 43, White to Derby, 24 May; FO 78/2486.

[60] Report No. 58, White to Elliot, 24 May; *Turkey No. 3 (1876)*, inclosure in Doc. No. 334.

[61] Report No. 59, White to Elliot, 24 May; *ibid.*, inclosure in Doc. No. 335.

[62] Political Report No. 51, White to Derby, 29 May; *ibid.*, Doc. No. 337. Report No. 70, Wrede to Andrássy, 25 May; *First Red Book*, Doc. No. 367.

a part of their final preparations. In April Prince Milan's uncle went to Bucharest to enlist the co-operation of Rumania in the task of throwing off their common bond of subjection to Turkey. The calculating Hohenzollern who sat on Rumania's princely throne saw the dangers of Milan's course and warned him against it; but Milan would not, or could not, listen. He replied that he had been obliged to choose between revolution and war and that he had elected the latter. Prince Charles, however, continued to be unsympathetic and, to Milan's expressed displeasure, declared that he proposed to remain neutral.[63]

At the same time the Serbian government proposed to send a special agent to Athens to reopen negotiations there. The agent went, but the Greek ministers were still so opposed to a revival of the old alliance that they refused to have any formal communication with him.[64] Unwilling to accept defeat, the Serb agent went to Salonika and established contact there with a local Greek war committee formed after the murder of the French and German consuls. This committee had for its set purpose the preparation of an insurrection in the Greek part of European Turkey which would eventually, it was hoped, force war on the Athens government. The intriguers, among whom was an ex-premier of Greece, were distrustful of the Serbian agent but in the end capitulated to his offer of a subvention from Beograd and, apparently with the approval of the Greek premier of the day, engaged in a discussion of common operations.[65] Even so, however, when the new Serbian ministry canvassed the foreign outlook in mid-May its members had to recognize that in embarking on war with Turkey they could not count on aid from Rumania and Greece.[66]

For a time the prospects of an understanding with Montenegro seemed no better. The negotiations which had been undertaken by Alimpich at Cetinje in February and early March had made some progress[67] until, as has been noted, the energetic interference of

[63] *Aus dem Leben König Karls von Rumänien*, III, 15, 21–22.

[64] Report No. 69, Stuart to Derby, Athens, 8 April; FO 32/464. Report No. 447, Elliot to Derby, 1 May; FO 78/2458.

[65] Stojanović, *op. cit.*, pp. 91–92.

[66] Lascaris, *La Politique extérieure*, pp. 31–32.

[67] At the end of February Prince Nicholas had accepted the Serbian alliance proposal in principle but hesitated to sign on account of Austrian and Russian opposition (Tel., Wrede to Andrássy, 29 February; SA, Beograd, 1876).

Andrássy had impelled Prince Milan to recall his agent.[68] Standing in the way of a Serbo-Montenegrin partnership in war on Turkey was not only the threat of the Great Powers but also that rivalry between the two principalities which could not be long forgotten. Each continued to be jealous and suspicious of the other; Prince Nicholas was resentful of Serbia's previous behavior, and Prince Milan was mortally afraid that Montenegro might be given some undue advantage.[69] With the advent of May the little states were aping the large ones by indulging in a press campaign of recrimination,[70] but as the days went by the common determination on war again brought the princes together. At the end of the month a new treaty was ready for signature in Cetinje and Nicholas, while professing reluctance to go counter to Russian wishes, warned St. Petersburg that he could not refuse an understanding.[71]

THE SWORD IS DRAWN

Toward the end of May, when Count Andrássy was putting his hopes in Turkey's acceptance of his armistice program, the alarming crescendo of Serbian preparations boded only disaster for the long-delayed pacification. Yet the Austrian minister had no effective means of stopping Serbia's progress toward war. In March he had done all that he could reasonably do when he called upon Milan to halt preparations and when he threatened intervention. His action had not been successful, and now after two and a half months he recognized that the only way to influence Beograd was through a

[68] Tel. No. 22, Langenau to Andrássy, 19 March; *First Red Book*, Doc. No. 271. *The Times* (London), 21 March 1876, p. 5, col. 2.

[69] Political Report No. 19, White to Derby, 20 March; *Turkey No. 3 (1876)*, Doc. No. 87, incomplete. Stojanović, *op. cit.,* p. 93.

[70] *The Times* (London), 9 May 1876, p. 10, col. 2.

[71] "Schatokhine telegraphs from Ragusa yesterday for transmission to your Excellency: 'Prince Nicholas telegraphs: "I beg you inform your Government that Servia, from pressure of circumstances, perseveringly proposes to me an alliance for common action. Although not in a position to act against the national duty, by declining a preliminary agreement, I do not wish to negotiate with Servia without informing Russia, in order not to incur the reproaches for similar appeals in former negotiations."'" (Tel., Novikov to de Giers, 17/29 May, communicated by Shuvalov to Derby, 27 June; FO 65/953.)

"Schatokhine telegraphs from Ragusa yesterday: 'The Prince requests me to transmit the following reply to the Chancellor: "I have as yet decided nothing with Servia, and I shall prolong the negotiations, but a formal refusal to come to an understanding is not possible. . . . ."'" (Tel., Novikov to Gorchakov, 20 May/1 June; *ibid.*)

menace of occupation that he was willing to carry out. Under existing circumstances it was out of the question for the Dual Monarchy to take upon itself the onus and responsibility of such an action. The one possible means of restraining the Serbs seemed a new remonstrance from Russia; and on 27 May Andrássy addressed a telegraphic appeal for such to Prince Gorchakov, suggesting as an additional inducement that a successful restraint on Milan would discomfit Great Britain.[72]

The Russian chancellor was at the time interested chiefly in carrying on with the Berlin memorandum and in coercing Turkey into its acceptance. Consequently, until he knew what resolution was to be taken at the Sublime Porte he was reluctant to interfere in Serbia. Indeed it would seem that it was part of Russian policy to use the Serbian danger as a means of intimidating Turkey.[73] When the new Austrian appeal was presented to Gorchakov on the twenty-ninth he expressed a reluctance to act, justifying himself on the uncertainty of what the Turks would do and on the apparent uselessness of another démarche. Kartzov was absent from Beograd for a short time and the chancellor thought that if Milan still was master of Serbia he would await the return of the Russian agent before his final decision, and that if he were not master, no remonstrance whatever would be of value.[74] The Austrian ambassador carried the ques-

[72] Tel. No. 4, Andrássy to Károlyi in Ems, 27 May; SA, Varia Turquie I, 1875.

[73] The British agent in Beograd, in reporting a talk with his Russian colleague, wrote as follows: ". . . . In fact I gathered from his conversation for the first time a full confirmation of my invariable suspicions that Russia has been during the last ten months designedly making use of Servia first with a view to exercise a constant pressure on the Porte, and ultimately to make her act, either now or a few years hence, as a docile tool in upsetting the Turkish Empire by means of a general rising of the Christians both Slav and Greek.

"Mr. Kartzoff said that there is no reason to think that the time has come for a general conflagration in the East, but he insinuated at the same time that should the Porte continue to throw difficulties in the adoption of what he is pleased to call the moderate demands and recommendations of Prince Gortchakoff it is not unlikely that Servia will be allowed to commence hostilities, but he added that these were his private views, mentioned in strict confidence, and that he had no Instructions from his Government for his guidance since the interview at Berlin. . . . .

"Mr. Kartzoff did not attempt to deny to me that he had recommended the Prince to be fully prepared, in accordance with the means available in a country so backward in military organization, but he pleaded that the advice proffered by him had no object in view but the defence of Servia against the possiblity of a Turkish aggression. . . . ." (Political Report No. 50, White to Derby, 27 May; FO 78/2486.)

[74] Tels. Nos. 6 and 7, Károlyi to Andrássy, 29 May; SA, Varia Turquie I, 1875.

398 DIPLOMATIC HISTORY OF THE BALKAN CRISIS 1875–1878

tion the next day directly to Alexander II himself, and the tsar, as was his custom in impasses between Andrássy and Gorchakov, decided against his chancellor. By imperial order new warnings were sent at once to both Beograd and Cetinje.[75] Again the two princes were told in plain language not to abandon their neutrality and not to interfere with the Great Powers' efforts toward pacification.[76]

Prince Nicholas replied with his usual deference that he still did not propose to undertake any action, but went on to say that he felt obliged none the less to continue his war preparations in order to be ready for all eventualities. Milan was less facile. The Russian chargé d'affaires reported on 30 May: "The Prince passed over in entire silence the advice of the emperor and thereupon closed the audience."[77] The tsar, thoroughly annoyed at such action, sent Kartzov back to Beograd to reaffirm the imperial message. The consul claimed in his report to the tsar that he had quite abandoned his intimacy with Prince Milan since the installation of the new bellicose ministry and the Chernaiev episode,[78] but White, his British colleague, had no faith in a leopard's ability to change its spots:

[75] Tel. No. 8, Károlyi to Andrássy, 30 May; SA, Germany, 1876. The printed version (*First Red Book,* Doc. No. 383) was changed from French to German and materially altered. On 5 June, after the formal recognition of Murad V, the Russian chancellor wished to proceed immediately with the Berlin memorandum and he urged as a reason for Austrian support his own adherence to Andrássy's propositions. "Le prince Gortchakoff compte sur Votre Excellence," Károlyi telegraphed on that day. "Il vous a fait de grandes concessions à Berlin, où vous lui avez dit que vous le lui prévaudriez. Sur notre demande il vient, contraire à son impression primitive, d'exercer une nouvelle pression sur la Serbie. . . ." (Tel. No. 14; SA, Varia Turquie I, 1875.)

[76] Draft No. 288, Derby to Buchanan, 10 June; *Turkey No. 3 (1876),* Doc. No. 405. Report No. 250, Loftus to Derby, 1 June; *ibid.,* Doc. No. 408. In the same days the tsar vetoed an attempt of Serbia to float a loan in Moscow (Tel. No. 12, Károlyi to Andrássy, 3 June; SA, Germany, 1876).

[77] Tel. No. 11, Károlyi to Andrássy, 2 June; SA, Germany, 1876. The quotation is from Tel., Novikov to Gorchakov, 20 May/1 June; FO 65/953.

[78] "Mes rapports personnels avec le Prince Milan se sont bien rapidement ressentis des influences funestes qu'il subit depuis l'avènement au pouvoir du Ministère Omladiniste actuel. Les entrevues fréquentes, je dirai presque quotidiennes, que j'avais eues auparavant avec Son Altesse servaient peut-être de contrepoids aux effets que ne manquaient de produire sur son impressionable nature les suggestions alarmantes et bien calculées des hommes de son nouvel entourage. Ceux-ci auront, à coup sûr, cherché à agir sur sa pusillanimité pour le menacer du pretendant Karagéorgévitch, toujours aux portes de la Serbie, ainsi que d'une révolution intérieure, s'il hésitait encore à embrasser franchement leurs tendances.

"Je ne tardai pas à m'en apercevoir à ma dernière visite au palais. A cette occasion je dois reconnaître que sans doute il répugna au Prince d'imiter l'exemple

. . . . The message which Mr. Kartzoff brought here for the Prince on behalf of his Sovereign was according to Monsieur Novikoff a very precise and positive one, but from the effect it appears to have produced here, it is not improbable that it lost some of its force by transmission. . . . .

Owing to the intimacy of the relations existing between Prince Milan and my Russian Colleague, and to the advanced state of Servian preparations for action, it is quite impossible to form a correct estimate of the exact nature of their conversations, but I have reason to believe that they had by no means as peaceful a tendency as is represented.

The prince has not even promised any delay, but merely to try and do his best, and when the signal is given to commence, all parties will pretend to have been taken unawares by some untoward event, and Russia will pretend surprise.[79]

The effect of the warning was indeed that which White observed. In Serbia the war preparations went rapidly forward and Russia merely earned the embittered charge of treachery to the Slavic cause by her admonitions and her remonstrances at a time when it was too late to halt the impending action.[80]

Count Andrássy, as the instigator of the tsar's message, was extremely irritated at its lack of result. In these first days of June not only was the Beograd government deaf to warnings but Ristich was now openly saying that the only means whereby war could be avoided was through Turkey's assigning the administration of Bosnia and Hercegovina to Serbia in return for an increased tribute.[81] Such an arrangement was still beyond the pale of the tolerable from the Austro-Hungarian point of view, and Andrássy had to look to further preventive measures. He turned first to the Turks and proposed to them a twofold program: he advocated still his armistice and nego-

de son Ministre des Affaires Étrangères, en souillant sa bouche par le mensonge; aussi fut-il avec moi d'une réserve insolite. Dès lors je crus inopportune de continuer avec lui des relations d'amitié purement personnelle qui auraient pû, aux yeux du public, m'exposer à être moralement solidaire d'une ligne de conduite que je ne cesse pas de désapprouver.

"En conséquence, malgré quelques réproches que Son Altesse a déjà bien voulu me faire parvenir par l'entremise d'un de ses intimes, je ne l'ai plus revu depuis plus de 15 jours, et son dernier procédé dans l'affaire Chernaieff ne me semble guère de nature à m'encourager dans l'abandon de la froide réserve que j'ai cru adopter à son égard" (Kartzov to Emperor Alexander II, Beograd, 14/26 May, communicated by Shuvalov to Derby, 27 June; FO 65/953).

[79] Political Report No. 59, White to Derby, 8 June; *Turkey No. 3 (1876)*, Doc. No. 437, incomplete.

[80] Report No. 86, Wrede to Andrássy, 14 June; SA, Beograd, 1876.

[81] Report No. 79, Wrede to Andrássy, 30 May; *First Red Book*, Doc. No. 379, incomplete.

tiations with the insurgents as the best means of removing any plausible pretext for Serbian action, and he urged upon the Porte the concentration of all possible troops on the frontier in preparation for Milan's attack.[82] And as a last and not hopeful resort, on 3 June he telegraphed requests to London, Paris, and Rome for new attempts to discourage the Serbs from hostile action.[83]

The governments concerned promptly responded[84] and within the ensuing week all of the agents of the Great Powers, except that of Austria-Hungary, who declared a repetition of his former action incompatible with the dignity of his country, formally waited upon Ristich and Prince Milan in the interest of peace.[85] The replies made by minister and prince were no more reassuring than previous replies. Both expressed the usual sincere respect for the wishes of the Great Powers, but neither would make a commitment for the future except for assuring Kartzov that they would refrain as long as possible from a declaration of war.[86]

[82] Tel., Buchanan to Derby, 3 June; FO 7/871. In reporting a conversation between Andrássy and the Turkish agent in Budapest the British consul wrote: "It appears that His Excellency allowed his vexation at Servia's proceedings to appear very clearly by saying, 'Servia is determined to attack you; if you can beat her, so much the better for us'" (Report No. 89, Harriss-Gastrell to Buchanan, 5 June; FO 7/880).

[83] Tel., Andrássy to Beust, Kuefstein, and Wimpffen, 3 June; First Red Book, Doc. No. 400.

[84] Tel. No. 18, Kuefstein to Andrássy, 4 June; ibid., Doc. No. 405. Report No. 397, Lyons to Derby, 6 June; Turkey No. 3 (1876), Doc. No. 385. Tel. No. 62, Wimpffen to Andrássy, 3 June; First Red Book, Doc. No. 406. Tel. No. 40, Beust to Andrássy, 6 June; ibid., Doc. No. 416. Draft No. 278, Derby to Buchanan, 7 June; Turkey No. 3 (1876), Doc. No. 386. Draft No. 7, Derby to White, 6 June; ibid., Doc. No. 378.

[85] The failure of the Austrian consul to take part in the admonitions created some confusion, since the instructions to the British and Italian agents had directed them to support Wrede's action (Political Report No. 56, White to Derby, 7 June; Turkey No. 3 [1876], Doc. No. 435. Derby to Beust, 10 June; ibid., Doc. No. 403. Beust to Derby, 15 June; ibid., Doc. No. 452). But both White and Joannini proceeded independently. White, however, exploited his opportunity: "I observed to my Austrian colleague that such language had been frequently employed by me unofficially here, but that the opportunity of giving it in an official form had been denied us by the action taken at Belgrade by two of the three Imperial Powers [besides which one did not like intruding]" (ibid., Doc. No. 435; the clause in brackets is deleted in the printed form).

The co-operation of Germany was asked on 7 June (Tel. No. 22, Andrássy to Trauttenberg; First Red Book, Doc. No. 426) and two days later the German agent in Beograd received his instructions (Tel., Wrede to Andrássy, 10 June; ibid., Doc. No. 447).

[86] Tel., White to Derby, 8 June; Turkey No. 3 (1876), Doc. No. 396. One sentence in the printed version of this telegram was suppressed: "My opinion is that

Before these sterile discussions in Beograd had run their brief course it was decided at the Sublime Porte to call upon Milan and Nicholas for an explanation of the war measures which they continued in spite of all the princely assurances of peaceful intentions. On 6 June a telegram to that effect was dispatched to Serbia, and five days later a comparable address was sent to Montenegro.[87] Milan replied promptly. After charging, as everyone expected, Turkish violations of Serbian territory and after making his usual defense of his armaments, the prince revealed the reason why he was able to tell Kartzov that he would delay an attack: a special agent, he informed the grand vizier, was to be sent immediately to Constantinople. He would allegedly "afford the Sublime Porte all necessary explanations, and will have orders to come to an understanding with the imperial government through an exchange of frank and loyal explanations so that our relations might be placed on a basis of absolute confidence."[88] Ristich announced that the instructions for the delegate would be confidential,[89] but it was a transparent secret that the minister in sending an embassy was making a final peaceful attempt to acquire the coveted land of Bosnia.[90] Prince Nicholas in turn gave his conventional response about the burden placed on his small country by the revolt and about the suspicions and menaces which, in spite of his loyal neutrality, forced him to resort to measures of precaution.[91]

the Russian Government having urged Servia to these ruinous preparations now restrain her for some ulterior plan." Political Report No. 58, White to Derby, 8 June; *ibid.,* Doc. No. 436. Report No. 81, Wrede to Andrássy, 7 June; *First Red Book,* Doc. No. 429, incomplete. Report No. 83, Wrede to Andrássy, 8 June; *ibid.,* Doc. No. 440, incomplete. Tel., Wrede to Andrássy, 8 June; *ibid.,* Doc. No. 434. The original form of this last document has an additional sentence at the end: "Weder Fürst Milan noch Ristič gaben eine bestimmte friedliche Erklärung und versprachen nur so lange möglich sich der Aggression zu enthalten."

[87] Zichy to Andrássy, 7 June; *First Red Book,* Doc. No. 423. Rashid to Musurus, 8 June; *Turkey No. 3 (1876),* Doc. No. 401. The Grand Vizier to Prince Nicholas, 11 June; *First Red Book,* Doc. No. 494, and *Turkey No. 3 (1876),* Doc. No. 516.

[88] Prince Milan to the Grand Vizier, 7 June; *Turkey No. 3 (1876),* Doc. No. 426, and *First Red Book,* Doc. No. 456.

[89] Political Report No. 67, White to Derby, 17 June; FO 78/2486.

[90] Tel., Wrede to Andrássy, 15 June; *First Red Book,* Doc. No. 459.

[91] Prince Nicholas to the Grand Vizier; *ibid.,* Doc. No. 494 and *Turkey No. 3 (1876),* Doc. No. 516. The Turks in giving out Nicholas' response dated it 21 June, but Elliot in a dispatch of 15 June (Report No. 628; *ibid.,* Doc. No. 508) gives a summary.

In Constantinople the grand vizier expressed himself as satisfied with Prince Milan's response and on 12 June made a reply as noncommittal and conciliatory as that which the prince had sent to him.[92] The Turkish authorities were not overly concerned with the menace from Serbia; they anticipated that an army of 40,000 men could repulse any attempt of the Serbs to cross the frontier.[93] Paradoxically, the smaller of the principalities gave the Turks the greater concern. While the sultan's ministers were quite ready to enter the trial by combat with Serbia, they were in mid-June preparing to purchase Montenegrin neutrality by promises of territorial concessions.

The idea of buying off Prince Nicholas from his covert support of the insurrection had been in the air for several months. In early February a rumor, denied both at the Porte[94] and in Cetinje,[95] was circulated by the press that negotiations were being conducted by Ali Pasha.[96] The Russians had taken up the rumor and sounded out Andrássy. Their effort, however, had been fruitless; the Austrian minister had not only condemned the idea in talking with Novikov[97] but had warned the Turks against making such an unfortunate bargain.[98] In Constantinople Andrássy's view had been thoroughly endorsed, but official Russia had persisted in favoring the idea. Ignatiev had become an immediate convert after hearing the sympathetic views of a British consul[99] and in March had broached the

[92] The Grand Vizier to Prince Milan, 12 June; *Turkey No. 3 (1876)*, Doc. No. 426 and *First Red Book,* Doc. No. 456.

[93] Tel., Zichy to Andrássy, 11 June; *First Red Book,* Doc. No. 448. Report No. 612, Elliot to Derby, 12 June; *Turkey No. 3 (1876)*, Doc. No. 478.

[94] Tel. No. 31, Zichy to Andrássy, 8 February; SA, Varia Turquie I, 1875. Ali also denied the authenticity of the rumor (Report No. 31, Wassitch to Andrássy, 13 March; *ibid.*).

[95] *The Times* (London), 12 February 1876, p. 5, col. 5; 24 February, p. 8, col. 2.

[96] *Ibid.,* 4 February, 1876, p. 5, col. 1. The dispatch in question, dated Ragusa, 3 February, read: "Ali Pasha is said to have offered to the Prince of Montenegro to cede Sutorina, Bagagni, Zubi, Erzegevina, and Spitza, bordering on the Albania Sea, on condition of the Montenegrins entering into an arrangement to withdraw from the insurgent armies and to suspend military operations."

[97] Dispatch, Andrássy to Langenau, 9 February; SA, Russia, 1876.

[98] Tel. No. 9, Andrássy to Zichy, 8 February; SA, Varia Turquie I, 1875.

[99] Report No. 221, Elliot to Derby, 20 February; *Turkey No. 3 (1876)*, Doc. No. 37, incomplete. The consul in question was none other than Holmes, who had come to Constantinople to report in person to his superior. Report No. 12B, Langenau to Andrássy, 1/13 March; SA, Varia Turquie I, 1875.

subject directly to the sultan himself.[100] Gorchakov, in the same month, it will be recalled, had refused to admonish Prince Nicholas without accompanying the rebuke with the offer of a territorial reward for good conduct.[101] In early May the Turks had been persuaded to abandon their former hostility to the proposition and renew the frontier negotiations then several months in abeyance.[102] No less notable had been the change of opinion in Vienna. After continuing to reiterate his objections until early May,[103] Andrássy had suddenly changed his mind and recommended to Rashid that he begin bargaining with Nicholas immediately.[104] By June there had been a compa-

[100] Report No. 297, Elliot to Derby, 20 March; *Turkey No. 3 (1876)*, Doc. No. 92. Ignatiev's attitude toward Montenegro was described by Elliot on 29 February (Report No. 250; FO 78/2456) as follows:

"The language held by General Ignatiew not only to his colleagues but to persons not likely to abstain from repeating it, leads to the certain conclusion that as far as depends upon him, he will endeavour to frustrate the attempts at pacification, unless concessions are made to Montenegro.

"The General's position and proceedings are so peculiar that it is impossible to form a confident opinion as to the extent to which he acts with the concurrence of his Government.

"My own impression is that he is allowed very great latitude and that his Government are not informed, and do not wish to be informed, of much that he does.

"He is in constant direct personal communication with the Prince of Montenegro, and when what he wishes does not agree with what is said from St. Petersburg, the Prince no doubt believes that, if the latter conveys the ostensible policy of Russia, her real policy is to be learnt from the Ambassador at Constantinople.

"The collapse of the Insurrection without benefit to Montenegro would be a severe, though probably momentary, blow to the Russian influence, but a still greater one to that of General Ignatiew himself, and, if the Emperor has determined loyally to support the present pacific efforts of Austria, his Ambassador is anxious that it should be known that he personally objects to the course.

"He wishes that the efforts of the Powers to induce the Insurgents to abandon the struggle should be made conditional on the cession to Montenegro of the Turkish districts which it covets.

"The Porte will not hear of this being even discussed at present; and after the acceptance of the Austrian proposals upon the understanding that the Powers would discourage the continuance of the Insurrection, a cession of territory could not with any decency be pressed upon its acceptance as the condition upon which their good will was to be obtained."

[101] Tel. No. 27 and Report No. 18AC, Langenau to Andrássy, 10 and 11 April, respectively; SA, Varia Turquie I, 1875.

[102] Tel. No. 112, Zichy to Andrássy, 6 May; *First Red Book*, Doc. No. 296, incomplete.

[103] Reports Nos. 156, 232, and 256, Buchanan to Derby, 23 March, 23 April, and 2 May; *Turkey No. 3 (1876)*, Docs. Nos. 82, 167, and 212, respectively. In the last of these reports Buchanan stated: ". . . . there appears to be little probability of his ever being disposed to recommend such a measure to the Porte. . . . ."

[104] Tel. No. 46, Andrássy to Zichy, 7 May; *First Red Book*, Doc. No. 305, incomplete. This same advice was reiterated with emphasis at the end of the month

rable swing of British opinion. Elliot, inclined in February to be sympathetic toward the proposition until he learned Turkish feeling,[105] had launched into a protracted campaign of opposition in spite of the views of the British consul who knew most about the insurrection[106] and in spite of Lord Derby's hesitant belief in April that there might be virtue in the plan.[107] But at the end of May, Elliot, now re-converted, had taken up with the grand vizier the possibility of a "direct understanding with the Prince of Montenegro without the intervention of any foreign power,"[108] and by the middle of June had arranged a scheme for negotiations to grow out of Prince Nicholas' congratulations to the new sultan.[109] Elliot's plan, however, had

---

when the dangers of a Serbian declaration of war had seriously increased (Tel. No. 57, Andrássy to Zichy, 29 May; ibid., Doc. No. 377, incomplete).

[105] Report No. 195, Elliot to Derby, 14 February; Turkey No. 3 (1876), Doc. No. 12, incomplete.

[106] The arguments given in the printed form of Elliot's report (No. 221) of 20 February (ibid., Doc. No. 37) are not the ambassador's, but those given by Holmes to Ignatiev. Elliot's own views were suppressed: "I remarked that the suggestion was far from being a new one, having often been brought forward before, but at this moment I did not think it was possible to expect that the Turkish Government would come forward to make a gift of territory to the Prince of whom they had so much reason to complain. . . . ."

The principal disadvantage which Elliot saw in an arrangement by the terms of which Montenegro would become an acknowledged vassal of the sultan was the restriction that a European guaranty would place on Turkish military operations against the Montenegrins: "Nothing could be said against a simple recognition of the Suzerainty of the Sultan, but if the intention is to propose to put the Principality in the same position as the other vassal States, under a guarantee of the six Powers, Her Majesty's Government might not regard it with equal favour.

"Against any advantage to be expected from an arrangement which should partially withdraw Montenegro from the exclusive Protectorate of Russia must be placed the probability that a European guarantee of its autonomy, such as is enjoyed by Servia and Roumania, would operate as an encouragement to acts which Turkey would be debarred from resenting except after concert with all the Powers. . . . ." (Report No. 222, Elliot to Derby, 20 February; ibid., Doc. No. 38. The second of the above-quoted paragraphs was deleted from the printed text.) Elliot in arguing to Zichy against a cession to Nicholas played upon his Austrian colleague's helpless suspicions of Ignatiev; he assured Zichy that if an arrangement were made all the credit for it would be given to Ignatiev and his government (Report No. 253, Elliot to Derby, 2 March; ibid., Doc. No. 61, incomplete).

[107] Draft No. 169, Derby to Buchanan, 26 April; ibid., Doc. No. 166.

[108] Report No. 541, Elliot to Derby, 27 May; ibid., Doc. No. 374.

[109] Tel. and Report No. 621, Elliot to Derby, 14 June (FO 78/2459): "If the Prince of Montenegro could be induced to follow the example of the Prince of Servia and send some one to Constantinople to congratulate the Sultan, great benefit would be likely to result from it. The Porte does not appear altogether indisposed to make some concessions to Montenegro but says naturally that it cannot make the first overtures."

not appealed to Andrássy, who feared that the conflict between Montenegro and Turkey over independence would offer an insuperable barrier to successful discussions.[110] The Austrian minister had come to the conclusion that a better means of separating Serbia and Montenegro would be an offer from the grand vizier to discuss sympathetically with Prince Nicholas the question of frontiers after Montenegro had aided in restoring tranquillity. On 15 June Andrássy had taken up his plan with a Montenegrin agent in Vienna, and four days later had sent it to London for support and to Constantinople for action.[111] The next day he had followed his first suggestion to the Porte with a warning that if Serbia and Montenegro got the upper hand a return to status quo would be impossible,[112] and two days later had again telegraphed that, although Serbia's action made war seem inevitable, there still might be hope of winning Prince Nicholas for peace.[113] Elliot had then abandoned his first proposal and endorsed the Andrássy suggestion.[114]

Hence it came about that, advised by the Austrian and British and French[115] ambassadors, the grand vizier on 25 June utilized a reply to Prince Nicholas' recent telegram to make an attempt to separate Montenegro and Serbia. But in characteristic manner the grand vizier reduced his overture to minimum proportions. Declar-

[110] Tel. and Report No. 409, Buchanan to Derby, 18 June; FO 7/871.

[111] Tel., Andrássy to Zichy, 15 June; SA, Varia Turquie I, 1875. Tel. No. 20, Andrássy to Beust, 19 June; SA, London, 1876. Tel. No. 74, Andrássy to Zichy, 19 June; SA, Varia Turquie I, 1875.

[112] Tel. No. 76, Andrássy to Zichy, 20 June; SA, Turkey, 1876.

[113] Tel. No. 78, Andrássy to Zichy, 22 June; ibid.

[114] Tel. and Report No. 657, Elliot to Derby, 23 June; FO 78/2459. Report No. 660, Elliot to Derby, 24 June; Turkey No. 3 (1876), Doc. No. 528. Elliot's home government had not ventured at the time beyond accepting in principle the Austrian recommendation and pointing out "that the language of Count Andrassy's communication to Count Zichy was extremely vague as to the nature and the extent of the concessions which it was suggested that the Porte should make in return for the Prince's assistance, and observed that the Porte might hesitate to commit itself without a clearer conception of the sacrifices which it might be called upon to incur" (Draft No. 308, Derby to Buchanan, Turkey No. 3 [1876], Doc. No. 484). When the foreign office learned by telegraph, however, of Elliot's advice to the Porte, his action was approved (Draft No. 310, Derby to Buchanan, 24 June; ibid., Doc. No. 488).

[115] The Duc Decazes had come out in April for a territorial cession to Montenegro (Decazes to Bourgoing, 28 April; First Yellow Book, p. 122. Draft No. 444, Derby to Adams, 3 May; Turkey No. 3 [1876], Doc. No. 192), and Bourgoing had subsequently put the proposal to the Turkish ministers (Report No. 448, Lyons to Derby, 23 June; Turkey No. 3 [1876], Doc. No. 486, incomplete).

ing himself persuaded that Mukhtar Pasha's latest march into Niksich without opposition was a proof of "the loyal sentiments of your Highness," he offered assurance that the sultan would "take into consideration in fitting time and season the line of conduct" followed by the prince.[116] This offer was essentially what Andrássy had suggested—but since it was an offer coming from the Turks it could not be taken very seriously in Cetinje.

Regardless of the merits of the proposal, however, events in Serbia had already made it useless. The representations of the various foreign agents in Beograd had gone entirely unheeded and the final military arrangements had been pushed forward. Before the middle of June various militia units had been called out and sent to the frontier. The treasury was already empty and money from the forced loan was coming in very slowly, but the Serbian government showed no signs of hesitating in its course.[117] On the twenty-first, mobilization orders went out for all the first-class militia[118] and Ristich confessed that the proposed mission to Constantinople would probably not be sent, since the plan had not been well received at the Porte.[119] Convinced that the threat of military action was not going to intimidate the sultan into delivering over Bosnia and Hercegovina, and equally convinced that the best way to deal with Russian opposition was to present Russia with a *fait accompli,* the Serbian foreign minister and his fellow members of the government decided on 22

---

[116] The Grand Vizier to the Prince of Montenegro, 25 June; *First Red Book,* Doc. No. 494 and *Turkey No. 3 (1876),* Doc. No. 516.

[117] Report No. 85, Wrede to Andrássy, 14 June; *First Red Book,* Doc. No. 458. Political Report No. 64, White to Derby, 12 June; *Turkey No. 3 (1876),* Doc. No. 440, incomplete. In the suppressed part of this dispatch the British consul wrote:
"The advice and counsels of the different foreign Representatives have hitherto gone unheeded, and the sincerity of the Russian recommendations can well be doubted; the Prince has been so artfully drawn into a net by the action of the Slavophil Agents and of the Omladina combined with the unfortunately unadvised means adopted by Austria to deter him from action and the occasionally offensive language employed by Agents of that Power, that it is much to be feared that he is no longer a free agent, and that matters have got beyond his control so that he cannot, even if he would, recede unless under positive orders from Russia and such as would be manifest to all his people and to the whole world. . . . . No very long delay is therefore possible and the financial situation must ere long inspire some desperate resolution, or in the absence of Foreign aid, a confession that the resources of the Country have been miscalculated."

[118] Tel., Wrede to Andrássy, 21 June; *First Red Book,* Doc. No. 479.

[119] Tel., Wrede to Andrássy, 21 June; *ibid.,* Doc. No. 478.

June that the time had come for action.[120] On that day war was declared—in an eloquent euphemism. The prince addressed a long letter
to the grand vizier, which, after disjointedly describing the menace of Turkish troops and frontier violations and the long-standing
grievances of the people of Bosnia and Hercegovina, announced that
Milan had found himself obliged "to examine the means whereby I
might be able to second the Porte in its efforts to put an end to this
state of affairs." The letter went on to explain that that means "consists of placing the forces of Serbia at the service of the common
interests of the empire and of the principality"—that is, an occupation of the insurgent provinces in the name of the tranquillity and
integrity of the Ottoman Empire. In terminating his announcement
Prince Milan called upon the grand vizier "to facilitate the mission
which I am undertaking by giving orders to the imperial authorities
to send to their homes the bands of pillagers and by enjoining upon
the imperial troops not to obstruct my efforts in order that I might
profess proudly, as I desire, the principle of the maintenance of the
empire."[121]

On the evening of the twenty-sixth a final theatrical performance
took place in Beograd. The play was a stirring national drama entitled "The Janissary." The scene was laid in those early times in
which the people of Serbia had had to pay tribute of their most
promising sons for the sultan's select corps and the story was an account of the sufferings inflicted upon a virtuous Serb family by
Turks of unspeakable wickedness, sufferings which in the end were
expiated by the massacre of the oppressors. As the curtain went
down, one attendant reported, "all reserve was thrown away by a

[120] In the following year Ristich wrote a pamphlet in defense of the declaration
of war. In it he stated his belief that Serbia's cause would be advanced regardless
of the outcome of military operations. Indeed, he apparently believed that a defeat
might do Serbia more eventual good than victory, since Serbia in defeat would inevitably provoke Russian sympathies and Russian sympathies in turn would force
official intervention (Trivanovitch, *Journal of Modern History*, III, 432, note 35).

On 1 July the British ambassador received a letter written by an unnamed correspondent, dated Beograd, 27 June. It read in part as follows: "I had an interview
today with M. Ristich who appeared less preoccupied than a fortnight ago. He still
has the idea that the Porte, seeing Serbia and Montenegro prepared to enter into
campaign, will cede at the last moment and make territorial concessions. . . . . If
the Porte does not give way at the last moment war will commence on 5 July"
(Report No. 423, Buchanan to Derby, 1 July; FO 7/872).

[121] The Prince of Serbia to the Grand Vizier, 10/22 June; *First Red Book*,
annex to Doc. No. 512; *First Green Book*, annex to Doc. No. CCXXXI; and *First
Yellow Book*, pp. 160–64.

simultaneous yell so full of the electricity of passion that hot and cold thrills of sympathy overran even the quietest of the onlookers."[122]

On the twenty-ninth Milan and his staff went to the headquarters of the army.[123] The next day the prince's war manifesto appeared. It was, of course, a Serbian version of the impassioned theme of high and virtuous resolution with which the current world is so familiar— the eternal trial by combat between an iniquitous enemy on the one hand and an innocent and outraged people on the other:

. . . . Serb soldiers, we go into this war driven not by hatred and revenge but by the imperative needs of ourselves and of our brothers, by the needs of general peace. Proud of the mission of civilization and freedom which has been given to you in the East by God's dispensation, go confidently and bravely forward, raising your arms only against those who oppose you. . . . .

Our movement is purely national. This movement must be closed to the elements of social revolution and of religious fanaticism. We carry with us no desire for revolution, no fire and destruction, only justice, order and security. . . . .

Forward then, my proud heroes, in the name of Almighty God the righteous father of all peoples, forward in the name of justice, freedom, and civilization.[124]

On 2 July Serbian troops crossed the frontier,[125] embittered against Austrian as well as Turk[126] and firm in their belief that mighty Russia would not abandon them.[127]

On the same day the prince of Montenegro, after a formal declaration of war, sent his army into action.[128]

Thus it came about that two small and backward principalities flaunted the wishes of the Great Powers of Europe and set out to satisfy their ambitions by the time-hallowed means of war.

---

[122] *The New York Times,* 22 July 1876, p. 1, cols. 1–2.

[123] Tel., White to Derby, 29 June; FO 78/2486.

[124] *First Red Book,* Doc. No. 528. *Turkey No. 3 (1876),* inclosure in Doc. No. 532. *British and Foreign State Papers,* 67: 1238–41. *First Green Book,* annex to Doc. No. CCXXXIII.

[125] Tel. and Report No. 696, Elliot to Derby, 2 July; FO 78/2460. Tel., Wrede to Andrássy, 2 July; *First Red Book,* Doc. No. 515.

[126] Report No. 101, Wrede to Andrássy, 1 July; *ibid.,* Doc. No. 512.

[127] Report No. 95, Wrede to Andrássy, 28 June; SA, Beograd, 1876.

[128] The Prince of Montenegro to the Grand Vizier, 2 July; *First Yellow Book,* pp. 164–66; *First Green Book,* annex to Doc. No. CCXL; Hertslet, *Map of Europe by Treaty,* IV, Doc. No. 464.

THE GREAT POWERS AND NON-INTERVENTION

The Russian government, during a year of developing Balkan crisis, had remained loyal to the alliance with Austria and had honestly sought to effect the pacification of Bosnia and Hercegovina without opening the door to the uncertainties of the old Eastern question. At the same time, the Russian government through its agents had given its benedictions to Serbian and Montenegrin war preparations, partly as a means of intimidating the Turks into making acceptable concessions and partly in the interest of having the principalities ready in case diplomacy should fail. In a world in which small states know that they can present great powers with *faits accomplis* and have a fairly good chance of success, the Russian policy of encouraging the two Slavic principalities to sharpen their swords was at best a dangerous one. In June as the final touches were given to the edges of the swords it became apparent that the policy had been a fatal one—fatal at least to pacification. At the last moment the tsar and his chancellor saw only one way to save peace, and that was through British support for Bosnian autonomy before Serbia and Montenegro plunged into war. In the last days of June Kartzov was again ordered to protest in Beograd, and appeals were sent to London for an immediate decision.[129]

Fearing that the Turks might precipitate the impending war by an attack, Gorchakov instructed Ignatiev to remind the Porte of the provisions of the Paris treaty which proscribed an invasion of Serbia[130] and he proposed to the European capitals that, in case the Turks did commit an act of aggression, the Great Powers should protest on the basis of treaty right. The chancellor was unwilling, however, to follow the same procedure in the case of the Serbo-Montenegrin aggression which, in late June, seemed more certain. It was one thing to attempt to restrain the principalities from entering upon a war but quite another to deprive them through diplomatic

[129] *Note verbale* of Novikov based on Tel., Gorchakov to Novikov, 14/26 June; SA, Russia, 1876. Gorchakov to Shuvalov, 15/27 June, 15/27 June, 16/28 June; *Slavonic Review*, III, 680–81, Docs. Nos. 53, 54, and 56, respectively.

[130] Report No. 669, Elliot to Derby, 26 June; FO 78/2460: ". . . . A Dragoman was sent by General Ignatiew to inform His Excellency [Safvet Pasha] that in consequence of the menacing attitude adopted towards Servia he had been instructed by Prince Gortchakow to remind the Porte of the provisions of the Treaty of Paris under which an armed intervention in the Principality cannot take place without a previous understanding with the Guaranteeing Powers. . . . ."

interference of the gains they might be able to win once the struggle had begun. Russian official policy could only wish advantages for them and Russian public opinion was pledged in advance to their cause. After the demoralized troops of Turkey had fought in vain during the greater part of a year to put down a small rebellion, it was easy for the Russian mind to anticipate certain defeat for Ottoman arms. Its interest, therefore, suggested allowing the contestants to settle their old scores for themselves; and, to that end, Gorchakov on the eve of the war proposed to Europe a declaration of absolute non-intervention.[131]

The Russian proposal created a difficult problem for Italy. As had been the case for a year, Italy was impotent in the face of the three united empires—but none the less ambitious and apprehensive. Austro-Italian relations, always potentially bad, had been improved by Emperor Francis Joseph's visit to King Victor Emmanuel in the spring of 1875, but in February of the next year irredentist agitation raised its head again and attempts were made to send volunteers into the insurgent area. Many of these foreign recruits were arrested by the Austrian authorities, with the result that the old animosities revived. In June Italy commemorated the league of the Lombard com-

---

[131] Tel., Gorchakov to Shuvalov, 15/27 June; *Slavonic Review*, III, 680, Doc. No. 54. The British ambassador in St. Petersburg summed up his view of the Russian outlook on 21 June in these words: "I am persuaded that Russia is most anxious to prevent the present insurrection from extending and assuming larger proportions, and that, should such be the case, Russia will not interfere herself, nor will she permit any other foreign Power to interfere.

"She will advocate the principle of non-intervention, and will be satisfied to let the parties fight it out, in the confident hope that the Christian element will come out victorious.

"Russia will not draw the sword herself, but she will withdraw the restraint she has hitherto exercised on Servia and Montenegro which has hitherto been to the advantage of Turkey. I am inclined to believe that this course is the one which would be most suitable to her own views and most in harmony with the national feeling, if she could be assured, that the conflagration would not extend beyond certain limits—and that it would cause no danger to the general peace of Europe.

"Russia is in no way prepared for war, and will not willingly be drawn into War: on the other hand she has interests which cannot be safely sacrificed even to her necessity for peace. Her Alliance with Austria is strictly based on the maintenance of the Status quo in the east, and it remains to be seen how far the interests of Austria and Russia could harmonize, if the present Status quo should be changed. A mistrust of Austria has already shewn itself in certain quarters here—even in official circles; but the perfect confidence of the two Emperors is unshaken, and so long as this continues the two Governments will continue to act in harmony." (Report No. 281, Loftus to Derby, 21 June; *Turkey No. 3 [1876]*, Doc. No. 494, incomplete.)

munes and the stimulated patriotism of the kingdom found a focal point in hostility to the old northern foe.[132] The ministers in Rome were increasingly inclined to share the attitude of the public, because the persisting disturbance to the east of the Adriatic gave ever greater promise of Austrian intervention. With ambitions of their own in that region, the Italians could not contemplate with any pleasure the appearance of Francis Joseph's troops in the hinterland of Dalmatia and in Albania. The foreign minister by June had come to the conclusion that Italy's best interests could be served—and the future least engaged—by some form of autonomy for Bosnia and Hercegovina. He recognized that the peculiar conditions obtaining in those provinces made the success of such an arrangement problematical, but

to one thing, IIis Excellency said, the Italian Government would be always opposed; viz., the creation of a Slav state *independent* of the Porte. Such a state if composed of Bosnia and Herzegovina would eventually be swallowed up by Austria; or if united with Servia and Montenegro would become dependent on Russia. In either case it would be a bone of contention between those two Powers, consequently a constant menace to the peace of Europe. In either case it would tend to the extension of the power of Austria or Russia along the shores of the Adriatic and this would be a result which would affect the most important interests of Italy.

In conclusion M. Melegari said that the fundamental policy of the Italian Government in regard to the East was the maintenance of the Turkish Empire, and provided this was upheld it did not very much matter to the Italian Government by what measures the Sultan secured the allegiance of his subjects. . . . .[133]

On 26 June the Russian proposal in anticipation of war was presented in Rome. The Austrian agent observed that there was little desire for a formal and binding declaration of non-intervention,[134] and, indeed, after a week of deliberation Melegari and his colleagues in the cabinet did not subscribe fully to the tsar's proposition. The minister on 3 July wrote to St. Petersburg "that the policy of Italy, in so far as we are concerned and in the present circumstances could only be one thing—non-intervention."[135] In anticipation, however, that those "present circumstances" might change, officers of the Ital-

---

[132] *The Memoirs of Francesco Crispi* (London, 1912–1914), II, 3–4.

[133] Report No. 229, Paget to Derby, Rome, 16 June; FO 45/286. Derby to Paget, 1 June; *Turkey No. 3 (1876)*, Doc. No. 332.

[134] Tel. No. 80, Wimpffen to Andrássy, 1 July; *First Red Book,* Doc. No. 511.

[135] Melegari to Nigra, 3 July; *First Green Book,* Doc. No. CCXXV.

ian general staff were soon exploring Albania and warships were sounding the waters along the coast.[136]

For the French as well as for the Italians the war between the principalities and Turkey was pregnant with future complications. The Duc Decazes responded affirmatively to the Russian proposal of non-intervention,[137] but the problem of French policy could not be disposed of so easily. How to hold in check a bloodthirsty Bismarck remained always the major anxiety of France and the best means to that end seemed to be the continuation of peace through the European concert. To the French way of thinking the Anglo-Russian interference in Berlin a year before had forestalled a return of the German army and the continuation of Anglo-Russian co-operation was manifestly a gauge of French security. Peace between Russia and Austria appeared equally desirable lest the scheming Iron Chancellor step in and annex the German part of the Dual Monarchy and thereby send France forever to the ranks of the secondary powers. Popular feeling was opposed to an alliance with any one country, and there was growing up a conviction that it had not been profitable to place so much hope in Russia as the French had done since 1870. But on one point there was no doubt: for the Paris officials British support continued to be a prime concern.[138]

---

[136] *Andrássy*, II, 386, note 1.

[137] Report No. 40AC, Kuefstein to Andrássy, 3 July; SA, France, 1876.

[138] Report No. 564, Lyons to Derby, Paris, 20 July; FO 27/2166: "The state of affairs in Turkey continues to cause great alarm in France. It is not, however, respecting the solution of the Eastern Question properly so-called, that anxiety is felt in this Country. The distribution of territory and the balance of influence in the Levant are not matters which deeply interest Frenchmen at this moment. They believe not merely French interests and French influence in the East, but the safety of France herself to be at stake.

"They are convinced that Prince Bismarck, in whom they personify all that is ambitious in Germany, and all that is hostile to France, is determined that France shall not restore her strength, and resume her high place in Europe, if he can prevent it. They conceive that he is on the watch for a favourable opportunity of attacking France before she has recovered from the effects of the last war. They perhaps undervalue the security which they derive from the manifest disinclination of the great body of German People to engage in a new contest. They are indeed nervously anxious that the French Government should not repeat the error of 1870, and itself provoke the enmity of Germany; but they seem to entertain little doubt that if Prince Bismarck thought the time for a new war was come, he would find the means of arousing the war spirit and again uniting Germany in hostility to France.

"Such being the sentiments prevalent in France, it is natural that the safety of the Country should be held to depend mainly upon the influence over Germany ex-

In response to these considerations the French foreign minister
had been laboring earnestly since the middle of May to bring England back into the European concert. He had tried first to secure
some agreement on a modified program in Turkey, but that had

erted in favour of peace by Foreign Powers. The French firmly believe that it was
the united action of England and Russia at Berlin which alone preserved France
from invasion last year. The special object of their fears now is that the complications in the East may produce a disagreement between England and Russia, which
may neutralize the influence of those Powers in favour of peace, or even range one
or the other of them on the opposite side.

"Hardly less apprehension is felt, lest the Eastern Question should produce a
breach between Russia and Austria. The French imagine that to embroil Austria
and Russia in the East might very well accord with the designs which they persist
in attributing to Prince Bismarck. By this means he might, they conceive, carry
into effect the plans for annexing the German Provinces of Austria to the German
Empire; and for completing the destruction of France as a Great Power.

"The Duc Decazes has in general conducted the Foreign Affairs of the country
in accordance with the public sentiment, and has shown great tact and judgment in
avoiding dangerous discussions, without apparently lowering the dignity of France.
He has, however, been charged lately with too decided a predilection for Russia, and
too restless a desire to play a conspicuous part in the affairs of Europe.

"In fact the general feeling is that France should carefully avoid entangling herself in a close and separate alliance with any one Power, lest by doing so she should
promote an opposite alliance between some other equally important Power and Germany. Moreover, the hopes that were fixed so entirely upon Russia for some time
after the War, have very much subsided in France, since it has become more and
more apparent that, at least during the lives of the Emperors William and Alexander, a breach between Germany and Russia is little to be expected. Public opinion
has in consequence turned very considerably towards England, and it would certainly not sanction at this moment any union with Russia so close as to give umbrage
to English feelings or to interfere with obtaining English support for France in
case of need.

"That the Duc Decazes has been, and is, extremely desirous of standing well
with Russia is certain; and it may perhaps be doubted whether he has not been on
some occasions over active, and too ready to try and play the part of mediator between Governments who were more likely to come to an understanding by direct
communication with each other.

"But, however this may be, it is certain that his activity has been directed
towards good objects., He has earnestly endeavoured to circumscribe the troubles in
Turkey; to promote a good understanding between all the Great Powers, and especially between England and Russia; to avoid giving offense to Germany, and above
all to contribute to the maintenance of the peace of Europe.

"And whether or no he has always confined himself within the limits which
public opinion, and, it may be added, prudence prescribe in the present state of
France, much allowance is to be made for the constant anxiety under which he has
laboured. Calmness and abstinence from action are not easy, on the part of a Minister for Foreign Affairs, who is under the impression that an error or an omission
on his part may expose his Country to an invasion which she has but small means
of resisting. . . . ."

failed. Then, on 23 June, he had launched a new plan for unanimity in the form of a new collective warning to Serbia,[139] and that scheme also had failed.[140] Before this second maneuver was demonstrably futile Decazes received Gorchakov's proposed declaration of non-intervention, and he immediately seized on it as the most promising means to his desired end. Only two weeks before the war began, Disraeli and Derby had made a somewhat comparable suggestion in their discussions with Shuvalov. The policy of bleeding advanced by the prime minister, it will be recalled, provided for a hands-off policy unless the insurgents were defeated. Decazes now attempted to capitalize this stand by proposing to London that all the powers, accepting the British views, pledge themselves to unselfish and concerted efforts for the general peace. Lord Derby could of course agree to such words without prejudicing anything, and he did so. Decazes then busied himself with attempting to secure other ratifications; but he soon ran into a snag—the unwillingness of Austria to be indifferent to the fate of Bosnia.[141] This third attempt to unite the powers was hardly launched before his zeal to arrange for all contingencies led Decazes into secret discussions with Vienna at utter variance with his program of non-intervention. On 8 July he suggested to the Austrian ambassador that the time had arrived to agree on a peaceful settlement that would provide for either a Turkish victory or a Turkish defeat. In case of victory he proposed, as before, a regime for Bosnia comparable to that set up in Crete. In case of defeat he favored agreement on autonomy for the insurgent area. Decazes went on to say that he looked on an Austrian occupation as the best solution of the problem; but, knowing Andrássy's desire to plead disinterestedness, he advanced the idea that autonomy would be a good

---

[139] Report No. 448, Lyons to Derby, 23 June; *Turkey No. 3 (1876)*, Doc. No. 486.

[140] All of the powers responded favorably to this suggestion except Russia, whose reply had not reached Paris when the war began (Report No. 39B, Kuefstein to Andrássy, 1 July; SA, France, 1876 and Report No. 40AB, Kuefstein to Andrássy, 3 July; *ibid.*). The British acquiescence was contingent: ". . . . if the other Powers, whose influence over Servia is so apparent, are also ready to do so, and to show the reality of their sentiments by firmly discouraging the incentives to hostile measures against Turkey, which Servia is receiving from foreign agitators and agents of Slav Committees" (Draft No. 645, Derby to Lyons, 27 June; *Turkey No. 3 [1876]*, Doc. No. 496, and Report No. 478, Lyons to Derby, 29 June; *ibid.*, Doc. No. 520).

[141] Decazes to Le Flô, 6 July; *Documents français*, II, Doc. No. 71. Report No. 40AB, Kuefstein to Andrássy, 3 July; SA, France, 1876.

transition to that final result.[142] In a subsequent discussion the French minister, disappointed that he had received no confidential communications and solicitous for the good-will of Austria, returned to his proposal for autonomy and hinted that he would support the appointment of a member of the Habsburg family as head of the new principality.[143]

In the chamber of deputies Decazes insisted that France, intent on internal recovery, was taking no active role other than that of promoting understanding, and he promised that neither the word nor the honor nor the interests of France would be compromised.[144]

In Berlin, as in Paris, the Russian proposal of non-intervention was accepted without hesitation. But realism prevailed in the Wilhelmstrasse, and the German foreign office, in order to avoid future

[142] Report No. 42, Kuefstein to Andrássy, Paris, 8 July; SA, France, 1876. The Austrian representative reported Decazes' words as follows: ". . . . Je reconnais parfaitement la situation difficile qui vous est faite. Vous ne pourrez jamais permettre la constitution d'un grand état serbe à vos frontières; mais l'autonomie de la Bosnie, sous la suzeraineté de la Porte, dans des conditions qui seraient encore à déterminer vous créerait moins d'embarras que l'annexion de la Bosnie à la Serbie.

"La meilleure solution eût été, à mon avis, l'occupation immédiate de la Bosnie par l'Autriche-Hongrie. Si une pareille décision avait pu sembler utile au gouvernement impériale et royal, celui-ci eût été assuré de notre assentiment et de notre appui le plus sympathique. Mais je comprends que dans ce genre de choses on préfère plaider le désintéressement, et peut-être l'autonomie de la Bosnie pourra-t-elle mieux servir de transition pour arriver au même résultat."

[143] Report No. 46 (secret), Wimpffen to Andrássy, 19 July; ibid. "Dans un entretien confidentiel le duc Decazes me dit qu'il a appris dans le temps par l'Empereur Guillaume qui en avait parlé à Mr. de Gontaut-Biron que nous étions contraires à l'annexion de la Bosnie à la monarchie austro-hongroise et que depuis il a su par la voie de Londres que nous nous opposions à l'annexion de la Bosnie à la Serbie.

"A ces paroles qui ressemblaient à des regrets de n'avoir reçu ces communications que par des voies indirectes le duc Decazes rattacha le désir exprimé dans ma dépêche d'aujourd'hui de pouvoir, le cas écheant, s'entendre directement avec nous. Il ajouta qu'il comprenait parfaitement que nous étions contraires à tous les projets d'annexion; aussi il espère que dans certaines éventualités Votre Excellence consentirait à l'autonomie de la Bosnie. A ma question, ce qu'il entendait par cette autonomie, il me répondit qu'il pouvait s'agir d'ériger la Bosnie en voyvodinat et il m'insinua qu'on pourrait peut-être lui donner comme chef un prince de la maison d'Autriche.

"Il me semble du reste que les paroles du duc Decazes ont eu pour but principal de me convaincre de ses bonnes dispositions à notre égard et de son désir de nous être utile, et aussi de me donner à entendre que malgré la réserve que lui impose sa situation, la France vise à jouer dans l'intérêt du maintien de la paix générale un rôle intermédiaire entre les puissances les plus intéressées dans les affaires d'orient."

[144] France, Assemblée nationale, Annales du Sénat et de la Chambre des députés, Session ordinaire de 1876, Tome III, 371–72 (13 July).

embarrassments, gave out the opinion that the policy should not be too loudly proclaimed.[145]

In London, where the Anglo-Russian negotiations had been terminated on 29 June by a rejection of every basis of understanding, a sympathetic response to Gorchakov's declaration was out of the question. On 1 July, when Shuvalov asked Derby about England's intentions, the foreign secretary replied that the cabinet undoubtedly would observe a policy of strict non-intervention but, still in a defiant mood toward Russia, he went on to warn the ambassador

that it must be clearly understood that Her Majesty's Government entered into no engagement to continue to abstain from intervention, in the event (which, however, I could not assume as probable) of a different course being pursued by other Powers.[146]

Queen Victoria had been distinctly unsympathetic toward the policy of her two ministers. She had protested against their isolating England, and she had failed to see why her cabinet had sent her fleet to the mouth of the Dardanelles.[147] In the hope of calming the rising Russophobe ardor of her chief minister she had taken it upon herself in June to invite a letter from Tsar Alexander.[148]

The royal message came at a time when Alexander and his chancellor were embittered over the failure of the Anglo-Russian negotiations to produce some tangible results[149] and when Ignatiev was trying to capitalize their irritation in favor of independent action. Citing the hostile intrigues of Elliot and the movements of the British fleet, the general urged a Russian demonstration in the Caucasus region. Shuvalov, however, defended the British against the charge of being intent on war. "The policy of England," he informed his sovereign, "is hesitant, it is tortuous, but it does not seem to me to be bellicose."[150] Unwilling to take the extreme advice of one of his ambassadors and encouraged perhaps by the moderation of the other,

[145] Report No. 29AB, Károlyi to Andrássy, 2 July; SA, Varia Turquie I, 1875.

[146] Draft No. 396, Derby to Loftus, 1 July; *Turkey No. 3 (1876)*, Doc. No. 521.

[147] Queen Victoria to Derby, 27 May; *Letters of Queen Victoria*, II, 455.

[148] Duke of Edinburgh to Queen Victoria, 31 July; *ibid.*, II, 473. The queen sent her message through her son, the Duke of Edinburgh, who was married to the tsar's daughter Marie.

[149] Dreux, *Dernières années de l'ambassade en Allemagne de M. Gontaut-Biron, 1874–1877*, p. 243.

[150] Shuvalov to Alexander II, 20 June/2 July; *Slavonic Review*, III, 681–82, Doc. No. 57.

Alexander in early July addressed a personal letter to his "dear sister," Queen Victoria, in response to her invitation. In it he made another attempt to establish good relations with Great Britain. He expressed his belief in the European concert and his sincere desire for peace. There was a dignified hint of remonstrance when he wrote of England's relation to the concert which, he maintained, was charged with preserving the general peace and the interests of humanity, but he cordially thanked his dear sister for her personal influence exerted in favor of co-operation.[151]

Disraeli was not mollified by the tsar's letter. On the eve of the war he had been convinced that Serbia would never move without Russian support, and he had wanted, as has been seen, to address a grave warning to St. Petersburg.[152] The plan was defeated by his inert colleague in the foreign office, and the result was what the prime minister called an "infamous invasion" of Turkey, an invasion which he hoped soon to see "properly punished."[153] When asked for advice in the preparation of a royal answer to the tsar, Disraeli was still in the mood in which he had written his letter to Shuvalov on 29 June. His "rough suggestions," for which he sent a flattering courtier's apologies to his sovereign, were put into French translation and dispatched to Russia on 9 July.[154] The queen informed her dear brother that she was happy to have been able to contribute to the maintenance of the peace of Europe in concert with her allies; she thought that the *six* powers might have intervened somewhat prematurely in the affairs of Turkey, but she observed that events had extricated them from a difficult position and had made possible a return to the principle of non-intervention, and consequently to a general neutrality, which she hoped would be strictly observed by all. In the future, if it became necessary to take further steps, Victoria thought that those further steps could be decided by common agreement of *all*.[155]

When this letter reached the tsar its *"sécheresse officielle"* created an *"impression pénible."* The prime minister, whose hand Gorchakov

[151] Emperor Alexander II to Queen Victoria, 22 June / 4 July; *Slavonic Review*, III, 683, Doc. No. 60, and *Letters of Queen Victoria*, II, 468.

[152] Disraeli to Derby, 28 June; *Disraeli*, VI, 36.

[153] Disraeli to Lady Chesterfield, 9 July; *ibid.*, VI, 37.

[154] Disraeli to Queen Victoria, 7 July; *Letters of Queen Victoria*, II, 468–69.

[155] Queen Victoria to Emperor Alexander II, 9 July; *ibid.*, II, 469–70.

detected in its composition, had achieved his purpose again.[156] Disraeli happily decided that all of the powers, including even Russia, wished to defer to England, and it appeared to him that "something like the old days of our authority" had returned.[157]

The prime minister's satisfaction with the course of European events was not shared by British public opinion. The spread of hostilities in the Balkans had created an atmosphere of uncertainty and fear of general war. In addition, as July went on, news was coming into England which was rapidly preparing the greatest storm of moral indignation that a nation has ever experienced in time of peace. On 23 June the *Daily News* printed its first account of the horrors which had been perpetrated in Bulgaria, but the attempts of the government to discredit "coffee-house babble" stayed the full force of the outburst until late in the summer. Before the true import of the news from Bulgaria was realized and the government's treatment of the problem was completely understood, British opinion was occupied with the war and its possible repercussions in the future. On 14 July

[156] Gorchakov to Shuvalov, 11/24 [*sic*] July; *Slavonic Review*, III, 682–83, Doc. No. 59.

Prince Gorchakov's views about English action were expressed to Loftus in mid-July: ". . . . Our conversation commenced with referring to the events which had taken place in the East since his departure.

"He [Gorchakov] referred to the Berlin Memorandum expressing the surprise with which he had received the refusal of Her Majesty's Government to adhere to it. He said that it was of so moderate a character that the only reproach which could be made to it was that it did not go far enough.

"It had been his wish and object to reserve for England what he termed a 'leading part' in its execution, namely, if necessary the maritime action, as the British Fleet was more numerous and more powerful than all the other fleets combined. He should even have proposed that the Command in Chief should have been given to the oldest Admiral, in order to ensure its being given to an English Admiral.

"In making these remarks I could perceive that His Highness had not yet recovered from his mortification at the refusal of England to adhere to the Berlin Memorandum, for he dwelt on this topic which is now distanced by subsequent events, and is still impressed with the belief of its having prejudicially influenced the pacific efforts of Europe.

"His Highness further observed that, in consequence of this refusal of England and of the reply made by Your Lordship in the House of Lords to a question as to the Treaty obligations of England towards Turkey in the event of internal disorders [speech of Lord Derby on 15 June, *Hansard,* 3d series, CCXXIX, 1888–1892] —it had been no longer possible to restrain Servia and Montenegro from action, and thence had arisen the present deplorable state of affairs. . . . ."

It will be recalled that on two different occasions Gorchakov, when talking to the French ambassador, declared that he had been anticipating that France would be given the chief maritime role (*vide supra*, pp. 300, 341).

[157] Disraeli to Lady Chesterfield, 9 July; *Disraeli,* VI, 37.

two deputations went to the Foreign Office to present memorials. The first, headed by John Bright, sought assurance that the country was in no immediate danger of war. The second was introduced by Lewis Farley, who had gained notoriety during the preceding autumn for his anti-Turkish activities. Farley's group, representing the League in Aid of the Christians in Turkey, besought moral support for the insurgents. In his replies to the deputations Lord Derby reviewed his policies and canvassed the prospects for war. With his usual skepticism the minister dismissed any apprehension about complications to come:

> It is very difficult to judge of anything beyond the immediate future. But so far as it is possible for anyone to forecast the future of events, I think it is the most improbable thing in the world that, in consequence of anything that is now passing within the limits of the Turkish Empire, a general European war should ensue. That seems to me one of those hypotheses which are so remote that it is scarcely worth while to speculate upon them. I do not see the quarter from which the war is to come. . . . .

France and Italy, he said, were not disposed to interfere in making a disturbance; Germany was not interested.

> Now, I cannot so insult your understandings as to speculate or to assume that there could be any one here who supposes that England wants to bring about a war. . . . . There is no party and no set of men in this country who would not regard a European war as the greatest of misfortunes.

Austria and Russia he then considered. Austria, he undiplomatically explained, was a ramshackle organization of many races and could not, without the greatest dangers, undertake an aggressive action. As for Russia, there were indeed many Russians who were strongly sympathetic toward the insurgents, but the tsar was a "sincere lover of peace" and Russia's financial condition and administration made war "utterly unsuited to the policy of the Russian Empire."

England had made two decisions, Derby continued, which had allegedly created an impression that the cabinet anticipated war—the rejection of the Berlin memorandum and the sending of ships to Besika Bay. Such an interpretation was unfounded: the memorandum was rejected because, as he had stated on previous occasions, it was deemed unworkable; and the fleet went to Turkish waters solely for the purpose of protecting British interests endangered by "the state of things in Constantinople and in the country near Constantinople."

In regard to the future Derby differentiated between Britain's role in a disturbance involving Turkey and an outside power on the one hand and the existing war between suzerain and subject on the other. For the former contingency he reserved his decision:

No one is more strongly for non-intervention within all reasonable and practical limits than I have been and am; but we must push no doctrine to an extreme, and an absolute declaration of non-intervention under all circumstances is a declaration of international anarchy, and I need not tell you that international anarchy does not mean either international peace or progress.

Intervention between the sultan and his vassals Derby held to be a proposal "which has never been so much as entertained," and he proposed to "impress that view upon others."

The utmost that can be asked of us is to see fair play. We undertook undoubtedly twenty years ago to guarantee the sick man against murder, but we never undertook to guarantee him against suicide or sudden death. . . . . We shall not intervene, we shall do our utmost, if necessary, to discourage others from intervening; but I don't believe that under the present circumstances it will be necessary. If an opportunity of mediation should offer itself—and that does not seem to be an unlikely event—we shall gladly avail ourselves of it. While we retain, as we are bound to do, our own freedom and our own independence of action and of judgment, we attach quite as much importance as those other Powers with whom we have acted to that general understanding among the great European States which is the best and surest guarantee of peace.[158]

The foreign secretary's speeches were reassuring, if not to Farley and his deputation, at least to those who had been apprehensive of war. John Bright wrote in his diary that Derby's reply was "re-

---

[158] *The Times* (London), 15 July 1876, p. 9, cols. 5–6. *Speeches and Addresses of Edward Henry, XVth Earl of Derby*, I, 281–89.
    Andrássy took strong exception to Derby's uncomplimentary reference to the Dual Monarchy and protested to Buchanan. The foreign secretary in reply explained that Andrássy had misunderstood his expressions. He declared that he did not mean that the dual system "would be a cause of disaffection and weakness in the face of an enemy. My words referred to the danger which would be created for the Cabinet of Vienna by the proclamation of a powerful Slavonic State on the Austrian frontier, as such a State would not fail to be a strong influence over the Sclave population both in Austria and Hungary; while if, on the other hand, the result of war should be the annexation of Sclave territory, the difficulty of keeping together so many various races under an Empire would be materially increased. I thought also that the Austrian Government had more to lose, and less to gain, than any other, by a war which must be waged in the name and for the sake of the principle of nationality. There was in these reflections nothing, I conceived, which would be construed as unfriendly or uncomplimentary to the Government of the Austro-Hungarian Empire. . . . ." (Draft No. 338, Derby to Buchanan, 26 July; FO 7/865.)

markable" and gave "much satisfaction,"[159] and a sedative effect was noted on public opinion.[160] Nevertheless there were ominous signs that the relative apathy of the British press was ending. *The Spectator,* always impatient with Derby, declared that "he is determined to have a reputation for having thrown equally-wet blankets on both the combatants,"[161] and ridiculed him for holding out possibilities of Turkish reform:

It is a mere imaginative coining of fairy money, to throw into the balance against solid coin of the realm. Lord Derby is so afraid to seem to favour the Christian rebels, that he invents dreamy apologies for the Turk, which have just as much to do with the actual condition of Eastern affairs as lark-pie conditional on the falling of the sky has to do with any one's bill of fare for his dinner to-day.[162]

The *Saturday Review,* which appeared on the same day, for the first time showed signs of departing from an unquestioning support of the Conservative government. Derby's explanation about the fleet was readily analyzed into its component parts of misrepresentation and confusion; but, even so, the author of the leading article was unable to see the pertinence of his own observations and he supposed that sending the fleet had some good explanation that could not be publicly avowed. He was none the less disturbed by what the prime minister might do in foreign affairs:

Lord Derby, though he exercises great power, is not absolutely supreme in his own department; and the exaggeration of caution and common sense tends to stimulate the antagonism of imagination and eccentricity.[163]

Before the end of July the swelling current of indignant opinion had put the government on the defensive and Disraeli had need of his endowment of imagination and eccentricity. On the thirty-first, as the press campaign was growing in bitterness, British policy was debated in the House of Commons and the cabinet heard some searching criticisms of its varying explanations about the fleet and of its hostility to Russia and of its treatment of the Berlin memorandum. The debate was begun by a Conservative member who introduced a resolution favoring British pressure on Turkey for reform in the

---

[159] R. A. J. Walling, editor, *The Diaries of John Bright* (New York, 1931), p. 383.

[160] Thompson, *Public Opinion and Lord Beaconsfield,* I, 347–49.

[161] *The Spectator,* 22 July 1876, pp. 909–10.

[162] "Lord Derby and Mr. Disraeli on the Bulgarian Atrocities," *ibid.,* pp. 912–13.

[163] "Lord Derby's Explanations,"*Saturday Review,* 22 July 1876, pp. 92–93.

interest of saving the Porte from outside intervention. But after a seconding speech in the same vein opponents of the government gained the floor and the tone of the discussion quickly changed to severe strictures on Turkey and sharp criticism of British policy. Gladstone entered the debate for the Liberals and his words were a forewarning of the impassioned utterances that were soon to be his. Speaking as the one member of the House officially connected with the Crimean War, he described British policy of 1853 as twofold: "first, to defend the Turkish Empire against assaults from without, and, secondly, to defend her from corruption and dissolution from within." The Crimean War, he insisted, destroyed Russia's individual right of interference in Turkey, but neither the war nor the peace took away from the concert of Europe the moral right to exact that decent administration from the sultan which he had formally promised twenty years before:

> To these promises we have entrusted the happiness of millions, and to these promises the interests and welfare of millions of the people of Turkey have been sacrificed. I contend that to these promises there must be an end, and if sensible to the obligations of duty and honour, and looking back a quarter of a century ago to the rights we then acquired and the obligations we then came under, we ought to insist that there should be some reality in the guarantees—if with guarantees we are to be content—given by the Turkish Government. We must make sure in one way or the other that this terrible state of things is not to be indefinite.

After demanding some special arrangements for the insurgent area, Gladstone went on to take the British government severely to task for its sins of omission and commission. In the early days of the revolt the government had permitted "the initiative of concert and intervention to pass from their hands" and to this blunder the speaker ascribed "most of the difficulties and inconveniences which have since been experienced."

> I think you have most unwisely abandoned and surrendered that principle of the concert of Europe which I hope henceforward you will do your utmost to re-establish. By the concert of Europe you may succeed in restoring tranquillity; without it you never can. You may take a side and you may stimulate passion in connection with any question; you may do much to disturb a subject that is sufficiently disturbed and embroiled already; but if your object is to compose and settle it you must beat back upon the course in which you have been engaged, and instead of the system of sole action [as in the Suez Canal purchase], you must return to the policy established by the Crimean War, and endeavour, whatever you do, to do it in concert with the Great Powers.

On the basis of such a principle the former Liberal leader found nothing in the policy of the government to commend. The government had repudiated the moral responsibility of joining with the other powers in making the sultan reform his administration; it had refused to support the Andrássy note and had rejected the Berlin memorandum; and the defeat of that second reform measure, depriving the Serbs and Montenegrins "of all reasonable hope," had inspired their declaration of war. For the future, Gladstone went on, the only rational program was a European concert effecting measures "conceived in the spirit and advancing in the direction of self government." Autonomy which preserved the integrity of the empire but which still spared the people the miseries of the sultan's direct rule appeared to Gladstone to be the only tolerable arrangement. He concluded:

Within these limits . . . . I most earnestly hope that Her Majesty's Government may be able to discover a solution of this question—a solution which may have the effect of giving us the consolatory assurance that all our efforts and sacrifices made at the time of the Crimean War were not made in vain—a solution which may adjourn, and perhaps adjourn for a long time, the raising of a greater question as to the presence of the Turkish Power in Europe, which we feel to be fraught with serious and grave considerations of uncertainty, and perhaps of danger; and a solution which, above all, may afford to a population that has suffered long and suffered much a hope of gaining at length the benefits of rational government and civilized life.

Disraeli then rose to reply, stating it to be his duty to explain rather than vindicate the policy which his government had pursued. That policy was fundamentally a policy of status quo:

You will find it difficult to maintain the territorial integrity of Turkey without acknowledging the principle of *status quo*. Let us see what the *status quo* in Turkey is. It is not an ancient order of society or political arrangement that has become obsolete. It has been tested in the severest manner and by the severest deeds only 20 years ago. It has been tested by a sanguinary war and by the Conferences of the great States; and the results of these material struggles and moral considerations had been expressed in solemn Treaties; and, therefore, the *status quo* is not a state or condition to be looked upon lightly or with disrespect; it is a *status quo* with which, in our opinion, it was not proper to interfere. If ever there was a case in which interference was to be deprecated it was, in our opinion, in the condition of Turkey, because it was quite obvious that, from the circumstances of the relations between Turkey and the other States of Europe, supported as they were by peculiar Treaties, the interference of other Powers would have been induced, and would have led to a perilous state of affairs. Therefore, to recognize and to wish to maintain the *status quo* of Turkey and to deprecate interference with its condition in order to allow

Turkey and its subjects in the course of time to find that condition which suited both of them best, seemed to us the policy desirable.

Because of that basic consideration the cabinet had hesitated to join in the mission of the consuls; because of it too the cabinet had hesitated to accept the Andrássy note. Subsequently the cabinet had isolated itself completely by rejecting the Berlin memorandum.

Why did we refuse to sanction the Berlin Memorandum? We did so because we knew that the Turkish Government and the Turkish nation could not fulfil the conditions which were laid down in the Berlin Memorandum, and because we knew that the Berlin Memorandum ended with an intimation that, if this effort failed, very different measures would be had recourse to. And, of course, the very failure by the Turks to fulfil the rash and reckless promises which, in their miserable state of despair, they were ready to make every day, would have been the foundation for that which we, who were advocating a policy of non-intervention, wished particularly to avoid. It was perfectly clear that as the Turks would necessarily fail to observe the conditions laid down, the Berlin Memorandum would have allowed active interference—an occupation, perhaps, and an occupation in a country like Turkey generally leads to war.

Gladstone's charge that the rejection of the memorandum in London had caused the war Disraeli vigorously rejected.

We drove Servia to war, he says, because she was in sheer despair at not getting redress for her grievances. But what had Turkey to do with the redress of the grievances of Servia? Servia was as independent a country, you might say, with regard to the Government of Turkey, as England herself. If Turkey had come forward and practically made all the changes which are included in all the Hatti-Sheriffs and Hatti-Humayouns in existence, it would not have affected Servia in the least. Nothing appears to me more unwarranted than to maintain that the policy of this country with regard to Turkey led to war with Servia. Servia could not be affected in any way. Servia required no redress. What Servia wanted was Provinces, a very different thing, and the Papers on the Table show that in the Spring she was preparing for war, on the supposition that she would commence it probably with the presence of some European Power.

The prime minister then turned to the condemnation of the cabinet for not advancing some counterproposal. He and his colleagues could not, he said, proffer their advice to other governments when such advice was not requested—although in truth repeatedly such requests had been made in London—and he felt certain that any opinions advanced would never have been accepted by foreign powers.

Their self-love, their just pride, their somewhat mortified feeling at the course which we had taken, all would have impelled them to reject our proposition. And my own opinion is that it is not a wise thing for a country, and a country like England, to make proposals which it has not the means of carrying into effect, and to sketch a policy, which is never difficult to do, but which a country like this ought certainly not to entertain unless it entertained it in a serious, practical, and determined manner.

After reasserting the lack of connection between Britain's rejection of the Berlin memorandum and the Serb declaration of war, Disraeli turned to the repeated charges made against the government for contradictory and misleading explanations as to why the fleet was sent to Besika Bay. He ascribed the beginning of the ship movements to the request made by Elliot in concert with his colleagues for the dispatch of squadrons to Turkish waters:

Three of our ships arrived in Besika Bay and the squadrons of the other nations were soon established there also. The state of affairs at Constantinople at that moment was most critical. Even in that city, which has been the scene of some of the most violent occurrences in history, I do not know whether there was ever a period when there was greater danger, and when that danger was so indefinite, and caused such general alarm and terror. After the arrival of the ships in Besika Bay that condition of affairs grew worse from day to day —I must say, however, for our English Ambassador in Constantinople that he always took a more sanguine and courageous view of the state of affairs than his Colleagues did, and that he did not believe from his own observation that there was any fear of the religious feud between the Mussulmans and the Christians which was generally accepted as impending, and which so alarmed many; but he warned the Government that we must be prepared for startling events. There was, however, existing at the moment an anxiety, a dread, and a general apprehension, the nature of which was communicated by our Ambassador to the Government. This, then, was the state of things we had to consider. . . . .

We know very well that these waters had in time of public disturbance ever been the scene of sudden and startling events, and we felt that three ships in Besika Bay were under the circumstances but a very scanty protection, when, perhaps, you might have an insurrection stirred up in Salonica or on the coast of Syria, which was completely denuded of any protection whatever. We thought, therefore, that the time had arrived when we ought to take care that the Mediterranean Squadron should be somewhat more powerful than it was then.

Without being any more specific, the prime minister went on to hint that the government saw involved great stakes of high policy:

Let us look at what is the policy of England. The policy of England has ever been that the Mediterranean Sea should be considered as one of the great highways of our Indian Empire, and we have always held, and do hold it, that the waters of that sea and all the waters connected with it should be free and secure. When we are asked what is our policy, I say our policy is to secure those great results. Well, then, under these circumstances, we felt it our duty to increase the strength of the Mediterranean Squadron. . . . . It was no threat to any one. The Mediterranean Fleet is the symbol and the guarantee of our power. We could not and we never attempted to conceal that we had in that part of the world great interests which we must protect and never relinquish, and it was no threat to any particular Power that we said at such a moment that the Mediterranean Fleet, which is the guarantee and the symbol of our authority, should be there, that the world should know, whatever might happen, there should be no great change in the distribution of territories in that part of the world without the knowledge and consent of England. . . . .

I believe that the Governments of Russia and Austria have from the first— though they might, like ourselves, have made a mistake in their means—sincerely and unreservedly endeavoured to terminate these disturbances in Turkey. They felt that it was their interest to do so, and they have been most anxious to maintain the *status quo*. But, unfortunately, the world consists not merely of Emperors and Governments; it consists also of secret societies and revolutionary committees, and secret societies and revolutionary committees have been unceasingly at work in these affairs, and they do bring about in an Empire like Turkey most unexpected consequences, which may have a most injurious effect on British interests. When we are told that we sent our Fleet to the Dardanelles in order to maintain the Turkish Empire I deny it. It is not to maintain the Turkish Empire, and the Turkish Government were never deceived on that point.

As he closed his speech there were in the mind of Disraeli no doubt about the correctness of British policy, no regrets or apologies for the manner in which that policy had been followed during the year then coming to its close, and no undue concern for the future:

I cannot see, so far as I can review our conduct, that the Government have taken any course in these proceedings but such as the interests of this country required, and we have certainly not committed the country to any rash undertaking. We have said from the first that we were in favour of non-interference; we have said from the first that we should observe a strict neutrality if that strict neutrality were observed by others. There has been a difference of opinion between us and the other Powers; there has been some controversy; in what has it all ended? It has all ended by the other Powers adopting our policy. They have all, in a manner most unmistakable, admitted that non-interference is the policy that ought to be pursued, and that neutrality is the process they ought to follow. . . . . I have no doubt when the opportunity offers we shall find ourselves in that position which becomes the dignity of this country, and we shall have every opportunity which is desired to contribute to the general welfare of the world. The course which we have taken is the one which we believe we were called upon to pursue for the sake of our interests, and for the sake of our Empire; it was the course which, in the second place, we were called upon to pursue because we believed it was most conducive to the maintenance of peace; and thirdly, also, the one which we believed would lead to the progressive improvement of the population of the Turkish Empire. If there is to be nothing but confusion, if we are to have nothing but struggles and war, if secret societies and revolutionary committees are to ride rampant over those fair Provinces, I shall cordially deplore such a result as much as Gentlemen who attack me very often for my want of sympathy with the sufferers by imaginary atrocities. . . . .

I cannot believe that the scenes which have taken place during the last six months in these Turkish Provinces can be maintained, and when the occasion arrives we shall be ready to take our responsible part in what I hope may be the pacification of these countries, their advancement in civilization, and their general improvement . . . . But if we feel that we have the confidence of our countrymen, great as may be the difficulties we may have to encounter—vast as may be the responsibility of public men under such circumstances—we shall not shrink from doing our duty. And I trust that in fulfilling it we shall not disappoint the expectations of the country.[164]

In the meantime the non-intervention question had been taken up in Vienna and temporarily settled in Austro-Russian discussions. When the obviously approaching war came, the program to be adopted by the Dual Monarchy had not been announced and had not, indeed, been decided. True it was that Andrássy had resorted to threats to forestall Serbian action, but he had been obliged to admit that he was not in a position to carry them out. In his discussions of policy before the delegations in May the minister limited himself to generalities, recalling his three objectives—preservation of European peace, maintenance of the interests of the monarchy, and prevention of the recurrence of comparable conditions—and claiming that he was then attaining them.[165] The means whereby he proposed to defend his objectives in the future he had refused to divulge beyond admitting that his program could not be rigidly fixed in the face of changing events.[166] In June, as has been seen, Andrássy had sponsored a final summons to Beograd and had urged upon the Turks the necessity of doing nothing to precipitate the war in order that they might have a free hand to undertake a vigorous action.[167]

[164] *Hansard,* 3d series, CCXXXI, 126–216.

[165] "Précis of Count Andrassy's Answers before the Budget Committee of the Austrian Delegation respecting his Oriental Policy"; *Turkey No. 3 (1876),* inclosure in Doc. No. 298. Report No. 67, Harriss-Gastrell to Buchanan, 24 May; *ibid.,* Doc. No. 309.

[166] Report No. 69, Harriss-Gastrell to Buchanan, 24 May; *ibid.,* Doc. No. 311. Viktor Bibl, *Der Zerfall Österreichs* (Vienna, 1922–1924), II, 357–58. Andrássy's words had been somewhat modified to characterize his program as a *Politik von Fall zu Fall* and the double sense of the German word *"Fall"* was capitalized by the minister's opponents to charge that his policy led him from misfortune to misfortune (*de chute en chute*).

[167] Tels. Nos. 81, 83, and 84, Andrássy to Zichy, 26, 27, and 27 June, respectively; SA, Turkey, 1876.

On the eve of the war those settlements of the Balkan problem which had been unacceptable to the Dual Monarchy a year before were still unacceptable. The Anglo-Russian discussions in June of a proposed autonomy evoked from Andrássy a determined opposition to such an idea[168] and he persisted in his resolution that Serbia should not be permitted to take possession of Bosnia.[169] If Austria was to be spared the expense and dangers of a military occupation of the insurgent area it was important that Prince Milan's forces receive a sound defeat. For that reason he had urged the Turks to be prepared for invasion; for that reason he had advised against any resolution at the Porte that would give Russia an excuse for intervention; for that reason he had agreed with the English that the powers should not prevent a Turkish invasion of Serbia once the principality had declared war.[170] As soon as hostilities began, the Austrian authorities, under direction of Andrássy, inaugurated their tangible preparations for the protection of the monarchy's interests. An infantry division and a cavalry regiment were moved up to the Save frontier; the consul in Sarajevo was charged with working especially on the Roman Catholics to draw them closer to Austria and to Hungary, and the commanding general in Agram received orders to begin a propaganda campaign against Serbia in Bosnia and in the old military frontier districts.[171]

Such were Austro-Hungarian policy and action when Prince Gorchakov presented his non-intervention proposal of 26 June in Vienna. The chancellor's arguments to Andrássy were the same as those which he had addressed to the other capitals: The Christians had obtained only theoretical concessions by the interference of Europe, an interference which had been actually in favor of the Turks; in case of war the powers should proclaim the principle of absolute non-intervention and allow the struggle to go on.[172]

[168] Buchanan to Derby, 28 June; *Turkey No. 1 (1877)*, Doc. No. 1. *Vide supra,* pp. 364, 370–74.

[169] Report No. 61B, Beust to Andrássy, 5 July; SA, England, 1876: ".... Hochdieselben [Andrássy] äusserten Sich dahin, dass wenn trotz aller aufrichtigen Versuche Serbien davon abzuhalten, dieses doch in den Kampf sich sturzen und es ihm gelingen sollte, die Türken aus Bosnien zu vertreiben, für die österreichungarische Monarchie die Notwendigkeit eintreten werde, militärisch einzuschreiten, und Bosnien in Besitz zu nehmen."

[170] Tel., Andrássy to Beust, 27 June; *ibid.*

[171] Mollinary, *Sechsundvierzig Jahre,* II, 300–302.

[172] *Note verbale* in the handwriting of Novikov without date; SA, Varia Russia, 1876. The conclusion of this document reads: ".... Le chancelier croit en

The Russian proposal was obviously unacceptable to a minister who had such a vital interest in the outcome of the war. Andrássy, however, was unwilling to confess his real reason for refusing to commit himself and he rejected absolute non-intervention on the general grounds that unspecified Austrian interests forbade it. Novikov's reports of the minister's words were not clear, and Gorchakov understood that Andrássy would accept the principle on condition that it be held secret. On 1 July the chancellor, under the effects of the cumulative irritations suffered in his dealings with the Austrian minister, wrote a long letter of reproach to Vienna. Gorchakov reminded Andrássy, as was becoming his custom, of the concessions which he had made in Berlin; he taxed Andrássy with private negotiations in London against Russia, negotiations which, he charged, had given Derby an opportunity to point out the hollowness of claims of Austro-Russian solidarity;[173] he returned again to his proposal for a forthright declaration of non-intervention and loftily proclaimed that secrecy was contrary to the dignity of the powers in general and of his august sovereign in particular. That declaration,

outre le moment venu de fermer Klek par où tout dernièrement encore ont passé des armes et munitions. Nous maintenons le désir de conserver l'empire ottoman dans les seules conditions possibles, celles d'une sérieuse amélioration du sort des chrétiens, mais ne pouvons pas continuer dans la voie des voeux stériles, et croyons le temps venu pour faire comprendre à la Porte, ne fût-ce que par l'adoption de la marche proposée ci-dessus—et cela comme minimum de ce qui selon nous pourrait être fait pour le moment—que l'Europe chrétienne ne voit pas avec indifférence la position déplorable des chrétiens de Turquie."

[173] The passage of the letter here concerned reads: "Nous voyons que cet accord a subi des atteintes ou qu'au moins cela en a l'apparence. Notre désir le plus sincère est de le faire ressortir de nouveau aux yeux de tous. Nous croyons que le meilleur moyen de dissiper ces malentendus est de nous expliquer avec une entière franchise.

"Le comte Andrássy n'est pas de notre avis quant à l'autonomie administrative et tributaire. Nous l'avons proposée parce que la marche des évènements, grâce aux lenteurs que l'on a apportées à les dominer, nous avait donné la conviction que les demi-mesures, convenues à Berlin, n'offraient plus de chances d'une issue pratique.

"Le cabinet anglais et, je crois, la majorité des puissances européennes penchent pour une solution de ce genre. Le comte Andrássy a une autre opinion dont nous n'avons pas seuls la confidence. Elle est connue à Londres et Lord Derby n'a pas manqué de signaler au comte Shouvalow que l'entente entre les trois, qui jusqu'ici avait été la pierre angulaire de notre action, est loin d'être aussi complète que nous nous attachions à la représenter. . . . ."

Gorchakov had no apology to make for his own abandonment of the pledged *action à trois* and no reason other than the inefficacy of the *demi-mesures* which Andrássy had imposed on him in Berlin. It was, of course, a flat fabrication when the chancellor on 1 July wrote that the English cabinet was inclined toward a "solution of this kind."

the chancellor added, would entail Austria's closing the port of Klek to Turkish transports, which were again bringing troops to Herce-govina. He concluded his letter with a hint that was sharp despite its diplomatic dress:

> Count Andrássy will recall that I have never abandoned the habit of speaking with him à cœur ouvert. I shall permit myself to add that the relations of the two empires have gained because I have met in the minister for foreign affairs of Austria-Hungary a complete reciprocity.[174]

Andrássy in his reply a week later agreed that the relations of the two powers had indeed suffered a blow and he professed that complete frankness which the chancellor was demanding. But his subsequent paragraphs belied his profession. Gorchakov's remonstrance for dealings with London Andrássy disposed of with a misstatement and a thrust at Russia's own infidelity:

> It is true that I have not left Lord Derby in ignorance of my views but it was only after I had learned from your Excellency that overtures having autonomy as a basis had been made to the English government through Count Shuvalov. I would never have taken the initiative, recalling very well that precisely in order not to give occasion for even the appearance of disagreement we had agreed to come to an understanding between ourselves before submitting a new idea to the appreciation of a third power. But asked by Lord Derby who desired to know our thoughts on the question which the cabinet of St. Petersburg had just presented to him, I had only two alternatives: either to make no response at the risk of being obliged to refuse later after an accord had been established between England and Russia, or to state openly my opinion with the frankness from which I shall never depart.

With regard to the practical problem of the moment Andrássy was no more frank. Disclaiming any desire for secrecy, he rejected entirely any declaration of non-intervention as an invariable rule of conduct. There were possibilities for the future in Turkey which the powers might not wish to tolerate, he told Gorchakov, and if they accepted the proposed principle they could do nothing. He cited as such contingencies, not a Serbian occupation of Bosnia, but Turkey's refusal to grant toleration and Turkey's desire to exterminate the Christians. Andrássy virtuously contended that it was not in the interest of either Austria or Russia or of Europe or humanity to bind its hands. His only concession was that he, like the Italians and the English and others, would agree to non-intervention in the cir-

---

[174] Gorchakov to Novikov, Jugenheim, 19 June/1 July; SA, Varia Turquie I, 1875.

cumstances as they then existed.[175] But that was a concession which meant nothing.

This exchange of views was a new proof of Bismarck's long-standing observation that Austria and Russia could act in harmony and confidence only so long as there was no need for action. Talk of frankness and loyalty and reciprocity could not hide the fundamental fact of divergent sympathies and interests when it became necessary to adopt policies toward the new war. It was fortunate for the relations of the two powers that Alexander and Francis Joseph and their chief ministers were scheduled to meet at Reichstadt in Bohemia on the day after Andrássy had a second time rejected absolute non-intervention.

Before going to iron out his difficulties with Gorchakov, Andrássy wrote what he claimed to be a statement of his policy for the benefit of the English whom the June negotiations had of necessity brought into closer relations with Vienna.[176] The theme of the minister's dispatch was the identity of English and Austrian objectives despite a difference in means. Those objectives he described as follows:

1. We wished to maintain as long as might at all be possible the *status quo* in Turkey, combining with our efforts in that direction those for the improvement of the position of the Christian subjects of the Porte.
2. As soon and in so far as it would become impossible to maintain the *status quo,* we were all along determined to prevent events taking a turn detrimental to our interests.

Andrássy explained that, while England with her millions of Mohammedans could afford to adopt a Turcophile policy pure and simple in the interest of status quo, Austria had to take into consideration her Slavic subjects when formulating a policy toward Turkey lest those

---

[175] Andrássy to Novikov, 7 July; SA, Varia Turquie I, 1875. When the French ambassador approached Andrássy in the interest of a declaration of non-intervention through which England might be brought back into the European concert, the minister gave a comparable refusal to formulate a binding program for the future (Vogüé to Decazes, 7 July; *Documents français,* II, Doc. No. 72).

[176] The various dispatches of Derby anent his negotiations with Shuvalov had been communicated to Andrássy and he had in turn continued his campaign against autonomy and urged the British not to prejudice the future by binding declarations (Reports Nos. —, 435, and 451, Buchanan to Derby, 4, 4, and 6 July; *Turkey No. 1* [*1877*], Docs. Nos. 1, 4, and 5, respectively). See also Drafts Nos. 319 and 324, Derby to Buchanan, 4 and 6 July; *ibid.,* Doc. No. 3 and *Turkey No. 3 (1876),* Doc. No. 527, respectively. It is not true that Derby asked Andrássy for an expression of opinion on autonomy as the latter claimed in his letter of 7 July to Novikov.

subjects and their relations across the frontier throw themselves into the arms of Russia. A minister in Vienna could not ignore the interests of the Christian Slavs of Turkey; but such a fact, Andrássy insisted, did not alter the fundamentally conservative character of his policy nor the identity of English and Austrian aims. In anticipation of his meeting on the morrow with a dissatisfied Russian chancellor, he continued:

A further explanation of the different mode of proceeding towards the same end followed by the two countries lies in England's exceptional position towards the general European politics. The insular position of Great Britain enables its government to follow to a certain extent a line of policy of its own independent from that of other Powers and only taking cognizance of every incident as it arrives without thereby endangering in any way the general peace of Europe. On the other hand we cannot without great risk of a general conflagration cease to keep up a friendly contact with Russia, as long as it does not become altogether impossible for us to act in harmony with her.

The readiness which exists on both sides to come to an understanding and a compromise as soon as any individual case arises is alone able to subordinate the latent antagonistic interests of the two empires to considerations of a higher order. Accordingly our going together with Russia in the way and to the extent above mentioned must be looked upon as a guarantee for the preservation of the peace of Europe. An opposite course would be the signal for a European war. It is this consideration which prompts us as long as there seems any chance of preserving the peace of Europe to make concessions to the Russian views, whilst England on account of her insular position is enabled to stand aloof, to isolate herself and often to exercise—even by such isolation itself—a salutary influence on the preservation of peace. . . . .[177]

The meeting at Reichstadt grew out of a desire expressed by Tsar Alexander to Andrássy in Berlin to meet Francis Joseph somewhere during his return journey to Russia.[178] In June, again at the tsar's cordial request, the Austrian Archduke Albert had visited his imperial friend at Jugenheim and there the details of the meeting

[177] Andrássy to Beust, 8 July, communicated to Derby on 13 July; FO 7/888. The original text in German is in SA, England, 1876. The quotations are from an English translation made by the Austrian embassy, with some modification of capitalization and punctuation. Andrássy goes on to say that, true to such a policy, he would be obliged to "exert our influence in favour of the Christians" in case Turkey won the war, but he was not ready to confess his intentions in case of a contrary outcome.

[178] Tel., Andrássy to Emperor Francis Joseph, Berlin, 14 May; SA, Prussia, 1876: "Ich vergass Ew. Maj. mitzuteilen, dass Kaiser Alexander mir Auftrag gegeben, zu sagen, dass Er sich sehr freuen würde, Allerhöchstdenselben auf Seiner Rückreise ungefähr wie im vorigen Jahre irgendwo zu begegnen und dass Er, wenn dies E. M. genehm wäre, mit Erzherzog Albrecht das Nähre über das Rendezvous verabreden würde. . . . ."

were settled.[179] The original plan of Emperor Alexander had anticipated merely a fraternal greeting; but toward the end of June, when new difficulties between Russia and Austria were arising, the tsar decided to bring his chancellor and requested the presence of Andrássy.[180] Urged on by Bismarck and Emperor William, the tsar and Gorchakov prepared themselves for a thoroughgoing discussion of eventualities. The Russians were still hoping that, despite England's rejection of their ideas and despite Andrássy's long-standing opposition, some arrangement could be made for a settlement which would be, without the name, the equivalent of autonomy.[181]

The externals of the meeting were the usual ones when sovereigns met—a decorated station, uniforms and insignia, and the *accolade à trois fois*. The discussions between Andrássy and Gorchakov and the tsar were a continuation of the negotiations over non-intervention which had been in progress for a week or more. If Gorchakov brought with him, as rumor had it,[182] long memoranda arguing some

[179] Private letter, Langenau to Andrássy, — March; SA, Russia, 1876. Archduke Albert to Emperor Francis Joseph, 17, 19, 21 [*sic*] June; SA, Kabinetskanzlei S. M.

[180] Tel., Emperor Francis Joseph to Andrássy, Ischl, 25 June; SA: "*Telegram des Erzherzogs Albrecht von heute: 'Fürst Gortchakow, welcher sich vor Tische etwas beunruhigt über die Nachrichten aus Wien, ohne sie zu bezeichnen, äusserte, sagte mir bald darauf, dass in diesem Falle daran nicht zu zweifeln sei.'*" Tel., Emperor Francis Joseph to Emperor Alexander II, 1 July; SA, Russia, 1876: "*Je Te remercie de tout mon cœur des excellentes communications que l'archiduc Albert, arrivé ici ce matin, m'a faites de Ta part. C'est avec bonheur que je vais au devant de notre prochaine entrevue. D'après Ton désir j'y amenerais le comte Andrássy.*"

[181] Tel., Károlyi to Andrássy, 4 July; SA, Prussia, 1876: "Wie Herr von Radowitz mir heute mitgeteilt, legten die beiden Kaiser in Ems und Jugenheim den grössten Wert und die grösste Hoffnung auf einen gründlichen Gedankenaustausch über die Eventualitäten der orientalischen Frage bei Gelegenheit der Zusammenkunft in Reichstadt. Russischerseits bereitet man sich eingehend darauf vor, um, wie Herr von Radowitz meint, eine Form zu finden, welche es uns ermöglichen würde, einer eventuellen autonomen Gestaltung der Verhältnisse in Bosnien und Herzegowina, wenn nicht dem Namen, jedoch annähernd der Sache nach, zuzustimmen.

"Kaiser Alexander wäre sehr peinlich impressioniert über mögliche Meinungsverschiedenheiten zwischen Russland und Österreich-Ungarn; er hege den aufrichtigen Wunsch, dieselben auszugleichen, und Kaiser Wilhelm habe ihn letzthin in Jugenheim auf das wärmste in diesem Streben unterstützt. . . . ."

The German chancellor's attitude toward Austro-Russian relations in July is well stated in Bismarck to King Ludwig II of Bavaria, Kissingen, 5 July; Otto Fürst von Bismarck-Schönhausen, *Gedanken und Erinnerungen* (Stuttgart, 1898), I, 359.

[182] Report No. 461, Buchanan to Derby, 11 July; FO 7/872: "I have reason to believe that Prince Gortchakoff arrived at Reichstadt armed with several long

434 DIPLOMATIC HISTORY OF THE BALKAN CRISIS 1875–1878

covert form of autonomy, his new documents fared no better than did the document which he carried to Berlin in May. Andrássy again took the initiative from the chancellor by stating, as he had during the negotiations for the December note and the Berlin memorandum, what he could not accept and what he demanded. Non-intervention he declared possible only on condition of Turkish victory. A defeat of the sultan's forces with an entailed collapse of Turkey in Europe, he now stated frankly, would necessitate an Austrian intervention. In such a case he proposed to annex a part of the insurgent area in order to prevent the neighboring principalities from expanding into a great Slavic state prejudicial to the security of the Habsburg Empire. If such a contingency arose he professed his willingness for Russia to claim compensation not only in Bessarabia, as agreed in Berlin, but also to take an equivalent of Austria's increase in Asiatic Turkey.[183]

---

memoranda on the present state of affairs in the Ottoman Empire, but that Count Andrassy expressed an unwillingness to enter into any discussion for the present, as to the course which it may be necessary to adopt, under circumstances which have not yet arisen:—and I am told that the Emperor and His Excellency [Francis Joseph and Andrássy], while expressing an earnest desire to maintain a cordial agreement with Russia, gave it clearly to be understood that such an agreement must depend upon their not being expected to adopt views incompatible with the interests of Austria-Hungary, and to which public opinion in the Monarchy is opposed."

Wertheimer (*Andrássy*, II, 321) relates that Gorchakov and Andrássy were hardly in the train for a brief ride together en route to the castle before the chancellor drew from his sack a memorandum and proposed to read it. Andrássy allegedly stopped him before he could begin, telling him that there were some preliminary questions that well might be dealt with without delay. The first question was, "Do you want Constantinople?" Gorchakov, taken somewhat by surprise, answered in the negative; whereupon Andrássy is reputed to have said, "*Gottlob,* otherwise we would have had war." The second alleged question was, "Would you like to have Bessarabia?" And Gorchakov, blushing with joy and shaking the minister's hand, confessed to such an ambition. Wertheimer bases his story on the testimony of Ludwig Dóczi ("Die Fahrt nach Reichstadt," *Neuer Pester Journal,* 3 January 1909), who claimed to have heard it from Andrássy himself a few days after his return. As the story stands it has all the marks of being apocryphal, regardless of who started it. Andrássy's major consideration was far from being centered on Constantinople; at such a moment when there were serious and immediate difficulties to be regulated it does not seem plausible that the Austrian minister would have put a question of such remote and indirect concern. Nor is it more plausible that a second question should have been so framed as Wertheimer relates. During the discussions at Berlin in May it had been agreed between the two statesmen that Russia might recover Bessarabia in exchange for an Austro-Hungarian annexation at the expense of Turkey (*vide supra*, pp. 290–91, 292, 297).

[183] Annex II of letter, Gorchakov to Novikov, 23 November/5 December; SA, "Abmachung mit Russland," Doc. No. 14: "M. le comte Andrássy voudra bien se rappeler que dans l'entretien à Reichstadt c'est lui qui a pris l'initiative de proposer

Gorchakov had no quarrel with Andrássy's statement of the case, and the Austrians and Russians arrived at a general verbal understanding. In case of a Turkish victory it was agreed that status quo would be preserved with a slight modification through recognition by Austria of Montenegro's de facto independence. Both powers would respect the principle of non-intervention so long as Turkey was not guilty of excess violence against the Christians, and Austria would agree, as a further proof of neutrality, to close to both parties in the struggle the ports of Klek and Cattaro.[184] With regard to the insurgent provinces Andrássy still refused to go beyond his former concessions and Gorchakov was obliged to capitulate, although he continued to hope that a settlement comparable to that of Crete or, if possible, that some form of local autonomy could be arranged.

The dispositions to be made in case of a Turkish defeat were more delicate, and Andrássy approached them warily in his conversations with Gorchakov and the tsar. The minister, unable to deny Serbia and Montenegro some advantage from a successful war, consented to territorial increases, expressed in not too concrete terms, to both principalities. Those increases, however, he made the basis for his own demands for annexations which in turn would entail compensation for Russia. The fate of the remainder of the Balkan Peninsula was regulated largely by prohibitions. Constantinople was designated as a free city; and, because Austria forbade a large Slavic state and Russia a large Greek state, it was agreed that, although Greece was to expand, a series of autonomous political units would be the best solution.

As the two imperial trains separated that afternoon both parties were content with the agreement just made. Austria and Russia were prepared for future collaboration regardless of the Balkan contingency which might arise, and each was assured a vital advantage if Turkey should collapse. Andrássy had paved the way for the pro-

---

et de désigner l'annexion à laquelle nous aurions droit en réciprocité de celle que nous consentirions pour l'Autriche-Hongrie, c.-à-d., les territoires qui nous avaient été enlevés par le traité de Paris et Batoum en Asie. . . . ."

In his subsequent communication to Bismarck, Andrássy claimed that he had proposed all of the arrangements agreed upon at Reichstadt (Stolberg to Bismarck, 13 September; *Die Grosse Politik,* II, Doc. No. 233).

[184] Gorchakov had repeatedly, at Berlin and later, argued that real Austrian neutrality would entail closing the port of Klek to Turkish transports. The British, on the other hand, had protested that supplies for the insurgents had gone in through Cattaro. Andrássy felt obliged, therefore, when he at last gave way to Gorchakov's importunities about Klek, to close the other harbor as well.

tection of Austrian interests at the small price in Austrian coin of giving away Rumania's province of Bessarabia and some of the sultan's possessions in Asia. Gorchakov had betrayed certain of his Slavic brethren into the hands of the Magyars and Germans, but he had secured Austrian permission to wipe out the last great loss and humiliation which dated from the disaster in the Crimea.

The completeness of the understanding, however, was based on the completeness of the misunderstanding. No document describing the agreement was drawn up at the time and the specific points were obscured by cautious phraseology. Particularly was this true in that all-important discussion of the extent of Austria's projected annexation. Andrássy in talking with the tsar confined himself to designating on a small-scale map the territories which he was willing to give to the principalities and those which he wanted to take himself.[185] The result was that when he and Gorchakov sat down later to make separate memoranda of the agreement there were several divergencies in the two texts. The major one involved the fate of Bosnia and Hercegovina in case of Turkish defeat. The Russian document read:

> The powers will act together to regulate the consequences of the war.
> They will not favor the establishment of a great Slav state, but Montenegro and Serbia will be permitted to annex: the former, Hercegovina and a port on the Adriatic; the latter, certain parts of Old Serbia and of Bosnia.
> In such a case Austria will have the right to annex Turkish Croatia and certain parts of Bosnia contiguous to her frontiers according to a line to be agreed upon. . . . .

The Austrian document, on the other hand, specified that Serbia would be given territory toward the Drina in Bosnia, in Novi-Bazar and to the river Lim, whereas Montenegro would receive the port of Spizza, an adjacent part of Hercegovina, and additional territory up to the other side of the Lim, so that that stream would be the boundary between the two principalities. "The rest of Bosnia and Hercegovina," Andrássy's version read, "would be annexed to Austria-Hungary."[186] In the autumn the error was going to be discovered.

[185] Andrássy to Novikov, Budapest, 19 December 1876; SA, "Abmachung mit Russland," Doc. No. 20.

[186] The original text of the Austrian document—*Résumé des pourparlers secrets de Reichstadt*—in SA, "Geheime Verträge," bears the notation in Andrássy's hand: *"Niedergeschrieben gleich nach Reichstadt nach meiner dictée durch Novikow und dem russischen Cabinet mitgeteilt."* It is published in Pribram, *The Secret Treaties of Austria-Hungary*, II, 188–91. The Russian version may be found in *Krasni Arkhiv*, I, 36–43, along with a *promemoria* written by Gorchakov and dated 28

Gorchakov was going to claim that "neither the emperor nor I recall that the word Hercegovina was mentioned in this sense,"[187] and Andrássy was going to claim in turn that he had expressly designated on the map the two provinces of Bosnia and Hercegovina,[188] but

June/8 July. The Russian text is reproduced in N. V. Tcharykow, *Glimpses of High Politics, through War and Peace, 1855–1929* (New York, 1931), pp. 103–4. The editors of *Krasni Arkhiv* state (I, 37) that the original is not in the archives. Tcharykow explains (p. 98) that the Russian version was written down in a book into which Gorchakov's confidential secretary copied all his documents.

Before the documents were printed, three accounts of the Reichstadt agreement based on them were printed: Tatishchev, *Imperator Aleksandr II*, II, 315–16; Goriainov, *Le Bosphore et les Dardanelles*, p. 318; and Wertheimer, *Andrássy*, II, 322–34. For a discussion of the relation of these studies to the texts, see George Hoover Rupp, "The Reichstadt Agreement," *American Historical Review*, XXX (April 1925), 503–10. A document which makes much of his speculation no longer necessary is partially given *infra*, note 188.

The accounts given by Diplomaticus ("Secret Treaty of Reichstadt," *Fortnightly Review*, XC [November 1908], 828–37) and by Jean Larmeroux (*La Politique extérieure de l'Autriche-Hongrie, 1875–1914* [Paris, 1918], I, 43–44) are not to be taken seriously. Nor is that of Alexander Karathéodory Pasha (*Le Rapport secret sur le congrès de Berlin* . . . . [Paris, 1919], p. 130) to the effect that the Rumanian minister Cogalniceano had had in his hands copies of pencil-written documents exchanged by Gorchakov and Andrássy at Reichstadt. (There is an English translation of Karathéodory's statement in Hanotaux, *Contemporary France*, IV, 361, note 1.) The Rumanian agent in Vienna most certainly knew nothing more than he was supposed to know (Iorga, *Correspondance*, p. 133, Doc. No. 300; p. 134, Doc. No. 303), although Iorga, who found no proof of the assertion in the Rumanian documents, is apparently inclined to give the story some credence (*ibid.*, p. xxx).

During the course of the conversations between Andrássy and Gorchakov at Reichstadt, the former renewed the attempt which he had made in Berlin to dislodge General Ignatiev from Constantinople. He told the chancellor that public opinion—that old and handy phantom—could hardly believe in a complete understanding with Russia so long as the redoubtable ambassador remained at his post, and he offered to recall Zichy, whom he alleged to be entirely satisfactory, if Gorchakov would replace Ignatiev. Gorchakov again refused the request, stating that the general's recall would at that time give the Turks and English too much satisfaction. He did, however, intimate that it was possible in case Sir Henry Elliot was also supplanted. Andrássy forwarded the proposition to London (19 July; SA, England, 1876), but it is not certain whether or not Beust presented it to Derby; at all events nothing came of it.

[187] Annex II of letter, Gorchakov to Novikov, 23 November/5 December; SA, "Abmachung mit Russland"; ". . . . Quant aux vues de l'Autriche, il nous semble qu'il y a un malentendu. A Reichstadt M. le comte Andrássy ne nous a parlé que d'une partie de la Bosnie et de la Croatie turque. Il m'avait même dit qu'il m'enverrait une carte où seraient indiquées les limites de ces acquisitions. Ni l'Empereur ni moi nous ne nous souvenons que le mot même de l'Herzégovine ait été prononcé dans ce sens. . . . ."

[188] Andrássy to Novikov, 19 December; *ibid:* ". . . . Quant au malentendu relatif aux annexions éventuelles de l'Autriche-Hongrie dont le prince chancelier

those controversies were on 8 July problems for the future. At that time Austria and Russia in the persons of their monarchs and their chief ministers had seemingly agreed in their attitude toward the war recently declared on Turkey by Serbia and Montenegro.

Before quitting Reichstadt Prince Gorchakov drew up a statement describing the agreement reached, and that statement, with slight variations, made the rounds of Europe in the next few days as an authentic account of the interview:

> The two emperors have departed in the best accord, resolved to proclaim the principle of non-intervention at this time. They anticipate a subsequent understanding with the great Christian powers if circumstances demonstrate the necessity for it.[189]

---

parle à Votre Excellence, je ne peux me rendre compte de ce qui a pu y donner lieu. Je ne disconviens pas qu'au début de l'entretien que j'ai eu l'honneur d'avoir à Berlin avec Sa Majesté l'Empereur Alexandre et Son Altesse le prince de Gortchacow, en parlant d'une manière générale des remaniements territoriaux qui pourraient devenir inévitables et des droits que nos Croates croyaient avoir sur la partie de la Bosnie qu'on appelle la Croatie turque, je n'aie pas fait mention de l'Herzégovine. Mais lorsque plus tard à Reichstadt l'Empereur Alexandre me fit l'honneur de me demander des renseignements plus précis, je désignais expressément à Sa Majesté sur la carte les deux provinces ottomanes—la Bosnie et l'Herzégovine—qui séparent la Dalmatie du reste de l'Autriche-Hongrie. Cette carte étant à petite échelle, je promis au prince, sur sa demande, de lui désigner exactement les limites du territoire en question sur une carte plus détaillée.

"L'Herzégovine est en outre mentionnée en toutes lettres dans l'aide-mémoire sur les résultats de l'entrevue, que vous avez écrit sous ma dictée immédiatement après l'entrevue. Je vous ai prié de vouloir bien placer un double de cette pièce sous les yeux du prince chancelier. Jusqu'à ce jour elle n'avait provoqué aucune observation de sa part. Il y a donc évidemment un malentendu et j'aime à espérer que le prince voudra bien se souvenir de ces détails. . . ."

[189] Pribram, op. cit., II, 190. Andrássy to Kuefstein, Beust, and Gravenegg, 9 July; First Red Book, Doc. No. 539, a German translation of Gorchakov's text. R. W. Seton-Watson, "Russian Commitments in the Bosnian Question," Slavonic Review, VIII, 582, note 1. Seton-Watson publishes correspondence between Andrássy and Beust and shows how misleading the Austrian statements were. Tel. and Report No. 456, Buchanan to Derby, 10 July; Turkey No. 3 (1876), Doc. No. 529. Derby to Buchanan, 10 July; ibid., Doc. No. 530. Tel. No. 61, Beust to Andrássy, 10 July; First Red Book, Doc. No. 540.

The same misleading account the Austrian minister sent to his ally in Berlin (Andrássy to Károlyi, 9 July; SA, "Abmachung mit Russland"); but in September, when his problems were more serious, Andrássy sent a confidential confession to the German chancellor (Stolberg to Bismarck, 13 September; Die Grosse Politik, II, Doc. No. 233). Schweinitz asserted that Bismarck took so seriously Andrássy's request for discretion that he did not reveal the secret even to Emperor William (Denkwürdigkeiten, II, 335).

Gorchakov sent a copy of his statement en clair to Ignatiev, and it, as Elliot reported, "consequently passed through the hands of the Porte." He continued— with apparent indignation: "The expression that the Great 'Christian' Powers might

SUMMARY

In July the Balkan crisis had gone through its first year. One expedient after another designed for its solution had been proposed and one after another their failures had left the problem more complicated than before. With the Great Powers hopelessly divided on any constructive program, the principalities of Serbia and Montenegro had marched forward with their military preparations and had finally, in the face of remonstrances which Andrássy had not been able to convert into convincing threats, declared their long-awaited war on Turkey. The Russian government, anticipating a Slavic victory, had then proposed a European policy of strict non-intervention but no foreign office had been willing to commit itself so sweepingly in the uncertain future. The French minister had tried again to reconcile England to the Continent; but the London cabinet, unmindful of the first storm clouds on the horizon of public opinion, had continued to be indifferent to the French importunities and defiant toward all things Russian. Count Andrássy had refused to allow Balkan affairs to take their own course but, moved by the desire for co-operation with Russia so long as agreement was at all possible, had met with Prince Gorchakov and they, together with Tsar Alexander, had arrived at what they thought was a clear understanding regarding Turkey's eventual victory or collapse.

The future, however, was not easily harnessed in July of 1876. European history was sprinkled with accounts of the miscarriage of plans between sovereign states, of wars that went contrary to expectation, of the caprice of public opinion; and to the record was destined to be added one more, having its own peculiarities of time and

---

have to come to an understanding amongst themselves has been taken as implying that the intention of the Northern Governments is that the measures to be adopted with regard to the insurgent provinces shall be concerted without consultation with the Turkish Government, upon whom it is intended to enforce compliance with their decision" (Report No. 795, Elliot to Derby, 27 July; FO 78/2461).

Andrássy in his notification to the Porte was much more diplomatic toward Turkey and much less generous toward Russia: "Eröffnen Sie Pforte zu ihrer Beruhigung vertraulich, dass wir in Reichstadt ubereingekommen sind an Nichtintervention unter gegenwärtigen Verhältnissen festzuhalten, wodurch selbstverständlich jede Gefahr einer militärischen Intervention Russlands ausgeschlossen erscheint. Alle neueren Vorschläge bezüglich Bosniens und der Herzegovina sind aufgegeben, und man behält sich lediglich vor, wenn die Umstände es fordern sollten, ein vertrauliches Einvernehmen zwischen den Grossmächten herbeizuführen, bis dahin aber den Ereignissen freien Lauf zu lassen" (Tel. No. 93, Andrássy to Zichy, 9 July; SA, Turkey, 1876).

circumstance. But for the moment there was a pause in the maneuvers of diplomacy; Europe looked back over a year's failure in the attempts of sovereign states to cope with a disturbance begun by a small band of Hercegovinians, and Europe looked forward with uncertainty to further attempts on the part of those same sovereign states whose interests dictated a vital concern for what happened in the Balkan Peninsula and whose sole morality was to define and defend those interests as each of itself saw fit.

Appendix

APPENDIX A

THE ACTIVITIES OF WESSELITSKY-BOJIDAROVICH

During the same time that Baron Rodich was attempting his work of pacification there was also busy in Hercegovina a Russian agent who assumed in
suspicious eyes—and there were many—the role of a man of mystery. Gabriel
de Wesselitsky-Bojidarovich, descendant of a Hercegovinian family settled for
several generations in Russia, had gone to his ancestral home soon after the
outbreak of the rebellion to organize and direct a relief organization. In January 1876 he went to Russia, at least ostensibly to collect funds for his charitable work. Stopping for a visit in Vienna, he called on Novikov, the Russian
ambassador, and discussed with him the question of the revolt and possible
means of settlement. According to Wesselitsky's own story, written when he
was an old man, Novikov asked him to draw up a memorandum on a peaceful
solution, and the ambassador was so pleased with it when finished that he sent
it to St. Petersburg. In the Russian capital Wesselitsky was received by the
tsar and Gorchakov. The latter, according to the memoir, welcomed the relief
worker, graciously praised his memorandum, and gave him the commission to
return to Hercegovina and use his influence toward persuading the insurgents
to accept the dispositions of the Great Powers.[1] Wesselitsky's own words
have it that he warned the chancellor that the Hercegovinians would not submit until the Turkish troops were withdrawn, but that Gorchakov responded
that it would not at that time be possible to garrison the province with local
troops and to give over the administration to a Hercegovinian. On 10 February, at the chancellor's request, Wesselitsky drew up a new memorandum,
summarizing the conversation which had taken place between them some days
earlier. The document recapitulated Gorchakov's expressed desire that the insurgents should submit, recorded the mission assigned to the writer, and re-
stated Wesselitsky's own views on the necessity for the withdrawal of Turkish
troops and for an *administration provinciale particulière*.[2] The British ambassador in St. Petersburg wrote of Wesselitsky and his mission as follows:

> In regard to M. Wassiletzky, I may inform Your Lordship that he is a private
> person domiciled for some years in Russia but originally a native of the Herzegovine.
> He has interested himself in the cause of his countrymen, and during the winter held
> meetings with a view to collect money for the relief of the sick and wounded in the
> Herzegovine. Before leaving St. Petersburg as a member of the Red Cross for the
> Herzegovine, he was received by Prince Gortchakow, who charged him to inform
> the Insurgent Chiefs that, if they resisted the counsels of Europe, they had nothing
> to expect from Russia. To this may be attributed the report that he was an agent

---

[1] G. de Wesselitsky-Bojidarovich, *Dix mois de ma vie*, pp. 92–107; hereafter
cited as *Dix mois*.

[2] Wesselitsky-Bojidarovich, *La Bosnie-Herzégovine* (Paris, 1919), pp. 68–69;
text of the memorandum, pp. 86–87.

of the Russian government, whereas Prince Gortchakow had only profited of his position and influence with the insurgents to make known to them the wishes of the Imperial Government. I am informed that M. Wassiletzky is very moderate and conciliatory although his sympathies are with the Insurgents and that he is very anxious to aid in bringing about a Pacification.[3]

According to the two accounts related by Wesselitsky, when he was again in Vienna en route to the scene of the rebellion *"une mutuelle et soudaine sympathie"* took possession of him and Andrássy. The latter allegedly threw down his reserve and branded Rodich not only his own principal enemy but the principal enemy of the Dual Monarchy as well. The mission of the governor-general of Dalmatia, Andrássy supposedly told his visitor, was ordered by Emperor Francis Joseph and inspired by the aristocratic court circle, when those elements in Vienna, intent on expansion, began to fear that Wesselitsky's mission of peace was almost certain of success. But Andrássy, for his own part, fearing the intrigues of Rodich, formally asked Wesselitsky to speak in his name also to the insurgents.[4] Wesselitsky's statements are only partially confirmed by Andrássy: ". . . . Bozidarovic-Wesselicki hat Mission Fürsten Nicolaus zur Pacification zu bewegen, und scheint mit gutem Willen daranzuarbeiten. Ich habe ihm Ihre Unterstützung versprochen. . . . ."[5]

The peace emissary first went to Cetinje to interview Prince Nicholas. According to the memoirs, the prince was somewhat defiant and suspicious toward him as a new factor which might undermine the exclusive control over the insurgents which Nicholas professed to have. Wesselitsky tried to mollify him by telling him that he had taken the initiative of attempting to persuade the Great Powers to grant an extension of territory for Montenegro. From Cetinje, Wesselitsky went over the frontier into Hercegovina, and on 4 April —two days before Rodich's first interview—gave the insurgents the messages he had received in St. Petersburg and Vienna.[6] After his speech he returned to Cattaro, mysteriously meeting Rodich and an elaborately uniformed suite en route. Wesselitsky had himself apparently prepared a list of four conditions for pacification in elaborating the ideas which he had presented to Novikov and Gorchakov. They were, according to his memoirs: (1) *administration provinciale particulière;* (2) gradual withdrawal of troops recruited in other parts of Turkey and their replacement by native soldiers; (3) assistance in the form of reconstruction of destroyed buildings and of food and seed until the next harvest; and (4) a general amnesty.[7] These points, he states, were

[3] Report No. 138, Loftus to Derby, 12 April; FO 65/936, suppressed from *Turkey No. 3 (1876)*, Doc. No. 138.

[4] *Dix mois,* pp. 139–40, 151–52; *La Bosnie-Herzégovine,* pp. 69–70.

[5] Andrássy to Rodich, 8 March; SA, Varia Turquie I, 1875.

[6] *The Times* (London), 7 April 1876, p. 5, col. 2.

[7] *Dix mois,* pp. 155–56. In a letter dated Ragusa, 5/17 March, Wesselitsky gave to Andrássy a statement of four points which he characterized as the wishes of the insurgents and which vary somewhat from the four points which appear in the memoirs of a man approaching ninety years: (1) withdrawal of the Turkish troops during the repatriation work with the exception of those in certain fortresses; (2) material proof that provisions and materials would be furnished until the next harvest; (3) surveillance of reforms and especially of repatriation by European com-

agreed upon as the substance of the written reply which the insurgents promised to give him on the following day. When the reply came to him, however, he found to his painful surprise that it had been elaborated into the seven points which were to be given to Baron Rodich two days later. It was a text, he writes, "dont la rédaction diffuse contenait quelques exigences additionnelles plus offensantes pour les Turcs que nécessaires aux Herzégoviniens."[8]

In addition to stating their demands in their reply, the leaders, addressing Wesselitsky as a "son of our country," asked him to present their conditions to Turkey and the Great Powers and to be the representative of their interests. A few days later he received an address from the Bosnian leaders giving him full power as their agent. The conditions laid down by this latter group, however, did not coincide with those of their Hercegovinian brethren. They were essentially a restatement of the four points which Wesselitsky had represented to Andrássy on 5/17 March as the insurgent demands—not the *"points Wesselitsky"* which evidently he later imagined.[9] The quondam philanthropist accepted this commission and on 11 April left Ragusa en route to Vienna, St. Petersburg, and Constantinople.[10] Wesselitsky subsequently recalled an enthusiastic reception in Vienna where Ambassador Novikov gave him "the most sincere support" and where Andrássy, enthusiastic about his alleged victory over Rodich and allegedly sympathetic toward the insurgent demands, urged him to persuade the Turks.[11] The contemporary documents record another story. Novikov declared that Wesselitsky's mission was at an end when he made his declaration and that his subsequent actions were his own private affair in which the ambassador had no interest.[12] The British ambassador found that the new agent was persona non grata in Vienna and suspected of overweening ambitions to be made governor or prince of Hercegovina,[13] while

missioners; and (4) the privilege to the Christians of maintaining arms on terms of equality with the Mohammedans (Tel., Andrássy to Rodich, 27 March; SA, Varia Turquie I, 1875). See also *Turkey No. 3 (1876)*, inclosure in Doc. No. 122.

[8] *Dix mois,* p. 167. The text of the letter to Wesselitsky may be found in *ibid.,* pp. 162–65, and in *La Bosnie-Herzégovine,* pp. 88–90, in slightly varying phraseology. Wesselitsky's claim (*Dix mois,* p. 155) that the *"points Wesselitsky"* had been accepted by the Turks in a circular to the Great Powers in March must be attributed to that flourishing megalomania which characterizes both of his books. The same may be said of his statement that the question of his mission was debated and arranged by the ambassadors in Constantinople (*ibid.,* pp. 152–53). The list of corrections, however, is too long.

[9] *La Bosnie-Herzégovine,* pp. 92–94. This Bosnian address was published in the Belgian *Nord* and reproduced in *The Times* of 27 May and subsequently copied in the English translation in *Turkey No. 3 (1876)*, inclosure in Doc. No. 313.

[10] *The Times* (London), 13 April 1876, p. 5, col. 3; 20 April, p. 10, cols. 2–3. A letter written by Wesselitsky to the *Nord,* in which he briefly reviews his commission from Gorchakov and his negotiations with the insurgents, appears in *ibid.,* 25 April, p. 7, cols. 5–6. See also Report No. 206, Buchanan to Derby, 13 April; *Turkey No. 3 (1876)*, Doc. No. 139.

[11] *Dix mois,* pp. 183–85; *La Bosnie-Herzégovine,* p. 72.

[12] Report No. 221, Buchanan to Derby, 20 April; *Turkey No. 3 (1876)*, Doc. No. 155, incomplete.

[13] Report No. 215, Buchanan to Derby, 20 April; *ibid.,* Doc. No. 153.

the criticisms which Andrássy made of the insurgent conditions were much more than the meaningless conventionality which Wesselitsky subsequently asserted him to be.[14]

The remainder of the memoir of the "representative of the Bosnians and the Hercegovinians" is excellent melodrama. The next scene was enacted at the Turkish embassy, where Aarifi Pasha was suddenly transmuted from a violent denunciator into a warm friend and convert to the plan of an *administration provinciale particulière* which Wesselitsky had proposed in February to Gorchakov—with the hope, it seems fairly certain, of being placed at the head of the new principality. The proposed journey to Russia was abandoned when Ignatiev urged him to come immediately to Constantinople. He went with the warm approval of Novikov and Andrássy and was received with pleasure by both Ignatiev and the grand vizier. Mahmud, so the reminiscence goes, declared that he had already sent a circular to the Great Powers announcing that the Ottoman government was ready to ratify *"les points Wesselitsky,"* and then proceeded to invite his guest to supervise the work of repatriation and, when that task was finished, to become governor-general of the united province of Bosnia and Hercegovina! Wesselitsky recalls that he accepted the first labor but asked for time to consider the second and greater offer. Back in Vienna he was feted as the representative of the oppressed Slavs; rumors began to circulate about a new post, and the world sought his favor. A wine company wanted to name a new brand of champagne Wesselitsky-Bojidarovich; financiers wanted him to collaborate in establishing a new Monte Carlo in Hercegovina; rich and high-born ladies dreamed of marrying their daughters to him. But in the end, despite Vienna's swirl at his feet, despite the tsar's congratulations to one of his regiments for its having had Wesselitsky once upon a time as lieutenant, the agent of peace declined the office of governor-general of Bosnia and Hercegovina[15] and sank into obscurity.[16]

[14] *Dix mois*, p. 185. Report No. 222, Buchanan to Derby, 20 April; *Turkey No. 3 (1876)*, Doc. No. 156.

[15] *Dix mois*, pp. 168 ff.

[16] For a review of the life of this interesting character see R. W. Seton-Watson, "Gabriel Wesselitsky," *Slavonic Review*, IX (1931), 732–35.

APPENDIX B

DOCUMENTS CONCERNING THE BERLIN MEMORANDUM

1. TEXT OF THE MEMORANDUM BROUGHT BY PRINCE GORCHAKOV TO BERLIN[1]

La question de la pacification de l'Herzégovine est entrée dans la phase suivante :

Les réfugiés ont répondu aux pressantes recommandations qui leur ont été faites de la part de l'Autriche-Hongrie et de la Russie qu'ils appréciaient l'utilité des améliorations consignées en leur faveur dans la dépêche de M. le comte Andrássy du 30 décembre, et qu'ils étaient prêts à s'en contenter et à rentrer dans leurs foyers, si leur sécurité personnelle et l'exécution de ces réformes leur étaient garanties.

Quelles peuvent être ces garanties ?

Selon le plan primitif de M. le comte Andrássy elles résidaient dans le fait *moral* que les Puissances avaient par une démarche identique fait parvenir à la Porte la demande formelle de certaines réformes destinées, dans leur opinion, à remédier à la situation déplorable de la Bosnie et de l'Herzégovine, et à mettre ainsi un terme aux agitations continuelles qui troublaient la tranquillité publique au détriment du repos de l'Europe et de la Turquie elle-même.

La Porte ayant déclaré déférer à cette demande, il en résultait un engagement positif contracté par elle envers les cabinets et, par conséquent, pour ceux-ci l'obligation morale de veiller à l'exécution de cette promesse qui devait avoir pour corollaire une pression morale à exercer sur les insurgés pour les engager à poser les armes.

On pensait que les réfugiés et les insurgés devaient seconder de leur côté les efforts d'apaisement des cabinets et rentrer dans leurs foyers en se confiant à la protection des Puissances, qui avaient acquis le droit, possédaient la force, et rempliraient certainement le devoir d'assurer l'accomplissement des réformes promises, constituant pour eux toute la somme d'améliorations réelles que les circonstances permettaient d'obtenir.

Cependant les chefs insurgés ont objecté que l'expérience du passé leur interdisait la possibilité de s'en remettre à la bonne foi des autorités turques dans une question où il s'agissait de leur existence à moins d'un contrôle efficace et de garanties matérielles de la part des Puissances.

Ils ont formulé ces garanties d'abord en quatre points. L'ambassadeur de Russie à Constantinople s'efforça de les faire admettre par la Porte au moyen de quelques atténuations. Ces modifications avaient rencontré un accueil favorable près de Rachid Pacha. Mais plus tard, sous l'influence de diverses

---

[1] "Original des ursprünglichen Vorschlages welcher vom Fürsten Gortschakoff in Berlin gemacht wurde und im Namen der drei Mächte den Grossmächten mitgeteilt werden sollte," SA, Varia Russia, 1876.

circonstances, les chefs insurgés ont formulé avec plus de précision et d'extension leurs conditions en sept points.

Ces conditions ont été différemment appréciées. Le Cabinet Impérial de Russie a jugé qu'elles pouvaient être une base de discussion. Le Cabinet de Vienne a trouvé qu'elles dépassaient le programme accepté par les Puissances, présenté par elles à la Porte et auquel celle-ci avait adhéré. Il a pensé en conséquence qu'il n'avait pas le droit de les soutenir à Constantinople et il a invité les chefs insurgés à s'adresser directement à la Porte.

Toutefois après mûre réflexion, M. le comte Andrássy a jugé possible d'appuyer auprès de la Porte les demandes des insurgés, réduites aux points suivants : Les matériaux pour la reconstruction des maisons et des églises seront fournis aux réfugiés rentrants, leur subsistance sera assurée, jusqu'à ce qu'ils puissent vivre de leur travail. En tant que la distribution des secours relèverait du commissaire turc, celui-ci devrait s'entendre sur les mesures à prendre avec la commission mixte, mentionnée dans la note du 30 décembre, afin de garantir l'application sérieuse des réformes et d'en contrôler l'exécution. Cette commission sera présidée par un Herzégovinien chrétien, composée d'indigènes représentant fidèlement les deux religions du pays ; ils seront élus à la fin des hostilités. A l'effet d'éviter toute collision, le conseil sera donné à Constantinople de concentrer les troupes turques au moins jusqu'à l'apaisement des esprits, sur quelque point au choix de la Porte. Les Chrétiens garderont leurs armes comme les Mussulmans. Les consuls ou délégués des Puissances exerceront leur surveillance sur l'application des réformes en général et sur les faits relatifs au repatriement en particulier.

Tel est l'état de la question. Il semble en résulter : (1) qu'en tout cas les conditions formulées par les chefs insurgés, sans être toutes acceptables, peuvent être toutes discutées, comme ouvrant une voie possible vers l'apaisement ; (2) qu'il y aurait par conséquent avantage à obtenir de la Porte une suspension d'armes et l'ouverture des pourparlers directs avec les délégués herzégoviniens ; (3) que la plupart de ces conditions seraient susceptibles de transactions qui les rendraient acceptables par les deux parties ; (4) qu'elles ont moins pour but d'étendre le programme des réformes que d'en garantir la fidèle exécution ; (5) que le fond essentiel de la question, et en même temps le principal obstacle, résident dans le contrôle et la garantie extérieure réclamés par les chefs insurgés, vu que d'un côté la Porte rejette ces exigences comme une atteinte à sa souveraineté et une offense à sa dignité, tandis que de l'autre les insurgés déclarent que sans ces conditions ils ne peuvent avoir aucune confiance, ni dans la sécurité, ni dans les secours, ni dans les réformes promises par la Porte. C'est donc sur ce point spécial que doit se porter l'attention des Cabinets.

Le contrôle européen peut être moral ou matériel.

Le programme de M. le comte Andrássy n'implique qu'un contrôle moral. Il résulte du droit acquis par les Puissances par le fait qu'elles ont demandé à la Porte certaines réformes dans un intérêt européen, et que la Porte leur a fait connaître officiellement sa ferme résolution d'exécuter ces réformes. Il résulte en outre du fait qu'en échange de cette communication les Cabinets ont usé d'une pression énergique sur les insurgés de l'Herzégovine et sur les Principautés voisines pour amener la pacification.

Comment ce droit aurait-il à s'exercer? C'est ce qui n'est pas précisé. Dans l'état actuel des choses les consuls résidant sur place surveilleraient avec soin la marche des affaires et rendraient compte de la situation à leurs ambassades. Celles-ci useraient de remontrances amicales auprès des ministres turcs. La Porte ne se refuse pas à ce genre de contrôle auquel elle est habituée. Mais il est à remarquer qu'il existe depuis longtemps sans avoir remédié aux abus. Les enquêtes consulaires se sont toujours faites, quelquefois avec solemnité. Les représentations des ambassadeurs n'ont pas manqué. Les faits ont démontré leur peu d'efficacité. La démarche provoquée par la dépêche de M. le comte Andrássy n'a fait que confirmer le droit moral de remontrance et d'intervention diplomatique déjà constaté par le protocôle de la Conférence de 1861 à l'occasion des affaires de Syrie. Les représentations des ambassadeurs pourront en acquérir plus d'autorité, elles pourront être collectives, et la Porte ne sera pas fondée en droit à y opposer la clause des traités écartant toute ingérence dans les affaires intérieures.

Toutefois l'efficacité pratique d'un pareil contrôle reste douteuse. C'est pourquoi les chefs insurgés, instruits par une longue expérience n'y ont pas confiance, d'autant plus qu'à l'heure qu'il est il ne s'agit pas seulement de vexations chroniques à rendre plus ou moins tolérables, il s'agit pour eux de savoir si, en rentrant dans leurs foyers détruits, eux et leurs familles ne seront pas exposés à périr de faim, de misère ou sous le couteau des mussulmans.

Devant une défiance aussi légitime il n'y a guère à espérer qu'une garantie jugée illusoire puisse amener la pacification désirée. Ce résultat ne pourrait être finalement atteint que si les Cabinets persistaient dans leur pression actuelle sur les insurgés, les forçaient par épuisement et désespoir à se livrer aux autorités turques. Mais une pareille solution répugne aux sentiments d'humanité et même à l'honneur des Grandes Puissances qui assumeraient une grave responsabilité. Elle ne répondrait d'ailleurs pas davantage à leurs intérêts, car l'apaisement effectif dans ces conditions ne serait pas durable et la menace de nouvelles explosions continuerait à peser indéfiniment sur la paix et la prosperité financière de l'Europe.

Les chefs insurgés ont evidemment agi dans cette conviction en demandant que ce contrôle fût renforcé par une commission européenne. L'idée d'une commission consulaire implique la supposition que les consuls résidant sur place agiraient collectivement et non isolément. Leur action ne serait plus directe et aurait plus d'autorité. Cette combinaison n'est pas nouvelle. Elle a été appliquée notamment en Syrie en 1860. Mais à cette époque elle s'est appuyée sur une occupation militaire française par délégation de l'Europe et cette circonstance a certainement contribué à en assurer l'efficacité.

Une commission consulaire dans les conjunctions actuelles rencontrerait deux obstacles. D'abord le manque d'unité et les rivalités personnelles qui caracterisent habituellement ces réunions de consuls. Ensuite l'opposition de la Porte, qui n'a jamais admis cette ingérence directe que sous la pression d'une absolue nécessité. Le premier obstacle pourrait être écarté par l'accord entre les Grandes Puissances. Comme il ne s'agirait point de modifier le *statu quo* politique, mais de le consolider en veillant simplement à l'exécution scrupuleuse de réformes dont les bases sont déjà posées et acceptées, il est permis d'espérer qu'une commission consulaire pourrait fonctionner avec l'ensemble nécessaire. Quant à l'opposition de la Porte, elle exigerait pour être vaincue une pression énergique résultant de la volonté unanime de l'Europe, émanant d'une conférence formelle.

Mais même dans ce cas, il faudrait prévoir les efforts constants des autorités turques pour paralyser et annuler l'activité de la commission. C'est ce que M. le comte Andrássy a déjà signalé, quant au contrôle à exercer sur la distribution des secours aux réfugiés, en faisant remarquer que la Porte pourrait fournir à la commission tout, excepté l'argent. Cette mauvaise volonté s'appliquerait probablement à toute la sphère d'activité de la commission. Elle aura des inconvénients plus sérieux encore, lorsqu'il s'agirait pour les consuls de s'interposer pour empêcher les actes de violence des Mussulmans ou en poursuivre la répression et pour assurer aux Chrétiens l'égalité promise.

Le seul fait qui en Syrie a pu donner aux autorités turques la force et l'énergie nécessaire pour punir les auteurs des massacres de Damas et indemniser les victimes a été l'occupation militaire française. Il serait à craindre que, sans une sanction matérielle analogue une commission consulaire en Herzégovine ne fût plus compromettante qu'efficace. Les mêmes objections s'appliquent à la combinaison d'une commission européenne spéciale. Afin de la rendre plus pratique quelques nuances pourraient y être introduites afin d'éviter de froisser la dignité souveraine du Sultan par une ingérence officielle et directe des Puissances dans l'administration du pays. En dehors de diverses combinaisons énumérées ci-dessus, il ne resterait plus qu'une intervention directe et une occupation, mesures que les Cabinets ont le désir d'éviter aussi longtemps que ce sera possible.

Toutefois en conclusion il semble nécessaire de remarquer que, quelque soit la solution qui serait arrêtée entre les Cabinets, il serait utile d'y ajouter la sanction d'un concert en vue d'une coërcition éventuelle. Jusqu'à présent la Porte envisage l'entente des Cabinets comme purement *négative*. Elle ne croit pas à la possibilité d'une entente active. Tant qu'elle gardera cette conviction, la diplomatie n'aura que peu de prise sur elle, d'autant plus qu'après le précédent de l'intervention en Syrie elle devrait en conclure que l'Europe dans sa situation actuelle est moins résolue et moins à même de faire prévaloir ses volontés même dans une question qui touche à ses intérêts directs qu'elle ne l'a été en 1860. La Porte y puiserait la certitude d'une complète impunité.

Il semble donc indispensable qu'en se concertant sur les meilleurs moyens d'apaiser la crise présente, d'en prévenir le retour périodique, les Puissances s'entendent également sur le principe d'une coërcition éventuelle, afin d'affirmer aux yeux des Turcs leur ferme résolution de ne point laisser la paix générale à la merci de leur incurie ou de leur fanatisme.

2. RUSSELL TO DERBY, BERLIN, 15 MAY 1876[2]

My Lord,

After the Conference on Saturday was over, of which I sent Your Lordship the result in my Despatch No 204 of the 13th instant, both Prince Gortchacow and Count Andrassy asked me privately and separately to come and see them on the following day.

[2] Report No. 209, secret; FO 64/852.

I called first on Count Andrassy at the Austrian Embassy. He shewed me the last Telegrams he had received from Count Zichy at Constantinople. They contained the same information exactly as those Your Lordship has received from Sir Henry Elliot and communicated to me.

Indeed Count Zichy says in one of them that he entirely shares the views taken by Sir Henry Elliot of recent events, and thinks those held by General Ignatieff exaggerated and personal.

Count Andrassy observed that he had not himself always been able to his regret to agree with Sir Henry Elliot,—but that he fully agreed in the present instance with Count Zichy and Sir Henry, and thought General Ignatieff's spirit of intrigue had had a mischievous influence at Constantinople.

He would tell me in strict confidence that he had not concealed his opinion from Prince Gortchacow and had proposed to him to recall Count Zichy and send a new Ambassador, if he would do the same and recall General Ignatieff, but Prince Gortchacow would not agree, and he had therefore not thought himself in a position to speak of this proposition to the Czar.

He was, however, still convinced that the removal of General Ignatieff would tend largely to simplify matters at Constantinople.

General Ignatieff, he said, had never forgiven him for refusing to receive him as Ambassador at Vienna, and for having asked for Mr de Novikoff in preference, who was an honest, truthful Agent with whom he was able to entertain the most intimate and satisfactory relations.

Count Andrassy then went on to repeat most of the Statements he had recently made to Her Majesty's Ambassador at Vienna on the subject of the insurrection, the attitude of Montenegro, the weakness of the Porte, and the secret pretensions of the King of Greece, all of which appear in Sir Andrew Buchanan's report to Your Lordship. He asserted his conviction that the principles laid down in his Note of the 30 December which had met with the support of the European Powers, would with time and patience be carried out, and would finally bring about the desired pacification,—whilst any attempt at autonomy or redistribution of territory would only awaken national passions more likely to increase than to quell the excitement it was the object of the Northern Powers to extinguish in the interest of the Christians, the Turks, and humanity in general.

The occupation of Herzegovine or Bosnia by a foreign Power he looked upon as a temporary measure, but not as a solution to the question and as far as he was concerned he would never consent to it.

The result of his Conferences with Prince Bismarck and Prince Gortchacow which had been communicated to us yesterday,—would facilitate the carrying out by the Porte of the Principles of his Note of the 30th December and he most sincerely hoped it would meet with the approval and support of Her Majesty's Government.

I said that Her Majesty's Government would always be ready to support peace and the integrity of the Turkish Empire,—but that there was a passage in the Memorandum the Conference had communicated to us, which in my opinion was somewhat obscure and required explanation. I alluded to the last sentence which said, that if the armistice expired without having brought about the desired result,—"les trois Cours Impériales sont d'avis qu'il deviendrait nécessaire d'ajouter à leur action diplomatique la sanction d'une entente, en vue des mesures efficaces qui paraîtraient réclamées dans l'intérêt de la paix générale pour arrêter le mal et en empêcher le développement."

Count Andrassy replied that it simply meant that if the proposed measures failed, other ones would become necessary.

What measures? I asked.

After a moment's hesitation Count Andrassy replied that circumstances might so alter the situation of affairs that it was impossible to foretell what measures might be thought necessary by the guaranteeing Powers two months hence,—he therefore preferred not to enter upon conjectures and speculations for the present.

Count Andrassy then changed the subject and spoke in the highest praise of his friend Lord Lytton, and of the pleasure with which he had heard of his appointment as Governor General of India. After some further general conversation I took my leave and called on Prince Gortchacow at the Russian Embassy.

Prince Gortchacow received me with his usual demonstrations of benevolent friendliness and then read me his last telegrams from General Ignatieff.

They recounted the same events as Sir Henry Elliot's and Count Zichy's telegrams, but in very sensational language, and dwelt on the great danger to which he, General Ignatieff was personally exposed at the hands of the enemies of Russia in Stamboul.

Prince Gortchacow said that Turkey was a Powder Magazine, which a spark might blow up. Anything and everything might occur at Constantinople and we must be prepared for surprises. He certainly did not wish Turkey to break up, and the present Conferences which he had asked for proved his sincere desire to maintain peace and the territorial "Status quo," but recent events led him to fear that the Turkish Empire was weaker and further advanced in general decay than he had himself believed possible. We stood before the unknown (*l'inconnu*) and the united action based on a cordial and intimate understanding and agreement of the great Powers alone could save Turkey from crumbling to pieces. No doubt all that could be done was a mere replastering—"*replâtrage*"—but if it made the Edifice last a few years longer, our efforts would be well repaid.

For this reason he attached the greatest importance to the support of England and the other great Powers France and Italy. He had all along insisted on an "*entente à 6 et pas seulement à 3*" and then lowering his voice Prince Gortchacow added: "more so than my allies, who do not see the importance of it, as I do."

The Russian Chancellor then explained that the measures submitted by the Conference to the approval of Her Majesty's Government, for he was anxious for Your Lordship's opinion and advice, were very mild, perhaps too mild; but it was essential at this moment not to propose anything that the Porte in her present difficulties could not at once accept, and all the guaranteeing Powers subscribe to without hesitation. If the Porte were asked too much and if the Great Powers could not at once cordially agree, time would be wasted in discussion. In a crisis like the present one, every hour was precious to prevent bloodshed and the spread of religious fanaticism.

He took a very serious view of the impending danger,—far more so than Count Andrassy who was an optimist. He had told him so, and had shewed him General Ignatieff's reports which had evidently made an impression on the Count, and had opened his eyes to the calamities which threatened Turkey and which he had not before sufficiently realized, from an innate tendency to believe that things settled themselves by leaving them alone. I repeated the same question to Prince Gortchacow which I had put to Count Andrassy respecting the last sentence of the Memorandum communicated to us by the Conference and said I did not understand what future measures were alluded to.

Prince Gortchacow also replied that they were measures to be concerted by all the guaranteeing Powers according to the requirements of the moment. A measure for instance which had occurred to him as useful would be to station ships in all the Ports of Turkey, and agree that in the event of the Turkish authorities demanding assistance against an outburst of fanaticism, a portion of the crew should be allowed to land to support the authority of the Turkish Governors in case of need.

The Ships of all nations would become Temples of refuge for the persecuted Christians in the East sailing under the Red Cross of Geneva.

Time, of course, would shew what was required. What he asked for, was unity in thought and purpose on the part of the six guaranteeing Powers, so as to compel the Turkish Government to do what was necessary for their own salvation.

In the further course of conversation, Prince Gortchacow said he was not a Pan-slavist, which was a Republican idea, but a Russian, which was the embodiment of peace, progress and order. He further said that he would remain at Ems with the Czar, and would go to Wildbad while His Majesty was at Jugenheim, so as to be within call, if wanted.

I took my leave, and as Prince Bismarck was not visible, I called on Herr von Bülow. He said that the German Government had great confidence in Count Andrassy's knowledge of Eastern affairs, and that they thought the practical measures proposed by him for the pacification of the Herzegovine would lead finally, though perhaps slowly, to the desired end. The cooperation of France and Italy was already promised, and that of England was anxiously and most sincerely hoped for.

His Excellency further said that a portion of the German Fleet would be sent to Salonica, and a second Gunboat to Constantinople for the protection of the German Residents in case of need.

On my asking him how he interpreted the last sentence of the Memorandum of the Conference, and what measures were alluded to, he replied that it simply meant that the Northern Powers would invite the other Great Powers to join in a general Conference to discuss the best means of giving renewed vitality to the Turkish Empire, and of improving the condition of the Christians in the Herzegovine.

That is all I have been able to learn from the Members of the Berlin Conference. The impression prevailing among persons who are generally well-informed is, that Prince Gortchacow had a plan of his own for dealing with the question which he could not prevail upon his colleagues to accept,—Prince Bismarck and Count Andrassy having met previously and determined to resist any policy suggested by General Ignatieff. Be that as it may, no one can say what Prince Gortchacow's plan may have been.

Certain it is that he must have expected the Conferences to last longer than they did, as well as the treatment of subjects which do not appear to have been discussed at all, for he had sent for Monsieur de Novikoff, and one of his Secretaries from Vienna, for Mr Wassilitz, the Herzegovinian Agent, for the Russian Consul General from Ragusa, and for the Senator Petrovich from Montenegro, as well as for several Cabinet Messengers to await his orders in Berlin.

Monsieur de Novikoff found nothing to do, Monsieur Wassilitz was never consulted, the Consul General arrived too late, and the Senator Petrovich was telegraphed to to remain at Vienna.

Of the Messengers, only one was sent to Constantinople. Prince Bismarck was never alluded to in conversation with me either by the Russian or the Austrian Chancellor, and during the Conference, he was unusually reserved and serious.

I have the honour . . . .

3. RUSSELL TO DERBY, BERLIN, 26 MAY 1876[3]

My Lord,

I found an opportunity of mentioning personally to Prince Bismarck before his departure for Lauenburg the regret Her Majesty's Government experienced in having to separate themselves from the action of the German Government in regard to the proposals submitted to them by the three Northern Powers for the pacification of Bosnia and Herzegovina,—and in obedience to Your Lordship's instruction No 386 "very confidential and secret" of the 19th instant, already previously communicated in substance to me by telegraph, I repeated that Her Majesty's Government would be glad to act in concert with the German Government in all matters, so far as it may be possible to do so, since they believe that the interests of Germany and of Great Britain are equally directed to the maintenance of the territorial "Status quo," and the preservation of European Peace.

The objections of Her Majesty's Government entertained to the Berlin proposals in question, which they had no reason to suppose originated with the German Government, were founded on general principles. Your Lordship had told the German Ambassador at the earliest moment what they were, in order that His Highness should receive timely intimation of them.

Prince Bismarck replied that he was gratified by Your Lordship's message, but he nevertheless regretted that Her Majesty's Government had separated themselves from the united action of the other five Powers. No one could contest the right of England to follow the course best calculated to serve her interests, and as to Germany, her interests would not be affected by the ultimate fate of Turkey, but Germany like England, as Your Lordship said, was interested in the maintenance of peace,—and peace, as matters now stood, depended on the continuance of the friendly understanding existing between Austria and Russia, which the general concert of the six great Powers tended to confirm and consolidate, but which the withdrawal of the support of England might weaken and disturb.

Russia was better prepared than Austria to bear the consequences of a

[3] Report No. 234, "very confl & secret"; FO 64/852.

quarrel, whilst Austria was not in a condition to stand a conflict with Russia without serious damage to herself.

If a difference of opinion arose between them, the position of Germany would become extremely difficult,—with every wish for a neutral position, Germany might be compelled in her efforts to maintain peace to take the part of either Russia or Austria, and then would come the moment when the moral support of England might be advantageously put forward in the interest of peace. For this reason, he welcomed the proffered cooperation of Her Majesty's Government, and tendered his thanks to Your Lordship for the message I had conveyed to him.

He regretted that Your Lordship had not, in January last, when he invited an understanding on Eastern Affairs, initiated some more detailed line of policy, but he thought that the present situation might even facilitate an agreement as to what was really wanted for the preservation of peace, in case of danger.

In the first instance, he could not but hope that Her Majesty's Government might be able to lend their moral support to Austria, because he looked upon the independence and strength of Austria as essential to the peace of Europe.

Count Andrassy, who was the author of the memorandum of the 13th of May, had sustained a severe defeat by the refusal of Her Majesty's Government to support the proposals of the Berlin Conference.

The traditional policy of England was favourable to Austria, and he had no doubt it would continue so,—he therefore also hoped that Count Andrassy would, if unduly pressed by Russia, receive some support and encouragement at Your Lordship's hands. Count Andrassy needed it and deserved it, and (to use Prince Bismarck's own words) "it would be kind and useful to pat him on the back, and send him a few soothing telegrams."

In reply to a question of mine, Prince Bismarck said that Prince Gortchakow had a broader plan for the pacification of European Turkey, which Count Andrassy had firmly opposed from the outset, and that he had carried his point, after a long discussion with the Czar, against the Russian Chancellor, an achievement he might well be proud of. Prince Gortchakow had then yielded, and promised his support to the memorandum dictated by Count Andrassy to Baron Jomini and submitted to the Governments of England, France and Italy for their consideration.

I asked if it was true that Prince Gortchakow had recommended a foreign occupation of the Herzegovina? Prince Bismarck replied that he had not, that his plan was, on the contrary, based on the establishment of the autonomy of the revolted Provinces under Turkish governors, which Count Andrassy entirely declined to consent to. The refusal of Her Majesty's Government to support the proposals of the Berlin Conference at Constantinople was therefore "a severer blow" to Count Andrassy than to Prince Gortchakow.

As to the proposals themselves, he did not deny that they might be open both to objection and improvement, but he supported them because they kept up, continued and cemented the good understanding between Austria and Russia, to which he attached greater importance than to anything else in this question.

He regretted Her Majesty's Government could not support the other five

Powers in recommending an armistice at Constantinople, but Her Majesty's Government would always find him ready to consider and support any better proposals they thought more likely to bring about the pacification of European Turkey and to secure the maintenance of peace in general.

On taking leave Prince Bismarck begged that what he had said about Austria and Russia might, for obvious reasons, be considered a secret.

I have the honour . . . .

APPENDIX C

BIBLIOGRAPHY OF MATERIALS CITED

UNPUBLISHED DOCUMENTS

Austro-Hungarian Monarchy, *Haus-, Hof-, und Staatsarchiv.*
The political correspondence of the Austro-Hungarian ministry of foreign affairs is arranged normally by years and by countries. In addition to the files of telegrams and dispatches to and from the imperial agencies abroad, there are separate collections of diverse materials under the title of "Varia." Much of the correspondence pertaining to the period covered in this study is to be found in Varia Turquie I, 1875 and Varia Turquie II, 1875. These two collections are in turn divided into correspondence with agencies and individuals. Certain correspondence pertaining to confidential and secret negotiations has been arranged in a special file with subdivisions labeled as in the citations.

Great Britain, Public Record Office. The correspondence of the Foreign Office·has been arranged in series according to countries and bound in volumes. In the citations given the first figure after FO indicates the series and the second the volume.

PUBLISHED DOCUMENTS

Austro-Hungarian Monarchy, *Ministerium des k. und k. Hauses und des äussern. Auswärtige Angelegenheiten, Correspondenzen des kaiserlich-königlichen Ministeriums des äussern, No. 1, vom November 1866 bis Ende 1867.* Vienna, 1868.
———. *Auswärtige Angelegenheiten, Correspondenzen des kais. kön. gemeinsamen Ministeriums des äussern, No. 2, vom Januar bis November 1868.* Vienna, 1868.
———. *Auswärtige Angelegenheiten, Correspondenzen des kais. und kön. gemeinsamen Ministeriums des äussern, No. 6.* Vienna, 1872.
———. *Actenstücke aus den Correspondenzen des kais. und kön gemeinsamen Ministeriums des äussern über orientalische Angelegenheiten (vom 16. Mai 1873 bis 31. Mai 1877).* Vienna, 1877.
Cited as *First Red Book.*
France, *Assemblée nationale. Annales du Sénat et de la Chambre des députés, session ordinaire de 1876, tome III (du 12 juin au 13 juillet 1876).* Paris, 1876.
France, *Ministère des affaires étrangères. Documents diplomatiques: affaires d'Orient, 1875–1876–1877.* Paris, 1877.
Cited as *First Yellow Book.*
France, *Ministère des affaires étrangères, Commission de publication des documents relatifs aux origines de la guerre de 1914. Documents diplomatiques français (1871–1914).* Paris, 1929—.
Cited as *Documents français.*
Germany, *Auswärtiges Amt. Die Grosse Politik der europäischen Kabinette, 1871–1914, Sammlung der diplomatischen Akten des Auswärtigen Amtes (im Auftrage des Auswärtigen Amtes, herausgegeben von Johannes*

Lepsius, Albrecht Mendelssohn-Bartholdy, Friedrich Thimme). 40 vols. Berlin, 1922–27.
Cited as *Die Grosse Politik.*

Great Britain, Parliament, Lords. *Parliamentary Papers: Reports Received from Her Majesty's Consuls Relating to the Conditions of Christians in Turkey, 1860 (C. 2810)*. 1861, vol. xv-xvii. London, 1861.

Great Britain, Parliament, Commons. *Parliamentary Papers*, 1876, Vol. LXXXIV:

    Turkey No. 2 (1876). *Correspondence Respecting Affairs in Bosnia and the Herzegovina.*
    Cited as *Turkey No. 2 (1876)*.

    Turkey No. 3 (1876). *Correspondence Respecting the Affairs of Turkey, and the Insurrection in Bosnia and the Herzegovina.*
    Cited as *Turkey No. 3 (1876)*.

    Turkey No. 4 (1876). *Correspondence Respecting the Murder of the French and German Consuls at Salonica.*
    Cited as *Turkey No. 4 (1876)*.

———. *Parliamentary Papers*, 1877, Vol. XC.

    Turkey No. 1 (1877). *Correspondence Respecting the Affairs of Turkey.*
    Cited as *Turkey No. 1 (1877)*.

HANSARD. *Parliamentary Debates*. Third series.

HARRIS, DAVID. "Bismarck's Advance to England, January, 1876." *The Journal of Modern History*, III (Sept. 1931), 441–56.

HERTSLET, SIR EDWARD. *British and Foreign State Papers.*

———. *The Map of Europe by Treaty; Showing the Various Political and Territorial Changes Which Have Taken Place since the General Peace of 1814.* 4 vols. London, 1875–1891.

HOLLAND, THOMAS ERSKINE. *The European Concert in the Eastern Question.* Oxford, 1885.

IORGA, NICOLAE. *Correspondance diplomatique roumaine sous le roi Charles I (1866–1880), publiée sous les auspices du ministère des affaires étrangères de Roumanie.* Paris, 1923.

Italy, *Ministero degli affari esteri*. *Documenti diplomatici concernenti gli affari d'oriente presentati dal ministro degli affari esteri (Melegari) nella tornata del 3 marzo 1877.* [Rome, 1877.]
Cited as *First Green Book.*

LASCARIS, S. TH. "La première alliance entre la Grèce et la Serbie, le traité de Voeslau du 14/26 août 1867," *Le Monde slave*, Sept. 1926, pp. 390–437.

LHÉRITIER, MICHEL. "Le Traité d'alliance secret entre la Grèce et la Serbie (1867–1868)," *Revue des Etudes napoléoniennes*, XXIII (Sept.–Oct. 1924), 133–41.

MEYENDORFF, A. "Conversations of Gorchakov, Andrássy and Bismarck in 1872," *Slavonic Review*, VIII (Dec. 1929), 400–408.

NORADOUNGHIAN, GABRIEL. *Recueil d'actes internationaux de l'empire ottoman.* 4 vols. Paris, 1897–1903.

ONOU, ALEXANDER. "Correspondance inédite du baron Jomini (1817–1889)," *Revue d'histoire moderne*, September–October 1935, pp. 373–89.

PRIBRAM, ALFRED FRANZIS. *The Secret Treaties of Austria-Hungary, 1879–*

1914. 2 vols. English edition by Archibald Cary Coolidge. Cambridge, 1920–21.

Rumania, Academia Română. *Politica externă a României, intre anii 1873– 1880, privita dela agentia diplomatică din Roma de R. V. Bossy.* Bucharest, 1928.

Russia. *Krasnyi Archiv.* Vol. I. Moscow, 1922.

SCHOPOFF, A. *Les Réformes et la protection des chrétiens en Turquie, 1673– 1904, firmans, bérats, protocoles, traités, capitulations, conventions, arrangements, notes, circulaires, règlements, lois, mémorandums, etc.* Paris, 1904.

SETON-WATSON, R. W. "Russo-British Relations during the Eastern Crisis," *Slavonic Review,* III, 422–34, 657–83; IV, 177–97, 433–62, 733–59; V, 413–34; VI, 423–33.

TAFFS, WINIFRED. "Conversations between Lord Odo Russell and Andrássy, Bismarck and Gorchakov in September, 1872," *Slavonic Review,* VIII (March 1930), 701–707.

United States, Department of State. *Papers Relating to the Foreign Relations of the United States Transmitted to Congress with the Annual Message of the President* . . . . Washington, D.C., 1876.

CONTEMPORARY MATERIALS

Annual Register.

Augsburger Allgemeine Zeitung.

Blackwood's Edinburgh Magazine.

DANILEVSKII, N. I. *Russland und Europa, eine Untersuchung über die kulturellen und politischen Beziehungen der slawischen zur germanisch-romanischen Welt, übersetzt und eingeleitet von Karl Nötzel.* Stuttgart und Berlin, 1920.

EVANS, ARTHUR J. *Through Bosnia and the Herzegovina on Foot during the Insurrection, August and September 1875* . . . . London, 1876.

Fraser's Magazine.

FUAD. "The Political Testament of Fuad Pasha (addressed to the Sultan Abdul Aziz in 1869, one day before the death of its author)," *Nineteenth Century,* LIII (1903), 190–97.

GALLENGA, A. *Two Years of the Eastern Question.* 2 vols. London, 1877.

IRBY, A. P. "Bosnia in 1875," *Littell's Living Age,* CXXVII (1875), 643–51.

KLACZKO, JULIAN. "Le Congrès de Moscou et la propagande panslaviste," *Revue des deux mondes,* V (1867), 132–81.

———. *The Two Chancellors, Prince Gortchakof and Prince Bismarck,* translated from the French by Mrs. Tait. London, 1876.

London Quarterly Review.

MACKENZIE, G. MUIR, and IRBY, A. P. *Travels in the Slavonic Provinces of Turkey in Europe.* Second edition revised. 2 vols. London, 1877.

MIJATOVICS (MIYATOVIĆ), E. L. "Panslavism: Its Rise and Decline." *Fortnightly Review,* XX (July 1873), 94–112.

The New York Herald.

The Saturday Review.

SCHULTHESS, H. *Europäischer Geschichtskalender.* Nördling, 1860—.

The Spectator.
STILLMAN, W. J. *Herzegovina and the Late Uprising.* London, 1877.
THOMPSON, GEORGE CARSLAKE. *Public Opinion and Lord Beaconsfield, 1875–1880.* 2 vols. London, 1886.
The Times. London.
YRIARTE, CHARLES. "Une excursion en Bosnie et dans l'Herzégovine pendant l'insurrection," *Revue des deux mondes,* 1 March 1876, pp. 167–200; 1 May 1876, pp. 177–99; 1 June 1876, pp. 596–631.

BIOGRAPHIES AND MEMOIRS

Aus dem Leben König Karls von Rumänien. 4 vols. Stuttgart, 1894–1900.
BARKLEY, H. C. *Bulgaria before the War; during Seven Years' Experience of European Turkey and Its Inhabitants.* London, 1877.
BEUST, FRIEDRICH FERDINAND GRAF VON. *Memoirs of F. F. Count von Beust, Written by Himself.* Second edition. 2 vols. London, 1887.
BISMARCK, OTTO FÜRST VON. *Gedanken und Erinnerungen.* 2 vols. Stuttgart, 1898.
————. *Bismarck, the Man and the Statesman, Being the Reflections and Reminiscences of Otto, Prince von Bismarck, Written and Dictated by Himself after His Retirement from Office,* translated from the German under the supervision of A. J. Butler . . . . 2 vols. New York and London, 1899.
BUCKLE, GEORGE EARLE, editor. *The Letters of Queen Victoria, Second Series, a Selection from Her Majesty's Correspondence and Journal between the Years 1862 and 1878.* 2 vols. New York, 1926.
CECIL, LADY GWENDOLEN. *Life of Robert, Marquis of Salisbury.* 4 vols. London, 1921–32.
CHARYKOV, NIKOLAĬ V. *Glimpses of High Politics, through War and Peace, 1855–1929; the Autobiography of N. V. Tcharykow, Serf-owner, Ambassador, Exile.* New York, 1931.
CRISPI, FRANCESCO. *The Memoirs of Francesco Crispi, Compiled from Crispi's Diary and Other Documents by Thomas Palamenghi-Crispi,* translated by Mary Prichard-Agnetti. 3 vols. London, 1912–1914.
DREUX, ANDRÉ. *Dernières années de l'ambassade en Allemagne de M. Gontaut-Biron, 1874–1877, d'après ses notes et papiers diplomatiques.* Paris, 1907.
ECKARDSTEIN, HERMANN FREIHERR VON. *Lebens-Erinnerungen und Politische Denkwürdigkeiten.* 2 vols. Leipzig, 1919–20.
ELLIOT, SIR HENRY GEORGE. *Some Revolutions and Other Diplomatic Experiences.* London, 1922.
————. "The Death of Abdul Aziz and Turkish Reform," *Nineteenth Century,* XXIII (1888), 276–96.
GABRIAC, MARQUIS DE. *Souvenirs diplomatiques de Russie et d'Allemagne (1870–72).* Paris, 1896.
GARDINER, A. G. *The Life of Sir William Harcourt.* 2 vols. New York, 1923.
GATHORNE-HARDY, ALFRED E., editor. *Gathorne-Hardy, First Earl of Cranbrook, a Memoir, with Extracts from His Diary and Correspondence.* 2 vols. London, 1910.

GLAISE-HORSTENAU, EDMUND VON. *Franz Josephs Weggefährte, das Leben des Generalstabschefs Grafen Beck, nach seinen Aufzeichnungen und hinterlassenen Dokumenten.* Vienna, 1930.

GONTAUT-BIRON, ÉLIE VICOMTE DE. *Mon ambassade en Allemagne (1872–1873).* Third edition. Paris, 1906.

HARDINGE, SIR ARTHUR. *The Life of Henry Howard Molyneux Herbert, Fourth Earl of Carnarvon, 1831–1890.* 3 vols. London, 1925.

HOHENLOHE-SCHILLINGSFÜRST, FÜRST CHLODWIG ZU. *Denkwürdigkeiten des Fürsten Chlodwig zu Hohenlohe-Schillingsfürst.* 2 vols. Stuttgart und Leipzig, 1907.

IGNATIEV, COUNT NICHOLAS P. "Zapiski Grafa N. P. Ignatyeva," *Istoricheski Vyesnik* (St. Petersburg), CXXXV, 50–75, 441–62, 805–36; CXXXVI, 50–84, 430–67, 825–63; CXXXVII, 54–92.

———. "Zapiski Grafa N. P. Ignatyeva, 1867–1874," *Izvestiia ministerstva inostrannikh diel,* 1914, I, 93–135; II, 66–105; III, 92–121; IV, 75–103; VI, 147–68; 1915, I, 142–74; II, 164–89; III, 160–75; IV, 223–36; VI, 109–27.

ISMAIL KEMAL. *The Memoirs of Ismail Kemal Bey, edited by Sommerville Story* .... London, 1920.

KARATHÉODORY, ALEXANDER. *Le Rapport secret sur le Congrès de Berlin, adressé à la Sublime Porte par Karathéodory pacha.* Paris, 1919.

LANG, ANDREW. *Life, Letters, and Diaries of Sir Stafford Northcote, First Earl of Iddesleigh.* 2 vols. London, 1890.

LEE, SIR SIDNEY. *King Edward VII, a Biography.* 2 vols. New York, 1925–27.

LOFTUS, LORD AUGUSTUS. *The Diplomatic Reminiscences of Lord Augustus Loftus* .... *1862–79.* Second series. 2 vols. London, 1894.

MIDHAT, ALI HAYDAR. *The Life of Midhat Pasha, a Record of His Services, Political Reforms, Banishment, and Judicial Murder, Derived from Private Documents and Reminiscences by His Son, Ali Haydar Midhat Bey.* London, 1903.

MIJATOVICH (MIYATOVIĆ), COUNT CHEDOMIL. *The Memoirs of a Balkan Diplomatist.* London, 1917.

MITTNACHT, HERMANN FREIHERR VON. *Erinnerungen an Bismarck.* Sixth edition. Stuttgart und Berlin, 1904.

MOLLINARY, ANTON FREIHERR VON. *Sechsundvierzig Jahre im österreich-ungarischen Heere, 1833–1879.* 2 vols. Zürich, 1905.

MONYPENNY, W. F., and BUCKLE, G. E. *The Life of Benjamin Disraeli, Earl of Beaconsfield.* 6 vols. New York, 1913–20.

NELIDOV, A. "Souvenirs d'avant et d'après la guerre de 1877–1878," *Revue des deux mondes,* XXVII (1915), 302–39; XXVIII, 241–77; XXX, 241–70.

NEWTON, THOMAS WODEHOUSE LEGH, 2d Baron. *Lord Lyons, a Record of British Diplomacy.* 2 vols. London, 1913.

POSCHINGER, HEINRICH VON. *Fürst Bismarck: Neue Tischgespräche und Interviews.* 2 vols. Stuttgart, 1895–99.

RADOWITZ, JOSEPH MARIA VON. *Aufzeichnungen und Erinnerungen aus dem Leben des Botschafters Joseph Maria von Radowitz.* 2 vols. Berlin, 1925.

RASCHDAU, L. "Aus dem politischen Nachlass des Unterstaatssekretärs Dr. Busch," *Deutsche Rundschau,* CXXXVII (Dec. 1908), 368–405.

RUMBOLD, SIR HORACE. *Recollections of a Diplomatist.* 2 vols. Second impression. London, 1902.
SANDERSON, SIR T. H., and ROSCOE, E. S., editors. *Speeches and Addresses of Edward Henry XVth Earl of Derby, K.G.* 2 vols. London, 1894.
SCHWEINITZ, HANS LOTHAR VON. *Briefwechsel des Botschafters General v. Schweinitz.* Berlin, 1928.
———. *Denkwürdigkeiten des Botschafters General v. Schweinitz.* 2 vols. Berlin, 1927.
STILLMAN, W. J. *The Autobiography of a Journalist.* 2 vols. Boston and New York, 1901.
TATISHCHEV, S. S. *Imperator Aleksandr II, ego zhizn i tsarstvovania.* 2 vols. St. Petersburg, 1903.
WALLING, R. A. J., editor. *The Diaries of John Bright.* New York, 1931.
WEMYSS, MRS. ROSSLYN. *Memoirs and Letters of the Right Hon. Sir Robert Morier, G.C.B., from 1826 to 1876.* 2 vols. London, 1911.
WERTHEIMER, EDUARD VON. *Graf Julius Andrássy, sein Leben und seine Zeit, nach ungedruckten Quellen.* 3 vols. Stuttgart, 1910–13.
WESSELITSKY-BOJIDAROVITCH, GABRIEL DE. *Dix mois de ma vie, 1875–1876.* Paris, 1929.
———. *La Serbie; son rôle dans l'histoire et la civilisation. La Bosnie-Herzégovine.* Traduit de l'anglais par M. de Vaux Phalipau. Paris, 1919.
ZETLAND, MARQUIS OF. *The Letters of Disraeli to Lady Bradford and Lady Chesterfield.* 2 vols. London, 1929.

SECONDARY MATERIALS

BAMBERG, FELIX. *Geschichte der orientalischen Angelegenheit im Zeitraume des Pariser und des Berliner Friedens.* Berlin, 1892.
BEAMAN, A. HULME. *M. Stambuloff.* London, 1895.
BIBL, VIKTOR. *Der Zerfall Österreichs.* 2 vols. Vienna, 1922–24.
BLAISDELL, DONALD C. *European Financial Control in the Ottoman Empire.* New York, 1929.
BLUM, HANS. *Fürst Bismarck und Seine Zeit.* 6 vols. and supplement. Munich, 1894–99.
DEVAS, GEORGES Y. "Les Origines de l'unité yougoslave," *Le Monde slave,* April 1918, pp. 532–49.
DIPLOMATICUS. "Secret Treaty of Reichstadt," *Fortnightly Review,* XC (November 1908), 828–37.
ENGELHARDT, ED. "La Confédération balkanique," *Revue d'histoire diplomatique,* VI (1892), 29–55.
———. *La Turquie et le Tanzimat, ou histoire des réformes dans l'empire ottoman depuis 1826 jusqu'à nos jours.* 2 vols. Paris, 1882–84.
FISCHEL, ALFRED. *Der Panslawismus bis zum Weltkrieg, ein geschichtlicher Überblick.* Stuttgart und Berlin, 1919.
FLEURY, GENERAL COUNT. *La France et la Russie en 1870.* Paris, 1902.
FLOROVSKY, ANTON. "Dostoyevsky and the Slavonic Question," *Slavonic Review,* IX (December 1930), 411–23.
FOURNIER, AUGUST. *Wie wir zu Bosnien kamen.* Vienna, 1909.
FRAHM, FRIEDRICH. "England und Russland in Bismarcks Bündnispolitik," *Archiv für Politik und Geschichte,* Jhg. 5, Teil I (1927), 365–431.

GORIAINOV, SERGE. *Le Bosphore et les Dardanelles, étude historique sur la question des détroits, d'après la correspondance diplomatique déposée aux archives centrales de Saint-Pétersbourg et à celles de l'empire.* Paris, 1910.

HALLBERG, CHARLES W. *The Suez Canal: Its History and Diplomatic Importance.* New York, 1931.

HANOTAUX, GABRIEL. *Contemporary France.* 4 vols. Translated from the French by E. Sparvel-Bayly. New York, 1903–1909.

HAUMANT, EMILE. *La Formation de la Yougoslavie (XVe–XXe siècles).* Paris, 1930.

——. "Les Origines de la lutte pour la Macédoine (1855–1872)," *Le Monde slave,* III (1926), 52–66.

HAUSER, HENRI, director. *Histoire diplomatique de l'Europe (1871–1914).* 2 vols. Paris, 1929.

HOSCHILLER, MAX. "La Russie sur le chemin de Byzance," *Revue de Paris,* XXII (August 1915), 590–616, 766–96.

HUSZÁR, EMMERICH VON. "Die Memoiren des Grafen N. P. Ignatiew," *Österreichische Rundschau,* XLI (November 1915), 166–74.

HYDE, ARTHUR MAY. *A Diplomatic History of Bulgaria from 1870 to 1886.* Urbana, Ill., 1931.

IORGA, NICOLAE. *Geschichte des osmanischen Reiches.* 5 vols. Gotha, 1908–1913.

——. "Origines des idées d'indépendance balkanique," *Le Monde slave,* IV (July 1927), 73–93.

JAPIKSE, NICOLAAS. *Europa und Bismarcks Friedenspolitik.* Berlin, 1927.

JOVANOVIĆ, SLOBODAN. "Serbia in the Early 'Seventies," *Slavonic Review,* IV (December 1925), 384–95.

LA JONQUIÈRE, LE VICOMTE DE. *Histoire de l'empire ottoman depuis les origines jusqu'à nos jours.* 2 vols. Paris, 1914.

LANGER, WILLIAM L. *European Alliances and Alignments, 1871–1890.* New York, 1931.

LARMEROUX, JEAN. *La Politique extérieure de l'Autriche-Hongrie, 1875–1914.* 2 vols. Paris, 1918.

LASCARIS, S. TH. *La Politique extérieure de la Grèce avant et après le Congrès de Berlin (1875–1881).* Paris, 1924.

LEE, DWIGHT E. *Great Britain and the Cyprus Convention Policy of 1878.* Cambridge, 1934.

LEGER, LOUIS P. M. *Le Panslavisme et l'intérêt français.* Paris, 1917.

LHÉRITIER, MICHEL. *Histoire diplomatique de la Grèce de 1821 à nos jours.* Vol. 3. Paris, 1925.

MASARYK, THOMAS GARRIGUE. *The Spirit of Russia: Studies in History, Literature and Philosophy* .... translated from the German original by Eden and Cedar Paul. London, 1919.

MERTZ, HEINRICH. *Die Schwarze-Meer Konferenz von 1871.* Stuttgart, 1927.

MIJATOVICH (MIYATOVIĆ), CHEDOMIL. *Servia and the Servians.* London, 1908.

MILLER, WILLIAM. "Bosnia before the Turkish Conquest," *English Historical Review,* XIII (October 1898), 643–66.

——. *The Ottoman Empire and Its Successors, 1801–1922, Being a Revised and Enlarged Edition of the Ottoman Empire, 1801–1913.* Cambridge, 1923.

ONOU, ALEXANDER. "The Memoirs of Count N. Ignatyev," *Slavonic Review,* X, 386–407, 627–40; XI, 108–25.

PITTARD, EUGENE. *Race and History, an Ethnological Introduction to History.* New York, 1926.

PLATZHOFF, WALTER. "Die Anfänge des Dreikaiserbundes (1867–1871)," *Preussische Jahrbücher,* CLXXXVIII (1922), 283–306.

RACHFAHL, FELIX. *Deutschland und die Weltpolitik.* Stuttgart, 1923.

RADEFF, SIMÉON. *La Macédoine et la renaissance bulgare aux XIXe siècle.* Sofia, 1918.

RHEINDORF, KURT. *Die Schwarze-Meer Frage, 1856–1871.* Berlin, 1925.

RIKER, T. W. "Michael of Serbia and the Turkish Occupation," *Slavonic Review,* XII (1933–34), 133–54, 409–29.

RUPP, GEORGE HOOVER. "The Reichstadt Agreement," *American Historical Review,* XXX (April 1925), 503–10.

SETON-WATSON, R. W. "Gabriel Wesselitsky," *Slavonic Review,* IX (March 1931), 732–75.

———. "Les Relations de l'Autriche-Hongrie et de la Serbie entre 1868 et 1874: la mission de Benjamin Kállay à Belgrade," *Le Monde slave,* February 1926, pp. 210–30; May 1926, pp. 186–204; August 1926, pp. 273–88.

———. *The Role of Bosnia in International Politics (1875–1914).* Reprint from the *Proceedings of the British Academy,* Volume XVII. London, 1931.

———. *Disraeli, Gladstone and the Eastern Question, a Study in Diplomacy and Party Politics.* London, 1935.

SOSNOSKY, THEODOR VON. *Die Balkanpolitik Österreich-Ungarns seit 1866.* 2 vols. Stuttgart, 1913–14.

STOJANOVIC, MIHAILO D. "Serbia in International Politics, from the Insurrection in Herzegovina (1875) to the Congress of Berlin (1878)." Manuscript dissertation (1930) at the University of London.

SUMNER, B. H. "Ignatyev at Constantinople, 1864–74," *Slavonic Review,* XI (1933), 341–53, 556–71.

TAFFS, WINIFRED. "The War Scare of 1875," *Slavonic Review,* IX (1930–31), 335–49, 632–49.

TEMPERLEY, HAROLD. *The Bulgarian and Other Atrocities, 1875–8, in the Light of Historical Criticism.* Reprint from the *Proceedings of the British Academy,* Volume XVII. London, 1931.

———. *History of Serbia.* London, 1919.

TRIVANOVITCH, VASO. "Serbia, Russia, and Austria during the Rule of Milan Obrenovich, 1868–78," *The Journal of Modern History,* III (September 1931), 414–40.

TRUBETZKOI, PRINCE GREGORY. "La Politique russe en Orient: le schisme bulgare," *Revue d'histoire diplomatique,* XXI (1907), 161–98, 394–426.

———. "Les Préliminaires de la conférence de Londres," *Revue d'histoire diplomatique,* XXIII (1909), 108–38, 271–90, 359–96.

WARD, SIR ADOLPHUS WILLIAM, editor. *The Cambridge History of British Foreign Policy.* 3 vols. Cambridge, 1922–23.

WIRTHWEIN, WALTER G. *Britain and the Balkan Crisis, 1875–1878.* New York, 1935.

Index

INDEX

Aarifi Pasha (Turkish Ambassador to Austria-Hungary), protest against intervention, Jan. 1876, 212

Abdul Aziz (Sultan of Turkey, 1861–1876): character of man and of his rule, 6–7; private arrangement with Russia, offered by (Sept. 1875), 138; renewed willingness for Russian entente (Nov. 1875), 155; Andrássy note, 226–29; orders for treatment of insurgents and refugees revoked (Feb. 1876), 236; apprehensive of Berlin conference, 325; deposition, 334–35

Alexander II (Tsar of Russia, 1855–1881): attitude toward Crimean War and Peace of Paris, 40; desire to visit Berlin (Sept. 1872), 50; approval of Ignatiev's plan (Sept. 1875), 135; rejects Ignatiev's plea for isolated role (Oct. 1875), 146; reaction to Turkish threat of war on Montenegro (April 1876), 272; at Berlin conference, 295–96; reaction to British rejection of Berlin Memorandum, 318; appeal for French support (June 1876), 341; Gorchakov overridden on intervention in Serbia (May 1876), 398; exchange of letters with Queen Victoria, 416–17

Ali Pasha: appointed governor of Bosnia-Hercegovina, 233; Stillman's interview, 237 (n. 29); renewed attack on insurgents, 247; amnesty proclamation (March 1876), 250–51

Andrássy, Count Julius (Austro-Hungarian Minister for Foreign Affairs, 1871–1879): background, 26; inaugural circular (1871), 26; Balkan policy before 1875, 27–28; Andrássy pre-1875 attitude toward annexation of Bosnia and Hercegovina, 28–29; attitude toward Serbia before 1875, 28–31; pre-1875 attitude toward Germany, 49; attitude toward Russia (1871–72), 50; agreement with Gorchakov (Sept. 1872), 53; role in war scare of May 1875, 60–61; program at outbreak of the revolt, 69–72; re-

action to Russian mediation proposal (July 1875), 74–75; admonitions to Prince Milan, 104; attitude toward Serbian war threat, 114–16; response to Ignatiev reform plan (Sept. 1875), 140–41; counter-proposals to Russia, 143–45; rejection of Jomini's proposal for military occupation (Nov. 1875), 151–52; insistence on his own program (Nov. 1875), 152–53; criticism of Ignatiev, 153; attempt to forestall Turkish reform initiative (Nov.–Dec., 1875), 157–61; reserve toward non-allied powers during autumn 1875, 194–95; protest against Anglo-Russian confidences (Nov. 1875), 195; resentment of Derby's attempt to divide Austria and Russia (Dec. 1875), 196; attitude toward British consideration of the Andrássy note, 205, 207; opinion of Ignatiev, 215 (n. 179); instructions to Zichy for presenting note, 222–24, 226; plan for repatriation of refugees advanced (Jan. 1876), 240–41; orders to Austrian officials for pacification work, 242–43; optimism (March 1876), 251; rejection of insurgent demands (April 1876), 256–57; negotiations with Russia concerning insurgent demands, 256–57, 261–64; treatment of war threat against Montenegro, 270–72, 273; attempt to arrange new truce, 276–77, 278–79; attempt to stay Mukhtar's march to Nicksich (April 1876), 282–83; understanding sought with Bismarck before Berlin conference, 289; attempt to dissuade Gorchakov from raising autonomy issue (March 1876), 289 (n. 7); preliminary conference with Bismarck, 291–92; victory at Berlin conference, 297; attack on British rejection of Berlin memorandum, 312–14; acceptance of Gorchakov's desire to revive Berlin memorandum (June 1876), 340; acceptance of Gorchakov's compromise proposal as a substitute for Berlin

321–23; Turks asked to invite British support of Berlin memorandum, 322; attempt to evoke British co-operation in question of recognizing Murad, 338; treatment of Gorchakov's desire to revive Berlin Memorandum, 340–46; compromise proposals sent to Britain (June 1876), 343–44; his projects (May 1876), 413–15

Derby, Earl of (British Secretary of State for Foreign Affairs): characterization, 21–22; attitude toward outbreak of the revolt, 86–87; outlook in autumn of 1875, 191–92; interview with Shuvalov (Oct. 1875), 193–94; Edinburgh speech (18 Dec. 1875), 197; relations with Beust (Nov.–Dec., 1875), 197; reaction to Andrássy note, 202; international admonition to Nicholas proposed by, 282; outlook in April–May, 1876, 304; condemnation of Berlin memorandum, 306–7; dispatches regarding the Berlin memorandum, 310–11; treatment of Turkish protest against Berlin memorandum, 333–34; speeches to Bright and Farley delegations (July 1876), 419–21; reaction to the deposition of Abdul Aziz, 352–53

Dervish Pasha: first reaction to the revolt, 63; dismissal of, 65; advance of Mukhtar supported by (April 1876), 280

Disraeli, Benjamin (Prime Minister of Great Britain, 1874–1880): advent of his government in 1874, 19–20; desire to break league of the three emperors, 23; consular mission, 88; outlook in Sept.–Oct., 1875, 188–89; Lord Mayor's banquet (9 Nov. 1875), 189–90; purchase of Suez Canal shares, 191; condemnation of the Andrássy note, 203–4; reaction to Berlin conference, 305–6; condemnation of Berlin memorandum, 307–8; his naval projects (June 1876), 349–51; inauguration of Anglo-Russian negotiations (June 1876), 354–57; reaction to the deposition of Abdul Aziz, 352–53; opinion of Serbian declaration of war, 417; draft of Victoria's reply to Alexander II, 417; defense of government policy in House of Commons debate (July 1876), 423–27

Doscos (Greek consul-general in Beograd), share in alliance negotiations, 379 (n. 9)

Elliot, Sir Henry George (British Ambassador to Turkey, 1867–77): attitude toward ministerial change (Aug. 1875), 65–66; character of, 83–84; influence in Turkey, 84–85; attitude toward outbreak of revolt, 85; approval of consular mission, 86; admonitions to the Sultan to effect reforms (Aug. 1875), 138, 156; condemnation of Andrássy note, 203; see n. 125; intervention on behalf of Mahmud, 227; advice against an attack on Montenegro, 268; suspicions of Montenegro (April 1876), 270; changing views regarding Turkish-Montenegrin settlement, 404–5

Fadeiev, Rostislav, *Opinion on the Eastern Question*, 37

Farley, Lewis, Russian subvention for propaganda sought by, 186 (n. 64); delegation to Foreign Office (July 1876), 419

Ferman of December 1875, proclamation in insurgent area, 232

France: attitude toward negotiations for consular mission, 78–80; acceptance of Andrássy note, 181–83; war threat against Montenegro (April 1876) protested by, 273; approval of Berlin memorandum, 303; agreement to proceed with Berlin memorandum without England, 321–23; recognition of Murad, 338; response to Russian nonintervention proposal, 412–15; public opinion (June–July, 1876), 412 (n. 138)

Francis Joseph (Emperor of Austria-Hungary, 1848–1916): attitude toward Germany (1866–1871), 25; attitude toward annexation of Bosnia, 31; Dalmatian journey (May 1875), 32; reconciliation with Germany, 48; Berlin visit (Sept. 1872), 49; in St. Petersburg (Jan. 1874), 56–57

Gathorne-Hardy, reaction to imperial league's treatment of Britain, 308

Gavard (French chargé d'affaires in London), his estimate of British policy, 190–91